GAAS
GUIDE
1997

MILLER

GAAS GUIDE
1997

A comprehensive restatement of
**Standards for Auditing, Attestation,
Compilation and Review, and the
Code of Professional Conduct**

LARRY P. BAILEY, Ph.D., CPA

HARCOURT BRACE PROFESSIONAL PUBLISHING

A Division of

Harcourt Brace & Company
SAN DIEGO   NEW YORK   LONDON

Contents

Preface   vii

About the Author   x

Accounting Resources on the Web   xi

Cross-Reference   xiii

Part I. Audited Financial Statements
    Overview   1.01
    Responsibility and Function of the Independent
      Auditor   2.01
    Generally Accepted Accounting Principles   3.01
    Generally Accepted Auditing Standards   4.01
    Pre-Engagement Planning   5.01
    Planning the Engagement   6.01
    Internal Control, Errors, and Irregularities 7.01
    Evidence   8.01
    Sampling Techniques and Procedures   9.01
    Completing the Audit   10.01
    Auditor's Reports   11.01
    Auditor's Special Reports   12.01

**Part II. Interim Reviews, Condensed Financials, Filings
Under Federal Securities Statutes, and Letters to
Underwriters**   13.01

Part III. Compilation and Review Engagements   14.01

Part IV. Prospective Financial Statements   15.01

Part V. Attest Engagements   16.01

Part VI. Agreed-Upon Procedures Engagements   17.01

**Part VII. Specialized Industry Accounting and
Auditing Practices**
    Audits of Construction Contractors   18.01
    Audits of Credit Unions   19.01
    Audits of Employee Benefit Plans   20.01

Audits of Health Care Providers 21.01
Audits of Not-for-Profit Organizations 22.01
Audits of State and Local Governmental Units 23.01

Part VIII. Code of Professional Conduct 24.01

Self-Study CPE Program 25.01

Topical Index 26.01

Preface

The 1997 *Miller GAAS Guide* has been revised to bring you more practical information on generally accepted auditing standards. In addition, the *Guide* has been completely updated for the most recent pronouncements, including the following:

- New pronouncements on internal control—Statement on Auditing Standards No. 78 (Consideration of Internal Control in a Financial Statement Audit: An Amendment to SAS No. 55) and Statement on Standards for Attestation Engagements No. 6 (Reporting on an Entity's Internal Control Over Financial Reporting: An Amendment to Statement on Standards for Attestation Engagements No. 2 [December 1995])

- Exposure Draft issued by the Auditing Standards Board (ASB) on fraud—Consideration of Fraud in a Financial Statement Audit (May 1996)

- New pronouncements on auditing standards—Statement on Auditing Standards No. 77 (Amendments to Statements on Auditing Standards No. 22, "Planning and Supervision," No. 59, "The Auditor's Consideration of an Entity's Ability to Continue as a Going Concern," and No. 62, "Special Reports") and Statement on Auditing Standards No. 79 (Amendments to Statement on Auditing Standards No. 58, "Reports on Audited Financial Statements")

- New Statements on Quality Control Standards—SQCS-2 (System Quality Control for a CPA Firm's Accounting and Auditing Practice) and SQCS-3 (Monitoring a CPA Firm's Accounting and Auditing Practice)

- Additional detail on the AICPA Code of Professional Conduct and in the Cross-Reference to make researching particular issues easier

- More detailed coverage of Auditing and Attestation Interpretations

The *GAAS Guide* describes the auditing standards, practices, and procedures in use today. These include generally accepted auditing standards, Statements on Auditing Standards and Interpretations, Statements on Standards for Attestation Engagements and Interpretations, Statements on Standards on Accounting and Review Services and Interpretations, Specialized Industry Audit Guides, Statements on Quality Control Standards, and the Code of Professional Conduct.

The parts in this *Guide* are classified by the type of auditing or accounting engagement an independent auditor or accountant may render to a client. Within each part of the book, a particular topic is reviewed in a comprehensive, easily understood format. In-depth illustrations of specific auditing topics and opinions are used generously to aid the reader in grasping a particular subject. All auditing and accounting pronouncements covering the same topic have been compiled and integrated in the same place, regardless of the date of their origin.

Perhaps the most important feature of this *Guide* is its readability. The utmost care has been exercised to avoid unintelligible language. Sentence structure has been deliberately simplified as much as possible to foster the maximum understanding.

Observation paragraphs are used to stress important information and possible conflicts. Although no attempt is made to resolve apparent errors and conflicts in the promulgated pronouncements, these items are brought to the reader's attention.

The quality of future revisions of the *GAAS Guide* will benefit significantly from the input and constructive suggestions the author receives from readers. With this in mind, the author respectfully requests that readers submit their comments to the publisher.

Acknowledgments

The author would like to thank Dan M. Guy, Vice President, Professional Standards and Technical Services, American Institute of Certified Public Accountants, for his recommendations to improve this edition of the *GAAS Guide*. Mr. Guy is the lead author of a college textbook, *Auditing*, Third Edition, published by The Dryden Press, a division of Harcourt Brace & Company.

The author and publisher thank the following contributors to the *GAAS Guide*:

Ray Whittington, Director, School of Accountancy, San Diego State University, for his work on "Completing the Audit."

Robert A. Davidson, CPA, and Whitley B. Forehand, CPA, Davidson & Golden, Nashville, Tennessee, for their work on "Audits of Construction Contractors."

Rhett D. Harrell, CPA, Marietta, Georgia, for his work on "Audits of State and Local Governmental Units."

Susan Paulsen, CPA, Paulsen, Megaard & Company, Bothell, Washington, for her work on "Audits of Health Care Providers."

Warren Ruppel, CPA, New York, New York, for his work on "Audits of Not-for-Profit Organizations."

David M. Walker, Partner, Arthur Andersen LLP, Atlanta, Georgia, for his work on "Audits of Employee Benefit Plans."

Larry P. Bailey
c/o Harcourt Brace Professional Publishing
525 B Street, Suite 1900
San Diego, CA 92101
Attn: GAAS Editor

About the Author

Larry P. Bailey is a Professor of Accounting at Rider University in Lawrenceville, N.J., where he teaches auditing and financial accounting. Dr. Bailey earned a B.S. degree in business from Concord College and a Masters and Ph.D. from the University of Pennsylvania. He is a Certified Public Accountant (Virginia) and has worked in public accounting (Arthur Young & Company), in government (intern for the State of New Jersey), and as an educational consultant.

Professor Bailey is a member of the American Institute of Certified Public Accountants and the American Accounting Association. His research interests include auditing and governmental financial reporting, and he has published numerous articles in such journals as *Management Accountant, The CPA Journal,* and *Government Accountants Journal.* He is also the author of four books (including the Miller *Governmental GAAP Guide* and Miller *Compilations and Reviews*), the Miller *Governmental GAAP Update Service,* and various pamphlets.

Accounting Resources on the Web

The following World Wide Web addresses are just a few of the resources on the Internet that are available to practitioners. Because of the evolving nature of the Internet, some addresses may change. In such a case, refer to one of the many Internet search engines, such as Yahoo! (http://www.yahoo.com).

AICPA   http://www.aicpa.org/

American Accounting Association   http://www.rutgers.edu/accounting/raw/aaa/

FASB   http://www.rutgers.edu:80//accounting/raw/internet/

Federal Tax Code Search   http://www.tns.lcs.mit.edu:80/

Fedworld   http://www.fedworld.gov/uscode/

GASB   http://www.financenet.gov/

General Accounting Office   http://www.gao.gov/

Harcourt Brace Professional Publishing   http://www.hbpp.com

House of Representatives   http://www.house.gov/

IRS Digital Daily   http://www.irs.ustreas.gov/prod/

Library of Congress   http://lcweb.loc.gov/homepage/

Office of Management and Budget   http://www.qns.com/~ombokc/intro.htm

Securities and Exchange Commission   http://www.sec.gov/

Thomas Legislative Research   http://thomas.loc.gov/

Cross-Reference

ORIGINAL PRONOUNCEMENTS TO GAAS GUIDE CHAPTERS

This locator provides instant cross-reference between original pronouncements and the chapters in this publication where the pronouncements appear and with the AICPA Codification. Original pronouncements are listed chronologically on the left and the chapters in which the pronouncements appear in the *GAAS Guide* are listed on the right. Primary Codification references are shown in parentheses. Where an original pronouncement has been superseded, cross-reference is made to the succeeding pronouncement.

STATEMENTS ON AUDITING PROCEDURES

> Statements on Auditing Procedures Nos. 1–54 were codified or superseded by Statement on Auditing Standards No. 1 in November 1972.

STATEMENTS ON AUDITING STANDARDS

> Statements on Auditing Standards are interpretations of generally accepted auditing standards. Statements on Auditing Standards are issued by the Auditing Standards Board. Rule 202 of the Code of Professional Conduct requires that members of the AICPA adhere to generally accepted auditing standards. A member must be prepared to justify a departure from a Statement on Auditing Standards.

ORIGINAL PRONOUNCEMENT	GAAS GUIDE REFERENCE
SAS-1 (throughout)	
Codification of Auditing Standards and Procedures	
• Introduction	Audited Financial Statements, p. **1.03**
• General Standards	Responsibility and Function of the Independent Auditor, p. **2.03**
	Generally Accepted Auditing Standards, p. **4.05**
• Standards of Fieldwork	Generally Accepted Auditing Standards, p. **4.08**
• First, Second, and Third Standards of Reporting	Generally Accepted Auditing Standards, p. **4.10**
• Fourth Standard of Reporting	Generally Accepted Auditing Standards, p. **4.12**
• Other Types of Reports	Auditor's Special Reports, p. **12.03**
• Special Topics	Auditor's Special Reports, p. **12.03**
• Special Reports of the Committee on Auditing Procedure	Evidence, p. **8.06**

SAS-2

Reports on Audited Financial Statements   Superseded by SAS-58

SAS-3

The Effects of EDP on the Auditor's Study and
Evaluation of Internal Control   Superseded by SAS-48

SAS-4

Quality Control Considerations for a Firm of
Independent Auditors   Superseded by SAS-25

SAS-5

The Meaning of "Present Fairly in Conformity
with Generally Accepted Accounting Prin-
ciples" in the Independent Auditor's Report   Superseded by SAS-69

SAS-6

Related Party Transactions   Superseded by SAS-45

SAS-7 (AU 315)

Communications Between Predecessor and Suc-
cessor Auditors   Pre-Engagement Planning, p. **5.04**

SAS-8 (AU 550)

Other Information in Documents Containing
Audited Financial Statements   Auditor's Reports, p. **11.41**

SAS-9

The Effect of an Internal Audit Function on the
Scope of the Independent Auditor's Examination   Superseded by SAS-65

SAS-10

Limited Review of Interim Financial Information   Superseded by SAS-24

SAS-11

Using the Work of a Specialist   Superseded by SAS-73

SAS-12 (AU 337)

Inquiry of a Client's Lawyer Concerning Liti-
gation, Claims, and Assessments   Completing the Audit, p. **10.05**

SAS-13

Reports on a Limited Review of Interim Financial Information   Superseded by SAS-24

SAS-14

Special Reports   Superseded by SAS-62

SAS-15

Reports on Comparative Financial Statements   Superseded by SAS-58

SAS-16
The Independent Auditor's Responsibility for
the Detection of Errors or Irregularities   Superseded by SAS-53

SAS-17
Illegal Acts by Clients   Superseded by SAS-54

SAS-18
Unaudited Replacement Cost Information   Withdrawn

SAS-19 (AU 333)
Client Representations   Evidence, p. **8.76**
                                                  Completing the Audit, p. **10.12**

SAS-20
Required Communication of Material Weak-
nesses in Internal Accounting Control   Superseded by SAS-60

SAS-21 (AU 435)
Segment Information   Evidence, p. **8.53**

SAS-22 (AU 311)
Planning and Supervision   Pre-Engagement Planning, p. **5.03**
                                                   Planning the Engagement, p. **6.03**
SAS-23
Analytical Review Procedures   Superseded by SAS-56

SAS-24
Review of Interim Financial Information   Superseded by SAS-36

SAS-25 (AU 161)
The Relationship of Generally Accepted Audit-   Responsibility and Function of the Indepen-
ing Standards to Quality Control Standards   dent Auditor, p. **2.06**

SAS-26 (AU 504)
Association with Financial Statements   Auditor's Reports, p. **11.08**

SAS-27
Supplementary Information Required by the
Financial Accounting Standards Board   Superseded by SAS-52

SAS-28
Supplementary Information on the Effects of
Changing Prices   Superseded by SAS-52

SAS-29 (AU 551)
Reporting on Information Accompanying the
Basic Financial Statements in Auditor-Submit-
ted Documents   Auditor's Reports, p. **11.48**

SAS-30
Reporting on Internal Accounting Control   Superseded by SSAE-2

SAS-31 (AU 326)
Evidential Matter   Evidence, p. **8.08**

SAS-32 (AU 431)
Adequacy of Disclosure in Financial Statements   Auditor's Reports, p. **11.15**

SAS-33
Supplementary Oil and Gas Reserve Information   Superseded by SAS-45

SAS-34
The Auditor's Considerations When a Question Arises About an Entity's Continued Existence   Superseded by SAS-59

SAS-35
Special Reports—Applying Agreed-Upon Procedures to Specified Elements, Accounts, or Items of a Financial Statement   Superseded by SAS-75

SAS-36
Review of or Performing Procedures on Interim Financial Information   Superseded by SAS-71

SAS-37 (AU 711)
Filings Under Federal Securities Statutes   Interim Reviews, p. **13.27**

SAS-38
Letters for Underwriters   Superseded by SAS-49

SAS-39 (AU 350)
Audit Sampling   Evidence, p. **8.11**
    Sampling Techniques and Procedures, p. **9.03**

SAS-40
Supplementary Mineral Reserve Information   Superseded by SAS-52

SAS-41 (AU 339)
Working Papers   Internal Control, p. **7.72**
    Evidence, p. **8.23**

SAS-42 (AU 552)
Reporting on Condensed Financial Statements and Selected Financial Data   Interim Reviews, p. **13.55**

SAS-43 (throughout)
Omnibus Statement on Auditing Standards
- Generally Accepted Auditing Standards   Generally Accepted Auditing Standards, p. **4.03**
- The Auditor's Study and Evaluation of Internal Control   No reference
- Inventories Held in Public Warehouses   Evidence, p. **8.38**
- Consistency of Application of Generally Accepted Accounting Principles   Auditor's Reports, p. **11.19**
- Reports on Audited Financial Statements   No reference
- The Meaning of "Present Fairly in Conformity with GAAP" in the Independent Auditor's Report   Superseded by SAS-69
- Letter for Underwriters   No reference

SAS-44
Special-Purpose Reports on Internal Account-
ing Control at Service Organizations   Superseded by SAS-70

SAS-45 (AU 313; AU 334)
Omnibus Statement on Auditing Standards—
1983
  • Substantive Tests Prior to the Balance Sheet
    Date   Evidence, p. **8.15**
  • Related Parties   Evidence, p. **8.64**

SAS-46 (AU 390)
Consideration of Omitted Procedures After the
Report Date   Completing the Audit, p. **10.23**

SAS-47 (AU 312)
Audit Risk and Materiality in Conducting an
Audit   Evidence, p. **8.18**

SAS-48 (AU 326)
The Effects of Computer Processing on the Examination of Financial Statements   Superseded

SAS-49
Letters for Underwriters   Superseded by SAS-72

SAS-50 (AU 625)
Reports on the Application of Accounting Prin-
ciples   Auditor's Special Reports, p. **12.28**

SAS-51 (AU 534)
Reporting on Financial Statements Prepared for
Use in Other Countries   Auditor's Special Reports, p. **12.33**

SAS-52 (AU 558)
Omnibus Statement on Auditing Standards—
1987
  • The Meaning of "Present Fairly in Confor-
    mity with Generally Accepted Accounting
    Principles" in the Independent Auditor's
    Report   Superseded by SAS-69
  • Required Supplementary Information   Completing the Audit, p. **10.17**
                                              Auditor's Reports, p. **11.42**
  • Reporting on Information Accompanying
    the Basic Financial Statements in Auditor-
    Submitted Documents   No reference

SAS-53 (AU 316)
The Auditor's Responsibility to Detect and Re-
port Errors and Irregularities   Internal Control, Errors, and Irregularities, p.
                                                 7.40, 7.75

SAS-54 (AU 317)
Illegal Acts by Clients   Internal Control, Errors, and Irregularities, p.
                                                 7.47

Cross-Reference

SAS-55 (AU 319)
Consideration of the Internal Control in a Financial Statement Audit (as amended)

Internal Control, Errors, and Irregularities, p. **7.07**

SAS-56 (AU 329)
Analytical Procedures

Evidence, p. **8.59**
Completing the Audit, p. **10.05**

SAS-57 (AU 342)
Auditing Accounting Estimates

Evidence, p. **8.42**

SAS-58 (AU 508)
Reports on Audited Financial Statements

Auditor's Reports, p. **11.05**

SAS-59 (AU 341)
The Auditor's Consideration of an Entity's Ability to Continue as a Going Concern

Evidence, p. **8.69**
Auditor's Reports, p. **11.37**

SAS-60 (AU 325)
Communication of Internal Control Structure Related Matters Noted in an Audit

Internal Control, Errors, and Irregularities, p. **7.31**

SAS-61 (AU 380)
Communication with Audit Committees

Completing the Audit, p. **10.24**

SAS-62 (AU 623)
Special Reports

Auditor's Special Reports, p. **12.04**

SAS-63
Compliance Auditing Applicable to Governmental Entities and Other Recipients of Governmental Financial Assistance

Superseded by SAS-68

SAS-64 (AU 341; 508; AU 543)
Omnibus Statement on Auditing Standards— 1990

Evidence, p. **8.74**
Auditor's Reports, p. **11.34**

SAS-65 (AU 322)
The Auditor's Consideration of the Internal Audit Function in an Audit of Financial Statements

Internal Control, Errors, and Irregularities, p. **7.52**
Evidence, p. **8.52**

SAS-66
Communication of Matters About Interim Financial Information Filed or to Be Filed with Specified Regulatory Agencies—An Amendment to SAS No. 36, Review of Interim Financial Information

Superseded by SAS-71

SAS-67 (AU 330)
The Confirmation Process

Evidence, p. **8.28**

SAS-68

Compliance Auditing Applicable to Governmental Entities and Other Recipients of Governmental Financial Assistance

Superseded by SAS-74

SAS-69 (AU 411)

The Meaning of "Present Fairly in Conformity with Generally Accepted Accounting Principles" in the Independent Auditor's Report

Generally Accepted Accounting Principles, p. **3.13**

SAS-70 (AU 324)

Reports on the Processing of Transactions by Service Organizations

Internal Control, Errors, and Irregularities, p. **7.58**

SAS-71 (AU 722)

Interim Financial Information

Interim Reviews, p. **13.04**

SAS-72 (AU 634)

Letters for Underwriters and Certain Other Requesting Parties

Interim Reviews, p. **13.31**

SAS-73 (AU 336)

Using the Work of a Specialist

Evidence, p. **8.46**

SAS-74 (AU 801)

Compliance Auditing Considerations in Audits of Governmental Entities and Recipients of Governmental Financial Assistance

Audits of State and Local Governmental Units, p. **23.19**

SAS-75

Engagements to Apply Agreed-Upon Procedures to Specified Elements, Accounts, or Items of a Financial Statement

Agreed-Upon Procedures Engagements, p. **17.04**

SAS-76

Amendments to Statement on Auditing Standards No. 72, Letters for Underwriters and Certain Other Requesting Parties

Interim Reviews, p. **13.32**

SAS-77

Amendments to Statements on Auditing Standards No. 22, "Planning and Supervision," No. 59, "The Auditor's Consideration of an Entity's Ability to Continue as a Going Concern," and No. 62, "Special Reports"

Evidence, p. **8.05**, Auditor's Report, p. **11.03**, and Auditor's Special Reports, p. **12.03**

SAS-78

Consideration of Internal Control in a Financial Statement Audit: An Amendment to SAS No. 55

Internal Control, Errors, and Irregularities, p. **7.05**

SAS-79

Amendments to Statement on Auditing Standards No. 58, "Reports on Audited Financial Statements"

Auditor's Report, p. **11.03**

AUDITING INTERPRETATIONS

Auditing Interpretations* provide guidance to the independent auditor in interpreting Statements on Standards (SASs) issued by the Auditing Standards Board (ASB). Auditing Interpretations are issued by the Audit Issues Task Force of the ASB and are reviewed by the ASB. Auditing Interpretations are not considered as authoritative as the SASs; however, a member of the AICPA may have to justify a departure from an Auditing Interpretation if the quality of the member's work is questioned.

ORIGINAL PRONOUNCEMENT	GAAS GUIDE REFERENCE
Section 311: Planning and Supervision (SAS-22)	
1. Communications Between the Auditor and Firm Personnel Responsible for Non-Audit Services (AU 9311.01–.03) (February 1980)	No reference
2. Planning Considerations for an Audit of a Federally Assisted Program (AU 9311.04–.34)	Withdrawn March 1989
3. Responsibility of Assistants for the Resolution of Accounting and Auditing Issues (AU 9311.35–.37) (February 1986)	Planning the Engagement, p. **6.07**
Section 315: Communications Between Predecessor and Successor Auditors (SAS-7)	
1. Determining the Predecessor Auditor (AU 9315.01–.05) (May 1985)	Pre-Engagement Planning, p. **5.06**
2. Restating Financial Statements Reported on by a Predecessor Auditor (AU 9315.06–.07) (September 1986)	Pre-Engagement Planning, p. **5.05**
3. Audits of Financial Statements That Had Been Previously Audited by a Predecessor Auditor (AU 9315.08–.18) (April 1995)	Pre-Engagement Planning, p. **5.06**
Section 317: Illegal Acts by Clients (SAS-54)	
1. Consideration of the Internal Control Structure in a Financial Statement Audit and the Foreign Corrupt Practices Act (AU 9317.01–.02) (October 1978)	No reference
2. Material Weaknesses in the Internal Control Structure and the Foreign Corrupt Practices Act (AU 9317.03–.06) (October 1978)	Internal Control, Errors, and Irregularities, p. **7.74**

---

* In the GAAS Guide Reference column, "No reference" is listed for those Auditing Interpretations that contain duplicate material already included elsewhere in this publication or that are directed to isolated events.

Section 324: Reports on the Processing of Transactions by Service Organizations (SAS-70)

1. Describing Tests of Operating Effectiveness and the Results of Such Tests (AU 9324.01–.03) (April 1995)

Internal Control, Errors, and Irregularities, p. **7.71**

2. Service Organizations That Use the Services of Other Service Organizations (Subservice Organizations) (AU 9324.04–.18) (April 1995)

Internal Control, Errors, and Irregularities, p. **7.72**

Section 325: Communication of Internal Control Structure Related Matters Noted in an Audit (SAS-60)

1. Reporting on the Existence of Material Weaknesses (AU 9325.01–.07) (February 1989)

Internal Control, Errors, and Irregularities, p. **7.36**

Section 326: Evidential Matter (SAS-31)

1. Evidential Matter for an Audit of Interim Financial Statements (AU 9326.01–.05) (February 1974)

No reference

2. The Effect of an Inability to Obtain Evidential Matter Relating to Income Tax Accruals (AU 9326.06–.17) (March 1981)

Completing the Audit, p. **10.14**
Auditor's Reports, p. **11.30**

3. The Auditor's Consideration of the Completeness Assertion (AU 9326.18–.21) (April 1986)

Evidence, p. **8.10**

Section 332: Long-Term Investments (SAS-1)

1. Evidential Matter for the Carrying Amount of Marketable Securities (AU 9332.01–.14) (January 1975)

No reference

2. Management Representations When Current Management Was Not Present During the Period Under Audit (Au 9333.05–.06) (October 1995)

Completing the Audit, p. **10.14**

Section 333: Client Representations (SAS-19)

1. Management Representations on Violations and Possible Violations of Laws and Regulations (AU 9333.01–.04) (March 1979)

Completing the Audit, p. **10.14**

Section 334: Related Parties (SAS-45)

1. Evaluating the Adequacy of Disclosure of Related Party Transactions (AU 9334.01–.05)

Withdrawn August 1983 by SAS-45

2. Disclosure of Commonly Controlled Parties (AU 9334.06–.09)

Withdrawn August 1983 by SAS-45

3. Definition of "Immediate Family" (AU 9334.10–.11)

Withdrawn August 1983 by SAS-45

4. Exchange of Information Between the Principal and Other Auditor on Related Parties (AU 9334.12–.13) (April 1979) — Evidence, p. **8.64**

5. Examination of Identified Related Party Transactions with a Component (AU 9334.14–.15) (April 1979) — Evidence, p. **8.65**

6. The Nature and Extent of Auditing Procedures for Examining Related Party Transactions (AU 9334.16–.21) (May 1986) — Evidence, p. **8.66**

Section 337: Inquiry of a Client's Lawyer Concerning Litigation, Claims, and Assessments (SAS-12)

1. Specifying Relevant Date in an Audit Inquiry Letter (AU 9337.01–.03) (March 1977) — Completing the Audit, p. **10.08**

2. Relationship Between Date of Lawyer's Response and Auditor's Report (AU 9337.04–.05) (March 1977) — Completing the Audit, p. **10.08**

3. Form of Audit Inquiry Letter When Client Represents That No Unasserted Claims and Assessments Exist (AU 9337.06–.07) (March 1977) — No reference

4. Documents Subject to Lawyer–Client Privilege (AU 9337.08–.09) (March 1977) — Completing the Audit, p. **10.07**

5. Alternative Wording of the Illustrative Audit Inquiry Letter to a Client's Lawyer (AU 9337.10–.14) (June 1983) — No reference

6. Client Has Not Consulted a Lawyer (AU 9337.15–.17) (June 1983) — Completing the Audit, p. **10.07, 10.13**

7. Assessment of a Lawyer's Evaluation of the Outcome of Litigation (AU 9337.18–.23) (June 1983) — Completing the Audit, p. **10.09**

8. Use of the Client's Inside Counsel in the Evaluation of Litigation, Claims, and Assessments (AU 9337.24–.27) (June 1983) — No reference

9. Use of Explanatory Language About the Attorney–Client Privilege or the Attorney Work-Product Privilege (AU 9337.28–.30) (February 1990) — Completing the Audit, p. **10.08**

Section 339: Working Papers (SAS-41)

1. Providing Access to or Photocopies of Working Papers to a Regulator (AU 9339.01–.15) (July 1994) — Evidence, p. **8.24**

Section 341: The Auditor's Consideration of an Entity' Ability to Continue as a Going Concern (SAS-59)

1. Eliminating a Going-Concern Explanatory Paragraph from a Reissued Report (9341.01–.02) (August 1995) — Evidence, p. **8.07, 8.69**

Section 342: Auditing Accounting Estimates (SAS-57)

1. Performance and Reporting Guidance Related to Fair Value Disclosures (AU 9342.01–.10) (February 1993) Evidence, p. **8.46**

Section 350: Audit Sampling (SAS-39)

1. Applicability of SAS-39 (AU 9350.01–.02) (January 1985) Sampling Techniques and Procedures, p. **9.03**

Section 380: Communication with Audit Committees (SAS-61)

1. Applicability of Section 380 (AU 9380.01–.03) (August 1993) Completing the Audit, p. **10.25**

Section 410: Adherence to Generally Accepted Accounting Principles (SAS-1)

1. Accounting Principles Recommended by Trade Associations (AU 9410.01–.03) Withdrawn August 1982 by SAS-43

2. The Impact of FASB Statement No. 2 on Auditor's Report Issued Prior to the Statement's Effective Date (AU 9410.04–.12) Superseded October 1979 by Interpretation No. 3

3. The Impact on an Auditor's Report of an FASB Statement Prior to the Statement's Effective Date (AU 9410.13–.18) (October 1979) Auditor's Reports, p. **11.17**

Section 411: The Meaning of "Present Fairly in Conformity with Generally Accepted Accounting Principles" in the Independent Auditor's Report (SAS-69)

1. The Auditor's Consideration of Accounting Principles Set Forth in Industry Audit and Accounting Guides (AU 9411.01–.04) Deleted September 1984

2. The Auditor's Consideration of Accounting Principles Promulgated by the Governmental Accounting Standards Board (AU 9411.05–.10) Withdrawn April 1988 by SAS-52

Section 420: Consistency of Application of Generally Accepted Accounting Principles (SAS-1)

1. The Effect of APB Opinion No. 30 on Consistency (AU 9420.01–.10) Superseded October 1979 by Interpretation No. 5

2. The Effect of APB Opinion No. 28 on Consistency (AU 9420.11–.15) (February 1974) Auditor's Reports, p. **11.19**

3. Impact on the Auditor's Report of FIFO to LIFO Change in Comparative Financial Statements (AU 9420.16–.21) (January 1975) Auditor's Reports, p. **11.19**

4. The Effect of FASB Statement No. 13 on Consistency (AU 9420.24–.27) Withdrawn March 1989

5. The Effects of Changes in Accounting Principles and Classification on Consistency (AU 9420.28–.31) Withdrawn December 1992

6. The Effect of FASB Statement No. 34 on Consistency (AU 9420.32–.43) Withdrawn March 1989

7. The Effect of FASB Statement No. 31 on Consistency (AU 9420.44–.51) Withdrawn March 1989

8. The Effect of Accounting Changes by an Investee on Consistency (AU 9420.52–.54) (July 1980) Evidence, p. **8.41**

9. The Effect of Adoption of FASB Statement No. 35 on Consistency (AU 9420.58–.63) Withdrawn March 1989

10. Change in Presentation of Accumulated Benefit Information in the Financial Statements of a Defined Benefit Pension Plan (AU 9420.64–.65) (December 1980) No reference

11. The Effect of the Adoption of FASB Statement No. 36 on Consistency (AU 9420.66–.68) Withdrawn March 1989

Section 504: Association with Financial Statements (SAS-26)

1. Annual Report Disclosure of Unaudited Fourth Quarter Interim Data (AU 9504.01–.07) (November 1979) Auditor's Reports, p. **11.45**

2. Association of the Auditor of an Acquired Company with Unaudited Statements in a Listing Application (9504.08–.12) Deleted May 1980

3. Association of the Auditor of the Acquiring Company with Unaudited Statements in a Listing Application (AU 9504.13–.14) Deleted May 1980

4. Auditor's Identification with Condensed Financial Data (AU 9504.15–.18) (November 1979) Interim Reviews, p. **13.58**

5. Applicability of Guidance on Reporting When Not Independent (AU 9504.19–.22) (November 1979) No reference

6. Reporting on Solvency (AU 9504.23–.35) Rescinded May 1988

Section 508: Reports on Audited Financial Statements (SAS-58)

1. Report of an Outside Inventory-Taking Firm as an Alternative Procedure for Observing Inventories (AU 9508.01–.06) (July 1975) Evidence, p. **8.38**

2. Reporting on Comparative Financial Statements of Nonprofit Organizations (AU 9508.07–.10) Superseded June 1977 by SAS-15

3. Reporting on Loss Contingencies (AU 9508.11–.14) — Superseded January 1989 by SAS-58

4. Reports on Consolidated Financial Statements That Include Supplementary Consolidating Information (AU 9508.15–.20) — Superseded December 1980 by SAS-29

5. Disclosures of Subsequent Events (AU 9508.21–.24) — Superseded January 1989 by SAS-58

6. The Materiality of Uncertainties (AU 9508.25–.28) — Superseded January 1989 by SAS-58

7. Reporting on an Uncertainty (AU 9508.29–.32) — Withdrawn August 1982 by SAS-43

8. Reporting on Financial Statements Prepared on a Liquidation Basis of Accounting (AU 9508.33–.38) (December 1984) — Auditor's Special Reports, p. **12.03**

9. Quantifying Departures from Generally Accepted Accounting Principles (AU 9508.39–.43) — Superseded January 1989 by SAS-58

10. Updated Reports Resulting from the Retroactive Suspension of Earnings per Share and Segment Information Disclosure Requirements (AU 9508.44–.48) — Withdrawn March 1989

11. Restating Financial Statements Reported on by a Predecessor Auditor (AU 9508.49–.50) — Withdrawn

12. Reference in Auditor's Standard Report to Management's Report (AU 9508.51–.52) (January 1989) — Auditor's Reports, p. **11.07**

Section 543: Part of Audit Performed by Other Independent Auditors (SAS-1)

1. Specific Procedures Performed by the Other Auditor at the Principal Auditor's Request (AU 9543.01–.03) (April 1979) — Evidence, p. **8.58**

2. Inquiries of the Principal Auditor by the Other Auditor (AU 9543.04–.07) (April 1979) — Evidence, p. **8.56**

3. Form of Inquiries of the Principal Auditor Made by the Other Auditor (AU 9543.08–.10) (April 1979) — Evidence, p. **8.56**

4. Form of Principal Auditor's Response to Inquiries from Other Auditors (AU 9543.11–.14) (April 1979) — Evidence, p. **8.57**

5. Procedures of the Principal Auditor (AU 9543.15–.17) (April 1979) — Evidence, p. **8.57**

6. Application of Additional Procedures Concerning the Audit Performed by the Other Auditor (AU 9543.18–.20) (December 1981) — Evidence, p. **8.57**

7. Reporting on Financial Statements Presented on a Comprehensive Annual Financial Report of a Governmental Entity When One Fund Has Been Audited by Another Auditor (AU 9543.21–.24) — Withdrawn December 1992

Section 550: Other Information in Documents Containing Audited Financial Statements (SAS-8)

1. Reports by Management on Internal Accounting Control (AU 9550.01–.06)

Superseded May 1994 by Interpretation Nos. 2 and 3

2. Reports by Management on the Internal Control Structure Over Financial Reporting (AU 9550.07–.11) (May 1994)

Internal Control, Errors, and Irregularities, p. **7.39**

3. Other References by Management to the Internal Control Structure Over Financial Reporting, Including References to the Independent Auditor (AU 9550.12–.15) (May 1994)

Internal Control, Errors, and Irregularities, p. **7.39**

Section 558: Required Supplementary Information (SAS-52)

1. Supplementary Oil and Gas Reserve Information (AU 9558.01–.06) (February 1989)

Completing the Audit, p. **10.19**

Section 561: Subsequent Discovery of Facts Existing at the Date of the Auditor's Report (SAS-1)

1. Auditor Association with Subsequently Discovered Information When the Auditor Has Resigned or Been Discharged (AU 9561.01–.02) (February 1989)

Completing the Audit, p. **10.23**

Section 623: Special Reports (SAS-62)

1. Auditor's Report Under Employee Retirement Income Security Act of 1974 (AU 9623.01–.08)

Withdrawn February 1983

2. Reports on Elements, Accounts, or Items of a Financial Statement That Are Presented in Conformity with GAAP (AU 9623.09–.10)

Withdrawn March 1989 by SAS-62

3. Compliance with the Foreign Corrupt Practices Act of 1977 (AU 9623.11–.14)

Deleted October 1993

4. Reports on Engagements Solely to Meet State Regulatory Examination Requirements (AU 9623.15–.16)

Deleted April 1981 by SAS-35

5. Financial Statements Prepared in Accordance with Accounting Practices Specified in an Agreement (AU 9623.17–.25)

Withdrawn March 1989 by SAS-62

6. Reporting on Special-Purpose Financial Presentations (AU 9623.26–.31)

Withdrawn March 1989 by SAS-62

7. Understanding of Agreed-Upon Procedures (AU 9623.32–.33)

Deleted April 1981 by SAS-35

8. Adequacy of Disclosure in Financial Statements Prepared on a Comprehensive Basis of Accounting Other Than Generally Accepted Accounting Principles (AU 9623.34–.39)

Withdrawn March 1989 by SAS-62

9. Auditors' Special Reports on Property and Liability Insurance Companies' Loss Reserves (AU 9623.40–.46) (May 1981)
Auditor's Special Reports, p. **12.14**

10. Reports on the Financial Statements Included in Internal Revenue Form 990, "Return of Organizations Exempt from Income Tax" (AU 9623.47–.54) (July 1982)
Auditor's Special Reports, p. **12.25**

11. Reporting on Current-Value Financial Statements That Supplement Historical-Cost Financial Statements in a General-Use Presentation of Real Estate Entities (AU 9623.55–.59) (July 1990)
Auditor's Special Reports, **12.06**

12. Evaluation of the Appropriateness of Informative Disclosures in Insurance Enterprises' Financial Statements Prepared on a Statutory Basis (AU 9623.60–.79) (December 1991)
Auditor's Special Reports, p. **12.08**

13. Reporting on a Special-Purpose Financial Statement That Results in an Incomplete Presentation But Is Otherwise in Conformity with Generally Accepted Accounting Principles (AU 9623.80–.87) (May 1995)
Auditor's Special Reports, p. **12.19**

Section 634: Letters for Underwriters and Certain Other Requesting Parties (SAS-72)

1. Letters to Directors Relating to Annual Reports on Form 10-K (AU 9634.01–.09) (April 1981)
Interim Reviews, p. **13.31**

2. Negative Assurance on Unaudited Condensed Interim Financial Statements Attached to Comfort Letters (AU 9634.10–.12)
Deleted April 1993 by SAS-72

Section 642: Reporting on Internal Accounting Control

1. Pre-Award Surveys (AU 9642.01–.03)
Deleted October 1993

2. Award Survey Made in Conjunction with an Audit (AU 9642.04–.05)
Deleted October 1993

3. Reporting on Matters Not Covered by Government-Established Criteria (AU 9642.06–.07)
Deleted October 1993

4. Limited Scope (AU 9642.08–.09)
Deleted October 1993

5. Compliance with the Foreign Corrupt Practices Act of 1977 (AU 9642.10–.13)
Deleted October 1993

6. Reports on Internal Accounting Control of Trust Departments of Banks (AU 9642.14–.17)
Deleted October 1993

7. Report Required by U.S. General Accounting Office (AU 9642.18–.25)
Superseded by SAS-60

8. Form of Report on Internal Accounting Control Based Solely on a Study and Evaluation Made as Part of an Audit (AU 9642.26–.32)
Superseded January 1989 by SAS-60

9. Reporting on Internal Accounting Control Based Solely on an Audit When a Minimum Study and Evaluation Is Made (AU 9642.33–.34)　　　Superseded January 1989 by SAS-60

10. Report Required by U.S. General Accounting Office Based on a Financial and Compliance Audit When a Study and Evaluation Does Not Extend Beyond the Preliminary Review Phase (AU 9642.35–.36)　　　Superseded January 1989 by SAS-60

11. Restricted Purpose Report Required by Law to Be Made Available to the Public (AU 9642.37–.38)　　　Superseded January 1989 by SAS-60

12. Reporting on Internal Accounting Control "Compliance with the Currency and Foreign Transactions Reporting Act" (AU 9642.39–.41)　　　Deleted October 1993

Section 711: Filings Under Federal Securities Statutes (SAS-37)

1. Subsequent Events Procedures for Shelf Registration Statements Updated After the Original Effective Date (AU 9711.01–.11) (May 1983)　　　Interim Reviews, p. **13.29**

2. Consenting to Be Named as an Expert in an Offering Document in Connection with Securities Offerings Other Than Those Registered Under the Securities Act of 1933 (AU 9711.12–.15) (June 1992)　　　Interim Reviews, p. **13.30**

3. Consenting to the Use of an Audit Report in an Offering Document in Securities Offerings Other Than One Registered Under the Securities Act of 1933 (AU 9711.16–.17) (June 1992)　　　Interim Reviews, p. **13.30**

STATEMENTS ON STANDARDS FOR ACCOUNTANTS' SERVICES ON PROSPECTIVE FINANCIAL INFORMATION

> Statements on Standards for Accountants' Services on Prospective Financial Information are issued by the Auditing Standards Board. These Statements are issued under the authority of Rules 201 and 202 of the AICPA's Code of Professional Conduct. A member of the AICPA must be prepared to justify departures from guidelines established by a Statement on Standards for Accountants' Services on Prospective Financial Information.

ORIGINAL PRONOUNCEMENT	GAAS GUIDE REFERENCE
Financial Forecasts and Projections (AT 200)[1]	Prospective Financial Statements, p. **15.03**

---

[1] In April 1993, the Statement on Standards for Accountants' Services on Prospective Financial Information (Financial Forecasts and Projections) was recodified as part of SSAE-1.

[2] In April 1993, these three pronouncements were recodified as SSAE-1.

STATEMENTS ON STANDARDS FOR ATTESTATION ENGAGEMENTS

Statements on Standards for Attestation Engagements are issued jointly by the Auditing Standards Board, the Accounting and Review Services Committee, and the Management Consulting Executive Committee. These Statements are issued under the authority of Rules 201 and 202 of the AICPA's Code of Professional Conduct. A member of the AICPA must be prepared to justify departures from guidelines established by a Statement on Standards for Attestation Engagements.

ORIGINAL PRONOUNCEMENT	GAAS GUIDE REFERENCE
SSAE-1 (AT 100; AT 200; AT 300)	
Codification of Statements on Standards for Attestation Engagements	
• Attestation Standards (AT 100) (March 1986)[2]	Attest Engagements, p. **16.05, 16.07**
• Financial Forecasts and Projections (AT 200) (December 1987)[2]	Prospective Financial Statements, p. **15.03** Attest Engagements, p. **16.06** Agreed-Upon Procedures Engagements, p. **17.28**
• Reporting on Pro Forma Financial Information (AT 300) (September 1988)[2]	Attest Engagements, p. **16.06, 16.28**
SSAE-2 (AT 400)	
Reporting on an Entity's Internal Control Structure Over Financial Reporting (May 1993)	Attest Engagements, p. **16.37** Agreed-Upon Procedures Engagements, p. **17.28**
SSAE-3 (AT 500)	
Compliance Attestation (December 1993)	Attest Engagements, p. **16.65**
SSAE-4 (AT 100; AT 200; AT 400; AT 500; AT 600)	
Agreed-Upon Procedures Engagements (September 1995)	Agreed-Upon Procedures Engagements, p. **17.17**
SSAE-5 (AT 100)	
Amendment to Statement on Standards for Attestation Engagements No. 1, Attestation Standards (November 1995)	Attest Engagements, p. **16.67**
SSAE-6 (AT 400)	
Reporting on an Entity's Internal Control Over Financial Reporting: An Amendment to Statement on Standards for Attestation Engagements No. 2 (December 1995)	Agreed-Upon Procedures Engagements, p. **17.17**

ATTESTATION INTERPRETATIONS

Statements on Standards for Attestation Engagements Interpretations provide guidance to the accountant in interpreting the Statements on Standards for Attestation Engagements issued by the Auditing Standards Board (ASB). Statements on Standards for Attestation Engagement Interpretations are issued by the Audit Issues Task Force of the ASB and are reviewed by members of the ASB. Statements on Standards for Attestation Engagements Interpretations are not considered as authoritative as the actual Statements on Standards for Attestation Engagements. However, a member of the AICPA may have to justify a departure from an Interpretation if the quality of the work is questioned.

ORIGINAL PRONOUNCEMENT	GAAS GUIDE REFERENCE
AT Section 100: Attestation Standards	
1. Defense Industry Questionnaire on Business Ethics and Conduct (AT 9100.01–.32) (August 1987)	Attest Engagements, p. **16.08**
2. Responding to Requests for Reports on Matters Relating to Solvency (AT 9100.33–.44) (May 1988)	Attest Engagements, p. **16.26** Agreed-Upon Procedures Engagements, p. **17.05**
3. Applicability of Attestation Standards to Litigation Services (AT 9100.47–.55) (July 1990)	Attest Engagements, p. **16.05**

INDUSTRY AUDIT GUIDES

An Audit Guide is published for the guidance of members of the AICPA in a particular area. It does not have the authority of a pronouncement issued by the Auditing Standards Board. However, an Audit Guide represents the considered opinion of a committee, subcommittee, or task force that has been charged with the responsibility to address the area and, as such, contains the best thoughts of the profession of the best practices in an area. The AICPA Accounting Standards Executive Committee and members of the AICPA Auditing Standards Board believe that the recommendations established by the guides are consistent with existing standards and principles covered by Rules 202 and 203 of the AICPA Code of Professional Conduct. A member of the AICPA may have to justify a departure from a guide if the quality of the work is questioned.

ORIGINAL PRONOUNCEMENT	GAAS GUIDE REFERENCE
Audit Sampling	Sampling Techniques and Procedures, p. **9.03**
Audits of Certain Nonprofit Organizations	Audits of Not-for-Profit Organizations, p. **22.03**

Audits of Construction Contractors

Audits of Construction Contractors, p. **18.03**

Audits of Credit Unions

Audits of Credit Unions, p. **19.03**

Audits of Employee Benefit Plans

Audits of Employee Benefit Plans, p. **20.03**

Audits of Providers of Health Care Services

Audits of Health Care Providers, p. **21.03**

Audits of State and Local Governmental Units

Audits of State and Local Governmental Units, p. **23.03**

Consideration of the Internal Control Structure in a Financial Statement Audit

Internal Control, Errors, and Irregularities, p. **7.05**

Guide for Prospective Financial Information

Prospective Financial Statements, **15.03**

STATEMENTS OF POSITION OF THE ACCOUNTING STANDARDS DIVISIONS

Statements of Position (SOPs) of the Accounting Standards Division are issued by the AICPA Accounting Standards Executive Committee. An AICPA SOP is an authoritative source of generally accepted accounting principles if the accounting issue is not addressed by a pronouncement covered by Rule 203 of the AICPA Code of Professional Conduct. A member who decides not to follow the guidance established by a SOP should be prepared to justify such departure.

SOP 78-10

Accounting Principles and Reporting Practices for Certain Nonprofit Organizations (as a-mended)

Audits of Not-for-Profit Organizations, p. **22.03**

SOP 81-1

Accounting for Performance of Construction-Type and Certain Production-Type Contracts

Audits of Construction Contractors, p. **18.03**

SOP 82-1

Accounting and Financial Reporting for Personal Financial Statements

Compilation and Review Engagements, p. **14.71**

SOP 87-2

Accounting for Joint Costs of Informational Material and Activities for Not-for-Profit Organizations That Include a Fund Raising Appeal

Audits of Not-for-Profit Organizations, p. **22.13**

Cross-Reference

SOP 90-3

Definition of the Term *Substantially the Same* for Holders of Debt Instruments, as Used in Certain Audit Guide and a Statement of Position
Audits of Credits Unions, p. **19.04**

SOP 92-3

Accounting for Foreclosed Assets
Audits of Credit Unions, p. **19.04**

SOP 94-2

The Application of Requirements of Accounting Research Bulletins, Opinions of the Accounting Principles Board, and Statements and Interpretations of the Financial Accounting Standards Board to Not-for-Profit Organizations
Generally Accepted Accounting Principles, p. **3.13**

SOP 94-3

Reporting of Related Entities by Not-for-Profit Organizations
Audits of Not-for-Profit Organizations, p. **22.06**

SOP 94-4

Reporting of Investment Contracts Held by Health and Welfare Benefit Plans and Defined-Contribution Pension Plans
Audits of Employee Benefit Plans, p. **20.03**

STATEMENTS OF POSITION OF THE AUDITING STANDARDS DIVISION

Statements of Position (SOPs) are issued by designated committees of the AICPA and address application of generally accepted auditing standards to specific industries, transactions, or other auditing issues. The recommendations made in a SOP have been reviewed by the AICPA Auditing Standards Board for consistency with existing auditing standards. A member who decides not to follow the guidance established by a SOP should be prepared to justify such departure.

SOP 92-4

Auditing Insurance Entities' Loss Reserves
Audits of Employee Benefit Plans, p. **20.03**
Evidence, p. **8.47**

SOP 92-2

Questions and Answers on the Term "Reasonably Objective Basis" and Other Issues Affecting
Prospective Financial Statements Prospective Financial Statements, p. **15.03**

SOP 92-9

Audits of Not-for-Profit Organizations Receiving Federal Awards (as revised)
Audits of Health Care Providers, p. **21.20**

STATEMENTS ON STANDARDS FOR ACCOUNTING AND REVIEW SERVICES

Statements on Standards for Accounting and Review Services are issued by the Accounting and Review Services Committee in connection with unaudited statements or information of a nonpublic entity. Under Rule 202 of the Code of Professional Conduct, a member must be prepared to justify departures from Statements on Standards for Accounting and Review Services.

ORIGINAL PRONOUNCEMENT	GAAS GUIDE REFERENCE
SSARS-1 (AR 100)	
Compilation and Review of Financial Statements	Compilation and Review Engagements, p. **14.05, 14.11**
SSARS-2 (AR 200)	
Reporting on Comparative Financial Statements	Compilation and Review Engagements, p. **14.57**
SSARS-3 (AR 300)	
Compilation Reports on Financial Statements Included in Certain Prescribed Forms	Compilation and Review Engagements, p. **14.11, 14.46**
SSARS-4 (AR 400)	
Communication Between Predecessor and Successor Accountants	Compilation and Review Engagements, p. **14.11, 14.14, 14.62**
SSARS-5	
Reporting on Compiled Financial Statements	Deleted by SSARS-7
SSARS-6 (AR 600)	
Reporting on Personal Financial Statements Included in Written Personal Financial Plans	Compilation and Review Engagements, p. **14.69**
SSARS-7	
Omnibus Statement on Standards for Accounting and Review Services—1992	Compilation and Review Engagements, p. **14.10**

ACCOUNTING AND REVIEW SERVICES INTERPRETATIONS

Accounting and Review Services Interpretations provide guidance to the accountant in interpreting the Statements on Standards for Accounting and Review Services (SSARS) issued by the AICPA. Accounting and Review Services Interpretations are issued by the staff of the Accounting and Review Services Committee of the AICPA and are reviewed by members of that Committee. Accounting and Review Services Interpretations are not considered as authoritative as the actual Statements on Standards for Accounting and Review Services. However, a member of the AICPA may have to justify any departure from an Accounting and Review Services Interpretation, if the quality of the work is questioned.

ORIGINAL PRONOUNCEMENT   GAAS GUIDE REFERENCE

AR Section 100: Compilation and Review of Financial Statements

1. Omission of Disclosures in Reviewed Financial Statements (AR 9100.01–.02) (December 1979)

    Compilation and Review Engagements, p. **14.51**

2. Financial Statements Included in SEC Filings (AR 9100.03–.05) (December 1979)

    Compilation and Review Engagements, p. **14.20**

3. Reporting on the Highest Level of Service (AR 9100.06–.12) (December 1979)

    Compilation and Review Engagements, p. **14.35**

4. Discovery of Information After the Date of the Accountant's Report (AR 9100.13–.15) (November 1980)

    Compilation and Review Engagements, p. **14.45, 14.53**

5. Planning and Supervision (AR 9100.16–.17) (August 1981)

    Compilation and Review Engagements, p. **14.12, 14.32**

6. Withdrawal from Compilation or Review Engagement (AR 9100.18–.22) (August 1981)

    Compilation and Review Engagements, p. **14.38**

7. Reporting When There Are Significant Departures from Generally Accepted Accounting Principles (AR 9100.23–.26) (August 1981)

    Compilation and Review Engagements, p. **14.05**

8. Reports on Specified Elements, Accounts, or Items of a Financial Statement (AR 9100.27–.28) (November 1981, as amended)

    Compilation and Review Engagements, p. **14.06**

9. Reporting When Management Has Elected to Omit Substantially All Disclosures (AR 9100.29–.30) (May 1982)

    Compilation and Review Engagements, p. **14.40**

10. Reporting on Tax Returns (AR 9100.31–.32) (November 1982)

    Compilation and Review Engagements, p. **14.09**

11. Reporting on Uncertainties (AR 9100.33–.40) (December 1982)

    Compilation and Review Engagements, p. **14.42**

12. Reporting on a Comprehensive Basis of Accounting Other Than Generally Accepted Accounting Principles (AR 9100.41–.45) (December 1982, as revised)

    Compilation and Review Engagements, p. **14.43**

13. Additional Procedures (AR 9100.46–.49) (March 1983)

    Compilation and Review Engagements, p. **14.26**

14. Reporting on Financial Statements When the Scope of the Accountant's Procedures Has Been Restricted (AR 9100.50–.53)

    Withdrawn April 1990

15. Differentiating a Financial Statement Presentation from a Trial Balance (AR 9100.54–.57) (September 1990)

    Compilation and Review Engagements, p. **14.07**

16. Determining if the Accountant Has "Submitted" Financial Statements Even When Not Engaged to Compile or Review Financial Statements (AR 9100.58–.60)

    Withdrawn November 1992 by SSARS-7

17. Submitting Draft Financial Statements (AR 9100.61–.62) (September 1990)

Compilation and Review Engagements, p. **14.06, 14.35**

18. Special-Purpose Financial Presentations to Comply with Contractual Agreements or Regulatory Provisions (AR 9100.63–.72) (September 1990)

Compilation and Review Engagements, p. **14.19**

19. Reporting When Financial Statements Contain a Departure from Promulgated Accounting Principles That Prevents the Financial Statements from Being Misleading (AR 9100.73–.75) (February 1991)

Compilation and Review Engagements, p. **14.05**

20. Applicability of Statements on Standards for Accounting and Review Services to Litigation Services (AR 9100.76–.79) (May 1991)

Compilation and Review Engagements, p. **14.10**

AR Section 200: Reporting on Comparative Financial Statements

1. Reporting on Financial Statements That Previously Did Not Omit Substantially All Disclosures (AR 9200.01–.04) (November 1980)

Compilation and Review Engagements, p. **14.40**

AR Section 300: Compilation Reports on Financial Statements Included in Certain Prescribed Forms

1. Omission of Disclosures in Financial Statements Included in Certain Prescribed Forms (AR 9300.01–.03) (May 1982)

Compilation and Review Engagements, p. **14.48**

AR Section 400: Communication Between Predecessor and Successor Accountants

1. Reports on the Application of Accounting Principles (AR 9400.01–.05) (August 1987)

Compilation and Review Engagements, p. **14.69**

AR Section 600: Reporting on Personal Financial Statements Included in Written Personal Financial Plans

1. Submitting a Personal Financial Plan to a Client's Advisers (AR 9600.01–.03) (May 1991)

Compilation and Review Engagements, p. **14.70**

STATEMENTS ON QUALITY CONTROL STANDARDS

Statements on Quality Control Standards are issued by the AICPA's Quality Control Standards Committee. The standards apply to audit, compilation, review, and other services governed by standards issued by the Auditing Standard Board or the Accounting Review and Services Committee. Members who do not observe the standards established by Statements on Quality Control Standards may be called upon to justify such departures.

Cross-Reference

ORIGINAL PRONOUNCEMENT   GAAS GUIDE REFERENCE

SQCS-1
System of Quality Control for a CPA Firm   Superseded

SQCS-2 (QC-10)
System Quality Control for a CPA Firm's Accounting and Auditing Practice   Responsibility and Function of the Independent Auditor, p. **2.06**

SQC-3 (QC-10)
Monitoring a CPA Firms' Accounting and Auditing Practice   Responsibility and Function of the Independent Auditor, p. **2.06**

QUALITY CONTROL INTERPRETATIONS

Interpretations of quality control standards are issued by the AICPA's Quality Control Standards Committee. Interpretations do not have the authority of statements on quality control standards issued by the AICPA Quality Control Standards Committee. However, members should be aware that they may be called upon to justify departures from interpretations.

ORIGINAL PRONOUNCEMENT   GAAS GUIDE REFERENCE

QC Section 10-1: System of Quality Control for a CPA Firm

1. The Relationship Between Inspection and Monitoring (QC 10-1.01–.02) (July 1980)   Superseded by SQCS–2

2. Implementation of Inspection in CPA Firms (QC 10-1.03–.19) (July 1980)   Superseded by SQCS–2

3. Documentation of Compliance with a System of Quality Control (QC 10-1.20–.21) (June 1982)   Superseded by SQCS–2

CODE OF PROFESSIONAL CONDUCT

A member engaged in the practice of public accounting must observe all the Rules of Conduct. A member not engaged in the practice of public accounting must observe Rule 102 (Integrity and Objectivity) and Rule 501 (Acts Discreditable).

ORIGINAL PRONOUNCEMENT   GAAS GUIDE REFERENCE

Rule 101 (ET 101)
Independence   Code of Professional Conduct, p. **24.05**

Rule 102 (ET 102)
Integrity and Objectivity   Code of Professional Conduct, p. **24.20**

Rule 201 (ET 201)
General Standards   Code of Professional Conduct, p. **24.22**

Rule 202 (ET 202)
Compliance with Standards   Code of Professional Conduct, p. **24.24**

Rule 203 (ET 203)
Accounting Principles   Code of Professional Conduct, p. **24.26**

Rule 301 (ET 301)
Confidential Client Information   Code of Professional Conduct, p. **24.28**

Rule 302 (ET 302)
Contingent Fees   Code of Professional Conduct, p. **24.30**

Rule 401
Encroachment (Revoked 1977)   No reference

Rule 402
Offers of Employment (Revoked 1979)   No reference

Rule 501 (ET 501)
Acts Discreditable   Code of Professional Conduct, p. **24.33**

Rule 502 (ET 502)
Advertising and Other Forms of Solicitation Code of Professional Conduct, p. **24.35**

Rule 503 (ET 503)
Commissions and Referral Fees   Code of Professional Conduct, p. **24.36**

Rule 504
Incompatible Occupations (Revoked 1988)   Code of Professional Conduct, p. **24.38**

Rule 505 (ET 505)
Form of Organization and Name   Code of Professional Conduct, p. **24.38**

INTERPRETATIONS OF RULES OF CONDUCT

Interpretations of Rules of Conduct of the Code of Professional Conduct are prepared by the professional ethics division's executive committee to provide guidelines as to the scope and application of the Rules but are not intended to limit such scope or application. A member who departs from such guidelines shall have the burden of justifying such departure in any disciplinary hearing.

ORIGINAL PRONOUNCEMENT   GAAS GUIDE REFERENCE

RULE 101

101-1
Interpretation of Rule 101   Code of Professional Conduct, p. **24.08**

Cross-Reference

101-2

Former Practitioners and Firm Independence
Code of Professional Conduct, p. **24.09**

101-3

Accounting Services
Code of Professional Conduct, p. **24.09**

101-4

Honorary Directorships and Trusteeships of Not-for-Profit Organizations
Code of Professional Conduct, p. **24.09**

101-5

Loans from Financial Institution Clients and Related Terminology
Code of Professional Conduct, p. **24.10**

101-6

The Effect of Actual or Threatened Litigation on Independence
Code of Professional Conduct, p. **24.12**

101-7

Application of Rule 101 to Professional Personnel
Deleted

101-8

Effect on Independence of Financial Interest in Nonclients Having Investor or Investee Relationships with a Member's Client
Code of Professional Conduct, p. **24.12**

101-9

The Meaning of Certain Independence Terminology and the Effect of Family Relationships on Independence
Code of Professional Conduct, p. **24.14**

101-10

The Effect on Independence of Relationships with Entities Included in the Governmental Financial Statements
Code of Professional Conduct, p. **24.16**

101-11

Independence and the Performance of Professional Services under the Statements on Standards for Attestation Engagements and Statement on Auditing Standards No. 75, "Engagements to Apply Agreed-upon Procedures to Specified Elements, Accounts, or Items of a Financial Statement"
Code of Professional Conduct, p. **24.18**

101-12

Independence and Cooperative Agreements with Clients
Code of Professional Conduct, p. **24.20**

RULE 102

102-1

Knowing Misrepresentations in the Preparation of Financial Statements or Records
Code of Professional Conduct, p. **24.21**

102-2
Conflicts of Interest — Code of Professional Conduct, p. **24.21**

102-3
Obligations of a Member to His or Her Employer's External Accountant — Code of Professional Conduct, p. **24.21**

102-4
Subordination of Judgment by a Member — Code of Professional Conduct, p. **24.21**

102-5
Applicability of Rule 102 to Members Performing Educational Services — Code of Professional Conduct, p. **24.22**

102-6
Professional Services Involving Client Advocacy — Code of Professional Conduct, p. **24.22**

RULE 201
201-1
Competence — Code of Professional Conduct, p. **24.23**

201-2
Forecasts — Deleted

201-3
Shopping for Accounting and Auditing Standards — Deleted

201-4
Definition of the Term *Engagement* as Used in Rule 201—General Standards — Deleted

RULE 203
203-1
Departures from Established Accounting Principles — Code of Professional Conduct, p. **24.27**

203-2
Status of FASB and GASB Interpretations — Code of Professional Conduct, p. **24.27**

203-3
FASB Statements that Establish Standards for Disclosure Outside of the Basic Financial Statements — Deleted

203-4
Responsibility of Employees for Preparation of Financial Statements in Conformity with GAAP — Code of Professional Conduct, p. **24.28**

Cross-Reference

RULE 301

301-1

Confidential Information and Technical Standards Deleted

301-2

Disclosure of Confidential Client Information in Certain Circumstances Deleted

301-3

Confidential Information and the Purchase, Sale, or Merger of a Practice Code of Professional Conduct, p. **24.29**

RULE 302

302-1

Contingent Fees in Tax Matters Code of Professional Conduct, p. **24.32**

RULE 501

501-1

Retention of Client Records Code of Professional Conduct, p. **24.34**

501-2

Discrimination in Employment Practices Code of Professional Conduct, p. **24.34**

501-3

Failure to Follow Standards and / or Procedures or Other Requirements in Governmental Audits Code of Professional Conduct, p. **24.34**

501-4

Negligence in the Preparation of Financial Statements or Records Code of Professional Conduct, p. **24.34**

501-5

Failure to Follow Requirements of Governmental Bodies, Commissions, or Other Regulatory Agencies in Performing Attest or Similar Services Code of Professional Conduct, p. **24.34**

501-6

Solicitation or Disclosure of CPA Examination Questions and Answers Code of Professional Conduct, p. **24.35**

RULE 502

502-1

Informational Advertising Deleted

502-2

False, Misleading, or Deceptive Acts in Advertising or Solicitation Code of Professional Conduct, p. **24.36**

502-3

Other Forms of Solicitation   Deleted

502-4

Self-Designation as Expert or Specialist   Deleted

502-5

Engagements Obtained Through Efforts of
Third Parties   Code of Professional Conduct, p. **24.36**

Rule 503

503-1

Fees in Payment for Services   Deleted

Rule 505

505-1

Investment in Accounting Organization   Code of Professional Conduct, p. **24.40**

505-2

Application of Rules of Conduct to Members
Who Operate a Separate Business   Code of Professional Conduct, p. **24.40**

ETHICS RULINGS—CODE OF PROFESSIONAL CONDUCT

Ethics rulings are formal rulings made by the executive committee of the AICPA professional ethics division. These rulings summarize the application of Rules of Conduct and
Interpretations to a particular set of circumstances. AICPA members who depart from
such rulings in similar circumstances will be requested to justify such departures.

ORIGINAL PRONOUNCEMENT	GAAS GUIDE REFERENCE
Rules 101 and 102	
1 — Acceptance of a Gift	Code of Professional Conduct, p. **24.41**
2 — Association Membership	Code of Professional Conduct, p. **24.41**
3 — Member as Signer or Cosigner of Checks	Code of Professional Conduct, p. **24.41**
4 — Payroll Preparation Services	Code of Professional Conduct, p. **24.41**
5 — Deleted	No reference
6 — Member's Spouse as Accountant of Client	Code of Professional Conduct, p. **24.41**
7 — Member Providing Contract Services	Code of Professional Conduct, p. **24.41**
8 — Member Providing Advisory Services	Code of Professional Conduct, p. **24.42**
9 — Member as Representative of Creditor's Committee	Code of Professional Conduct, p. **24.42**
10 — Member as Legislator	Code of Professional Conduct, p. **24.42**
11 — Member as Executor or Trustee	Code of Professional Conduct, p. **24.42**
12 — Member as Trustee	Code of Professional Conduct, p. **24.42**

13 — Deleted	No reference
14 — Member on Board of Directors of Federated Fund-Raising Organization	Code of Professional Conduct, p. **24.42**
15 — Deleted	No reference
16 — Member on Board of Directors of Non-profit Social Club	Code of Professional Conduct, p. **24.42**
17 — Member of Social Club	Code of Professional Conduct, p. **24.43**
18 — Deleted	No reference
19 — Member on Deferred Compensation Committee	Code of Professional Conduct, p. **24.43**
20 — Member Serving on Governmental Advisory Unit	Code of Professional Conduct, p. **24.43**
21 — Member as Director and Auditor of the Entity's Profit Sharing Trust	Code of Professional Conduct, p. **24.43**
22–27— Deleted	No reference
28 — Cash Account with Brokerage Client	Superseded by Ethics Ruling No. 59
29 — Member as Bondholder	Code of Professional Conduct, p. **24.43**
30 — Deleted	No reference
31 — Financial Interest in a Cooperative, Condominium Association, Planned Unit Development, Homeowners Association, Timeshare Development, or Other Common Interest Realty Association	Code of Professional Conduct, p. **24.44**
32 — Deleted	No reference
33 — Member as a Participant in Employee Benefit Plan	Code of Professional Conduct, p. **24.44**
34 — Deleted	No reference
35 — Stockholder in Mutual Funds	Code of Professional Conduct, p. **24.44**
36 — Participant in Investment Club	Code of Professional Conduct, p. **24.44**
37 — Deleted	No reference
38 — Member as Co-Fiduciary with Client Bank	Code of Professional Conduct, p. **24.44**
39 — Member as Officially Appointed Stock Transfer Agent or Registrar	Code of Professional Conduct, p. **24.44**
40 — Deleted	No reference
41 — Member as Auditor of Insurance Company	Code of Professional Conduct, p. **24.44**
42–43— Deleted	No reference
44 — Past Due Billings	Superseded by Ethics Ruling No. 52
45 — Deleted	No reference
46 — Member as General Counsel	Superseded by Ethics Ruling No. 51
47 — Deleted	No reference
48 — Faculty Member as Auditor of a Student Fund	Code of Professional Conduct, p. **24.45**
49 — Investor and Investee Companies	Superseded by Interpretation 101-8
50 — Deleted	No reference
51 — Member Providing Legal Services	Code of Professional Conduct, p. **24.45**
52 — Unpaid Fees	Code of Professional Conduct, p. **24.45**
53 — Deleted	No reference

54 — Member Providing Appraisal, Valuation, or Actuarial Services — Code of Professional Conduct, p. **24.45**

55 — Independence During Systems Implementation — Code of Professional Conduct, p. **24.45**

56 — Executive Search — Code of Professional Conduct, p. **24.46**

57 — Deleted — No reference

58 — Member as Lessor — Code of Professional Conduct, p. **24.46**

59 — Deleted — No reference

60 — Employee Benefit Plans—Member's Relationships with Participating Employer(s) — Code of Professional Conduct, p. **24.46**

61 — Participation of Member's Spouse in Client's Stock Ownership Plans (Including an ESOP) — Code of Professional Conduct, p. **24.46**

62–63— Deleted — No reference

64 — Member on Board of Organization for Which Client Raises Funds — Code of Professional Conduct, p. **24.46**

65 — Use of the CPA Designation by Member Not in Public Practice — Code of Professional Conduct, p. **24.47**

66 — Member's Retirement or Savings Plan Has Financial Interest in Client — Code of Professional Conduct, p. **24.47**

67 — Servicing of Loan — Code of Professional Conduct, p. **24.47**

68 — Blind Trust — Code of Professional Conduct, p. **24.47**

69 — Investment with a General Partner — Code of Professional Conduct, p. **24.47**

70 — Member's Depository Relationship with Client Financial Institution — Code of Professional Conduct, p. **24.47**

71 — Use of Nonindependent CPA Firm on an Engagement — Code of Professional Conduct, p. **24.47**

72 — Member on Advisory Board of Client — Code of Professional Conduct, p. **24.48**

73 — Meaning of the Period of a Professional Engagement — Code of Professional Conduct, p. **24.48**

74 — Audits, Reviews, or Compilations and a Lack of Independence — Code of Professional Conduct, p. **24.48**

75 — Member Joining Client Credit Union — Code of Professional Conduct, p. **24.48**

76 — Deleted — No reference

77 — Individual Considering or Accepting Employment with the Client — Code of Professional Conduct, p. **24.48**

78 — Deleted — No reference

79 — Member's Investment in a Partnership That Invests in a Member's Client — Code of Professional Conduct, p. **24.49**

80 — The Meaning of a Joint Closely Held Business Investment — Code of Professional Conduct, p. **24.49**

81 — Member's Investment in a Limited Partnership — Code of Professional Conduct, p. **24.49**

82 — Campaign Treasurer — Code of Professional Conduct, p. **24.49**

83–84— Deleted — No reference

85 — Bank Director — Code of Professional Conduct, p. **24.50**

86 — Partially Secured Loans — Code of Professional Conduct, p. **24.50**

87 — Loan Commitment or Line of Credit — Code of Professional Conduct, p. **24.50**

88 — Loans to Partnership in Which Members Are Limited Partners — Code of Professional Conduct, p. **24.50**

89 — Loan to Partnership in Which Members Are General Partners — Code of Professional Conduct, p. **24.50**

90 — Credit Card Balances and Cash Advances — Code of Professional Conduct, p. **24.51**

91 — Member Leasing Property from a Client — Code of Professional Conduct, p. **24.51**

92 — Joint Interest in Vacation Home — Code of Professional Conduct, p. **24.51**

93 — Service on Board of Directors of Federated Fund-Raising Organization — Code of Professional Conduct, p. **24.51**

94 — Indemnification Clause in Engagement Letters — Code of Professional Conduct, p. **24.51**

95 — Agreement with Attest Client to Use ADR Techniques — Code of Professional Conduct, p. **24.51**

96 — Commencement of ADR Proceeding — Code of Professional Conduct, p. **24.51**

97 — Performance of Certain Extended Audit Services — Code of Professional Conduct, p. **24.52**

98 — Member's Loan from a Nonclient Subsidiary or Parent of an Attest Client — Code of Professional Conduct, p. **24.52**

99 — Member Providing Services for Company Executives — Code of Professional Conduct, p. **24.52**

100 — Actions Permitted When Independence Is Impaired — Code of Professional Conduct, p. **24.52**

101 — Client Advocacy and Expert Witness Services — Code of Professional Conduct, p. **24.53**

102 — Member's Indemnification of a Client — Code of Professional Conduct, p. **24.53**

Rules 201, 202, 203, and 204

1–6 — Deleted — No reference

7 — Non-CPA Partner — Superseded by Ethics Ruling No. 190

8 — Subcontractor Selection for Management [Advisory] Service Engagements — Code of Professional Conduct, p. **24.53**

9 — Supervision of Technical Specialist on Management [Advisory] Service Engagements — Code of Professional Conduct, p. **24.53**

10 — Preparation and Transmittal of Financial Statements by a Member in Public Practice — Code of Professional Conduct, p. **24.53**

11 — Applicability of Rule 203 to Members Performing Litigation Support Services — Code of Professional Conduct, p. **24.54**

Rules 301 and 302

1 — Computer Processing of Clients' Returns — Code of Professional Conduct, p. **24.54**

2 — Distribution of Client Information to Trade Associations — Code of Professional Conduct, p. **24.54**

3 — Information to Successor Accountant about Tax Return Irregularities — Code of Professional Conduct, p. **24.54**

4 — Deleted — No reference

5 — Records Retention Agency — Code of Professional Conduct, p. **24.54**

6 — Revealing Client Information to Competitors — Code of Professional Conduct, p. **24.55**

7 — Revealing Names of Clients — Code of Professional Conduct, p. **24.55**

8–13 — Deleted — No reference

14 — Use of Confidential Information on Management [Advisory] Service Engagements — Code of Professional Conduct, p. **24.55**

15 — Earlier Similar Management [Advisory] Service Study with Negative Outcome — Code of Professional Conduct, p. **24.55**

16 — Disclosure of Confidential Client Information — Code of Professional Conduct, p. **24.55**

17 — Definition of the Receipt of a Contingent Fee or a Commission — Code of Professional Conduct, p. **24.56**

18 — Bank Director — Code of Professional Conduct, p. **24.56**

19 — Receipt of Contingent Fees or Commissions by a Member's Spouse — Code of Professional Conduct, p. **24.56**

20 — Disclosure of Confidential Client Information to Professional Liability Insurance Carrier — Code of Professional Conduct, p. **24.56**

21 — Member Providing Services for Company Executives — Code of Professional Conduct, p. **24.56**

Rules 501, 502, 503, 504, and 505

1 — Retention of Records — Superseded by Interpretation 501-1

2 — Fees: Collection of Notes Issued in Payment — Code of Professional Conduct, p. **24.57**

3 — Employment by a Non-CPA Firm — Code of Professional Conduct, p. **24.57**

4–32 — Deleted — No reference

33 — Course Instructor — Code of Professional Conduct, p. **24.57**

34–37 — Deleted — No reference

38 — CPA Title, Controller of Bank — Code of Professional Conduct, p. **24.57**

39–44 — Deleted — No reference

45 — CPA Title on Agency Letterhead — Superseded

46–62 — Deleted — No reference

63 — Directory Listing, White Pages — Superseded

64–77 — Deleted — No reference

78 — Letterhead: Lawyer—CPA — Code of Professional Conduct, p. **24.57**

79–81 — Deleted — No reference

82 — Newsletter — Code of Professional Conduct, p. **24.58**

83–90 — Deleted — No reference

91 — Press Release on Change in Staff — Superseded

92 — Press Release on Change in Staff — Superseded

93–107 — Deleted — No reference

108 — Member Interviewed by the Press — Code of Professional Conduct, p. **24.58**

109–115 — Deleted — No reference

116 — Bank Director — Superseded

117 — Consumer Credit Company Director — Code of Professional Conduct, p. **24.58**

118–133 — Deleted — No reference

134 — Association of Accountants Not Partners — Code of Professional Conduct, p. **24.58**

135 — Association of Firms Not Partners   Code of Professional Conduct, p. **24.58**

136 — Audit with Former Partner   Code of Professional Conduct, p. **24.59**

137 — Nonproprietary Partners   Code of Professional Conduct, p. **24.59**

138 — Partner Having Separate Proprietorship   Code of Professional Conduct, p. **24.59**

139 — Partnership with Non-CPA   Code of Professional Conduct, p. **24.59**

140 — Political Election   Code of Professional Conduct, p. **24.59**

141 — Responsibility for Non-CPA Partner   Code of Professional Conduct, p. **24.59**

142–143 — Deleted   No reference

144 — Title: Partnership Roster   Code of Professional Conduct, p. **24.59**

145 — Firm Name of Merged Partnerships   Code of Professional Conduct, p. **24.60**

146 — Membership Designation   Code of Professional Conduct, p. **24.60**

147–157 — Deleted   No reference

158 — Operation of Separate Data Processing Business by a Public Practitioner   Code of Professional Conduct, p. **24.60**

159–161 — Deleted   No reference

162 — CPA Designation on Professional Organization Letterhead   Superseded   No reference

163–167 — Deleted   No reference

168 — Audit Guides Issued by Governmental Agencies   Superseded by Interpretation 501-3

169–174 — Deleted   No reference

175 — Bank Director   Superseded by Ethics Ruling Nos. 85 and 18

176 — Newsletters and Publications Prepared by Others   Code of Professional Conduct, p. **24.60**

177 — Data Processing: Billing Services   Code of Professional Conduct, p. **24.60**

178 — Deleted   No reference

179 — Practice of Public Accounting Under Name of Association or Group   Code of Professional Conduct, p. **24.61**

180–181 — Deleted   No reference

182 — Termination of Engagement Prior to Completion   Code of Professional Conduct, p. **24.61**

183 — Use of the AICPA Accredited Personal Financial Specialist Designation   Code of Professional Conduct, p. **24.61**

184 — Definition of the Receipt of a Contingent Fee or Commission   Code of Professional Conduct, p. **24.61**

185 — Sale of Products to Clients   Code of Professional Conduct, p. **24.61**

186 — Billing for Subcontractor's Services   Code of Professional Conduct, p. **24.61**

187 — Receipt of Contingent Fees or Commissions by Member's Spouse   Code of Professional Conduct, p. **24.61**

188 — Referral of Products of Others   Code of Professional Conduct, p. **24.62**

189 — Requests for Client Records and Other Information   Code of Professional Conduct, p. **24.62**

190 — Non-CPA Partner   Code of Professional Conduct, p. **24.62**

PART I
Audited Financial Statements

AUDITED FINANCIAL STATEMENTS
Overview

Contents

Citations to Auditing Standards   1.03

AUDITED FINANCIAL STATEMENTS
Overview

An audit is a methodical review and objective examination of an item, including the verification of specific information as determined by the auditor or as established by general practice. Generally, the purpose of an audit is to express an opinion on or reach a conclusion about what was audited.

In financial accounting, it is usually the financial statements of an enterprise that are the subject of an audit. The independent auditor generally expresses an opinion, in the form of an audit report, on the fairness of the financial statements.

The financial statements of an enterprise are the representations of the management of the enterprise, not of the independent auditor. The financial statements are the product and property of the enterprise, and the independent auditor merely audits them and expresses an opinion on them. The independent auditor's expression of the opinion is known as the *attest function*.

Governments, corporations, small businesses, financial institutions, investors, and the general public rely on the independence and objectivity of the certified public accountant. If audit reports are not properly prepared, monetary losses can result both to the audited entity and to those who rely on its financial statements. The regulation of the accounting profession by state governments is generally based on the attest function. The general public can be threatened if those providing the attest function are not regulated.

Without a report from an independent auditor, a company's financial statements would have little meaning because the company would be reporting on itself. Thus, the role of the independent auditor is well established in the business and financial community.

Citations to Auditing Standards

In November 1972, the Auditing Standards Executive Committee (now the Auditing Standards Board) of the American Institute of Certified Public Accountants (AICPA) issued Statement on Auditing Standards (SAS) No. 1 (Codification of Auditing Standards and

Procedures), which contained a codification of previously issued Statements on Auditing Procedures (SAPs) Nos. 1 through 54. Only the SAPs that were of continuing interest to the auditing profession were included in SAS-1. Thus, all the currently effective SAPs as of November 1972 were included in SAS-1.

Since November 1972, the Auditing Standards Board has issued promulgated auditing standards in the form of Statements on Auditing Standards. These Statements communicate promulgated auditing standards to all interested parties.

Citations to SAPs in this publication refer to the sections in SAS-1 that include the codification of all currently effective SAPs as of November 1972. All other promulgated auditing and related standards are referred to by their original citations.

The *1997 Miller GAAS Guide* incorporates standards issued through August 1, 1996, which includes SAS-79 (Amendment to Statement on Auditing Standards No. 58, "Reports on Audited Financial Statements") and SSAE-6 (Reporting on an Entity's Internal Control Over Financial Reporting: An Amendment to Statement on Standards for Attestation Engagements No. 2).

RESPONSIBILITY AND FUNCTION OF THE INDEPENDENT AUDITOR

CONTENTS

Overview	**2.03**
Role of the Independent Auditor	**2.03**
General Standard No. 1	**2.04**
General Standard No. 2	**2.05**
General Standard No. 3	**2.05**
Quality-Control Standards	**2.06**
Independence, Integrity, and Objectivity	**2.07**
Personnel Management	**2.07**
Acceptance and Continuation of Clients and Engagements	**2.08**
Engagement Performance	**2.08**
Monitoring	**2.08**
Administration of the Quality-Control System	**2.09**
Assignment of Responsibilities	**2.09**
Communication	**2.09**
Documentation of Quality Controls	**2.09**
Documentation of Compliance with Quality Controls	**2.09**
Monitoring a Firm's System of Quality Control	**2.09**
Inspection Procedures	**2.10**
Pre-issuance or Post-issuance Review of Selected Engagements	**2.10**

RESPONSIBILITY AND FUNCTION OF
THE INDEPENDENT AUDITOR

Overview

The purpose of an independent audit is to determine whether the client's financial statements are presented fairly, in all material respects, in accordance with generally accepted accounting principles (GAAP). This determination can be made only after the independent auditor has performed an audit in accordance with generally accepted auditing standards (GAAS). An auditing firm has the responsibility to design a quality-control system that reasonably ensures that professional standards will be followed in the conduct of an audit engagement. The following Statements on Auditing Standards (SAS) and their related Interpretations are discussed in this chapter in the sequence in which they appear below:

- SAS-1 (Codification of Auditing Standards and Procedures)
- SAS-25 (The Relationship of Generally Accepted Auditing Standards to Quality Control Standards)

SAS-1 establishes three general standards that address (1) the training and proficiency of an auditor, (2) the concept of independence, and (3) the standard of due care as it applies to an audit engagement (AU 150.2).

SAS-25 establishes the requirement that a firm of independent auditors must design a system of controls to provide reasonable assurance that generally accepted auditing standards are being observed in each engagement. The specific controls to be established are discussed in the Quality Control Standards Series of the American Institute of Certified Public Accountants (AICPA) (AU 161).

Role of the Independent Auditor

The adequacy of a client's internal control will directly affect the accuracy of the client's financial statements. In other words, the more effective the internal control, the less chance that material errors or irregularities will appear in the financial statements. The design, maintenance, and monitoring of an adequate internal control and the resulting financial statements are solely the responsibility of the management of an enterprise.

> **OBSERVATION:** *Even though the client has the ultimate responsibility for the adequacy of its internal control, SAS-60 (Communication of Internal Control Structure Related Matters Noted in an Audit) requires the auditor to notify the client of any reportable conditions discovered in the internal control.*

As the financial statements are prepared, the auditor may recommend changes in the format, terminology, or content of the statements or may actually assist in their preparation. The client must decide whether to accept the auditor's recommendations. If the client decides not to accept the recommendations, the auditor must determine whether the financial statements are materially misstated. If they are, the auditor must not issue an unqualified opinion.

In the conduct of the audit and the issuance of the report, the auditor exercises a considerable amount of professional judgment. Professional judgment is based on and limited by the auditor's professional expertise and experience. In no event is the auditor permitted to act in the capacity of an appraiser, lawyer, actuary, or other expert.

> **OBSERVATION:** *Although the auditor is not expected to be an expert in nonaccounting fields, SAS-73 (Using the Work of a Specialist) and SAS-12 (Inquiry of a Client's Lawyer Concerning Litigation, Claims, and Assessments) clearly require the auditor to be aware of situations that might require the use of an expert to determine whether financial statements are prepared in accordance with GAAP.*

The auditor's responsibility for the conduct of a professional engagement extends to the client, outsiders who rely on the financial statements, and the accounting profession. The three general standards embodied in GAAS provide guidance for the auditor in assessing these responsibilities.

General Standard No. 1 The first general standard requires that the auditor be adequately trained and proficient as an auditor. Adequate training includes exposure to technical accounting material as well as a sound general education. Proficiency as an auditor is gained through appropriate professional experience. Each state, through its state board of accountancy, establishes the required education and practical experience that must be completed before a person can be licensed to practice (AU 210).

> **OBSERVATION:** *Although the state board of accountancy determines the requirements for licensing, each auditor in charge of an engagement must assess the work of subordinates to determine whether professional and firm standards have been achieved.*

Professional training is a continuous process. An integral part of this process demands that an auditor stay abreast of current developments in accounting and auditing, which includes continuing professional education.

General Standard No. 2 The second general standard requires that an auditor be independent. *Independence* refers to the impartiality of the auditor with respect to the client and to those who rely on the financial statements. There are two dimensions of independence: independence in fact and independence in appearance (AU 220).

As a professional, an auditor strives for independence in fact, which represents the mental attitude of the auditor. That is, the auditor favors neither the client nor those who read the financial statements. However, the accounting profession must also be concerned with whether other parties believe that the auditor is independent. In this case, the auditor must avoid relationships that might suggest that independence has been lost.

Since it is impossible to evaluate the actual independence of the auditor (independence in fact), professional rules and guidelines have been concerned with independence in appearance. For example, an auditor cannot be an employee of his or her client. These rules are part of the Code of Professional Conduct, which is discussed in the chapter entitled "Code of Professional Conduct."

> **OBSERVATION:** *The concept of independence is so fundamental to an audit engagement that SAS-26 (Association with Financial Statements) requires that the auditor disclaim an opinion on the financial statements when he or she is not independent, even if all other generally accepted auditing standards have been observed.*

General Standard No. 3 The third general standard requires that due professional care be exercised in the conduct of the engagement, including the preparation of the audit report. An auditor may be competent and independent, but if the engagement is not conducted in a professional manner, the conclusions expressed in the auditor's report may be suspect (AU 230).

Due professional care in an audit is achieved by observing standards of fieldwork and reporting. For example, the first standard of fieldwork is concerned with the planning and supervision of an engagement. If an auditor can demonstrate that this standard as well as the other standards have been achieved, it is unlikely that a court of law could find the auditor guilty of negligence.

> **OBSERVATION:** *Although legal liability can be avoided by the observation of GAAS, it must be remembered that it is a matter of judgment exercised by the court or a peer review group that determines whether the standards have been achieved. An auditor's first line of defense is the preparation and maintenance of workpapers that clearly demonstrate and document the compliance with these standards.*

Quality-Control Standards

An accounting firm must adopt a system of controls to provide reasonable assurance that generally accepted auditing standards are being followed by the professional staff of the firm (SAS-25). The AICPA Auditing Standards Board has the authority to issue pronouncements on quality-control standards for CPA firms that are members of the AICPA (AU 161).

The actual design of the system of quality controls will vary from firm to firm, depending on such factors as the size of the professional staff, the number of offices, and the geographical location of the offices.

Quality-control standards are based on Statement on Quality Control Standards (SQCS) No. 2 (System of Quality Control for a CPA Firm's Accounting and Auditing Practice) and SQCS-3 (Monitoring a CPA Firm's Accounting and Auditing Practice). The concepts and guidance discussed in SQCS-2 and SQCS-3 are summarized below.

> **OBSERVATION:** *SQCS-1 (System of Quality Control for a CPA Firm) was superseded by SQCS-2.*

The standards established by SQCSs apply to a firm's accounting and auditing practice, which is defined as follows by SQCS-2:

> Accounting and auditing practice refers to all audit, attest, accounting and review, and other services for which standards have been established by the AICPA Auditing Standards Board or the AICPA Accounting and Review Services Committee under Rules 201 or 202 of the AICPA Code of Professional Conduct.

The components of a quality-control system include the following:

- Independence, integrity, and objectivity
- Personnel management
- Acceptance and continuance of clients and engagements
- Engagement performance
- Monitoring

Although these components are discussed separately in the following analysis, an effective system of quality control recognizes that all of the components are interrelated.

Independence, integrity, and objectivity Policies and procedures should be established to reasonably assure that personnel are independent. For example, a firm may distribute a client list periodically to staff members and have them acknowledge that they have no financial interest in the client businesses or that none of their relatives holds a key position with a client. What constitutes independence, integrity, and objectivity is more fully addressed in the chapter entitled "Code of Professional Conduct."

Personnel management Quality-control policies and procedures related to personnel management should encompass "hiring, assigning personnel to engagements, professional development, and advancement activities." SQCS-2 specifically states that controls should be designed to reasonably assure that the following are achieved:

- Employees possess the appropriate characteristics to enable them to perform competently.
- Work is assigned to personnel who have the technical training and proficiency required to complete the assignment.

- Professional personnel participate in general and industry-specific continuing professional education (CPE) and other professional development activities that enable personnel to fulfill their responsibilities and to satisfy applicable CPE requirements of the AICPA and regulatory agencies.

- Personnel selected for advancement have the qualifications necessary to fulfill their new responsibilities.

Acceptance and continuance of clients and engagements   Controls should be in place to determine whether the firm should continue to be associated with clients and prospective clients. These controls should be designed to assess the integrity of management. For example, a firm may require a thorough investigation of the integrity of the principals associated with existing and prospective clients. Although the firm must be concerned with the integrity of management, the evaluation performed by the firm does not vouch for the integrity of its management.

In addition to requiring an assessment of management, SQCS-2 requires that controls be established to provide reasonable assurance that the following objectives related to an engagement are achieved:

- Undertake only those engagements that the firm can reasonably expect to be completed with professional competence.

- Appropriately consider the risk associated with providing professional services in a particular circumstance.

Engagement performance   Quality-control policies and procedures should be designed to reasonably assure that an engagement is performed in a manner that satisfies "professional standards, regulatory requirements, and the firm's standards of quality." These control policies and procedures should encompass all phases of the engagement—from its initial acceptance to the preparation of the accountant's report. An integral part of engagement performance includes consultation that ranges from reference to authoritative literature to discussions with personnel who have expertise relevant to the engagement.

Monitoring   Controls should be established to determine whether quality controls discussed earlier are being observed by the firm. SQCS-3, which is addressed later in this chapter, more fully describes the role of monitoring a firm's quality-control system.

Administration of the Quality-Control System

Once established, controls can achieve their objectives only with an effective system of administration. SQCS-2 lists the following as components that should be considered in the design of an effective administration system.

Assignment of responsibilities The responsibility for the design and maintenance of quality controls should be assigned to a competent individual(s) who has been given adequate authority to administer the quality-control system.

Communication A firm must communicate its quality controls (as well as changes to those controls) to its personnel on a timely and comprehensible basis.

Documentation of quality controls The firm's documentation of specific quality controls should be dependent on the characteristics of the firm and its practice.

> *OBSERVATION: SQCS-2 does not require that quality controls be documented, but it does require the documentation to reflect the "size, structure, and nature of the practice of the firm." In addition, the standard concludes that "although communication ordinarily is enhanced if it is in writing, the effectiveness of a firm's system of quality control is not necessarily impaired by the absence of documentation of established quality-control policies and procedures."*

Documentation of compliance with quality controls Personnel must document their compliance with the firm's quality controls. The form of documentation is dependent on the characteristics of the firm and its practice.

> *OBSERVATION: Although SQCS-2 does not require that quality controls be documented (as noted in the previous Observation), the standard does require documentation that controls were observed.*

Monitoring a Firm's System of Quality Control

SQCS-2 specifically states that monitoring a firm's system of quality control encompasses the following:

- Relevance and adequacy of the firm's controls
- Appropriateness of the firm's guidance materials and any practice aids
- Effectiveness of professional development activities
- Compliance with the firm's controls

Although the specific procedures that constitute effective monitoring of a firm's quality-control system are dependent on "the firm's management philosophy and the environment in which the firm practices," SQCS-3 concludes that such procedures may include (a) inspection procedures and (b) pre-issuance or post-issuance review of selected engagements.

Inspection procedures   Specific inspection procedures for monitoring a firm's quality controls should be designed to determine whether the firm's quality controls are being observed by the firm's personnel. Inspection procedures could include reviewing administrative and personnel records, reviewing workpapers, and having conversations with the firm's personnel. In addition, SQCS-3 notes that inspection procedures may encompass (a) a periodic summarization of weakness discovered during the monitoring process, (b) recommendations to eliminate or minimize the occurrence of such weaknesses, (c) communication of weaknesses and related recommendations to the firm's appropriate management personnel, and (d) follow-up procedures conducted by the firm's appropriate management personnel to ensure that recommendations are implemented on a timely basis.

Pre-issuance or post-issuance review of selected engagements   Monitoring procedures could include a review of an engagement before a report is issued or after a report is issued. Review procedures are considered inspection procedures if they satisfy the following criteria:

- The review is sufficiently comprehensive to enable the firm to assess compliance with all applicable professional standards and the firm's quality controls.
- Findings from the reviews that indicate the need to improve compliance with or modify the firm's quality controls are periodically summarized, documented, and communicated to the firm's management personnel who have the responsibility and authority to make changes in those controls.

- The firm's management considers on a timely basis the systemic causes of findings that indicate improvements are needed and determines appropriate actions to be taken.

- The firm implements planned actions on a timely basis, communicates changes to personnel who might be affected, and follows up to determine that the planned actions were taken.

In order for reviews to be considered monitoring procedures, they must be conducted by reviewers who "are not directly associated with the performance of the engagement." The one exception to this rule is if a firm has a "limited number of qualified management-level individuals." In such instances, a post-issuance review may be conducted by the person with final responsibility for the engagement. Although SQCS-3 allows this exception, it does note that reviewing one's own work is generally not as effective as a review performed by someone who was not associated with the engagement. For this reason, SQCS-3 suggests that a firm consider hiring someone outside of the firm to perform inspection procedures.

> **OBSERVATION:** *Although a peer review is not a substitute for a firm's monitoring procedures, SQCS-3 concludes that a peer review that satisfies the standards established by the AICPA may substitute for "some or all of its inspection procedures for the period covered by the peer review."*

GENERALLY ACCEPTED ACCOUNTING PRINCIPLES

CONTENTS

Overview	3.03
Basic, or Pervasive, Principles	3.05
Separate Entity	3.05
Matching	3.05
Representational Faithfulness	3.05
Materiality	3.06
Conservatism	3.06
Continuity (Going Concern)	3.06
Full Disclosure	3.06
Operating Cycle	3.06
Consistency (Comparability)	3.07
Objectivity (Neutrality)	3.07
Current Operating Performance Versus All-Inclusiveness	3.07
Expense Recognition Principles	3.08
Broad Principles	3.09
Basic Financial Statements	3.09
Detailed Principles	3.11
Accounting Research Bulletins	3.11
Opinions of the Accounting Principles Board	3.11
Statements of the Accounting Principles Board	3.11
FASB Statements and Interpretations	3.12
Other FASB Publications	3.12
Accounting Standards Executive Committee	3.12
GASB Statements and Interpretations	3.12
Support for Accounting Principles	3.13
Determining Authoritative Support for GAAP	3.13
Exhibit I: Private-Sector Accounting Hierarchy	3.15
Exhibit II: Public-Sector Accounting Hierarchy	3.16

National Automated Accounting Research System
  (NAARS)   **3.17**
Departure from GAAP   **3.18**
GAAP and Consistency   **3.18**
Correction of Errors   **3.20**
GAAP and Regulated Industries   **3.20**
GAAP and Specialized Industries   **3.21**

GENERALLY ACCEPTED
ACCOUNTING PRINCIPLES

Overview

The purpose of an audit engagement is to determine whether financial statements are fairly presented in accordance with generally accepted accounting principles (GAAP). Furthermore, the first reporting standard of GAAS requires that the report explicitly state whether the financial statements are prepared in accordance with GAAP (AU 411.01).

GAAP are defined as technical accounting principles, methods, and procedures that are generally accepted at a particular time. Accounting principles include both written and unwritten rules.

GAAP are dynamic: they are constantly changing. Future changes may be accelerated by the need for more meaningful financial information resulting from a rapidly changing economic and social environment.

There is some confusion about the sources of generally accepted accounting principles. Although it would be convenient to have a single authoritative source of generally accepted accounting principles, they now exist in a wide variety of publications in the form of standards, conventions, assumptions, principles, rules, and so forth, all of which are referred to as GAAP (AU 411.02).

The most authoritative sources of GAAP are listed below:

- American Institute of Certified Public Accountants (AICPA)
  - Accounting Principles Board (APB) Opinions
  - Accounting Research Bulletins (ARBs)
  - Accounting Interpretations
  - Industry Audit and Accounting Guides
  - Statements of Position
- Financial Accounting Standards Board (FASB)
  - Statements
  - Interpretations

- — Technical Bulletins
- — Emerging Issues Task Force Consensuses
- Governmental Accounting Standards Board (GASB)
  - — Statements
  - — Interpretations
  - — Technical Bulletins
  - — Implementation Guides
- Pronouncements of the Securities and Exchange Commission (SEC) (usually in the form of Accounting Series Releases, S-X Regulations, and Staff Accounting Bulletins)
- Various publications of professional organizations
- Various up-to-date textbooks, reference books, accounting articles, and committee reports that contain authoritative expressions of GAAP

GAAP may be classified as (1) basic or pervasive, (2) broad, and (3) detailed principles. Basic principles are the foundation of much of the accounting process. Besides being the means of implementing the accrual basis of accounting, basic principles encompass the following assumptions:

- Separate entity
- "Matching"
- Representational faithfulness
- Materiality
- Conservatism
- Continuity (going concern)
- Full disclosure
- Operating cycle
- Consistency (comparability)
- Objectivity (neutrality)
- Current operating performance versus all-inclusiveness

Broad principles are used to determine the selection, measurement, and method of reporting events in the financial accounting process.

Detailed principles are directed toward specific events or transactions and how they should be recorded and presented. They are used to implement the basic and broad principles. In the past, detailed principles were published by the AICPA (opinions of the APB and ARB), but most are now issued by the FASB and the GASB. Detailed principles published by the AICPA's Accounting Standards Executive Committee (AcSEC) are reviewed by the FASB and GASB.

Basic and broad principles evolve over long periods; detailed principles change more rapidly.

Basic, or Pervasive, Principles

Separate entity   The separate entity concept requires that each financial accounting unit be separately identified. The accounting equation of assets minus liabilities equals owner's equity is an expression of the separate entity principle. The assets, liabilities, and operations of each separate entity are segregated from the individual owners and from other separate accounting units.

Matching   The matching concept requires that revenue and related costs be *matched* in determining net income for a specific period. If revenue is deferred to a future period, the associated costs of that revenue must also be deferred. It frequently is necessary to estimate revenue and/or costs to achieve a proper matching. The result of using the matching concept in determining income or loss is called the *earning process*. When the earning process is complete and an exchange has occurred, only then is the realization of revenue recognized. The realization principle requires that revenue be earned before it is recognized.

When properly measured and realized in conformity with GAAP, revenues will cause a gross increase in assets or a gross decrease in liabilities; and costs will cause a gross decrease in assets or a gross increase in liabilities.

The measurement principle involves the measurement and valuation of resources and obligations. Time must be measured and valuations made of nonmonetary exchanges. Time periods are usually determined to enhance comparability, and valuations must be made in recording and presenting financial information. Cost in conformity with GAAP is usually the historical or acquisition valuation. Estimates and allocations must be measured in the financial accounting process and require informed professional judgment.

Representational faithfulness   GAAP require that the economic substance of an event take precedence over its legal form when it is recorded or measured. Although this is a recognized concept, it is difficult to apply in practice because, as noted in FASB Concepts Statement (FASB CON) No. 2 (Qualitative Characteristics of Accounting Information), the representational faithfulness concept is a "rather vague idea that defies precise definition."

Materiality Evaluations and decisions in financial reporting should be based on materiality, the determination of which requires informed professional judgment. The basic principle of materiality is directly related to full disclosure, which is concerned only with significant information.

Conservatism The concept of conservatism has evolved over the years because accountants preferred that estimates or errors in judgment result in an understatement, rather than an overstatement, of net income and/or net assets. Conservatism is reflected in the practice that inventories should be valued at *the lower of cost or market* and by the recognition of losses on firm purchase commitments. Extreme conservatism, such as arbitrary writeoffs of assets and excessive provisions for liabilities, is unacceptable.

Continuity (going concern) An enterprise is viewed as a continuing operation, possessing the resources to meet its obligations and commitments. However, if liquidation is imminent or if the entity cannot continue in existence to meet its current plans and obligations, financial information may be prepared on the assumption that operations will cease and/or liquidation will occur.

Full disclosure Financial statements, including accompanying footnotes, should contain adequate disclosure of all pertinent data necessary for a fair presentation in conformity with GAAP. If there is any doubt about disclosing an item or event, it is probably better to make the disclosure.

Operating cycle In the ordinary course of business, capital continually circulates within the current assets. For example, with a manufacturer, cash is expended for materials, labor, and factory overhead, which are converted into finished inventory. After being sold, the inventory is usually converted into a trade receivable and, on collection of the receivable, back into cash. The average time elapsing between originally expending the cash and receiving the cash back from the trade receivable is called an operating cycle. When the operating cycle occurs more frequently than once a year, one year is used as a basis for segregating current assets. When the operating cycle is longer than one year, as it is with the lumber, some tobacco products, and distillery businesses, the longer period should be used as the operating cycle. If a business clearly has no operating cycle, the one-year rule is used.

Frequently, businesses have a natural business year, at the end of which the company's activity, inventory, and trade receivables are at their lowest point.

Consistency (comparability)   Comparable financial statements reveal considerably more information than noncomparable statements. Comparability furnishes useful data about differences in the results of operations for the periods involved or in the financial position at the comparison dates. Consistency is a major factor in creating comparability. Consistency between entities, time periods, and accounting data presentation is necessary for comparability.

Objectivity (neutrality)   Financial accounting data should not be recorded or reported in accordance with the desires of any individual or organization. Data should be presented objectively in conformity with GAAP and prepared for the common needs of all users. Preparing financial accounting data to satisfy a few users to the detriment of others who may have opposing views is a violation of the concept of neutrality.

Current operating performance versus all-inclusiveness   There is some difference of opinion on what is the most useful concept of income for a given time period. Proponents of the all-inclusive concept believe that all items affecting net increases in owners' equity, except dividends and capital transactions, should be included in computing net income. They support their position with the following reasons:

- Extraordinary items are part of income, and annual income statements over the life of an entity, when combined, should represent total net income as reported.
- Omission of extraordinary items will distort the total financial position of an enterprise.
- Extraordinary items may be manipulated or possibly overlooked if not included on a regular basis.
- An income statement that includes all charges or credits arising during the year is simple to prepare, easy to understand, and not subject to variations based on judgment.

Proponents of the current operating performance concept, who advocate excluding extraordinary items from net income, maintain the following positions:

- Net income should emphasize the normal operations of an enterprise and should exclude nonrecurring extraordinary items.

- The annual income statement's primary purpose is to inform those interested in what an entity was able to earn under the current year's operating conditions.

- Net income for the year should reflect, as clearly as possible, what happened under that year's conditions, so that the year's performance may be compared with that of prior years and with the performance of other enterprises in the same industry.

- When extraordinary items are included in the computation of net income, readers of financial statements are frequently unable to determine net income from normal operations.

- A material extraordinary item included in net income may be so distorting in its effect as to lead to unsound judgment about the current operating performance of the company.

Although the two schools of thought still exist, present-day GAAP support the all-inclusive concept. Net income should include all items of income and loss during a reporting period, except prior-period adjustments, dividends, and capital transactions. All extraordinary items should be segregated and shown separately in the income statement.

Expense recognition principles   Although the expense recognition principles are not traditionally considered one of the basic principles of accounting, they are very important. The three basic expense recognition principles used in GAAP are:

- Associating cause and effect
- Systematic and rational allocation
- Immediate recognition

When a cost is related to specific revenue, a cause-and-effect relationship is established. An example of this method of expense recognition is sales commissions, which are directly related to the revenue generated by the sale.

If an asset provides benefits for more than one period, its cost should be allocated in a systematic and rational manner. This method is used in the absence of a direct basis for associating cause and effect. An example of this method of expense recognition is the depreciation of fixed assets.

There are three bases for recognizing an expense immediately in the current period:

- Cost incurred provides no future benefits.

- Costs recorded as assets in prior periods no longer provide any future benefits.

- Allocating the cost to future periods or directly associating it to revenue serves no useful purpose.

An example of an expense recognized in the current period is the writeoff of obsolete inventory.

Broad Principles

Broad principles are the bridge between basic and detailed principles. They provide the guidelines for selecting, recording, and communicating financial events produced by the accounting process. Broad principles may be categorized as follows:

Selecting, analyzing, and measuring—Internal and external events must be selected, analyzed, and measured in accordance with GAAP.

Classifying, recording, and summarizing—The selected events must be properly classified and recorded as assets, liabilities, owners' equity, revenue, or expenses and then summarized in a workable format.

Adjusting and communicating—The summarized events are adjusted, as necessary, and are communicated in the form of financial statements.

Basic financial statements   The minimum requirements for fairly presenting the financial position, changes in cash flows, and results of operations of an enterprise in conformity with GAAP are listed below. (The corporate form is used in our example, but the terminology may differ for other types of separate accounting entities.)

- Balance sheet (statement of financial position)
- Statement of operations (income)
- Statement of cash flows
- Statement of changes in retained earnings
- Disclosure of any other changes in stockholders' equity
- Any other necessary related notes for adequate disclosure

These basic financial statements are usually prepared for two or more time periods to enhance their usefulness and to provide comparability.

Working capital Working capital (also referred to as net working capital) is the difference between current assets and current liabilities. Working capital is usually disclosed by classifying current assets and current liabilities separately. Proper disclosure of the components of working capital is presumed to be useful for most business enterprises.

Capital changes It is necessary to disclose capital changes in the period in which they occur, in the form of a separate statement, as part of the basic financial statements, or as accompanying footnotes.

Offsetting of assets and liabilities It is improper to offset assets and liabilities in a balance sheet, unless the right of offset exists. An exception to this general rule is a security that in substance is an advance payment of taxes that will be paid in the near future. In such a case, the purchase is tantamount to the prepayment of taxes.

Gains and losses A material item of gain or loss, other than a prior-period adjustment, should be included in the determination of net income for the period but segregated from income from continuing operations if it is not typical of the business activities of the enterprise and if it is nonrecurring. Gains and losses that are typical of the customary business activities of an enterprise may be disclosed separately if their effects are material.

Other disclosures Besides the informative classification and segregation of data, financial statements should disclose all additional information necessary for a *fair presentation* in conformity with GAAP. Notes that are necessary for an adequate disclosure are considered an integral part of the financial statements. Financial statements are restricted to numbers associated with very few words and are essentially summaries of much detailed information. They usually require amplification through the use of footnotes to make the information more meaningful and to provide additional disclosure.

Detailed Principles

Detailed accounting principles change more frequently and are the means of implementing the basic and broad principles. No comprehensive authoritative list of detailed accounting principles is available, but the major sources of GAAP are reviewed below.

Accounting Research Bulletins   From 1939 to 1953, the AICPA issued 42 Accounting Research Bulletins (ARBs), of which 8 concerned accounting terminology and 34 dealt with problems the accounting profession was most concerned with at the time. In June 1953, the AICPA issued ARB-43 (Restatement and Revision of Accounting Research Bulletins), which, excluding the ARB on terminology, condensed all prior ARBs. It eliminated what was no longer applicable, condensed and clarified what continued to be of value, and arranged the retained material by subjects. Subsequently, ARB-44 through ARB-51 were issued between October 1954 and August 1959. Accounting Research Bulletins are a source of GAAP.

Opinions of the Accounting Principles Board   Opinions of the Accounting Principles Board (APB) of the AICPA present the conclusions of at least two-thirds of the board members. These opinions need not be applied to items that are not material (principle of materiality). The substance of transactions and the principles set forth in the opinions promulgated by the APB should control the accounting for transactions not expressly covered.

The APB went out of existence in 1973 and was replaced by the FASB. However, those APB opinions that have not been superseded continue to be an important source of promulgated GAAP.

Statements of the Accounting Principles Board   Four APB *Statements* were issued between 1962 and 1970. These Statements were rescinded by Statement of Position (SOP) 93-3 (Recision of Accounting Principles Board Statements). The four APB Statements never established generally accepted accounting principles, and according to the SOP, their withdrawal "should have no effect on financial reporting and should eliminate any confusion over the status of the pronouncements."

FASB Statements and Interpretations   As a result of the report issued in 1972 by the Wheat Committee (a committee established by the AICPA), the Accounting Principles Board was abolished and replaced with the Financial Accounting Standards Board.

Since 1973, the FASB has issued numerous Statements and Interpretations in the area of financial accounting. Each new FASB Statement is preceded by an Exposure Draft identifying and analyzing the issues to be considered. An Exposure Draft is sometimes preceded by a Discussion Memorandum or Invitation to Comment, and may be followed by public hearings, after which a final Statement is issued. A FASB Statement (FAS) establishes new, or modifies existing, GAAP; a FASB Interpretation (FIN) clarifies or explains previously issued promulgated GAAP.

Other FASB publications   In November 1978, the FASB issued the first of a series of Statements of Financial Accounting Concepts, which contain the objectives of financial reporting by business enterprises. The purpose of the series is to establish the objectives and concepts that the FASB will use to develop standards of financial accounting and reporting.

In December 1979, the FASB issued the first of its Technical Bulletins. These Bulletins provide guidance to accountants and enterprises in applying FASB Statements and Interpretations. The staff of the FASB issues these Bulletins without formal approval of the Board.

Accounting Standards Executive Committee   The Accounting Standards Executive Committee (AcSEC), a committee of the AICPA, establishes accounting principles by issuing Statements of Position, Audit and Accounting Guides, and AICPA Practice Bulletins.

GASB Statements and Interpretations   The Financial Accounting Foundation (FAF), after considerable debate within the profession, designated the Governmental Accounting Standards Board as the body that establishes accounting principles for all state and local governmental entities, including public benefit corporations and authorities, public employee retirement systems, governmental utilities, governmental hospitals and other health care providers, and public colleges and universities.

The GASB follows essentially the same due process that is followed by the FASB and establishes governmental accounting principles through the issuance of Statements, Interpretations, and Technical Bulletins.

Before the creation of the GASB, governmental accounting principles were established by the National Council on Governmental Accounting. In July 1984, shortly after its creation, the GASB issued GASB-1 (Authoritative Status of NCGA Pronouncements and AICPA Industry Audit Guide), which identified certain pre-GASB pronouncements as the basis for accounting principles for governmental entities.

Support for Accounting Principles

GAAP are those principles that have substantial authoritative support. Substantial authoritative support is a question of fact and a matter of judgment. The CPA is responsible for determining whether accounting principles have substantial authoritative support.

ARBs, APB Opinions, and the Statements and Interpretations of the FASB are given greater weight than other single sources.

Authoritative support can exist for accounting principles that differ from those recommended by ARBs, APB Opinions, and the Statements and Interpretations of the FASB.

Determining Authoritative Support for GAAP

To determine how a particular transaction or event should be accounted for and reported in the financial statements, the auditor must refer to the GAAP hierarchy in SAS-69, which establishes a private-sector accounting hierarchy and a public-sector accounting hierarchy. The private-sector accounting hierarchy should be used in the preparation of financial statements of commercial enterprises and not-for-profit organizations. The public-sector accounting hierarchy should be used in the preparation of statements for state and local governmental entities (AU 411.16).

> *OBSERVATION: SAS-69 notes that state and local governmental entities include public benefit corporations and authorities, public employee retirement systems, governmental utilities, governmental hospitals and other governmental health care providers, and public colleges and universities (AU 411.12).*

> *OBSERVATION: SOP 94-2 (The Application of the Requirements of Accounting Research Bulletins, Opinions of the Accounting Principles Board, and Statements and Interpretations of the*

*Financial Accounting Standards Board to Not-for-Profit Organizations) requires that ARBs, APB Opinions, and FASB Statements and Interpretations be applied by not-for-profit organizations unless the pronouncements specifically exclude them, are not relevant to the kinds of transactions entered into by not-for-profit organizations, or address topics also addressed in the AICPA Audit and Accounting Guides **Audits of Colleges and Universities, Audits of Providers of Health Care Services, Audits of Voluntary Health and Welfare Organizations, and Audits of Not-for-Profit Organizations.***

The private-sector and public-sector accounting hierarchies are presented in Exhibits I and II, respectively. In these hierarchies, the specific sources of generally accepted accounting principles are ranked by their level of authoritative support. Thus, for example, an accounting principle established by a FASB Statement would be more authoritative than an accounting principle identified in an AICPA Accounting or Audit Guide (AU 411.07).

OBSERVATION: For public companies, Level A would include rules and interpretive releases of the Securities and Exchange Commission (SEC). SAS-69 notes that the SEC staff issues Staff Accounting Bulletins, which deal with SEC disclosure requirements, but SAS-69 does not specifically identify where Staff Accounting Bulletins should be classified in the accounting hierarchy. Presumably, it is Level A. Also, SAS-69 notes that the SEC will challenge any accounting method that differs from a consensus established by the FASB Emerging Issues Task Force (AU 411.10).

OBSERVATION: SAS-69 does not refer to the fifth levels as Level E in the two accounting hierarchies, but rather labels the categories as "other accounting literature." This clearly establishes Levels A–D as "must know" GAAP, departures from which violate Rule 203 or 202 of the AICPA Code of Professional Conduct (AU 411.11).

The absence of official pronouncements or unofficial writings forces an enterprise to review other actual accounting and reporting practices. Specific practices may be identified by reviewing surveys and reports published by professional organizations. For example, the AICPA annually publishes *Accounting Trends and Techniques,* which summarizes accounting practices followed by 600 large busi-

EXHIBIT I
PRIVATE-SECTOR ACCOUNTING HIERARCHY

Authoritative GAAP

Level A
- FASB Statements
- FASB Interpretations
- APB Opinions
- AICPA Accounting Research Bulletins

Level B
- FASB Technical Bulletins
- AICPA Industry Audit and Accounting Guides
- AICPA Statements of Position

Level C
- FASB Emerging Issues Task Force consensus positions
- AICPA Practice Bulletins

Level D
- AICPA Accounting Interpretations
- Implementation Guides (Qs and As) published by the FASB staff
- Practices widely recognized and prevalent generally or in industry

Other Nonauthoritative Accounting Literature

- FASB Statements of Financial Accounting Concepts
- APB Statements
- AICPA Issues Papers
- International Accounting Standards of the International Accounting Standards Committee
- GASB Statements
- GASB Interpretations
- GASB Technical Bulletins
- Pronouncements of other professional associations or regulatory agencies
- AICPA Technical Practice Aids
- Accounting textbooks
- Handbooks
- Articles

EXHIBIT II
PUBLIC-SECTOR ACCOUNTING HIERARCHY

Authoritative GAAP

Level A
- GASB Statements
- GASB Interpretations
- FASB pronouncements made applicable by a GASB Statement or GASB Interpretation
- AICPA pronouncements made applicable by a GASB Statement or GASB Interpretation

Level B
- GASB Technical Bulletins
- AICPA Industry Audit and Accounting Guides made applicable by the AICPA
- AICPA Statements of Position made applicable by the AICPA

Level C
- AICPA Practice Bulletins made applicable by the AICPA
- GASB Emerging Issues Task Force consensus positions (if created)

Level D
- GASB Implementation Guides (Qs and As)
- Practices widely recognized and prevalent in state and local governments

Other Nonauthoritative Accounting Literature

- GASB Concepts Statements
- Sources identified in Levels A through D in the private-sector accounting hierarchy that have *not* been made applicable by the action of the GASB
- APB Statements
- FASB Statements of Financial Accounting Concepts
- AICPA Issues Papers
- International Accounting Standards of the International Accounting Standards Committee
- Pronouncements of other professional associations or regulatory agencies
- AICPA Technical Practice Aids
- Accounting textbooks
- Handbooks
- Articles

ness enterprises. Periodically the AICPA publishes a *Financial Report Survey,* which discusses the actual reporting practices of many companies for a specific accounting topic. Many accounting firms maintain departments that answer questions raised by professional staff members or clients about accounting methods or practices. As specific problems are solved, they are documented by the firm. This serves as a basis for the selection of accounting methods in similar situations. Some accounting firms have an informal arrangement whereby they share experiences and technical opinions with other accounting firms (AU 411.11).

National Automated Accounting Research System (NAARS)

Research into accounting practices has been greatly enhanced by the development of a data retrieval service called *National Automated Accounting Research System* (NAARS). Key terms that are relevant to the research topic are typed on a NAARS console installed in the accountant's office. Then the main data bank automatically searches and displays the number of documents containing the key word. At this point, the researcher decides the amount of material and the number of documents that are to be displayed or printed by the computer. The NAARS system is being used by large CPA firms, governmental regulatory agencies, industrial organizations, and universities. Anyone can use the system for a fee.

Departure from GAAP

Management is responsible for the selection and the application of accounting principles and practices. If, after the collection and evaluation of appropriate evidential matter, the auditor decides that the financial statements are not prepared in accordance with GAAP, and if the deviation is significant, the auditor's report must be modified (AU 110.02).

The report modification requires that an explanatory paragraph(s) fully describing the violation or departure from GAAP (including effects on financial statements, if practical) be added to the standard report. If the auditor concludes that the financial statements as a whole can still be relied on, even with the deviation, he or she may issue a qualified opinion. If the auditor concludes that the financial statements cannot be relied on, he or she should express an adverse opinion (AU 508.49).

GAAP and Consistency

A change in an accounting principle is the result of changing from one acceptable accounting principle to another acceptable accounting principle. A change in an accounting practice or method is also considered a change in accounting principle (AU 420.04).

There is a presumption in GAAP that, once adopted, an accounting principle should not be changed in accounting for events or for transactions of a similar nature. However, an accounting principle can be changed if the alternative principle is preferable (rule of preferability).

The consistency principle does not prohibit a company from changing accounting principles. However, the company must justify the adoption of a new accounting principle in a note to the financial statements and must disclose the effects of the newly adopted principle, practice, or method. Obviously, the new accounting principle, practice, or method must be a generally accepted one.

The manner in which accounting changes are reported and disclosed in financial statements is established by APB Opinion No. 20 (Accounting Changes). That opinion requires that an accounting change be reported by either (1) including the effects of the accounting change by restating each prior year's financial statement that is presented for comparative purposes or (2) disclosing the total *cumulative effect* of the change in accounting principle on all prior years in the income statement for the period in which the change is adopted.

The general conclusion in APB Opinion No. 20 is that an accounting change shall be accounted for by disclosing the *cumulative effect* of the change in the income statement for the period in which the change is adopted. However, there are several important exceptions in APB Opinion No. 20 that require the *retroactive restatement* of each prior year's financial statement presented for comparative purposes. The exceptions are as follows:

- A change from the LIFO inventory method to another method
- A change in the method of accounting for long-term construction-type contracts
- A change to or from the *full cost* method of accounting in the extractive industries
- A one-time change for closely held corporations in connection with a public offering of its equity securities, or when such a company first issues financial statements for (1) obtaining additional capital from investors, (2) effecting a business combination, or (3) registering securities

- A change from the retirement-replacement-betterment method of accounting to the depreciation method of accounting

APB Opinion No. 20 did not change the method of reporting the effects of changes in accounting principles that result from the application of new GAAP or new Audit and Accounting Guides. The method of reporting the effects of these changes in accounting principle is prescribed by the new GAAP or new Audit and Accounting Guide.

A change in an accounting estimate is usually the result of new events, changing conditions, more experience, or additional information, any of which would require the revision of previous estimates (AU 420.14).

Estimates are necessary in determining uncollectible receivables, salvage values, useful lives, provisions for warranty, and a multitude of other items involved in preparing financial statements (AU 420.14).

A change in a depreciation method for a previously recorded asset is a change in an accounting principle. A change in the estimated useful life or in the salvage value of a previously recorded asset is a change in an accounting estimate (AU 420.14).

A change in an accounting estimate should not be accounted for by restating prior years' financial statements. The effects of a change in accounting estimate are accounted for (1) in the period of change, if the change affects only that period, or (2) in the period of change and in future periods, if the change affects both periods (AU 420.14).

A change in an accounting estimate caused in part or in whole by a change in an accounting principle must be reported as a change in an accounting estimate (AU 420.14).

Disclosure in current-period financial statements of the effects of a change in an accounting estimate on income before extraordinary items, net income, and related per share data is required.

If a change in an accounting estimate affects future periods, the estimated effect, if material, on income before extraordinary items, net income, and the related per share information must be disclosed in the income statement.

Ordinary accounting estimates for uncollectible accounts or inventory adjustments, made each period, do not have to be disclosed unless they are material.

The auditor must be satisfied that the change in an accounting estimate is reasonable. If the auditor makes this determination and is satisfied that the change in estimate does not also include a change in an accounting principle, the matter is not mentioned in the audit report (AU 420.14).

Correction of Errors

Prior-period errors in financial statements discovered subsequently should be reported as prior-period adjustments. FAS-16 (Prior Period Adjustments) limits prior-period adjustments to the following:

1. Correction of errors in financial statements of prior periods
2. Adjustments resulting from the realization of income tax benefits of preacquisition operating-loss carryforwards of purchased subsidiaries

Errors result from mistakes in mathematics, in the application of an accounting principle, or from misjudgment in the use of facts. A change in an accounting estimate is the result of new information, changing conditions, more experience, or additional information that requires the revision of previous estimates. A change from an unacceptable accounting principle to a generally accepted one is a correction of a prior-period error (APB Opinion No. 20) (AU 420.11).

The nature of the error and the effect of its correction on income before extraordinary items, net income, and the related per share data must be fully disclosed in the period the error is discovered and corrected.

Prior-period errors in financial statements are corrected by restating the prior years' financial statements that are presented on a comparative basis with the current year's statements.

The correction of errors by restating financial statements is not a violation of the consistency concept; therefore, the auditor's report is not qualified (AU 420.15).

GAAP and Regulated Industries

Accounting principles as defined in the preceding discussion are applicable to all profit-seeking enterprises. However, many companies must conform to accounting rules established by governmental regulatory authorities or commissions.

> **OBSERVATION:** *Companies in regulated industries are required to use GAAP, with appropriate recognition of the **regulatory rate-making process**. Thus, financial statements issued for public dissemination by companies in regulated industries must be in conformity with GAAP (FAS-71 [Accounting for the Effects of Certain Types of Regulation]).*

When financial statements are prepared for general distribution and not exclusively to fulfill the statutory filing requirements, generally accepted accounting principles are applicable. In this case, the auditor must determine the impact of any regulatory accounting rules that are in violation of GAAP. If the effect of the deviation is material, the auditor should issue a qualified opinion or an adverse opinion.

When statutory financial statements containing permitted or required GAAP departures are prepared exclusively for filing with a regulatory agency, the auditor should not issue a qualified or adverse opinion. The auditor *may* issue an unqualified opinion; in such a case, the basis for the opinion is not conformity with GAAP, but rather conformity with a comprehensive basis of accounting other than GAAP. Such a restricted report is referred to as a *special report* (AU 623.04). (For a more complete discussion, see the chapter entitled "Auditor's Special Reports.")

GAAP and Specialized Industries

Some trade associations or groups may recommend that certain accounting methods be used in the preparation of financial statements. Recommendations of accounting methods by trade associations or groups do not necessarily constitute acceptable accounting methods. In the final analysis, the auditor must determine whether a method has general acceptance. If an auditor concludes that an accounting method recommended by a trade association has general acceptance, the report is not qualified. If the auditor concludes that the recommended method is inconsistent with GAAP, the auditor must issue either a qualified opinion or an adverse opinion, depending on the effect of the deviation on the financial statements.

GENERALLY ACCEPTED AUDITING STANDARDS

CONTENTS

Overview   4.03

Generally Accepted Auditing Standards   4.04

Statements on Auditing Standards   4.04

Auditing Interpretations   4.04

Statements on Quality Control Standards   4.04

Code of Professional Conduct   4.05

General Standards   4.05

General Standard No. 1: The audit is to be performed by a person or persons having adequate technical training and proficiency as an auditor   4.05

General Standard No. 2: In all matters relating to the assignment, an independence in mental attitude is to be maintained by the auditor or auditors   4.07

General Standard No. 3: Due professional care is to be exercised in the performance of the audit and the preparation of the report   4.07

Standards of Fieldwork   4.08

Standard of Fieldwork No. 1: The work is to be adequately planned and assistants, if any, are to be properly supervised   4.08

Standard of Fieldwork No. 2: A sufficient understanding of internal control is to be obtained to plan the audit and to determine the nature, timing, and extent of tests to be performed   4.09

Standard of Fieldwork No. 3: Sufficient competent evidential matter is to be obtained through inspection, observation, inquiries, and confirmations to afford a reasonable basis for an opinion regarding the financial statements under audit   4.10

Standards of Reporting   4.10

   Reporting Standard No. 1: The report shall state
     whether the financial statements are presented
     in accordance with generally accepted accounting
     principles   4.10

   Reporting Standard No. 2: The report shall identify
     those circumstances in which such principles
     have not been consistently observed in the current
     period in relation to the preceding period   4.11

   Reporting Standard No. 3: Informative disclosures
     in the financial statements are to be regarded as
     reasonably adequate unless otherwise stated in
     the report   4.12

   Reporting Standard No. 4: The report shall contain
     either an expression of opinion regarding the
     financial statements taken as a whole, or an
     assertion to the effect that an opinion cannot be
     expressed   4.12

The Broad Nature of GAAS   4.13

Attestation Standards   4.13

GENERALLY ACCEPTED AUDITING STANDARDS

Overview

Professional auditing standards are viewed and interpreted in at least two different ways, as the minimum level of performance required to measure the quality of an audit by an independent auditor and as minimum guidelines for the performance of an audit engagement. Under the first view, professional auditing responsibilities would be achieved if the independent auditor performs an audit in accordance with generally accepted auditing standards (GAAS). However, the independent auditor recognizes that most professional auditing standards are broad and seldom specifically address the actual problems that arise in individual audit engagements. Therefore, under the second view, the auditor would meet professional auditing responsibilities by using existing professional auditing standards that require the constant exercise of professional judgment. Many auditing experts believe that professional auditing standards should be viewed in the second context because there is simply no way to establish standards in such detail that professional judgment is minimized or eliminated. Because they seldom provide the exact answer, professional auditing standards should be viewed as minimum guidelines that set the tone for the auditing profession.

The following Statement on Auditing Standards is discussed in this chapter:

- SAS-1 (Codification of Auditing Standards and Procedures)

SAS-1 provides a broad discussion of the professional responsibilities of the independent auditor. These responsibilities are described in the context of the three general standards, the three standards of fieldwork, and the four standards of reporting (AU 110.01).

The logical starting place for a discussion of professional auditing standards is a brief review of the auditing pronouncements that constitute this body of knowledge. These pronouncements are also discussed in much greater detail later in the book.

Generally accepted auditing standards Auditing standards deal with the quality of the audit performed by the independent auditor. Ten generally accepted auditing standards have been approved and adopted by the members of the AICPA. GAAS are divided into three groups: (1) general standards, (2) standards of fieldwork, and (3) standards of reporting. Under Rule 202 of the Code of Professional Conduct, every member of the AICPA must comply with GAAS (ET 202).

To the extent that they are relevant in the circumstances, the ten generally accepted auditing standards are applicable to all services governed by Statements on Auditing Standards, unless the Auditing Standards Board specifies otherwise (AU 160.06).

Statements on Auditing Standards Statements on Auditing Standards (SAS) are issued by the Auditing Standards Board (ASB) of the AICPA and are recognized as interpretations of the ten generally accepted auditing standards. SAS generally apply only in situations where auditing services are being performed.

Under Rule 202 of the Code of Professional Conduct, every member of the AICPA must comply with all applicable SAS (ET 202).

Auditing Interpretations Auditing Interpretations are issued by the ASB. These Interpretations are somewhat less authoritative than SAS and do not come under Rule 202 of the Professional Code of Conduct (ET 202).

Statements on Quality Control Standards Statements on Quality Control Standards (SQCSs) are issued by the Auditing Standards Board of the AICPA. The Statements are related to the audit function, but are not in themselves auditing standards (i.e., they are not part of GAAS). The standards established by SQCSs apply to a firm's accounting and auditing practice, which is defined as follows:

> Accounting and auditing practice refers to all audit, attest, accounting and review, and other services for which standards have been established by the AICPA Auditing Standards Board or the AICPA Accounting and Review Services Committee under Rules 201 or 202 of the AICPA Code of Professional Conduct.

Quality-control standards are discussed in the chapter entitled "Responsibility and Function of the Independent Auditor."

Code of Professional Conduct   The Code of Professional Conduct is not in itself an auditing standard. However, it does provide members of the AICPA and others with guidelines for behavior in the conduct of their professional affairs. It also provides assurance to the public that the profession intends to maintain high standards and to enforce compliance with these professional standards by its members. The Code of Professional Conduct applies to all types of services performed in the practice of public accounting, including auditing.

GENERAL STANDARDS

The most important factor in any profession is the people who make up that profession. The personal characteristics of an auditor are described below in a discussion of the three general standards. Desirable traits are difficult to describe in any individual, much less a profession. Therefore, these general standards are quite broad and open to a considerable degree of interpretation.

General Standard No. 1

> The audit is to be performed by a person or persons having adequate technical training and proficiency as an auditor.

The first standard addresses two characteristics that an auditor should possess: adequate technical training and proficiency as an auditor.

A technical body of accounting and auditing knowledge must be mastered as a prerequisite for the successful practice of auditing. This body of knowledge encompasses an understanding of generally accepted accounting principles and generally accepted auditing standards. Much of this knowledge can be acquired by the completion of an accounting degree at a college or university (AU 210.03).

Adequate technical training goes beyond the completion of certain accounting courses. Accounting educators or practitioners do not agree on what specific courses should be completed by a prospective auditor. In one respect, the practitioner's problem of technical training has been solved by action taken by state boards of accountancy. These boards establish the minimum number of credits that must be completed before a candidate can take the CPA examination (AU 210.03).

For a number of reasons, the practitioner should not take a passive role in accepting the state boards' prescribed course requirements. Not all newly hired auditors will take the CPA examination; some may never meet the state-mandated requirements. In addition, the needs of a particular firm may require that an employee have specialized accounting or auditing training. But most importantly, adequate technical training is a dynamic concept and should not be applied only to newly hired employees. Passing the CPA examination ten years ago does not necessarily mean that a CPA is adequately trained today. Thus, a CPA firm must view technical training in the context of its clientele and (1) establish minimum courses that should be completed by an employee and (2) design a training program that reflects changes in the accounting profession.

Adequate technical training for an auditor does not go beyond the bounds of accounting and auditing knowledge. A firm may encounter a situation in which technical training in other disciplines is needed to successfully complete an audit engagement. For example, the fairness of the financial statements may be dependent on geological conclusions or actuarial computations. SAS-73 (Using the Work of a Specialist) recognizes the technical limitations of an auditor and establishes guidelines for the use of members of other disciplines. In much the same way, SAS-12 (Inquiry of a Client's Lawyer Concerning Litigation, Claims, and Assessments) provides guidelines for the use of a lawyer in applying Financial Accounting Standards Board Statement (FAS) No. 5 (Accounting for Contingencies).

Although adequate technical training is concerned with accounting and auditing, the electronic processing of data has presented the profession with a perplexing problem. Computer processing is a discipline distinct from auditing; however, computer procedures cannot be ignored by auditors. Computer procedures and concepts have become an integral part of an entity's accounting system and must be understood, to varying degrees, by an auditor. The auditing profession has not yet selected a single solution to the computer dilemma, but typically, auditing firms obtain computer expertise by (1) hiring computer experts, (2) training auditors to be specialists in the computer field, or (3) providing computer training to all members of the audit staff.

No matter what course is taken, an audit firm must possess a level of computer knowledge sufficient to meet the needs of its clients.

The second part of the first general standard refers to an auditor's need for proficiency. Success in auditing goes beyond the need for education and training. An auditor should be able to apply his or her knowledge in an actual engagement. Thus, proficiency is gained through on-the-job experience. It should be noted that the basis for proficiency is adequate training and education. Therefore, the first general standard must be applied on an integrated basis, recognizing the interrelationship of training and proficiency.

> **OBSERVATION:** *If the first general standard is applied literally to an engagement, only experienced auditors can be used because of the proficiency requirement. However, General Standard No. 1 must be evaluated in conjunction with the first standard of fieldwork, which notes that assistants must be properly supervised. Thus, professional standards can be achieved if a firm matches the background of its staff with the complexities of a particular engagement and designs a plan of supervision that reflects both the background and the complexities.*

General Standard No. 2

In all matters relating to the assignment, an independence in mental attitude is to be maintained by the auditor or auditors.

Although every profession should demand that its members be trained and proficient, the second general standard is unique to the auditing profession. This standard states that an auditor must be independent. The need for independence is a result of the auditor's responsibility to users of the financial statements. Since the users of financial statements have no way of verifying the fairness of the statement, they must rely on the work of an independent auditor. If it is suspected that the auditor is not independent, then the integrity and fairness of the financial statements are questionable (AU 220.02).

Independence is discussed in more detail in the chapter entitled "Code of Professional Conduct."

General Standard No. 3

Due professional care is to be exercised in the performance of the audit and the preparation of the report.

The final general standard requires that the auditor exercise due professional care in the conduct of an audit engagement, including the preparation of the auditor's report. This general standard recognizes that even if an auditor is competent and independent, these qualities alone will not necessarily result in a successful audit. In addition to possessing these qualities, an auditor must be conscientious in the conduct of the engagement (AU 230.02).

In some respects, the standard of due professional care encompasses the other nine generally accepted auditing standards. The auditor must observe the standards of fieldwork and reporting to achieve the concept of due professional care. The fieldwork and reporting standards can be achieved only if the auditor is adequately trained and experienced and has an independent mental attitude (AU 230.02).

On the other hand, the standard of due professional care is more than just the observance of the other nine standards. This standard is the synthesizer for the entire engagement. The auditor is expected to pull together all the facts gathered during the engagement and to use his or her experience and professional judgment to reach a conclusion about the fairness of the financial statements or some other specific facet of the engagement. Factors such as the ability to recognize problems, inquisitiveness, and professional skepticism are all part of the concept of due professional care.

STANDARDS OF FIELDWORK

Before an opinion on the financial statements can be formulated, an auditor must be convinced about the fairness of the statements. The standards of fieldwork provide the auditor with a basis for judging the quality of the financial statements. The three standards of fieldwork are briefly described below and are comprehensively discussed in subsequent sections.

Standard of Fieldwork No. 1

> The work is to be adequately planned and assistants, if any, are to be properly supervised.

The first standard of fieldwork partly recognizes that the successful completion of an audit engagement is a difficult task and, like most difficult tasks, requires proper planning. Adequate planning of an audit encompasses features such as understanding the basic characteristics of the client, determining personnel requirements, and determining how to use a firm's resources in an effective manner (AU 310.03).

Part of the first standard of fieldwork also requires that staff assistants be properly supervised. In most audit engagements, several auditors with varying degrees of experience will be used. When two or more auditors are involved in an engagement, there must be a system of review and supervision. The degree of supervision will depend on a variety of factors, such as the background of the assistant and the nature of the work being performed by the assistant (AU 311.11).

> **OBSERVATION:** *Although the first standard of fieldwork refers to supervision of assistants, it must be interpreted more broadly so that supervision and review procedures are designed for all organizational levels of an accounting firm.*

Standard of Fieldwork No. 2

> A sufficient understanding of internal control is to be obtained to plan the audit and to determine the nature, timing, and extent of tests to be performed.

The second standard of fieldwork relates to a client's internal control. Policies and procedures of an internal control should be designed in a manner that enables the entity to record, process, summarize, and report financial data consistent with assertions reflected in its financial statements. For example, an assertion in the financial statements may state that inventories are measured using the lower of FIFO cost or market inventory method. The client must establish policies and procedures that reasonably assure that inventories are costed at recent purchase prices and that inventory items are reduced to estimated replacement cost when appropriate (AU 319.06).

The auditor's responsibility is to understand a client's internal control to a degree that allows the auditor to determine the nature, extent, and timing of audit procedures in a manner that ensures the audit will be effective (AU 319.16).

Standard of Fieldwork No. 3

> Sufficient competent evidential matter is to be obtained through inspection, observation, inquiries, and confirmations to afford a reasonable basis for an opinion regarding the financial statements under audit.

Auditing may be defined as the process of collecting and evaluating evidence. The third standard of fieldwork requires that the auditor collect sufficient and competent evidential matter as a basis for drawing a conclusion about the reliability of a client's financial statements. The sufficiency of evidential matter relates to the quantity of evidence acquired through confirmations, observations, inquiries, and the use of other audit techniques. Competent evidential matter refers to the quality of the evidence gathered. Ultimately, what constitutes sufficient and competent evidence is a matter of professional judgment (AU 326.02).

STANDARDS OF REPORTING

A critical part of the auditor's role is communicating the results of the engagement to a variety of financial statement users. The communication of information and opinions is always a formidable task. The four standards of reporting briefly discussed below are very specific, unlike the six other generally accepted auditing standards. These reporting standards are extensively discussed and illustrated in a subsequent section.

Reporting Standard No. 1

> The report shall state whether the financial statements are presented in accordance with generally accepted accounting principles.

The first standard of reporting requires that the auditor's report state whether the financial statements are prepared in accordance with generally accepted accounting principles. GAAP are defined as technical accounting terms encompassing accounting rules and procedures that are generally accepted at a particular time. There is no comprehensive list of GAAP, since acceptable accounting practice is composed of written as well as unwritten accounting principles. Rule 203 of the AICPA'S Code of Professional Conduct prohibits an auditor from issuing an unqualified opinion on the financial statements when a client has not followed promulgated accounting principles (ET 203).

Reporting Standard No. 2

> The report shall identify those circumstances in which such principles have not been consistently observed in the current period in relation to the preceding period.

The consistent application of accounting principles is required by the second standard of reporting. The consistency standard enhances the comparability of financial statements from year to year. When accounting principles are not consistently applied, APB Opinion No. 20 (Accounting Changes) must be followed to determine how the change is to be accounted for and what disclosures must be made (AU 420.04).

If there is no violation of the consistency standard, there is no reference to consistency in the standard auditor's report. However, if there is a consistency violation, a paragraph similar to the following should be added to the report after the opinion paragraph (AU 508.35).

As discussed in Note X to the financial statements, the Company changed its method of computing inventories and cost of goods sold in 19X5.

Although a paragraph similar to the one above is added to the report when a consistency violation occurs, the auditor's report is considered to be unqualified because the opinion paragraph of the report is not modified.

Reporting Standard No. 3

> Informative disclosures in the financial statements are to be regarded as reasonably adequate unless otherwise stated in the report.

The third standard of reporting may be referred to as an exception standard, since it does not require an explicit reference in the auditor's report. This standard requires a reference to disclosure in the auditor's report only if informative disclosures in the financial statements are not reasonably adequate. What constitutes reasonably adequate informative disclosure for a particular event or for the financial statements as a whole is a matter of professional judgment (AU 508.55).

Reporting Standard No. 4

> The report shall contain either an expression of opinion regarding the financial statements taken as a whole, or an assertion to the effect that an opinion cannot be expressed. When an overall opinion cannot be expressed, the reasons therefor should be stated. In all cases where an auditor's name is associated with financial statements, the report should contain a clear-cut indication of the character of the auditor's work, if any, and the degree of responsibility the auditor is taking.

The fourth and final reporting standard requires that the auditor express an opinion in the report on financial statements or explain why an opinion cannot be expressed. When an unqualified opinion cannot be issued, the auditor's report must explain the substantive reasons for the deviation from the standard auditor's report. Whenever an auditor's name is associated with financial statements, the auditor's report must carefully describe the character of the auditor's work and the degree of responsibility taken by the auditor with respect to the financial statements (AU 508.04).

An auditor may express an unqualified opinion on all financial statements presented, or the auditor's opinion may be split. For example, the auditor may express an unqualified opinion on the balance sheet and a qualified opinion on the statement of income and statement of cash flows. Thus, the expression "taken as a whole" in the fourth standard of reporting is equally applicable to a complete set of financial statements and to each individual financial statement (AU 508.05).

THE BROAD NATURE OF GAAS

Although generally accepted auditing standards provide guidance in the conduct of an audit engagement, the standards are extremely broad. If these standards were the only basis for professional guidance, there would be a variety of interpretations of the standards. More specific guidance is found in Statements on Auditing Standards that are promulgated by the Auditing Standards Board. All SAS issued by the board are incorporated in this publication.

When specialized problems unique to a particular industry are encountered, SAS often are not specific enough to provide guidance for the collection of evidential matter or the structure of the auditor's report. Rather than issue an SAS that would be applicable to all audit engagements, the AICPA, through appropriate industry committees, issues Industry Audit and Accounting Guides.

ATTESTATION STANDARDS

Generally accepted auditing standards apply to engagements in which the auditor will express an opinion on the financial statements. These types of engagements often are referred to as *attestation engagements*. An auditor can be hired to perform a wide variety of other attestation work as well. For example, a client or other party may request an auditor to report on its description of internal control that relates to the preparation of financial statements or on its compliance with various statutory, regulatory, and contractual requirements. In general, an attestation engagement is one in which an auditor is engaged to issue an opinion about the reliability of another party's written assertion. An *assertion* is a declaration, or a set of related declarations taken as a whole, that is made by another party.

To provide guidance for accountants performing attestation engagements (other than those in which the accountant expresses an opinion on the financial statements), the AICPA established Statements on Standards for Attestation Engagements (SSAE). The attestation standards are as follows (AT 100.06–.52):

General Standards

- The engagement shall be performed by a practitioner or practitioners having adequate technical training and proficiency in the attest function.
- The engagement shall be performed by a practitioner or practitioners having adequate knowledge on the subject matter of the assertion.
- The practitioner shall perform an engagement only if he or she has reason to believe that the following two conditions exist:
  - The assertion is capable of evaluation against reasonable criteria that either have been established by a recognized body or are stated in the presentation of the assertion in a sufficiently clear and comprehensive manner for a knowledgeable reader to be able to understand them.
  - The assertion is capable of reasonably consistent estimation or measurement using such criteria.
- In all matters relating to the engagement, an independence in mental attitude shall be maintained by the practitioner or practitioners.
- Due professional care shall be exercised in the performance of the engagement.

Standards of Fieldwork

- The work shall be adequately planned and assistants, if any, shall be properly supervised.
- Sufficient evidence shall be obtained to provide a reasonable basis for the conclusion that is expressed in the report.

Standards of Reporting

- The report shall identify the assertion being reported on and state the character of the engagement.
- The report shall state the practitioner's conclusion about whether the assertion is presented in conformity with the established or stated criteria against which it was measured.
- The report shall state all of the practitioner's significant reservations about the engagement and the presentation of the assertion.

- The report on an engagement to evaluate an assertion that has been prepared in conformity with agreed-upon criteria or on an engagement to apply agreed-upon procedures should contain a statement limiting its use to the parties who have agreed upon such criteria or procedures.

Attestation standards are discussed in the chapter entitled "Attest Engagements."

PRE-ENGAGEMENT PLANNING

CONTENTS

Overview	**5.03**
New Client Evaluation	**5.03**
Communication with Predecessor Auditor	**5.04**
Audit of Financial Statements Previously Audited by a Predecessor Auditor	**5.06**
Predecessor Auditor That Has Ceased Operations	**5.07**
Communication with a Predecessor Auditor That Has Ceased Operations	**5.07**
Unavailability of the Workpapers of a Predecessor Auditor That Has Ceased Operations	**5.07**
Significant Audit Procedures Performed by a Predecessor Auditor That Has Ceased Operations	**5.08**
Part of Audit Performed by Another Independent Auditor That Has Ceased Operations	**5.08**
Successor Auditor Becomes Aware of Information That Leads Him or Her to Believe That Financial Statements Reported on by a Predecessor Auditor That Has Ceased Operations May Be Materially Misstated	**5.08**
Independence	**5.09**
Accepting a Client	**5.09**
Documentation	**5.11**
Continuing Audits	**5.11**

PRE-ENGAGEMENT PLANNING

Overview

Pre-engagement planning includes procedures that are employed before the auditor begins to obtain an understanding of the client's internal control structure or to collect evidential matter. It begins with the evaluation of the prospective client or, in the case of a continuing audit, the reassessment of whether the auditor wants to continue performing professional services for an existing client. The following Statements on Auditing Standards are discussed in this chapter in the sequence in which they appear below:

- SAS-22 (Planning and Supervision)

- SAS-7 (Communications Between Predecessor and Successor Auditors)

SAS-22 provides guidance for acquiring an adequate knowledge of a new client as part of pre-engagement planning (AU 310).

SAS-7 establishes guidance for the successor auditor in communicating with the predecessor auditor. SAS-7 requires that the successor auditor communicate with the predecessor auditor, if any, to determine whether there are factors that should be taken into consideration in determining whether to accept the client (AU 315).

New Client Evaluation

Statement on Quality Control Standards (SQCS) No. 2 states that an accounting firm should establish procedures to determine whether a client should be accepted. Although the firm must evaluate the integrity of the client's management, the firm is not required to *vouch* for it.

An accounting firm must evaluate its ability to service the prospective client. Rule 201 of the Code of Professional Conduct requires that an accounting firm accept only those clients that the firm can reasonably expect to serve in a competent manner (ET 201.01).

Rule 201 does not suggest that an accounting firm must possess complete technical knowledge before accepting an engagement. The acceptance of a client on the basis that additional training or knowledge will be acquired before completion of the engagement does not represent a lack of competence (ET 201.02).

> **OBSERVATION:** *SAS-22 implies that appropriate knowledge of a business may be obtained by (1) a review of the audit workpapers from prior years, (2) an interview of key client personnel, (3) a review of publications on accounting and auditing matters, and (4) a review of industry publications (AU 311.08).*

Quality-control standards related to the evaluation of a prospective client are discussed in the chapter entitled "Responsibility and Function of the Independent Auditor."

Communication with Predecessor Auditor

SAS-7 requires that an auditor attempt to communicate with the predecessor auditor before accepting an engagement. This communication is necessary to determine whether there are prior client-auditor problems that might cause the successor auditor to refuse the engagement. However, Rule 301 of the Code of Professional Conduct prohibits an auditor from disclosing confidential information except when the client agrees to the disclosure. To reconcile the requirements of SAS-7 with Rule 301, the successor auditor should ask the prospective client to grant permission to discuss the impending engagement with the predecessor auditor. The client should not place any restrictions on the exchange of information between the successor and predecessor auditors. If the successor auditor cannot obtain required information from the predecessor auditor because of client restrictions, the successor auditor should consider the reasons for the restrictions and consider the implications when deciding whether to accept the client (AU 315.04–.05).

> **OBSERVATION:** *Although SAS-7 does not require that the client's authorization to the predecessor auditor be in writing, it is good*

practice for the predecessor auditor to require written authorization (see Rule 301 for certain exemptions) (AU 315.02).

Questions raised by the successor auditor should be sufficiently specific to help determine whether the engagement should be accepted. Following are some of the questions that the successor auditor should consider asking the predecessor auditor before accepting the engagement (AU 315.06):

- Have there been situations in which management has manipulated financial information in a fraudulent manner or committed illegal acts?
- Have there been incidents of management intervention or circumvention of internal control?
- Have you had significant disagreements with the client over the application of accounting principles?
- Does the client attempt to restrict or direct the scope of the audit?
- Does management accept the concept that it is primarily responsible for the content of the financial statements?
- Does management encourage its key employees to cooperate fully with the independent auditor?

> **OBSERVATION:** *An Auditing Interpretation of SAS-7 entitled "Restating Financial Statements Reported on by a Predecessor Auditor" (September 1986) states that a successor auditor should discuss with the predecessor auditor information discovered by the successor auditor that might require the restatement of financial statements reported on by the predecessor auditor. The communication should provide the predecessor auditor with information that will allow the predecessor auditor to comply with the auditing standards established by Section 561 of SAS-1 (Subsequent Discovery of Facts Existing at the Date of the Auditor's Report) (AU 9315.06–.07).*

In most instances, the predecessor auditor should respond to inquiries requested by the successor auditor. If the predecessor auditor refuses to respond or if the responses are limited, the successor auditor should carefully consider whether to accept the engagement (AU 315.07).

> **OBSERVATION:** *An Auditing Interpretation of SAS-7 entitled "Determining the Predecessor Auditor" (May 1985) states that a successor auditor may be replaced before the engagement is complete and the successor auditor's report is issued. Under this circumstance, the "next" successor auditor is required to communicate with both the original predecessor auditor and the successor auditor being replaced (AU 9315.01–.05).*

Audit of Financial Statements Previously Audited by a Predecessor Auditor

An Interpretation of SAS-7 entitled "Audits of Financial Statements That Had Been Previously Audited by a Predecessor Auditor" (April 1995) addressees a number of issues related to an audit of financial statements that previously had been audited by a predecessor auditor. These audits are referred to as *reaudits*. When the successor auditor communicates with the predecessor auditor, the successor auditor should make it clear that the purpose of the communication is to determine whether a reaudit should be accepted. If the reaudit engagement is accepted, the successor auditor must obtain sufficient competent evidential matter on which to express an opinion on the previously audited financial statements. While the successor auditor may review the workpapers of the predecessor auditor, the work performed by the predecessor auditor does not constitute sufficient competent evidential matter for the reaudit. The Interpretation also notes that the predecessor auditor is not a specialist (as defined in SAS-73 [Using the Work of a Specialist]) or an internal auditor (as defined in SAS-65 [The Auditor's Consideration of the Internal Audit Function in an Audit of Financial Statements]). Furthermore, the successor auditor's report should not be based on shared responsibility for the opinion on the previously audited financial statements (AU 9315.08–.18).

As part of the planning of the reaudit, the Interpretation concludes, the successor auditor should request access to the workpapers for the previously audited financial statements and for the prior period.

The successor auditor should apply appropriate audit procedures to the inventory amount presented in the previously audited financial statements. Although the successor auditor cannot observe the inventories reported in the previously audited financial statements, he or she must observe the current inventory count (generally as part of the current audit engagement) and perform appropriate tests of inventory transactions during the intervening period.

Predecessor Auditor That Has Ceased Operations

The pre-engagement planning of an audit is complicated when a predecessor auditor has ceased operations. In 1991, the Auditing Standards Division provided guidance for this circumstance by issuing a Notice to Practitioners entitled "Audit, Review, and Compilation Considerations When a Predecessor Accountant Has Ceased Operations."

> **OBSERVATION:** *A Notice to Practitioners is nonauthoritative guidance prepared by the AICPA staff in consultation with members of the Auditing Standards Board. Notices generally are published in "The CPA Letter." They are not approved, disapproved, or otherwise acted on by a senior technical committee of the AICPA.*

> **OBSERVATION:** *Members of the SEC Practice Section of the AICPA must notify a client and the SEC in writing within five days of becoming aware of the end of the client–auditor relationship. In addition, members must notify the Quality Control Inquiry Committee in writing within 30 days of service of a lawsuit.*

Communication with a predecessor auditor that has ceased operations In some instances, a predecessor auditor will have ceased operations before the successor auditor accepts an engagement. In this circumstance, the successor auditor should nonetheless attempt to communicate with the predecessor auditor to obtain information concerning the acceptance of the engagement. Rather than contacting the predecessor accounting firm, it may be possible to contact the engagement partner who was responsible for the engagement. If no response or a limited response is received from the predecessor auditor, that fact should be considered by the successor auditor in determining whether it is appropriate to accept the engagement.

Unavailability of the workpapers of a predecessor auditor that has ceased operations Information contained in the predecessor auditor's workpapers is often useful in conducting the current engagement. However, workpapers may not be available when a predecessor auditor has ceased operations. If the successor auditor is unable to gain access to the predecessor auditor's workpapers, other audit procedures must be performed to obtain sufficient evidential matter required by the current engagement. The required evidence could relate to matters such as amounts of beginning balances and existence of contingencies. If sufficient evidential matter cannot be acquired by using other audit procedures, the successor auditor must determine whether an unqualified opinion can be expressed in the current engagement.

Significant audit procedures performed by a predecessor auditor that has ceased operations   In some engagements, a predecessor auditor will perform significant audit procedures before the accounting firm's operations have ceased. Because the predecessor auditor has not issued a report on the client's financial statements, the successor auditor can neither assume responsibility for the work of the predecessor auditor nor prepare a report that describes the shared responsibility of reporting on the financial statements. However, the successor auditor may inspect the predecessor auditor's workpapers when determining the nature, timing, and extent of procedures to be used in the current engagement.

Part of audit performed by another independent auditor that has ceased operations   Part of an audit (subsidiary, division, branch, component, or investment in another enterprise) may be performed by another auditor that has ceased operations. The principal auditor may refer to the audit of the other auditor or assume responsibility for the other auditor's work only if (1) the other auditor has issued a separate audit report and (2) the procedures required by SAS-1, Section 543 (Part of Audit Performed by Other Independent Auditors), have been completed *before* the other auditor ceased operations. If both of these conditions do not exist, the principal auditor must perform appropriate procedures in order to express an opinion on the financial statements; however, the work of the other auditor can be used in determining the nature, timing, and extent of the procedures.

Successor auditor becomes aware of information that leads him or her to believe that financial statements reported on by a predecessor auditor that has ceased operations may be materially misstated   A successor auditor may believe that financial statements audited by a predecessor auditor that has ceased operations could be materially misstated. In this circumstance, the successor auditor should inform management of the apparent problem and request that management determine whether the financial statements are materially misstated. Management, as part of its investigation, may find it helpful to discuss the matter with the previous engagement partner of the defunct CPA firm. If management concludes that the financial statements are materially misstated, that information should be conveyed to the individual(s) responsible for concluding the operations of the predecessor firm. Also, the successor auditor should consider whether management action is necessary so that the misstated financial statements will not be relied on in the future. If management does not respond to the problem in a satisfactory manner, the successor auditor should inform the audit committee (or equivalent party) of the matter. If the audit committee does not respond in an appropriate manner, the successor auditor should consider withdrawing from the engagement. Actions contemplated by the auditor should be discussed with legal counsel.

Independence

As a preliminary step before the engagement is accepted, an accounting firm should make inquiries of its professional staff to determine if there is any relationship between a partner or staff member and the client that might impair the firm's independence.

Accepting a Client

Once the auditor has determined (1) that its firm is independent and competent to conduct the audit, (2) that the client's reputation is one of integrity, and (3) that appropriate responses have been received from the predecessor auditor, if any, he or she should request a preliminary conference with the client. At this conference, the auditor and the client must agree on certain issues, including the following:

1. Specific services to be rendered
2. Cooperation and work expected to be performed by the client's personnel
3. Expected starting and completion dates of the engagement
4. Possibility that the completion date may be changed if unforeseen audit problems arise or if adequate cooperation from the client's personnel is not received
5. Nature and limitations of an audit engagement
6. Estimate of the fee to be charged for the engagement

The issues enumerated above, as well as others, should be clearly explained in an engagement letter. The following is an example of an engagement letter.

Mr. Robert J. Bray, President
The West End Company
1800 Carolina Avenue
Cherry Hill, NJ 08003

Dear Mr. Bray:

In accordance with the agreement reached in our conference on October 14, 19X5, we are to perform an audit of the balance sheet of The West End Company as of December 31, 19X5, and of the related statements of income, retained earnings, and cash flows for the fiscal year then ended. The audit report will be mailed to you and the Board of Directors.

We are also to prepare the federal and state income tax returns for the fiscal year ending December 31, 19X5.

Our audit will be made in accordance with generally accepted auditing standards and, accordingly, will include such tests of the accounting records and such other auditing procedures as we consider necessary to enable us to express an opinion regarding your financial statements. Our engagement cannot be relied upon to disclose all errors, irregularities, or illegal acts, including fraud or defalcations, that may exist. However, we will inform the appropriate level of management of any material errors that come to our attention and any irregularities or illegal acts that come to our attention, unless they are clearly inconsequential.

Our audit will include gaining an understanding of your company's internal control over financial reporting. The purpose of that understanding is to enable us to determine the nature, timing, and extent of our auditing procedures, not to provide any assurance about internal control. If we discover matters that, in our judgment, represent significant deficiencies in the design or operation of your internal control, we will communicate these to you in writing by the conclusion of the audit.

The fair presentation of the financial statements is the responsibility of your company. In addition, your company is responsible for the development, implementation, and maintenance of adequate internal control over financial reporting and for the accuracy of the financial statements. Although we may advise you about appropriate accounting principles and their application, the selection and method of application are solely the responsibility of your company.

Based on our discussion with your personnel and the predecessor auditor and a preliminary review of your accounting records, we estimate the cost of the audit engagement, including the preparation of the related tax returns, will be between $75,000 and $80,000. It should be recognized that the estimated fee could be affected by unusual circumstances we cannot foresee at this time. However, if we should encounter such problems, we will contact you to discuss the implications of the new developments.

Whenever possible, we will attempt to use your company's personnel. This effort should substantially reduce our time requirements and help us perform an efficient audit.

We appreciate the opportunity to serve your company. Do not hesitate to contact us if you have questions about the engagement or desire other professional services.

If the terms designated in this letter are satisfactory, please sign in the space provided below and return the duplicate copy of the letter to us.

Sincerely,

Penny J. Nichols, CPA

Accepted by:

Title:

Date:

> **OBSERVATION:** *A good question for the auditor to consider when evaluating a continuing client is, "Knowing what we know now, would we accept the client as a new client?"*

Documentation

The acceptance of an audit engagement should be well documented. The documentation should clearly show that the necessary pre-engagement planning procedures were properly completed. The documentation should also include copies of communications with the client, memoranda of the exchanges between the successor auditor and the predecessor auditor, if any, and other pertinent information concerning pre-engagement planning.

Continuing Audits

Once an audit engagement is accepted, the professional relationship between the client and the independent auditing firm should be evaluated from year to year. This requirement is explicitly mandated by SQCS-2. Thus, the independent auditing firm should continue to evaluate the integrity of management and should periodically determine the firm's ability to service the client.

PLANNING THE ENGAGEMENT

CONTENTS

Overview	6.03
Appointment of Independent Auditor	6.03
Engagement Planning in a Computer Environment	6.04
Nature, Timing, and Extent of Procedures	6.06
Engagement Supervision	6.07
Analytical Procedures	6.08
Engagement Planning Checklist	6.08

PLANNING THE ENGAGEMENT

Overview

The first standard of fieldwork requires that an engagement be properly planned and supervised. As noted in the chapter entitled "Pre-Engagement Planning," planning an audit engagement begins before the engagement is accepted. Specifically, Statement on Quality Control Standards (SQCS) No. 2 requires that an accounting firm establish policies and procedures to periodically evaluate existing clients and also to evaluate prospective clients before they are accepted. The following Statements on Auditing Standards and their related Interpretations are discussed in this chapter:

- SAS-7 (Communications Between Predecessor and Successor Auditors)
- SAS-22 (Planning and Supervision)
- SAS-55 (Consideration of the Internal Control Structure in a Financial Statement Audit as amended by SAS 78)

SAS-7 establishes guidance for communications between a successor auditor and predecessor auditor that relate to the acceptance of a client (AU 315).

SAS-22 provides broad guidance for implementing the first standard of fieldwork. In addition, this SAS identifies various factors that may have an effect on planning an audit engagement (AU 311).

SAS-55 describes how various factors affect the planning of an audit engagement.

Appointment of Independent Auditor

Ideally, an auditor should be appointed early enough to allow efficient planning of an engagement. SAS-22 lists the following factors that may have an effect on the engagement planning (AU 311.03):

- The client's organization and operating characteristics
- Accounting policies and methods used by the client
- Methods used to process significant accounting information, including the use of other parties such as service centers
- Planned assessed level of control risk
- Establishment of materiality criteria
- Accounts that are likely to require adjustment
- Unique conditions that may require special audit procedures
- Purpose of the engagement (for example, a special report based on a comprehensive set of accounting rules other than GAAP)

Early appointment of the auditor also benefits the client, because the auditor can plan his or her work in a manner that will save time. Moreover, an early appointment will increase the likelihood that the auditor will complete the engagement and deliver the report on time (AU 310.03).

Although early appointment of the auditor is advantageous to both the auditor and the client, an auditor may be engaged near or after the end of the accounting period. However, before the auditor accepts such an engagement, preliminary steps should be taken to determine whether it is likely that an unqualified opinion can be expressed. For example, the auditor may not be satisfied with the physical inventory on hand because of weak internal control. When the auditor is unsure about the adequacy of the scope of the engagement, the client should be informed of the circumstances and the type of opinion that may have to be issued (AU 310.04).

SAS-7 requires that the successor auditor (with permission of the client) make inquiries of the predecessor auditor, if any, before an engagement is accepted (AU 315.03).

Engagement Planning in a Computer Environment

The design of an accounting system and the nature of the related internal control procedures are influenced by the methods that an entity uses to process significant accounting information. These methods may include the use of service organizations, such as outside service centers. Thus, in planning an engagement, an auditor must consider the methods used by an entity to process significant accounting information. In addition, the nature, timing, and extent of audit procedures performed by the auditor also may be influenced by the extent of computer processing that is used for significant accounting applications. Significant accounting applications are those that relate to accounting information that can materially affect the financial statements that the auditor is examining (AU 311.09).

In an examination of financial statements, the following matters should be considered by the auditor in evaluating the effects of an entity's use of computer processing (AU 311.09):

- The degree that computers are used to process accounting information that could materially affect the client's financial statements

- The organization of an entity's computer processing activities

- The availability of evidential matter, such as input documents, transaction files, and master files, and the length of time that the information is accessible by the auditor

- The availability of computer-generated information that may be used in substantive testing, especially for analytical review purposes

- The use of computer-assisted audit techniques to increase efficiency or as the only alternative to obtain essential evidential matter

> **OBSERVATION:** *Guidance for the use of outside service centers can be found in SAS-70 (Reports on the Processing of Transactions by Service Organizations) and its related Auditing Procedure Study.*

Computerization of the accounting system can affect the auditor's consideration of internal control and the performance of substantive tests. The auditor should consider whether it is necessary to seek assistance from computer specialists. The specialists may be part of the CPA firm's in-house staff or may work for another organization. In either case, the auditor is still primarily responsible for work performed by a computer specialist. Thus, the auditor's understanding of computerized accounting systems must be sufficient to (1) communicate the objectives of the work to the computer specialist, (2) determine whether the work to be performed by the specialist will achieve the desired audit objectives, and (3) determine how the work of the specialist will affect the nature, timing, and extent of other audit procedures (AU 311.10).

> **OBSERVATION:** *Standards established by SAS-73 (Using the Work of a Specialist) are not applicable to the work of a computer specialist as described above, because the specialist's work must be reviewed and supervised like any other staff assistant, as required by SAS-22. Under SAS-22, the auditor's responsibility is to review the work of each assistant "to determine whether it was adequately performed and to evaluate whether the results are consistent with the conclusions to be presented in the auditor's report."*

Nature, Timing, and Extent of Procedures

Proper planning of an engagement allows the auditor to make an initial design of the audit approach. This design encompasses (1) the type of audit procedures to be performed (confirmation, vouching, etc.), (2) the timing of procedures (interim, year-end, etc.), and (3) the extent to which procedures will be employed (number of confirmations to be mailed). The following are typical planning procedures that can be employed to facilitate the design of audit procedures (AU 311.04):

- Stay abreast of current business conditions that relate to the client.
- Read interim financial statements for the current year.
- Discuss the audit approach with management, the board of directors, and the audit committee.
- Evaluate new audit and accounting pronouncements as they relate to the client.
- Discuss the use of client personnel in the preparation of data to be used by the auditor.
- Determine whether nonaudit specialists within the accounting firm will be needed (for example, a tax specialist or a computer specialist).
- Determine whether work of other parties is appropriate (for example, specialists or internal auditors).
- Prepare an audit budget to show personnel requirements and timing of the engagement.
- Review client's correspondence file, prior years' working papers, and annual report if the engagement is a continuing engagement.

The general description of the client and related auditing and accounting problems may be summarized in a memo, often referred to as an audit plan. Specific instructions on the nature, extent, and timing of audit procedures should be identified in a set of written audit programs. These specific instructions are tentative and may be changed as the engagement progresses (AU 311.04).

Engagement Supervision

The first standard of fieldwork refers not only to planning but also to engagement supervision. Thus, it is recognized that planning the engagement must be supplemented by determining whether the audit plan is being executed as designed. Supervision also involves the review of the audit effort and related audit judgments made by assistants to determine whether these judgments are appropriate. Specifically, SAS-22 states that instructing assistants, staying abreast of audit results, and reviewing workpapers are examples of supervision (AU 311.11).

During the conduct of an engagement, differences of opinion are likely to occur regarding the significance or implications of audit findings. These differences may surface during the supervision phase of the engagement. The supervision phase may be structured, such as the review of workpapers, or it may be informal, such as discussions between an assistant and a supervisor. Both the auditor responsible for the engagement and any assistants should be aware of the procedures to be followed when differences exist. SAS-22 specifically states that procedures should allow assistants to document their positions if they disagree with how a particular audit question was resolved (AU 311.11).

> **OBSERVATION:** *An Auditing Interpretation entitled "Responsibility of Assistants for the Resolution of Accounting and Auditing Issues" (February 1986) states that paragraph 14 of SAS-22 requires that during an audit, if differences of opinion relating to accounting and auditing issues arise between the firm's personnel, the in-charge auditor and all assistants should be familiar with the procedure that should be observed. The Interpretation concludes that each assistant has a responsibility to bring disagreements or concerns to the attention of the appropriate person in the firm. The assistant has the right to document any position taken if he or she chooses not to be associated with the final resolution of the matter (AU 9311.35–.37).*

Analytical Procedures

Analytical procedures should be used in the planning of the audit engagement. Analytical procedures, tests of the financial information through study and comparison of relationships among data, may be used during the planning phase of the engagement. The relationships among certain data may be reasonably expected to exist and to continue from period to period. Thus, the auditor may be able to detect unexpected relationships and trends. In this event, the auditor may elect to perform additional audit procedures to determine the reason for the unexpected relationships and trends. For example, if the auditor is aware that the client's industry is in a business slump, he or she would not expect an increase in the inventory turnover rate. Analytical procedures can also be used during other phases of the audit; these procedures are discussed in the chapter entitled "Evidence" (AU 329.02).

> *OBSERVATION: Caution must be used when preliminary accounting numbers are part of the analytical technique employed in the planning phase of the engagement. At this point in the engagement, the numbers are not audited and may lead to an invalid conclusion. In the example in the preceding paragraph, the ending inventory numbers may be understated because of a number of counting and pricing errors.*

Engagement Planning Checklist

When planning an engagement, the independent auditor should consider performing the following procedures:

- Obtain an understanding of the client's operating characteristics.
- Obtain an understanding of the current economic conditions that may affect the client.
- Evaluate technological changes, if any, that may have occurred in the client's industry since the conclusion of the prior engagement.
- Evaluate current government regulations that may affect the client.
- Discuss current operating conditions of the client with key personnel, such as the chief financial officer, controller, etc.

- Perform analytical procedures, including computations of trends and ratios, and determine whether the results are consistent with respect to expectations.
- Review prior years' workpapers.
- Review current correspondence file.
- Determine whether new accounting pronouncements could have an effect on the client's financial statements.
- Determine whether new auditing pronouncements could have an effect on the design of the audit approach.
- Consider whether specialized accounting or auditing topics require consultation with other professional members of the firm.
- Consider whether the work of a specialist is necessary to complete the engagement.
- Review the engagement letter to determine whether the objectives stated in the letter are consistent with the design of the audit approach.
- Review the special characteristics of the audit engagement and determine whether the appropriate audit personnel have been assigned to the engagement.
- Discuss the use of client personnel in the conduct of the engagement with appropriate officials of the client.
- Prepare a time budget classified by major audit tasks and time periods.
- Evaluate the client's internal audit function and, if appropriate, determine how it may be used in the engagement.
- Instruct assistants who will be involved in the engagement to read the audit plan, prior years' workpapers, and the current correspondence file.
- Establish broad guidelines for materiality and discuss these guidelines with assistants.
- During the review of prior years' workpapers, identify areas that may require adjustments to the financial statements or that may result in the use of extended audit procedures.
- Determine whether it will be necessary to use the report of another auditor.
- Identify areas that pose the greatest audit exposure because of such factors as dollar value of the account, weaknesses in internal control, and susceptibility to asset misappropriation.

- Review the current year's interim financial statements.

- Review reports prepared by the internal audit department or governmental agencies that may have accounting or audit implications.

- Review audit programs to determine whether they should be revised.

- Prepare a list of officers, principals, affiliated companies, etc., to be distributed to audit staff members, which should be used as a basis of identifying possible related party transactions.

- Identify correspondence that must be mailed early in the engagement.

- Determine whether the client has any special requests as to the timing, nature, and extent of audit procedures. Also, evaluate the client's response regarding any limitations on the scope of the audit engagement.

- Prepare an audit plan or update the prior period's audit plan.

- Have a final meeting with all audit personnel assigned to the engagement.

INTERNAL CONTROL, ERRORS, AND IRREGULARITIES

Contents

Overview	**7.05**
Nature of Internal Control	**7.07**
Control Environment	**7.08**
Risk Assessment	**7.11**
Control Activities	**7.11**
Information and Communication	**7.12**
Monitoring	**7.13**
The Application of Internal Control Concepts to Small and Midsized Entities	**7.13**
Other Factors to Be Considered in the Design of Internal Control	**7.15**
Limitations of Internal Controls	**7.15**
Implementing the Second Standard of Fieldwork	**7.16**
Understanding Internal Controls	**7.16**
Financial Statement Assertion	**7.16**
Relevant Controls	**7.18**
Developing an Understanding	**7.18**
Obtaining an Understanding of the Control Environment	**7.19**
Obtaining an Understanding of Risk Assessment	**7.19**
Obtaining an Understanding of Control Activities	**7.19**
Obtaining an Understanding about Information and Communication	**7.20**
Obtaining an Understanding about Monitoring	**7.20**
Procedures Used to Obtain an Understanding of Components	**7.20**
Documenting the Auditor's Understanding of the Internal Control	**7.21**
Flowcharts	**7.21**

Internal Control Questionnaire   **7.22**

Narrative Descriptions   **7.22**

Determine the Planned Assessed Level of Control Risk   **7.23**

Perform Tests of Controls   **7.24**

    Identification of Internal Control Policies and Procedures   **7.25**

       Breadth of Influence   **7.25**

       Degree of Relevance   **7.25**

    Tests of Controls   **7.25**

       Evaluation of Effectiveness of Design   **7.25**

       Evaluation of Operational Effectiveness   **7.26**

Evaluate the Planned Level of Control Risk   **7.27**

    Type of Evidential Matter   **7.27**

    Source of Evidential Matter   **7.27**

    Timeliness of Evidential Matter   **7.27**

    Interrelationship of Evidential Matter   **7.29**

Documenting the Assessed Level of Control Risk   **7.29**

Designing Substantive Tests Based on Assessed Level of Control Risk   **7.30**

Reportable Conditions   **7.31**

    Agreed-Upon Criteria   **7.34**

    Reporting Format   **7.34**

Management Letter   **7.38**

Reports by Management   **7.38**

Errors and Irregularities   **7.40**

    Nature of Errors and Irregularities   **7.41**

    Planning the Engagement   **7.42**

    Mental Attitude of Auditor   **7.44**

    Discovery of Errors or Irregularities   **7.45**

    Communication of Errors and Irregularities to the Audit Committee   **7.45**

    Auditor's Report   **7.46**

    Other Engagements   **7.47**

Illegal Acts   7.47

  Illegal Acts with Direct Effects on the Financial
    Statements   7.47

  Illegal Acts with Indirect Effects on the Financial
    Statements   7.48

  Audit Procedures—No Suspicion of Illegal Acts   7.49

  Audit Procedures—Suspicion of Illegal Acts   7.49

  Discovery of Illegal Acts   7.50

    Communication with Audit Committee   7.50

    Audit Report   7.51

    Other Engagements   7.52

Internal Audit Function   7.52

  Assessing Objectivity and Competence of Internal
    Auditors   7.53

  Effect of the Internal Audit Function on Audit Planning   7.54

    Understanding the Internal Control   7.54

    Assessing Risk   7.54

    Designing Substantive Procedures   7.55

  Degree of Reliance on the Internal Audit Function   7.55

  Evaluating Internal Audit Work   7.56

Reports on the Processing of Transactions by Service
  Organizations   7.57

  Role of the User Auditor   7.58

    Planning   7.59

    Control Risk Assessment   7.60

    Substantive Tests   7.60

  Evaluating the Service Auditor   7.61

  Role of the Service Auditor   7.62

  Written Representations   7.71

Documenting   7.72

Foreign Corrupt Practices Act   7.72

  Maintenance of Books and Records   7.73

  System of Internal Controls   7.73

  Accounting Standards Provisions   7.73

  Antibribery Provisions   7.74

Appendix: Consideration of Fraud in a Financial
    Statement Audit (Exposure Draft)   **7.75**
    The Auditor's Current Responsibility with
        Respect to Fraud   **7.75**
    Risk Assessment   **7.77**
    Risk Assessment and the Audit Plan   **7.78**
    Evaluation Test Results   **7.78**
    Proposed Effective Date   **7.80**

INTERNAL CONTROL, ERRORS, AND IRREGULARITIES

Overview

To perform an effective and efficient audit, the independent auditor must gain an understanding of the client's internal control. The degree of reliance that an auditor can place on the internal control of an enterprise depends on a number of factors, including the control environment and the design of the accounting system. The following Statements on Auditing Standards and AICPA Audit Guides are discussed in this chapter:

- SAS-55 (Consideration of the Internal Control Structure in a Financial Statement Audit)
- SAS-78 (Consideration of Internal Control in a Financial Statement Audit: An Amendment to SAS No. 55)
- AICPA Audit Guide, *Consideration of the Internal Control Structure in a Financial Statement Audit*
- SAS-47 (Audit Risk and Materiality in Conducting an Audit)
- SAS-60 (Communication of Internal Control Structure Related Matters Noted in an Audit)
- SAS-53 (The Auditor's Responsibility to Detect and Report Errors and Irregularities)
- SAS-54 (Illegal Acts by Clients)
- SAS-65 (The Auditor's Consideration of the Internal Audit Function in an Audit of Financial Statements)
- SAS-70 (Reports on the Processing of Transactions by Service Organizations)
- SAS-41 (Working Papers)

SAS-55, as amended by SAS-78, requires that an auditor obtain an understanding of a client's internal control as a basis for planning the audit engagement. The auditor's assessment of the client's internal control, in part, determines the nature, timing, and extent of substantive auditing procedures (AU 319).

The AICPA Audit Guide entitled *Consideration of the Internal Control Structure in a Financial Statement Audit* provides expanded explanations and numerous illustrations of the concepts introduced in SAS-55.

> **OBSERVATION:** *The AICPA issued SAS-78, which amends SAS-55 and the related AICPA Audit Guide to incorporate the concepts developed by the Committee of Sponsoring Organizations of the Treadway Commission (COSO). The COSO report provides a broader definition of internal control than that initially established in SAS-55. SAS-78 is effective for audits of financial statements for periods that begin on or after January 1, 1997.*

SAS-47 provides a discussion of inherent risk. Inherent risk is an element that should be considered in assessing control risk (AU 312).

SAS-60 provides definitions for reportable conditions and material weaknesses in a client's internal control. In addition, SAS-60 discusses the report format that should be used to communicate reportable conditions and material weaknesses to the client's audit committee (or group of individuals with responsibilities similar to the audit committee) (AU 325).

SAS-53 defines errors and irregularities and discusses the auditor's responsibilities with respect to their discovery. Included in these responsibilities are the strategy for planning of an engagement, effects of discovering errors and irregularities, and the reporting of irregularities to the client's audit committee (or group of individuals with responsibilities similar to the audit committee) (AU 316).

SAS-54 discusses the auditor's responsibility for discovering illegal acts. In general, the auditor should plan the engagement to take into consideration illegal acts that have a direct and material effect on the financial statements. On the other hand, illegal acts with indirect effects on the financial statements should be evaluated as contingent liabilities when they come to the attention of the auditor (AU 317).

SAS-65 discusses the possible effect an internal audit function can have on the evaluation of internal control and the design (nature, timing, and extent) of subsequent audit procedures (AU 322).

SAS-70 provides guidance for reporting on internal control of an organization that processes transactions or accounts for assets or liabilities of another entity. A special report on the service organization's internal control may be prepared by the *service auditor* and evaluated by the *user auditor* to assess control risk for the *client organization* (AU 324).

SAS-41 requires the auditor to prepare workpapers that specifically demonstrate that the second standard of fieldwork has been satisfied (AU 339) Nature of Internal Control

Nature of Internal Control

The second standard of fieldwork requires that "a sufficient understanding of internal control is to be obtained to plan the audit and to determine the nature, timing, and extent of tests to be performed." SAS-55 was issued to provide specific guidance for achieving the objective established in the second standard. SAS-55 describes internal control as follows (AU 319.06):

> Internal control is a process—effected by an entity's board of directors, management, and other personnel—designed to provide reasonable assurance regarding the achievement of objectives in the following categories: (a) reliability of financial reporting, (b) effectiveness and efficiency of operations, and (c) compliance with applicable laws and regulations.

Once objectives are established by management, it must also establish a process that encourages employees to follow and meet the established objectives. Thus, a critical part of the success of the internal control process is the following five components:

> *Control environment*—It sets the tone of an organization, which influences the control consciousness of its employees. The control environment is the foundation for all other components of internal control because it provides discipline and structure.

> *Risk assessment*—Risk assessment is the process that an entity must conduct to identify and assess any relevant risks to its objectives. Once this is done, management must determine how the risks should be managed.

> *Control activities*—Control activities are the polices and procedures that help ensure that management directives are carried out.

> *Information and communication*—These two key elements help management carry out its responsibilities. Management must

establish a timely and effective process for relaying information.

Monitoring—Monitoring is a process that an entity uses to assess the quality of its internal control performance over time.

SAS-55 provides a broad definition of *internal control*, ranging from financial-reporting matters to the efficient execution of operational activities. However, the purpose of an audit of financial statements is narrow: determine whether the financial statements are prepared in accordance with generally accepted accounting principles (or any other comprehensive basis of accounting). For this reason, the auditor is concerned with the internal control process and its components as they relate to the reliability of financial reporting. The following discussion of the five components of internal control is limited to the internal control objective related to financial reporting (AU 319A.84.1–.84.20).

Control environment The success or failure of implementing internal controls will depend on the environment in which the internal control process takes place. It is unlikely that specific internal control activities, no matter how well designed, can be effective if those activities must be executed in a flawed control environment (AU 319.25–.27). SAS-55 identifies several elements, as discussed below, that affect an entity's control environment.

Integrity and ethical values Internal controls are usually executed by people. SAS-55 concludes that "integrity and ethical behavior are the product of the entity's ethical and behavioral standards, how they are communicated, and how they are reinforced in practice" and should be of concern to the auditor.

> **OBSERVATION:** *The conclusion in SAS-55 that ethical behavior is a product of policies and procedures instituted by a client is simplistic and narrow. How integrity and ethical values are instilled in a society and its institutions is a matter that is constantly debated and is often politically sensitive. It is unlikely that ethical behavior is developed in the sterile manner described in SAS-55. Recognizing that the assessment of integrity and ethical values is indeed a daunting task, the auditor should nonetheless be sensitive to formal policies and the general behavior of a client's personnel. For example, a formal policy that bases a significant portion of divisional management's compensation on profitability may estab-*

lish circumstances in which key employees search for "unacceptable" financial reporting practices of a division's operating results. On the other hand, the personal life-styles of key employees may raise questions about whether questionable business practices are occurring. Providing guidance for the assessment of human behavior is fraught with danger, but an auditor who refuses to at least informally assess the personal characteristics of key personnel is not properly assessing this element of the control environment.

Commitment to competence Internal control policies and procedures can generally be executed successfully only if personnel are adequately trained. The auditor should be aware of how the client evaluates job requirements and how employees' skills are matched with the demands of their jobs.

Participation of board of directors or audit committee A potential weakness of the internal control concept is that sometimes internal controls are overridden by key management personnel. There is often no way to stop this from happening, but one way to address the problem is to create a board of directors or an audit committee that takes its fiduciary responsibilities to stockholders seriously. However, an auditor should also keep in mind that a board of directors that is dominated by an entity's chief executive officer or other key management personnel reduces the effectiveness of the control environment.

Management's philosophy and operating style The attitude of key management personnel has a significant effect on an organization's internal control. For example, a management team with a cavalier attitude toward its fiduciary responsibilities may have a negative effect on the degree to which internal controls are adopted, implemented, and monitored. A team with an excessive entrepreneurial attitude may emphasize the operational aspects of the entity but not give adequate consideration to internal control. At the other end of the organizational spectrum, a management team in a bureaucratic entity may be dominated by the need to achieve budgeted goals at the expense of reporting accurate information.

Organizational structure An organizational structure establishes a vehicle by which an entity can achieve its various objectives, including those related to internal control. Important concepts that an entity should consider when developing an organizational structure include "key areas of authority and responsibility and appropriate lines of reporting." These concepts are broad, and the identification of specific internal control features related to organizational structure will depend on factors such as the nature of the entity and its size.

Assignment of authority and responsibilities A client enhances its control environment by paying appropriate attention to how it assigns authority and responsibility. SAS-55 notes that the following factors relate to the assignment of authority and responsibility:

- The process for assigning authority and responsibility for operating activities
- The establishment of reporting relationships and authorization hierarchies
- The process for identifying appropriate business practices
- Consideration of knowledge and experience possessed by key personnel
- The provision of resources necessary to complete assigned duties
- The process for communicating the entity's objectives, the relationship of each employee to the achievement of the entity's objectives, and the scope of accountability for each employee

For example, if management documents the role of employees and departments by clearly explaining their level of authority and degree of responsibility, management has strengthened the entity's control environment by implementing the concept of segregation of duties and responsibilities and by increasing departmental autonomy. On the other hand, when roles are ill-defined, the control environment does not contribute to the likelihood that adequate internal control can be implemented or maintained by a client.

Human resource policies and practices Perhaps the most important element of internal control is the personnel who perform and execute the control activities. For this reason, the client should adopt personnel policies that reasonably ensure that only capable and honest people are hired and retained. Effective policies for employee selection, training, promotion, and supervision should be adopted and put in place. The selection of competent and honest personnel does not automatically ensure that errors or fraud will not occur; however, adequate personnel policies, coupled with the design concepts suggested earlier in this section, enhance the likelihood that the client's internal control will function effectively.

Risk assessment   The design of internal controls related to financial reporting should include management's assessment of risk factors that may prevent financial statements from being prepared in accordance with generally accepted accounting principles. When designing internal controls, management should consider "external and internal events and circumstances that may occur and adversely affect an entity's ability to record, process, summarize, and report financial data consistent with the assertions of management in the financial statements." Risk assessment is an ongoing process and SAS-55 notes that the initial assessment of risk can change for the following reasons (AU 319.28–.30):

- Changes in operating environment
- New personnel
- Information system(s) may change
- The entity may experience rapid growth
- New technologies may be introduced into the production process or information processing systems
- New products or services may be introduced by the client
- Corporate restructuring may occur
- Foreign operations may be introduced or expanded
- New accounting pronouncements may be adopted

Control activities   In addition to creating an effective control environment and a risk-assessment process, the client's internal controls should include specific control activities (policies and procedures). SAS-55 classifies control activities as (a) performance reviews, (b) physical controls, and (c) segregation of duties (AU 319.32–.33)

Performance reviews   Control activities include specific policies and procedures that relate to the performance evaluation of the entity (either a portion of the entity or the entity as a whole). For example, a performance review could involve the comparison of (a) budgeted financial information to actual results or (b) previous year's operational results to the current year's results. A performance review incorporates not only the comparison of sets of information and data but also critical analysis and recommendations for improvements.

Information processing   Control activities related to information processing are concerned with the accuracy, completeness, and authorization of transactions. These controls can be classified as general controls and application controls. General controls usually relate to the following activities in the entity's information systems:

- Data center operations
- System software acquisition and maintenance
- Access security
- Application system development and maintenance

Application controls relate to specific applications, such as the processing of payroll information or purchase transactions. Application controls include input controls (related to the integrity of data moving from one point to another point), processing controls (related to proper processing of all authorized transactions), and output controls (related to the accuracy of data processed and their controlled distribution).

Physical controls   Control activities related to physical controls are concerned with the physical security of assets, including limited or controlled access to assets (including documentation that authorizes the movement of assets), and periodic counts, along with comparisons between recorded amounts and counted amounts.

Segregation of duties   The concept of segregation of duties is based on the need to separate custodial responsibility, accounting responsibility, and operational responsibility. This approach provides a system of checks on the competency and integrity of personnel, because it is not possible for a single department or individual to control a transaction without creating a need for interdepartmental reviews.

Information and communication   Internal control features related to the information and communication component focus on the entity's information systems and the "methods and records established to record, process, summarize, and report entity transactions (as well as events and conditions) and to maintain accountability for the related assets, liabilities, and equity." SAS-55 notes that an entity's accounting information system should include methods and records that satisfy the following objectives (AU 319.34–.36):

- Identify and record all valid transactions.
- Provide a timely description of transactions so they can be properly classified.
- Properly measure recorded transactions.
- Record transactions in the appropriate accounting period.

As part of the communication process, individuals who have internal control responsibilities within the accounting system should understand how their activities relate to the activities performed by other individuals within the organization. That is, the accounting system should not be viewed as a separate activity but rather as an integral part of the process by which the organization achieves its objectives. For example, individuals who have responsibilities related to the accounting system should know what constitutes an exception to the normal informational process and who should be informed when an exception occurs. Effective communication may be achieved by preparing accounting manuals and policy statements and by oral statements made by management.

Monitoring   Once internal controls are implemented, management will need to assess the controls (both from a design and an operational perspective) on a timely basis and to make modifications when appropriate. SAS-55 notes that ongoing monitoring should be part of the routine activities of effective internal control. In some entities the routine monitoring will be supplemented by the internal auditor function, which does not have to be performed by a formal internal audit department. In such instances, strengths and weaknesses of internal controls are identified and communicated to appropriate managerial personnel. In addition, external parties can have an important role in monitoring internal controls. For example, as part of its role a regulatory agency may evaluate internal controls or the client's customers may complain about billing errors or incorrect shipment of materials. All of these factors make up the monitoring component of internal control (AU 319.37–.39).

The Application of Internal Control Concepts to Small and Midsized Entities

Internal control is a critical element in helping the client to prepare financial statements that reflect generally accepted accounting principles. However, SAS-55 recognizes that internal control for a large, publicly held company will be different from internal control for a small company or even a midsized company. The five components of internal control should be present in every client's internal control, but how control objectives are achieved can vary from client to client. For example, the following features of a small or midsized entity's internal control may be as effective as the features adopted by a public company.

> *Control environment*—Policies and procedures related to the control environment may not be as extensively documented in a formal manner but rather may be orally communicated to affected personnel. However, although a formal code of conduct may not be formally documented, the essence of such a code may be part of the culture of the entity (AU 319.84.4).

> *Risk assessment*—Risk assessment related to the preparation of financial statements may be less formal in a small company; however, key managerial personnel (including owner-managers), because of their involvement in the day-to-day operations of the entity, may be fully aware of the relationship between various operational activities and financial reporting objectives (AU 319.84.7).

> *Control activities*—Control activities may be concentrated, to some extent, in a relatively small number of personnel; however, managerial personnel may have an extensive awareness of "normal" levels of activity and would likely become aware of transactions that appear questionable (AU 319.84.10).

> *Information and communication*—Documentation of the information system and communication of related control features may not be extensive or formal in a small company; however, extensive involvement by a relatively small number of managerial personnel may not require formal accounting manuals or involved accounting records (AU 319.84.15).

> *Monitoring*—There may be limited ongoing monitoring of daily activities; however, management's day-to-day involvement in operational activities may provide an adequate separate evaluation of the effectiveness of the design and operations of internal controls (AU 319.84.20).

Other Factors to Be Considered in the Design of Internal Control

Although the five components of internal control apply to all entities, the concepts are broad and must be applied in a manner that reflects the characteristics of a particular entity. In addition to the size of the entity, SAS-55 concludes that the following factors should be considered by the auditor when evaluating internal controls of a particular client (AU 319.15):

- The organization and ownership characteristics of the client
- The nature of the client's business
- The diversity and complexity of the client's activities
- The data processing methods used by the client to transmit, process, maintain, and access information
- The legal and regulatory environment in which the client operates

Limitations of Internal Controls

The basic characteristics of internal controls provide a reasonable assurance that the entity's objectives will be achieved; however, the controls cannot provide absolute assurance that those objectives will be attained. No matter how well internal controls are designed, they do have inherent limitations. For example, one of the design principles of internal controls is that the duties and responsibilities of departments and individuals need to be properly segregated. If collusion exists, the effectiveness of this principle may be completely invalidated. Additionally, internal controls can be circumvented by management. Other factors, such as employee carelessness, misunderstanding of instructions, and errors in judgment, have a similar impact on the effectiveness of internal controls. Finally, a basic concept in the design of internal controls is the realization that policies and procedures must be cost effective. That is, the benefits derived from an internal control procedure should exceed the cost of adopting the procedure. When designing internal controls, an entity cannot measure the cost-benefit relationship precisely, but a reasonable analysis combined with appropriate judgment and estimates can be useful (AU 319.16–.18).

IMPLEMENTING THE SECOND STANDARD OF FIELDWORK

In order to satisfy the second standard of fieldwork and the related guidance established by SAS-55, the following steps may be followed by the auditor:

1. Understand (relevant/related to financial statement assertions) internal control and determine whether related policies and procedures are in operation.

2. Document the understanding of the internal controls.

3. Determine the planned assessed level of control risk.

4. Perform tests of controls to provide support for the planned assessed level of control risk.

5. Evaluate whether the planned assessed level of control risk is supported by the results of tests of controls.

6. Document the assessed level of control risk and the basis if it is assessed at less than the maximum level.

7. Design substantive tests based on assessed level of control risk.

UNDERSTANDING INTERNAL CONTROLS

In all audit engagements, the auditor must adequately understand those policies and procedures of internal control relevant to the audit of the financial statements. As noted earlier, relevant policies and procedures are concerned with the recording, processing, summarizing, and reporting of financial data consistent with the assertions embodied in the financial statements. Thus, the auditor needs to understand internal control policies and procedures that increase the likelihood that the financial statements will be prepared in accordance with generally accepted accounting principles (AU 319.10).

Financial statement assertion   SAS-31 (Evidential Matter) identifies the following financial statement assertions (AU 326.03):

> *Existence or occurrence*—The auditor should determine whether assets or liabilities of the entity exist at a given date and whether recorded transactions have occurred during a given period.

Completeness—The auditor should determine whether all transactions and accounts that should be presented in the financial statements are so included.

Rights and obligations—The auditor should determine whether assets are the rights of the entity and liabilities the obligations of the entity at a given date.

Valuation or allocation—The auditor should determine whether assets, liabilities, revenue, and expense components have been included in the financial statements at appropriate amounts.

Presentation and disclosure—The auditor should determine whether particular components of the financial statements are properly classified, described, and disclosed.

The interrelationship of assertions embodied in the financial statements and relevant internal controls for inventory is illustrated below.

Assertions in the Financial Statements Related to Inventories	Relevant Internal Controls
Inventory is held for resale (existence).	Portions of the inventory are counted every four months. Counts are compared to the perpetual inventory amounts.
Purchases of inventory for the period are recorded (completeness).	Prenumbered receiving reports are prepared and used for the receipt of all inventory. Receiving reports are accounted for every two months.
Inventory on hand is owned (rights).	A perpetual inventory system is maintained for goods received from consignors. Every three months, recorded amounts are compared to actual counts.
Inventory is valued at FIFO (valuation).	Perpetual inventory system is maintained for both quantities and cost.
Inventory is a current asset (presentation and disclosure).	Inventory turnover rates on a test basis for certain inventory items are computed to identify slow-moving and obsolete inventory.

Relevant controls   Generally, relevant internal controls are concerned only with financial data; however, policies and procedures related to nonfinancial data also may be of interest to the auditor. For example, quality control data may be useful for testing the assertion in the financial statement that the allowance for returned goods is properly valued. On the other hand, policies and procedures that relate to effectiveness, economy, and efficiency are usually not useful in testing assertions embodied in the financial statements (AU 319.10–.11).

Developing an understanding   SAS-55 concludes that the auditor must obtain an understanding of the design of internal controls for all five control components in every audit engagement. The auditor's understanding must be sufficient to plan the audit engagement to achieve the following (AU 319.19):

- Identify misstatements that could occur in the financial statements

- Identify factors that affect the degree of risk for misstatements in financial statements

- Identify factors relevant to the design of substantive tests

Although the auditor is required to obtain an understanding of all five components of the client's internal controls, the specific nature, timing, and extent of the audit procedures used to obtain such an understanding will not be the same for all engagements. Specifically, SAS-55 notes that the following factors will have an impact on the extent of the auditor's understanding of a client's internal controls during the planning stage of the audit engagement (AU 319.20):

- The size and complexity of the client

- Previous client engagements, if any

- The nature of the specific controls implemented by the client

- The degree to which specific controls are documented by the client

During the planning stage of the audit engagement, the auditor's responsibility to gain an understanding of internal controls is limited to determining whether internal controls are in place; it does not include determining whether those control are being used effectively (Determining whether controls are being used effectively is part of tests of controls, which are discussed later.) (AU 319.21).

While the auditor is developing an understanding of internal controls, he or she may encounter circumstances indicating that the financial statements cannot be audited. These circumstances include (AU 319.22):

- The lack of management integrity raises doubts about the overall reliability of internal controls
- The accounting records are inadequate and do not provide sufficient competent evidential matter on which an opinion may be based

Obtaining an understanding of the control environment   SAS-55 concludes that the auditor should develop an understanding of the client's control environment "to understand management's and the board of directors' attitude, awareness, and actions concerning the control environment considering both the substance of controls and their collective effect." The auditor should develop a broad view of the control environment, taking into consideration how various elements of the environment relate to other components of the client's internal control. For example, SAS-55 points out that while a client may have effective hiring practices that relate to financial and accounting personnel, those practices may be invalidated by "a strong bias by top management to overstate earnings" (AU 319.23–.27).

Obtaining an understanding of risk assessment   The auditor should acquire an understanding of how the client identifies risks related to the possible occurrence of errors for particular transactions, events, and balances. For example, if the client receives a significant amount of returned goods, the auditor should understand how management identifies such goods and similar financial reporting risks and how risks of this nature are managed so that the financial statements will not be materially misstated (AU 319.28 and .29).

Obtaining an understanding of control activities   The auditor should obtain an understanding of control activities so that he or she can reasonably assure that management's objectives related to financial reporting are achieved. As noted earlier, control activities relate to (a) performance reviews, (b) information processing, (c) physical controls, and (d) segregation of duties. SAS-55 notes that "ordinarily, auditing planning does not require an understanding of the control activities related to each account balance, transaction class, and disclosure component in the financial statements or to every assertion relevant to them."

Although the auditor is required to obtain an understanding of all five components of internal control, that does not suggest that this gathering of information is accomplished as five distinct tasks. The auditor, for example, may develop an understanding of some control activities as part of obtaining information about the information and communication component of internal control (AU 319.32 and .33).

Obtaining an understanding about information and communication The auditor should gain an understanding of the information and communication component of internal control so that the following will be achieved (AU 319.34–.36):

- Understand the classes of transactions in the entity's operations that are significant to its financial statements.
- Understand how those transactions are initiated.
- Understand the accounting records, supporting documents, machine-readable and machine-transmitted information, and specific accounts in the financial statements involved in the processing and reporting of transactions.
- Understand the accounting process—from the initiation of a transaction to its inclusion in the financial statements, including how the computer is used to process data.
- Understand the financial reporting process for preparing financial statements, including significant accounting estimates and disclosures.

Finally, the auditor should acquire an understanding of how the client communicates "financial reporting roles and responsibilities and significant matters relating to financial reporting" to appropriate personnel.

Obtaining an understanding about monitoring The auditor should develop an understanding of how the client monitors its internal controls to see whether those controls are effective. SAS-55 notes that obtaining an understanding about monitoring activities should be based on guidance established by SAS-65 (The Auditor's Consideration of the Internal Audit Function in an Audit of Financial Statements) (AU 319.37–.39).

Procedures used to obtain an understanding of components The auditor may use the following procedures to obtain an understanding of an entity's internal controls (AU 319.41–.43):

- Review workpapers from previous assignments.
- Make inquiries of appropriate management, supervisory, and staff personnel.
- Inspect relevant documents and records.
- Observe the entity's activities and operations.

The extent to which such procedures are used depends on the characteristics of the engagement. Characteristics that should be considered include the following:

- Size and complexity of the entity
- Level of previous experience with the entity
- Nature of relevant policies and procedures identified
- Manner of documentation of relevant polices and procedures used by the entity
- Assessments of inherent risks
- Judgments about materiality levels with respect to specific accounts and transactions

DOCUMENTING THE AUDITOR'S UNDERSTANDING OF THE INTERNAL CONTROL

Once the auditor has gained an adequate understanding of the entity's internal control, that understanding should be documented in the workpapers. Methods of documentation include the preparation of flowcharts, internal control questionnaires, and narrative descriptions. The auditor must use professional judgment to determine which method(s) should be used to document the understanding (AU 319.44).

Flowcharts

As used by the independent auditor, a flowchart is a symbolic diagram of a specific part of an internal accounting control system indicating the sequential flow of data and/or authority. A properly prepared flowchart should reflect all operations, movements, delays, and filing procedures associated with whatever is being charted, and should also indicate the conversion of source documents into accounting information—for example, ledgers, journals, or computer-generated documents. Flowcharting is an excellent method for the independent auditor to use for collecting the necessary information for the study and review of controls and their subsequent evaluation. Flowcharting is also an effective method of visual communication and can bring to the attention of the independent auditor the absence of necessary controls.

Internal Control Questionnaire

The second tool used in the documentation of the auditor's understanding of the internal control is the internal control questionnaire. Most internal control questionnaires are designed to yield affirmative or negative answers to the questions. An affirmative answer generally indicates a satisfactory degree of internal control; a negative answer indicates a possible weakness in control or at least indicates that further investigation is required. For example, the client may follow some alternative procedure that yields a negative answer on the questionnaire but actually results in adequate control. In these circumstances, the negative answer on the internal control questionnaire should be supported with a written supplemental statement explaining the circumstances. When negative answers do indicate a weakness in a control, they should be compiled on a separate weakness investigation worksheet. Space should be provided on this worksheet to describe the possible effects of the weakness and to indicate whether such effects could lead to material errors. Space also should be provided for recommendations of changes in the audit program as a result of a particular weakness.

Narrative Descriptions

An auditor may document his or her understanding of the internal control by preparing a narrative description of the system. Following the auditor's discussion with appropriate client personnel, a written description of the system is prepared. Flexibility is the primary advantage of the memorandum, since all systems can be described verbally. However, the success of this technique depends on the writing proficiency of the auditor. A poorly written internal control narrative can lead to a misunderstanding of the system, thus resulting in the improper design and application of tests of controls.

> **OBSERVATION:** *While professional standards permit the auditor complete freedom in the use of internal control questionnaires, flowcharts, or narrative descriptions, it is probable that the more complex a system becomes, the more appropriate the use of flowcharting becomes. Narrative descriptions of complex accounting systems with numerous "branching" routes can tax even auditors with strong communication skills.*

DETERMINE THE PLANNED ASSESSED LEVEL OF CONTROL RISK

Once the auditor has obtained an understanding of the internal control, he or she must determine the planned assessed level of control risk. Such an approach is based on the interrelationship of audit risk and other risk factors defined below (AU 319.45–.46).

Audit risk refers to the probability that an auditor will not detect a material error that exists in the financial statements and includes inherent risk, control risk, and detection risk. SAS-55 defines these risks as follows:

Inherent risk—The susceptibility of an assertion to a material misstatement assuming there are no related internal control structure policies or procedures

Control risk—The risk a material misstatement that could occur in an assertion will not be prevented or detected on a timely basis by an entity's internal control structure policies and procedures

Detection risk—The risk the auditor will not detect a material misstatement that exists in an assertion

Once the auditor has obtained an understanding of the client's internal control, it is possible to assess the level of control risk for a particular engagement. At this point, the assessment is primarily analytical. The auditor has documented the system and, based on the documentation, has identified potential strengths and weaknesses in the internal control.

The assessment of the level of control risk provides the auditor with a general strategy for planning the remaining internal control evaluation. If the auditor believes the internal control is well designed, the level of control risk will be assessed at a relatively low level for a given assertion. On the other hand, if the internal control appears to be poorly designed, a higher level of control risk will be assigned to the internal control.

In circumstances where the auditor believes the internal control is not reliable, the auditor should ignore a substantial portion of the structure and depend almost exclusively on evidential matter collected as part of the performance of substantive tests. When the control risk is assessed at a relatively low level, the auditor will perform tests of controls (discussed below).

> *OBSERVATION: SAS-55 discusses an intermediate step before determining the planned assessed level of control risk. Once the auditor has obtained an adequate understanding of the entity's internal control, control risk for an assertion embodied in the financial statements is assessed at the maximum level.* **Maximum** *level is defined as "the greatest probability that a material misstatement that could occur in a financial statement assertion will not be prevented or detected on a timely basis by an entity's internal control." The maximum level of control risk assumes that (1) internal control policies and procedures are unlikely to apply to an assertion, (2) internal control policies and procedures are unlikely to be effective, or (3) the evaluation of the effectiveness of relevant policies and procedures would be inefficient. Likewise, the discussion in this chapter assumes a similar approach and frames the discussion in terms of the planned assessed level of control risk.*

PERFORM TESTS OF CONTROLS

Generally, an audit is more efficient when the auditor can rely to some degree on the client's internal control structure. However, that reliance can occur only under the following circumstances (AU 319.61–.63):

- Specific internal control policies and procedures related to specific assertions can be identified.
- Tests of controls are performed.

> *OBSERVATION: SAS-55 refers to this strategy as "assessing control risk at a level less than the maximum."*

Identification of Internal Control Policies and Procedures

The auditor must identify specific internal control policies and procedures relevant to the prevention or detection of material misstatements in specific assertions embodied in the financial statements. Internal control policies and procedures may be evaluated based on their breadth of influence and degree of relevance. The auditor should consider both of these factors when determining whether he or she is justified in identifying policies and controls that may serve as a basis for the reduction of the assessed level of control risk.

Breadth of influence   Some internal control policies and procedures have a pervasive effect on accounts and classes of transactions. Generally, policies and procedures related to the control environment and the accounting system have a pervasive effect. For example, methods of assigning authority and responsibility have implications for all assertions embodied in the financial statements. Control procedures, on the other hand, tend to be directed to specific assertions related to account balances and classes of transactions.

Degree of relevance   Some policies and procedures are directly related to specific assertions while other policies and procedures are related only indirectly to specific assertions. The more direct the relationship between policies and procedures and an assertion, the more likely that policies and procedures can provide a basis for reducing the level of assessed control risk.

Tests of Controls

The performance of tests of controls is the second step in the process of determining whether the planned assessed level of control risk is appropriate. Tests of controls are used to determine the effectiveness of the (1) design of policies and procedures and (2) operations of policies and procedures (AU 319.45–.56).

Evaluation of effectiveness of design   To evaluate the effectiveness of design, the auditor determines whether policies and procedures are adequate to prevent or detect material misstatements of financial statement assertions. The process of evaluating the design of policies and procedures is more analytical in nature than corroborative; that is, the auditor is concerned with the design rather than the operational effectiveness of policies and procedures. Audit procedures generally used to evaluate the effectiveness of design include the following:

- Inquiries of appropriate personnel (possibly through the preparation of an internal control questionnaire)
- Inspection of documents and reports to determine how information is collected
- Observation of the application of specific policies and procedures to determine which policies and procedures are in place
- Evaluation of documentation

Evaluation of operational effectiveness   The evaluation of the operational effectiveness of internal control policies and procedures requires the collection of corroborative evidence to determine (1) who performed the procedures, (2) whether procedures were performed correctly, and (3) the extent to which procedures were performed throughout the accounting period. Audit procedures generally used to evaluate the operational effectiveness of policies and procedures include the following:

- Inquiries of appropriate personnel to determine who performed a procedure
- Inspection of documents and reports to determine how a procedure was executed and who executed the procedure
- Observation of the application of specific policies and procedures to determine who performed a procedure
- Reperformance of the procedure to substantiate that the procedure was correctly performed

In practice, both elements of the tests of controls (effective design and operational effectiveness) will be performed concurrently. The auditor is not concerned with the classification of specific audit procedures but rather with the evaluation and substantiation of internal control policies and procedures.

> **OBSERVATION:** *The tests of details of transactions are classified as substantive tests; however, the auditor may use tests of details of transactions as tests of controls when they are useful in determining the effectiveness of internal control policies and procedures.*

EVALUATE THE PLANNED LEVEL OF CONTROL RISK

If an auditor decides to perform tests of controls, the results of the tests should be used to determine whether the planned assessed level of control risk can be justified. The auditor must obtain sufficient competent evidential matter to support the assessment of control risk at the planned assessed level. Professional judgment must be used to determine what constitutes sufficient competent evidential matter; the following factors should be used in making this judgment (AU 319.64–.65):

- Nature (type) of evidential matter
- Source of evidential matter
- Timeliness of evidential matter
- Interrelationships of evidential matter
- Extent of evidential matter

Type of Evidential Matter

The competency of evidential matter varies. Some policies and procedures may be substantiated through the inspection of documents, whereas other policies and procedures must be substantiated through observation. The auditor must consider the type of evidential matter that is obtained and, using professional judgment, determine its degree of competency (AU 319.66–.67).

Source of Evidential Matter

The source of evidential matter must be determined to assess whether competent evidential matter has been obtained. In general, evidence directly acquired by the auditor (for example through observation) is more competent than evidence acquired indirectly (for example through inquiry). SAS-55 concludes that evidential matter acquired only through inquiry is not adequate to provide a basis for assessing control risk at a level less than the maximum (AU 319.68–.69).

Timeliness of Evidential Matter

Ideally, tests of controls (effective design or operation of internal control policies and procedures) should be performed so that a judgment can be made about policies and procedures applicable to the entire period covered by the audit. In many engagements, tests of controls will be performed at an interim date. In this circumstance, the auditor must decide what additional procedures must be applied to the period from the interim date to the year-end date of the financial statements. When making this decision, the auditor should consider the following factors (AU 319.70–.73):

- Significance of assertions related to tests of controls
- Specific policies and procedures evaluated and tested during the interim period
- Effectiveness of the policies and procedures evaluated during the interim period
- Time lapse between year-end date and interim date
- Evidence about policies and procedures gathered from substantive tests performed between the interim date and year end

The auditor should also determine if there have been significant changes in the design and operation of internal control policies and procedures subsequent to the performance of tests of controls at the interim date. Such changes should be evaluated to determine the possible implications for the performance of substantive tests.

The results of tests of controls from prior audits may be used to assess control risk. To determine whether the prior audit results are relevant to the current assessment of control risk, the following factors should be evaluated:

- Significance of assertions related to policies and procedures tested in prior periods
- Specific policies and procedures evaluated and tested during prior periods
- Extent to which policies and procedures were evaluated in prior periods and the result of tests of controls
- Evidence about policies and procedures gathered from substantive tests in the current period

In general, the longer the time period between the performance of tests of controls in prior periods and the current engagement, the less assurance that can be drawn from the performance of tests of controls in prior periods.

Interrelationship of Evidential Matter

There is seldom, if ever, a perfect one-to-one relationship between the results of performing a single test of controls procedure and a single assertion embodied in the financial statements. To properly evaluate evidence gathered as part of tests of controls, the auditor must recognize that interrelationships exist among evidential matter. Generalizations about these interrelationships are summarized below (AU 319.74–.78):

- Assessment of risk concerning an assertion usually will be based on evidence gathered from various audit (tests of controls) procedures.
- Evidence gathered through tests of controls must be evaluated in the context of the control environment and the accounting system.
- Various types of evidence that support a similar conclusion increase the assurance about the effectiveness of policies and procedures.
- Various types of evidence that support dissimilar conclusions decrease the assurance about the effectiveness of policies and procedures.
- Evidence is accumulated throughout an engagement and it may be necessary for the auditor to reassess the level of control risk.

DOCUMENTING THE ASSESSED LEVEL OF CONTROL RISK

The assessment of control risk for a particular assertion (or group of assertions related to an account balance or class of transactions) must be documented. The assessment must be related to the results of the performance of tests of controls. While specific documentation methods and levels cannot be established, SAS-55 notes that the following factors will influence the auditor's documentation (AU 319.57):

- Assessed level of control risk
- Nature of the entity's internal control
- Nature of the entity's documentation of its internal control

> *OBSERVATION: A variety of control risks can be assessed in a single engagement. As demonstrated in the discussion in this chapter, the auditor can assess a maximum level and a level less than the maximum. In practice, it is likely that different control risks will be assessed for different account balances and classes of transactions and for different assertions related to the same account balance or class of transactions.*

DESIGNING SUBSTANTIVE TESTS BASED ON ASSESSED LEVEL OF CONTROL RISK

Based on the auditor's (1) assessment of inherent risk and (2) assessment of control risk resulting from the understanding of the entity's internal control and perhaps tests of control, the auditor determines an acceptable level of detection risk. Detection risk is the risk that the auditor will not detect a material misstatement in an assertion. The lower the assessment of inherent risk and control risk, the higher the acceptable detection risk. In other words, the auditor is willing to accept a relatively higher detection risk when other risk factors (inherent and control) are relatively low (AU 319.79–.82).

Substantive tests are defined as "tests of details and analytical procedures performed to detect material misstatements in the account balance, transaction class, and disclosure components of financial statements." The establishment of a level of acceptable detection risk is used as a basis for determining the nature, timing, and extent of substantive tests. For example, as the level of detection risk is decreased:

- Audit procedures that create more competent evidential matter are employed (nature of procedures).

- Audit procedures are more likely to be applied to year-end balances than to interim balances (timing of procedures).

- The size of the sample selected for testing becomes larger (extent of procedures).

The above generalizations are reasonable: If the auditor desires a lower level of detection risk, the quality and/or quantity of audit evidence collected through substantive tests must increase.

As suggested earlier, there is interplay among the risk factors. By establishing an overall audit risk and assessing inherent risk and control risk, the auditor selects an appropriate level of detection risk that when combined with inherent and control risks will result in the attainment of the overall audit risk sought by the auditor. However, under no circumstances could assessed low levels of inherent risk and control risk suggest that there is no need to perform substantive tests to achieve the overall audit risk.

> **OBSERVATION:** *Tests of details of transactions are principally substantive tests and therefore are concerned with the identification of material misstatements in the financial statements. Tests of details of transactions may be applied secondarily as tests of controls to evaluate the design and operational effectiveness of internal control policies and procedures. In order for tests of details of transactions to simultaneously function as substantive tests and tests of controls, the auditor must consider carefully whether tests of details of transactions have been adequately designed to satisfy both purposes.*

REPORTABLE CONDITIONS

During an audit engagement, the auditor may discover matters related to the entity's internal control that should be reported to the entity's audit committee or to individuals with responsibilities equivalent to an audit committee. SAS-60 (Communication of Internal Control Structure Related Matters Noted in an Audit) refers to these matters as *reportable conditions* and defines such conditions as follows (AU 325.02):

> Reportable conditions are matters coming to the auditor's attention that, in his [or her] judgment, should be communicated to the audit committee because they represent significant deficiencies in the design or operation of the internal control, which could adversely affect the organization's ability to record, process, summarize, and report financial data consistent with the assertions of management in the financial statements.

> **OBSERVATION:** *SAS-60 supersedes SAS-20 (Required Communication of Material Weaknesses in Internal Accounting Control) and introduces a new, lower threshold of communication for **reportable conditions**. The main purpose of SAS-60 is to require the communication of conditions that are less significant than those identified in SAS-20. In fact, SAS-60 notes that some conditions may not be considered reportable but may nonetheless be communi-*

*cated to management or other appropriate parties. The standards
established by SAS-60 apply to **all** engagements, regardless of
whether the client has an audit committee. Reportable conditions
related to the client's internal control structure must be communicated to someone (e.g., owner/manager).*

In an appendix to SAS-60, the following were listed as possible
reportable conditions (AU 325.21):

- Deficiencies in internal control design
  — Inadequate overall internal control design
  — Absence of appropriate segregation of duties consistent with
    appropriate control objectives
  — Absence of appropriate reviews and approvals of transac-
    tions, accounting entries, or systems output
  — Inadequate procedures for appropriately assessing and ap-
    plying accounting principles
  — Inadequate provisions for safeguarding assets
  — Absence of other control techniques considered appropriate
    for the type and level of transaction activity
  — Evidence that a system fails to provide complete and accu-
    rate output that is consistent with objectives and current
    needs because of design flaws

- Failures in the operation of internal control
  — Evidence of failure of identified controls in preventing or
    detecting misstatements of accounting information
  — Evidence that a system fails to provide complete and accu-
    rate output consistent with the entity's control objectives
    because of the misapplication of control procedures
  — Evidence of failure to safeguard assets from loss, damage, or
    misappropriation
  — Evidence of intentional override of internal control by those
    in authority to the detriment of the overall objectives of the
    system
  — Evidence of failure to perform tasks that are part of internal
    control, such as reconciliations not prepared or not pre-
    pared in a timely manner
  — Evidence of willful wrongdoing by employees or manage-
    ment

— Evidence of manipulation, falsification, or alteration of accounting records or supporting documents

— Evidence of intentional misapplication of accounting principles

— Evidence of misrepresentation by client personnel to the auditor

— Evidence that employees or managers lack the qualifications and training to fulfill their assigned functions

- Other

— Absence of a sufficient level of control consciousness within the organization

— Failure to follow up and to correct previously identified internal control deficiencies

— Evidence of significant or extensive undisclosed related party transactions

— Evidence of undue bias or lack of objectivity by those responsible for accounting decisions

An audit is not structured to identify all reportable conditions. Once discovered, however, the reportable condition should be communicated to the audit committee (or to "individuals with a level of authority and responsibility equivalent to an audit committee in organizations that do not have one, such as the board of directors, the board of trustees, an owner in an owner-managed enterprise, or others who may have engaged the auditor"). What constitutes a reportable condition is a matter of professional judgment. Factors to consider in making such a judgment include size and complexity of the entity, organizational structure, and characteristics of ownership. In some instances, management may be aware of reportable conditions but decide to accept the risk associated with the deficiency rather than incur the cost of additional control procedures. If the audit committee (or equivalent individuals) is aware of the deficiency and has acknowledged an understanding of the risk related to the condition, there is no need for the auditor to report the condition. Nonetheless, at subsequent dates, the auditor may decide periodically to remind the audit committee (or equivalent individuals) of the reportable condition (AU 325.04–.06 and .09).

Reportable conditions may be discovered during various phases of the engagement, including during the evaluation of the internal control structure and the tests of financial statement balances. Deficiencies may be related to any of the five components of internal control. In addition, deficiencies may arise because of poor design or poor execution within the control structure. For example, a reportable condition could be related to lack of proper segregation of duties and responsibilities (design within the control structure) or lack of timely preparation of bank reconciliations (execution within the control structure) (AU 325.02).

Agreed-upon criteria   A client may request that an auditor communicate control structure related matters that are not necessarily reportable conditions as defined in SAS-60. Such agreed-upon arrangements include reporting deficiencies that may not be as significant as reportable conditions or reporting results from applying additional procedures when the client is already aware of a deficiency. The auditor should expand the audit approach in an appropriate manner to satisfy the agreed-upon requirements (AU 325.07–.08).

> *OBSERVATION: SAS-60 does not prohibit the auditor from informing the client of conditions that may increase the efficiency or effectiveness of the client's operations, even when there is no understanding that the auditor will do so.*

Reporting format   Reportable conditions or conditions related to agreed-upon criteria should be communicated in writing; however, if the conditions are communicated orally, the communication should be adequately documented in the workpapers (AU 325.09).

The written report should include a scope paragraph, which is a paragraph(s) that describes the reportable condition, and a paragraph stating that the report is only for the use of the audit committee, management, and others within the organization. An example of a report is presented below (AU 325.10–.11).

In planning and performing our audit of the financial statements of the X Company for the year ended December 31, 19X5, we considered its internal control in order to determine our auditing procedures for the purpose of expressing our opinion on the financial statements and not to provide assurance on the internal control. However, we noted certain matters involving the internal control and its operation that we consider to be reportable conditions under standards established by the American Institute of Certified Public Accountants. Reportable conditions involve matters coming to our attention relating to significant deficiencies in the design or operation of internal control that, in our judgment, could adversely affect the organization's ability to record, process, summarize, and report financial data consistent with the assertions of management in the financial statements.

[Describe reportable condition in separate paragraph(s).]

This report is intended solely for the information and use of the audit committee [board of directors, board of trustees, or owners in owner-managed enterprises], management, and others within the organization [or specified regulatory agency or other specified third party].

If governmental regulations require submission of the report, the report should contain a reference to the regulatory agency (AU 325.10).

The standard report format may be expanded to include, for example, a description of the inherent limitations of internal control or other matters that describe the basis for the report (AU 325.13).

When the auditor discovers no reportable conditions during the engagement, a report to the audit committee (or equivalent individuals) stating that fact should *not* be prepared because of the possible misunderstanding of the report and the assurance provided by the report (AU 325.17).

> **OBSERVATION:** *Government Auditing Standards require a written report on the internal control in all audits. When no reportable conditions have been discovered during the engagement, an auditor complies with Government Auditing Standards by issuing a report that essentially states that no material weaknesses were discovered. The form of the report is discussed in SAS-74 (Compliance Auditing Considerations in Audits of Governmental Entities and Recipients of Governmental Financial Assistance).*

When the report describes both reportable conditions and other conditions identified as part of the agreed-upon criteria, the auditor may find it appropriate to identify which comments are applicable to which category (AU 325.14).

A reportable condition may have such a potentially detrimental effect on an entity's internal control that it may be considered a material weakness. SAS-60 defines a *material weakness* as follows (AU 325.15):

> A reportable condition in which the design or operation of the specific internal control elements do not reduce to a

relatively low level the risk that errors or irregularities in amounts that would be material in relation to the financial statements being audited may occur and not be detected within a timely period by employees in the normal course of performing their assigned functions.

The auditor may choose or the entity may request that the material weakness be separately identified and reported to the audit committee (or equivalent individuals) (AU 325.15).

At the discretion of the auditor or at the request of the entity, the auditor may report on a reportable condition while also reporting that the reportable condition is not considered to be a material weakness. Under this reporting circumstance, the following two paragraphs (placed before the last standard paragraph) would be added to the standard, three-paragraph report illustrated earlier (AU 325.16).

A material weakness is a reportable condition in which the design or operation of one or more of internal control components does not reduce to a relatively low level the risk that errors or irregularities in amounts that would be material in relation to the financial statements being audited may occur and not be detected within a timely period by employees in the normal course of performing their assigned functions.

Our consideration of internal control would not necessarily disclose all matters in the internal control structure that might be reportable conditions and, accordingly, would not necessarily disclose all reportable conditions that are also considered to be material weaknesses as defined above. However, none of the reportable conditions described above is believed to be a material weakness.

The auditor should issue a report on reportable conditions or other matters on a timely basis. In some instances, this may require issuance of the report before the completion of the engagement. The timing of the issuance of the report will depend on such factors as the nature and significance of the reportable condition and the need for immediate remedial action (AU 325.18).

An Auditing Interpretation of SAS-60 entitled "Reporting on the Existence of Material Weaknesses" (February 1989) concludes that an auditor is not prohibited from issuing a report on material weaknesses that is separate from the report on reportable conditions. A separate report on material weaknesses should be consistent with the following guidelines (AU 9325.01–.03):

- State that the purpose of the audit was to report on the financial statements and not to provide assurances concerning internal control.
- Provide a definition of a material weakness.
- State that the report is to be used solely by the audit committee, management, and others within the organization. (If the report is required by a governmental agency, reference may be made to the governmental agency.)
- Do not state that no reportable conditions were discovered.

An example of a *separate* report on material weaknesses is illustrated below (AU 9325.04).

In planning and performing our audit of the financial statements of X Company for the year ended December 31, 19X5, we considered its internal control in order to determine our auditing procedures for the purpose of expressing our opinion on the financial statements and not to provide assurance on the internal control structure. Our consideration of internal control would not necessarily disclose all matters in internal control that might be material weaknesses under standards established by the American Institute of Certified Public Accountants.

A material weakness is a condition in which the design or operation of the specific internal control does not reduce to a relatively low level the risk that errors or irregularities in amounts that would be material in relation to the financial statements being audited may occur and not be detected within a timely period by employees in the normal course of performing their assigned functions. However, we noted no matters involving internal control and its operation that we consider to be material weaknesses as defined above.

This report is intended solely for the information and use of the audit committee, management, and others within the organization.

The auditor may add the following sentence to the above report:

These conditions were considered in determining the nature, timing, and extent of the procedures to be performed in our audit of the 19X5 financial statements, and this report does not affect our report on these financial statements dated February 15, 19X6.

If material weaknesses are discovered, the last sentence in the first paragraph of the above illustration should be changed to read: *However, we noted the following matters involving internal control and its operation that we consider to be material weakness as defined above.* A description of the material weaknesses should follow (AU 9325.05).

In some instances, the auditor may be asked to issue a separate report on material weaknesses and also comment on matters relating to internal control or other matters. For example, the auditor may be asked to comment on specific internal control procedures. Under this circumstance, the separate report on material weaknesses should be modified as follows (AU 9325.06):

• Clearly identify the internal control feature or other matter that is the subject of the report.

• Distinguish the additional matter being reported on from internal control.

• Describe in reasonable detail the scope of the investigation of the additional matter.

• Express a conclusion in language that is comparable to the language used in the separate report on material weaknesses illustrated above.

In wording the separate report, the auditor should be careful not to report on the internal control structure (AU 9325.07).

MANAGEMENT LETTER

Although the purpose of an audit engagement is to formulate an opinion on the financial statements, auditors are often requested to prepare a management letter at the conclusion of the consideration of internal control. The management letter often identifies weaknesses in the accounting system and operational inefficiencies discovered by the auditor. Professional standards do not dictate the format of the management letter. On the other hand, an auditor may be engaged to report on a client's internal control, in which case the reporting format is established by SSAE-2.

REPORTS BY MANAGEMENT

Management may include a report on assertions about the effectiveness of its internal control over financial reports in a document that also includes its audited financial statements and the auditor's report on those financial statements. If the auditor has not been engaged to report on management's assertions about its internal control, the guidance established by SAS-8 (Other Information in Documents Containing Audited Financial Statements) should be observed. Under SAS-8, the auditor is required to read the "other" information for possible material inconsistencies and material misstatements of fact (AU 550.04).

> *OBSERVATION: From a practical perspective it is unlikely that the auditor will discover a material inconsistency between the audited financial statements and assertions made by management because, generally, the financial statements do not include references to the client's internal control. On the other hand, an auditor may discover a material misstatement concerning internal control made by management. These can be detected because, as part of the engagement, the auditor is required to obtain an understanding of the client's internal control.*

An Auditing Interpretation of SAS-8 entitled "Reports by Management on the Internal Control Structure Over Financial Reporting" (May 1994) allows (but does not require) the auditor to include the paragraph shown below in the auditor's report on the client's financial statements (AU 9550.10).

We were not engaged to examine management's assertion about the effectiveness of its internal control over financial reporting as of December 31, 19X5, included in the accompanying Management Report on Internal Control and, accordingly, we do not express an opinion thereon.

> *OBSERVATION: When the auditor has been engaged to report on management assertions about the effectiveness of its internal control, the guidance established SSAE-2 should be observed.*

In addition to making statements about its internal control in a document that contains its audited financial statements, management may make similar or related statements in other communications directed to external parties. If the auditor reads the other communications, the statements made by management should be evaluated to determine whether the auditor's role with respect to the client's internal control has been misinterpreted or misstated. When the auditor concludes that management's reference to the role of the auditor is incorrect, the Interpretation (May 1994) states that the auditor should discuss the matter with management and follow the guidance established by SAS-8 with respect to the discovery of material inconsistencies and misstatements of fact (AU 9550.11).

> *OBSERVATION:* Some clients tend to make broad statements about the role of the auditor with respect to its internal control and about the subtleties of the internal control itself. For this reason, the auditor should carefully consider any comments made by management. The example in the Interpretation assumes that management states, "X Company's external auditors have reviewed the company's internal control in connection with their audit of the financial statements." However, this is an incorrect statement because SSAE-2 does not allow for a "review" engagement covering an entity's internal control.

ERRORS AND IRREGULARITIES

To satisfy generally accepted auditing standards, an engagement should be conducted to detect material misstatements (or omissions) in the financial statements. Material misstatements may arise because of errors or irregularities. An audit should be designed to provide reasonable assurance that both will be detected (AU 316.05).

In SAS-53 (The Auditor's Responsibility to Detect and Report Errors and Irregularities), errors are defined as *unintentional* misstatements in the financial statements, while irregularities are *intentional* misstatements. For example, an inadvertent omission of a disclosure in the financial statements is an error; however, a disclosure intentionally made to deceive a user of the financial statements is an irregularity. Because of the difficulty in determining intent, in practice it is sometimes difficult to correctly determine whether an action is an error or an irregularity (AU 316.02–.03).

Even when an auditor adequately plans and executes an engagement in such a way as to detect material errors and irregularities, there is no guarantee that financial statements will be free from material errors or irregularities. An auditor can offer only a *reasonable assurance* that material errors or irregularities do not exist. Thus, the subsequent discovery of material errors or irregularities does not, by itself, demonstrate that generally accepted auditing standards were not observed (AU 316.06–.08).

Nature of Errors and Irregularities

Although an auditor must plan an engagement to detect both errors and irregularities, it is often more difficult to evaluate the possibility that material irregularities could occur and to design specific audit procedures to test for the occurrence of irregularities. A client's control structure has a significant effect on the assessment of the probability that a material error will occur, and generally corroborative evidence can be obtained to detect whether an error has occurred. For example, returned accounts receivable confirmations may lead to the detection of various posting errors to the subsidiary ledger. On the other hand, the detection of fictitious receivables in the same subsidiary ledger is usually more difficult and requires considerably more ingenuity on the part of an auditor.

Some factors relevant to the detection of material irregularities that should be considered by the auditor include (1) level of occurrence, (2) method of concealment, (3) internal control, and (4) impact on financial statements.

An irregularity that is committed by an employee of a client usually has an immaterial effect on the financial statements, and the possibility of such an occurrence is based on the strengths and weaknesses of internal control. On the other hand, an irregularity committed by a member of senior-level management (or an owner-manager) is more likely to be material, and furthermore internal control is less capable of preventing this type of irregularity because the perpetrator may be in a position to override specific controls. Thus, when planning and executing audit procedures, the auditor should evaluate the integrity of management.

The likelihood that an auditor can detect an irregularity is generally related to the type of method used to conceal the irregularity. For example, irregularities that involve collusion generally are very difficult to detect, whereas irregularities concealed by altering documents may be easier to discover if the transactions are subject to validation by contacting uninvolved third parties. In general, the likelihood of detecting irregularities depends on the scheme used, the frequency of the irregularities, and the relative magnitude of the irregularities (AU 316.07).

Internal control should be designed to prevent the occurrence of errors and irregularities that could have a material effect on the financial statements. If internal control is not designed in this manner, the auditor must perform appropriate tests to determine whether errors or irregularities have occurred. More difficult is the anticipation of a breakdown in an adequately designed internal control because of unusual transactions or circumstances. An auditor should evaluate the likelihood of this type of unusual occurrence and plan the audit approach accordingly.

When planning the engagement, an auditor should anticipate the possible effects of errors and irregularities on the financial statements. In general, overstated amounts are easier to detect than understated amounts. Also, errors and irregularities that affect a single financial statement are generally more difficult to detect than those that affect both the balance sheet and the income statement.

Planning the Engagement

As part of planning, an auditor should consider the risk of material misstatements occurring in a particular engagement. The assessment of audit risk should be evaluated at the financial statement level and at the account balance or class of transaction level (AU 316.09).

At the financial statement level, SAS-53 notes that the following factors may be relevant in assessing the audit risk of material misstatements (AU 316.10):

- Characteristics of management
  - A single individual dominates management operating and financial decisions.
  - There is an aggressive attitude with respect to financial reporting.
  - There is a high turnover rate, particularly for senior accounting management.
  - There is an undue emphasis on achieving earnings projections.
  - The reputation of management in the business community is poor.
- Characteristics of industry and entity
  - There is inadequate or inconsistent profitability exhibited by the entity in relation to the industry.
  - Profitability is highly sensitive to economic factors.
  - There is a high rate of change in the industry.

— There is a high failure rate within the industry.

— The entity is decentralized without adequate monitoring of operations.

— There is a question about the continued existence of the entity (see discussion of SAS-59 [The Auditor's Consideration of an Entity's Ability to Continue as a Going Concern]).

• Characteristics of engagement

— There are several contentious or difficult accounting issues.

— Several significant balances or transactions are difficult to audit.

— There is a history of significant misstatements in the financial statements of prior periods.

— There are significant and unusual related party transactions.

— The client is a new client and the information obtained from the predecessor auditor is limited.

In addition to the factors listed above, the strengths and weaknesses of the client's internal control should be considered in assessing the audit risk related to the occurrence of material misstatement. For a public company, the role of the board of directors and the audit committee in overseeing the financial reporting and disclosure process for which management is responsible should be considered. For a nonpublic company, the role of the owner-manager should be evaluated (AU 316.11).

On the basis of an understanding of specific risk factors related to management characteristics, operating and industry characteristics, and engagement characteristics, the auditor should establish an audit plan that reflects an assessment of these risk factors. Such factors may have an effect on the nature, timing, and extent of audit procedures employed. In addition, the experience level of personnel assigned to the engagement and the degree of supervision also may be affected (AU 316.12–.14).

At the account balance or class of transaction level, the risk related to the possibility of the occurrence of a material irregularity is based on the assessment of inherent risk and control risk. Inherent risk relates to the nature of the account balance or class of transaction and is assessed by referring to factors such as the complexity of accounting issues related to the account or transaction, the availability of corroborative evidential matter, and the extent to which estimates are used to determine the amount of the balance or transaction. In addition, factors identified at the financial statement level may have an effect on inherent risk or an effect related to specific account balances or classes of transactions. Control risk is a function of the client's internal control and is determined for each accounting subsystem as part of the evaluation of the internal control (AU 316.15).

Mental Attitude of Auditor

An auditor should approach an engagement with professional skepticism; that is, the auditor should reserve judgment about a particular condition, event, or transaction until sufficient competent evidential matter is available to draw an objective conclusion. Such an attitude does not imply that the auditor assumes the worst possible outcome for all situations. Instead, the auditor takes into consideration all factors related to a particular item to determine what degree of skepticism is appropriate. For example, the auditor does not assume that collusion exists unless factors identified by the auditor suggest that the risk of material misstatements occurring is relatively high. Professional skepticism should be exercised in both the planning phase and the corroborative phase of an engagement (AU 316.16–.20).

When the auditor concludes there is a significant audit risk that material misstatements could occur, audit planning should reflect an increased level of professional skepticism. In general, the auditor demands more competent evidential matter or a greater amount of evidential matter, or a combination of both. For example, transactions normally vouched may be substantiated through direct confirmation with an unrelated third party (more competent evidential matter), or the number of items sampled from a population may be increased (greater amount of evidential matter) (AU 316.18).

During the performance of audit procedures, the auditor should maintain an appropriate level of skepticism and be alert for the identification of conditions significantly different from expectations. These conditions may include results from analytical procedures that differ markedly from expected results, balances that are not reconciled on a timely basis, missing documentation or accounting records, and known but uncorrected errors. The nature and extent of unexpected results should be evaluated to determine whether the initial assessment of audit risk related to the possible occurrence of material misstatements during the planning stage of the engagement is still appropriate. Such a reassessment of audit risk may result in changing the nature, extent, and timing of audit procedures that have been or are scheduled to be performed (AU 316.21).

Discovery of Errors or Irregularities

Differences between recorded amounts and substantiated amounts should be analyzed to determine whether the differences are errors or irregularities. When it appears the difference is an irregularity, the auditor should consider whether the financial statements are materially affected. If it is concluded that the effects of the irregularity are not material, SAS-53 states that the following actions should be taken (AU 316.22–.24):

- Notify management of the irregularity (at least one level above the level involved in the irregularity).

- Determine whether there are implications for other phases of the engagement based on the level at which the irregularity was perpetrated.

If the auditor concludes that an audit adjustment has or may have a material effect on the financial statements, or if the effect cannot be evaluated, the following steps should be taken (AU 316.25):

- Identify implications for other phases of the engagement.

- Discuss the irregularity, including the method that may be used to investigate the matter with management (at least one level above the level involved in the irregularity).

- Attempt to obtain evidential matter to substantiate the irregularity and its effect on the financial statements.

- Advise the client to discuss the matter with its legal counsel if it appears laws have been violated.

Communication of Errors and Irregularities to the Audit Committee

The auditor should be satisfied that the entity's audit committee (or equivalent individuals) is aware of irregularities (except inconsequential ones) that the auditor has become aware of during the engagement. All irregularities (consequential and inconsequential ones) that involve the entity's senior management should be communicated directly to the audit committee by the auditor (AU 316.28).

SAS-53 notes that irregularities that are individually immaterial may be reported on an aggregated basis to the audit committee. The auditor may reach an understanding with the audit committee about what is considered to be a reportable irregularity (AU 316.28).

Notification of the occurrence of irregularities to parties other than management and the audit committee is not required; however, under the following circumstances, the auditor may be called on to inform another party of an irregularity (AU 316.29):

- SEC disclosure requirements based on a change of auditors
- Inquiries received from a successor auditor
- Subpoena issued by a court
- Governmental audit requirements applicable to entities that have received financial aid

Because of the confidential relationship between the entity and the auditor, the auditor may find it advisable to contact legal counsel before irregularities are disclosed to outside parties (AU 316.29).

Auditor's Report

An unqualified opinion is expressed if the client properly revises the financial statements to reflect the effects of the discovered irregularity. If the financial statements are not revised, a qualified or adverse opinion may be expressed. When the auditor is not allowed to perform procedures related to the investigation of an irregularity or is unable to determine whether an irregularity has a material effect on the financial statements, a qualified opinion or a disclaimer of opinion should be expressed. In addition, the auditor should communicate the findings to the audit committee or board of directors.

If the entity refuses to accept the modified auditor's report, the auditor should withdraw from the engagement. The audit committee or board of directors should be informed of the reason for the withdrawal. The auditor may decide to withdraw from an engagement for other reasons. This decision will depend on the circumstances surrounding the irregularity, including the degree of cooperation received from management and the board of directors.

Other Engagements

An auditor may be engaged to perform a service that results in an increased or decreased responsibility to detect irregularities. For example, an auditor may perform an audit subject to governmental requirements that are different from engagements subject to generally accepted auditing standards, or the scope of an engagement may be limited to a specified element or account in a financial statement. The auditor should assess the risk of the occurrence of irregularities in the context of the requirements of each special engagement (AU 316.30–.32).

ILLEGAL ACTS

Although the purpose of an audit is not to detect illegal acts, an auditor should be aware that such acts could occur. SAS-54 (Illegal Acts by Clients) defines *illegal acts* as "violations of laws or governmental regulations," including acts committed by management and the entity's employees acting on behalf of the entity. An illegal act, for purposes of SAS-54, does not include acts arising from the personal conduct of an employee of the entity unrelated to business activities (AU 317.02).

An entity must observe many laws and regulations. In general, the auditor lacks the expertise to identify and evaluate all illegal acts. For purposes of determining the auditor's responsibilities for detecting illegal acts, illegal acts are classified as either those with a direct effect on the financial statements or those with an indirect effect on the financial statements (AU 317.03).

Illegal Acts with Direct Effects on the Financial Statements

Some laws and regulations directly apply to the financial statements and are, therefore, taken into consideration when the auditor plans his or her audit procedures. For example, the auditor may determine whether a provision for income taxes has been properly reflected in the financial statements to comply with Internal Revenue Code and related regulations. The auditor's responsibility for detecting illegal acts relating to laws and regulations having a direct and material effect on the financial statements is the same as the responsibility relating to the detection of errors and irregularities (see previous discussion of SAS-53). The auditor must design the audit to provide reasonable assurance of detecting such acts (AU 317.04–.05).

Illegal Acts with Indirect Effects on the Financial Statements

Most laws and regulations have only an indirect effect on the financial statements; that is, when an illegal act related to this type of law or regulation has occurred, the effects are often indirect in that they require disclosure in the financial statements based on their classification as a contingent liability. Illegal acts of this type are generally related to the operations of the organization rather than to the financial and accounting aspects of the entity. Furthermore, under many circumstances, the auditor has no basis for determining whether this type of law or regulation has been violated (AU 317.06).

SAS-54 addresses illegal acts relating to laws and regulations that have an indirect effect on the financial statements. The following discussion refers to them as illegal acts. Although the auditor is not responsible for the detection of illegal acts, during various phases of the engagement specific information may be discovered that raises questions about whether these illegal acts occurred. SAS-54 lists the following as examples of specific information that may raise questions about the existence of illegal acts (AU 317.09):

- Unauthorized transactions, improperly recorded transactions, or transactions not recorded in a complete or timely manner in order to maintain accountability for assets

- Investigation by a governmental agency, an enforcement proceeding, or payment of unusual fines or penalties

- Violations of laws or regulations cited in reports of examinations by regulatory agencies made available to the auditor

- Large payments for unspecified services to consultants, affiliates, or employees

- Sales commissions or agents' fees that appear excessive in relation to those normally paid by the client or to the services actually received

- Unusually large payments in cash, purchases of bank cashiers' checks in large amounts payable to bearer, transfers to numbered bank accounts, or similar transactions

- Unexplained payments made to government officials or employees

- Failure to file tax returns or pay government duties or similar fees common to the entity's industry or the nature of its business

Audit Procedures—No Suspicion of Illegal Acts

Typically, the engagement does not include audit procedures specifically directed to identifying illegal acts when no specific information has come to the attention of the auditor that would suggest that any illegal acts occurred. Nonetheless, the following inquiries of management should be made (AU 317.08):

- Entity's compliance with laws and regulations
- Entity's policies that may prevent illegal acts
- Entity's directives and periodic representations obtained by the entity concerning compliance with laws and regulations

Also, the auditor should request a written representation from the entity stating no violations or possible violations of laws or regulations have occurred that may require accrual or disclosure in the financial statements (AU 317.08).

Audit Procedures—Suspicion of Illegal Acts

If an auditor is aware of information concerning an illegal act, the auditor should (1) understand the nature of the act, (2) understand the circumstances surrounding the act, and (3) obtain sufficient information to evaluate the effects of the act on the financial statements. If possible, the auditor should deal with management at least one level above those involved in the act (AU 317.10).

When management cannot provide sufficient information to demonstrate that an illegal act did not take place, the auditor should (AU 317.11):

- Consult with the entity's legal counsel or other specialists (the entity should make the arrangements for meeting with its legal counsel).
- If necessary to obtain a further understanding of the act, perform additional procedures such as the following:

— Inspect supporting documentation and compare with accounting record.

— Confirm information with other parties and intermediaries.

— Determine if the transaction has been properly authorized.

— Consider whether similar transactions have occurred and attempt to identify them.

Discovery of Illegal Acts

When an illegal act has occurred or probably occurred, the auditor should evaluate the effects of the act (AU 317.12).

The possible loss arising from the illegal act should be evaluated to determine whether the amount is material. All costs related to the loss, such as penalties and fines, should be considered. The need for accrual and / or disclosure in the financial statements should be evaluated in the context of guidelines established by FAS-5 (Accounting for Contingencies) (AU 317.13–.15).

The illegal act should also be evaluated to determine whether other aspects of the engagement are affected. This is particularly applicable to the evaluation of the reliability of management representations. Such facts as the perpetrators involved, the methods of concealment, and the nature of internal control procedures overridden should be considered in the evaluation (AU 317.16).

Communication with audit committee   An auditor should ensure that an illegal act has been communicated to the client's audit committee (or to "individuals with a level of authority and responsibility equivalent to an audit committee in organizations that do not have one, such as the board of directors, the board of trustees, an owner in an owner-managed enterprise, or others who may have engaged the auditor"). The communication should include the following (AU 317.17):

- Description of the illegal act
- Circumstances surrounding the illegal act
- Auditor's evaluation of the effects of the illegal act on the financial statements

If members of senior management are involved in the illegal act, the auditor should communicate directly with the audit committee (or equivalent individuals). The communication can be written or oral, and in both cases it should be adequately documented in the workpapers (AU 317.17).

Notification of the occurrence of an illegal act to parties other than management and the audit committee (or equivalent individuals) is not required; however, SAS-54 notes that under the following circumstances the auditor may be called on to inform another party of an illegal act (AU 317.23):

- SEC disclosure requirements based on a change of auditors

- Inquiries received from a successor auditor

- Subpoena issued by a court

- Governmental audit requirements applicable to entities that have received financial aid

Because of the confidential relationship between the entity and the auditor, the auditor may find it advisable to contact legal counsel before illegal acts are disclosed to outside parties (AU 317.23).

Audit report   If the effects of an illegal act are not properly accrued for or disclosed in the financial statements, either an adverse opinion or a qualified opinion should be expressed. If the entity does not allow the auditor to collect sufficient competent evidential matter to determine whether an illegal act has taken place or whether an illegal act has a material effect on the financial statements, a disclaimer of opinion generally should be expressed. If the entity refuses to accept the modified auditor's report, the auditor should withdraw from the engagement and notify the board of directors and the audit committee (or equivalent individuals) of the reason for the withdrawal (AU 317.18–.20).

In some circumstances, it may not be possible to determine whether an illegal act has occurred because evidential matter does not exist to resolve the issue or there is disagreement about the interpretation of the law or regulation. In this case, the auditor is faced with an uncertainty and must determine whether the auditor's report should be modified (see discussion in the chapter entitled "Auditor's Reports") (AU 317.21).

> **OBSERVATION:** *The Auditing Standards Board is considering whether to eliminate the circumstances under which the auditor's report should be modified because of an uncertainty.*

Other engagements SAS-54 establishes professional standards relating to the auditor's responsibility for detecting illegal acts in the course of the audit of the entity's financial statements. An auditor may accept other engagements that impose a different responsibility for detecting illegal acts. Such engagements may include professional services subject to governmental auditing standards or special engagements designed to determine compliance with specific laws or regulations. A special engagement would be governed by the attestation standards discussed in the chapter entitled "Attest Engagements" (AU 317.24).

INTERNAL AUDIT FUNCTION

As suggested earlier, an internal audit function, if it exists, is part of the client's internal control. SAS-65 (The Auditor's Consideration of the Internal Audit Function in an Audit of Financial Statements) describes how the auditor should evaluate the internal audit function in order to plan the audit engagement (designing the nature, timing, and extent of subsequent audit procedures) (AU 322.01).

An internal audit function may consist of a variety of activities, some or all of which may not be related to the recording, processing, and reporting of financial information. The auditor should obtain an understanding of the internal audit function as part of obtaining an understanding of the client's internal control. While special circumstances of each engagement will dictate the specific audit approach, the auditor should initially develop an understanding of the purpose and scope of the internal audit function and its location in the organizational hierarchy. In addition, the auditor may read reports prepared by internal auditors, determine how staff members are allocated within the internal audit function (operational versus financial audit activities), and refer to assessments of internal audit activities that were part of previous audits of the client's financial statements (AU 322.02–.05).

If the auditor concludes that relevant activities are being performed by internal auditors, and it appears that it would be efficient to rely on those activities in assessing internal control risk, the auditor should assess the objectivity and competence of internal auditors (AU 322.06–.08).

OBSERVATION: SAS-65 requires that, in all engagements, the auditor develop some understanding of the internal audit function and determine whether that function is relevant to the assessment of control risk. Thus, if there is an internal audit function, it must be evaluated. The evaluation is not optional (AU 322.05).

Assessing Objectivity and Competence of Internal Auditors

Objectivity of internal auditors should be evaluated by determining the organizational status of the internal audit function and by examining the policies that may enhance the likelihood that the internal auditors are objective (AU 322.10).

> **OBSERVATION:** *The standard of objectivity is different from the standard of independence. Although it could be argued that it is simply a matter of semantics, the differentiation is based on the reasonable assumption that an internal auditor could not achieve independence because he or she is an employee of the client.*

SAS-65 states that factors relevant to determining organizational status of the internal audit function include the following (AU 322.10):

- Direct reporting to an officer, which implies broad audit coverage and adequate consideration of audit findings
- Direct access and reporting to the board of directors, the audit committee, or the owner/manager
- Oversight responsibility for internal audit employment decisions that rests with the board of directors, the audit committee, or the owner/manager

In addition, policies that minimize the placement of internal auditors in situations where they have an existing relationship (for example, auditing a department where a spouse works), or may have a future relationship (possible assignment to a department once the internal audit stint is completed), can contribute to the objectivity of the internal audit function and should be considered by the auditor.

In assessing competence of the internal auditors, the auditor should review background information on the internal auditors such as their educational achievements (degrees, certifications, continuing education) and professional experience. In addition, the auditor should consider operational practices such as the assignment of internal auditors, supervision and review of personnel within the department, quality of workpapers, and specific performance evaluations (AU 322.09).

In some instances SAS-65 concludes that it may be necessary to test the effectiveness of the client's policies and procedures on objectivity and competency. For example, rather than simply accept an assertion that the audit committee is involved in the hiring of internal auditors, the auditor may decide to interview members of the committee and ask them specifically about their roles in hiring a particular internal auditor. The degree to which the effectiveness of policies and procedures will be tested should be based on the anticipated degree to which the internal audit function will be a factor in the planning of subsequent audit procedures: the greater the reliance on the internal audit function, the greater the degree to which the policies and procedures should be tested (AU 322.11).

Effect of the Internal Audit Function on Audit Planning

If the auditor concludes that the internal audit function possesses an acceptable level of objectivity and competence, the role of internal auditors may affect the following three phases of an audit engagement (AU 322.12):

- Understanding the internal control
- Assessing risk
- Designing substantive procedures

Understanding the internal control The understanding of the client's internal control generally consists of an analytical phase and a tests-of-controls phase. Work performed by internal auditors may affect one or both of the phases of the engagement. For example, internal auditors may have documented the cash disbursements system by preparing a flowchart and supportive narrative descriptions. In addition, the internal auditors may have inspected canceled voucher packages to determine whether certain specific control procedures depicted on the flowchart were followed. The auditor could rely on this documentation to gain an initial understanding of the cash disbursement system (analytical phase) and review the number and type of control deviations discovered by the internal auditors (tests-of-controls phase) (AU 322.13).

Assessing risk Risk is assessed by the auditor at the financial statement level and the account balance or class of transaction level. Risk at the financial statement level is broad in nature in that it applies to assessing the risk of material misstatement in one of the financial statements. Generally, factors related to the control environment have a broad effect on risk assessment. Thus, an evaluation of the internal audit function as an element of the client's internal control can have an effect on the auditor assessment's of risk at the financial statement level.

Risk at the account balance or class of transaction level is directed to specific control activities and the related assertions that appear in the financial statements. The performance of tests of controls by internal auditors may influence the level of risk assessed at the account balance or class of transaction level. For example, if internal auditors have tested the cash disbursement system, the auditor reviewing the tests may decide that control risk as it relates to assertions concerning certain operating expenses (such as advertising expense and utilities expense) can be assessed at a level less than maximum (AU 322.16).

Designing substantive procedures   Work completed by internal auditors may be used as part of the auditor's substantive tests. For example, internal auditors may have analyzed and vouched a substantial portion of line items that make up travel and entertainment expenses. The auditor may decide to significantly reduce the number of items in the account to be vouched because of the work performed by internal auditors (AU 322.17).

> **OBSERVATION:** *The design of substantive procedures described above is not the same as using internal auditors to provide direct assistance to the auditor. The latter topic is discussed in the chapter entitled "Evidence" (AU 322.17).*

Degree of Reliance on the Internal Audit Function

Although the role of the internal audit function can be considered in understanding internal control, assessing risk, and designing substantive procedures, the independent auditor is solely responsible for the opinion expressed on the financial statements. For this reason, the auditor should carefully consider the extent to which the internal audit function should influence the audit approach. In determining the role the internal audit function should play in the audit, the fundamental guidance is simple: evidential matter obtained indirectly from an internal auditor is less reliable than the same evidential matter developed directly by the independent auditor (AU 322.18–.19).

SAS-65 concludes that three factors—(1) the materiality of balances or classes of transactions, (2) the degree of inherent risk and control risk, and (3) the degree of subjectivity needed to evaluate evidence to support assertions in the financial statements—should be considered in determining the degree of reliance on the internal audit function. As each one of these factors increases, the degree of reliance on work performed by internal auditors should decrease (and vice versa) (AU 322.20).

When assertions related to material amounts are characterized by a high risk of material misstatement or a high degree of subjectivity (or both), SAS-65 reiterates that the auditor must be in a position to accept sole responsibility for satisfying the standards of fieldwork with respect to these assertions and the related internal control. Furthermore, the work of the internal auditors cannot solely be used as a basis for eliminating the performance of substantive tests by the auditor on those assertions. SAS-65 suggests that the following assertions may have either a high degree of risk or a high degree of subjectivity in evaluating audit evidence (AU 322.21–.22):

- Significant accounting estimates that are the basis for valuing assets or liabilities
- Existence and disclosure of related party transactions
- Existence and disclosure of contingencies and other uncertainties
- Existence and disclosure of subsequent events

While the work of internal auditors may be used in a variety of circumstances, SAS-65 concludes that the following judgments should be made by the auditor and not by internal auditors:

- Assessments of inherent risk and control risk
- Sufficiency of audit tests performed
- Evaluation of significant accounting estimates

Other similar judgments also should be made exclusively by the auditor (AU 322.19).

Evaluating Internal Audit Work

When the auditor concludes that the work of internal auditors may be used to determine an understanding of internal control, to assess risk, or as substantive procedures, the auditor should evaluate the quality of that work. Factors that may be considered in assessing the work of internal auditors include the following (AU 322.24–.25):

- Consistency of the scope of the work with audit objectives
- Adequacy of internal audit programs
- Adequacy of workpaper documentation, including evidence of supervision and review
- Appropriateness of conclusions drawn
- Consistency of internal audit reports with nature of work performed

The auditor's evaluation of the effectiveness of the procedures conducted by internal auditors should include the testing of the internal auditors' work related to significant financial statement assertions. Such evaluation can be satisfied either by (1) examining controls, transactions, or balances examined by the internal auditors or (2) examining similar controls, transactions, or balances not actually examined by the internal auditors. The auditor should then compare his or her own results to those of the internal auditors. The degree to which the auditor performs such tests is a matter of professional judgment (AU 322.26).

REPORTS ON THE PROCESSING OF TRANSACTIONS BY SERVICE ORGANIZATIONS

In some instances, a client may use the services of another organization in which (1) transactions are executed and accountability is maintained or (2) transactions are recorded and processed by the other organizations. For example, a mortgage company may use the services of another entity to receive and process monthly mortgage payments from its customers, or a company may engage a computer processing service to record and process routine transactions related to payroll, trade receivables, and trade payables (AU 324.03).

The activities performed by the other company may be considered part of the client's internal control and therefore may require that the auditor develop a sufficient understanding of the controls in place at the other company's facilities. However, it may be costly to have the client's auditor visit the other organization to obtain such an understanding. Also, it could be disruptive to the other organization to have several of its customers' auditors review and test its control structure (AU 324.06).

To provide a reasonable solution to this problem, the AICPA issued SAS-70 (Reports on the Processing of Transactions by Service Organizations). SAS-70 identifies and defines the following four parties relative to reporting on processing of transactions by service organizations (AU 324.02):

1. *User organization*—The entity that has engaged a service organization and whose financial statements are being audited.

2. *User auditor*—The auditor who reports on the financial statements of the user organization.

3. *Service organization*—The entity (or segment of an entity) that provides services to the user organization.

4. *Service auditor*—The auditor who reports on the processing of transactions by a service organization.

> **OBSERVATION:** *The standards established by SAS-70 are also applicable to service organizations that develop, provide, and maintain the software used by user organizations. On the other hand, the standards are not applicable to the audit of a client's transactions that arise from financial interests in partnerships, corporations, and joint ventures, when the entity's proprietary interest is accounted for and reported. In addition, SAS-70 would not apply when the service organization executes transactions based on specific authorization granted by the user organization. For example, the user auditor would not consider the control procedures of a broker that simply executes security transactions for the user organization (AU 324.03).*

Role of the User Auditor

When a user organization employs a service organization, the user organization's ability to institute effective internal controls over the activities performed by the service organization can vary (AU 324.06).

In many instances, internal controls of the service organization is an extension of the user organization's accounting system. Generally, transactions authorized by the user organization are transferred to the service organization for additional processing, and internal control policies and procedures are maintained by both the user and the service organizations. In other instances, the service organization may execute transactions and maintain related accountability, and the user organization may not have effective internal controls over such transactions (AU 324.06).

Planning In determining whether, and to what degree, the user auditor should obtain an understanding of the service organization's internal control, SAS-70 concludes that the following factors should be considered (AU 324.08):

- Materiality of assertions in the user organization's financial statements that are affected by internal control policies and procedures maintained by the service organization

- Inherent risk related to the assertions described

- Nature of the services performed by the service organization (i.e., routine accounting services or highly specialized services that are used by only a few customers)

- Degree to which the internal control policies and procedures of the user and service organizations are interrelated

- Specific internal control policies and procedures of the user organization that apply to transactions affected by the service organization

- Level of discretion granted to the service organization with respect to transactions

- Capabilities of the service organization (such as performance record, insurance coverage, and financial stability)

- Experience of the user auditor with respect to the service organization

- Amount of auditable information maintained by the user organization

- Existence and applicability of governmental auditing regulations in addition to GAAS

- Availability of information concerning the internal control policies and procedures of the service organization, including:

  — Manuals and descriptions of systems

  — Internal control reports such as those prepared by service auditors, internal auditors, or regulatory authorities

On the basis of these factors, and others that the user auditor may consider relevant, the user auditor should decide whether the service organization should be contacted. If the user auditor concludes that there is sufficient information about the service organization's internal control to plan the audit, there is no need to contact the service organization. If, however, it is concluded that the information is insufficient for adequate planning of the audit, the user auditor should consider contacting the service organization (through the client). The user auditor could (1) request additional information from the service organization, (2) request that a service auditor be engaged by the service organization (see later discussion entitled "Role of the Service Auditor"), or (3) visit the service organization and obtain the desired information (AU 324.09–.10).

Control risk assessment When assessing control risk, the user auditor should consider controls employed by the service organization, as well as those established by the user organization. SAS-55 concludes that control risk can be assessed at a level below the maximum level only when (1) specific controls relate to specific financial statements assertions and (2) those procedures are subject to tests of controls. Evidence arising from tests of controls may be obtained by the user auditor in the following ways (AU 324.11–.12):

- The user auditor may perform tests of controls at the user organization's location.
- The user auditor may perform tests of controls at the service organization.
- The user auditor may obtain a service auditor's report on controls placed in operation, as well as tests of operating effectiveness.
- The user auditor may obtain a service auditor's report on the application of agreed-upon procedures that describes appropriate tests of controls.

Although the user auditor may obtain information about tests of controls in a variety of ways, the information should be carefully evaluated to determine whether it is relevant to and sufficient for the assessment of control risk at a level that is less than the maximum level (AU 324.13–.16).

Substantive tests The service auditor may perform audit procedures that substantiate transactions and balances that appear in the user organization's financial statements. Such procedures should be agreed to by the user organization, user auditor, service organization, and service auditor. Similarly, governmental auditing regulations or other arrangements may require the service auditor to perform specific substantive tests. The user auditor may take into consideration the results of performing such procedures (AU 324.17).

Evaluating the Service Auditor

As suggested earlier, the user auditor may obtain a service auditor's report on (1) controls placed in operations (used to obtain an understanding of internal control in order to plan the engagement) or (2) controls placed in operation and tests of operating effectiveness (used to obtain an understanding of internal control in order to plan the engagement and assess control risk). Before either of these reports is relied on, the user auditor should make inquiries concerning the service auditor's professional reputation. Guidance for making such inquiries can be found in SAS-1, Section 543 (Part of Audit Performed by Other Independent Auditors) (AU 324.18).

> *OBSERVATION: Although the user auditor may rely on the work of the service auditor, there should be no reference to such work in the user auditor's report on the financial statements of the user organization. This is not a "division of responsibility" reporting circumstance as described in SAS-1, Section 543.*

If it is concluded that the service auditor's professional reputation is acceptable, there should be a determination of whether the work performed by the service auditor is sufficient to achieve the user auditor's objectives. To make this determination, the user auditor should consider performing one or more of the following procedures (AU 324.19):

- Communicate with the service auditor and discuss the application and results of audit procedures performed.
- Review the audit programs used by the service auditor.
- Review the audit workpapers of the service auditor.

If it is concluded that the work of the service auditor does not fully meet the needs of the user auditor, (1) the user auditor may request (with the permission of the user organization and the service organization) that the service auditor perform agreed-upon procedures or (2) the user auditor may perform appropriate procedures at the service organization's location (AU 324.19).

Role of the Service Auditor

When a service auditor reports on the processing of transactions by a service organization, the general standards, and the relevant standards of fieldwork and reporting, should be observed. Although the service auditor must be independent with respect to the service organization, it is not necessary to be independent from every user organization (AU 324.22).

If the service auditor becomes aware of illegal acts, irregularities, or uncorrected errors (that are other than inconsequential) that affect a user organization, the service auditor should determine whether the user organization has been informed of the matter. If such matters have not been communicated to the user organization, the service auditor should inform the service organization's audit committee (or equivalent party) of the matter. If, after being informed of the matter, the audit committee does not take appropriate action, the service auditor should consider withdrawing from the engagement.

The service organization should determine what type of engagement should be performed by the service auditor; however, in an ideal situation, the user organization would discuss the matter with the service organization and its auditors to ensure that all parties will be satisfied with the service auditor's report. SAS-70 identifies the following types of reports on a service organization that can be issued by a service auditor (AU 324.24):

- Reports on controls placed in operation
- Reports on controls placed in operation and tests of operating effectiveness

SAS-70 defines a report on policies and procedures placed in operation (PPPO report) as follows (AU 324.24):

> A service auditor's report on a service organization's description of its control structure policies and procedures that may be relevant to a user organization's internal control structure, on whether such policies and procedures were suitably designed to achieve specified control objectives, and on whether they had been placed in operation as of a specific date.

A report on controls placed in operation and tests of operating effectiveness (PPPO/TOE report) is defined as follows:

> A service auditor's report on a service organization's description of its controls that may be relevant to a user organization's internal control, on whether such controls were suitably designed to achieve specified control objectives, on whether they had been placed in operation as of a specific date, and on whether the controls that were tested were operating with sufficient effectiveness to provide reasonable, but not absolute, assurance that the related control objectives were achieved during the period specified.

The user auditor may use the PPPO report to obtain an understanding of the user organization's internal control as it relates to the activities performed by the service organization. It may be used to plan tests of controls and substantive tests in the audit of the user organization's financial statements, but it *cannot* be the basis for reducing the user auditor's assessment of control risk below the maximum level. A PPPO/TOE report, however, *can* be used by the user auditor to reduce the assessment of control risk below the maximum level, as well as to obtain an understanding and plan tests.

The service auditor issuing a PPPO or a PPPO/TOE report should obtain an adequate description of the relevant controls of the service organization's internal control that is sufficient to satisfy the needs of the user auditor. To determine whether the controls have been placed in operation by the service organization, the service auditor should consider the following audit procedures (AU 324.25–.27):

- Refer to results from previous experience with the service auditor (may include results from the audit of the service organization's financial statements).

- Make inquiries of appropriate service organization personnel.

- Inspect relevant documents and records of the service organization.

- Observe activities conducted by the service organization.

When issuing a PPPO/TOE report, the service auditor should complete the above procedures and should also perform tests of controls based on guidance established in SAS-55 and SAS-39 (Audit Sampling) to determine the effectiveness of the relevant policies and procedures identified (AU 324.27).

The service auditor should make inquiries about changes in controls that may have occurred before fieldwork was begun. If there have been significant changes in controls (limited to changes within the last 12 months), those controls should be included in the description of the service organization's controls. If such changes are not included in the description of the service organization's controls, the service auditor should include them in his or her report (AU 324.28).

For PPPO reports and PPPO/TOE reports, the description of relevant controls placed in operation at the service organization may be prepared by the service organization or by the service auditor. In either case, the representations made in the description are those of the management of the service organization. In order for the service auditor to express an opinion on the description, the following conditions must exist (AU 324.34):

- There must be an appropriate identification and description of control objectives and the relevant controls.

- The service auditor must evaluate the relationships between the control objective and the relevant controls.

- Sufficient evidence must be obtained by the service auditor to provide a basis for expressing an opinion on the description.

During the engagement, the service auditor should consider whether there are significant deficiencies in the service organization's controls that suggest that control objectives could not be satisfied. In addition, the service auditor should consider any additional information, whether or not it is related to specific control objectives, that (1) questions the ability of the service organization to record, process, summarize, or report financial data to user organization without error and (2) indicates the user organizations would generally not have controls in place to discover errors (AU 324.32).

The service auditor should evaluate the control objectives (unless they are established by an outside party) to determine whether they are reasonable and consistent with the service organization's contractual obligations (AU 324.35).

In addition to including a description of relevant controls, a service auditor's PPPO/TOE report on the processing of transactions by the service organization should be accompanied by a separate description of tests of specified service organization controls designed to obtain evidence about the operating effectiveness of the relevant controls. That description should include the following:

- Controls that were tested

- Control objectives that the controls were intended to achieve
- Tests applied to the controls
- Results of the tests applied
- Description of the nature, timing, and extent of tests (presented in sufficient detail to enable user auditors to determine the effect on the assessment of control risk for the user organizations)
- Relevant information about exceptions discovered by the service auditor, including causative factors and corrective actions taken

The service organization determines which control objectives will be subjected to tests of controls. The service auditor determines which controls are relevant to achieving specific control objectives and then establishes the nature, timing, and extent of audit procedures to test their effectiveness. The test period for relevant controls should generally cover a period of not less than six months and sample items should be selected over the entire period.

SAS-70 establishes the following procedures for preparing PPPO and PPPO/TOE reports (AU 324.29):

- Refer to the applications, services, products, or other aspects of the service organization covered by the report.
- Describe the scope and nature of the procedures performed.
- Identify the party that specified the control objectives.
- Indicate the purpose of the engagement.
- State an opinion on whether the description presents fairly, in all material respects, the relevant aspects of the service organization's controls that had been placed in operation as of a specific date.
- State the inherent limitations of the potential effectiveness of controls and the risk of projecting to future periods any evaluation of the description.
- Identify the parties for which the report is intended.

A PPPO report should also state an opinion as to whether the controls were suitably designed to provide reasonable assurance that the specified control objectives would be achieved if those controls were complied with satisfactorily, and it should disclaim an opinion on the operating effectiveness of the policies and procedures.

A PPPO/TOE report, on the other hand, should also state an opinion on whether the controls tested were operating with sufficient effectiveness to provide a reasonable assurance that the related control objectives were achieved during the period. Therefore, in this type of report, the service auditor must also:

- Refer to the description of tests of specified service organization controls.
- Disclose the period covered by tests of specified controls.
- State an opinion on whether controls tested were operating with sufficient effectiveness to provide a reasonable assurance that the related control objectives were achieved during the period.
- State that the effectiveness of specific service organization controls depends on their interaction with individual user organizations' policies, procedures, and other factors.
- If all control objectives listed in the description of controls were not covered by tests of operating effectiveness, state that the opinion is not applicable to those control objectives not listed in the description of tests performed.
- State that the service auditor has not performed procedures to determine the effectiveness of controls for user organizations.

According to SAS-70, PPPO reports and PPPO/TOE reports should be addressed to the service organization. Presented below is a sample PPPO report as illustrated in SAS-70 (AU 324.38).

We have examined the accompanying description of the [identify service applications] of X Service Organization. Our examination included procedures to obtain reasonable assurance about whether (1) the accompanying description presents fairly, in all material respects, the aspects of X Service Organization's policies and procedures that may be relevant to a user organization's internal control structure, (2) the control structure policies and procedures included in the description were suitably designed to achieve the control objectives specified in the description, if those policies and procedures were complied with satisfactorily, and (3) such policies and procedures had been placed in operation as of [identify specific date]. The control objectives were specified by [identify party that specified control objectives]. Our examination was performed in accordance with standards established by the American Institute of Certified Public Accountants and included those procedures we considered necessary in the circumstances to obtain a reasonable basis for rendering our opinion.

We did not perform procedures to determine the operating effectiveness of policies and procedures for any period. Accordingly, we express no opinion on the operating effectiveness of any aspects of X Service Organization's policies and procedures, individually or in the aggregate.

In our opinion, the accompanying description of the aforementioned application presents fairly, in all material respects, the relevant aspects of X Service Organization's policies and procedures that had been placed in operation as of [identify date]. Also, in our opinion, the policies and procedures, as described, are suitably designed to provide reasonable assurance that the specified control objectives would be achieved if the described policies and procedures were complied with satisfactorily.

The description of policies and procedures at X Service Organization is as of [identify date] and any projection of such information to the future is subject to the risk that, because of change, the description may no longer portray the system in existence. The potential effectiveness of specific policies and procedures at the Service Organization is subject to inherent limitations and, accordingly, errors or irregularities may occur and not be detected. Furthermore, the projection of any conclusions, based on our findings, to future periods is subject to the risk that changes may alter the validity of such conclusions.

This report is intended solely for use by the management of X Service Organization, its customers, and the independent auditors of its customers.

A sample PPPO/TOE report illustrated in SAS-70 is presented below.

We have examined the accompanying description of the [identify service applications] of X Service Organization. Our examination included procedures to obtain reasonable assurance about whether (1) the accompanying description presents fairly, in all material respects, the aspects of X Service Organization's policies and procedures that may be relevant to a user organization's internal control structure, (2) the control structure policies and procedures included in the description were suitably designed to achieve the control objectives specified in the description, if those policies and procedures were complied with satisfactorily, and (3) such policies and procedures had been placed in operation as of [identify specific date]. The control objectives were specified by [identify party that specified control objectives]. Our examination was performed in accordance with standards established by the American Institute of Certified Public Accountants and included those procedures we considered necessary in the circumstances to obtain a reasonable basis for rendering our opinion.

In our opinion, the accompanying description of the aforementioned application presents fairly, in all material respects, the relevant aspects of X

Service Organization's policies and procedures that had been placed in operation as of [identify date]. Also, in our opinion, the policies and procedures, as described, are suitably designed to provide reasonable assurance that the specified control objectives would be achieved if the described policies and procedures were complied with satisfactorily.

In addition to the procedures we considered necessary to render our opinion as expressed in the previous paragraph, we applied tests to specific policies and procedures, listed in Schedule A, to obtain evidence about their effectiveness in meeting the control objectives, described in Schedule A, during the period from [identify period covered]. The specific policies and procedures and the nature, timing, extent, and results of the tests are listed in Schedule A. This information has been provided to user organizations of X Service Organization and to their auditors to be taken into consideration, along with information about the internal control structure at user organizations, when making assessments of control risk for user organizations. In our opinion the policies and procedures that were tested, as described in Schedule A, were operating with sufficient effectiveness to provide reasonable, but not absolute, assurance that the control objectives specified in Schedule A were achieved during the period [identify period covered].

The relative effectiveness and significance of specific policies and procedures at X Service Organization and their effect on assessments of control risk at user organizations are dependent on their interaction with the policies, procedures, and other factors present at individual user organizations. We have performed no procedures to evaluate the effectiveness of policies and procedures at individual user organizations.

The description of policies and procedures at X Service Organization is as of [identify date], and information about tests of the operating effectiveness of specified policies and procedures covers the period from [identify period covered]. Any projection of such information to the future is subject to the risk that, because of change, the description may no longer portray the system in existence. The potential effectiveness of specified policies and procedures at the Service Organization is subject to inherent limitations and, accordingly, errors or irregularities may occur and not be detected. Furthermore, the projection of any conclusions, based on our findings, to future periods is subject to the risk that changes may alter the validity of such conclusions.

This report is intended solely for use by the management of X Service Organization, its customers, and the independent auditors of its customers.

OBSERVATION: If all of the control objectives identified in the description of policies and procedures were not subject to tests of controls, the following should be added as the last sentence to the third paragraph in the preceding example: However, the scope of our engagement did not include tests to determine whether control objectives not listed in Schedule A were achieved; accordingly, we express no opinion on the achievement of control objectives not included in Schedule A.

If the service auditor concludes that the description that accompanies the PPPO or PPPO/TOE report is inaccurate or incomplete, the report should state so and provide additional details to provide the user auditor with an appropriate understanding of the policies and procedures (AU 324.39).

An effective design of internal controls at the service organization may be based on the assumption that complementary controls are in place at the user organization. Under this circumstance, the user organization's complementary controls should be part of the description of the service organization's relevant control structure. Also, when the user organization's controls are considered necessary to achieve the stated control objectives, the report should be modified by adding an additional statement to the phrase "complied with satisfactorily" in the scope paragraph (first paragraph) and the opinion paragraph (third paragraph in the PPPO report, second paragraph in the PPPO/TOE report). The additional phrase is shown below (AU 324.38).

And user organizations applied the internal control structure policies and procedures contemplated in the design of the Service Organization's policies and procedures.

When the service auditor concludes that the description of controls is inaccurate or incomplete, the report should be changed by adding an explanatory paragraph (placed immediately before the opinion paragraph) that describes the deficiency and by qualifying the opinion paragraph. SAS-70 presents the following as an example of a qualified PPPO or PPPO/TOE report on a service organization's policies and procedures (AU 324.39).

[Explanatory Paragraph]

The accompanying description states that X Service Organization uses operator identification numbers and passwords to prevent unauthorized access to the system. Based on inquiries of staff personnel and inspections of activities, we determined that such procedures are employed in Applications A and B but are not required to access the system in Applications C and D.

[Opinion Paragraph]

In our opinion, except for the matter referred to in the preceding paragraph, the accompanying description of the aforementioned application presents fairly, in all material respects, the relevant aspects of X Service Organization's policies and procedures that had been placed in operation as of [identify date]. Also, in our opinion, the policies and procedures, as described, are suitably designed to provide reasonable assurance that the specified control objectives would be achieved if the described policies and procedures were complied with satisfactorily.

When the service auditor concludes that there are significant deficiencies in the design or operation of relevant controls, the report should be changed by adding an explanatory paragraph (placed immediately before the opinion paragraph) that describes the deficiency and by qualifying the opinion paragraph. SAS-70 presents the following as an example of a qualified PPPO or PPPO/TOE report on a service organization's policies and procedures (AU 324.40).

[Explanatory Paragraph]

As discussed in the accompanying description, from time to time the Service Organization makes changes in application programs to correct deficiencies or to enhance capabilities. The procedures followed in determining whether to make changes, designing the changes, and implementing them do not include review and approval by authorized individuals who are independent from those involved in making the changes. There are also no specified requirements to test such changes or to provide test results to an authorized reviewer prior to implementing the changes.

[Opinion Paragraph]

In our opinion, the accompanying description of the aforementioned application presents fairly, in all material respects, the relevant aspects of X Service Organization's policies and procedures that had been placed in operation as of [identify date]. Also, in our opinion, except for the deficiency referred to in the preceding paragraph, the policies and procedures, as described, are suitably designed to provide reasonable assurance that the specified control objectives would be achieved if the described policies and procedures were complied with satisfactorily.

Written Representations

The service auditor should obtain written representation from the service organization that includes the following matters (AU 324.57):

- Acknowledge that management is responsible for establishing and maintaining appropriate controls related to the processing of transactions for user organizations.
- Acknowledge the appropriateness of the control objectives specified.
- State that the description of controls presents fairly, in all material respects, the aspects of the service organization's controls that may be relevant to a user organization's internal control.
- State that controls, as described, had been placed in operation as of a specified date.
- State that management has disclosed any significant changes in controls that have occurred since the service organization's last examination.
- State that management has disclosed any illegal acts, irregularities, or uncorrected errors that may affect one or more user organizations.
- State that management has disclosed all design deficiencies in controls of which it is aware, including those for which the costs may exceed the benefits.
- State that management has disclosed all instances, of which it is aware, when controls have not operated with sufficient effectiveness to achieve the specified control objectives (required only for PPPO/TOE reports).

OBSERVATION: An Auditing Interpretation of SAS-70 entitled "Describing Tests of Operating Effectiveness and the Results of Such Tests" (April 1995) concludes that the report on the controls placed in operation and tests of operating effectiveness should provide a sufficient description of the tests performed and their results to enable the user auditor to adequately assess control risk for financial statement assertions related to the tasks performed by the service organization (AU 9324.01–.03).

OBSERVATION: Another Interpretation of SAS-70 entitled "Service Organizations That Use the Services of Other Service Organizations (Subservice Organizations)" concludes that the user auditor must consider evaluating controls of a subservice organization that performs work for the service organization (AU 9324.04–.18).

DOCUMENTING

SAS-41 (Working Papers) requires that workpapers demonstrate that the second standard of fieldwork has been observed. Proper documentation would include completed internal control questionnaires, flowcharts, narrative descriptions, and audit programs. An important concept of the second standard of fieldwork is the effect of the study and assessment of control risk on the nature, timing, and extent of substantive testing. It is therefore advisable that an auditor prepare so-called "bridging" workpapers. This type of workpaper typically would include headings (1) for the identification of weaknesses, (2) for the possible effect on the financial statements, and (3) for the impact on subsequent audit procedures. The bridging workpapers should also identify strengths in the system that will possibly permit the auditor to curtail some audit procedures (AU 339).

OBSERVATION: A constant comment heard from auditors involved in peer reviews is that work performed by a firm often is not adequately documented. In many instances the work has been completed but there is no support to demonstrate this fact. Obviously such an approach is an invitation for disaster in the form of a deficient report from the peer review team, or for embarrassing moments in a court of law.

FOREIGN CORRUPT PRACTICES ACT

The Foreign Corrupt Practices Act (FCPA) was enacted in 1977 as an amendment to the 1934 Securities Exchange Act. Any corporation subject to the 1934 Act is therefore covered by the FCPA. The primary purpose of the FCPA is to prohibit U.S. businesses from giving bribes or making other corrupt payments to officials of foreign governments. Severe penalties may be imposed against corporations and individual directors, officers, or agents who engage in such conduct.

All companies that must file annual audited financial statements with the SEC under the Securities Exchange Act of 1934 are now required to maintain reasonably complete and accurate books and records and also to devise "sufficient" systems of internal controls.

The FCPA of 1977 consists of accounting standards provisions and antibribery provisions.

Maintenance of books and records   The FCPA requires that each company's books, records, and accounts accurately and fairly reflect, in reasonable detail, the transactions and dispositions of the company's assets.

System of internal controls   The FCPA requires that each company devise and maintain a system of internal controls sufficient to provide reasonable assurance that:

- Transactions are executed in accordance with management's general or specific authorization.

- Transactions are recorded as necessary (1) to permit preparation of financial statements in conformity with GAAP and (2) to maintain accountability for assets.

- Access to assets is permitted only in accordance with management's general or specific authorization.

- The recorded accountability for assets is compared with the existing assets at reasonable intervals, and appropriate action is taken with respect to any differences.

The concept of reasonable assurance recognizes that the cost of a system of internal control should not exceed the expected benefits and that the evaluation of costs and benefits requires estimates and judgments made by management.

Accounting standards provisions   Any company or individual found to have willfully violated the accounting standards provisions may be fined $10,000, and an individual may be imprisoned for a period of not more than five years. A company may be sued by a third party for failing to comply with the accounting standards provisions or for failing to disclose any material facts.

> **OBSERVATION:** *An Auditing Interpretation of SAS-54 entitled "Material Weaknesses in the Internal Control Structure and the Foreign Corrupt Practices Act" (October 1978) states that in audits of entities subject to the Foreign Corrupt Practices Act of 1977, the auditor should consult with the client's management and legal counsel if he or she finds a material weakness in internal control. If no corrective action is taken by the client, the auditor should consider withdrawing from the engagement (AU 9317.03–.06).*

Antibribery provisions   The Act prohibits *any* company from offering a bribe to a foreign official for the purpose of obtaining, retaining, or directing business to *any* person.

A foreign official includes any officer or employee of a foreign government or any department, agency, or instrumentality thereof, and any person acting on behalf of, or in any official capacity for, a foreign government or department, agency, or instrumentality thereof. An employee of a foreign government whose functions are basically clerical is *not* considered a foreign official.

These antibribery provisions apply to every U.S. business that either is organized under the laws of a state or territory of the United States or has its principal place of business in the United States.

The FCPA provides for severe penalties for violations of either the accounting standards provisions or the antibribery provisions. A violation of the antibribery provisions of the Act is a criminal offense. Companies may be fined up to $1,000,000. Individuals may be fined up to $10,000 and may be imprisoned for up to five years.

APPENDIX

CONSIDERATION OF FRAUD IN A FINANCIAL STATEMENT AUDIT (EXPOSURE DRAFT)

Over the years there has been a significant difference between the auditor's responsibility with respect to fraudulent financial statements and the role of the auditor as perceived by external parties, such as investors, creditors, regulatory agencies, and the general public. During this period, the profession has been subjected to unprecedented litigation, some warranted and some misguided. In order to clarify the role of the auditor in the detection of fraud, the Auditing Standards Board issued an Exposure Draft entitled "Consideration of Fraud in a Financial Statement Audit" in May 1996.

The Auditor's Current Responsibility with Respect to Fraud

The auditor's current responsibility for the detection of fraud is based on SAS-53 (The Auditor's Responsibility to Detect and Report Errors and Irregularities), which states the following:

> The auditor should assess the risk that errors and irregularities may cause the financial statements to contain a material misstatement. Based on that assessment, the auditor should design the audit to provide reasonable assurance of detecting errors and irregularities that are material to the financial statements.

SAS-53 defines an *error* as an unintentional misstatement in the financial statements, and an *irregularity* is characterized as an intentional misstatement. For example, an inadvertent omission of a disclosure in the financial statements is an error, but the omission of a disclosure in order to mislead a user of the financial statements is an irregularity. Because the difference between an error and an irregularity is intent, from a practical point of view it is difficult, perhaps impossible, to differentiate between an error and an irregularity. Nonetheless, current auditing standards require that the auditor plan the engagement so that he or she can provide reasonable assurance that material errors and irregularities do not exist.

> **OBSERVATION:** *In the past, the AICPA has been reluctant to use the term **fraud**, even though there is no difference between fraud and an irregularity. However, the AICPA has decided to use the term **fraud** instead of irregularity in the proposed standard.*

The Exposure Draft concludes that the auditor is concerned with two broad categories of material fraud: *fraudulent financial reporting* and *misappropriation of assets*. Fraudulent financial reporting results from financial statements that have been misstated in order to deceive those who might rely on the statements. The Exposure Draft provides the following as examples of acts that involve fraudulent financial reporting:

- Manipulation, falsification, or alteration of accounting records or supporting documents from which financial statements are prepared

- Misrepresentation in or intentional omission from the financial statements of events, transactions, or other significant information

- Intentional misapplication of accounting principles relating to amounts, classification, manner of presentation, or disclosure

The misappropriation of assets (defalcation) is concerned with the theft of a business's assets and involves acts such as (a) embezzling assets, (b) stealing assets, (c) misusing assets, or (d) having the business pay for assets or services that are never received.

Although the proposed standard clarifies the definition of *fraud*, it does not change the auditor's responsibility for detecting fraud. That is, no matter how diligently an auditor performs and executes an engagement, he or she cannot provide absolute assurance that materially misstated financial statements will be detected during the engagement. Thus, the auditor provides only a reasonable assurance that material misstatements will be detected, which is the same standard that applies in a current audit and is the same standard that applies to errors.

Risk Assessment

Although the Auditing Standards Board did not change the level of assurance that an auditor can offer with respect to fraud in an audit engagement, the proposed standard requires that the auditor specifically assess the risk of material misstatements in financial statements due to fraudulent activities. While the Exposure Draft notes that there is no single approach for identifying risk factors that increase the likelihood that fraud can occur, it lists the following as examples of risk factor categories that may be considered:

Factors related to fraudulent financial reporting:

> *Management characteristics*—Management characteristics pertain to management's abilities, pressures, style, and attitudes relating to internal control and the financial reporting process.

> *Industry conditions*—Industry conditions involve the economic and regulatory environment in which the entity operates.

> *Operating characteristics and financial stability*—These two factors pertain to the nature and complexity of the entity and its transactions, the financial condition of the entity, and the profitability of the entity.

Factors related to misappropriation of assets:

> *Susceptibility of assets to misappropriation*—This factor pertains to the nature of an entity's assets and the degree to which they are subject to theft.

> *Employee relationships or pressures*—These factors pertain to the extent of financial stress among employees and whether there are adverse relationships between employees and the entity—especially employees who have access to assets susceptible to misappropriation.

> *Controls*—Controls involve the lack of controls designed to prevent or detect misappropriation of assets.

Risk Assessment and the Audit Plan

There is at least some possibility of material fraud occurring in every engagement, irrespective of the characteristics of a particular engagement. For that reason, the Exposure Draft proposes that an auditor conduct a risk assessment for every engagement. Once that assessment is made, the auditor is faced with a number of options, which are as follows:

- Make no change in planned audit procedures, because the planned procedures are adequate to address the present risk factors related to fraud

- Change planned audit procedures to address risk factors identified as part of the assessment (under this approach the auditor must also determine whether the modified audit approach should be broad-based or directed to a specific account balance, class of transactions or assertion, or both)

- Withdraw from the engagement, because it is not feasible to change the planned audit procedures in a manner that addresses the level of risk assessed

When the auditor concludes that the planned audit approach should be modified because of the risk assessment related to fraud, the changes would have an effect on the planned audit approach, specifically, the nature, timing, and extent of substantive tests.

> **OBSERVATION:** *Although the Exposure Draft discusses fraud risk assessment as a distinct component of an audit engagement, it recognizes that risk assessment is an ongoing process and that evidence obtained during the audit engagement may change the initial risk assessment.*

Evaluation Test Results

When the auditor discovers a misstatement in the financial statements, the basis for the misstatement should be evaluated to determine whether the situation arose from an error or from possible fraud. If it is concluded that the misstatement was based on fraud, the implication of the fraud should be evaluated by the auditor even when the effect is immaterial. In some instances the existence of fraud will have an insignificant effect on the engagement because of the nature of the fraud. For example, the Exposure Draft points out that fraudulent transactions in a petty cash fund would generally be inconsequential because of the size of the fund and the level at which the fraud occurred. On the other hand, if the auditor concludes that the fraud or possible fraud could have a material effect on the financial statements, the auditor should do the following:

- Consider the effect on other elements of the engagement, including the nature, timing, and extent of tests; the assessment of control risk (if it has been initially assessed at a level less than maximum); and the appropriateness of personnel used in the engagement.

- Discuss the situation with (a) senior management and (b) an employee who is in a management position and who is at least one level above the point of the fraud.

- Attempt to obtain sufficient competent evidence to determine the materiality of the fraud and its effect.

- Recommend that the client consider consulting with its legal counsel.

If the auditor concludes that the fraud involves senior management and that it has a material impact on the financial statements, the audit committee should be informed of the matter. However, the Exposure Draft notes that the auditor ordinarily is not required to inform others (except senior management and the audit committee) of the matter, except perhaps in the following circumstances:

- Communication of the matter is required by law or regulation.

- Communication of the matter may be appropriate when an inquiry is received by a successor auditor as described in SAS-7 (Communications Between Predecessor and Successor Auditors).

- The information is subject to a subpoena.

- For audits of entities that receive governmental financial assistance, communication is specified by a funding agency or other specified agency.

Proposed Effective Date

The proposed effective date of the standard is for audits of financial statements for periods ending on or after December 15, 1997, although earlier application is allowed.

EVIDENCE

CONTENTS

Overview	**8.05**
Characteristics of Evidence	**8.07**
Competent Evidential Matter	**8.08**
Sufficient Evidential Matter	**8.08**
Evidence and the Audit Process	**8.09**
Sampling (Determining the Sufficiency of Evidence)	**8.10**
Audit Risk	**8.11**
Sampling and Tests of Controls	**8.12**
Sampling and Substantive Tests	**8.13**
Timing of Substantive Tests	**8.14**
Factors That Affect the Timing of Principal Substantive Tests	**8.16**
Extending Audit Conclusions to the Balance Sheet Date	**8.17**
Materiality and Audit Risk	**8.17**
Consideration of Materiality	**8.18**
Consideration of Audit Risk	**8.19**
Inherent Risk	**8.19**
Control Risk	**8.20**
Detection Risk	**8.20**
Assessing Audit Risk	**8.21**
Workpapers	**8.22**
Access to Workpapers by Regulators	**8.24**
Evidence and Procedures Required by Statements on Auditing Standards	**8.28**
Confirmation Process	**8.28**
Design of Confirmation Request	**8.29**
Confirmation Request Form	**8.30**
Prior Auditor Experience	**8.31**

Information Being Confirmed   8.31

Characteristics of Respondents   8.32

Performance of Confirmation Procedures   8.32

Evaluation of Information Received from the
    Third Party   8.34

    Unconfirmed Balances Do Not Appear to Be
        Unique   8.34

    Unconfirmed Balances Are Immaterial   8.34

Confirmation of Accounts Receivable   8.35

Evidence for Inventories   8.36

Inventories Counted by Others   8.38

Evidence for Long-Term Investments   8.39

Long-Term Investments—Equity Method   8.39

Long-Term Investments—Cost Method   8.41

Other Long-Term Investments   8.42

Evidence for Accounting Estimates   8.42

    Management's Internal Control   8.43

    Collection and Evaluation of Evidence   8.44

Substantive Evidence Obtained from a Specialist   8.46

    Qualifications of the Specialist   8.48

    Effect on Audit Evidence   8.49

    Using the Specialist's Work   8.50

    Effect on the Auditor's Report   8.51

Evidential Matter and Internal Auditors   8.52

Evidence for Segment Information   8.52

Using the Work of Another Auditor   8.55

    Basic Audit Procedures   8.56

    Procedures When No Reference Is Made   8.57

    Reporting When Reference Is Made   8.58

Evidence from Analytical Procedures   8.59

    Planning Audit Procedures   8.60

    Overall Review   8.61

    Substantive Tests   8.61

    Significant Deviations   8.63

Related Party Transactions   **8.64**
   Identifying Related Party Transactions   **8.64**
   Audit Approach   **8.66**
   Related Party Disclosures   **8.68**
Going-Concern Concept   **8.69**
   Evaluate Information Related to Substantial Doubt   **8.70**
   Identify and Evaluate Management's Plans   **8.71**
   Draw a Conclusion Concerning Substantial Doubt   **8.73**
Subsequent Events   **8.76**
Representation Letters   **8.76**
Reasonableness   **8.76**
Dual-Purpose Tests   **8.77**

EVIDENCE

Overview

The third standard of fieldwork requires that the auditor gather sufficient competent evidential matter as a basis for formulating an opinion on the financial statements. Evidence can be defined as any information that has an impact on determining whether financial statements are fairly presented in accordance with generally accepted accounting principles. A variety of professional standards have been published to provide guidance in the collection and evaluation of evidential matter. The following Statements on Auditing Standards and their related interpretations are discussed in this chapter:

- SAS-31 (Evidential Matter)
- SAS-39 (Audit Sampling)
- SAS-45 (Omnibus Statement on Auditing Standards—1983)
- SAS-47 (Audit Risk and Materiality in Conducting an Audit)
- SAS-41 (Working Papers)
- SAS-67 (The Confirmation Process)
- SAS-57 (Auditing Accounting Estimates)
- SAS-12 (Inquiry of a Client's Lawyer Concerning Litigation, Claims, and Assessments)
- SAS-73 (Using the Work of a Specialist)
- SAS-65 (The Auditor's Consideration of the Internal Audit Function in an Audit of Financial Statements)
- SAS-21 (Segment Information)
- SAS-56 (Analytical Procedures)
- SAS-59 (The Auditor's Consideration of an Entity's Ability to Continue as a Going Concern)
- SAS-64 (Omnibus Statement on Auditing Standards—1990)

- SAS-77 (Amendments to Statements on Auditing Standards No. 22, "Planning and Supervision," No. 59, "The Auditor's Consideration of an Entity's Ability to Continue as a Going Concern," and No. 72, "Special Reports")

SAS-31 discusses the qualities of evidential matter and establishes the concept that financial statements reflect various explicit and implicit assertions that must be substantiated by the auditor. The assertions identified in SAS-31 may be classified in the following broad categories: (1) existence or occurrence, (2) completeness, (3) rights and obligations, (4) valuation and allocation, and (5) presentation and disclosure (AU 326).

SAS-39 discusses factors that should be considered in determining sample sizes for tests of controls and tests of balances. In addition, this SAS concludes that the same fundamental approach is applicable to both statistical sampling and nonstatistical sampling and that the auditor must use professional judgment in deciding when statistical and nonstatistical sampling techniques should be used in an engagement (AU 350).

SAS-45 provides guidance on the application of substantive tests to accounting data that are presented for a date (an interim date) prior to the balance sheet date. The performance of principal substantive tests on interim data increases audit risk; however, audit risk can be reduced by applying appropriate tests to relevant data processed between the interim date and the balance sheet date (AU 313).

SAS-47 discusses the interrelationship between materiality and audit risk, and defines the component elements of audit risk (inherent risk, control risk, and detection risk). SAS-47 concludes that audit risk should be established at an appropriate low level (AU 312).

SAS-41 concludes that the work performed by the auditor should be substantiated through the preparation of audit workpapers. However, SAS-41 also notes that the audit workpapers required for a specific engagement are dependent on a number of factors, including the nature of the engagement (AU 339).

SAS-1 establishes the specific requirement that inventories must be observed. SAS-1 also establishes guidance for audits of entities whose inventories are held in a public warehouse or by other outside custodians (AU 331 and AU 901).

SAS-67 provides guidance on the confirmation process (AU 330).

SAS-57 concludes that it is management's responsibility to design an internal control structure that will produce accounting estimates consistent with generally accepted accounting principles. The auditor's responsibility is to collect sufficient competent evidence that supports the reasonableness of management's estimates (AU 342).

SAS-12 establishes professional guidance on how the auditor is to interact with the client's independent counsel in evaluating litigation, claims, and assessments (AU 337).

SAS-73 recognizes that the auditor may encounter situations that require the expertise of a specialist to substantiate information that is the basis for certain assertions in the financial statements. The auditor must evaluate the reputation, integrity, experience, and qualifications of the specialist. SAS-73 is not applicable to specialists who work for the auditing firm (AU 336).

SAS-65 discusses the effect of the internal audit function on the independent auditor's approach. The auditor should evaluate the competence and objectivity of the internal audit group before determining to what extent, if any, the internal auditors may be used to collect evidence (AU 322).

SAS-21 provides guidance for auditing segment information presented in accordance with reporting standards established by Financial Accounting Standards Board (FASB) Statement No. 14 (Financial Reporting for Segments of a Business Enterprise) (AU 435).

SAS-59 requires the auditor to evaluate conditions and events that raise questions about the client's ability to continue as a going concern. If the auditor concludes that substantial doubt exists about the ability of the client to continue as a going concern, this condition should be discussed in an additional paragraph to be added to the standard auditor's report (AU 341).

SAS-64 clarifies the language that should be used in the auditor's report when the question of an entity's ability to continue as a going concern arises (AU 341.12).

SAS-77 requires that a written audit program(s) be prepared for every audit engagement, prohibits the auditor from using conditional language when the report includes a going-concern explanatory paragraph, and prohibits the general distribution of audited financial statements that are prepared on a basis of accounting established by a regulatory authority.

CHARACTERISTICS OF EVIDENCE

Although a variety of information may have some effect on the auditor's decision process, it is recognized that both the quality and quantity of evidence must be evaluated. The third standard of fieldwork refers to these two characteristics as *competent* (quality) and *sufficient* (quantity). Thus, the auditor must collect competent evidential matter of a sufficient quantity (AU 341.01).

Competent Evidential Matter

SAS-31 (Evidential Matter) states that evidential matter is competent when it is both valid and relevant. The Statement notes that generalizing about what constitutes reliable evidence is difficult, because the particular circumstances of each audit must be considered. However, recognizing the possibility that exceptions exist, SAS-31 lists the following generalizations (AU 326.19):

• Evidence is more reliable if it is obtained from an independent source.

• The more effective the internal control, the more reliable the evidence.

• Evidence obtained directly by the auditor through physical examination, observation, computation, and inspection is more persuasive than information obtained indirectly.

Sufficient Evidential Matter

The term *sufficient* refers to the amount of evidence collected. Audit judgment is used to determine when sufficiency is achieved, as it is to determine the competency of evidential matter. The concept of sufficiency recognizes that the auditor can never reduce audit risk to zero, and SAS-31 emphasizes that the accumulation of evidence should be persuasive rather than convincing. This concept is consistent with the idea that the auditor is not free to collect unlimited amounts of evidence, since he or she must work within economic limits. Cost cannot, however, be the sole basis for the quantity or quality of audit procedures (AU 326.20–.22).

Evidential matter can be classified as underlying accounting data and corroborating evidence. Underlying accounting data consist of general and specialized journals, ledgers, manuals, and supporting worksheets and other analyses. Generally, underlying accounting data are tested by retracing transactions through the accounting system, recomputing allocations, and performing other mathematical calculations. Although underlying accounting data are an important part of evidential matter, such data are not adequate to determine whether financial statements are fairly presented in accordance with generally accepted accounting principles. Therefore, it is necessary for the auditor to collect corroborating evidence before an opinion on the financial statements can be expressed. Corroborating evidence consists of documentary evidence, such as vendor's invoices, confirmations, and observations (AU 326.14–.17).

EVIDENCE AND THE AUDIT PROCESS

The collection and evaluation of sufficient competent evidential matter can be described, and should be applied, as a logical process. SAS-31 attempts to provide the logical framework for the audit process. Conceptually, the auditor should design a substantive tests audit program by relating assertions made in the financial statements to specific audit procedures that are designed to test the validity of the assertions. Five assertions are generally identified with a balance sheet account and its related accounts on the income statement (AU 326.03–.08).

Existence or occurrence—The financial statements assert that an asset or a liability exists at the balance sheet date and that a nominal account represents transactions that occurred during an accounting period.

Completeness—The financial statements assert that all items that comprise an asset, a liability, or a nominal account are represented.

Rights and obligations—The financial statements assert that assets properly represent rights owned by the client and that liabilities represent obligations of the client.

Valuation and allocation—The financial statements assert that all accounts are valued in accordance with generally accepted accounting principles.

Presentation and disclosure—The financial statements assert that accounts and related information are properly classified, described, and disclosed.

Using the five broad assertions in SAS-31 as a starting point, the auditor can identify related audit objectives. Generally, a single assertion will lead to more than one audit objective. For example, a balance sheet may represent that inventories are valued at a particular amount. In turn, this single financial statement assertion may lead to the following audit objectives: (1) inventories are stated at FIFO cost and (2) defective inventories are stated at net realizable value.

Having identified an audit objective, audit procedures are selected to achieve the particular audit objective. Of course, an audit objective may require that more than one audit procedure be employed. Likewise, a single audit procedure may, in part, contribute information to the evaluation of other audit objectives (AU 326.09–.10).

> *OBSERVATION: An Auditing Interpretation entitled "The Auditor's Consideration of the Completeness Assertion" (April 1986) states that an auditor's reliance on the internal control structure and the written representations of management does not provide sufficient audit evidence to support the assertion that all account balances and transactions have been properly included in the financial statements (completeness assertion, paragraph 3 of SAS-31).*
>
> *An auditor must evaluate the audit risk of omission and whether any accounts and/or transactions have been improperly omitted from the financial statements. Substantive tests that are designed to obtain evidence about the completeness assertion are used to reduce the audit risk of omission. These substantive tests should include analytical procedures and tests of details of related account balances. The type and quantity of substantive tests may vary depending on the auditor's assessment of control risk (AU 9326.18–.21).*

SAMPLING (DETERMINING THE SUFFICIENCY OF EVIDENCE)

On the basis of facts known by the auditor, it may be decided that all transactions or balances that make up a particular account must be reviewed to obtain sufficient evidence. In most instances, however, the auditor will test at a level of less than 100%. Audit sampling is covered by SAS-39 (Audit Sampling). To provide guidance in applying the provisions of SAS-39, the AICPA Statistical Sampling Committee issued an Auditing Procedure Study (APS) entitled *Audit Sampling*. That APS is discussed in the chapter entitled "Sampling Techniques and Procedures."

Sampling can be applied on a nonstatistical or statistical basis. It is interesting to note that before the issuance of SAS-39, the standards discussed statistical sampling in detail but devoted little discussion of nonstatistical sampling or sampling in general. SAS-39 recognizes that from a conceptual perspective, statistical sampling and nonstatistical sampling are very similar. In fact, SAS-39 discusses sampling in general and makes few references to concepts or procedures unique to either statistical or nonstatistical sampling (AU 350.03).

Audit Risk

In every audit engagement a degree of risk is always present, even when all transactions and balances are tested 100%. This uncertainty is referred to in SAS-39 as *audit risk* and is a combination of the following factors (AU 350.07–.08):

- The probability that a material misstatement will occur during the accounting process (that is, processing transactions through the accounting system)
- The probability that a material misstatement will not be discovered by the auditor in the performance of substantive tests

The first risk is a function of a client's internal control. In general, the stronger the internal control, the lower the likelihood that a material misstatement will occur. The second risk is controlled, to a degree, by the auditor's quality of performance in testing the details of transactions and balances and performing analytical procedures. Two factors have an effect on the second risk and are referred to as *sampling risk* and *nonsampling risk*. Sampling risk occurs because less than 100% of the sample units in a population are reviewed. For this reason, sampling risk can be reduced by increasing the size of the sample. Unfortunately, nonsampling risk is much harder to control, since it deals with the nature, timing, and execution of audit procedures rather than with the extent of audit procedures. The following are some examples of nonsampling risks (AU 350.08–.11):

- Using an inappropriate audit procedure (nature)
- Performing an audit procedure at an inappropriate date (timing)
- Failing to detect a misstatement on a document being examined (execution)

> **OBSERVATION:** *Nonsampling errors are indeed a part of an audit and should be recognized as such. Research conducted by the Commission on Auditors' Responsibilities discovered that 58% of the respondents to a questionnaire had signed for completing audit steps but had not actually performed the work (see p. 116 of the final*

> *report). Proper staff training, effective planning, and the use of realistic budgets for engagements can have an effect on the number of nonsampling errors committed by staff personnel. SAS-39 points out that nonsampling risk can be reduced to a negligible level through planning, supervision, and quality control.*

As suggested above, the level of sampling risk is influenced by the size of the sample. Achieving an acceptable level of sampling risk is the result of a trade-off between trying to avoid overauditing on the one hand and underauditing on the other. The risks associated with overauditing and underauditing can be discussed in the context of the performance of the tests of controls and substantive tests. During the performance of the tests of controls, there is a risk of assessing control risk too low. Conversely, there is a risk of assessing control risk too high. During the performance of the substantive tests, the auditor faces the risk of incorrect acceptance of a balance when, in fact, the balance is materially misstated, and the risk of incorrect rejection of a balance when, in fact, the balance is not materially misstated (AU 350.10).

Sampling and Tests of Controls

Tests of controls are performed to determine whether internal control is functioning in the manner prescribed. Generally, the control features that are associated with the concept of segregation of duties are not susceptible to sampling. On the other hand, internal control features that are verified by vouching, recomputation, or retracing transactions or procedures are susceptible to sampling (AU 350.32).

When the auditor performs a test of controls, the size of the sample depends on the establishment of (1) the tolerable deviation rate, (2) the expected deviation rate, and (3) the allowable risk of assessing control risk too low. Factors that are considered in setting the tolerable deviation rate are (1) the specific accounting records under review, (2) any related internal control features, and (3) the auditor's specific purpose for testing the control procedure. The expected deviation rate is the likely rate of deviation from the prescribed internal control procedure. Prior years' workpapers may serve as a basis for estimating the likely deviation rate in a population. Finally, the allowable risk of setting control risk too low, based on SAS-39, should be established at a low level (AU 350.31–.34).

Once the sample size is determined, the sample itself must be selected. SAS-39 states that the actual sample should be chosen in a way that is expected to be representative of the entire population. This means that each item in the population should have a chance of selection. For example, it would be inappropriate to test only sales invoices from a particular month. SAS-39 notes that a random selection method is one way of reasonably assuring that a representative sample is obtained. Random selection means that each item in the population has an equal chance of being selected. The use of random number tables, computer-generated random numbers, and sequential sampling (with one or more random starts) are widely used random selection methods (AU 350.39).

Once selected, the sample is tested to determine whether the control is operating effectively. For example, a customer order may be inspected to determine if it was properly approved for sale or credit. On the basis of the sample tested, the auditor draws a conclusion about the entire population. If the auditor concludes that the sample deviation rate is too great, then the planned assessment of the internal control feature must be changed. For example, if the auditor expected a deviation rate of 3% but the sample deviation rate is 8%, he or she would have to change the planned substantive tests by modifying the nature, timing, and/or extent of subsequent audit procedures (AU 350.40–.41).

Noncompliance analysis should not be confined simply to the establishment of a sample deviation rate. SAS-39 points out that each deviation should be reviewed individually to determine whether it has other audit implications. For example, noncompliance may actually be an irregularity rather than a routine deviation, and the auditor should consider what further action must be taken as a result of discovering the irregularity (AU 350.42).

Sampling and Substantive Tests

Substantive tests are performed to determine the validity and propriety of transactions and balances and are usually concerned with dollar values rather than with error or deviation rates. Generally, an account balance is reviewed to determine whether all the items that make up the balance should be examined 100%. For the part of the balance that is sampled, the size of the sample is determined by considering (1) the characteristics of the population, (2) the tolerable misstatement, and (3) the allowable risk of incorrect acceptance (AU 350.16–.21).

The homogeneity of a particular population has an effect on the size of the sample that is selected. For example, a particular population that is composed of similar items with similar dollar values requires a smaller sample size than a population composed of different items that have significantly varying dollar values. In the planning phase of sampling, the auditor establishes the allowable tolerable misstatement. The tolerable misstatement is the dollar amount of misstatement that could exist without the financial statements being materially misstated. As the allowable tolerable misstatement decreases, the size of the sample should increase. For example, if the auditor decreases the allowable tolerable misstatement from 10% to 5%, the sample size should be increased. Finally, the allowable risk of incorrect acceptance is, as stated earlier, the probability that the auditor may accept an incorrect balance. The allowable risk of incorrect acceptance is related to the auditor's assessment of internal control. There is an inverse relationship between the adequacy of internal control and the allowable risk of incorrect acceptance. For example, the stronger the internal control, the higher the established level of allowable risk of incorrect acceptance. That is, the auditor is willing to accept more risk in the performance of the substantive tests if the client has strong internal controls. The size of the sample increases as the allowable risk of incorrect acceptance decreases. Logically, if the auditor wants to reduce risk, he or she generally must increase the sample size (AU 350.16–.23).

> *OBSERVATION: The concepts established in SAS-39 are applicable to statistical and nonstatistical sampling, but neither approach is explicitly endorsed. However, SAS-39 notes that statistical sampling helps the auditor (1) design an efficient sample, (2) measure the sufficiency of the evidential matter obtained, and (3) evaluate the sample results. Without identifying them as such, these are the primary advantages of statistical sampling over nonstatistical sampling. The disadvantages, as noted in SAS-39, are costs of training auditors and of designing a sample plan. Again, although SAS-39 does not endorse one sampling approach over the other, it appears to suggest that statistical sampling is superior to nonstatistical sampling when a sampling approach is warranted by the engagement characteristics (AU 350.45–.46).*

Timing of Substantive Tests

Audit planning, the consideration of internal control, and the application of substantive tests are frequently conducted by the auditor prior to the balance sheet date. In this manner, the auditor may become aware of significant matters that affect the year-end financial statements, including (1) related party transactions, (2) changing economic conditions, (3) recent accounting pronouncements, and (4) other items that may require adjustment at the balance sheet date (AU 313.02).

SAS-45 (Omnibus Statement on Auditing Standards—1983) provides guidance on the application of substantive tests as of a date that is prior to the balance sheet date. SAS-45 distinguishes between *principal substantive tests* of the details of a particular asset or liability account and *other types of substantive tests*, including the following (AU 313.08):

- Tests of details of the additions to and reductions from accounts such as property, investments, debt, and equity

- Tests of details of transactions affecting income and expense accounts

- Tests of accounts that are not to be audited by testing the details of items composing the balance, such as warranty reserves, clearing accounts, and certain deferred charges

- Analytical procedures applied to income and expense accounts

Substantive tests can be applied to the above types of transactions for any selected dates prior to the balance sheet date and completed as part of the year-end audit procedures. However, certain factors must be considered by the auditor before *principal substantive tests* can be applied to the details of particular asset or liability accounts as of a date (interim date) that is prior to the balance sheet date (AU 313.04).

The performance of principal substantive tests prior to the balance sheet date increases audit risk because misstatements that could exist at the balance sheet date may not be detected by the auditor as of the interim audit date. This potential audit risk increases as the period increases between the date of the interim date substantive tests and the balance sheet date. However, the auditor can control the increased audit risk by properly designing the substantive tests that are applied during the period between the interim date substantive tests and the balance sheet date (AU 313.03).

Before applying principal substantive tests to the details of asset or liability accounts at an interim date, the auditor should consider the following factors (AU 313.04):

- The cost of the additional substantive tests during the period between the interim date of the principal substantive tests and the balance sheet date

- The difficulty of controlling the increased audit risk

Factors that affect the timing of principal substantive tests The auditor should first determine whether the performance of principal substantive tests to the details of balance sheet accounts at an interim date is cost effective. If the auditor can assess control risk as low during the period between the interim date of the principal substantive tests and the balance sheet date, the additional substantive tests that are necessary during this period may be restricted to the extent that they are cost effective. In this event, the auditor may have a reasonable basis for extending the audit conclusions from the interim date of the principal substantive tests to the balance sheet date. On the other hand, if the auditor cannot assess control risk as low during the period between the interim date of the principal substantive tests and the balance sheet date, the additional substantive tests that are necessary during this period may not be restricted to the extent that they are cost effective (AU 313.04–.05).

To achieve a reasonable basis of extending the audit conclusions from the interim date of the principal substantive tests to the balance sheet date, the auditor does not have to assess control risk as low. In this event, the auditor must exercise care in determining the effectiveness of the substantive tests performed during the period from the interim date of the principal substantive tests to the balance sheet date. If the auditor concludes that the effectiveness of the tests is impaired, the tests should be performed at the balance sheet date (AU 313.05).

Because of rapidly changing business conditions or other circumstances occurring during the period between the interim date of the principal substantive tests and the balance sheet date, the auditor must consider the possibility of management misstating the financial statements. If these conditions exist, the auditor may conclude that the principal substantive tests should not be performed at the interim audit date (AU 313.06).

The nature of the balance sheet account should be considered by the auditor to determine whether the interim-audit-date balance is likely to be similar to the balance-sheet-date balance. The auditor must consider the predictability of the amount and the significance and composition of the particular balance sheet account that is selected for interim principal substantive tests. Finally, the client's accounting procedures must be sufficiently adequate to permit the auditor to analyze the year-end account balances and the transactions occurring in the account between the interim date of the principal substantive tests and the balance sheet date (AU 313.07).

Extending audit conclusions to the balance sheet date   When the auditor decides to perform principal substantive tests to the details of a balance sheet account at an interim date, additional substantive tests should be applied to the transactions that occurred in the account between the interim date and the balance sheet date. The additional substantive tests must be selected to ensure that the overall audit objective for the particular balance sheet account is achieved. Generally, the tests should include the comparison of details of the interim and year-end balances in the account. In addition, analytical procedures and/or substantive tests of details should be performed to provide a basis for extending to the balance sheet date the audit conclusion reached at the interim date of the principal substantive tests. If significant monetary misstatements are discovered at the interim date of the principal substantive tests, the auditor may be required to modify the nature, timing, or extent of the additional substantive tests that are performed during the period between the interim date and the balance sheet date. Under these circumstances, the auditor must exercise professional judgment (AU 313.08–.09).

The performance of principal substantive tests to the details of a balance sheet account at an interim date must be coordinated with other audit procedures related to the same balance sheet account. Coordinating auditing procedures should be based on the auditor's planned assessed level of control risk related to the particular balance sheet account (AU 313.10).

MATERIALITY AND AUDIT RISK

In determining the nature, timing, and extent of audit procedures, the auditor should consider, among other factors, materiality and audit risk. *Materiality* is defined in the FASB's Statement of Financial Accounting Concepts No. 2 (Qualitative Characteristics of Accounting Information) as "the magnitude of an omission or misstatement of account information that, in the light of surrounding circumstances, makes it probable that the judgment of a reasonable person relying on the information would have been changed or influenced by the omission or misstatement." *Audit risk* refers to the possibility that financial statements are materially misstated even when the auditor issues an unqualified opinion on the statements. SAS-47

(Audit Risk and Materiality in Conducting an Audit) explains how the auditor should integrate the concepts of materiality and audit risk into the planning and execution of an audit engagement (AU 312.01).

Consideration of Materiality

SAS-47 reiterates the well-established concept that considerable professional judgment is used to establish a materiality factor for an audit engagement. There is a qualitative as well as a quantitative element that must be considered when the auditor establishes the materiality factor. From a quantitative point of view, the auditor usually relates materiality to many different amounts that appear on the financial statements. For example, an auditor may decide that a material error is one that has a 5% impact on net income or a 10% impact on total assets. However, SAS-47 notes that an immaterial error from a quantitative perspective may nevertheless be considered material because of the qualitative nature of the error (AU 312.03–.07).

> *OBSERVATION: SAS-47 states that qualitative factors should be considered when determining the materiality of an item. The discussion of qualitative factors uses the following example: An illegal payment of an otherwise immaterial amount could be material if there is a reasonable possibility that it could lead to a material contingent liability or a material loss of revenue.*

Even though an item should be evaluated quantitatively and qualitatively, SAS-47 notes that for practical reasons only the quantitative nature of the item can be considered during the planning phase of an engagement. The quantitative threshold(s) might be based on the enterprise's prior years' financial statements or annualized interim financial statements. When this approach is used, the initial basis for determining materiality should be compared to the actual financial statements for the period. If circumstances change significantly and it is obvious that a lower materiality level should have been used, the auditor must consider whether sufficient evidential matter has been obtained to substantiate the lower level of materiality. In other words, when materiality is defined at too high an amount during the planning stage, the auditor runs the risk of underauditing (AU 312.12–.15).

Consideration of Audit Risk

As noted earlier, *audit risk* refers to the possibility that financial statements may be materially misstated even though an unqualified opinion has been expressed by the auditor. SAS-47 concludes that audit risk should be established at an appropriate low level for issuing an opinion on the financial statements. There is an inverse relationship between audit risk and materiality, which can be expressed in the following generalizations (AU 312.17):

- The risk that an item could be misstated by an extremely large amount is generally low.
- The risk that an item could be misstated by an extremely small amount is generally high.

Although audit risk is generally related to the financial statements taken as a whole, it also should be evaluated at the individual account balance and class of transaction level. To evaluate audit risk at this level, the auditor must consider the following three types of risk:

- Inherent risk
- Control risk
- Detection risk

Inherent risk   The nature of the account balance or class of transactions and the fundamental characteristics of the entity being audited determine the level of inherent risk. *Inherent risk* is defined by SAS-47 as the likelihood of a misstatement existing in an account balance or class of transactions that would be material when aggregated with misstatement(s) in other accounts or classifications, assuming that there were no related internal controls. There are many factors that can affect inherent risk. Factors to be considered include the need for estimates, sensitivity to external forces, and characteristics of the industry in which the company operates. As a general rule, there is less risk associated with an account that is based on actual transactions than one based on estimates. For example, there is less risk associated with rent expense than with warranty expense based on this single factor, and there is more risk associated with the inventory of a company that is part of an industry that is experiencing rapid technological changes (AU 312.20).

Control risk   The client's design of internal control will have an impact on the level of audit risk. *Control risk* is defined as the possibility of a misstatement occurring in an account balance or class of transactions that (1) could be material when aggregated with misstatement(s) in other balances or classes and (2) will not be prevented or detected on a timely basis by the system of internal control. Control risk, like inherent risk, cannot be changed by the auditor. The client's design of internal control that produces the current financial statements must be treated as a given factor. Of course the auditor can make recommendations for improving the system, which may affect the audit engagement of the next period. In general, the stronger the internal control, the more likely that material misstatements will be prevented or detected by the system (AU 312.20).

Detection risk   Even though the auditor performs a variety of audit procedures, it is possible that a material misstatement will not be detected. SAS-47 defines *detection risk* as the risk that an auditor's procedures will lead to the conclusion that a misstatement in an account balance or class of transactions that could be material when aggregated with a misstatement in other accounts or classes does not exist when in fact such a misstatement does exist. Detection risk arises because all items that comprise an account balance are not examined (sampling misstatement) and audit procedures are not properly applied (nonsampling misstatement) (AU 312.20).

> *OBSERVATION: To control sampling misstatements the auditor may refer to professional standards established in SAS-39 and the related APS. Guidance for controlling nonsampling misstatements may be found in SAS-22 (Planning and Supervision), SAS-25 (The Relationship of Generally Accepted Auditing Standards to Quality Control Standards), and the Statement on Quality Control Standards series. Quality control standards are discussed in the chapter entitled "Responsibility and Function of the Independent Auditor."*

During the planning phase of the engagement, the auditor must consider the inherent risk, control risk, and detection risk and select an audit strategy that will result in a low level of audit risk once the engagement is complete. The level of control risk will be based on the auditor's preparation of internal control questionnaires, flowcharts, and so forth. Of course, considerable professional judgment must be exercised to assess these levels of risk (AU 312.21–.24).

There is an inverse relationship between the auditor's assessment of inherent and control risks and the level of detection risk. If the inherent risk and control risk are high, the auditor should establish a low level of detection risk. The level of detection risk would have an impact on the design of the auditor's substantive tests. In general, if a low level of detection risk is established, the auditor would (1) expand the sample of substantive tests (extent of procedures), (2) be less likely to perform substantive tests at interim dates (timing of procedures), and (3) perform audit procedures that result in more *competent* evidential matter (nature of procedures) (AU 312.25).

Assessing Audit Risk

Once substantive tests have been performed, the auditor must assess the audit risk in the context of the definition of materiality. Initially the auditor should identify the known misstatement amount based on the performance of audit procedures. Next, the known misstatement should be used as a basis to estimate the likely misstatement amount. In a simple example, an auditor may identify a known misstatement of $20,000 based on testing and may project a likely misstatement of $80,000 if the sample tested represents 25 percent of the total account balance. In addition, the auditor would combine the quantitative results of his or her misstatement analysis with relevant qualitative factors to determine the risk that material misstatements exist (AU 312.27–.28).

As noted earlier, there is more potential audit risk for an account balance or class of transactions that is based on estimates. A projected balance or class of transactions based on audit sampling will seldom be equal to the actual amounts shown in the financial statements. Generally, this difference should not be treated as a misstatement as long as the auditor believes the difference is reasonable. However, if the auditor believes the difference is *not* reasonable, the difference between the amount on the financial statements and the closest reasonable estimate should be treated as a misstatement and aggregated with other likely misstatements in determining whether a material misstatement exists (AU 312.29).

Also, when the auditor deals with estimates in the financial statements, he or she must be alert to possible biases on the part of management. For example, if the client consistently makes estimation misstatements that always increase net assets or net income, the auditor should consider this tendency and its overall effect on the financial statements taken as a whole (AU 312.29).

Once the aggregate misstatement amount is estimated, it should be compared to materiality. If the likely misstatement amount is greater than the amount designated as material, additional investigation must be conducted or the financial statements must be modified. If the likely misstatement amount is less than the materiality amount, audit risk must be assessed. As the likely misstatement amount approaches the materiality amount, the level of audit risk rises. As noted earlier, SAS-47 concludes that the audit risk should be established at a relatively low level. Thus, the comparison and the analysis of the relationship of the likely misstatement and the level of materiality is critical. For example, if the auditor has estimated the aggregate likely misstatement to be $90,000 and the level of materiality is $100,000, it is likely that audit risk is too great to conclude that the financial statements are fairly stated. On the other hand, if the estimated aggregate likely misstatement had been $10,000 rather than $90,000, it is likely that the auditor would conclude that a low level of audit risk had been achieved (AU 312.31–.32).

WORKPAPERS

The work performed and the conclusions reached by the auditor should be adequately documented in the audit workpapers. Professional standards regarding workpapers are discussed in SAS-41 (Working Papers) (AU 339).

> **OBSERVATION:** *Workpapers are the property of the auditor, and appropriate procedures should be established to protect the confidentiality of the information. Workpapers should be retained for a period that meets the legal requirements and the needs of the auditor.*

SAS-41 recognizes that the actual quantity and nature of the workpapers for any particular engagement will differ depending on the specific circumstances of the engagement. The following circumstances may have an effect on the content of workpapers (AU 339.04):

- Nature of engagement
- Nature of auditor's report

- Nature of financial data subject to auditor's report, including the financial statements, schedules, and other financial information
- Nature and condition of client's records
- Assessed level of control risk
- Degree of supervision and review required

In general, workpapers must demonstrate that the three standards of fieldwork have been achieved and that the accounting records agree or reconcile with the financial statements being reported on. Workpapers may include memos, audit programs, flowcharts, completed internal control questionnaires, confirmations, and other documents that demonstrate the accumulation of evidence by the auditor. Finally, workpapers are an essential product of an audit. They aid in the control of an engagement and serve as a basis for performing a review of the work completed (AU 339.05).

Although SAS-41 does not attempt to prescribe the detailed content of an auditor's workpapers, it should be remembered that some SASs require that certain items be included in the auditor's workpapers. These requirements and related standards are listed below:

- Letter of inquiry sent to the client's lawyer (SAS-12 [Inquiry of a Client's Lawyer Concerning Litigation, Claims, and Assessments])

- Client representation letters (SAS-19 [Client Representations])

- Notation in the workpapers, or a copy of the written communication sent to the client, that describes reportable conditions in the internal control structure (SAS-60 [Communication of Internal Control Structure Related Matters Noted in an Audit])

- Written audit programs (SAS-22)

- Understanding of internal control (SAS-55)

- Oral communication of illegal acts (SAS-54)

- Oral communication to an audit committee (SAS-61)

- Explanation of why accounts receivable were not confirmed (SAS-67)

> **OBSERVATION:** *In a summary accompanying the Exposure Draft that preceded SAS-41, the Auditing Standards Board (ASB) noted*

that the main purpose of the draft was "to make it clear that workpapers are required." Although it may seem that such a statement is self-evident and that no action was necessary by the ASB, results of peer reviews demonstrate that many firms do not prepare adequate workpapers. In many cases it seems that the auditor has performed the necessary procedures. However, a violation of professional standards occurs when an independent auditor does not accumulate sufficient competent evidential matter.

OBSERVATION: When a regulator requests access to or photocopies of workpapers based on a law, regulation, or audit contract requiring that access, the auditor should inform the client of the request and make appropriate arrangements with the regulator to comply. If the regulator engages another accounting firm to perform the investigation, the auditor should obtain a description of the other accounting firm's role and should obtain from the accounting firm an acknowledgment that it is bound by the same confidentiality restrictions imposed on the regulator. Generally, the auditor should not provide information to the regulator until the audit is complete. If the request for the information is not based on a law, regulation, or audit contract, the auditor may with to consult legal counsel concerning the request.

Access to Workpapers by Regulators

Although workpapers are the property of the auditor, governmental regulators may have the right to them based on law, regulation, or the audit contract. An Auditing Interpretation of SAS-41 entitled "Providing Access to or Photocopies of Working Papers to a Regulator" (July 1994) states that when regulators have requested access to workpapers, the auditor should observe the following guidance (AU 9339.02–.05):

- Consider notifying the client that regulators have requested access to the workpapers and state that the auditor intends to comply with the request.
- Make arrangements (time, date, place, etc.) with the regulators concerning access to the workpapers.
- Establish procedures that allow the auditor to maintain control over the workpapers.

In addition to the above procedures, the auditor should consider sending a letter to the regulatory agency (probably requesting a signed acknowledgment of receipt of the letter) that explains the role of the auditor and the nature of the workpapers. An example of such a letter is presented below (AU 9339.05–.06).

Your representatives have requested access to our workpapers in connection with our audit of the December 31, 19X5, financial statements of X Company. It is our understanding that the purpose of your request is to facilitate your regulatory examination.

Our audit of X Company's December 31, 19X5, financial statements was conducted in accordance with generally accepted auditing standards, the objective of which is to form an opinion on whether the financial statements, which are the responsibility and representations of management, present fairly, in all material respects, the financial position, results of operations and cash flows in conformity with generally accepted accounting principles. Under generally accepted auditing standards, we have the responsibility, within the inherent limitations of the auditing process, to design our audit to provide reasonable assurance the errors and irregularities that have a material effect on the financial statements will be detected, and to exercise due care in the conduct of our audit. The concept of selective testing of the data being audited, which involves judgment both as to the number of transactions to be audited and as to the areas to be tested, has been generally accepted as a valid and sufficient basis for an auditor to express an opinion on financial statements. Thus, our audit, based on the concept of selective testing, is subject to the inherent risk that material errors or irregularities, if they exist, would not be detected. In addition, an audit does not address the possibility that material errors or irregularities may occur in the future. Also, our use of professional judgment and the assessment of materiality for the purpose of our audit means that matters may have existed that would have been assessed differently by you.

The workpapers were prepared for the purpose of providing the principal support for our report on X Company's December 31, 19X5, financial statements and to aid in the conduct and supervision of our audit. The workpapers document the procedures performed, the information obtained, and the pertinent conclusions reached in the engagement. The audit procedures that we performed were limited to those we considered necessary under generally accepted auditing standards to enable us to formulate and express an opinion on the financial statements taken as a whole. Accordingly, we make no representation as to the sufficiency or appropriateness, for your purposes, of either the information contained in our workpapers or our audit procedures. In addition, any notations, comments, and individual conclusions appearing on any of the workpapers do not stand alone, and should not be read as an opinion on any individual amounts, accounts, balances, or transactions.

Our audit of X Company's December 31, 19X5, financial statements was performed for the purpose stated above and has not been planned or conducted in contemplation of your regulatory examination or for the purpose of assessing X Company's compliance with laws and regulations. Therefore, items of possible interest to you may not have been specifically addressed. Accordingly, our audit and the workpapers prepared in connection therewith should not supplant other inquiries and procedures that should be undertaken by the [name of regulatory agency] for the purpose of monitoring and regulating the financial affairs of X Company. In addition, we have not audited any financial statements of X Company since December 31, 19X5, nor have we performed any audit procedures since February 22, 19X6, the date of our auditor's report, and significant events or circumstances may have occurred since that date.

The workpapers constitute and reflect work performed or information obtained by [name of CPA firm] in its capacity as independent auditor for X Company. The documents contain trade secrets and confidential commercial and financial information of our firm and X Company that is privileged and confidential, and we expressly reserve all rights with respect to disclosures to third parties. Accordingly, we request confidential treatment under the Freedom of Information Act or similar laws and regulations when requests are made for the workpapers or information contained therein or any documents created by the [name of regulatory agency] containing information derived therefrom. We further request that written notice be given to our firm before distribution of the information in the workpapers (or photocopies thereof) to others, including other governmental agencies, except when such distribution is required by law or regulation.

The above illustrative letter should be appropriately modified to reflect the circumstances of the engagement. Some of the modifications that may be needed include the following:

- When the audit has been conducted in accordance with GAAS and other established auditing procedures (such as generally accepted governmental auditing standards), the letter should be appropriately modified.

- When the audit was conducted in accordance with the Single Audit Act of 1984, and other federal audit requirements, the letter should be modified to explain the object of the audit.

- When the letter is sent to the regulatory agency at the request of management (rather than by law, regulation, or audit contract), the letter should state that "the management of X Company has authorized us to provide you access to our workpapers in order to facilitate your regulatory examination."

- When the financial statements are based on regulatory accounting principles, the letter should be appropriately modified.

- When the regulatory agency has asked for photocopies of the workpapers, the letter should state "any photocopies of our workpapers we agree to provide you will be identified as 'Confidential Treatment Request by [name of auditor, address, telephone number].'"

- When the audit engagement has not been completed, the letter should be modified to describe that fact and to put the regulatory agency on guard that the workpapers may change based on the performance of additional audit procedures (generally, the auditor should not agree to supply the regulatory agency with incomplete workpapers).

The auditor should not agree to transfer the ownership of the workpapers to the regulatory agency.

When a regulatory agency requests the auditor's workpapers but there is no legal basis for the request (no applicable law, regulation, or audit contract requirement), the auditor should evaluate the purpose for the request. That evaluation may include consultation with legal counsel. If the auditor agrees with the request, permission for access to the workpapers should be obtained from the client (preferably in writing). In some instances the client may request an inspection of the workpapers before granting the regulatory agency access to them. If the auditor agrees to the client's request, the auditor should maintain control over the workpapers (AU 9339.11–.15).

Some regulatory agencies may hire a third party to inspect workpapers. Under this circumstance, the auditor should follow the same procedures that would apply if the regulatory agency itself were inspecting the workpapers. In addition, the auditor should obtain from the regulatory agency a statement (preferably in writing) that the third party is "acting on behalf of the regulator and agreement from the third party that he or she is subject to the same restriction on disclosure and use of workpapers and the information contained therein as the regulator" (AU 9339.09–.10).

> **OBSERVATION:** *The guidance established by the Interpretation does not apply to requests from (1) the Internal Revenue Service, (2) peer review programs (and similar programs) established by the AICPA or state societies of CPAs, (3) proceedings arising from alleged violations of ethical standards, or (4) subpoenas.*

EVIDENCE AND PROCEDURES REQUIRED BY STATEMENTS ON AUDITING STANDARDS

There is no list available of audit procedures that must be performed to constitute an audit engagement. An audit engagement is too complex to expect such a simple solution. However, several Statements on Auditing Standards pertain to the collection of evidence. These pronouncements are discussed in the remainder of this chapter.

Confirmation Process

Evidential matter may be obtained by confirming or acquiring information directly with or from third parties. The confirmation process can be used as part of the audit of a number of account balances, transactions, and other information. For example, accounts receivable and payable may be confirmed with customers and vendors, respectively, a complex transaction may be confirmed with the counterparty, and the relationship between two (related) parties may be explained by the other party (AU 330.04).

In general, audit evidence obtained through the confirmation process is considered very reliable. SAS-31 reinforces this position by stating that "when evidential matter can be obtained from independent sources outside an entity, it provides greater assurance of reliability for the purposes of an independent audit than that secured solely within the entity" (AU 326.19).

For the confirmation process to provide reliable evidence, that process must be appropriately applied in an audit of financial statements. SAS-67 (The Confirmation Process) addresses the confirmation process and identifies the following as elements of that process:

- Selection of items for confirmation
- Design of confirmation request
- Performance of confirmation procedures
  - Communication of information to the third party
  - Obtaining information from the third party
- Evaluation of information received from the third party

> *OBSERVATION: Audit planning involves the nature, timing, and extent of audit procedures. For the most part, SAS-67 dis-*

cusses only the nature of the confirmation process. Guidance for timing audit procedures is provided in SAS-45, and guidance for determining the extent of audit procedures is provided in SAS-39 and SAS-47.

Design of Confirmation Request

When designing a confirmation request, the auditor should identify related audit objectives and then format the confirmation request so that those objectives will be achieved. Audit objectives are established to test the numerous assertions (both explicit and implicit) that are included in a client's financial statements. SAS-31 identifies the following five categories of assertions (AU 330.11):

1. Existence and occurrence
2. Completeness
3. Rights and obligations
4. Valuation or allocation
5. Presentation and disclosure

Although confirmation requests may be designed to obtain evidence to support all five assertions, evidence acquired through confirmation generally is either not relevant to all five assertions or more persuasive in testing one assertion than the others. For example, when an account receivable is confirmed, the evidential matter created through confirmation is very persuasive with respect to the existence assertion, but is almost irrelevant to the valuation assertion. Thus, when evaluating the evidence from confirmation requests the auditor should recognize the limitations of the confirmation process. If an important assertion will not be tested as part of the confirmation process, the auditor must select other audit procedures that will satisfactorily test the remaining assertions (AU 330.13–.14).

In designing the confirmation request, SAS-67 suggests that factors such as the following be considered by the auditor (AU 330.16):

- Confirmation request form
- Prior auditor experience
- Information being confirmed
- Characteristics of respondents

Confirmation request form   An auditor may use either a positive confirmation form or a negative confirmation form (AU 330.17).

A positive confirmation form may be designed in two ways. The information to be confirmed may be indicated in the confirmation request, or the request may be blank, requiring the respondent to fill in the missing information. There is a trade-off in the selection of the complete or incomplete format. When an incomplete form is completed and returned by a respondent, more competent evidence is created than when the respondent is simply asked to sign a complete confirmation form. However, when the incomplete form is used, the response rate generally will be lower (sufficiency of evidence matter) and it may be necessary to perform alternative audit procedures to supplement the confirmation process. When a positive confirmation is used and the request is not returned, no evidence is created (AU 330.18–.19).

A negative confirmation form requires the respondent to return the confirmation only if there is disagreement. When negative confirmations are not returned, the evidence generated is different from that generated when positive confirmations are used. That is, the lack of returned negative confirmations provides only *implicit* evidence that the information is correct. SAS-67 describes this limitation as follows (AU 330.22):

> Unreturned negative confirmations do not provide explicit evidence that the intended third parties received the confirmation requests and verified that the information contained on them is correct.

Because of the limitation described above, the negative confirmation form should be used only when all of the following conditions are met (AU 330.20):

- The combined assessed level of inherent and control risk is low.
- The audit population contains a large number of relatively small individual balances.
- There is no reason to believe that respondents will not give adequate attention to confirmation requests.

Even under the conditions described above, SAS-67 expresses a concern that the use of negative confirmations will not generate sufficient competent evidential matter and concludes that "the auditor should consider performing other substantive procedures to supplement the use of negative confirmations." For example, if the auditor uses negative confirmations to test the existence of accounts receivable, it may also be advisable to use additional tests (such as reviewing subsequent cash collections and vouching) to determine with reasonable assurance that accounts receivable do exist (AU 330.20).

When a response is received from a negative confirmation, the auditor should investigate the reason for the disagreement. If there are a number of disagreements or the disagreements appear to be significant, the auditor should reconsider the original assessment of the level of inherent and control risk. This reassessment may lead to the conclusion that the combined assessed level of inherent and control risk is not low, in which case the auditor should appropriately modify the originally planned audit approach (AU 330.21).

Prior auditor experience   In designing confirmation requests, the auditor should consider prior experience with the client and with similar clients. Prior experience may suggest, for example, that a confirmation form was improperly designed or that previous response rates were so low that audit procedures other than confirmations should be considered (AU 330.23).

Information being confirmed   The auditor should consider the capabilities of the respondent in determining what should be included in the confirmation request. Respondents can confirm only what they are capable of confirming, and there will be a tendency to confirm only what is relatively easy to confirm. For example, in designing an accounts receivable confirmation, consideration should be given to whether respondents are more capable of verifying an individual account balance or transactions that make up a single receivable balance. The auditor's understanding of the nature of transactions as they relate to respondents is fundamental to determining what information should be included in a confirmation request (AU 330.24).

Information to be confirmed with respondents should not be limited to dollar or other amounts. For example, in complex transactions it may be appropriate to confirm terms of contracts or other documentation that support such transactions. In addition, it may be appropriate to confirm information that is based on oral modifications and therefore not part of the formal documentation. SAS-67 provides the following guidance with respect to oral modifications (AU 330.25):

> When the auditor believes there is a moderate or high degree of risk that there may be significant oral modifications, he or

she should inquire about the existence and details of any such modifications to written agreements.

If the client responds to the auditor's inquiry that there are no oral modifications to an agreement, the auditor should consider confirming with the other party to the agreement that no oral modifications exist (AU 330.25).

Characteristics of respondents   Confirmation requests should be addressed to respondents who, when they respond to the requests, will generate meaningful and competent evidential matter. Factors to be considered include the following (AU 330.26–.27):

- Competence of respondent
- Knowledge of respondent
- Objectivity of respondent

If information concerning the above factors (as well as other relevant factors) comes to the auditor's attention and that information suggests that meaningful and competent evidential matter will not result from the confirmation process, the auditor should consider using other audit procedures to test financial statement assertions (AU 330.27).

SAS-67 specifically warns that under some circumstances, the level of professional skepticism should be increased, resulting in a closer scrutiny of the respondent. Two examples presented in SAS-67 include the occurrence of an unusual transaction or the existence of a significant balance or transaction (AU 330.27).

> **OBSERVATION:** *For these as well as other circumstances, SAS-67 does not state specifically what the actions of the auditor should be. Presumably, the auditor could decide to investigate more closely the characteristics of the respondents or to employ other audit procedures to reduce the risk of material misstatements in the financial statements.*

Performance of Confirmation Procedures

The confirmation process should be executed so that the client does not have an opportunity to intercept requests when they are mailed or when they are returned from respondents. However, the work of internal auditors may be used in the confirmation process if the guidance established by SAS-65 (The Auditor's Consideration of the Internal Audit Function in an Audit of Financial Statements) is observed (AU 330.28).

The confirmation process ideally involves the auditor mailing a confirmation request directly to a respondent and receiving directly from the respondent the returned confirmation. When positive confirmations are used, and there is no response, the auditor should consider sending second and possibly third requests (AU 330.28).

SAS-67 does recognize that other means of confirmation may be used but notes that the auditor must consider using additional audit procedures to reasonably ensure that a response is authentic and relevant. Specifically, SAS-67 discusses the use of facsimile and oral responses (AU 330.29).

When a facsimile is received from a respondent as part of the confirmation process, the same degree of uncertainty concerning the source of the information arises. To reduce that risk, procedures such as the following may be employed (AU 330.29):

- Verify the source and content of the facsimile through a telephone call to the respondent.

- Request the respondent to mail the original confirmation directly to the auditor.

When information is confirmed orally, the content of and circumstances surrounding the confirmation should be documented in the workpapers. If the information confirmed orally is significant, SAS-67 requires that the auditor request the respondent to confirm the information in writing (AU 330.29).

> **OBSERVATION:** *Information may be received from a respondent via a fax machine. As with other evidential matter, the auditor must take precautions reasonably to ensure that the fax is authentic. For example, a fax received directly by the client is similar to a returned confirmation that has been opened by the client. To avoid this problem the auditor may receive the fax on an auditor-controlled telephone line, or reconfirm the information contained on the fax through a telephone conversation with the respondent. In general, the auditor must be careful not to reduce his or her level of professional skepticism because technology has changed the way evidence is created.*

Evaluation of Information Received from the Third Party

The auditor often is unable to obtain a 100% response rate when positive confirmations are used. When information has not been confirmed, alternative audit procedures must frequently be used. The specific nature of alternative procedures depends on the account balance or transaction and the adequacy of the client's internal control structure. For example, when a customer will not confirm an account receivable, the existence of the account could be substantiated through the review of a subsequent cash collection(s) or the inspection of documentation for the transaction(s) that created the year-end balance (AU 330.30 and .33).

SAS-67 concludes that it may be acceptable to omit the use of alternative procedures if *both* of the following circumstances exist (AU 330.31):

- Unconfirmed balances do not appear to be unique.

- Unconfirmed balances are immaterial when projected as 100% misstatements.

Unconfirmed balances do not appear to be unique The auditor should review those accounts that respondents will not confirm to determine whether they are unusual. While it is difficult to define *unusual*, transactions that are complex and not routine, or balances that do not follow a dollar-value pattern, would increase the level of audit risk and would generally preclude the auditor from omitting alternative procedures. For example, most auditors would be skeptical if most of the unconfirmed accounts receivable were from customers that also had other relationships with the client (AU 330.31).

Unconfirmed balances are immaterial The auditor may treat all accounts that respondents do not confirm as misstatements if collectively those misstatements could not have a material effect on the financial statements. In determining the misstatements, the auditor must project the assumed misstatements from the unconfirmed balances to the total population (AU 330.31).

Based on the evidence obtained through the confirmation process and the use of alternative audit procedures, the auditor should determine whether related assertions have been sufficiently tested. SAS-67 concludes that the auditor should consider the following factors when making this determination (AU 330.33):

- Reliability of evidence obtained through the confirmation process and alternative procedures

- The nature and implications of exceptions discovered

- Evidence that may have been obtained through the use of procedures other than confirmation and alternative audit procedures

If the auditor concludes that evidential matter obtained through the confirmation process, alternative audit procedures, and other audit procedures is not sufficient to substantiate relevant assertions in the financial statements, additional evidence must be obtained. The additional evidence may be acquired by employing whatever procedures the auditor may deem appropriate, including additional confirmations, tests of details, and analytical procedures (AU 330.33).

> *OBSERVATION: Auditors must be cautious when confirming the fair value of assets with parties that originally were involved in the acquisition of the assets being investigated. Because the respondent party may not provide objective evidence, the auditor should consider whether it is necessary to communicate with a party not involved in the transaction to collect competent evidential matter concerning the fair value of an asset.*

Confirmation of Accounts Receivable

In addition to providing standards for employing the confirmation process, SAS-67 specifically addresses the confirmation of accounts receivable. The term *accounts receivable* is defined as follows (AU 330.34):

1. The entity's claims against customers that have arisen from the sale of goods or services in the normal course of business.
2. A financial institution's loans.

> *OBSERVATION: Although SAS-67 defines the term **accounts receivable**, that definition also encompasses notes receivable and other receivables that use descriptive terms, assuming the account*

balance arose from the sale of goods or services in the normal course of business.

SAS-67 states that the confirmation of accounts receivable is a generally accepted auditing procedure and should be employed in all audit engagements except under one or more the following circumstances (AU 330.34):

- The accounts receivable balance is immaterial.
- It is expected that the use of confirmations would be ineffective (for example, prior experience may suggest that the response rate is too low or responses are expected to be unreliable).
- Confirmation is not necessary to reduce audit risk to an acceptably low level.

The last circumstance arises when the combined assessed level of inherent and control risk is low, and the expected evidence created from analytical procedures and other substantive tests of details results in the achievement of an acceptable level of audit risk (AU 330.34).

> **OBSERVATION:** *Although the confirmation of accounts receivable is not necessary when audit risk can otherwise be reduced to an "acceptably low level," SAS-67 appears to warn auditors that such a situation is unusual by stating that "in many situations, both confirmation of accounts receivable and other substantive tests of details are necessary to reduce audit risk to an acceptably low level for the applicable financial statement assertions" (AU 330.34).*

When the auditor concludes that it is not necessary to confirm accounts receivable, that position must be documented in the workpapers. Thus, the workpapers must include a full explanation based on one or more of the three circumstances listed above (AU 330.35).

Evidence for Inventories

The observation of inventories is a mandatory generally accepted auditing procedure. The observation requirement may be achieved in a number of ways. If the inventory quantity is determined entirely by a physical count, the count should be made on or near the balance sheet date and the auditor must be present to observe the count. If the client has an effective internal control structure, including perpetual inventory records, the inventory can be observed at the balance sheet date, before the balance sheet date, or after the balance sheet date. Finally, the inventory may be estimated by the client through the use of statistical sampling. When statistical sampling is used, the auditor must determine the validity and application of the statistical plan and observe such counts as he or she deems necessary (AU 331.01–.11).

An auditor may not be able to observe the inventory count on the balance sheet date. For example, the auditor may have been appointed to the engagement after the physical count was completed. In this event, the auditor must use alternative audit procedures to support the existence of the inventory at the balance sheet date. Alternative audit procedures consist of the auditor making or observing inventory counts at a date subsequent to the balance sheet date and reviewing intervening transactions at or near the balance sheet date to reconcile the subsequent count to the client's count. The auditor should also test and review the documentation created by the client's physical count. When the auditor does not observe the physical count of inventory and is not satisfied with the use of alternative audit procedures, the audit report must be modified (AU 331.12–.13).

Inventories may be held in public warehouses or by other outside custodians. Generally, the direct confirmation of the inventory held by outside custodians provides sufficient evidence to validate the existence and ownership of the inventory. However, if the inventory held by outside custodians is significant in relation to current assets and total assets, confirmation must be supplemented with the performance of the following procedures (AU 331.14):

- Discuss with the client (owner of the goods) the client's control procedures in investigating the warehouseman, including tests of related evidential matter.

- Observe the warehouseman's or client's count of goods whenever practical and reasonable.

- If warehouse receipts have been pledged as collateral, confirm details with the lenders to the extent deemed necessary by the auditor.

- Obtain an independent auditor's report on the warehouseman's control procedures relevant to custody of goods and, if applicable, pledge receipts; or apply alternative procedures at the warehouse to gain reasonable assurance that information received from the warehouseman is reliable (SAS-43 [Omnibus Statement on Auditing Standards]).

Although these procedures are required by GAAS, when the inventory of the auditor's client is held by a public warehouse, the public warehouse's auditor must also be concerned with the inventories owned by others but held by the public warehouse. In a special report issued by the Committee on Auditing Procedures (predecessor of the Auditing Standards Board) and incorporated as part of SAS-1 (Codification of Auditing Standards and Procedures), the following recommendations were made (AU 901.43):

- Study and evaluate the system relating to the goods held for others.
- Test the system described above.
- Test the warehouse's accountability for recorded outstanding warehouse receipts.
- Observe physical counts whenever practical and reasonable.
- Confirm accountability with owners of the goods to the extent deemed necessary.
- Follow other audit procedures considered appropriate in the circumstances.

Inventories Counted by Others

Some companies are in the business of counting, recording, and pricing inventories. The auditor's responsibility for the count and other tasks performed by an inventory-taking company is similar to the responsibility for tasks normally performed directly by the client. Therefore, the auditor should (1) review the client's inventory-counting program, (2) make or observe a test of physical counts, (3) make appropriate mathematical checks, and (4) test the valuation of the inventory.

> **OBSERVATION:** *An Auditing Interpretation entitled "Report of an Outside Inventory-Taking Firm as an Alternative Procedure for Observing Inventories" (July 1975) states that the report from an outside company that takes independent inventory counts is not by itself a satisfactory substitute for the auditor's own observation of the physical count of inventory. The auditor should examine the*

procedures and programs of the outside inventory-counting firm
and test its calculations and intervening transactions (AU 9508.01–
.06).

Evidence for Long-Term Investments

Long-term investments may be in the form of investments in common stocks, joint ventures, other investments such as bonds, and similar debt obligations that resemble an investment. As with audit objectives related to all assets, the auditor must be concerned with the existence, ownership, cost, and market value of these types of investments and their related income, which must be recognized in a particular accounting period. A unique problem associated with these types of investments arises because some of the evidence that supports their carrying value is generated by the investee. For discussion purposes, investments may be classified as those accounted for by (1) the equity method, (2) the cost method, or (3) other methods (AU 332.01).

The Auditing Standards Board has issued an Exposure Draft (Investments in Debt and Equity Securities) that would supersede the guidance established in AU 332 (and Interpretation No. 1 of that section). The Exposure Draft proposes new auditing standards that are consistent with recent accounting standards established by the FASB, especially FAS-115 (Accounting for Certain Investments in Debt and Equity Securities).

Long-Term Investments—Equity Method

When the equity method (APB Opinion No. 18 [The Equity Method of Accounting for Investments in Common Stock] and FASB Interpretation (FIN) No. 35 [Criteria for Applying the Equity Method of Accounting for Investments in Common Stock]) is employed, the investor recognizes his or her proportionate share of the investee's income by debiting the investment account and crediting income from the investment. The carrying value of the investment is reduced when cash dividends are paid by the investee. A long-term investment in common stock should be accounted for by the equity method if the investor exercises significant influence over the operating and financial policies of the investee. APB Opinion No. 18 lists the following factors that may indicate that an investor has the ability to exercise influence over an investee (AU 332.06–.09):

- Representation on the investee's board of directors
- Participation in the investee's policy-making processes
- Material intercompany transactions
- Interchange of managerial personnel
- Technological dependency on the investor company

To promote uniformity, APB Opinion No. 18 concludes that a 20% or more ownership of the outstanding voting stock of an investee indicates a presumption that the investor has the ability to exercise significant influence over the investee, unless evidence to the contrary exists. The auditor must make inquiries to determine whether the equity method is appropriate in accounting for long-term investments (AU 332.06–.09).

The existence and ownership of common stock is determined by inspecting the actual securities. When the securities are held by other parties, the details of the shares held should be confirmed in writing by the auditor with the other party. The carrying value of the investment may be determined by references to audited financial statements of the investee. In this event the investor's auditor acts as principal auditor and must follow the audit procedures discussed later in this chapter. In addition, the investor's auditor must also decide whether to make reference to the work of the investee's auditor. (The report format under these circumstances is discussed in the chapter entitled "Auditor's Reports.") In some instances the investee may issue unaudited financial statements, or a regulatory body or similar authority may issue an examination report on the investee. These reports do not constitute sufficient evidential matter to support the carrying value of the investment. The investor's auditor, directly or through the investee's auditor, if any, may apply audit procedures to the unaudited financial statements to obtain evidential matter to support the carrying value of the investment. The extent and nature of audit procedures employed by the investor's auditor are dependent on the materiality of the investment (AU 332.10–.12).

When the equity method is used, there may be a difference between the original cost of the investment and the investor's interest in the underlying equity in the net assets of the investee at the date of acquisition. This may result in positive or negative goodwill, which must be recognized in the investor's financial statements. However, part or all of the difference may be attributable to understated assets at the date of acquisition, in which case that portion is not considered goodwill. Thus, the investor may be required to amortize goodwill and depreciate the understated amount of assets in determining net income for the period. SAS-1 states that the valuation of assets made by the investor or investee may be acceptable to the auditor, but also notes that an independent appraisal of the investee provides more competent evidential matter (AU 332.05).

> **OBSERVATION:** *Presumably, the use of valuations made by personnel of the investor or the investee or by an independent expert would require that the guidelines established by SAS-73 (Using the Work of a Specialist) be followed.*

If an auditor is unable to substantiate the carrying value of a material investment by reviewing audited financial statements and applying procedures to unaudited financial statements, there is a scope limitation. The scope limitation should be described in an explanatory paragraph in the auditor's report. Depending on the materiality of the investment, a qualified opinion or disclaimer of opinion may have to be expressed (AU 332.16).

> **OBSERVATION:** *An Auditing Interpretation entitled "The Effect of Accounting Changes by an Investee on Consistency" (July 1980) states that an auditor must refer in his or her report to a consistency violation when there has been a change in accounting principle by an investee accounted for by the equity method that causes a material lack of comparability in the financial statements of an investor (AU 9420.52–.54).*

Long-Term Investments—Cost Method

The cost method requires that income be recognized by the investor when the investee declares a cash dividend. If the investment in common stock is a marketable security, the investment must be accounted for at the lower of aggregate cost or market as prescribed by FAS-115 (Accounting for Certain Investments in Debt and Equity Securities) (AU 332.04).

APB Opinion No. 18 states that the cost method should be used by an investor who does not have significant influence over an investee. It is presumed by APB Opinion No. 18 that investments of less than 20% be accounted for by the cost method, unless evidence substantiates that the investor has the ability to exercise significant influence over the investee (AU 332.06–.08).

Existence and ownership of common stock is substantiated by the inspection of the securities, unless the securities are held by a third party, in which case their existence should be confirmed in writing. Generally, under the cost method the carrying value of the investment is its original cost. The original cost should be vouched. If the securities are marketable securities (basically a broad and active market), market value can be determined by reference to market quotations at the balance sheet date (AU 332.04).

Other Long-Term Investments

Long-term investments may be represented by investments in bonds, loans, and advances that are in the nature of investments and joint ventures. APB Opinion No. 18 requires that the equity method be used to account for a joint venture. The three groups of investments mentioned above should be accounted for at their original cost except for discounts or premiums associated with the investment, which should be amortized using the interest method as required by APB Opinion No. 21 (Interest on Receivables and Payables).

The existence and ownership of investments in bonds and notes can be determined by physical inspection at the balance sheet date. Loans, advances, and registered bonds should be confirmed in writing with the debtor or the trustee. The carrying value of the investment may be substantiated by vouching the original transaction and making appropriate recomputations when a discount or premium is involved. SAS-1 states that it may be necessary to obtain audited financial statements of the investee to determine whether investments in bonds and similar debt obligations, as well as loans and advances in the nature of investments, are recorded at an appropriate carrying value (lower of cost or net realized value) (AU 332.04–.05).

Evidence for Accounting Estimates

SAS-57 (Auditing Accounting Estimates) defines an *accounting estimate* as "an approximation of a financial statement element, item, or account." Accounting estimates are made to measure past transactions or events (loss contingency arising from pending lawsuits) or to measure assets (net realizable value of accounts receivable) or liabilities (accrual related to warranty contracts) (AU 342.02).

It is the responsibility of management to establish reasonable accounting estimates. Such estimates are established by reviewing past experiences and evaluating these experiences in the context of current and expected future conditions. Thus, accounting estimates are based on both objective factors (past transactions and events) and subjective factors (projecting the likely outcome of future transactions and events). Although management is responsible for accounting estimates, an auditor must collect sufficient evidential matter to determine that accounting estimates are reasonable. Because of the uncertainty related to accounting estimates and the higher possibility of misstatement, an auditor must have a greater degree of skepticism when planning and performing procedures related to the audit of accounting estimates (AU 342.03–.04).

Management's internal control structure   As for all classes of transactions and events that affect the financial statements, management should adopt, either formally or informally, a process for developing accounting estimates. The process should include identifying circumstances that require accounting estimates, and collecting and evaluating information that leads to the development of reasonable accounting estimates (AU 342.05).

Many factors, such as the availability of reliable data and the required complexity of the evaluation process, have an effect on the risk of material misstatement in the financial statements because of unreasonable accounting estimates. In addition, when assessing the risk factor for misstatement the auditor should consider the entity's internal control structure relating to the development of accounting estimates. The entity's internal control structure should include the following elements (AU 342.06):

- Use of policies and procedures that allow the entity to identify circumstances requiring the development of accounting estimates
- Development of sufficient and reliable data
- Use of competent personnel
- Review and approval of accounting estimates by appropriate personnel (including the review of relevant factors and assumptions and the need for specialists)
- Comparison of previous accounting estimates with actual results
- Determination that accounting estimates are consistent with management's plans

Collection and evaluation of evidence   The audit of accounting estimates should include a determination of whether (1) all circumstances that give rise to accounting estimates have been identified by the entity, (2) accounting estimates are reasonable, and (3) accounting estimates are presented in accordance with generally accepted accounting principles (GAAP), including adequate disclosure (AU 342.08–.09).

Circumstances giving rise to accounting estimates   To determine whether the entity has identified all circumstances that require accounting estimates, the auditor should consider the entity's operating characteristics and the industry in general—including any new pronouncements that affect the industry. On the basis of a review of these factors, the auditor should consider performing the following procedures (AU 342.08):

- Read the financial statements and identify those assertions implied in the financial statements that may require an accounting estimate.
- Refer to evidence gathered in other parts of the engagement, including the following:
  - Changes made or contemplated by the entity or the industry that would affect the operations of the business
  - Changes made in the manner in which information is accumulated
  - Identified litigation and other contingencies
  - Relevant information contained in minutes of the board of directors, stockholders, and other significant committees
  - Relevant information contained in regulatory reports, supervisory correspondence, and similar information from relevant regulatory agencies
- Discuss with management situations that may require an accounting estimate.

Evaluating reasonableness of estimates   To determine which specific accounting estimates are reasonable, an auditor should concentrate on fundamental factors and assumptions that are material to an estimate and for which changes in the factor or assumption would have a significant effect on the accounting estimate. In addition, attention should be directed to factors and assumptions that are different from past patterns or that are highly subjective (AU 342.09).

The audit approach should encompass an understanding of the entity's process for developing accounting estimates. Having gained such an understanding, one or a combination of the following approaches should be adopted (AU 342.10):

- Review and test the accounting estimation process.
- Develop an independent estimate.
- Review subsequent events or transactions.

Procedures that should be considered when the auditor decides to review and test the accounting estimation process include the following (AU 342.11):

- Identify management controls and supporting data.
- Identify sources of data and factors used by management.
- Consider whether data and factors are relevant, reliable, and sufficient to support the estimate.
- Determine whether other factors or assumptions are appropriate.
- Determine if assumptions are internally consistent with other assumptions and supporting data.
- Determine that historical data used are comparable and consistent with data of the period under audit and that such data are reliable.
- Determine whether changes during the current period require that other factors be considered in developing assumptions.
- Review documentation supporting assumptions used to make accounting estimates.
- Inquire about other plans that may have been adopted by management that could have an effect on assumptions related to accounting estimates.
- Determine whether a specialist is needed to evaluate assumptions.
- Recompute calculations made to convert assumptions and key factors into the accounting estimate.

The auditor may test the reasonableness of accounting estimates by making an independent calculation. In making the calculation, the auditor should use other factors or alternative assumptions that he or she considers relevant (AU 342.12).

Finally, the auditor may decide to test the reasonableness of an accounting estimate by reviewing subsequent events or transactions that occur after the date of the balance sheet but before the completion of fieldwork. Such information may make it unnecessary to evaluate factors and assumptions related to the accounting estimate. In other circumstances, the uncertainty related to the evaluation of factors and assumptions may be significantly reduced (AU 342.13).

As stated earlier, the purpose of the audit of accounting estimates is to determine whether estimates are reasonable. Thus, an auditor might conclude that an estimate is reasonable although it is not the best estimate. The difference between the reasonable estimate and best estimate should not necessarily be treated as a misstatement; however, if most estimates appear to reflect a particular bias, such as the tendency to understate expenses, the auditor should consider whether all misstatements combined result in a material misstatement (AU 342.14).

Accounting estimates are presented in accordance with GAAP Once the auditor has determined that an accounting estimate has been identified and properly valued, the auditor must determine whether the accounting estimate is properly presented and disclosed in the financial statements. The nature of the accounting estimate, relevant accounting and reporting standards, and the general rule of disclosure must be considered when making this determination (AU 342.07).

> **OBSERVATION:** *An Auditing Interpretation of SAS-57 entitled "Performance and Reporting Guidance Related to Fair Value Disclosures" (February 1993) concludes that, when auditing estimates related to FAS-107 (Disclosures About Fair Value of Financial Instruments), the auditor should collect sufficient competent evidential matter to reasonably assure that (1) valuation methods are acceptable, are applied consistently, and are adequately documented; and (2) estimation methods and significant assumptions are disclosed (AU 9342.01–.10).*

Substantive Evidence Obtained from a Specialist

In some instances the dollar amounts reflected in the financial statements are based on evidential matter that an auditor is not capable of evaluating. For example, pension costs depend on an actuarial analysis that is usually beyond the expertise of an auditor. SAS-73, which supersedes SAS-11 (Using the Work of a Specialist), was issued to provide guidance in an engagement requiring the services of a specialist. Although there is no complete list of circumstances that require the use of a specialist, SAS-73 provides the following examples (AU 336.06–.07):

- Valuation of inventories, property, plant, and equipment, financial instruments, and works of art for which the question of a writedown due to the application of the lower of cost or market rule or the cost recoverability rule is relevant
- Valuation of an environmental contingency
- Physical measurements (tons, barrels, etc.) of raw materials
- Dollar valuations based on specialized measurement techniques such as actuarial computations
- Interpretation of technical material such as legal documents and regulatory standards and guidance

> **OBSERVATION:** *SAS-73 did not change the requirement established by SOP 92-4 (Auditing Insurance Entities' Loss Reserves) that a "loss reserve specialist," not an employee or officer of the client, must be used to audit the loss reserve for property and liability insurance companies.*

> **OBSERVATION:** *SAS-73 concludes that the auditor has the necessary expertise to consider the financial statement implications (accrual, disclosure, and presentation) of income tax matters (AU 336.01). This presupposes an understanding of income tax laws and regulations that apply to a particular client and the standards established by FAS-109 (Accounting for Income Taxes) and other related pronouncements.*

SAS-73 does not provide guidelines for the use of a lawyer who is requested to make representations concerning litigation, claims, or assessments (see SAS-12); however, the standard does apply to using the expertise of a lawyer in other circumstances (AU 336.02).

The standards established by SAS-73 apply to the audit of financial statements prepared in accordance with GAAP as well as to engagements discussed in SAS-62 (Special Reports); however, they do not apply to specialists employed by the auditor when those specialists are part of the audit team. When a auditor employs a specialist as a member of the audit team in an engagement, the standards established by SAS-22 must be observed (AU 336.04–.05).

An auditing firm must apply the standards established by SAS-73 in the following circumstances (AU 336.03):

- When management employs a specialist and the auditor is considering using the work of the specialist as part of substantive testing
- When management employs a specialist to perform advisory services, and the specialist is employed by the auditor to perform services related to substantive testing (Under this circumstance, the auditor should consider the effect on independence.)
- When the auditor employs a specialist as part of substantive testing

> **OBSERVATION:** *SAS-73 was issued in part to clarify when professional standards apply to the work of a specialist. Based on the above list, it is obvious that such standards apply only as part of substantive testing. Thus, the standards apply when it is necessary to use the work of a specialist to determine whether specialized inventory must be written down below its original cost or purchase or production. On the other hand, the standards would not apply when a real estate appraisal is part of a mortgage company's internal control procedures used to determine whether a loan should be made.*

Once an auditor determines that a specialist is appropriate in an engagement, the following factors should be considered (AU 336.08):

- Qualifications of the specialist
- Effect on audit evidence
- Using the specialist's work
- Effect on the auditor's report

Qualifications of the specialist Initially, the auditor must determine the nature of the work to be performed by a specialist as it relates to substantive testing. That is, the auditor should identify the assertions (as defined by SAS-31) in the financial statements (either explicitly or implicitly) that can be substantiated only through evidence obtained or developed by a specialist. For example, presentation and disclosure assertions related to the projected benefit obligation that appears in a note to the financial statements (as required by

FAS-87 [Employers' Accounting for Pensions]) requires the expertise of an actuary. Specifically, SAS-73 requires that the auditor obtain an understanding of the following with respect to nature of the services to be provided by a specialist (AU 336.09):

- The objectives and scope of the specialist's services
- The relationship of the specialist and the client
- The methods and assumptions to be used in the work
- A comparison of the methods and assumptions proposed for the current engagement with those used in the previous engagement
- The appropriateness of the work of the specialist in relationship to the assertions to be substantiated
- The form and content of the results of work of the specialist and how they relate to the auditor's need to evaluate that work

> **OBSERVATION:** *SAS-73 notes that it may be necessary to inform the specialist that his or her work will be used to substantiate certain assertions in the financial statements. Although SAS-73 does not provide any guidance on when this contact may be appropriate, it generally would be necessary to ensure that the specialist understands the need to provide a "usable link" between the specialist's work and the assertions to be substantiated. Essentially, the prudent auditor must make sure that the technical nature of the specialist's work makes sense in the context of the audit engagement (AU 336.09).*

Before reliance is placed on the work of a specialist, the qualifications and experience of the specialist should be established. Qualifications can be established by identifying the professional designations (certification, license, etc.) and the professional reputation earned by the specialist. In addition, professional work experience provides insight into whether the qualifications of the specialist are acceptable.

Effect on audit evidence   Perhaps the most sensitive aspect of using the work of a specialist is the relationship between the specialist and the client, and the effect of that relationship on an auditor's collection of competent and sufficient evidential matter. If the specialist is biased in favor of the client, the information created by the specialist and used as evidence by the auditor will be tainted.

Ideally, the specialist would not have a relationship with the client that could provide an opportunity for the client to "directly or indirectly control or significantly influence the specialist." The concept of a relationship is broad and encompasses such circumstances as that of an employer/employee or a member of the same family. If no relationship between the client and the specialist exists (that is, the specialist is hired by the auditor and there are no other direct or indirect relationships between the client and the specialist), there is a higher chance that the work performed by the specialist will be reliable (AU 336.10–.11).

> *OBSERVATION: SAS-73 notes that the term **relationship** includes (but is not limited to) those relationships included in Note 1 of SAS-45. The SAS-45 note is based on the definition of **related parties** contained in SAS-57.*

If a relationship between the client and the specialist does exist, the auditor is required to obtain an understanding of the relationship, as the existence of a relationship does not in itself preclude the auditor from relying on the specialist's work. In this circumstance, SAS-73 requires that the auditor "assess the risk that the specialist's objectivity might be impaired." If the auditor concludes that the specialist's objectivity might be impaired, the auditor must perform additional procedures. These procedures should focus on "some or all of the specialist's assumptions, methods, or findings." When the results of performing the additional procedures do not dispel the auditor's concern with the specialist's objectivity, the auditor should engage another specialist (AU 336.11).

Using the specialist's work   The auditor's role in the evaluation of the evidence created by a specialist is to determine whether the specialist's findings are reasonable. SAS-73 concludes that the following approach should be used to assess the findings' reasonableness (AU 336.12):

- Obtain an understanding of the specialist's methods and assumptions.

- Test the data provided to the specialist by the client. (The nature, timing, and extent of the testing should be based on the auditor's assessment of the client's control risk.)

- Evaluate whether the relevant assertions in the financial statements are substantiated by the specialist's findings.

If, on the basis of the above and other procedures deemed appropriate by the auditor, the auditor concludes that the findings are reasonable, the evidence can be relied on as the basis for forming an opinion on the financial statements. On the other hand, if the auditor's evaluation does not suggest that the findings are reasonable, SAS-73 requires that the auditor perform additional procedures. If the matter still is unresolved after the performance of additional procedures, the auditor should obtain the opinion of another specialist (AU 336.12).

Effect on the auditor's report When the auditor concludes that the specialist's findings support the particular assertions in the financial statements, the third standard of fieldwork has been satisfied. An unqualified opinion, without reference to the work of the specialist, can be expressed (AU 336.13).

On the other hand, when the findings of the specialist do not support the relevant assertions in the financial statements, the auditor should perform additional procedures to try to resolve the problem. If the issue cannot be resolved through the performance of additional procedures or through obtaining the services of another specialist, the auditor must determine whether the circumstance is (1) a deviation from GAAP or (2) a scope limitation.

A deviation from GAAP arises when the auditor concludes that the relevant assertions in the financial statements are not supported by findings of the specialist and other procedures (perhaps, including the work of another specialist) that may be performed by the auditor. Under this circumstance, the auditor should express either a qualified or an adverse opinion on the financial statements.

A scope limitation arises when the auditor concludes that the performance of additional audit procedures would not provide a reasonable basis for either substantiating or refuting the relevant assertions in the financial statements. Under this circumstance, the auditor should either express a qualified opinion or disclaim an opinion on the financial statements (AU 336.13–.14).

SAS-73 concludes that, generally, the auditor's report, whether unqualified or modified, should not make reference to the findings of a specialist, because the reference may be interpreted as (1) a qualification or (2) an attempt to divide the responsibility for the report between the auditor and the specialist. However, SAS-73 allows the auditor to add explanatory language to an unqualified report or a modified report if "the auditor believes such reference will facilitate an understanding of the reason for the explanatory paragraph or the departure from the unqualified opinion." Thus, the auditor may decide to express an unqualified opinion and add an explanatory paragraph (after the opinion paragraph but with no reference in the opinion paragraph to the explanatory paragraph) that refers to the findings of a specialist. In addition, the auditor may decide to express an opinion that is other than unqualified, and the paragraph that describes the basis for the report modification could then refer to the findings of a specialist. In each circumstance, the explanatory paragraph may refer to and identify the specialist (AU 336.15–.16).

Evidential Matter and Internal Auditors

If the client has an internal audit function, the auditor may decide to use internal auditors to perform specific audit tasks directly. For example, the auditor could request that internal auditors assist in developing an understanding of the client's internal control structure, perform tests of controls, or perform substantive tests. If internal auditors are requested to directly assist the auditor, SAS-65 states that the following guidelines should be followed (AU 322):

- Assess the competence and objectivity of internal auditors.
- Supervise, review, evaluate, and test work performed by internal auditors.
- Describe to the internal auditors their responsibilities.
- Describe the objective of the work performed.
- Describe circumstances that could affect the nature, timing, and extent of audit procedures.
- Direct internal auditors to inform the auditor of all significant accounting and auditing issues that arise during the performance of their work.

> *OBSERVATION: Specific guidance for using the work of internal auditors is more fully described in the chapter entitled "Internal Control, Errors, and Irregularities."*

Evidence for Segment Information

FAS-14 (Financial Reporting for Segments of a Business Enterprise) requires a company to disclose information about the company's operations in different industries, its foreign operations and sales, and its major customers. A year and a half after FAS-14 was issued, the FASB decided to restrict the scope of the standard and issued FAS-21 (Suspension of the Reporting of Earnings Per Share and Segment Information by Nonpublic Enterprises), which states that nonpublic enterprises do not have to comply with FAS-14 or APB Opinion No. 15 (Earnings Per Share). FAS-21 defines a *nonpublic enterprise* as an enterprise other than one whose debt or equity securities trade in a public market, on a foreign or domestic stock exchange, or in the over-the-counter market (including securities quoted only locally or regionally) or one that is required to file financial statements with the Securities and Exchange Commission. SAS-21 (Segment Information) provides guidance in the audit of segment information (AU 435.01–.02).

When segment information is presented, it is part of the financial statements. The auditor must collect sufficient competent evidential matter to be reasonably assured that the disclosures are made in accordance with generally accepted accounting principles. An auditor expresses an opinion on the financial statements taken as a whole and does not, per se, express a separate opinion on segment information. For this reason, the audit procedures employed to test segment information are selected on the basis of the concept of the materiality of the segment information in relation to the financial statements taken as a whole. Materiality of an element is determined by considering the quantitative (dollar value) and qualitative (significance, pervasiveness, and impact of a matter) aspects of an item (AU 435.03–.05).

SAS-21 emphasizes that, like other phases of an audit, the testing of segment information should be properly planned. Basically, the auditor must change the normal audit procedures to determine whether transactions and line items in an account are properly classified as to industry, foreign or domestic, and major customer. For example, an auditor typically vouches a sales transaction by inspecting a customer order, sales invoice, and bill of lading. The inclusion of segment information in the financial statements would require that the documentation also be inspected to determine whether the sale is appropriately classified as to industry, origin, and customer. The following factors have an effect on the design of audit procedures for the testing of segment information (AU 435.04–.06):

- The adequacy and structure of the client's internal control structure with respect to segment information
- The number and size of segments
- The number and nature of operating units in each industry segment and geographical area

- Accounting principles used for the industry segments and geographical areas

The following audit procedures should be employed to test segment information (AU 435.07):

- Inquire about management's methods of determining segment information, and determine if these methods are in conformity with GAAP.
- Inquire about the bases of accounting for transactions between industry segments, and test, to the extent necessary, for conformity to those bases.
- Test the disaggregation of the company's financial statements into segment information.
- Inquire about the methods of allocating operating expenses and identifiable assets used by two or more segments. Determine if these methods are reasonable, and test allocations as deemed necessary.
- Determine if segment information has been classified on a basis consistent with prior periods.

FAS-14 states that a client does not have to report segment information by industry if the client operates predominantly (90% or more) in a single industry. Under these circumstances, the client would have a *dominant segment*, which must be identified in the financial statements, but none of the detail segmental disclosures of FAS-14 would need to be reported. Furthermore, the client may claim that by the nature of its business it does not have to disclose information associated with foreign operations, export sales, or major customers. When a client makes these representations, an auditor must collect evidence to support the exceptions to FAS-14. The auditor's knowledge of the client's operations will usually be sufficient to substantiate the client's basis for nondisclosure of segment information. However, if the client fails, or is unable, to develop information to support its position, there is a scope limitation in the engagement, and a qualified opinion should be expressed. In a similar fashion, if the auditor is unable to apply audit procedures to test segment information because of the circumstances of the audit environment or restrictions imposed by the client, a qualified opinion should be expressed (AU 435.08 and .15).

> *OBSERVATION: The reporting requirements established by SAS-21 conflict in two ways with the basic reporting concepts of SAS-58 (Reports on Audited Financial Statements). First, according to SAS-21, scope limitations resulting from the circumstances of the audit may lead to a qualified opinion only. SAS-58 states that scope limitations of this nature may lead to either a qualified opinion or a disclaimer of opinion. Secondly, and more importantly, SAS-21 requires that a qualified opinion be expressed when the scope of the audit is limited by the client. SAS-58 states that a significant scope limitation imposed by the client should generally result in the auditor's expressing a disclaimer of opinion. Even though the segment information is self-contained in the financial statements and even though scope limitations should generally result in a qualified opinion, the auditor should not be required to express such an opinion. For example, the auditor may suspect that segment information may have been manipulated to enhance the profitability of a particularly sensitive business segment. Conservatism dictates that the guidelines established by SAS-58 be followed instead of those promulgated by SAS-21 when this type of scope problem is encountered.*

When the client refuses to disclose segment information or discloses the information in a manner inconsistent with FAS-14, there is a violation of GAAP. Such a violation may lead to a qualified opinion or an adverse opinion. When the segment information is omitted, the auditor is not required to provide the information in the report (AU 435.09).

> *OBSERVATION: It is interesting to note that a violation of GAAP with respect to segment information may be so material that a qualified opinion is not appropriate and that an adverse opinion may have to be expressed. Yet, as discussed in the preceding Observation, the same information may not be subject to testing, and only a qualified opinion is warranted.*

Using the Work of Another Auditor

An auditor must decide whether to make reference to the report of another auditor when part of the examination is made by another auditor. When part of an examination, such as the audit of a subsidiary, has been performed by another auditor, the principal auditor must decide whether participation permits him or her to act as the principal auditor. If so, the auditor must decide whether or not reference should be made to the other auditor. This decision is a matter of professional judgment and should be based on the materiality of the portions examined by each auditor. After a decision is reached about who is the principal auditor, the principal auditor must decide whether to refer to the other auditor in the report or to assume sole responsibility of the report. However, regardless of the decision of the principal auditor, the other auditor remains responsible for his or her own work and report (AU 543.01–.05).

Basic audit procedures Whether the principal auditor decides to make reference to another auditor or not, the following basic audit procedures must be performed (AU 543.10):

- Determine the professional reputation and standing of the other auditor.
- Obtain a representation from the other auditor that he or she is independent of the client.
- Notify the other auditor that his or her audited financial statements may be included in the consolidated or combined financial statements reported on by the principal auditor.
- Notify the other auditor that his or her report may be relied on and, if appropriate, referred to by the principal auditor.
- Determine whether the other auditor is familiar with GAAP and GAAS and whether he or she uses these standards in engagements and the resulting reports.
- If necessary, determine whether the other auditor is familiar with SEC reporting practices.
- Notify the other auditor that there may be a review of adjusting and eliminating intercompany transactions.

> *OBSERVATION: An Auditing Interpretation entitled "Inquiries of the Principal Auditor by the Other Auditor" (April 1979) states that it may be necessary for the other auditor to make inquiries of the principal auditor. Inquiry may be appropriate when the other auditor is making inquiries concerning related parties. In addition, the other auditor may make inquiries of the principal auditor about any matter considered significant to his or her examination. The inquiry should usually be made in writing and should note that the*

response should be made in writing. Also, the inquiry should specify the date by which the principal auditor should respond. The principal auditor should identify what stage of completion the examination is in as of the date of the reply. Also, the principal auditor should state that all the information requested by the other auditor would not necessarily be revealed by procedures used by the principal auditor. The principal auditor is not required to perform any procedures directed toward identifying matters that would not affect his or her audit (AU 9543.04–.07).

If the principal auditor concludes that the report of the other auditor cannot be relied on, a scope limitation exists, and a qualified opinion or a disclaimer of opinion should be expressed (AU 543.11).

Procedures when no reference is made   When the principal auditor decides not to refer to the report of another auditor, it may be appropriate for the principal auditor to perform one or more of the following procedures (AU 543.12):

- Visit the other auditor and discuss the audit procedures employed and the results obtained during the engagement.
- Review the other auditor's audit program.
- Review the other auditor's workpapers.
- Consider whether instructions should be given to the other auditor as to the scope of work.
- Consider whether the principal auditor should discuss relevant matters directly with personnel of the consolidating or combining entity and/or should perform additional tests.

OBSERVATION: An Auditing Interpretation of Section 542 of SAS-1, "Application of Additional Procedures Concerning the Audit Performed by the Other Auditor" (December 1981), states that a principal auditor who decides not to make reference to the audit of another auditor may consider various factors when determining whether to apply procedures to obtain information about the adequacy of the other auditor's examination. One factor that may be taken into consideration includes knowledge of the other auditor's quality control policies and procedures that provide the other auditor with reasonable assurance of conformity with GAAS. Other factors that may be considered are (1) past experience with

> the other auditor, (2) the materiality of the financial statements examined by the other auditor in relationship to the combined or consolidated financial statements, (3) the degree of control exercised by the principal auditor over the work performed by the other auditor, and (4) the results of audit procedures performed by the principal auditor that may suggest that additional procedures may have to be performed by the other auditor (AU 9543.18–.20).

Generally, an auditor decides not to refer to another auditor when (1) the other auditor is an associate or correspondent, (2) the principal auditor actually engages the other auditor, or (3) the financial statements examined by the other auditor are immaterial in relation to the consolidated or combined group (AU 543.04–.05).

Reporting when reference is made   If the principal auditor decides to refer to the other auditor's examination, the report should, in both the scope and opinion paragraphs, clearly indicate the degree of responsibility and the portions of the financial statements examined by each. (This may be done in percentages, total assets, total revenue, or other appropriate criteria.) In addition, the other auditor may be named by the principal auditor only with his or her *express permission* (AU 543.07).

Reference to another auditor by the principal auditor does not constitute a qualification of opinion, but rather a description of responsibility between the two auditors (AU 543.08).

If the other auditor's opinion is qualified, the principal auditor must decide whether the subject of the qualification is material in relation to the consolidated statements. If it is not, the principal auditor does not need to refer to the qualification in the report (AU 543.15).

> **OBSERVATION:** *Another Interpretation of Section 543, "Specific Procedures Performed by the Other Auditor at the Principal Auditor's Request" (April 1979), states that when a principal auditor requests that the other auditor perform specific procedures, the principal auditor is responsible for determining the extent of the procedures to be performed (AU 9543.01–.03).*

When the principal auditor decides to refer to the report of another auditor, the basic audit procedures described previously must be performed (AU 543.10).

> **OBSERVATION:** *An auditor is placed in the role of a principal auditor when a long-term investment is accounted for by the equity method. Furthermore, an auditor may be placed in the role of a principal auditor even if the cost method is used to account for a long-term investment. The latter circumstance may arise when the work of the other auditor constitutes a major element of evidence with respect to the investment account. Presumably, this occurs when there is some question whether there has been a permanent impairment in the carrying value of the investment (AU 543.14).*

Evidence from Analytical Procedures

Analytical procedures are used to determine whether information is consistent with the auditor's expectations. For example, if an auditor is aware that a client has invested heavily in new machinery, depreciation expense would be expected to be significantly greater in the current period than in the prior period. To successfully employ analytical procedures, an auditor must have a thorough knowledge of the client and the industry in which it operates. Because analytical procedures are applied in a broad manner in the collection of evidence and such an approach has limitations in achieving audit objectives, SAS-56 (Analytical Procedures) concludes that analytical procedures should be employed by experienced staff (AU 329.02–.03).

Expectations concerning financial information and assumptions that affect financial information may be developed from sources such as the following (AU 329.05):

- Prior-period financial information (if appropriate, modified for new conditions and events)
- Budgeted, forecasted, and projected financial information
- Interrelationships of financial information
- Industrial characteristics
- Nonfinancial information that may affect financial information

Analytical procedures may be applied during the following three phases of an audit engagement (AU 329.04):

- Planning audit procedures
- Overall review of financial information
- Performance of substantive tests

SAS-56 concludes that analytical procedures must be used in planning the nature, timing, and extent of audit procedures and in conducting an overall review of the financial information. The auditor must use professional judgment to determine whether analytical procedures should be used as a substantive test to collect evidential matter related to account balances or classes of transactions (AU 329.04).

> **OBSERVATION:** *Although SAS-56 does not require that analytical procedures be used as part of substantive testing, it does imply that it may be difficult to achieve certain audit objectives efficiently without applying them as a substantive test.*

Planning audit procedures An auditor must perform analytical procedures to provide a basis for determining the nature, timing, and extent of subsequent audit procedures. Analytical procedures are employed to reduce to an acceptable level the possibility that a material misstatement or omission in the financial statements may occur (detection risk). When establishing an acceptable level of detection risk, the auditor must consider the susceptibility of an account to be misstated (inherent risk), the control structure related to the account (control risk), and materiality. Analytical procedures applied early in the engagement can help the auditor understand factors that must be used to establish a satisfactory level of detection risk (AU 329.06).

The planning phase of an engagement should include review of financial information that is generally aggregated to identify unexpected relationships or trends. This may be accomplished by comparing general ledger balances with similar balances from prior periods and with budgeted or forecasted balances. Various ratios or trends may be computed to facilitate the analysis; however, the evaluation should be sensitive to changing conditions that may explain unexpected variations or may raise expectations that variations should in fact be present in the financial information. For example, the balance in the current legal expense account may be consistent with both last year's amount and the budgeted amount, but such expense stability may be unwarranted because the client has experienced unanticipated legal problems. In planning subsequent audit procedures, the auditor should select procedures to determine whether the client's legal counsel is billing its services on a timely basis (AU 329.07).

In addition to financial information, nonfinancial data may be taken into consideration as part of the performance of analytical procedures. For example, quality control reports prepared near year-end may identify production problems, which may suggest that significant amounts of inventory sold during the latter part of the year may be returned or may significantly increase future warranty claims (AU 329.08).

Overall review An auditor must perform analytical procedures as part of the final review of the audited financial information to determine whether the anticipated opinion on the financial statements appears to be warranted (AU 329.22).

Substantive tests Analytical procedures may be used as part of substantive tests (tests of financial statement balances) to achieve desired audit objectives or achieve those objectives in an efficient manner. In general, analytical procedures are used as part of substantive testing by evaluating aggregated information to form conclusions about specific assertions contained in the financial statements. For example, an aged trial balance may be prepared and analyzed to test the assertion that accounts receivable are presented at net realizable value. In many instances both analytical procedures and tests of details will be used to examine financial statement balances and classes of transactions (AU 329.09–.10).

SAS-56 concludes that in determining whether and to what extent analytical procedures should be used, an auditor should consider the following factors (AU 329.11):

- Nature of the assertion being tested
- Plausibility and predictability of the relationship
- Reliability and availability of the data used to develop the expectation
- Precision of the expectation

These four factors should be considered in assessing the relative efficiency and effectiveness of analytical procedures as compared to tests of details (AU 329.11).

The nature of the assertion being tested should be evaluated to determine whether analytical procedures may satisfy the related audit objective in a more efficient and effective way than tests of details. In general, it may be more appropriate to test assertions related to the completeness assertion (all transactions and accounts are reflected in the financial statements) by using analytical procedures. For example, the validity of an allowance for returned merchandise may be more effectively tested by using analytical procedures (review of sales volume, history of returned goods, maintenance of production standards, etc.) than by using tests of details (vouching actual sales returned) (AU 329.12).

The applicability of analytical procedures depends on the plausibility and predictability of the relationship between data. There is seldom a one-to-one relationship between data; however, the stronger the relationship, the more likely analytical procedures can satisfy some audit objectives. The following generalizations may be useful in identifying plausible relationships (AU 329.13–.14):

- Relationships in a relatively stable environment tend to be more predictable than those in an unstable environment. (For example, bad debts expense and credit sales tend to be closely related to a stable economic environment.)

- Relationships among data on the income statement tend to be more predictable than relationships among data on the balance sheet. (For example, sales and sales commission expense tend to be more closely related than trade accounts payable and inventories.)

- Relationships that are subject to management discretion are less predictable. (For example, loss contingency accruals associated with the number of pending lawsuits tend not to be predictable.)

To draw an inference about an account balance or a class of transactions based on applying analytical procedures, the data on which the inference is made must be reliable and available. In evaluating the reliability of data, the following generalizations are useful (AU 329.15–.16):

- Audited data (current or prior years) are more reliable than unaudited data.

- Internal data tend to be more reliable when developed from records maintained by personnel who are not responsible for the audited amount.

- Internal data tend to be more reliable when developed under an adequate control structure.

- Data from an external source tend to be more reliable.

- Reliability of expectations increases as sources of data increase.

Because analytical procedures generally lead to fairly broad conclusions about assertions in the financial statements, an auditor should consider the precision of the established expectation. In some instances, an auditor may be satisfied with a fairly imprecise expectation. For example, expectations concerning the relationship between warranty expense and sales subject to warranty may be imprecise (say, from 1% to 8% of sales) if significant changes in warranty expenses are unlikely to have a material effect on the financial statements. On the other hand, a more precise expectation may be demanded for sales returns when the client is in an industry that experiences significant returns and a change of a percentage point or two could have a material effect on the financial statements. Some of the factors that affect the precision of an expectation include (AU 329.17–.19):

- The number of relevant variables that affect a relationship (the more variables, the more precise the expectation)

- The number of relevant variables that are evaluated by the auditor (the more variables evaluated, the more precise the expectation)

- The level of detail in the data used to construct the expectation (the more detailed the data, the more precise the expectation)

Significant deviations   When planning analytical procedures, the auditor should set the *materiality thresholds* for acceptable deviations from expected amounts. The amount of an acceptable deviation from the expected amount should be less than what is considered material when those deviations are combined with other errors in other account balances and classes of transactions (AU 329.20).

When a significant deviation from an expected amount is encountered, the auditor should attempt to identify and corroborate reasons to explain the deviation. The corroborative process may include the following (AU 329.21):

- Use of information obtained in other parts of the examination

- Explanation provided by the client

- Use of extended audit procedures

The corroborative process is employed to reasonably ensure that the significant deviation is caused by factors other than errors. The more precise and reliable an expectation, the lower the probability that a significant deviation is the result of factors other than errors. Under this latter circumstance, an auditor must be more skeptical about explanations that seek to justify a significant deviation (AU 329.21).

Related Party Transactions

An auditor must be alert for the possible occurrence of related party transactions and should evaluate them with a higher degree of skepticism than transactions that are executed by parties that are not related (AU 334.04). SAS-45 establishes guidelines for evaluating related party transactions that are discovered during an audit engagement (AU 334.01).

An accounting transaction generally reflects the resources exchanged and obligations incurred when parties to a transaction are unrelated. The values assigned to the accounts may be verified by the auditor through the examination of supporting documentation. For example, if a client purchases machinery for $10,000 cash, the inspection of the vendor invoice will usually satisfy the auditor that the fair value of the asset acquired at the transaction date was $10,000. However, if the parties to the transaction are related, it cannot always be assumed that the recorded amounts properly reflect the true economic substance of the transaction. Moreover, the inspection of supporting documentation may not provide the auditor with competent evidential matter. Professional guidelines for related party transactions were established in SAS-45 and FAS-57 (Related Party Disclosures) (AU 334.02).

> **OBSERVATION:** *An Auditing Interpretation of SAS-45, "Exchange of Information Between the Principal and Other Auditor on Related Parties" (April 1979), states that the principal auditor and other auditors of related entities should exchange information on the names of known related parties in the early stages of their examinations (AU 9334.12–.13).*

Identifying related party transactions   A related party transaction occurs when one party to a transaction has the ability to impose contract terms that would not have occurred if the parties had been unrelated. FAS-57 concludes that related parties consist of all affiliates of an enterprise, including (1) its management and their immediate families, (2) its principal owners and their immediate families,

(3) investments accounted for by the equity method, (4) beneficial employee trusts that are managed by the management of the enterprise, and (5) any party that may, or does, deal with the enterprise and has ownership, control, or significant influence over the management or operating policies of another party to the extent that an arm's-length transaction may not be achieved (AU 334.01).

> **OBSERVATION:** *Another Interpretation of SAS-45, "Examination of Identified Related Party Transactions with a Component" (April 1979), states that principal auditors ordinarily should allow access to the relevant portions of their workpapers to other auditors who are auditing a component or subsidiary of the entity. This enables other auditors to understand the related party transactions (AU 9334.14–.15).*

In addition to relationships that may lead to the auditor's identification of a related party transaction, certain transactions suggest that the parties may be related. SAS-45 lists the following as examples (AU 334.03):

- Contracts that carry no or an unrealistic interest rate
- Real estate transactions that are made at a price significantly different from appraised values
- Nonmonetary transactions that involve the exchange of similar assets
- Loan agreements that contain no repayment schedule

Finally, certain conditions may increase the possibility that a related party transaction may occur. These conditions include the following (AU 334.06):

- Inadequate working capital or lines of credit
- Management's desire for strong earnings to support the market price of the company's stock
- Earnings forecast that was too optimistic
- A declining industry
- Excess capacity
- Significant legal problems
- Exposure to technological changes

Although these conditions do not usually result in related party transactions, they indicate that the auditor must be more alert to the increased possibility (AU 334.06).

Audit approach   FAS-57 covers related party transactions and how they should be identified and disclosed in the financial statements. FAS-57 is reviewed at the end of this section. SAS-45 concludes that until special accounting rules are promulgated, the auditor should evaluate related party transactions in the context of existing generally accepted accounting principles and consider whether material transactions are adequately disclosed in the financial statements (AU 334.11).

> *OBSERVATION: The Interpretation of SAS-45 entitled "The Nature and Extent of Auditing Procedures for Examining Related Party Transactions" (May 1986) states that the auditor should apply sufficient audit procedures to provide reasonable assurance that related party transactions are adequately disclosed in the financial statements and that material misstatements associated with identified related party transactions do not exist. Since the audit risk associated with management's assertions concerning related party transactions is generally higher than that of other transactions, the audit procedures that are applied to related party transactions should be more extensive or effective. For example, to obtain additional evidence or a better understanding of a related party transaction, an auditor may apply selected audit procedures to, or actually audit, the financial statements of the related party (AU 9334.16–.19).*

Initially the auditor should select audit procedures that are likely to identify transactions with related parties. These procedures are as follows (AU 334.08):

- Supply the names of known related parties of the client and its divisions, segments, etc., to all audit personnel.
- Read the minutes of the board of directors meetings and executive or operating committee meetings.
- Review proxy and other material filed with the SEC and comparable data filed with other regulatory agencies for information on material related party transactions.
- Read conflict-of-interest statements prepared by the client's key personnel.

- Review major transactions for indications of previously undisclosed relationships.
- Consider if any transactions are not being recorded.
- Review significant or nonroutine transactions, especially those occurring near the end of the accounting period.
- Review confirmations of compensating-balance agreements for suggestions that balances are or were maintained for or by related parties.
- Review invoices from law firms to see whether a related party is involved.
- Review loan confirmations to determine if guarantees exist.

> **OBSERVATION:** *"The Nature and Extent of Auditing Procedures for Examining Related Party Transactions" states that the auditor should consider obtaining written representations from senior management of an entity and its board of directors, regarding whether they or other related parties were involved in transactions with the entity (AU 9334.20–.21).*

When a related party transaction is identified, the auditor should consider performing the following procedures (AU 334.09):

- Understand the purpose of the transaction.
- Read documentation that supports the transaction.
- Test the reasonableness of numbers compiled for possible disclosure in the financial statements.
- If appropriate, arrange for the audit of intercompany account balances. Use the same audit date cutoff for all balances.
- If appropriate, arrange for the examination of transactions by the auditors for each of the parties.
- Determine the transferability and value of collateral, if any.

If the auditor is not satisfied with the results of the above procedures, additional procedures may be selected to obtain a complete understanding of the nature of the transaction. These procedures may include confirming data with the other party, discussing transactions with banks or other parties, inspecting documents held by others, or verifying the existence of the other party by referring to trade journals or other sources (AU 334.10).

Related party disclosures   The FASB requires disclosure of related party transactions that (1) are not eliminated in consolidated or combined financial statements and (2) are necessary to understand the entity's financial statements (AU 334.11).

If separate financial statements of an entity that had been consolidated are presented in a financial report that includes the consolidated financial statements, duplicate disclosure of the related party transactions is not necessary. Thus, disclosure of the related party transactions in the consolidated statements is all that is required. However, disclosure of related party transactions is required in separate financial statements of (1) a parent company, (2) a subsidiary, (3) a corporate joint venture, or (4) an investee that is less than 50% owned. The minimum financial statement disclosures required by FAS-57 for related party transactions that (1) are not eliminated in consolidation or combination and (2) are necessary to the understanding of the financial statements are as follows:

1. The nature of the related party relationship. The name of the related party should also be disclosed if it is essential to the understanding of the relationship.

2. A description of the related party transactions, including amounts and other pertinent information for each period in which an income statement is presented.

   Related party transactions of no amount, or nominal amounts, must also be disclosed. In other words, all information that is necessary for an understanding of the effects of the related party transactions on the financial statements must be disclosed.

3. The effects of any change in terms between the related parties from terms used in prior periods. In addition, the dollar amount of transactions for each period in which an income statement is presented must be disclosed.

4. If not apparent in the financial statements, (a) the terms of related party transactions, (b) the manner of settlement to related party transactions, and (c) the amount due to, or from, related parties must all be disclosed.

5. The nature of any control relationship, even if there were no transactions between the related parties, must be disclosed in all circumstances.

The amount of detail disclosed for related party transactions must be sufficient for the user of the financial statements to be able to understand the related party transaction. Thus, the disclosure of the total amount of a specific type of related party transaction, or the effects of the relationship between the related parties, may be all that is necessary.

One cannot assume that a related party transaction is consummated in the same manner as an arm's-length transaction. Disclosures or other representations of related party transactions in financial statements should not, under any circumstances, indicate that the transaction was made on the same basis as an arm's-length transaction.

Going-Concern Concept

Financial statements are usually prepared on the assumption that the entity will continue as a going concern. When a company decides or is forced to liquidate, the going-concern concept is not appropriate, and assets should be presented at their estimated net realizable values and legally enforceable liabilities should be classified according to priorities established by law (AU 341.01).

SAS-59 (The Auditor's Consideration of an Entity's Ability to Continue as a Going Concern) concludes that as part of an examination, the auditor should evaluate conditions or events discovered during the engagement that raise questions about the appropriateness of the going-concern concept. Such conditions or events may be identified at various points during the engagement, including the performance of analytical procedures, reading of responses received from the entity's legal counsel, and evaluating the entity's compliance with restrictions imposed by loan agreements (AU 341.02).

Information that raises questions about going concern generally relates to the entity's ability to meet its maturing obligations without selling operating assets, restructuring debt, or revising operations based on outside pressures or similar strategies. SAS-59 concludes that the projection of the going-concern concept is limited to a *reasonable period of time,* which is defined as not exceeding one year beyond the date of the audited financial statements (AU 341.01).

To satisfy the standards related to the going-concern concept established by SAS-59, the following steps should be followed (AU 341.03):

- Evaluate information obtained during the course of the engagement to determine whether substantial doubt has been raised about the entity's continued existence as a going concern for a reasonable period of time.

- When substantial doubt has been raised, identify and evaluate management's plans for dealing with the conditions or events that prompted the substantial doubt conclusions.

- Draw a conclusion concerning the existence of substantial doubt and consider the effect of this conclusion on disclosures in the financial statements and the format of the auditor's report.

Evaluate information related to substantial doubt Although the auditor is not specifically required to employ procedures to identify conditions or events that might raise a substantial doubt question, the auditor should be sensitive to evidential matter collected and implications relative to going concern (AU 341.05).

SAS-59 provides the following as examples of conditions and events that may raise a substantial doubt question (AU 341.06).

Condition or Event	Specific Example
Negative trends	• Recurring operating losses • Working capital deficiencies • Negative cash flows from operations • Adverse key financial ratios
Other indications of possible financial difficulties	• Default on loan or similar agreements • Arrearages in dividends
Other indications of possible financial difficulties	• Denial of usual trade credit from vendors • Restructuring of debt • Noncompliance with statutory capital requirements • Need to seek new sources of financing • Need to sell substantial assets
Internal matters	• Labor difficulties, such as work stoppages • Substantial dependence on the success of a particular project • Uneconomic long-term commitments • Need to significantly revise operations

Condition or Event	Specific Example
External matters	• Legal proceedings, legislation, or similar matters that might affect the entity's ability to continue operations
	• Loss of key franchise, license, or patent
	• Loss of principal customer or vendor
	• Occurrence of uninsured catastrophe

When the evidential matter raises a substantial doubt question, the auditor may obtain additional evidence that may remove the question of substantial doubt (AU 341.07).

Identify and evaluate management's plans   If it is concluded that there is substantial doubt about the continued existence of the entity as a going concern for a reasonable period of time, the auditor should identify and evaluate management's plans to mitigate the effects of the adverse conditions or events. SAS-59 identifies the following as examples of plans and factors that are relevant to the evaluation of those plans (AU 341.07).

Planned Action	Factors Relevant to Evaluation of Planned Action
Sale of assets	• Restrictions on the sale of assets
	• Likely marketability of assets
	• Effects from sale of assets
Borrow or restructure debt	• Likelihood of raising funds based on existing or committed debt arrangements
	• Existing or committed arrangements for restructuring debt or obtaining guarantees for loans
	• Restrictions on ability to borrow or use assets as collateral

Planned Action	Factors Relevant to Evaluation of Planned Action
Reduce or delay expenditures	• Feasibility of reducing or postponing expenditures • Effects of reducing or postponing expenditures
Increase ownership equity	• Feasibility of increasing equity based on existing or committed arrangements • Flexibility of dividend policy • Ability to raise funds from affiliates or other investors

The auditor should consider obtaining evidential matter to support planned actions that are significant to the substantial doubt question (AU 341.08).

Some management strategies may in part be evaluated through the auditor's investigation of management's prospective financial statements. The specific audit procedures that may be employed include the following (AU 341.09):

• Read the prospective financial statements.

• Identify fundamental assumptions used to prepare the prospective financial statements.

• Evaluate the prospective financial statements on the basis of the auditor's familiarity with the client's operations.

• Compare the prospective financial statements for prior periods with actual results.

• Compare the prospective financial statements for the current period with actual results to date.

During the evaluation of fundamental assumptions used to prepare the prospective financial statements, special emphasis should be directed to the following assumptions (AU 341.09):

• Assumptions that have a material effect on the prospective financial statements

- Assumptions that have a high degree of uncertainty
- Assumptions that are inconsistent with past patterns

If the auditor discovers material factors that are not reflected in the preparation of the prospective financial statements, such discoveries should be discussed with management with the understanding that the statements may have to be revised (AU 341.09).

Draw a conclusion concerning substantial doubt Once the auditor has evaluated management's strategies designed to mitigate the adverse effects of conditions or events that raise a question about continued existence, a determination must be made of whether substantial doubt about the going-concern concept exists (AU 341.10).

If substantial doubt does not exist, there is no need to modify the auditor's report. However, the auditor should consider whether the conditions or events that originally created the question about going concern should be disclosed in the financial statements. The disclosure might include the possible effect of the conditions or events and mitigating factors (including management's plans) (AU 341.11).

If the auditor concludes that substantial doubt exists, the effects of conditions or events should be considered as they relate to (1) adequate disclosures in the financial statements and (2) modification to the auditor's report (AU 341.10).

Adequate disclosures If an auditor concludes that substantial doubt exists about the client's ability to continue in existence, care must be taken to ensure that presentations and related disclosures in the financial statements properly reflect the (1) recoverability and classification of assets and (2) amount and classification of liabilities. In addition, an auditor should consider whether disclosures related to the possible discontinuation of operations are adequate in the financial statements. SAS-59 notes the disclosure might include the following (AU 341.10):

- Conditions or events that gave rise to the substantial doubt concerning continued existence
- Possible effects of the conditions or events
- Management's assessments concerning the significance of the conditions or events
- Other factors that may aggravate or mitigate the conditions or events

- Management's strategies that will attempt to deal with the adverse conditions or events

- Possible discontinuance of operations

> **OBSERVATION:** *The financial statement effects described above are relevant when there is substantial doubt about continued existence. If it is concluded that the going-concern concept is not applicable, the financial statements must be prepared on a liquidation basis. Guidance for reporting on liquidation-based financial statements can be found in an Auditing Interpretation entitled "Reporting on Financial Statements Prepared on a Liquidation Basis of Accounting" (December 1984) (AU 9508.33–.38).*

Report modifications   If an auditor concludes that substantial doubt exists about the continued existence of the client, the audit report should be modified. When the auditor believes that the financial statements can still be relied on, the report modification is limited to a reference to the going-concern matter in the report, but the opinion expressed is *unqualified* (AU 341.12).

The substantial doubt question is discussed in an explanatory paragraph following the opinion paragraph. SAS-64 (Omnibus Statement on Auditing Standards—1990) requires that the explanatory paragraph include the phrase "substantial doubt about its [the entity's] ability to continue as a going concern," or similar wording. If similar wording is used, the terms *substantial doubt* and *going concern* must be used in the phrase.

When an auditor concludes that there is substantial doubt about an entity's ability to continue as a going concern, the audit report should not use language that suggests that the conclusion is conditional on future events. Specifically, SAS-77 notes that the use of conditional terminology, such as "if the company is unable to obtain refinancing, there may be substantial doubt about the company's ability to continue as a going concern," is precluded.

The introductory, scope, and opinion paragraphs make no reference to the explanatory paragraph. An example of an explanatory paragraph based on a substantial doubt question is presented below (AU 341.12–.13).

The accompanying financial statements have been prepared assuming that the Company will continue as a going concern. As discussed in Note X to the financial statements, the Company is involved in litigation concerning alleged patent infringement. Because operations of the Company could be substantially impeded if the charges are upheld, the pending litigation raises substantial doubt about its ability to continue as a going concern. Management's plans in regard to the litigation are also described in Note X. The financial statements do not include any adjustments that might result from the outcome of this uncertainty.

> *OBSERVATION: An auditor can no longer express a "subject to" qualified opinion because of an uncertainty.*

When the auditor concludes that the uncertainty related to the substantial doubt question is so significant that an opinion cannot be expressed on the financial statements, a disclaimer of opinion may be expressed (AU 341.12).

The modification of the auditor's report because of a substantial doubt question in the current year does not imply that the auditor's report on a prior year's financial statements (presented on a comparative basis) should also be modified (AU 341.15).

During the current year, a question of substantial doubt contained in an auditor's report on a prior year's financial statements may no longer be applicable. Under this circumstance, the explanatory paragraph should not be repeated in the auditor's report on the comparative financial statements (AU 341.16).

> *OBSERVATION: The noninclusion of the explanatory paragraph is not a change in the opinion expressed by the auditor and therefore does not require the observance of the report guidelines established in SAS-58 concerning changes of opinions.*

Although the auditor is responsible for including an explanatory paragraph in the auditor's report when a substantial doubt question arises, the auditor is not responsible for predicting the outcome of future events. Thus, the liquidation of an entity (even within one year of the date of the financial statements) does not imply that the audit was substandard when an explanatory paragraph has not been included in the auditor's report. Similarly, the lack of including an explanatory paragraph in the auditor's report should not be taken as an assurance that the entity will continue as a going concern within a reasonable period of time (AU 341.04).

Subsequent Events

SAS-1 describes two types of subsequent events. The first type relates to "events that provide additional evidence with respect to conditions that existed at the date of the balance sheet and affect the estimates inherent in the process of preparing financial statements." Evidence available to the auditor before the issuance of the financial statements should be used to evaluate estimates used by management. The auditor evaluates these estimates in light of subsequent events by making inquiries of management and having a current knowledge of the technological factors that affect the client's operations (AU 560.02–.04).

The second type of subsequent event relates to "events that provide evidence with respect to conditions that did not exist at the date of the balance sheet being reported on but arose subsequent to that date." An example of this type of subsequent event would be fire or flood damages to property, plant, and equipment that occurred after the date of the balance sheet. The auditor may discover this type of subsequent event by reviewing the minutes of the board of directors meetings after the balance sheet date, making inquiries of management, and obtaining written representations from management (AU 560.05).

Representation Letters

SAS-19 (Client Representations) requires that written representations be obtained from the client to confirm oral representations and to reduce the likelihood of misunderstandings between the client and the auditor. Most written representations are broad in nature, and examples include representations concerning the availability of all records, related party disclosures, and unrecorded transactions (AU 333).

Written representations are part of the auditor's tests of assertions made in the financial statements concerning proper classification, descriptions, and disclosures.

Reasonableness

The auditor must exercise professional judgment concerning the overall presentation of each set of accounts. To test for reasonableness the auditor uses analytical review procedures, which are considered substantive tests made by studying the comparison of relationships among data.

Examples of analytical procedures to test the overall reasonableness of property, plant, and equipment follow:

- Compare balances in property, plant, and equipment and related accounts this year with balances in the previous year.
- Compare balances in property, plant, and equipment and related accounts with budgeted amounts.
- Study the relationship between property, plant, and equipment and depreciation expense taking into consideration depreciation methods, sales, and dispositions.
- Evaluate the effect of management policies, such as changes in capitalization policies or depreciation methods, on property, plant, and equipment and related accounts.

Dual-Purpose Tests

In an engagement, corroborative evidential matter is obtained by performing tests of controls and substantive tests. Tests of controls are performed to provide reasonable assurance that a client's internal control is functioning as prescribed. On the other hand, substantive tests are employed by the auditor to determine the validity and the propriety of accounting transactions and balances. SAS-55 (Consideration of Internal Control Structure in a Financial Statement Audit) states that although the purposes of tests of controls and substantive tests are different, both purposes are often achieved simultaneously through the tests of details (substantive tests other than analytical review). For example, a credit sales transaction may be evaluated by the auditor to determine whether the sale was recorded in accordance with generally accepted accounting principles by examining supporting documentation, including a customer order approved for credit. The test would be both a substantive test (validity of transaction) and a test of controls (an approved customer order is needed before a sales transaction is executed). In this case, the test of details would be a *dual-purpose test* (AU 319.64).

SAMPLING TECHNIQUES AND PROCEDURES

Contents

Overview	**9.03**
Statistical Sampling Plans	**9.04**
Audit Risk	**9.05**
Sampling Tests of Controls	**9.06**
Step 1—Determine the Objectives of the Test	**9.07**
Step 2—Define the Deviation Conditions	**9.08**
Step 3—Define the Population	**9.09**
Step 4—Determine the Method of Selecting the Sample	**9.10**
Step 5—Determine the Sample Size	**9.11**
Exhibit I: Audit Judgment Factors Used to Determine Sample Size for Tests of Controls	**9.13**
Table I: Statistical Sample Sizes for Tests of Controls with a 5% Risk of Assessing Control Risk Too Low	**9.16**
Step 6—Perform the Sampling Plan	**9.17**
Step 7—Evaluate the Sample Results	**9.17**
Table II: Statistical Sample Results Evaluation Table for Tests of Controls	**9.19**
Step 8—Document the Sampling Procedures	**9.21**
Sampling in Substantive Tests of Details	**9.21**
Step 1—Determine the Audit Objective of the Test	**9.22**
Step 2—Define the Population	**9.22**
Step 3—Choose an Audit Sampling Technique	**9.23**
Step 4—Determine the Sample Size	**9.24**
Exhibit II: Audit Judgment Factors Used to Determine Sample Size for Substantive Tests	**9.26**
Step 5—Determine the Method of Selecting the Sample	**9.28**
Step 6—Perform the Sampling Plan	**9.28**
Step 7—Evaluate the Sample Results	**9.29**
Step 8—Document the Sampling Procedures	**9.30**

SAMPLING TECHNIQUES AND PROCEDURES

Overview

The third standard of fieldwork requires that sufficient competent evidential matter be gathered by the auditor as a basis for formulating an opinion on the financial statements. Evidence may be defined as any information that has an effect on determining whether the financial statements are presented in accordance with generally accepted accounting principles (AU 326.14).

Examining the documentation for every transaction of a business is costly and time-consuming. Since most audit objectives do not require that amount of evidence, an auditor will frequently use sampling techniques and procedures. Statement on Auditing Standards (SAS) No. 39 (Audit Sampling) notes that there may be reasons other than sampling for which an auditor would examine less than all of the items in a given population, such as (1) to gain an understanding of the nature of an entity's operations or (2) to clarify his or her understanding of the design of the entity's internal control. Under these circumstances, guidelines established in SAS-39 are not applicable (AU 350.01).

> *OBSERVATION: An Auditing Interpretation on audit sampling entitled "Applicability" (January 1985) states that the following circumstances would not be considered sampling when less than 100% of the items in a given population are not examined: (1) it is not the auditor's intent to extend the conclusion reached by examining less than 100% of the items to the remainder of the items in the population; (2) although he or she might not be examining all of the items in the population, the auditor might be examining 100% of the items that make up a subgrouping of the entire population; (3) the auditor is performing tests of controls on a procedure not documented (e.g., observing the client counting his or her inventory); and (4) the auditor is not performing a substantive test of details (e.g., applying analytical procedures) (AU 9350.01–.02).*

The purpose of sampling is to examine less than 100% of the items in a given population. On the basis of the sampling results, an auditor can draw a conclusion about certain characteristics of the total population. For example, a sample of customer credit orders may be examined to determine whether appropriate credit approval has been made on each order. If the results of the sample reveal that 5% of the orders do *not* have appropriate approval, an auditor may conclude that 95% (plus or minus a precision factor) of all customer credit orders *do* have appropriate credit approval (AU 350.01).

Sampling can be applied on a nonstatistical or statistical basis. However, statistical sampling has the following advantages (AU 350.45–.46):

- Statistical sampling facilitates the design of an efficient sample.
- Statistical sampling measures the sufficiency of the evidential matter.
- Statistical sampling facilitates the evaluation of the sample results.
- Statistical sampling permits the quantification of sampling risk.

SAS-39 was issued to provide guidance for the auditor's design and implementation of audit sampling plans. SAS-39 endorses both a nonstatistical approach and a statistical approach to sampling by concluding that either approach can provide sufficient evidential matter, as required by the third standard of fieldwork (AU 350.03).

The standards established by SAS-41 (Working Papers) must be observed to properly document the sampling plan, sample results, and audit conclusions.

Statistical Sampling Plans

Attribute sampling measures the frequency of a specific occurrence in a particular population. This sampling technique is used to discover how often exceptions occur in the population under examination. Thus, attribute sampling is concerned with the qualitative characters of a sample. Generally, attribute sampling is associated with tests of controls, which are intended to provide reasonable assurance that internal control procedures are being followed by the client's personnel.

Variable sampling is used to estimate the dollar value of a population and to determine the reasonableness of specific balances on the financial statements. Thus, variable sampling is concerned with the quantitative characteristics of a population. Generally, variable sampling is associated with substantive tests, which are performed to gather evidential matter concerning the validity and the propriety of specific transactions and balances.

Depending on the circumstances, an auditor may employ an attribute sampling plan or a variable sampling plan.

Audit Risk

Even when every transaction and balance is examined 100%, there is always a degree of audit risk present in an audit. This degree of audit risk is referred to in SAS-39 as a combination of *nonsampling risk* and *sampling risk.* Examples of nonsampling risk are (1) the selection of inappropriate auditing procedures or (2) the failure to identify an error on a document that is examined by the auditor. Nonsampling risk cannot be measured, but it can be reduced to an acceptable level by the auditor's implementation of an effective quality control system (AU 350.09–.11).

Sampling risk occurs because less than 100% of the sample units in a population are reviewed. For this reason, sampling risk can be reduced by increasing the size of the sample. Sampling risks are classified as follows (AU 350.12):

- *Risk of Assessing Control Risk Too Low (Tests of Controls)*—The risk that the assessed level of control risk based on the sample is less than the true operating effectiveness of the control structure policy or procedure. In other words, the internal control is not as effective as the auditor believes it to be.

- *Risk of Assessing Control Risk Too High (Tests of Controls)*—The risk that the assessed level of control risk based on the sample is greater than the true operating effectiveness of the control policy or procedure. In other words, the internal control is more effective than the auditor believes it to be.

- *Risk of Incorrect Acceptance (Substantive Tests)*—The risk that the selected sample supports the auditor's conclusion that the recorded account balance is not materially misstated when in fact the recorded account balance is materially misstated. In other words, on the basis of the selected sample, the auditor concludes that the recorded account balance is not materially misstated when in fact, based on the total population, the recorded account balance is materially misstated.

- *Risk of Incorrect Rejection (Substantive Tests)*—The risk that the selected sample supports the auditor's conclusion that the recorded account balance is materially misstated when in fact the recorded account balance is not materially misstated. In other words, on the basis of the selected sample, the auditor concludes that the recorded account balance is materially misstated when in fact, based on the total population, the recorded account balance is not materially misstated.

The risk of incorrectly assessing control risk too high and the risk of incorrect rejection of a recorded account balance are both associated with the efficiency of the audit. For example, when an auditor assesses control risk at a high level (when in fact the control risk is lower), the extent of substantive testing may be increased unnecessarily by the auditor. Thus, the audit was not performed efficiently because the auditor could have selected, for example, a smaller sample for substantive testing (AU 350.13).

The risk of incorrectly assessing control risk too low on internal control and the risk of incorrect acceptance of a recorded account balance are both associated with the effectiveness of the audit. For example, when an auditor concludes that a recorded account balance is correct when in fact the balance is not correct, the effectiveness of the audit is impaired (AU 350.14).

Thus, the risk of assessing control risk too high and the risk of incorrect rejection may affect the efficiency of an audit, whereas the risk of assessing control risk too low and the risk of incorrect acceptance may affect the effectiveness of an audit. An auditor is more concerned with the risk of assessing control risk too low and the risk of incorrect acceptance than with the risk of assessing control risk too high and the risk of incorrect rejection, because the effectiveness of the audit is more important than the efficiency of the audit. For this reason, the risk of assessing control risk too low and the risk of incorrect acceptance of an incorrectly recorded account balance are emphasized in SAS-39 (AU 350.13–.14).

SAMPLING TESTS OF CONTROLS

As stated earlier, attribute sampling measures the frequency of a specific occurrence in a particular population. This sampling technique is used to discover how often exceptions occur in the population under examination. Thus, attribute sampling is concerned with the qualitative characteristics of a sample. Attribute sampling is associated with tests of controls, which are intended to provide insight into the effectiveness of the client's internal control. The auditor may use the following steps to apply attribute sampling to tests of controls (AU 350.31–38):

1. Determine the objectives of the test.
2. Define the deviation conditions.
3. Define the population.
   a. Define the period covered by the test.
   b. Define the sampling unit.
   c. Consider the completeness of the population.
4. Determine the method of selecting the sample.
   a. Random-number sampling
   b. Systematic sampling
   c. Other sampling
5. Determine the sample size.
   a. Consider the allowable risk of assessing control risk too low.
   b. Consider the maximum rate of deviations from prescribed internal control policies or procedures that would support the auditor's planned assessed level of control risk (tolerable rate).
   c. Consider the expected population deviation rate.
   d. Consider the effect of the population size.
   e. Consider statistical or nonstatistical sampling methods.
6. Perform the sampling plan.
7. Evaluate the sample results.
   a. Calculate the deviation rate.
   b. Consider the sampling risk.
   c. Consider the qualitative aspects of the deviations.
   d. Reach an overall conclusion.
8. Document the sampling procedures.

Step 1—Determine the Objectives of the Test

The use of sampling techniques in tests of controls is applicable only to those internal control features that generate documentary evidence. Thus, sampling techniques usually cannot be used in tests of controls for segregation of duties or the competency of personnel.

Tests of controls are concerned with determining whether a client's internal control is operating in accordance with prescribed policies. Each internal control procedure has an objective and prescribed rules to obtain that objective. For example, in the credit department of a business, a control may state that orders must be appropriately approved for acceptance of credit risk before being processed. The objective of this control is to ensure that credit is approved before an order is accepted. This control must also include the prescribed rules for attaining the objective. One of the rules for attaining this particular objective for the credit department may state that no additional credit may be granted to any customer who has an outstanding balance older than sixty days. The head of the credit department will be charged with the responsibility that this control and its prescribed rules are consistently followed.

Every single control objective must have one or more stated control techniques, which are designed to achieve the control objective. As with control objectives, all stated control techniques must be clearly defined and communicated to the appropriate personnel. Procedure manuals are usually used to define and communicate the control techniques.

Controls may be classified as preventive or detective. Preventive controls are established to prevent errors from occurring. Detective controls are established to detect errors that have occurred.

When performing tests of controls, the auditor must determine whether a specific internal control procedure is operating as designed and whether the control objective is being achieved. In this respect the auditor may be concerned with (1) who performed the control procedure, (2) where the control procedure was performed, and (3) whether the procedure was performed in accordance with prescribed policy.

The audit objective must be defined in terms of specific compliance characteristics that can be tested.

Step 2—Define the Deviation Conditions

A *deviation* is a departure from the prescribed internal control procedure. The auditor must identify any significant deviation conditions that exist in a control procedure. A significant deviation condition exists when a necessary step to achieve a particular internal control objective is not performed as prescribed. Some internal control procedures may be considered unimportant by the auditor, such as multiple approvals, and need not be tested (AU 350.33).

Step 3—Define the Population

The population selected for examination must be complete and provide the auditor with the opportunity to satisfy the established audit objective. A sample should be selected in a manner that is representative of the population from which it is selected. If the population is not complete in all respects, the selected sample will not be representative of the complete population. For example, the audit objective may be to determine whether all goods that are shipped are properly billed. For this audit objective, the auditor should define the population as bills of lading prepared during the audit period, rather than sales invoices, which may or may not represent goods that have been shipped (AU 350.39).

Step 3a—Define the Period Covered by the Test

A conclusion can be drawn about a population only if all items in the population have a chance of being selected for examination. The population from which the sample is selected should include all transactions for the accounting period under examination. However, professional standards recognize that it may be appropriate to perform tests of controls at interim dates and review subsequent transactions when the auditor performs year-end audit procedures.

Step 3b—Define the Sampling Unit

A population consists of a number of sampling units, such as canceled checks or sales invoices. For example, if the audit objective is to determine whether vouchers have been properly approved, the sampling items may be the line items in the voucher register rather than the checks used to pay the vouchers. Once the auditor adequately defines the population, the sample unit should not be difficult to define.

Step 3c—Consider the Completeness of the Population

The physical representation of the population must be consistent with the definition of the population. For example, the auditor may be concerned with all cash disbursements made during the period and define the population as all canceled checks during the period.

The auditor must determine that the defined population is complete in all respects.

Step 4—Determine the Method of Selecting the Sample

Sampling units must be selected from the defined population so that each sampling unit has a chance of being selected. Generally, the auditor's objective is to select a representative sample of all items from the population (AU 350.39).

Step 4a—Random-Number Sampling

A sample may be selected from the population on a random basis using random numbers generated by a computer or numbers chosen from a random-number table. Random selection means that each sampling unit has an equal chance of being selected from the population.

Step 4b—Systematic Sampling

A random sample may be selected using the systematic-selection method whereby every *nth* item is selected. Systematic selection is also referred to as sequential sampling. The following steps should be observed when systematic selection is used:

- Determine the population (*N*).
- Determine the sample size (*n*).
- Compute the interval size by dividing *N* by *n*.
- Select a random start (a random-number table can be used to determine the starting point).
- Determine the sample items selected by successively adding the interval to the random starting point.

To illustrate the systematic-selection method, assume that the auditor has defined the population as 3,000 sales invoices listed in the sales journal (*N*) and would like to select 100 sales invoices for testing (*n*). Thus, the interval is every 30th sales invoice (3000/100). If it is assumed that the auditor selects the number 12 as a random starting point, the first sales invoice selected would be the twelfth invoice, the second would be the forty-second invoice (12 + 30), and so on, until the sample of 100 items is selected.

A client may summarize or group a population in a specific order, and thus such a population would not be random. A sample selected from a nonrandom population using the systematic-selection method may not be appropriate for drawing statistical conclusions about a population, unless the auditor takes steps to solve the problem. The auditor should examine the population to determine whether it has been grouped or summarized in a particular order. Inquiries of client personnel may also be made to ascertain how individual transactions are accumulated or individual balances listed. If the population is in a specific order, it should be stratified and proportional samples drawn from each stratum. In this event, the auditor may want to test one or more of the strata more extensively.

Even if the population is not in a specific order, it usually is advisable for the auditor to have two or more random starts.

Step 4c—Other Sampling

Block sampling refers to selecting contiguous sampling units, such as all checks numbered from 420 to 440. Generally, block sampling cannot be used when a statistical sampling approach is used by the auditor. When the auditor uses only a few blocks to select the sample, block sampling also would be inappropriate for a nonstatistical sampling approach.

Haphazard sampling consists of selecting sampling units without any conscious bias. For example, the selection would be biased if the auditor had a tendency to select vendor folders that had the most vendor invoices in them. If properly applied, haphazard sampling can be used for nonstatistical sampling but not for a statistical sampling approach.

Step 5—Determine the Sample Size

A considerable amount of professional judgment is necessary to determine the proper sample size. The method for reaching a decision for determining the sample size is the same for nonstatistical sampling as it is for statistical sampling. In statistical sampling, the auditor will quantify the factors that are used to determine the sample size; in nonstatistical sampling, the factors will be described in subjective terms. For example, in statistical sampling, the auditor may conclude that a 10% factor should be assigned to the risk of assessing control risk too low. In nonstatistical sampling, the auditor may conclude that the client's control procedures appear to be well designed. Both conclusions are highly subjective and are based on the same fundamental analysis, although the conclusion associated with statistical sampling is more precise.

The audit decision process as described in SAS-39 is summarized in Exhibit I.

Step 5a—Consider the Allowable Risk of Assessing Control Risk Too Low

The level of sampling risk is influenced by the size of the sample. There is always a risk that the auditor will not draw a representative sample. The larger the sample, the more audit hours it takes to test the sample. Achieving an acceptable level of sampling risk is the result of a trade-off between trying to avoid overauditing on the one hand and underauditing on the other.

Establishing an allowable risk of assessing control risk too low is a function of the degree of assurance indicated by the evidential matter selected as part of the sample process. If the auditor desires a high degree of assurance, it is necessary to establish a relatively small risk of assessing control risk too low. Establishing a small risk of assessing control risk too low will require that (assuming all other factors remain constant) the auditor increase the size of the sample. The larger the sample size, the higher the degree of assurance the auditor can offer about the effectiveness of internal control. For example, if the auditor is using statistical sampling, a larger sample size must be selected if the auditor desires to make a statement about the maximum error rate at a 99% confidence level rather than at a 90% confidence level (AU 350.37).

Step 5b—Consider the Tolerable Rate

The *tolerable rate* is the maximum percentage of deviations (errors) in a population that an auditor will tolerate without changing the planned assessed level of control risk. SAS-39 concludes that the establishment of a tolerable rate in an engagement is based on (1) the planned assessed level of control risk and (2) the degree of assurance indicated by the evidential matter in the sample (AU 350.34).

The planned assessed level of control risk results from obtaining an understanding of the client's internal control. Thus, having gained an understanding of the client's internal control, the auditor establishes the planned level of control risk, which in turn is a factor in determining the sample size for tests of control. For example, if an internal control procedure (or related procedure) is considered highly relevant to a critical financial statement assertion, the auditor initially would plan to rely relatively heavily on the control procedure and there would be a tendency to establish a small tolerable rate (AU 350.34).

Step 5c—Consider the Expected Population Deviation Rate

The purpose of attribute sampling is to estimate the deviation rate of a particular characteristic in a population. However, before sampling can begin, the auditor must make a preliminary estimate of the deviation rate. The expected population deviation rate is the anticipated deviation rate in the entire population. Ideally, the estimate should be based on the results of audits of prior years, taking into consideration any subsequent modifications of the client's internal control. The auditor may review working papers for the last few years to obtain an idea of the expected population deviation rate. In a new engagement, the expected population deviation rate can be estimated by selecting and auditing a preliminary sample of about 25 items. The results of the test should be properly documented because the preliminary sample becomes part of the final sample (AU 350.38).

As the expected population deviation rate approaches the tolerable rate established by the auditor, the required sample size increases because the auditor must make an allowance for sampling risk. If the expected population deviation rate for a particular internal control procedure is equal to or greater than the tolerable rate, the auditor should establish the control risk at its maximum level (AU 350.38).

> *OBSERVATION: SAS-55 describes assessing control risk at the maximum level as "the greatest probability that a material misstatement that could occur in an assertion will not be prevented or detected on a timely basis by an entity's internal control structure" (AU 319.29).*

EXHIBIT I

Audit Judgment Factors Used to Determine Sample Size for Tests of Controls

Basis for Audit Judgment in Determining Factors Affecting Sample Size

Factors Affecting Sample Size

Degree of Assurance Desired

Planned Assessed Level of Control Risk

Prior Years' Working Papers or Pre-Audit Sample Rate

Allowable Risk of Assessing Control Risk Too Low

Consider the Tolerable Rate

Consider the Expected Population Deviation Rate

Consider the Effects of Population Size

Using Professional Judgment, Determine the Required Sample Size

Step 5d—Consider the Effect of the Population Size

In most circumstances, the size of the population has little or no effect on the determination of the required sample size. A population size of 5,000 sampling units or more will have practically no effect on the size of the sample.

Step 5e—Consider a Statistical or Nonstatistical Sampling Method

The auditor may use either a statistical sampling method or a nonstatistical sampling method.

Sample size and statistical sampling When the auditor uses statistical sampling, tables can be used to determine the appropriate sample size. Table I is based on a 5% risk of assessing control risk too low. To use Table I the following procedures should be observed:

- Find the table with the risk of assessing control risk too low established by the auditor. (Table I is based on a 5% risk of assessing control risk too low.)
- Refer to the column in Table I that corresponds to the auditor's tolerable rate.
- Refer to the row in Table I that corresponds to the auditor's estimate of the expected population deviation rate.
- The sample size is located where the tolerable rate column and the expected population deviation row intersect. (The number in parentheses is the number of expected errors.)

To illustrate the above steps, assume that the risk of assessing control risk too low has been established at 5% (Table I is based on 5%), the tolerable rate is 9%, and the expected population deviation rate is 4%. The sample size is located where the tolerable rate column (9%) and the expected population deviation row (4%) intersect. Thus, the required sample size is 100.

Sample size and nonstatistical sampling When the auditor uses nonstatistical sampling, the risk of assessing control risk too low, the tolerable rate, and the expected population deviation rate are taken into consideration and the sample size is determined by professional judgment. The following generalizations should be observed by the

TABLE I
STATISTICAL SAMPLE SIZES FOR TESTS OF CONTROLS
WITH A 5% RISK OF ASSESSING CONTROL RISK TOO LOW
(WITH NUMBER OF EXPECTED ERRORS IN PARENTHESES)

Tolerable Rate

Expected Population Deviation Rate	2%	3%	4%	5%	6%	7%	8%	9%	10%	15%	20%
0.00%	149(0)	99(0)	74(0)	59(0)	49(0)	42(0)	36(0)	32(0)	29(0)	19(0)	14(0)
.25	236(1)	157(1)	117(1)	93(1)	78(1)	66(1)	58(1)	51(1)	46(1)	30(1)	22(1)
.50	*	157(1)	117(1)	93(1)	78(1)	66(1)	58(1)	51(1)	46(1)	30(1)	22(1)
.75	*	208(1)	117(1)	93(1)	78(1)	66(1)	58(1)	51(1)	46(1)	30(1)	22(1)
1.00	*	*	156(2)	93(1)	78(1)	66(1)	58(1)	51(1)	46(1)	30(1)	22(1)
1.25	*	*	156(2)	124(2)	78(1)	66(1)	58(1)	51(1)	46(1)	30(1)	22(1)
1.50	*	*	192(3)	124(2)	103(2)	66(1)	58(1)	51(1)	46(1)	30(1)	22(1)
1.75	*	*	227(4)	153(3)	103(2)	88(2)	77(2)	51(1)	46(1)	30(1)	22(1)
2.00	*	*	*	181(4)	127(3)	88(2)	77(2)	68(2)	46(1)	30(1)	22(1)
2.25	*	*	*	208(5)	127(3)	88(2)	77(2)	68(2)	61(2)	30(1)	22(1)
2.50	*	*	*	*	150(4)	109(3)	77(2)	68(2)	61(2)	30(1)	22(1)
2.75	*	*	*	*	175(5)	109(3)	95(3)	68(2)	61(2)	30(1)	22(1)
3.00	*	*	*	*	195(6)	129(4)	95(3)	84(3)	61(2)	30(1)	22(1)
3.25	*	*	*	*	*	148(5)	112(4)	84(3)	61(2)	30(1)	22(1)
3.50	*	*	*	*	*	167(6)	112(4)	84(3)	76(3)	40(2)	22(1)
3.75	*	*	*	*	*	185(7)	129(5)	100(4)	76(3)	40(2)	22(1)
4.00	*	*	*	*	*	*	146(6)	100(4)	89(4)	40(2)	22(1)
5.00	*	*	*	*	*	*	*	158(8)	116(6)	40(2)	30(2)
6.00	*	*	*	*	*	*	*	*	179(11)	50(3)	30(2)
7.00	*	*	*	*	*	*	*	*	*	68(5)	37(3)

*Sample size is too large to be cost-effective for most audit applications.

NOTE: This table assumes a large population.

Copyright © 1983 by the American Institute of Certified Public Accountants, Inc. (The title of the table has been changed to conform to the terminology used in SAS-55.)

auditor in determining the sample size when nonstatistical sampling is employed:

- As the risk of assessing control risk too low increases, the required sample size decreases.
- As the risk of assessing control risk too low decreases, the required sample size increases.
- As the tolerable rate increases, the required sample size decreases.
- As the tolerable rate decreases, the required sample size increases.
- As the expected population deviation rate increases, the required sample size increases.
- As the expected population deviation rate decreases, the required sample size decreases.

Step 6—Perform the Sampling Plan

After the sample has been selected, audit procedures should be applied to each sampling unit to determine whether there has been a deviation from the established internal control procedure. Usually, a deviation occurs if the auditor is unable to perform an audit procedure or apply alternative audit procedures to a sampling unit. As a general rule, sampling units that are selected but not examined, such as voided transactions or unused documents, should be replaced with new sampling units. Voided transactions or unused documents are not considered deviations if the established procedure of accounting for these items has been properly followed (AU 350.40).

Step 7—Evaluate the Sample Results

After the audit procedures have been applied to each sampling unit, and the deviations, if any, from the prescribed internal control procedure have been summarized, the results of the sampling must be evaluated.

Step 7a—Calculate the Deviation Rate

The deviation rate is computed by dividing the number of deviations by the number of units in the sample. The sample deviation rate is the auditor's best estimate of the population deviation rate (AU 350.41).

Step 7b—Consider the Sampling Risk

The auditor must consider the degree of sampling risk involved in the sample results. Sampling risk arises because the auditor does not examine all of the sampling units in a population. An auditor can reach an entirely different conclusion on the basis of sample results than if the entire population is examined. When the auditor's estimate of the population deviation is less than the tolerable rate for the population, there is still a possibility that the true deviation rate in the population (maximum population deviation) is greater than the tolerable rate. The auditor can determine the degree of sampling risk in the sample results by computing the maximum population deviation rate (AU 350.41).

Sampling risk and statistical sampling   When the auditor employs statistical sampling, tables can be used to measure the allowance for sampling risk. Table II is based on upper limits at a 5% risk of assessing control risk too low. By using Table II, an auditor can determine the maximum population deviation rate. To use Table II the following procedures should be observed:

- Find the table with the risk of assessing control risk too low established by the auditor. (Table II is based on a 5% risk factor, and tables are available for other percentages.)
- Refer to the column in Table II that corresponds to the number of actual deviations found in the sample.
- Refer to the row in Table II that corresponds to the sample size.
- The maximum population deviation rate is located where the column for the actual number of deviations found in the sample and the sample-size row intersect.

To illustrate the above procedures, assume that the risk of assessing control risk too low established by the auditor is 5% (Table II is based on 5%), the sample size established by the auditor is 100, the tolerable rate established by the auditor is 9%, and the expected population deviation rate established by the auditor is 4%. If the auditor examines the 100 sample units and discovers two errors, the maximum population deviation rate is 6.2% as shown on Table II

TABLE II
STATISTICAL SAMPLE RESULTS EVALUATION
TABLE FOR TESTS OF CONTROLS
UPPER LIMITS AT 5% RISK OF ASSESSING CONTROL RISK TOO LOW

Actual Number of Deviations Found

Sample Size	0	1	2	3	4	5	6	7	8	9	10
25	11.3	17.6	*	*	*	*	*	*	*	*	*
30	9.5	14.9	19.6	*	*	*	*	*	*	*	*
35	8.3	12.9	17.0	*	*	*	*	*	*	*	*
40	7.3	11.4	15.0	18.3	*	*	*	*	*	*	*
45	6.5	10.2	13.4	16.4	19.2	*	*	*	*	*	*
50	5.9	9.2	12.1	14.8	17.4	19.9	*	*	*	*	*
55	5.4	8.4	11.1	13.5	15.9	18.2	*	*	*	*	*
60	4.9	7.7	10.2	12.5	14.7	16.8	18.8	*	*	*	*
65	4.6	7.1	9.4	11.5	13.6	15.5	17.4	19.3	*	*	*
70	4.2	6.6	8.8	10.8	12.6	14.5	16.3	18.0	19.7	*	*
75	4.0	6.2	8.2	10.1	11.8	13.6	15.2	16.9	18.5	20.0	*
80	3.7	5.8	7.7	9.5	11.1	12.7	14.3	15.9	17.4	18.9	*
90	3.3	5.2	6.9	8.4	9.9	11.4	12.8	14.2	15.5	16.8	18.2
100	3.0	4.7	6.2	7.6	9.0	10.3	11.5	12.8	14.0	15.2	16.4
125	2.4	3.8	5.0	6.1	7.2	8.3	9.3	10.3	11.3	12.3	13.2
150	2.0	3.2	4.2	5.1	6.0	6.9	7.8	8.6	9.5	10.3	11.1
200	1.5	2.4	3.2	3.9	4.6	5.2	5.9	6.5	7.2	7.8	8.4

*Over 20%

NOTE: This table presents upper limits as percentages. This table assumes a large population.

where the actual number of deviations found (2) intersects with a sample size of 100. The maximum population deviation rate is also referred to as the upper limits or the upper precision limits.

In the above illustration, the auditor can be 95% certain that the maximum population deviation rate is 6.2%. The 95% certainty percentage is the complement of the 5% risk factor (100% minus 5%). Since the maximum deviation rate of 6.2% is less than the tolerable rate of 9% established by the auditor, the planned assessed level of control risk is not changed. However, when the maximum population deviation rate is greater than the tolerable rate established by the auditor, the planned assessed level of control risk is not justified.

Sampling risk and nonstatistical sampling When the auditor employs nonstatistical sampling, the sampling risk cannot be quantified. The following generalizations should be observed when the auditor evaluates the results of nonstatistical sampling:

- The auditor may rely on the planned assessed level of control risk when the auditor's best estimate of the population deviation rate (based on the sample results) is equal to or less than the expected population deviation rate.

- The auditor cannot rely on the planned assessed level of control risk when the auditor's best estimate of the population deviation rate is greater than the expected population deviation rate.

Step 7c—Consider the Qualitative Aspects of the Deviations

The auditor should consider the qualitative aspects of each deviation. The nature and cause of each deviation should be analyzed and deviations should be classified into errors (unintentional deviations) or irregularities (intentional deviations). A determination should be made about whether the deviation resulted from a misunderstanding of instructions or from carelessness. The discovery of an irregularity would generally require more attention from the auditor than the discovery of an error (AU 350.42).

Step 7d—Reach an Overall Conclusion

The auditor must determine whether the overall audit approach supports the planned assessed level of control risk. To make this overall evaluation, the auditor should consider the following factors:

- Sample results of tests of controls
- Results of inquiries about controls that do not leave an audit trail
- Results of observations concerning control procedures that are based on the segregation of responsibilities

Professional judgment is required in reaching a conclusion on how the results of the tests of controls will affect the nature, timing, and extent of the subsequent substantive tests.

Step 8—Document the Sampling Procedures

To satisfy the requirements of SAS-41, the following matters should be considered for documentation in the auditor's workpapers:

- Description of internal controls tested
- Objective of the tests of controls
- Definition of population and sampling unit
- Definition of deviation conditions
- Method of determining sample size
- Method of sample selection
- Description of audit procedures employed and list of deviations discovered by the auditor
- Evaluation of sample results and overall conclusions

SAMPLING IN SUBSTANTIVE TESTS OF DETAILS

Variable sampling is used in the performance of substantive tests of transactions and balances. Variable sampling is used to estimate the dollar value of a population and to determine the reasonableness of financial statement balances. The purpose of substantive tests is to obtain evidence of the validity and propriety of accounting transactions and balances. The auditor may use the following steps to apply variable sampling to substantive tests (AU 350.15–.16):

1. Determine the audit objective of the test.
2. Define the population.

    a. Define the sampling unit.

    b. Consider the completeness of the population.

    c. Identify individually significant items.

3. Choose an audit sampling technique.

4. Determine the sample size.

    a. Consider variations within the population.

    b. Consider the acceptable level of risk.

    c. Consider the tolerable misstatement.

    d. Consider the expected amount of error.

    e. Consider the population size.

5. Determine the method of selecting the sample.

6. Perform the sampling plan.

7. Evaluate the sample results.

    a. Project the misstatement to the population and consider sampling risk.

    b. Consider the qualitative aspects of misstatements and reach an overall conclusion.

8. Document the sampling procedures.

Step 1—Determine the Audit Objective of the Test

The audit objective of performing substantive tests is to determine whether the dollar value assigned by management to an account balance or group of transactions is reasonable (AU 350.18).

Step 2—Define the Population

The population defined by the auditor must include all items that are related to the audit objective of the test. If items relevant to the audit objective are omitted from the population, the audit objective of the test will not be achieved. For example, the audit objective may be to determine whether the repairs and maintenance expense account is reasonably stated. The definition of the population could be all line items that make up the detail of the account, but such a definition would probably be deficient because other accounts—especially property, plant, and equipment—could contain expenditures that were capitalized when they should have been expensed. A better definition of the population would be all repairs and maintenance work orders authorized during the period (AU 350.17).

Step 2a—Define the Sampling Unit

The population is made up of individual sampling units that may be individual transactions, documents, customer or vendor balances, or an individual entry. The auditor must consider the efficiency of the audit when selecting the sampling unit. For example, it may be more efficient to define the sampling unit as the individual sales invoice rather than the individual accounts receivable, which may be made up of several invoices.

Step 2b—Consider the Completeness of the Population

The physical representation of the population must be consistent with the definition of the population. For example, the auditor may be concerned with all cash disbursements made during the period and define the population as all canceled checks during the period. The auditor must determine that the defined population is complete in all respects.

Step 2c—Identify Individually Significant Items

The population should be reviewed for items that should be individually examined because of the audit exposure related to these items. Items that should be examined individually include large dollar items, related party transactions, and accounts with a history of errors. When items are examined individually, they are not part of the sampling results. There is, therefore, no sampling risk associated with these items (AU 350.21).

Step 3—Choose an Audit Sampling Technique

Initially the auditor must determine whether a nonstatistical or statistical sampling approach should be employed. When it is decided that a statistical approach should be used, there are many different types of statistical sampling techniques that can be employed for substantive tests. A variety of statistical sampling techniques are used in practice (AU 350.45–.46).

Step 4—Determine the Sample Size

The auditor must use professional judgment to determine the sample size. The decision process for determining the sample size is the same for nonstatistical sampling as it is for statistical sampling. In statistical sampling the auditor will quantify the relevant factors, whereas in nonstatistical sampling the factors will be described in a less structured manner (AU 350.16).

The audit decision process for determining the sample size as described in SAS-39 is summarized in Exhibit II (AU 350.16).

Step 4a—Consider Variations within the Population

A basic concept in statistical sampling is the need to obtain a representative sample from the population. If the population is composed of various items, the auditor must examine a sufficiently large sample to be reasonably assured that a representative sample has been selected (AU 350.22).

For accounting populations, the variation within a population may be expressed in dollar amounts. It is not unusual for an accounting population to be composed of a few large balances, several medium balances, and numerous smaller balances. The required sample size increases as the variation in the population increases (AU 350.22).

When a classical variable statistical sampling technique is employed, the variation in the population is measured by computing the estimate of the standard deviation of the sample mean. When nonstatistical sampling is employed, the auditor may review the population or prior years' workpapers to acquire an understanding of the variation within the population (AU 350.22).

It usually is necessary to stratify the population when a classical statistical sampling technique is used. Stratification simply means that the population is divided into groups (strata) of sampling units that have the same or approximately the same dollar values, and samples are selected from each group. Stratification is necessary to reduce the effect of the variation in the population. When PPS sampling is used, there is no need to consider the variation within the population because this technique automatically considers that factor (AU 350.22).

EXHIBIT II

Audit Judgment Factors Used to Determine Sample Size for Substantive Tests

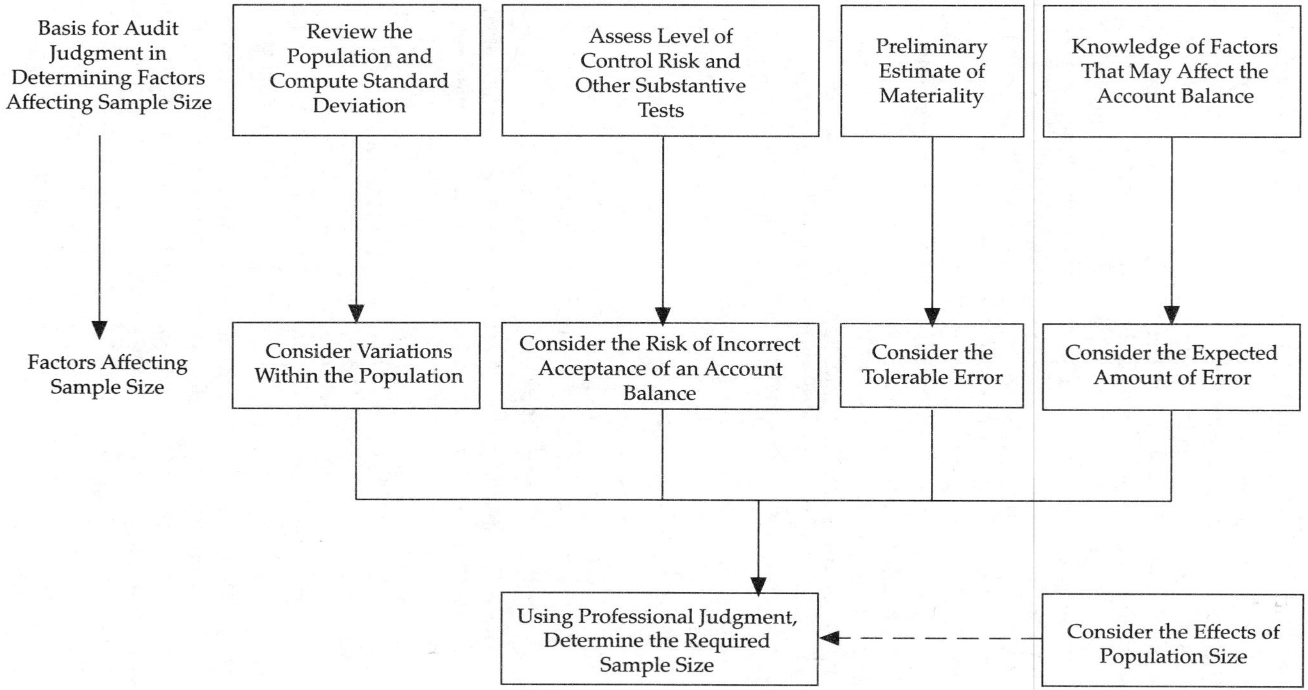

Step 4b—Consider the Acceptable Level of Risk

When considering whether to accept or reject the results of a sample, the auditor is faced with the risks of (1) incorrect rejection of a balance and (2) incorrect acceptance of a balance. The risk of incorrect rejection of a balance is the risk that the results of a sample will lead the auditor to conclude that the recorded account balance is materially misstated when, in fact, the recorded account balance is not materially misstated. The risk of incorrect acceptance of a balance is the risk that the results of a sample will lead the auditor to conclude that the recorded account balance is not materially misstated when, in fact, the recorded account balance is materially misstated (AU 350.19).

In determining an acceptable level of risk of incorrect acceptance for substantive tests of details, the auditor should consider (1) inherent risk, (2) control risk, and (3) the risk that other relevant substantive tests (including analytical procedures) would not detect a material misstatement. These relationships are illustrated in an appendix to SAS-39 in the following manner (AU 350.48):

$$TD = AR/(IR \times CR \times AP)$$

where AR = The allowable audit risk that monetary misstatements equal to tolerable misstatement might remain undetected for the account balance or class of transactions and related assertions after the auditor has completed all audit procedures deemed necessary.

IR = The susceptibility of an assertion to a material misstatement assuming there are no related internal controls.

CR = The risk that a material misstatement that could occur in an assertion will not be prevented or detected on a timely basis by the entity's internal controls. (The auditor may assess control risk at the maximum, or assess control risk below the maximum on the basis of the sufficiency of evidential matter obtained to support the effectiveness of internal controls.)

AP = The risk that analytical procedures and other relevant substantive tests would fail to detect misstatements that could occur in an assertion equal to tolerable misstatement, given that such misstatements occur and are not detected by the internal control.

TD = The allowable risk of incorrect acceptance for the substantive test of details, given that misstatements equal to tolerable misstatement occur in an assertion and are not detected by internal control or analytical procedures and other relevant substantive tests.

The above equation emphasizes relationships between the various factors that must be considered when determining the allowable risk of incorrect acceptance. For example, as control risk rises, the allowable risk of incorrect acceptance must decrease to achieve a stated level of audit risk. That quantitative relationship is based on the simple logic that as the perceived effectiveness of internal control decreases the auditor is less willing to establish a high allowable risk of incorrect acceptance of an account balance. Stated in terms of its effect on sample size, it is necessary to increase the size of the sample as control risk increases to reduce the level of risk of incorrect acceptance. Thus, from the perspective of sample size and all other factors remaining constant, there is an inverse relationship between control risk and the allowable risk of incorrect acceptance (AU 350.48).

While the relationships established in the above equation are intuitive, it is unlikely that an auditor would assign an absolute value to audit risk, but rather would evaluate the risk in an abstract manner. Even when statistical sampling is employed, most auditors would use the relationships established by the equation as a guide and would avoid a strict and comprehensive quantitative approach by simply "plugging in" risk factors. Even if an auditor insists on a strictly quantitative approach, that does not imply that judgment has been removed from the process. In the latter circumstance, the process may appear to be unbiased, but as discussed in this chapter, the risk factors are based on a number of decisions that depend heavily on professional judgment (AU 350.48).

Step 4c—Consider the Tolerable Misstatement

The tolerable misstatement is an estimate of the maximum monetary misstatement that may exist in an account balance or group of transactions when combined with misstatement in other accounts, without causing the financial statements to be materially misstated. The tolerable misstatement is based on the auditor's definition of *materiality*, or the maximum amount by which the financial statements could be misstated and still be in accordance with generally accepted accounting principles. There is an inverse relationship between the tolerable misstatement and the required sample size. Thus, the sample size must be increased when the tolerable misstatement is decreased (AU 350.18).

Step 4d—Consider the Expected Amount of Misstatement

An estimate of the expected amount of misstatement in a particular account balance or group of transactions is based on the following factors:

- Understanding of the entity's business
- Prior years' tests of the population
- Results of a pre-audit sample
- Results of tests of controls

The required sample size increases as the auditor's estimate of the expected amount of misstatement in the population increases.

An expected amount of misstatement in the population must be made when the auditor employs PPS sampling.

Step 4e—Consider the Population Size

The population size may have an effect on the sample size depending on which sampling technique is employed by the auditor.

Step 5—Determine the Method of Selecting the Sample

Sampling units must be selected from the defined population in such a way that each sampling unit has a known chance of being selected. The auditor's objective is to select a representative sample of all items from the population (AU 350.24).

Step 6—Perform the Sampling Plan

Once the sample has been selected, the auditor should apply appropriate audit procedures. If the auditor is unable to perform an audit procedure on a sampling unit selected for examination, alternative audit procedures should be considered. If the sampling unit does not have an effect on the conclusion reached by the auditor concerning the acceptability of the population, alternative audit procedures do not have to be applied, and the sampling unit may be treated as an misstatement for evaluation purposes. In addition, the auditor should determine whether the inability to apply an audit procedure has an effect on the assessed level of control risk or the assessment of risk on representations made by the client (AU 350.25).

Step 7—Evaluate the Sample Results

After the sample units have been tested, the sample results should be evaluated to determine whether the account balance or group of transactions is correct and in accordance with generally accepted accounting principles (AU 350.26–.30).

Step 7a—Project the Misstatement to the Population and Consider Sampling Risk

The misstatements discovered in the sampling units should be projected to the total population. In its simplest form, a $2,000 misstatement in a sample that represents 20% of the population would be projected as a total misstatement of $10,000 ($2,000/20%). The method of projecting the misstatement to the total population will depend on the type of sampling technique used by the auditor (AU 350.26).

If the projected misstatement is greater than the tolerable misstatement, the account balance cannot be accepted as correct. If the projected misstatement is significantly less than the tolerable misstatement, the auditor may conclude that the account balance is not materially misstated. As the projected misstatement approaches the tolerable misstatement, the risk of accepting an incorrect balance increases, and the auditor must use professional judgment in deciding whether to accept a balance as correct (AU 350.26).

Step 7b—Consider the Qualitative Aspects of Misstatements and Reach an Overall Conclusion

Each misstatement discovered by testing the sample should be evaluated to determine why the misstatement was made and whether the misstatement has an effect on other phases of the engagement. For example, the discovery of an irregularity would have broader implication to the auditor than the discovery of a routine misstatement (AU 350.27).

The results of the substantive tests may suggest that the assessed level of control risk was too low. Such a condition would require the auditor to consider whether substantive tests should be expanded (AU 350.28).

Step 8—Document the Sampling Procedures

To satisfy the requirements of SAS-41, the following matters should be considered for documentation in the auditor's workpapers:

- Description of audit procedures and objectives tested
- Definition of population and sampling unit
- Definition of a misstatement
- Basis for establishment of risk of incorrect acceptance, incorrect rejection, tolerable misstatement, and expected misstatement
- Audit sampling technique used
- Method of sampling selection
- Description of sampling procedures performed and list of misstatements discovered
- Evaluation of sample and summary of overall conclusions

COMPLETING THE AUDIT

CONTENTS

Overview	10.03
Audit Procedures for Completing the Audit	10.04
Performing Overall Analytical Procedures	10.05
Performing Procedures to Identify Litigation, Claims, and Assessments	10.05
Performing Procedures to Identify Subsequent Events	10.10
Obtaining the Representation Letter	10.12
Evaluating Audit Findings	10.15
Responsibilities for Information Included with the Financial Statements	10.17
Required Supplementary Information	10.17
Required Supplementary Oil and Gas Reserve Information	10.19
Information Outside the Financial Statements	10.21
Post-Audit Responsibilities	10.22
Information About the Appropriateness of the Auditor's Report	10.22
Omitted Audit Procedures	10.23
Communication with Audit Committees	10.24

COMPLETING THE AUDIT

Overview

A number of procedures are performed or extended by the auditor until the date of the audit report, and they are an important part of completing the audit. Completing an audit also involves evaluating the overall results of all of the audit procedures performed. These procedures and considerations are significant to the outcome of the audit and to determining the nature of the auditor's report. The following Statements on Auditing Standards and their related interpretations are discussed in this chapter in the sequence in which they appear below:

- SAS-56 (Analytical Procedures)
- SAS-12 (Inquiry of a Client's Lawyer Concerning Litigation, Claims, and Assessments)
- SAS-19 (Client Representations)
- SAS-47 (Audit Risk and Materiality in Conducting an Audit)
- SAS-52 (Omnibus Statement on Auditing Standards—1987)
- SAS-8 (Other Information in Documents Containing Audited Financial Statements)
- SAS-29 (Reporting on Information Accompanying the Basic Financial Statements in Auditor-Submitted Documents)
- SAS-1 (Codification of Auditing Standards and Procedures)
- SAS-46 (Consideration of Omitted Procedures After the Report Date)
- SAS-61 (Communication with Audit Committees)

SAS-56 describes how analytical procedures are used in an audit. It requires the use of analytical procedures in the planning stage of the audit and, near the end of the audit, in the overall review stage (AU 329).

SAS-12 provides guidance on the audit procedures designed to obtain information about litigation, claims, and assessments. The major part of this information is obtained from the letters of inquiry of the client's lawyer, which should be obtained or updated near the end of fieldwork (AU 337).

SAS-19 requires the auditor to obtain a representation letter from members of management who the auditor believes are responsible for and knowledgeable about the matters contained in the letter. Because the auditor is concerned about events occurring through the date of the audit report, the representation letter should be dated as of that date (AU 333).

SAS-47 provides guidance on the auditor's consideration of audit risk and materiality in planning and performing an audit. The standard also requires the auditor to evaluate audit findings by accumulating uncorrected known and likely misstatements to make an overall conclusion about whether the financial statements are fairly presented (AU 312).

SAS-52 describes procedures that should be adopted when a client presents supplementary information required by either the Financial Accounting Standards Board (FASB) or the Governmental Accounting Standards Board (GASB) (AU 558).

SAS-8 establishes guidance about the auditor's responsibility when information that is not part of the basic financial statements is included in a client-prepared document (AU 550).

SAS-29 provides guidance about the auditor's responsibility when information that is not part of the basic financial statements is included in an auditor-submitted document (AU 551).

SAS-1 describes the procedures that should be followed when the auditor subsequently discovers that a previously issued audit report may not have been appropriate (AU 561).

SAS-46 establishes procedures that should be followed when the auditor subsequently concludes that necessary audit procedures were not performed (AU 390).

SAS-61 concludes that certain matters not specifically addressed by other Statements on Auditing Standards should be evaluated for possible communication to the audit committee (AU 380).

AUDIT PROCEDURES FOR COMPLETING THE AUDIT

The auditor's opinion on the financial statements is based on all of the evidence gathered through the last day of fieldwork and any other information that comes to the auditor's attention up to the time the report is issued. Because of their nature, certain audit procedures cannot be completed until near the end of the audit, including:

- Performing overall analytical procedures
- Performing procedures to identify litigation, claims, and assessments
- Performing procedures to identify subsequent events
- Obtaining the representation letter

Performing Overall Analytical Procedures

According to SAS-56, analytical procedures are a required part of the overall review of the audit. At this stage, the objective of the procedures is to assess whether the financial statements appear to warrant the anticipated audit opinion. An approach to the overall review is described below (AU 329.22).

- Evaluate the adequacy of the data collected in response to unusual or unexpected balances identified as a part of the preliminary analysis.
- Identify any other unusual or unexpected balances not previously identified.

When the overall review identifies unusual or unexpected balances not addressed during other phases of the engagement, an auditor must determine whether additional inquiries or procedures should be performed before issuing the opinion on the financial statements (AU 329.22).

> **OBSERVATION:** *Overall analytical procedures may be documented in the working papers merely by signing off one or more audit program steps. The individual performing the procedures also may write a short memo describing any unusual items not adequately addressed and any additional procedures that were performed to investigate these items.*

Performing Procedures to Identify Litigation, Claims, and Assessments

SAS-12 provides guidance for the collection of evidential matter to determine whether litigation, claims, and assessments have been properly reflected in the financial statements in accordance with generally accepted accounting principles (GAAP). Financial reporting standards with respect to litigation, claims, and assessments were established by FAS-5 (Accounting for Contingencies). FAS-5 requires that a loss contingency be accrued if (1) information available before the issuance of the financial statements indicates that it is *probable* that an asset had been impaired or a liability incurred at the date of the financial statements and (2) the amount of loss can be reasonably estimated. If these two conditions are not both met but there is a *reasonable possibility* that a loss or an additional loss may be incurred, the loss contingency must be disclosed in the financial statements, usually in a note (AU 337B).

Although the point is not explicitly stated, SAS-12 recognizes that the auditor lacks the expertise to evaluate litigation, claims, and assessments in the context of the financial reporting requirements established by FAS-5. For this reason, the auditor must rely a great deal on the client's lawyer. The auditor's responsibility is to collect evidential matter (1) to identify circumstances that may result in a loss contingency, (2) to identify the period in which the event occurred that may lead to the loss contingency, (3) to support the probability of the loss, and (4) to support the estimated amount of the loss or the estimated range of the loss. To achieve these audit objectives, the following audit procedures should be employed (AU 337.04–.06):

- Discuss with the client the procedures used to identify and evaluate litigation, claims, and assessments.

- Obtain a list and evaluation of litigation, claims, and assessments from the client.

- Obtain a representation from the client, preferably in writing, that FAS-5 requirements have been observed with respect to litigation, claims, and assessments.

- Examine documents relative to legal liability matters, including correspondence and invoices from lawyers.

- Obtain from the client a statement in writing that the client has disclosed unasserted claims that the lawyer believes will probably be asserted.

- After obtaining permission from the client, notify the client's lawyer that the client has made the assurances described immediately above. Notification may be in the form of a separate letter or as part of the letter of audit inquiry.

- Ask the client to send letters of inquiry to lawyers who have been consulted concerning legal matters.

> **OBSERVATION:** *An Auditing Interpretation entitled "Client Has Not Consulted Lawyer" (June 1983) states that SAS-12 is expressly limited to inquiries of lawyers with whom management has consulted. If the client has not consulted a lawyer during the period, the auditor should rely on (1) the review of internal information available and (2) written representations from management stating it had not consulted a lawyer about litigation, claims, and assessments (AU 9337.15–.17).*

- Read minutes of meetings of stockholders, board of directors, and other executive committees.
- Read contracts, loan agreements, leases, and correspondence from taxing authorities.
- Obtain information from banks concerning loan agreements.
- Review other documents for possible guarantees made by the client.

> **OBSERVATION:** *An Auditing Interpretation of SAS-12, "Documents Subject to Lawyer–Client Privilege" (March 1977), states that it is not necessary for the auditor to examine documents held by the client that are subject to the lawyer–client privilege (AU 9337.08–.09).*

Representations made by the client with respect to litigation, claims, and assessments must be substantiated by letters of audit inquiry to the client's lawyers. Letters of audit inquiry should be sent to those lawyers who have the primary responsibility for and knowledge about particular litigation, claims, and assessments. In some circumstances the client's in-house counsel will be the recipient of the letter and may provide the auditor with the necessary corroboration concerning litigation, claims, and assessments. A letter of audit inquiry typically would include, but is not limited to, the following matters (AU 337.08–.09):

1. Identification of the client and the date
2. A list that describes and evaluates pending and threatened litigation, claims, and assessments, prepared by management or legal counsel
3. A list prepared by management that describes and evaluates unasserted claims

4. A request that the lawyer reply directly to the independent auditor if his or her views differ from management regarding Item 2 above

5. A statement that the client understands that whenever its lawyer has formed a professional conclusion concerning a possible claim or assessment, the lawyer has so advised the client and has consulted with the client concerning the question of disclosure provided for by GAAP

6. A request that the lawyer confirm Item 5 above

7. A request that the lawyer identify the nature of and reasons for any limitation in his or her response

Under special circumstances, representations made by the lawyer may be made orally. For example, the details and accounting implications of complex litigation may best be evaluated in a conference attended by the client, the lawyer, and the auditor (AU 337.10).

> **OBSERVATION:** *Another Interpretation of SAS-12, "Specifying Relevant Date in an Audit Inquiry Letter" (March 1977), states that the audit inquiry letter to a client's attorney should specify (1) the earliest acceptable effective date of the attorney's response and (2) the latest date for return to the auditor. A two-week period between the dates is recommended. If the attorney does not specify an effective date of the response, the effective date is assumed to be the date of the response (AU 9337.01–.03).*
> *A third Interpretation, "Relationship Between Date of Lawyer's Response and Auditor's Report" (March 1977), recommends that the effective date requested in a letter to the client's attorney be as close as possible to the date of the auditor's report (AU 9337.04–.05).*

> **OBSERVATION:** *The Interpretation of SAS-12 entitled "Use of Explanatory Language About the Attorney–Client Privilege or the Attorney Work-Product Privilege" (February 1990) notes that some clients state in their letter of audit inquiry that the letter is not intended to infringe on the attorney–client privilege or the attorney work-product privilege. Likewise, the response to the letter by legal counsel may state that counsel has been advised by the client that the request for information is not intended to waive the privileged relationship with the client. Such comments in the client letter of audit inquiry or counsel's response to the letter do not result in a limitation of the scope of an audit (AU 9337.28–.30).*

Under some circumstances a lawyer may not respond to the auditor's letter of audit inquiry. If the lawyer decides not to respond, there is a scope limitation and a qualified opinion or a disclaimer of opinion should be issued. When the lawyer cannot reasonably respond to the letter because of significant uncertainties surrounding the possible outcome of a certain legal matter, there is an uncertainty, and the auditor's report should be so modified (AU 337.13).

> **OBSERVATION:** *The Interpretation of SAS-12 entitled "Assessment of a Lawyer's Evaluation of the Outcome of Litigation" (June 1983) states that when the auditor is uncertain about the meaning of the lawyer's evaluation of litigation, claims, or assessments, he or she should request clarification either in a follow-up letter or in a conference with the client and lawyer. The clarification should be adequately documented in the auditor's workpapers (AU 9337.18–.23).*

> **OBSERVATION:** *There is an obvious difference between the role of the auditor and that of the lawyer with respect to disclosures of legal problems in the financial statements. In 1975, the Board of Governors of the American Bar Association approved a Policy Statement that presumably requires lawyers to respond to the letter of audit inquiry in a manner consistent with the philosophy of FAS-5. However, a review of the ABA's Policy Statement reveals that there are significant differences in the definition of terms associated with loss contingencies. For example, FAS-5 defines* **probable** *as "the future event or events that are likely to occur"; the ABA Policy Statement defines the term as "an unfavorable outcome for the client is probable if the prospects of the claimant not succeeding are judged to be extremely doubtful and the prospects for success by the client in the deference are judged to be slight." Even more important than the inconsistencies in definitions in the two documents is the tone of the ABA Policy Statement, which seems to encourage the lawyer to be extremely conservative in deciding how to respond to letters of audit inquiry. For example, the Policy Statement concludes that "it is appropriate for the lawyer to provide an estimate of the amount or range of potential loss . . . only if he believes that the probability of inaccuracy of the estimate of the amount or range of potential loss is slight."*

> **OBSERVATION:** *The lawyer's response to the auditor's letter of audit inquiry should be addressed to the auditor, should apply to*

circumstances that existed from the date of the balance sheet through the auditor's report date, and should have an effective date within two or three weeks of the report date.

Performing Procedures to Identify Subsequent Events

The auditor is responsible for collecting evidential matter pertaining to events that occur subsequent to the balance sheet date. Generally, the responsibility for identifying significant subsequent events continues through the date of the auditor's report, which is the last date of fieldwork. Subsequent events may affect the financial statements in two ways. First, the event may provide the basis for an adjusting entry at the date of the balance sheet. This occurs when the subsequent event affects the valuation of any account as of the balance sheet date. For example, the settlement of a lawsuit after the balance sheet date but before the issuance of the auditor's report would provide the evidence necessary to support an adjusting entry. Second, the event may not affect the valuations at the balance sheet date, because the event is not associated with assets or liabilities that existed at the balance sheet date. For this reason, the subsequent event does not require an accrual adjustment, but it is likely to be disclosed in the financial statements. Examples of subsequent events that do not require an accrual adjustment are the issuance of additional capital stock or losses resulting from fire or flood after the balance sheet date. The second type of subsequent event is usually disclosed in a note to the financial statements. If the event is material, however, it may be more appropriate to show the effects of the subsequent event in the form of pro forma financial statements supplementary to the financial statements. The pro forma statement is presented as if the subsequent event had occurred on the last day of the period being audited (AU 560.01–.06).

> **OBSERVATION:** *It is sometimes difficult to classify a subsequent event, because usually there is an informational lag period between the date the auditor becomes aware of the event and the actual identification of the economic event that affects the valuation of an account. For example, during the subsequent-event period, a competitor may announce a new product that may place a client's product at a significant disadvantage and probably require an inventory writedown. Although the product announcement occurred after the balance sheet date, it is likely that the technological breakthrough occurred on or before the balance sheet date. Of*

course, it becomes a little speculative to try to pinpoint the economic event, because the client and the auditor probably have limited information. For this reason, SAS-1 concludes that subsequent events that affect the realization of receivables and inventories and the settlement of estimated liabilities generally will require an adjustment to the financial statements (AU 560.07).

Audit procedures must be employed to obtain evidential matter associated with all subsequent events. These audit procedures may be classified as those associated with other phases of the audit engagement and those specifically designed to identify subsequent events. In many parts of the engagement, audit procedures are designed to determine whether an account is presented in accordance with GAAP by reviewing subsequent events. For example, cash collected on account subsequent to the balance sheet date is associated with subsequent events, but it provides evidence to support the collectibility of accounts receivable as of the balance sheet date. However, SAS-1 identifies the following audit procedures that should be performed to specifically identify possible subsequent events that may require an accrual adjustment or disclosure in the financial statements (AU 560.10–.12):

- Read the latest available interim financial statements.

- Inquire of and discuss with members of management who have financial accounting responsibility whether:

  — Any material contingent liabilities or commitments existed at the date of the balance sheet or shortly thereafter.

  — Any significant change in owners' equity, long-term debt, or working capital has occurred since the balance sheet date.

  — Any material adjustments have been made during the subsequent period.

- Inquire of and discuss with members of management who have financial accounting responsibility the status of items that were accounted for in the financial statements on the basis of tentative or preliminary data.

- Read the available minutes of stockholders, directors, and other committee meetings during the subsequent period.

- Obtain from client's legal counsel a description and evaluation of any impending litigation, claims, and contingent liabilities.

- Obtain a letter of representation from management (usually the chief financial officer) regarding any events occurring during the subsequent period that require adjustment to or disclosure in the financial statements.
- Follow any other procedures that are deemed appropriate depending on the results of the procedures described above.

> **OBSERVATION:** *SAS-58 (Reports on Audited Financial Statements) states that a note on a subsequent event that contains unaudited information, pro forma calculations, or other similar disclosures should not be labeled as unaudited (AU 508.46).*

Obtaining the Representation Letter

During the course of an engagement, the client's personnel make a variety of oral representations in response to questions raised by the auditor. SAS-19 requires that written representations be obtained from the client to confirm oral representations and to reduce the likelihood of misunderstandings between the client and the auditor. Most representations should be supported by corroborating evidential matter. In some instances, however, it may not be possible to substantiate a representation by management because of the nature of the representation. In these cases, SAS-19 states that it is acceptable to rely on the client representation unless there is evidence that contradicts such representation (AU 333.02).

Although there is no comprehensive list of items that must be included in a client representation letter, SAS-19 identifies the following items that should ordinarily be included (AU 333.04):

- Management's statement of responsibility for the financial statements
- Availability of all records, including minutes of directors and other meetings
- Statement that there are no significant misstatements in the statements and no unrecorded transactions
- Related party disclosures
- Client's noncompliance with any contracts
- Subsequent events

- Irregularities
- Various restrictive covenants
- Noncompliance with reporting requirements of regulatory agencies
- Various plans and intentions that affect amounts on the balance sheet
- Inventory representations regarding obsolete items
- Losses from sales commitments
- Title to assets, liens, or pledges as collateral
- Repurchase agreements
- Losses from purchase commitments
- Illegal acts and related loss contingencies
- Other liabilities and gain or loss contingencies
- Unasserted claims or assessments that counsel feels are likely to be asserted
- Various options, agreements, and restrictions on capital stock
- Statement that the representations in the letter pertain to consolidated financial statements and, if applicable, to separate financial statements of the parent company

Materiality, where the items can be quantified, should be used to determine which items should be included in the client representation letter (AU 333.05).

> **OBSERVATION:** *An Auditing Interpretation of SAS-12, "Client Has Not Consulted Lawyer" (June 1983), states that when a client has not consulted outside legal counsel concerning litigation, claims, and assessments, the auditor usually will rely on internal documentation and representations made by management. In this event, the* **client's representation** *may read as follows (AU 9337.15–.17):*
>
> > *We are not aware of any impending or threatened litigation, claims, or assessments, or unasserted claims or assessments, that are required to be accrued or disclosed in the financial statements in accordance with FAS-5. We have not consulted a lawyer concerning litigation, claims, or assessments.*

> **OBSERVATION:** *An Auditing Interpretation on evidential matter entitled "The Effect of an Inability to Obtain Evidential Matter Relating to Income Tax Accruals" (March 1981) requires the auditor to disclaim an opinion on the financial statements if the client limits the auditor's access to (1) tax accrual documentation and (2) the appropriate client personnel responsible for the tax calculations. The auditor must exercise professional judgment and expertise in obtaining and examining tax accrual information and cannot rely solely on the opinion of the client's outside or in-house legal or tax counsel (AU 9326.06–.10).*

The representation letter should be signed by client personnel who are responsible for and knowledgeable about the items enumerated in the letter. Generally, the chief executive officer and chief financial officer should sign the letter. To cover subsequent events, the letter should be dated as of the date of the auditor's report. If the client refuses to make representations in writing, there is a scope limitation, and a qualified opinion or disclaimer of opinion should be expressed (AU 333.09 and 333.11).

> **OBSERVATION:** *Management may not understand the technical terminology that is used in the illustrative representation letter included in SAS-19. Therefore, it is often effective for the auditor to either modify the terminology used or thoroughly discuss the letter with management.*

> **OBSERVATION:** *An Auditing Interpretation of SAS-19, "Management Representations when Current Management Was Not Present During the Period Under Audit" (October 1995), concludes that a representation letter should be obtained for all periods covered by the audit report. However, if current management is unable or unwilling to sign the representation letter for all periods covered, a scope limitation exists and the auditor should use AU 333.11 for guidance (AU 9333.05-.06).*

> **OBSERVATION:** *An Auditing Interpretation of SAS-19, "Management Representations on Violations and Possible Violations of Laws and Regulations" (March 1979), states that the auditor's request for written representations from management on significant violations or possible violations of laws and regulations*

need not include matters beyond those described in FAS-5 (AU 9333.01–.04).

EVALUATING AUDIT FINDINGS

The purpose of evaluating audit findings is to consider whether the results of all of the audit procedures performed support the position that the financial statements are fairly presented in accordance with generally accepted accounting principles. To issue an unqualified audit opinion, the auditor must conclude that there is a low risk that the financial statements are materially misstated. This evaluation may be completed using a workpaper on which aggregate misstatements are accumulated. The following two types of misstatements should be accumulated (AU 312.27–.28):

> *Known misstatements*—Actual misstatements found in performing audit procedures that are not corrected by the client. These are often accumulated on an "Adjusting Entries" workpaper.

> *Likely misstatements*—Estimated misstatements based on the results of the audit procedures. For example, if confirmation of accounts receivable is performed using audit sampling, the likely misstatement of the account is the amount of projected misstatement from the sample.

> **OBSERVATION:** *One likely source of misstatements is accounting estimates. For example, if the auditor believes that management's estimate of the allowance for uncollectible accounts receivable is understated and management will not adjust the estimate, the amount of estimated understatement is a likely misstatement that should be accumulated (AU 312.29).*

The workpaper used to accumulate misstatements usually has multiple columns used to accumulate the effect of the misstatements on key financial statement amounts, such as net income before taxes, total assets, total liabilities, and owners' equity. This allows the auditor to evaluate the effects of the misstatements on the separate financial statement amounts. An amount that is immaterial to total assets may be material to net income before taxes. An example of such a workpaper follows.

Financial Statement Effect

Overstatement/(Understatement)

W/P ref.	Description	Current Assets	Total Assets	Current Liabilities	Total Liabilities	Owners' Equity	Net Income (before taxes)
D-8	Error in prepaid expenses	$ 12,300	$ 12,300			$ 12,300	$ 12,300
F-6	Error—prior year's depreciation		(10,000)			(10,000)	
M-3	Unrecorded liabilities			$ (16,230)	$ (16,230)	16,230	16,230
C-6	Projected misstatement of accounts receivable	21,000	21,000			21,000	21,000
	Total known and likely misstatement	$ 33,300	$ 23,300	$ (16,230)	$ (16,230)	$ 39,530	$ 49,530
	Materiality	$ 200,000	$ 350,000	$ 200,000	$ 350,000	$ 400,000	$ 150,000

The amounts that the auditor considers material to each financial statement amount often are shown at the bottom of the schedule to facilitate comparison to the accumulated misstatement amounts. This comparison allows the auditor to evaluate the risk of material misstatement of the financial statements. If the amount of accumulated misstatement is not significantly less than the amounts considered to be material, the auditor generally will conclude that the risk of material misstatement is too high to issue an unqualified opinion on the financial statements.

> *OBSERVATION: The auditor must consider prior years' misstatements that have an effect on the current year's financial statements when determining whether the current year's financial statements are misstated.*

> *OBSERVATION: Many CPA firms have established rules of thumb regarding the relationship between materiality and accumulated misstatements. Generally, these rules indicate that audit findings are acceptable if the accumulated misstatement amount is less than 1/3 to 1/2 of the amount considered to be material.*

If the auditor concludes that the accumulated misstatement is too high in relation to materiality, the risk of material misstatement must be reduced. This can be accomplished by adjusting the financial statements for known misstatements or by obtaining additional evidence about accounts with likely misstatements. For example, if the auditor has a large projected misstatement from confirmation of a sample of accounts receivable, this likely misstatement may be reduced by (1) correcting the accounts for the actual misstatements found in the sample or (2) performing additional tests of accounts receivable to determine whether the projected misstatement actually exists (AU 312.31–.32).

RESPONSIBILITIES FOR INFORMATION INCLUDED WITH THE FINANCIAL STATEMENTS

Documents that contain audited financial statements may also contain other types of information. In completing the audit of the financial statements, the auditor must fulfill certain responsibilities regarding this information. These responsibilities vary depending on the nature of the information and the type of document.

Required Supplementary Information

The FASB and GASB have the authority to promulgate accounting and reporting standards, including required supplementary information. Although required supplementary information is not part of the basic financial statements, the information must be disclosed by certain entities designated by the FASB or GASB. The required supplementary information is considered to be an essential part of the financial report for the designated entities. This information does not have to be audited; however, certain limited procedures established by SAS-52 must be applied (AU 558.01).

> *OBSERVATION: The auditor also may be required to perform certain procedures on information as prescribed by the AICPA in an Audit Guide. For example, the Audit and Accounting Guide entitled* **Common Interest Realty Associations** *requires presentation of unaudited supplementary information about the funding of future major repairs and replacements of common property by these types of entities. It also sets forth procedures to be performed on this information by the auditor.*

> *OBSERVATION: SAS-52 is* **not** *applicable when the engagement includes the audit of the required supplementary information (AU 558.02).*

The auditor should apply the following procedures to supplementary information that an entity is required to include in its financial report (AU 558.07):

- Confirm that the required supplementary information is required by the FASB or GASB.
- Make inquiries of management concerning the methods used to prepare the required supplementary information, such as the following:

  — Is the information measured and presented as required?

  — Have measurement methods and presentation formats changed from those used in the previous year?

  — What are the significant assumptions or interpretations used to measure or present the information?

- Determine the required supplementary information's consistency with:

  — Answers to the inquiries received from management.

  — Audited financial statements.

  — Knowledge obtained as part of the audit of the financial statements.

- Determine whether written representations about the required supplementary information should be obtained from management.
- Apply other procedures, if any, that have been specified by other SAS, SAS Interpretations, Audit and Accounting Guides, or Statements of Position.
- Make additional inquiries if the application of procedures listed above raises questions about the measurement or presentation of the required supplementary information.

> **OBSERVATION:** *The reporting requirements applicable to required supplementary information are discussed in the chapter entitled "Auditor's Reports."*

When an entity *voluntarily* includes supplementary information that is required for other entities, the procedures established by

SAS-52 must be observed except in the following circumstances (AU 558.03):

- The entity has indicated in the financial report that the auditor has not applied limited procedures to the supplementary information.
- The auditor's report includes an explanatory paragraph that disclaims an opinion on the supplementary information. The explanatory paragraph would read as follows:

The [identify the supplementary information] on page X [or in Note X] is not a required part of the basic financial statements, and we did not audit or apply limited procedures to such information and do not express any assurance on such information.

If the auditor does not apply the limited procedures as required by SAS-52 to the voluntary presentation of the supplementary information, the standards established by SAS-8 must be observed (AU 558.03).

Required Supplementary Oil and Gas Reserve Information

FAS-19 (Financial Accounting and Reporting by Oil and Gas Producing Companies), as amended by FAS-25 (Suspension of Certain Accounting Requirements for Oil and Gas Producing Companies), requires that certain disclosures concerning oil and gas reserves and changes in the reserves be disclosed as information supplementary to the financial statements. This supplementary information is subject to the basic audit procedures established by SAS-52 and to the additional audit procedures established by SAS-45 (now found at AU 9558.01–.06), as follows:

- Determine the client's understanding of these factors:
  - Data used to compute reserve quantity information—The auditor should make inquiries of management concerning reserve quantity information, which includes (1) quantities

of proved oil and gas reserves owned net of interests of others, (2) reserves that are attributable to consolidated subsidiaries, (3) reserves that are attributable to investees (on a proportional basis), and (4) reserves related to royalty interests owned.

— Separate disclosure of sources of reserves—The auditor should make inquiries of management concerning separate disclosures such as (1) share of oil and gas produced from royalty interests for which reserve quantity information is not available, (2) reserves related to agreements with governments or authorities where the entity participates in the operations or serves as producer, (3) reserves that are attributable to investees (on a proportional basis), (4) information that may affect reserve quantities such as subsequent events or significant uncertainties, (5) whether reserves are located in entity's home country, and (6) disclosure that certain governments restrict the disclosure of reserve information or require that the information include other than proved reserves.

— Factors used to compute the standardized measure of discounted future net cash flows—The auditor should make inquiries of management concerning such factors.

- Determine if the client personnel who estimated reserves are appropriately qualified. (For example, the Society of Petroleum Engineers has prepared "Standards Pertaining to the Estimation and Auditing of Oil and Gas Reserve Information," which indicates the normal qualifications of a reserve estimator.)

- Compare recent production with reserve estimates for properties that have significant production or significant reserve quantities, and inquire about disproportionate ratios.

- Compare reserve information for supplementary information to information used to compute depletion and amortization, and investigate any differences.

- Inquire about methods and bases used to compute reserve information and whether they are documented and current.

- Inquire about methods used to calculate the standardized measure of discounted future net cash flows.

When the auditor is not certain that the oil and gas reserve information is presented in accordance with established guidelines, a paragraph similar to the following should be added to the auditor's report.

The oil and gas reserve information is not a required part of the basic financial statements, and we did not audit and do not express an opinion on such information. However, we have applied certain limited procedures prescribed by professional standards that raised doubts that we were unable to resolve regarding whether material modifications should be made to the information for it to conform with guidelines established by the Financial Accounting Standards Board.

The auditor may expand the above paragraph to include the reasons that led to the questions about the presentation of the reserve information.

Information Outside the Financial Statements

An entity may present a variety of information that is outside the financial statements in a document that also contains the financial statements. For example, an annual report may include both the financial statements and other information. The auditor does not have a responsibility to audit information presented outside the financial statements, but certain professional standards do apply, depending on the nature of the information and the document that contains the financial statements.

When information is presented outside the financial statements and the financial statements are included in a client-prepared document, the standards established by SAS-8 must be followed. When information is presented outside the financial statements and the financial statements are included in an auditor-submitted document, the standards established by SAS-29 must be followed. SAS-8 and SAS-29 are discussed in the chapter entitled "Auditor's Reports" (AU 550 and AU 551).

> **OBSERVATION:** *A document containing financial statements that has merely been reproduced by an auditor on the client's behalf is a client-prepared document.*

POST-AUDIT RESPONSIBILITIES

Information About the Appropriateness of the Auditor's Report

Usually, an auditor has no obligation to make continuing inquiries after the date of issuance of the report. If, however, an auditor becomes aware (1) of material information that would have affected the report and (2) that persons are currently relying, or are likely to rely, on the financial statements covered by the report, the auditor must take the following actions (AU 561.01–.06):

- The auditor should advise the client to immediately disclose the new information and its effect on the financial statements to persons currently relying, or likely to rely, on the financial statements.
- The auditor should issue revised financial statements and a new report as soon as practical, describing the reasons for revision.
- If financial statements, accompanied by an auditor's report for a subsequent period, are to be imminently issued, the auditor may make the necessary disclosures and revisions therein.
- The client should be advised to discuss the new disclosures or revisions with the SEC, stock exchanges, and appropriate regulatory agencies where applicable.
- The auditor must satisfy himself or herself that appropriate steps have been taken by the client.

If the client refuses to proceed as outlined above, the auditor should notify each member of the client's board of directors (1) that the client has refused and (2) in the absence of disclosure by the client, that the auditor will take the following additional steps to prevent further reliance on the report and the financial statements:

- Notify the client that the auditor's report must no longer be associated with the financial statements.
- Notify any regulatory agencies involved, if applicable, that the report should no longer be relied on.
- Notify persons known to be relying, or likely to rely, on the financial statements that the auditor's report should no longer be relied on.

These notifications should contain the following (AU 561.07–.08):

- A description of the effects of the newly discovered information on the auditor's report and on the financial statements
- The most precise and factual information available about the financial statement misstatement

If the client refuses to cooperate and, as a result, the auditor is unable to conduct an adequate investigation of the new information, the auditor's notifications need state only that new information has come to his or her attention and that if the new information is correct, the report should no longer be relied on or be associated with the financial statements (AU 561.09).

The auditor must carefully use professional judgment in the circumstances described above. Consultation with legal counsel usually is advisable (AU 561.02).

> *OBSERVATION: An Auditing Interpretation of SAS-1, Section 561, "Auditor Association with Subsequently Discovered Information When the Auditor Has Resigned or Been Discharged" (February 1989), concludes that the auditor's responsibility to investigate whether subsequently discovered information existed at the date of the auditor's report does not change even when the auditor has resigned or been discharged from the engagement (AU 9561.01–.02).*

Omitted Audit Procedures

SAS-46 provides guidance when the auditor concludes, subsequent to the date of the auditor's report, that one or more procedures were omitted from an engagement. This situation is different from the circumstance where the auditor, subsequent to the date of the report, discovers facts existing at the date of the auditor's report. The latter topic was discussed earlier in this chapter (AU 390.01).

> *OBSERVATION: Disclosure that procedures were omitted often comes as a result of a quality or peer review of the auditor's engagement.*

Initially, the auditor should assess the importance of the omitted audit procedure within the context of the engagement. This assessment may include a review of the workpapers and discussions with other personnel within the firm. The auditor must determine whether the third standard of fieldwork (evidential matter) was observed. If it is concluded that a significant audit procedure was omitted, and it is likely that the financial statements are being relied on or will be relied on by others, the auditor must take corrective action. If possible, the auditor should apply the omitted audit procedure or an alternative audit procedure. If the auditor is unable to apply the omitted or the alternative audit procedure, he or she should consult an attorney and discuss the appropriateness of the following actions (AU 390.02–.07):

- Notification of the client
- Notification of regulatory authorities (SEC, etc.)
- Notification of persons relying, or likely to rely, on the financial statements

The application of the omitted audit procedure or an alternative audit procedure may lead the auditor to conclude that facts did exist at the date of the report that could have had an effect on the audit approach or the auditor's report. In this circumstance, the auditor should follow the procedures discussed in the earlier section of this chapter entitled "Information About the Appropriateness of the Auditor's Report" (AU 390.06).

COMMUNICATION WITH AUDIT COMMITTEES

Another element that should be considered when a client designs its internal control system is the establishment of an audit committee. An audit committee should be composed mostly of board members who are not employees of the company. The role of the committee usually consists of nominating the independent auditor and reviewing the scope and the results of the audit. Selection of an audit committee may enhance the independence of the auditor, because the auditor can request the audit committee to encourage management to cooperate more fully, if necessary.

SAS-61 (Communication with Audit Committees) concludes that certain matters related to the audit should be communicated to those who have responsibility for oversight of the financial reporting process. The recipient of the communication will be the audit committee (or "individuals with a level of authority and responsibility equivalent to an audit committee in organizations that do not have one, such as the board of directors, the board of trustees, an owner in an owner-managed enterprise, or others who may have engaged the auditor"). Although the audit committee is to receive the communication, the auditor may also provide the information to the entity's management or others within the entity that may benefit from the communication (AU 380.01).

> **OBSERVATION:** *SAS-60, SAS-53, SAS-54, and SAS-71 (Interim Financial Information) also identify circumstances under which the auditor should communicate with the audit committee.*

The communication requirements established by SAS-61 apply to the following situations (AU 380.01):

- Engagements in which the client has established an audit committee or formally designated a group equivalent to an audit committee to have oversight responsibility with respect to the financial reporting process
- Engagements is which the client is a registrant that files periodic reports with the SEC under the Investment Company Act of 1940 or the Securities Exchange Act of 1934 (except a broker or dealer registered only because of section 15(a) of the 1934 Act).

> **OBSERVATION:** *An Auditing Interpretation of SAS-61 entitled "Applicability of Section 380" (August 1993) concludes that if the auditee's governing or oversight body has not established an audit committee or formally designated a group equivalent to an audit committee, the standards established by SAS-61 do not apply. For entities not classified in the above two categories and having a board of directors, the auditor may communicate the information required by SAS-61 to the board, but is not required to do so.*

The purpose of the communication is to provide the audit committee with additional information regarding the scope and results of the audit that may assist the audit committee in overseeing the financial reporting and disclosure process for which management is responsible. The communication with the audit committee may be written or oral. If written, the communication should indicate that it is intended only for the audit committee, board of directors, and, if appropriate, management. If the communication is oral, the matters communicated and other relevant factors related to the oral communication should be documented in the workpapers (AU 380.02–.03).

The communication with the audit committee should occur on a timely basis, either before or after the issuance of the auditor's report, depending on the circumstances (AU 380.04).

SAS-61 concludes that the following information should be communicated to the audit committee. In some cases, it may be more appropriate for management rather than the auditor to communicate some of the information; however, when the communication is made by management, the auditor must be satisfied that the communication was actually made (AU 380.05).

Topic of Communication	Nature of Communication
Auditor's responsibility under generally accepted auditing standards	• Level of assurance by the auditor with respect to engagements conducted in accordance with generally accepted auditing standards
	• The concept of reasonable assurance, including supporting concepts such as materiality and audit tests
	• Auditor's responsibility for detecting weaknesses in the control structure, errors, irregularities, and similar matters
Significant accounting policies	• Selection and application of significant accounting policies
	• Methods used to account for unusual transactions
	• Effects of significant accounting policies used to account for transactions and events when there is a lack of consensus about how the items should be accounted for and disclosed
Management judgments and estimates	• Process used to make accounting estimates
	• Auditor's basis for determining reasonableness of accounting estimates

Topic of Communication	Nature of Communication
Significant audit adjustments	• Implications of significant audit adjustments proposed and recorded • Implications of audit adjustments proposed but not recorded
Other information in documents containing audited financial statements	• Auditor's responsibility with respect to other information in documents that include the audited financial statements
Disagreements with management	• Significant disagreements with management concerning applicability of accounting principles, scope of engagement, or wording of audit report (does not include differences based on incomplete information that were later resolved)
Consultation with other accountants	• Auditor's view of management's consultation with other accountants concerning applicability of accounting principles, scope of engagement, or wording of audit report (see SAS-50)
Major issues discussed with management prior to retention	• Major issues discussed with management (such as applicability of accounting principles and audit standards) as part of the auditor retention process
Difficulties encountered in performing the audit	• Significant matters (such as availability of personnel and provision of information that impeded the audit process)

AUDITOR'S REPORTS

CONTENTS

Overview	**11.03**
Standard Auditor's Report	**11.04**
Association with Financial Statements	**11.08**
Modification of the Standard Auditor's Report	**11.09**
Accounting Conditions	**11.11**
Departure from GAAP	**11.11**
Departure from Promulgated GAAP	**11.14**
Inadequate Disclosures	**11.15**
Accounting Changes	**11.17**
Lack of Consistency	**11.17**
Retroactive Restatement	**11.18**
No Retroactive Restatement	**11.19**
FIFO to LIFO Change	**11.19**
Change in the Format of the Statement of Cash Flows	**11.19**
Accounting Changes—Segment Information	**11.20**
Changing to an Acceptable Principle	**11.21**
Correction of an Error	**11.22**
Changing to an Unacceptable Principle	**11.22**
Inappropriate Treatment of an Accounting Change	**11.23**
Lack of Reasonable Justification for Change	**11.24**
Change in Accounting Estimate	**11.25**
Change in Principle Inseparable from Estimate	**11.25**
Change in Reporting Entity	**11.26**
Change Arising from a Pooling of Interests	**11.26**
Substantially Different Transactions or Events	**11.27**
Change That May Have a Material Effect in the Future	**11.28**
Scope Conditions	**11.28**
Insufficient Competent Evidential Matter	**11.28**
Other Scope Limitations	**11.30**

Limited Reporting Engagements   **11.31**
Opinion Based on Another Auditor's Report   **11.32**
  Reporting by Successor Auditor for a Pooling of
    Interests   **11.34**
Unaudited Financial Statements—Public Companies   **11.35**
Uncertainty Conditions   **11.35**
  Uncertainties Unrelated to Going Concern   **11.35**
  Uncertainties Related to Going Concern   **11.37**
Other Conditions   **11.39**
  Emphasis of a Matter   **11.39**
  Reporting When Not Independent   **11.40**
  Other Data and Information in a Document Containing
    Audited Financial Statements   **11.41**
Required Supplementary Information   **11.42**
  Required Supplementary Information Is Omitted   **11.43**
  Deviation in Measurement or Presentation of
    Required Supplementary Information   **11.43**
  Limited Procedures Not Applied to Required
    Supplementary Information   **11.44**
  Substantial Doubt About Conformance of Required
    Supplementary Information   **11.44**
  Reporting on Fair Value Disclosures   **11.45**
  Reporting on Required Information   **11.46**
  Reporting on Required and Voluntary Information   **11.46**
  Complete Balance Sheet   **11.46**
  Incomplete Balance Sheet   **11.47**
  Reporting When Disclosures Are Not Audited   **11.47**
  Auditor-Submitted Documents   **11.48**
  Piecemeal Opinions   **11.51**
  Negative Assurance   **11.51**
Reporting on Comparative Financial Statements   **11.51**
  Updated Opinion Different from Previous Opinion   **11.53**
  Reporting by Predecessor Auditor   **11.54**
  Reporting When Predecessor Auditor Has Ceased
    Operations   **11.56**
  Special Reports   **11.62**

AUDITOR'S REPORTS

Overview

Once fieldwork is completed, the auditor is faced with the difficult task of communicating the results of the engagement to the client and third parties. Effective communication is a problem in all professions, and it should not be surprising that professional guidance for the preparation of the auditor's report is both technical in nature and voluminous in detail. The following Statements on Auditing Standards are discussed in this chapter in the sequence in which they appear below:

- SAS-58 (Reports on Audited Financial Statements)
- SAS-26 (Association with Financial Statements)
- SAS-32 (Adequacy of Disclosure of Financial Statements)
- SAS-59 (The Auditor's Consideration of an Entity's Ability to Continue as a Going Concern)
- SAS-8 (Other Information in Documents Containing Audited Financial Statements)
- SAS-29 (Reporting on Information Accompanying the Basic Financial Statements in Auditor-Submitted Documents)
- SAS-64 (Omnibus Statement on Auditing Standards—1990)
- SAS-79 (Amendments to Statement on Auditing Standards No. 58, Reports on Audited Financial Statements)
- SAS-77 (Amendments to Statements on Auditing Standards No. 22, Planning and Supervision; No. 59, The Auditor's Consideration of an Entity's Ability to Continue as a Going Concern; and No. 62, Special Reports)

SAS-58 establishes guidelines for preparing the standard auditor's report and modifications to the standard report. The standard report includes an introductory paragraph, a scope paragraph, and an opinion paragraph. The introductory paragraph identifies the financial statements and describes the basic responsibilities of management and the auditor for them. The scope paragraph provides a summarized description of the audit process. The auditor's opinion on the financial statements is expressed in the opinion paragraph. The standards established by SAS-58 eliminate the consistency violation as a basis for a qualified opinion (AU 508).

SAS-26 defines the meaning of *associated* in the phrase "associated with financial statements" (AU 504).

SAS-32 provides specific guidance for the implementation of the third standard of reporting (adequate disclosure). The auditor should expand the auditor's report to include informative disclosures omitted from the financial statements, if the disclosures are considered essential to the fair presentation of the financial statements (AU 431).

SAS-59 discusses the audit approach for evaluating an entity's ability to continue as a going concern. When the auditor concludes that there is substantial doubt about an entity's continued existence, a paragraph should be added to the standard auditor's report after the opinion paragraph. However, the addition of the paragraph is not the basis for the expression of a qualified opinion on the financial statements (AU 341).

SAS-8 establishes standards for information contained in a document that includes the audited financial statements. The standards require the auditor to read the other information to identify material inconsistencies or misstatements of fact (AU 550).

SAS-29 describes the auditor's responsibilities for auditor-submitted documents that include the audited financial statements (AU 551).

SAS-64 establishes specific language to be used for certain reporting situations (AU 508.83).

SAS-77 prohibits the use of "conditional" language when the report raises the issue of going concern (AU 341.13).

SAS-79 amends SAS-58 by prohibiting the issuance of an auditor's report that refers to uncertainties (other than an uncertainty related to the going-concern concept) (AU 508.29-.32).

Standard Auditor's Report

The format of the standard auditor's report is mandated by the four standards of reporting listed below (AU 550.02):

- The report shall state whether the financial statements are presented in accordance with generally accepted accounting principles.

- The report shall identify those circumstances in which such principles have not been consistently observed in the current period in relation to the preceding period.

- Informative disclosures in the financial statements are to be regarded as adequate unless otherwise stated in the report.

- The report shall contain either an expression of opinion regarding the financial statements, taken as a whole, or an assertion to the effect that an opinion cannot be expressed. When an overall opinion cannot be expressed, the reasons therefor must be stated. In all cases where an auditor's name is associated with financial statements, the report must contain a clear-cut indication of the character of the auditor's examination, if any, and the degree of responsibility the auditor is taking.

SAS-58 (Reports on Audited Financial Statements) concludes that the standard auditor's report should include the following (AU 508.08):

- Title that includes the word *independent*

- Statement that the financial statements identified in the report were audited

- Statement that the financial statements are the responsibility of the entity's management and that the auditor's responsibility is to express an opinion on the financial statements based on the audit

- Statement that the audit was conducted in accordance with generally accepted auditing standards

- Statement that generally accepted auditing standards require that the auditor plan and perform the audit to obtain reasonable assurance about whether the financial statements are free of material misstatement

- Statement that the audit included:

  — Examination of evidence supporting the amounts and disclosures in the financial statements on a test basis

  — Assessment of the accounting principles used and significant estimates made by management

  — Evaluation of the overall financial statement presentation

- Statement that the auditor believes that the audit provides a reasonable basis for his or her opinion

- Opinion of whether the financial statements present fairly, in all material respects, the financial position of the entity as of the balance sheet date and the results of its operations and its cash flows for the period then ended in conformity with generally accepted accounting principles

- Manual or printed signature of the auditor's firm

- Date of the audit report

The body of the standard auditor's report should include an introductory paragraph, a scope paragraph, and an opinion paragraph. In the introductory paragraph, the auditor (1) states that an audit has been performed and (2) describes the responsibility assumed by the entity's management and the auditor with respect to the financial statements (AU 508.08).

In the scope paragraph, the auditor states that generally accepted auditing standards were observed in the performance of the audit and briefly describes the audit. In the concluding sentence of the scope paragraph, the auditor states that the audit has provided a reasonable basis for expressing an opinion on the financial statements (AU 508.08).

In the opinion paragraph, the auditor states that the financial statements present fairly, in all material respects, the entity's financial position, results of operations, and cash flows. The auditor also states that the financial statements are presented in accordance with generally accepted accounting principles; however, the auditor does not refer to the consistent application of accounting principles (AU 508.08).

> **OBSERVATION:** *For a discussion of the meaning of the phrase* **present fairly** *see SAS-69 (The Meaning of "Present Fairly in Conformity with Generally Accepted Accounting Principles" in the Independent Auditor's Report). SAS-69 is discussed in the chapter entitled "Generally Accepted Accounting Principles" (AU 411).*

The following is an example of the standard auditor's report (AU 508.08).

Independent Auditor's Report

Penney and Nichols, CPAs
45789 Beachwood Drive
Centerville, New Jersey 08000

Board of Directors and Stockholders
X Company

We have audited the accompanying balance sheet of X Company as of December 31, 19X5, and the related statements of income, retained earnings, and cash flows for the year then ended. These financial statements are the responsibility of the Company's management. Our responsibility is to express an opinion on these financial statements based on our audit.

We conducted our audit in accordance with generally accepted auditing standards. Those standards require that we plan and perform the audit to obtain reasonable assurance about whether the financial statements are free of material misstatement. An audit includes examining, on a test basis, evidence supporting the amounts and disclosures in the financial statements. An audit also includes assessing the accounting principles used and significant estimates made by management, as well as evaluating the overall financial statement presentation. We believe that our audit provides a reasonable basis for our opinion.

In our opinion, the financial statements referred to above present fairly, in all material respects, the financial position of X Company as of December 31, 19X5, and the results of its operations and its cash flows for the year then ended in conformity with generally accepted accounting principles.

[Report Date]

[Signature]

OBSERVATION: An Auditing Interpretation on auditor's reports entitled "Reference in Auditor's Standard Report to Management's Report" (January 1989) concludes that the standard auditor's report should not elaborate on management's responsibilities for preparation of the financial statements. In addition, the standard auditor's report should not refer to management's report as it may erroneously provide assurances to users beyond the financial statements (AU 9508.51–.52).

The report is dated to coincide with the completion of fieldwork. Generally, the auditor is not required to perform audit procedures after the report date. The report is signed by a firm's partner (or sole proprietor), which legally binds the CPA firm to the assertions made in the report (AU 530.01).

The auditor's report may be addressed to the client, its board of directors, or its stockholders. For an unincorporated client, the report may be addressed to the partners or the sole proprietor. When an audit is performed at the request of a party other than the management or owners of the audited entity, the report should be addressed to the party that requested the audit (AU 508.09).

The standard report illustrated above is referred to as an unqualified report. When an unqualified report is issued, SAS-69 states that the following assurances are made by the auditor (AU 411.04):

- Accounting principles selected by the client have general acceptance.

- Accounting principles are appropriate for the client.

- Disclosures, such as financial statement notes, are adequate to allow the user to use, understand, and interpret the financial statements.

- Data presented in the financial statements are classified and summarized in a reasonable manner.

- Underlying events and transactions, within a range of acceptable limits, are reflected in the financial statements.

Association with Financial Statements

The fourth reporting standard establishes very definite reporting obligations when an auditor is *associated* with financial statements. SAS-26 (Association with Financial Statements) describes the meaning of *association* when the client is a public entity or a nonpublic entity whose financial statements are audited. Reporting requirements for a nonpublic entity whose financial statements are unaudited are established by Statements on Standards for Accounting and Review Services (SSARS). An auditor is *associated* with financial statements under the following circumstances (AU 504.03):

- The accountant agrees to the use of his or her name in a report or similar document that contains the financial statements.

- The accountant submits to the client or third parties financial statements that have been prepared by the accountant, or for which the accountant has assisted in the preparation. (Whether the accountant's name appears on the financial statements is irrelevant.)

> *OBSERVATION: SAS-26 refers specifically to financial statements and is not applicable to data presented in an alternative format. Although SAS-26 does not define the meaning of a financial statement, SAS-62 (Special Reports) states that financial statements would include information that purports to describe the assets and obligations of an organization or the changes of the assets and obligations over a period of time. In addition, SAS-62 recognizes that financial statements encompass those prepared in accordance with GAAP as well as those that reflect a comprehensive basis of accounting other than GAAP. Finally, SAS-26 states that a tax return prepared solely for a tax authority is beyond the scope of SAS-26 (AU 504.03; AU 623.02).*

MODIFICATION OF THE STANDARD AUDITOR'S REPORT

A variety of conditions may lead to a modification of the standard three-paragraph report.

Accounting Conditions

- There is a departure from GAAP (AU 508.49).
- There is a departure from an accounting principle promulgated by an authoritative body designated by the AICPA to promulgate such principles, and the auditor agrees with the departure (AU 508.14).
- Informative disclosures in the financial statements are not reasonably adequate (AU 508.55).

Accounting Changes

- There is lack of consistency.
- There is a change in the format of the statement of cash flows.
- Accounting principles used to present segment information have not been consistently applied or disclosed.

- There is a change from an unacceptable accounting principle to an acceptable accounting principle.
- There is a correction of an error.
- There is a change from an acceptable accounting principle to an unacceptable accounting principle.
- There is an inappropriate treatment in the accounting for a change in an accounting principle.
- Reasonable justification for a change in accounting principles has not been provided by management.
- There is a change in an accounting estimate.
- There is a change in an accounting principle that is inseparable from a change in an accounting estimate.
- There is a change in the reporting entity.
- There is a change arising from a pooling of interest.
- There is a change arising from substantially different transactions or events.
- There is a change that may give rise to a material effect in future financial statements (AU 508.59–.61).

Scope Conditions

- Sufficient competent evidential matter has not been collected (AU 508.40).
- There are other scope limitations (AU 508.45).
- The reporting engagement is limited (e.g., a report on the balance sheet only) (AU 508.47).
- Part of the engagement was conducted by another auditor (AU 508.12).
- The financial statements are unaudited (AU 504.05).

Uncertainty Conditions

- There are uncertainties related to going concern (AU 341.12).

Other Conditions

- An event, condition, or transaction affecting the financial statements is emphasized (AU 508.37).
- The auditor is not independent with respect to the financial statements (AU 504.09).

- Other information and data are presented in documents containing audited financial statements (AU 550.04).
- Required supplementary information is presented in the financial statements (AU 558.08).
- The auditor reports on fair value disclosures (AU 9342.01).
- Auditor-submitted documents containing information accompanying the basic financial statements are presented (AU 551.04).
- There is a piecemeal opinion (prohibited) (AU 508.73).
- There are negative assurances (prohibited) (AU 504.18).

ACCOUNTING CONDITIONS

Departure from GAAP

Generally accepted accounting principles include promulgated rules as well as unwritten rules that have gained acceptance through general usage. When generally accepted accounting principles are not observed by a client, the auditor must decide whether an unqualified, a qualified, or an adverse opinion should be issued. The selection of the appropriate opinion depends on the materiality of the departure, the effects of the departure, and the number of accounts affected by the departure. An unqualified opinion can be issued if the departure is not significant to the fair presentation of the financial statements. If the departure affects the fairness of the financial statements but overall the statements can be relied on, a qualified opinion can be issued. On the other hand, when the departure is so significant that the financial statements should not be relied on, an adverse opinion must be issued (AU 508.49–.50).

When a qualified or adverse opinion is issued, an explanatory paragraph must describe the departure and its effects, if determinable, on the financial statements. If a qualified opinion is issued, the opinion paragraph should specifically refer to the explanatory paragraph as illustrated below (AU 508.51–.52).

We have audited the accompanying balance sheet of X Company as of December 31, 19X5, and the related statements of income, retained earnings, and cash flows for the year then ended. These financial statements are the responsibility of the Company's management. Our responsibility is to express an opinion on these financial statements based on our audit.

We conducted our audit in accordance with generally accepted auditing standards. Those standards require that we plan and perform the audit to obtain reasonable assurance about whether the financial statements are free of material misstatement. An audit includes examining, on a test basis, evidence supporting the amounts and disclosures in the financial statements. An audit also includes assessing the accounting principles used and significant estimates made by management, as well as evaluating the overall financial statement presentation. We believe that our audit provides a reasonable basis for our opinion.

As more fully described in Note 12 to the financial statements, a net provision for loss on abandonment of certain property of $800,000 after related income taxes has been presented as an extraordinary charge against earnings for 19X5. In our opinion, generally accepted accounting principles require that the gross amount of such provision be included in the determination of income before income taxes and that the per share amount of the provisions ($.75) not be separately presented in the statement of income.

In our opinion, except for the effect of the matter described in the preceding paragraph on the statement of income, the financial statements referred to above present fairly, in all material respects, the financial position of X Company as of December 31, 19X5, and the results of its operations and its cash flows for the year then ended in conformity with generally accepted accounting principles.

If the auditor concludes that an adverse opinion is to be issued, language similar to that shown below would be used in the opinion paragraph (AU 508.69).

We have audited the accompanying balance sheet of X Company as of December 31, 19X5, and the related statements of income, retained earnings, and cash flows for the year then ended. These financial statements are the responsibility of the Company's management. Our responsibility is to express an opinion on these financial statements based on our audit.

We conducted our audit in accordance with generally accepted auditing standards. Those standards require that we plan and perform the audit to obtain reasonable assurance about whether the financial statements are free of material misstatement. An audit includes examining, on a test basis, evidence supporting the amounts and disclosures in the financial statements. An audit also includes assessing the accounting principles used and significant estimates made by management, as well as evaluating the overall financial statement presentation. We believe that our audit provides a reasonable basis for our opinion.

As disclosed in Note 12 to the financial statements, the Company reports all of its sales on the installment method for financial accounting purposes and on its tax return. In our opinion, generally accepted accounting principles require that sales be reported on the accrual basis with an appropriate provision for deferred taxes. As a result of these departures from generally accepted accounting principles, gross profit on sales is understated by $123,456 and income tax expense is understated by $14,222. The total effect of these departures on retained earnings is $109,234, which results in an increase in earnings per share of $1.42.

In our opinion, because of the effects of the matters discussed in the preceding paragraphs, the financial statements referred to above do not present fairly, in conformity with generally accepted accounting principles, the financial position of X Company as of December 31, 19X5, or the result of its operations or its cash flows for the year then ended.

OBSERVATION: If practicable, an auditor should provide information required by GAAP that has not been disclosed in the financial statements, unless the omission of the information from the auditor's report is recognized as appropriate by another SAS. If practicable means that the required information is reasonably obtainable from management's accounts and records and that by providing the information, the auditor is not required to assume the position of preparer of the financial information.

The above guidance also applies to those situations in which the auditor expresses a qualified or adverse opinion because of a departure from GAAP that is not related to disclosure (AU 431).

When generally accepted accounting principles have not been used to prepare the financial statements, a note to the financial statements may describe the nature and effects of the departure. Rather than repeat this information in an explanation paragraph, the auditor's report may incorporate the information in the note by reference. For example, the explanatory paragraph could read as follows (AU 508.52).

As more fully described in Note 12 to the financial statements, the Company reports all of its sales on the installment method for financial accounting purposes and on its tax return. In our opinion, generally accepted accounting principles require that sales be reported on the accrual basis with an appropriate provision for deferred taxes.

The opinion paragraph (either a qualified or an adverse opinion) would refer to the deviation described in the explanation (AU 508.51 and .69).

> **OBSERVATION:** *An auditor may incorporate the information in a note to the financial statements into the auditor's report by reference; however, the auditor must be careful that matters in the note that are inconsistent with the auditor's opinion are not also incorporated. For example, the note may attempt to justify the departure from generally accepted accounting principles in a manner that is inappropriate or misleading. Under this circumstance, it would be advisable to not make reference to the note and simply repeat the relevant information in the explanatory paragraph.*

Departure from Promulgated GAAP

Generally accepted accounting principles include written as well as unwritten accounting principles, methods, and procedures. Rule 203 of the AICPA Code of Professional Conduct states (AU 508.14):

> A member shall not (1) express an opinion or state affirmatively that the financial statements or other financial data of any entity are presented in conformity with generally accepted accounting principles or (2) state that he or she is not aware of any material modifications that should be made to such statements or data in order for them to be in conformity with generally accepted accounting principles, if such statements or data contain any departure from an accounting principle promulgated by bodies designated by Council to establish such principles that has a material effect on the statements or data taken as a whole. If, however, the statements or data contain such a departure and the member can demonstrate that due to unusual circumstances the financial statements or data would otherwise have been misleading, the member can comply with the rule by describing the departure, its approximate effects, if practicable, and the reasons why compliance with the principle would result in a misleading statement.

The AICPA Council has adopted resolutions designating the Financial Accounting Standards Board (FASB) and the Governmental Accounting Standards Board (GASB) as having the authority to promulgate accounting standards for commercial enterprises and governmental entities, respectively.

When an accounting principle is promulgated, there is a chance that strict interpretation and application of the rule may in some cases result in misleading financial statements. To prevent this situation, Rule 203 permits a client to use an alternative method. If the auditor agrees with the client's conclusion that the use of a promulgated rule would result in misleading financial statements, he or she may issue an unqualified opinion. However, an explanatory paragraph must be included in the standard report in which the nature, effect, and reason for the departure from the promulgated rule is described. The introductory, scope, and opinion paragraphs are not modified, and no reference is made to the explanatory paragraph in the opinion paragraph (AU 508.15).

> **OBSERVATION:** *Although Rule 203 may be needed to provide flexibility in the application of accounting principles, the rule must be used with a great deal of caution. When the rule is used, the auditor is, in effect, promulgating an accounting rule for a specific client, which is a heavy responsibility to undertake. Not surprisingly, there are very few examples where Rule 203 has been employed concerning the adaptation of different accounting methods.*

Inadequate Disclosures

The third standard of reporting states that informative disclosures in the financial statements are assumed sufficient unless specifically noted otherwise in the auditor's report. Informative disclosure includes the format and content of the financial statements, all related notes, terminology, account classification, parenthetical comments, and the degree of detail in the statements and related notes. In general, the financial information should not be abbreviated to the extent that informative disclosures are not communicated. On the other hand, the informative disclosures should not be detailed to the extent that they may be misunderstood (AU 508.55).

Information not adequately disclosed in the financial statements should be disclosed in an explanatory paragraph, if practical, when (1) informative disclosures are not considered adequate, (2) the report must be qualified, or (3) an adverse opinion is issued. SAS-32 (Adequacy of Disclosure of Financial Statements) defines *practical* to mean that (1) the information can be obtained from management's records and (2) the auditor's efforts in gathering the information do not constitute the actual preparation of the financial information. Thus, the auditor is not expected to actually prepare basic financial statements or any other financial information in an effort to include such data in the report. SAS-58 specifically states that when a client does not include a statement of cash flows, the auditor is not required to prepare and present such a statement in the report. However, an explanatory paragraph in the auditor's report must clearly state that the client has declined to include a statement of cash flows and that such a statement is required by GAAP. When such a statement is not presented in the financial statements, the auditor's report must be qualified. In all cases, when the auditor issues a qualified or adverse opinion, the explanatory paragraph in the report must be referred to in the opinion paragraph of the report (AU 508.56–.58).

The following example illustrates an auditor's report that is qualified because the client did not present a statement of cash flows (AU 508.58).

We have audited the accompanying balance sheet of X Company as of December 31, 19X5, and the related statements of income and retained earnings for the year then ended. These financial statements are the responsibility of the Company's management. Our responsibility is to express an opinion on these financial statements based on our audit.

We conducted our audit in accordance with generally accepted auditing standards. Those standards require that we plan and perform the audit to obtain reasonable assurance about whether the financial statements are free of material misstatement. An audit includes examining, on a test basis, evidence supporting the amounts and disclosures in the financial statements. An audit also includes assessing the accounting principles used and significant estimates made by management, as well as evaluating the overall financial statement presentation. We believe that our audit provides a reasonable basis for our opinion.

The Company did not present a statement of cash flows for the year ended December 31, 19X5. Presentation of such statement summarizing the Company's operating, investing, and financing activities is required by generally accepted accounting principles.

In our opinion, except that the omission of a statement of cash flows results in an incomplete presentation as explained in the preceding paragraph, the financial statements referred to above present fairly, in all material respects, the financial position of X Company as of December 31, 19X5, and the results of its operations for the year then ended in conformity with generally accepted accounting principles.

OBSERVATION: An Auditing Interpretation on adherence to GAAP, "The Impact on an Auditor's Report of an FASB Statement Prior to the Statement's Effective Date" (October 1979), states that it is necessary to evaluate the adequacy of the client's disclosure of the use of an accounting principle that is currently acceptable but will not be acceptable in the future based on the effective date of a new FASB Statement and the new FASB Statement requires the restatement of prior years' financial statements when it is adopted (AU 9410.13–.18).

ACCOUNTING CHANGES

Lack of Consistency

The second standard of reporting states that the report shall "identify those circumstances in which such principles have not been consistently observed in the current period in relation to the preceding period" (AU 420.01).

APB Opinion No. 20 (Accounting Changes) classifies accounting changes as (1) changes in an accounting principle, (2) changes in a reporting entity, and (3) changes in an accounting estimate. For each accounting change, APB Opinion No. 20 establishes appropriate accounting and reporting standards. In general, changes in accounting principles result in either a cumulative-effect adjustment that is reported on the statement of income (no restatement of prior-period financial statements) or an adjustment to the beginning balance of retained earnings (restatement of prior-period financial statements) (AU 420.04).

The auditor does not refer to the consistent application of accounting principles in the standard three-paragraph report under the following conditions (AU 508.34):

- There have been no changes in the application of accounting principles in the preparation of the current year's financial statements.

- There have been changes in the application of accounting principles in the preparation of the current year's financial statements, but the effects of the changes are considered immaterial.

When there has been a change in the application of an accounting principle and the effects of the change are considered material, an explanatory paragraph should be added to the standard auditor's report. The explanatory paragraph should immediately follow the opinion paragraph and include the following (AU 508.34):

- Reference to the note to the financial statements that discusses the change in accounting principle
- Discussion of the nature of the change in accounting principle

An example of an explanatory paragraph resulting from a change in an accounting principle is presented below.

As discussed in Note X to the financial statements, the Company changed its method of valuing inventories in 19X5.

Even though there has been a violation of the consistency standard, the auditor's report is *not* qualified, and there is no reference to the explanatory paragraph in the opinion paragraph (AU 508.34).

When the auditor's report covers only a single (current) year, the auditor must determine whether generally accepted accounting principles have been consistently applied in the current year and in the previous year. When the auditor's report covers two or more years, the auditor must determine whether generally accepted accounting principles have been applied on a consistent basis (1) between or among the financial statements reported on and (2) between the earliest set of financial statements reported on and the immediate previous year's set of financial statements (not reported on) if the previous year's statements are presented (AU 420.21).

Reporting a change in an accounting principle in a period after the change has occurred is dependent on whether (1) the change was accounted for through the retroactive restatement of prior years' financial statements and (2) the change was from FIFO to LIFO.

Retroactive restatement   When a change in an accounting principle is accounted for by the retroactive restatement of prior years' financial statements, there is comparability among the financial statements since all financial statements are prepared (after restatement) using the same accounting principles. For this reason, an explanatory paragraph (as illustrated earlier) describing a change in accounting principle needs to be added to the standard auditor's report only in the year of the change (AU 508.36).

No retroactive restatement When a change in an accounting principle is accounted for in a manner that does not result in the retroactive restatement of prior years' financial statements, there is a lack of complete comparability among financial statements due to the cumulative-effect adjustment reflected in the financial statements for the year of the change. For this reason, an explanatory paragraph describing the change in accounting principle must be added to the standard auditor's report for as long as the financial statements for the year of the change are presented with subsequent statements (AU 508.36).

FIFO to LIFO change APB Opinion No. 20 provides specific guidance when an entity changes from the FIFO to LIFO inventory method. A change from FIFO to LIFO requires neither a cumulative-effect adjustment nor a retroactive restatement of prior years' financial statements. An Auditing Interpretation on consistency entitled "Impact on the Auditor's Report of FIFO to LIFO Change in Comparative Financial Statements" (January 1975) concludes that a FIFO to LIFO accounting change would require an explanatory paragraph in the auditor's report for (1) the year of the change and (2) all subsequent years until the year of change is the earliest year reported on by the auditor (AU 9420.16–.20).

> **OBSERVATION:** *Another Interpretation on consistency, "The Effect of APB Opinion No. 28 on Consistency" (February 1974), states that the auditor should not add an explanatory paragraph in those circumstances in which accounting principles and practices used in preparing the annual financial information have been modified in accordance with APB Opinion No. 28 (Interim Financial Reporting) (AU 9420.11–.15).*

Change in the Format of the Statement of Cash Flows

FAS-95 (Statement of Cash Flows) allows some flexibility in the preparation of the statement of cash flows. For example, either the direct or the indirect method can be used to compute cash flows from operations. SAS-43 (Omnibus Statement on Auditing Standards) concludes that changes of this nature are not a violation of the consistency standard, and if prior years' financial statements are reclassified to conform to another format, the auditor's report need not refer to the change. These changes are considered to be reclassifications by SAS-43 (AU 420.13).

> **OBSERVATION:** *APB Opinion No. 20 is not applicable to re-classifications. When a reclassification occurs, prior years' financial statements should be reclassified so that all statements are comparable. However, if significant, the reclassifications should be disclosed in the financial statements or footnotes thereto.*

Accounting Changes—Segment Information

FAS-14 (Financial Reporting for Segments of a Business Enterprise) notes that an inconsistency in segment information may occur under the following circumstances (AU 435.11):

- The basis of accounting for sales or transfers between segments or between geographical areas, or the methods of allocating operating expenses or classifying identifiable assets, may change.

- The method of determining or presenting a measure of segment profitability may change.

- Accounting changes described by APB Opinion No. 20 may occur.

FAS-14 also requires that segment information for prior periods presented on a comparative basis be restated when (1) the financial statements are restated in accordance with APB Opinion No. 20 or (2) there has been a change in the way the client's products or services are grouped into segments (AU 435.12).

When there has been a change in an accounting principle as described in the previous paragraph, the nature and effect of the change must be disclosed in the financial statements. If the change is not adequately disclosed or the segment information is not retroactively restated as required by FAS-14, the auditor's report must be modified since the financial statements are not prepared in accordance with generally accepted accounting principles (inadequate disclosure). When an accounting change related to segment information has not been adequately described, the auditor's report should include the standard introductory and scope paragraphs and explanatory and opinion paragraphs similar to the ones illustrated below (AU 435.13).

In 19X5, X Company changed the manner in which it computes operating profits or losses for each segment. Prior to 19X5, operating expenses incurred by the Company and not directly traceable to a segment were allocated to each segment, except none of these costs were allocated to Division C. In 19X5, Division C was allocated a reasonable amount of these costs using the same basis as employed to allocate similar costs to the other three divisions. Division C's 19X5 operating income would have been 4% greater and Division A's, B's, and D's operating income would have been 1%, 5%, and 2% less, respectively, if the Company had not changed the manner in which traceable costs were allocated. The nature and effect of this change was not disclosed in the Company's financial statements. In our opinion, disclosure of the nature and effect of the change is required by reporting standards established in Statement No. 14 of the Financial Accounting Standards Board.

In our opinion, except for the omission of the information discussed in the preceding paragraph, the financial statements referred to above present fairly in conformity with . . .

An auditor's report is generally not modified because of the inconsistent application of accounting principles in the presentation of segment information. The report would be modified only if the change in accounting principle affected the financial statements taken as a whole (AU 435.14).

Nonpublic companies are not required to present segment information as described in FAS-14.

Changing to an Acceptable Principle

A change from an unacceptable accounting principle to a generally accepted accounting principle is considered to be a correction of an error in financial statements of a prior period. Prior-period errors in financial statements are corrected by restating the prior years' financial statements that are presented on a comparative basis with the current year's statements. The nature of the error and the effect of its correction on income before extraordinary items, net income, and the related per share data must be fully disclosed in the period the error is discovered and corrected (AU 420.11).

When there has been a change from an unacceptable to an acceptable accounting principle, a paragraph, similar to the one illustrated below, would be added to the standard auditor's report after the opinion paragraph.

As discussed in Note X to the financial statements, in 19X5 the Company changed from an unacceptable method of accounting for depreciation to an acceptable method. The change in accounting principles has been accounted for as a correction of an error and prior years' financial statements have been restated.

Correction of an Error

A correction of an error that arises from circumstances other than a change from an unacceptable accounting principle to an acceptable principle is not an accounting change. For this reason, the auditor's report does not refer to a consistency violation in the year the error is discovered and corrected (AU 420.15).

> **OBSERVATION:** *If the auditor has previously reported on the prior years' financial statements that are being corrected, standards established by SAS-1 (Section 561 — Subsequent Discovery of Facts Existing at the Date of the Auditor's Report) should be observed.*

Changing to an Unacceptable Principle

A newly adopted accounting principle must be evaluated to determine if it has general acceptance. If the auditor concludes that the accounting principle is not generally accepted, a decision must be made about whether a qualified opinion or an adverse opinion must be issued based on the deviation from generally accepted accounting principles. An explanatory paragraph(s), similar to the one presented below, should immediately precede the opinion (qualified or adverse) paragraph (AU 508.59).

During 19X5, the Company changed its method of valuing land held for investment from the cost method to the appraisal method. The increase resulting from the reevaluation amounted to $500,000 and is presented as an increase to stockholders' equity (appraisal capital). In our opinion, the newly adopted accounting principle (appraisal method) is not in conformity with generally accepted accounting principles.

There is no need to add an explanatory paragraph on consistency, because the change in accounting principle has been described adequately in the explanatory paragraph that discusses the selection of an unacceptable accounting principle (AU 508.61).

For the years following the adoption of the unacceptable accounting principle, the auditor should continue to express the qualified or adverse opinion on the financial statements for the year in which the change was made. In addition, the auditor must determine whether the effects of applying an unacceptable accounting principle also require the modification of opinion(s) on subsequent financial statements (AU 508.64–.65).

Inappropriate Treatment of an Accounting Change

As noted earlier, APB Opinion No. 20 provides standards for accounting for changes in accounting principles. A change in an accounting principle usually results in a cumulative-effect adjustment or a retroactive restatement of prior years' financial statements. If the standards established by APB Opinion No. 20 are not observed, the auditor must decide whether the auditor's report should be modified because of a deviation from generally accepted accounting principles. If it is concluded that the report should be modified, a paragraph similar to the one illustrated below should immediately precede the opinion (qualified or adverse) paragraph (AU 508.65):

During 19X5, the Company changed its method of accounting for depreciation, as described in Note X to the financial statements. The effects of the change to the new method were accounted for on a prospective basis. In our opinion, the change was not accounted for in accordance with generally accepted accounting principles in that the change should have resulted in a cumulative-effect adjustment being charged to the income statement. If the change had been accounted for as a cumulative-effect adjustment, net income would be decreased $70,000, and earnings per share would be decreased $.50. Additionally, net property, plant, and equipment would be decreased $100,000, and deferred income tax assets would be increased $30,000.

For the years following the incorrect treatment in accounting for the accounting change, the auditor should continue to express the qualified or adverse opinion on the financial statements for the year in which the change was made. If the accounting for the change in an accounting principle was accounted for prospectively when a cumulative-effect adjustment or a restatement of prior years' financial statements was appropriate, subsequent financial statements should be evaluated to determine whether a qualified or adverse opinion is appropriate (AU 508.64).

Lack of Reasonable Justification for Change

Once an accounting principle is adopted, the principle should not be changed unless it can be demonstrated that another accounting principle is preferable as well as acceptable. If management does not adequately justify the change in accounting principles, the auditor should determine whether the report should be modified. If it is concluded that the report should be modified, a paragraph similar to the one presented below should immediately precede the opinion paragraph (AU 508.66).

During 19X5, the Company changed its method of accounting for amortization, as described in Note X to the financial statements. In previous years, the Company used an accelerated amortization method but has now changed to the straight-line method. Although the straight-line method of amortization is in conformity with generally accepted accounting principles, in our opinion the Company has not provided reasonable justification for making this change as required by generally accepted accounting principles.

There is no need to add an explanatory paragraph on consistency, because the change in accounting principle has been described adequately in the explanatory paragraph that discusses the lack of reasonable justification for making the change in accounting principles (AU 508.61).

> *OBSERVATION: SAS-58 does not discuss whether a lack of reasonable justification for an accounting change could lead to an adverse opinion. Under most, if not all, circumstances, it would be difficult to argue that an adverse opinion should be expressed.*

For the years following the adoption of the new accounting principle, the auditor should continue to express the qualified opinion on the financial statements for the year in which the change was adopted. However, it is not appropriate to express a qualified opinion on subsequent financial statements since the newly adopted accounting principle is a generally accepted accounting principle (AU 508.66).

Change in Accounting Estimate

APB Opinion No. 20 concludes that a change in an accounting estimate must be accounted for prospectively. Thus, the effect of a change in an accounting estimate is accounted for (1) in the period of change, if the change affects only that period (for example, a change that affects the allowance for doubtful accounts), or (2) in the period of change and in future periods, if the change affects both periods (for example, a change in the remaining life of a depreciable asset). If the auditor is satisfied that the change in an accounting estimate is reasonable, the auditor's report is not qualified or otherwise modified (AU 420.14).

> *OBSERVATION: Although a change in an estimate is not considered to be a violation of the consistency standard, some auditors treat the effects of the change as a matter to be emphasized in the auditor's report. Emphasizing matters in the auditor's report is discussed in a later section of this chapter.*

Change in Principle Inseparable from Estimate

A change in an accounting estimate caused in part or entirely by a change in an accounting principle must be reported as a change in an accounting estimate. Although such a change is reported as a change in accounting estimate, it also involves a change in accounting principles for which the auditor's report must be expanded. In this case, an explanatory paragraph must be added to the auditor's report in which the accounting change is described; however, the opinion paragraph is unqualified with no reference to the explanatory paragraph (AU 420.12).

Change in Reporting Entity

The consistency standard is applicable when the reporting entity (1) presents consolidated or combined statements in place of statements of individual companies, (2) changes specific subsidiaries comprising the group of companies for which consolidated statements are presented, (3) changes the companies included in combined financial statements, or (4) changes from the cost, equity, or consolidation method of accounting to one of the other methods of accounting for subsidiaries or other investments in common stock (AU 420.07).

For the changes in the reporting entity described above, the auditor's report would include an explanatory paragraph immediately following the opinion paragraph, assuming that the change in the reporting entity is accounted for in accordance with generally accepted accounting principles. The opinion paragraph would be unqualified and there would be no reference to the explanatory paragraph. The following example illustrates an explanatory paragraph.

As described in Note X to the financial statements, the Company in 19X5 changed its method of accounting for investments in certain investee companies.

A change in a reporting entity does not occur when a subsidiary or other business component is purchased, sold, created, or liquidated (AU 420.10).

Change Arising from a Pooling of Interests

A pooling of interests is a business combination method that requires that the prior years' financial statements be restated to reflect the financial statements of the combining entities. Since comparability is achieved through the restatement of prior years' financial statements, there is no violation of the consistency standard and the auditor's report is not modified (AU 420.08).

If the current year's financial statements are presented comparatively with the prior years' and the prior years' financial statements do not reflect the combination of the pooled companies, the auditor's report must be modified to reflect (a) the inconsistent application of accounting principles to the prior years' statements and (b) a departure from GAAP, which may require a qualified or adverse opinion.

If the financial statements for the year in which the combination occurred are not presented on a comparative basis with the previous years' statements, the current year's financial statements should make the following disclosures:

- Describe the pooling transaction.
- Disclose revenues, extraordinary items, and net income for the prior years on a combined basis.

If the disclosures are not made, the audit report should be qualified. The auditor also may need to add an inconsistency paragraph to the report; however, a separate explanatory paragraph concerning consistency is not required if the explanatory paragraph related to the inadequate disclosure contains the information that is required in a consistency explanatory paragraph.

Substantially Different Transactions or Events

An accounting principle may be changed when transactions or events have a material effect on the financial statements. An accounting change of this nature is not a violation of the consistency standard and the auditor's report, therefore, is not modified. For example, a company may account for transactions on a cash basis because the affect on the financial statements is considered immaterial; however, in a subsequent year, the volume of transactions may increase, resulting in the need to adopt an accrual method. The adoption of the accrual method is not considered a change in an accounting principle (AU 420.18).

In addition, when an accounting principle is changed to account for transactions or events that are clearly different from previous transactions or events, the accounting change is not a violation of the consistency standard (AU 420.18).

Change That May Have a Material Effect in the Future

As noted earlier, the auditor's report is not modified when the effect of a change in an accounting principle is immaterial. If it is expected that the change may have a material effect on future financial statements, that expectation should be disclosed in a note to the financial statements; however, there is no need to refer to the change in accounting principle in the auditor's report in the current or future years (AU 420.19).

SCOPE CONDITIONS

Insufficient Competent Evidential Matter

The third standard of fieldwork requires that the auditor's opinion be based on sufficient competent evidential matter. If adequate evidence is not collected, a scope limitation occurs. In this case, the auditor should express a qualified opinion or issue a disclaimer of opinion on the financial statements. A scope limitation may result from circumstances of the engagement or restrictions imposed by the client. The significance of the restriction depends on the number of accounts affected by the scope limitation and their potential impact on the financial statements (AU 508.40–.41).

> *OBSERVATION: SAS-58 notes that when significant scope limitations are imposed by the client, the auditor generally should express a disclaimer of opinion on the financial statements (AU 508.42).*

When an auditor concludes that a qualified opinion should be expressed, there is no change in the introductory paragraph; however, the scope paragraph is modified by referring to the scope limitation that is described in an explanatory paragraph. The explanatory paragraph should contain a description of the nature of the scope limitation and the accounts involved. The description of the scope limitation should not be incorporated in the auditor's report by reference to a note to the financial statement, because the auditor, not the client, is responsible for the description of the scope limitation. Finally, the opinion paragraph should refer to the explanatory paragraph as the basis for the qualification and should contain the phrase *except for* in describing the qualification.

We have audited the accompanying balance sheet of X Company as of December 31, 19X5, and the related statements of income, retained earnings, and cash flows for the year then ended. These financial statements are the responsibility of the Company's management. Our responsibility is to express an opinion on these financial statements based on our audit.

Except as discussed in the following paragraph, we conducted our audit in accordance with generally accepted auditing standards. Those standards require that we plan and perform the audit to obtain reasonable assurance about whether the financial statements are free of material misstatement. An audit includes examining, on a test basis, evidence supporting the amounts and disclosures in the financial statements. An audit also includes assessing the accounting principles used and significant estimates made by management, as well as evaluating the overall financial statement presentation. We believe that our audit provides a reasonable basis for our opinion.

We were not able to confirm accounts receivable as of December 31, 19X5, stated at $500,000. The receivables were principally due from agencies of the U.S. government. In addition, we were unable to determine the validity of the accounts through the use of alternative procedures.

In our opinion, except for the effects of such adjustment, if any, as might have been determined to be necessary had we been able to determine the validity of accounts receivable, the financial statements referred to in the first paragraph above present fairly, in all material respects, the financial position of X Company as of December 31, 19X5, and the results of its operations and its cash flows for the year then ended in conformity with generally accepted accounting principles.

If the scope limitation requires the expression of a disclaimer of opinion, the following format should be used (AU 508.72).

We were engaged to audit the accompanying balance sheet of X Company as of December 31, 19X5, and the related statements of income, retained earnings, and cash flows for the year then ended. These financial statements are the responsibility of the Company's management.

No physical inventory was taken for merchandise held for sale by the Company as of December 31, 19X4, or December 31, 19X5, and inventory quantities are stated in the accompanying financial statements at $150,000 and $400,000, respectively.

Since the Company did not take physical inventories and we were not able to apply alternative auditing procedures to satisfy ourselves as to inventory quantities, the scope of our work was not sufficient to enable us to express, and we do not express, an opinion on the financial statements referred to above.

In addition, the second paragraph of the standard report is omitted and an explanatory paragraph is added to describe the scope limitation. If the auditor is aware of any departures from generally accepted accounting principles, these deficiencies should also be described in another separate explanatory paragraph. The opinion paragraph should refer to the explanatory paragraph that describes the scope limitation and also should state that an opinion is not expressed on the financial statements (AU 508.72).

Typical scope limitations include an inability to (1) observe the physical inventory, (2) confirm receivables, or (3) obtain financial statements related to an investment in another (investee) company. If the auditor is able to obtain sufficient competent evidential matter through alternative audit procedures (such as the review of subsequent cash receipts when a receivable is not confirmed), there is no scope limitation and the three-paragraph (unqualified) report should be issued (AU 508.42).

> *OBSERVATION: SAS-58 reiterates the point that although alternative procedures may be used when the auditor cannot observe the physical inventory count, "it will always be necessary for the auditor to make, or observe, some physical counts of the inventory and apply appropriate tests of intervening transactions" (AU 508.42).*

> *OBSERVATION: An Auditing Interpretation on evidential matter entitled "The Effect of an Inability to Obtain Evidential Matter Relating to Income Tax Accruals" (March 1981) requires the auditor to disclaim an opinion on the financial statements if the client limits the auditor's access to tax accrual documentation and access to the appropriate client personnel responsible for the tax calculation.*
>
> *The auditor is required to prepare tax working papers. If necessary, the evidential matter can take the form of a tax accrual memorandum. The auditor must exercise professional judgment and expertise in obtaining and examining tax accrual information and cannot rely solely on the opinion of the client's outside or in-house tax counsel (AU 9326.06–.17).*

Other Scope Limitations

When notes to the financial statements include unaudited information, the audit approach used depends on whether the information is essential to the fair presentation of the financial statements. If the information is considered essential to fair presentation, the auditor must perform procedures to determine whether the information is fairly presented. When the auditor is unable to apply the procedures considered necessary, a qualified opinion or a disclaimer of opinion should be expressed (AU 508.45–.46).

If the information is not considered essential for fair presentation of the financial statements, the disclosures may be "identified as unaudited or as not covered by the auditor's report." However, if the information is based on a subsequent event that occurs after the completion of fieldwork but before the financial statements are issued, the auditor must do one of the following:

- Dual date the report.
- Date the report as of the subsequent event.
- Extend procedures to enable the auditor to review all subsequent events to the extended date of the report.

In the above circumstances, the auditor cannot accept the labeling of the subsequent event as "unaudited" (AU 508.46).

Limited Reporting Engagements

An auditor may be engaged to audit one or more, but not all, of the financial statements. This type of engagement is not considered a limitation of the scope of an engagement. It is instead described as a limited reporting engagement. Of course, no scope limitation exists if the auditor is unrestricted in the performance of audit procedures considered necessary under the circumstances (AU 508.47).

In a limited reporting engagement, the auditor's report is modified so that only the financial statement(s) audited is identified. An example of a limited report on a balance sheet is presented below (AU 508.48).

We have audited the accompanying balance sheet of X Company as of December 31, 19X5. This financial statement is the responsibility of the Company's management. Our responsibility is to express an opinion on this financial statement based on our audit.

We conducted our audit in accordance with generally accepted auditing standards. Those standards require that we plan and perform the audit to obtain reasonable assurance about whether the balance sheet is free of material misstatement. An audit includes examining, on a test basis, evidence supporting the amounts and disclosures in the balance sheet. An audit also includes assessing the accounting principles used and significant estimates made by management, as well as evaluating the overall balance sheet presentation. We believe that our audit provides a reasonable basis for our opinion.

In our opinion, the balance sheet referred to above presents fairly, in all material respects, the financial position of X Company as of December 31, 19X5, in conformity with generally accepted accounting principles.

In a limited reporting engagement, the auditor must employ procedures to determine whether accounting principles have been applied consistently with those used in the previous year. If there has been a violation of the consistency standard, an explanatory paragraph should be added to the auditor's report (after the opinion paragraph). An unqualified opinion, however, is expressed on the financial statement(s) (AU 508.47).

Opinion Based on Another Auditor's Report

An auditor may report on the financial statements of a consolidated or combined entity, even if he or she does not audit every single entity in the consolidating or combining group. Under these circumstances, the auditor must decide whether or not to make reference to other auditors' reports. The amount and type of evidence required and the audit procedures the auditor should follow in deciding whether or not to refer to another auditor are discussed in the chapter entitled "Evidence." At this point, only the content of the auditor's report will be discussed (AU 543.02).

If the principal auditor decides not to refer to another auditor's report, the report on the consolidated or combined entity is not modified. However, the principal auditor must carefully evaluate any modifications in the other auditor's report to determine whether they are significant enough to be included in the principal auditor's report. Significance is based on the consolidated or combined financial statements. Thus, if the other auditor's modification is significant in relation to the consolidated or combined statements, the principal auditor should include the modification in the report (AU 543.04 and .15).

When the principal auditor decides to refer to the report of another auditor, the scope of work done by the other auditor must be described in the introductory paragraph of the principal auditor's report. This is accomplished by describing the amount of work performed by the other auditor in terms of percentage of sales, net income, total assets, or some other reasonable basis. In the opinion paragraph of the principal auditor's report it should be made clear that the opinion on the overall financial statements is based on the reports of both auditors. The name of the other auditor may be disclosed if he or she explicitly agrees to be named. When reference is made to another auditor's report, it does not constitute a qualification of the principal auditor's report. The reference is made to indicate the degree of responsibility that each auditor is assuming in the report (AU 543.07).

The following example illustrates an auditor's report where reference is made to the work of another auditor (AU 543.09).

We have audited the consolidated balance sheet of X Company as of December 31, 19X5, and the related consolidated statements of income, retained earnings, and cash flows for the year then ended. These financial statements are the responsibility of the Company's management. Our responsibility is to express an opinion on these financial statements based on our audit. We did not examine the financial statements of Z Company, a consolidated subsidiary whose statements reflect total assets and revenues constituting 15% and 12%, respectively, of the related consolidated totals. Those statements were audited by other auditors whose report has been furnished to us, and our opinion, insofar as it relates to the amounts included for Z Company, is based solely on the report of the other auditors.

We conducted our audit in accordance with generally accepted auditing standards. Those standards require that we plan and perform the audit to obtain reasonable assurance about whether the financial statements are free of material misstatement. An audit includes examining, on a test basis, evidence supporting the amounts and disclosures in the financial statements. An audit also includes assessing the accounting principles used and significant estimates made by management, as well as evaluating the overall financial statement presentation. We believe that our audit and the report of other auditors provide a reasonable basis for our opinion.

In our opinion, based on our audit and the report of other auditors, the consolidated financial statements referred to above present fairly, in all material respects, the financial position of X Company as of December 31, 19X5, and the results of its operations and its cash flows for the year then ended in conformity with generally accepted accounting principles.

Reporting by successor auditor for a pooling of interests When a pooling of interests occurs, the previous year's (or years') financial statements should be restated to incorporate the financial statements of all of the entities involved in the business combination. Subsequent to the pooling of the entities, an auditor may be requested to report on the previous year's restated (consolidated) financial statements; however, the auditor may not have audited all of the financial statements that form the basis for the restatement. Under this circumstance, the auditor must decide whether he or she has audited a sufficient part of the prior year's restated financial statements and therefore is in a position to report as the principal auditor on the restated financial statements of the previous year. If the auditor concludes that it is appropriate to serve as the principal auditor, the guidance discussed earlier with respect to formulating and expressing opinions based on another auditor's report should be observed (AU 543.16).

In some circumstances the auditor may conclude that it is not possible to serve as the principal auditor with respect to the restated financial statements. In this case, SAS-64 (Omnibus Statement on Auditing Standards—1990) concludes that the auditor (reporting on the current year's financial statements of the consolidated entity) may express an opinion limited to the *combining* of the prior year's financial statements. An example of an additional paragraph that may be added to the auditor's opinion on the current year's financial statements is illustrated below (AU 543.16).

We previously audited and reported on the consolidated balance sheet of X Company as of December 31, 19X4, and the related consolidated statements of income and cash flows for the year then ended, prior to their restatement for the 19X5 pooling of interests. The contribution of X Company and its subsidiaries to total assets, revenues, and net income represented 65%, 68%, and 70% of the respective restated totals. Separate financial statements of the other companies included in the 19X4 restated consolidated balance sheet and consolidated statements of income and cash flows were audited and reported on separately by other auditors. We also audited the combination of the accompanying consolidated balance sheets and consolidated statements of income and cash flows for the year ended December 31, 19X4, after restatement for the 19X5 pooling of interests. In our opinion, such consolidated statements have been properly combined on the basis described in Note A of the notes to the consolidated financial statements.

Unaudited Financial Statements—Public Companies

While SAS-58 describes the format of a disclaimer of opinion based on a scope limitation, SAS-26 describes the format of a disclaimer when the financial statements of a *public* company are unaudited (AU 504.05).

Presented below is an example of a disclaimer of an opinion that should be issued when the financial statements of a public company are unaudited (AU 504.05).

The accompanying balance sheet of X Company as of December 31, 19X5, and the related statements of income, retained earnings, and cash flows for the year then ended were not audited by us and accordingly, we do not express an opinion on them.

UNCERTAINTY CONDITIONS

Uncertainties Unrelated to Going Concern

During the preparation of financial statements, a client must make a variety of accounting estimates, such as the estimated useful life of depreciable assets, a provision for doubtful accounts receivable, and an accrual for a loss contingency. In most instances, the auditor is able to collect sufficient competent evidence to support the reasonableness of accounting estimates. In this case, the auditor's standard report is not modified.

FAS-5 (Accounting for Contingencies) provides accounting and reporting standards applicable to a type of uncertainty, namely loss contingencies. A *loss contingency* is defined as "an existing condition, situation, or set of circumstances involving uncertainty as to possible loss to an enterprise that will ultimately be resolved when one or more future events occur or fail to occur." Furthermore, the following classifications are used to categorize loss contingencies (AU 508.48–.49):

Probable—The future event or events are likely to occur.

Reasonably possible—The chance of the future event or events occurring is more than remote but less than likely.

Remote—The chance of the future event or events occurring is slight.

> **OBSERVATION:** *FAS-5 is not applicable to all uncertainties; however, the Statement provides the only broad guidance in this area and may be used as a general frame of reference when evaluating other uncertainties. Additional guidance is established by SOP 94-6 (Disclosure of Certain Significant Risks and Uncertainties).*

The accounting and reporting standards for loss contingencies are summarized below.

Characteristics of Loss Contingency	Presentation in the Financial Statements
Probable and a reasonable estimate (or range) of the loss can be made	Accrual of loss contingency
Probable but no reasonable estimate of the loss can be made	Disclosure of loss contingency
Reasonable estimate of the loss can be made but the loss is less than probable but more than remote	Disclosure of loss contingency
Remote likelihood of occurrence	No accrual or disclosure

With the issuance of SAS-79, the Auditing Standards Board no longer requires that an audit report be modified when uncertainties exist, assuming the accounting and reporting standards established by FAS-5 have been observed (AU 508.29).

> **OBSERVATION:** *The standards established by SAS-79 apply to reports issued or reissued on or after February 29, 1996. Per the Statement, the auditor should delete an uncertainty explanatory paragraph from an audit report that is being reissued, even if the uncertainty has not been resolved. If the auditor decides to add an "emphasis-of-a-matter paragraph," the paragraph may refer to the change required by the new auditing standard.*

OBSERVATION: The standards established by FAS-5 are highly judgmental and some would argue that, in general, businesses do not do an adequate job of reporting the results of uncertainties in their financial statements. The action taken by the Board places the auditor in the undesirable position of deciding whether accounting or disclosure standards have been violated, which is often difficult to do because of the subjectivity related to the application of the financial reporting standards. Before the issuance of SAS-79, the auditor could express an unqualified position and describe an uncertainty (under certain circumstances) in an explanatory paragraph. The new standards eliminate this option and force the auditor to conclude either that accounting and reporting standards have been observed or that they have not been observed. If the standards have not been observed, a qualified opinion or an adverse opinion must be expressed. The effect of the new standards may be that uncertainties that were previously highlighted in the auditor's report (and which put a financial-statement reader on alert) will no longer be communicated to interested parties. The narrowness of the Board's position can be circumvented by treating uncertainties as matters to be emphasized. The emphasis of a matter is discussed later in this chapter.

OBSERVATION: Matters of uncertainty should not be confused with scope limitations and deviations from generally accepted accounting principles. A scope limitation arises when evidential matter exists with respect to the uncertainty but had not been made available to the auditor. A deviation from generally accepted accounting principles occurs when (1) the uncertainty is not adequately disclosed, (2) an inappropriate accounting principle is used, or (3) an unreasonable accounting estimate is made. Scope limitations may lead to the expression of a qualified opinion or a disclaimer of opinion. Deviations from generally accepted accounting principles may lead to a qualified or adverse opinion (AU 508.29–.32).

Uncertainties Related to Going Concern

SAS-59 (The Auditor's Consideration of an Entity's Ability to Continue as a Going Concern) identifies a separate uncertainty condition referred to as a substantial doubt about an entity's ability to continue as a going concern. (The audit approach to identify substantial doubt circumstances is discussed in the chapter entitled "Evidence.")

If an auditor concludes that there is substantial doubt about an entity's continued existence as a going concern, an explanatory paragraph should be added to the standard report and placed after the opinion paragraph. SAS-64 requires that the explanatory paragraph include the phrase "substantial doubt about its [the entity's] ability to continue as a going concern," or similar wording. If similar wording is used, the terms *substantial doubt* and *going concern* must be used in the phrase. The introductory, scope, and opinion paragraphs should not refer to the explanatory paragraph. An unqualified opinion should be expressed. An example of a substantial doubt explanatory paragraph is presented below (AU 341.12–.13).

The accompanying financial statements have been prepared assuming that the Company will continue as a going concern. As discussed in Note X to the financial statements, the Company has experienced operating losses over the past seven years, resulting in a deficit equity position. The company's financial position and operating results raise substantial doubt about its ability to continue as a going concern. Management's plans in regard to these matters are also described in Note X. The financial statements do not include any adjustments that might result from the outcome of this uncertainty.

SAS-77 prohibits the use of conditional language when a substantial doubt explanatory paragraph is presented. Two examples of unacceptable language that are provided by SAS-77 are as follows (AU 341.13):

• If the company continues to suffer recurring losses from operations and continues to have a net capital deficiency, there may be substantial doubt about its ability to continue as a going concern.

• The company has been unable to renegotiate its expiring credit agreements. Unless the company is able to obtain financial support, there is substantial doubt about its ability to continue as a going concern.

The going-concern paragraph should be included in subsequent auditor's reports as long as substantial doubt about the entity's existence continues. Should the substantial doubt condition cease in a future period, there is no need to include the *substantial doubt* explanatory paragraph for reports that cover previous periods in which the substantial doubt condition was originally applicable (AU 341.16).

> *OBSERVATION: SAS-59 does not discuss the conditions related to substantial doubt about an entity's ability to continue as a going concern that may lead to a disclaimer of opinion; however, it does note that nothing in the Statement is intended to preclude an auditor from declining to express an opinion in cases involving uncertainties.*

Subsequent to the issuance of an auditor's report that referred to a going-concern issue, the client may request the auditor to reissue the report and remove the going-concern reference because the client believes the circumstances that led to the uncertainty have been changed. Since the request by the client is a new engagement, the auditor is not obligated to accept it. If the auditor accepts the engagement, the circumstances related to the going-concern issue should be examined to determine whether it is appropriate to revise the report.

Auditing Interpretation, "Eliminating a Going-Concern Explanatory Paragraph from a Reissued Report" (August 1995), notes that the auditor is not obligated to reissue a report; however, if the auditor decides to do so, he or she should perform the following procedures (AU 9341.01–.02):

- Audit the event or transaction that prompted the request to delete the going-concern paragraph.
- Perform procedures related to subsequent events as described in AU 560.11–.12.
- Consider the factors related to the going-concern concept as described in AU 341.06-.11.

In addition to the listed procedures, the auditor should conduct other procedures he or she deems appropriate. Based on the results of applying those procedures, the auditor should reassess the going-concern status of the client.

OTHER CONDITIONS

Emphasis of a Matter

Although reporting standards and rules are very detailed, it would be difficult to promulgate rules to provide guidance in every reporting situation. To provide some reporting flexibility, the auditor's report may emphasize a matter without qualifying the opinion. SAS-58 presents the following as possible matters that could be emphasized (AU 508.37):

- The entity reported on is a component of a larger entity.
- There have been significant transactions with a related party.
- A significant subsequent event has taken place.
- Comparability of financial statements has been affected by the accounting treatment of an event or transaction.

When the auditor decides to emphasize a matter, the auditing standards do not specify the placement of the emphasis paragraph, but do state that the introductory, scope, and opinion paragraphs should not refer to the explanatory paragraph. An unqualified opinion should be expressed. An example of an explanatory paragraph that emphasizes a matter is presented below (AU 508.37).

Company X, a wholly owned subsidiary of Z Company, sells 15% of its output to Z Company. As more fully described in Note Y to the financial statements, these intercompany sales are based on negotiated prices between the Company and Z Company, at approximate market prices that exist within the industry.

> **OBSERVATION:** *When an explanatory paragraph contains more information than the related financial statement disclosure, the auditor should consider whether the financial statements have been prepared in accordance with GAAP (inadequate disclosure).*

Reporting When Not Independent

The second general standard requires that the auditor be independent. Many of the relationships that should be avoided in order not to impair independence or not to suggest the loss of independence in the eyes of others are established by the Code of Professional Conduct. When the independent auditor concludes that he or she is no longer independent, a disclaimer of opinion must be expressed. Under these circumstances, no introductory, scope, or explanatory paragraphs are included in the auditor's report. The disclaimer of opinion should simply state that the auditor is not independent and that no opinion is expressed on the financial statements. The reason for the lack of independence *must not* be described in the auditor's report (AU 504.08–.09).

An example of a disclaimer of an opinion because the auditor is not independent is illustrated below (AU 504.10).

We are not independent with respect to X Company, and the accompanying balance sheet as of December 31, 19X5, and the related statements of income, retained earnings, and cash flows for the year then ended were not audited by us and, accordingly, we do not express an opinion on them.

When the auditor is not independent, and the client is a nonpublic entity, a review report cannot be issued. A compilation report may be issued if the standards established by Statements on Standards for Accounting and Review Services are observed. These standards are discussed in the chapter entitled "Compilation and Review Engagements."

Other Data and Information in a Document Containing Audited Financial Statements

The auditor's report may be included in a document that contains other information. For example, a company's annual report may include a message from the chief executive officer and descriptions of operations and future plans, as well as a variety of charts and graphs accompanied by explanations. SAS-8 (Other Information in Documents Containing Audited Financial Statements) establishes the review and reporting responsibilities of the independent auditor with respect to other information in (1) annual reports sent to holders of securities, (2) annual reports sent to charitable or philanthropic organizations, (3) annual reports filed with the SEC as required by the Securities Exchange Act of 1934, and (4) other documents reviewed by the auditor based on the client's request. Although the auditor is not required to audit the other information, he or she must read the information to determine whether there is (1) a material inconsistency or (2) a material misstatement of fact, as compared with the information presented in the financial statements (AU 550.01–.04).

In determining whether there is a material inconsistency, the auditor should compare other information in the document to the audited financial statements. For example, the president's letter may refer to sales for the current year, and the auditor should simply verify that the sales figure in the president's letter agrees with the sales amount reported on the income statement. When a material inconsistency is discovered, the auditor must determine which information is correct. If it is concluded that the client's other information is incorrect and the client refuses to change the other information, the auditor may choose to (1) withdraw from the engagement, (2) refuse to allow the client to include the auditor's report in the document, or (3) report on the material inconsistency. If the auditor decides to report on the material inconsistency, an explanatory paragraph containing a description of the inconsistency is included; however, the opinion paragraph is unqualified and makes no reference to the explanatory paragraph. The rationale for this conclusion is that the auditor's opinion is limited to the information that was audited in accordance with generally accepted auditing standards (AU 550.04–.05).

It is more difficult to identify a material misstatement of fact in an annual report because the nature of much of the other information will be nonaccounting and beyond the expertise of the auditor. SAS-8 simply states that judgment should be used, and that the auditor may consider (1) notifying the client in writing of the apparent material misstatement and (2) seeking legal advice concerning other steps to be taken (AU 550.06).

> **OBSERVATION:** *Apparently, SAS-8 is vague in this area of material misstatement because it emphasizes the auditor's limited expertise in relation to the other information. In other words, proceed with caution. However, if an auditor discovers a material misstatement of fact and the client refuses to change the other information and the auditor still issues a report, it may be wise for the auditor to follow the reporting format described when a material inconsistency is encountered.*

Required Supplementary Information

The FASB and GASB have the authority to promulgate reporting standards requiring that certain supplementary information be included with the basic financial statements. While required supplementary information must be presented by the affected entities, there is no requirement that the information be audited (AU 558.01). (Certain limited procedures that must be applied to required supplementary information are discussed in the chapter entitled "Evidence.")

An explanatory paragraph applicable to required supplementary information should not be added to the standard auditor's report except in the following circumstances (AU 558.08):

- Required supplementary information is omitted.

- Measurement or presentation of the required supplementary information deviates from guidelines established by the FASB or GASB.

- Auditor is unable to apply the limited procedures to the required supplementary information.

- Auditor has substantial doubt about whether the required supplementary information conforms to established guidelines.

Required supplementary information is omitted   When the supplementary information required by the FASB or GASB is omitted from the financial statements, an explanatory paragraph should be added to the standard report after the opinion paragraph. The introductory, scope, and opinion paragraphs should not refer to the explanatory paragraph and an unqualified opinion should be expressed on the basic financial statements. An example of an explanatory paragraph that is appropriate when required supplementary information is omitted is illustrated below (AU 558.08).

The [name of company or governmental entity] has not presented [describe supplementary information required by the FASB or GASB] that the [Financial Accounting Standards Board or Governmental Accounting Standards Board] has determined is necessary to supplement, although not required to be part of, the basic financial statements.

Deviation in measurement or presentation of required supplementary information   When the required supplementary information is not prepared or presented as prescribed, an explanatory paragraph should be added to the standard report. An example of such an explanatory paragraph is presented below (AU 558.08).

The [specifically identify the supplementary information] on page XX is not a required part of the basic financial statements, and we did not audit and do not express an opinion on such information. However, we have applied certain limited procedures, which consist principally of inquiries of management regarding the methods of measurement and presentation of the supplementary information. As a result of such limited procedures, we believe that [specifically identify the supplementary information] is not in conformity with guidelines established by the [Financial Accounting Standards Board or Governmental Accounting Standards Board] because [describe the material departures from the FASB or GASB guidelines].

Limited procedures not applied to required supplementary information   When the auditor is not able or allowed to apply limited procedures to the required supplementary information, an explanatory paragraph should be added to the standard report. An example for an explanatory paragraph of this nature is illustrated below (AU 558.08).

The [specifically identify the supplementary information] on page XX is not a required part of the basic financial statements, and we did not audit and do not express an opinion on such information. Further, we were unable to apply to the information certain procedures prescribed by professional standards because [describe reasons].

Even though the auditor was unable to apply the limited procedures, the auditor may be aware of deviations from the measurement or presentation of the supplementary required information. These deviations also should be described in an explanatory paragraph (AU 558.08).

Substantial doubt about conformance of required supplementary information   When the auditor has applied the limited procedures to the required supplementary information but is unable to resolve substantial doubts about the measurement or presentation of the information, an explanatory paragraph should be added to the standard report. Presented below is an example of an explanatory paragraph appropriate under this circumstance.

The [specifically identify the supplementary information] on page XX is not a required part of the basic financial statements, and we did not audit and do not express an opinion on such information. However, we have applied certain limited procedures prescribed by professional standards that raised doubts that we were unable to resolve regarding whether material modifications should be made to the information for it to conform with guidelines established by the [Financial Accounting Standards Board or Governmental Accounting Standards Board].

The auditor should consider including in the explanatory paragraph the reasons the substantial doubts were not resolved.

> **OBSERVATION:** *An Auditing Interpretation on association with financial statements, "Annual Report Disclosure of Unaudited Fourth Quarter Interim Data" (November 1979), states that the auditor has no obligation to audit disclosures of unaudited fourth quarter interim data. These disclosures are not essential for a fair presentation of annual financial statements (AU 9504.01–.07).*

Reporting on Fair Value Disclosures

FAS-107 (Disclosures About Fair Value of Financial Instruments) requires that "an entity shall disclose, either in the body of the financial statements or in the accompanying notes, the fair value of financial instruments for which it is practicable to estimate that value." Some companies may disclose only the information required by FAS-107, while others may voluntarily disclose the fair value of assets and liabilities not required by FAS-107. An Auditing Interpretation of SAS-57, "Performance and Reporting Guidance Related to Fair Value Disclosures" (February 1993), provides guidance for auditing and reporting on fair value disclosures (AU 9342.01–.10).

The auditor must collect sufficient evidential matter to satisfy the following (AU 9342.02):

- Valuation principles are acceptable.
- Valuation principles are consistently applied and their application is adequately documented.
- Estimation methods used and significant assumptions made are properly disclosed.

Reporting on required information   When a client reports only the disclosures required by FAS-107 and the auditor has satisfied the three conditions listed above, a standard auditor's report is issued with no reference to the fair value disclosures. If the required disclosures are not made, the auditor must decided whether to modify the standard report (qualified opinion or adverse opinion) depending on the assessment of the materiality of the disclosures omitted from the financial statements (AU 9342.04–.10).

> *OBSERVATION: The Interpretation notes that it may be appropriate to expand the standard report by adding an emphasis-of-a-matter paragraph when fair value is based on management's best estimate rather than on quoted market prices.*

Reporting on required and voluntary information   When voluntary information on fair values is presented, that information may be audited only when the following conditions are met (AU 9342.04).

1. Criteria used to measure and disclose the information are reasonable.

2. Application of the disclosure and measurement criteria by competent persons would result in similar information.

The Interpretation concludes that voluntary disclosures may result in the presentation of essentially a complete balance sheet or an incomplete balance sheet based on fair values (AU 9342.05).

Complete balance sheet   If the fair value disclosures (both required and voluntary) encompass all material items in the balance sheet, the Interpretation concludes that the auditor should expand the report by adding the paragraph below (AU 9342.06).

We have also audited in accordance with generally accepted auditing standards the supplemental fair value balance sheet of X Company as of December 31, 19X5. As described in Note X, the supplemental fair value balance sheet has been prepared by management to present relevant financial information that is not provided by the historical-cost balance sheets and is not intended to be a presentation in conformity with generally accepted accounting principles. In addition, the supplemental fair value balance sheet does not purport to present the net realizable, liquidation, or market value of X Company as a whole. Furthermore, amounts ultimately realized by X Company from the disposal of assets may vary significantly from the fair values presented. In our opinion, the supplemental fair value balance sheet referred to above presents fairly, in all material respects, the information set forth therein as described in Note X.

Incomplete balance sheet If the fair value disclosures do not include all of the material items in the balance sheet and the disclosures are made either on the face of the financial statements or in notes, the Interpretation concludes that there is no need to make reference to the disclosures in the auditor's report. However, if the disclosures are presented in a supplemental schedule or exhibit, the auditor should add the paragraph below to the report (AU 9342.07).

Our audit was conducted for the purpose of forming an opinion on the basic financial statements taken as a whole. The fair value disclosures contained in Schedule X are presented for purposes of additional analysis and are not a required part of the basic financial statements. Such information has been subjected to the auditing procedures applied in the audit of the basic financial statements and, in our opinion, is fairly stated in all material respects in relation to the basic financial statements taken as a whole.

Reporting when disclosures are not audited The auditor may not be requested to audit voluntary fair value disclosures or the auditor may be unable to audit the information because the conditions listed earlier may not be satisfied. When voluntary fair value disclosures are not audited but are presented in an auditor-submitted document, and appear in on the face of the financial statements, notes, or in a supplemental schedule to the basic financial statements, the disclosures should be labeled "unaudited" and the paragraph below should be added to the auditor's report (AU 9342.08).

Our audit was conducted for the purpose of forming an opinion on the basic financial statements taken as a whole. The fair value disclosures contained in Schedule X are presented for purposes of additional analysis and are not a required part of the basic financial statements. Such information has not been subjected to the auditing procedures applied in the audit of the basic financial statements, and, accordingly, we express no opinion on them.

> *OBSERVATION: When the unaudited voluntary disclosures are presented in a client-prepared document and the information is included on the face of the financial statements, the notes, or in a supplemental schedule, the disclosures should be labeled "unaudited." There is no need to disclaim an opinion on the information. If the unaudited voluntary disclosures are not presented on the face of the financial statements, the notes, or in a supplemental schedule, the information should be read by the auditor in a manner consistent with the guidance established by SAS-8 (Other Information in Documents Containing Audited Financial Statements) (AU 9342.09).*

Auditor-Submitted Documents

SAS-29 (Reporting on Information Accompanying the Basic Financial Statement in Auditor-Submitted Documents) replaces the professional guidelines associated with the so-called *long-form reports*. Specifically, SAS-29 is applicable to auditor-submitted documents that contain information accompanying basic financial statements. SAS-29 is also applicable to financial statements prepared in accordance with a comprehensive basis of accounting other than GAAP (AU 551.01).

> *OBSERVATION: The auditor's reporting responsibilities for client-prepared documents (for example, an annual report) and auditor-submitted documents (for example, a document bound in the CPA firm's cover) differ. In a client-prepared document, other information (that is, information other than the financial statements, related notes, and required supplementary information) included in the document is not referred to in the auditor's report. In an auditor-submitted document, the auditor must disclaim an opinion on the other information, unless the CPA has been engaged to audit, and has audited, it.*

Auditor-submitted documents may contain information outside the basic financial statements, such as statistical data concerning operating ratios and trends, historical financial summaries, descriptions of auditing procedures, and nonaccounting data. The additional information contained in the auditor-submitted document must be reported on by the auditor. The report should clearly identify the additional information and state that the information is not a required part of the basic financial statements and is presented as additional data for the user. The report should also state that the purpose of the examination is to form an opinion on the financial statements taken as a whole. Finally, the report should either disclaim an opinion on the additional information or note that information is fairly stated in relation to the financial statements taken as a whole. The auditor's opinion on the additional information may be incorporated in the standard report or may appear in a separate opinion elsewhere in the auditor-submitted document. The following example illustrates a paragraph added to the standard auditor's report applicable to additional information in an auditor-submitted document (AU 551.02–.03).

Our audit was made for the purpose of forming an opinion on the basic financial statements taken as a whole. The accompanying information presented on pages 14 through 16 is presented for purposes of additional analysis and is not a required part of the basic financial statements. Such information has been subjected to the procedures applied in the audit of the basic financial statements and, in our opinion, is fairly stated in all material respects in relation to the basic financial statements taken as a whole.

If the auditor concludes that the additional information is materially misstated, the report should be modified or the auditor should not agree to include the information in the auditor-submitted document (AU 551.09).

The auditor-submitted document may contain nonaccounting information that cannot be verified by the auditor. Under these circumstances, a disclaimer of opinion should be issued.

On the other hand, auditing procedures may be described as additional information. These procedures should be separated from other information, and care must be taken so that the additional information does not contradict or otherwise detract from the scope paragraph of the report (AU 551.11).

Auditor-submitted documents may contain consolidated or combined financial statements supplemented by consolidating or combining information. When the additional information has not been separately audited, an explanatory paragraph should state that (1) the purpose of the audit was to form an opinion on the financial statements taken as a whole, (2) the consolidating information is presented as additional data, and (3) the consolidating information is fairly stated in all material respects in relation to the consolidated financial statements (AU 551.16–.17). Presented below is an example of a paragraph added to the standard auditor's report that is applicable to consolidating or combining information included in an auditor-submitted document (AU 551.18).

Our audit was made for the purpose of forming an opinion on the consolidated financial statements taken as a whole. The consolidating information is presented for purposes of additional analysis of the consolidated financial statements rather than to present the financial position, results of operations, and cash flows of the individual companies. The consolidated information has been subjected to the procedures applied in the audit of the consolidated financial statements and, in our opinion, is fairly stated in all material respects in relation to the consolidated financial statements taken as a whole.

OBSERVATION: SAS-29 does not provide the auditor with the option to disclaim an opinion on the consolidating information. This is reasonable because an opinion on the consolidated financial statements could not be formed without subjecting the consolidating information to appropriate auditing procedures.

When an auditor-submitted document includes supplementary information required by the FASB or GASB, and the engagement did not include the audit of the supplementary information, the auditor should disclaim an opinion on the information. An example of a disclaimer of opinion on required supplementary information included in an auditor-submitted document is presented below (AU 551.15).

The [identify the supplementary information] on page XX is not a required part of the basic financial statements but is supplementary information required by the [Financial Accounting Standards Board or Governmental Accounting Standards Board]. We have applied certain limited procedures, which consisted principally of inquiries of management regarding the methods of measurement and presentation of the supplementary information. However, we did not audit the information and express no opinion on it.

An explanatory paragraph applicable to required supplementary information included in an auditor-submitted document should be added to the standard auditor's report under the following conditions (AU 551.15):

- Required supplementary information is omitted.
- Measurement or presentation of the required supplementary information deviates from guidelines established by the FASB or GASB.
- Auditor is unable to apply the limited procedures to the required supplementary information.
- Auditor has substantial doubt about whether the required supplementary information conforms to established guidelines.

Under these circumstances, the auditor should add an explanatory paragraph similar to the ones discussed in the section entitled "Required Supplementary Information."

Piecemeal Opinions

When an adverse opinion or a disclaimer of opinion is expressed, the auditor is prohibited from issuing a piecemeal opinion on some items that appear in the financial statements (AU 508.73).

Negative Assurance

When an auditor expresses a disclaimer of opinion on the financial statements, the disclaimer should not be contradicted by a negative assurance. A negative assurance implies that the financial statements, or other financial information, may be in accordance with generally accepted accounting principles, since nothing to the contrary was discovered during the engagement.

REPORTING ON COMPARATIVE
FINANCIAL STATEMENTS

Most financial statements are presented on a comparative basis. SAS-58 requires that prior-year financial statements presented with the current year be reported on by the continuing auditor or, when appropriate, by the predecessor auditor. When all financial statements presented have been audited by the same accounting firm, the introductory, scope, and opinion paragraphs refer to and report on all the financial statements. This simply means that plural terms are substituted for singular terms, so that reference will be made to balance sheets, income statements, and so forth. An example of an auditor's report that covers comparative statements for two years is illustrated below (AU 508.74).

We have audited the accompanying balance sheets of X Company as of December 31, 19X5 and 19X4, and the related statements of income, retained earnings, and cash flows for the years then ended. These financial statements are the responsibility of the Company's management. Our responsibility is to express an opinion on these financial statements based on our audits.

We conducted our audits in accordance with generally accepted auditing standards. Those standards require that we plan and perform the audit to obtain reasonable assurance about whether the financial statements are free of material misstatement. An audit includes examining, on a test basis, evidence supporting the amounts and disclosures in the financial statements. An audit also includes assessing the accounting principles used and significant estimates made by management, as well as evaluating the overall financial statement presentation. We believe that our audits provide a reasonable basis for our opinion.

In our opinion, the financial statements referred to above present fairly, in all material respects, the financial position of X Company as of December 31, 19X5 and 19X4, and the results of its operations and its cash flows for the years then ended in conformity with generally accepted accounting principles.

If one or more of the financial statements presented on a comparative basis require that the auditor's report be modified, the report modification guidelines section of this *Guide* should be observed. For example, the prior year's financial statements may be presented in accordance with GAAP and the current year's financial statements may not be presented in accordance with GAAP. In this event, (1) the introductory paragraph refers to both the current and prior years' financial statements, (2) an explanatory paragraph is added that contains an explanation of the deviation from GAAP in the current year's financial statements, and (3) the opinion paragraph contains an unqualified opinion on the prior year's financial statements and a qualified opinion (with reference to the explanatory paragraph) on the current year's financial statements (AU 508.76).

Presented below is an example of an auditor's report with different opinions on the comparative financial statements (AU 508.76).

We have audited the accompanying balance sheets of X Company as of December 31, 19X5 and 19X4, and the related statements of income, retained earnings, and cash flows for the years then ended. These financial statements are the responsibility of the Company's management. Our responsibility is to express an opinion on these financial statements based on our audits.

We conducted our audits in accordance with generally accepted auditing standards. Those standards require that we plan and perform the audit to obtain reasonable assurance about whether the financial statements are free of material misstatement. An audit includes examining, on a test basis, evidence supporting the amounts and disclosures in the financial statements. An audit also includes assessing the accounting principles used and significant estimates made by management, as well as evaluating the overall financial statement presentation. We believe that our audits provide a reasonable basis for our opinion.

As more fully described in Note 7 to the financial statements, a net provision for loss on abandonment of equipment of $14,000,000 after related income taxes has been presented as an extraordinary charge against earnings for 19X4. In our opinion, generally accepted accounting principles require that the gross amount of such provision be part of the determination of income from operations before taxes and that the per share amount of the provision not be separately presented in the statement of income.

In our opinion, except for the effects of the matter described in the previous paragraph on the 19X4 statement of income, the financial statements referred to above present fairly, in all material respects, the financial position of X Company as of December 31, 19X5 and 19X4, and the results of its operations and its cash flows for the years then ended in conformity with generally accepted accounting principles.

In this example, the auditor's opinion on the prior year's income statement is qualified because of a departure from generally accepted accounting principles, but an unqualified opinion is expressed on the current year's financial statements.

Updated Opinion Different from Previous Opinion

When a continuing auditor repeats a previous opinion on a prior year's financial statements, it is referred to as *updating* the report.

Updating means that the auditor has considered the appropriateness of the prior opinion in the context of the results of the current engagement. Thus, it must be determined whether the prior opinion is still applicable to the prior financial statements. If it is concluded that the prior opinion is still appropriate, the reporting guidelines applicable to comparative financial statements discussed above are followed (AU 508.77).

If the auditor believes the prior opinion is not appropriate, the current report (which covers both years) must include an explanatory paragraph stating why a different opinion on the prior financial statements is being expressed. The explanatory paragraph must disclose (1) that the updated opinion is different from the prior original opinion, (2) the reason the opinion is being revised, (3) the type of opinion previously issued, and (4) the date of the prior audit report. If the revised prior-year opinion is not unqualified, the current report must include an additional explanatory paragraph describing the deficiency (AU 508.78).

When an explanatory paragraph is added because of a change in the opinion expressed on a previous year's financial statements, the introductory, scope, and opinion paragraphs would not refer to the explanatory paragraph and an unqualified opinion is expressed on both years' financial statements (assuming that unqualified opinions are appropriate under the circumstances). An example of the explanatory paragraph is presented below (AU 508.78).

In our report dated February 18, 19X5, we expressed an opinion that the 19X4 statement of income did not fairly present the results of operations in conformity with generally accepted accounting principles because a net provision for loss on abandonment of equipment had been presented as an extraordinary charge against earnings for 19X4. As described in Note X, the Company has changed its presentation of the net provision by revising the 19X4 statement of income so that the statement is now presented in accordance with generally accepted accounting principles. Accordingly, our present opinion on the 19X4 financial statements, as presented herein, is different from that expressed in our previous report.

Reporting by Predecessor Auditor

In most circumstances, a predecessor auditor will be in a position to "reissue" the report. Reissuance is different from updating a report, in that the predecessor auditor is not in a position to evaluate his or her opinion in the context of the current year's examination. However, before reissuing the report, the predecessor auditor is required to (1) read and compare the current year's financial statements with the prior year's financial statements and (2) obtain a representation letter from the successor auditor. The representation letter should state whether current conditions have any effect on the prior year's opinion. If the predecessor auditor concludes, on the basis of these limited procedures, that the prior year's opinion is still appropriate, the prior year's report is reissued as it was originally, including the same original report date. If the predecessor auditor concludes that the prior year's opinion is no longer appropriate, he or she may issue a revised report. In an explanatory paragraph, the predecessor auditor must fully describe the type of original opinion issued and the reason for changing the opinion. The reissued report should be dual-dated, showing the original report date and the revised report date. Language such as the following should be used: "March 3, 19X5, except for Note 12 as to which the date is February 26, 19X6" (It is important to remember that an auditor is responsible for material subsequent events up to the date appearing on the report.) (AU 508.80–.82).

If the predecessor auditor's report is omitted from the current year's comparative financial statements, the successor auditor must modify the introductory paragraph of the current report. The introductory paragraph should state that the prior-year financial statements were audited by another CPA, also noting the type of opinion expressed and the date of the report. If the predecessor's report was not unqualified, the reason for the modification must also be explained. The successor auditor's opinion paragraph refers only to the current year's financial statements (AU 508.83).

> *OBSERVATION: Based on the standards established by SAS-70, the successor auditor's report should not refer to an uncertainty explanatory paragraph included in the predecessor's report.*

An example of a successor auditor's report in which the predecessor auditor's report is not presented appears below (AU 508.83).

We have audited the balance sheet of X Company as of December 31, 19X5, and the related statements of income, retained earnings, and cash flows for the year then ended. These financial statements are the responsibility of the Company's management. Our responsibility is to express an opinion on these financial statements based on our audit. The financial statements of X Company as of December 31, 19X4, were audited by other auditors whose report, dated February 18, 19X5, expressed an unqualified opinion on those statements.

We conducted our audit in accordance with generally accepted auditing standards. Those standards require that we plan and perform the audit to obtain reasonable assurance about whether the financial statements are free of material misstatement. An audit includes examining, on a test basis, evidence supporting the amounts and disclosures in the financial statements. An audit also includes assessing the accounting principles used and significant estimates made by management, as well as evaluating the overall financial statement presentation. We believe that our audit provides a reasonable basis for our opinion.

In our opinion, the 19X5 financial statements referred to above present fairly, in all material respects, the financial position of X Company as of December 31, 19X5, and the results of its operations and its cash flows for the year then ended in conformity with generally accepted accounting principles.

OBSERVATION: Reference to the predecessor auditor's name is prohibited in the successor auditor's report except when the predecessor auditor's practice has been acquired by or merged into the practice of the successor auditor (AU 508.83).

If the prior year's financial statements have been restated, the introductory paragraph of the successor auditor's report should state that the predecessor auditor reported on the previous year's financial statements before they were restated. When the successor auditor has been engaged to audit the restatement adjustments, and has applied sufficient procedures to determine that the adjustments are appropriate, the following paragraph may be added to the successor auditor's report (AU 508.83).

We also audited the adjustments described in Note X that were applied to restate the 19X4 financial statements. In our opinion, such adjustments are appropriate and have been properly applied.

Reporting When Predecessor Auditor Has Ceased Operations

Reporting complications arise when financial statements of a prior period have been reported on by a predecessor auditor that has ceased operations. In 1991, the Auditing Standards Division provided guidance under this circumstance by issuing a Notice to Practitioners entitled "Audit, Review, and Compilation Considerations When a Predecessor Accountant Has Ceased Operations."

> **OBSERVATION:** *A Notice to Practitioners is nonauthoritative guidance prepared by the AICPA staff in consultation with members of the Auditing Standards Board. Notices are generally published in the "CPA Letter." Notices to Practitioners are not approved, disapproved, or otherwise acted on by a senior technical committee of the AICPA.*

Reports on audited financial statements presented with prior-period financial statements audited by a predecessor auditor that has ceased operations When prior-period financial statements have been audited by a predecessor auditor that has ceased operations, the reporting requirements depend on (1) whether the financial statements have been restated and (2) whether the financial statements are filed with the SEC.

When prior-period financial statements have not been restated, the successor auditor should add the following to the introductory paragraph of the current year's audit report:

- State that the prior-period financial statements were audited by another auditor that has ceased operations.

- Disclose the date of the predecessor auditor's report.

- Disclose the type of report issued by the predecessor auditor.

- If the predecessor auditor's report was other than a standard report, explain the basis for modification.

The name of the predecessor auditor should not be referred to in the successor auditor's report.

It should be noted that the information described above should be included in the successor auditor's introductory paragraph even when the predecessor auditor's report is reprinted and presented with the current auditor's report. Reprinting a previous audit report is not the same as reissuing a report.

When prior-period financial statements have been restated, the successor auditor should add the same information to the introductory paragraph as required when the statements have not been restated and, in addition, state that the predecessor auditor reported on the financial statements before restatement. When the successor auditor's engagement encompasses the restatement adjustments that apply to the prior-period financial statements, the following paragraph may be added to the end of the current-period audit report.

We also audited the adjustments described in Note X that were applied to restate the 19X1 financial statements. In our opinion, such adjustments are appropriate and have been properly applied.

A successor auditor may believe that financial statements audited by a predecessor auditor that has ceased operations could be materially misstated. Under this circumstance the successor auditor should inform management of the apparent problem and request that management determine whether the financial statements are materially misstated. Management, as part of its investigation, may find it helpful to discuss the matter with the previous engagement partner of the defunct CPA firm. If management concludes that the financial statements are materially misstated, it should convey that information to the individual(s) responsible for concluding the operations of the predecessor firm. Also, the successor auditor should consider whether management action is necessary so that the misstated financial statements will not be relied on in the future. If management does not respond to the problem in a satisfactory manner, the successor auditor should inform the audit committee (or equivalent party) of the matter. If the audit committee does not respond in an appropriate manner, the successor auditor should consider withdrawing from the engagement. Actions contemplated by the auditor should be discussed with legal counsel.

> *OBSERVATION: In planning audit procedures to determine the reasonableness of restatement adjustments, the successor auditor should recognize that the predecessor auditor will be unable to observe the standards established by SAS-1, Section 561 (Subsequent Discovery of Facts Existing at the Date of the Auditor's Report).*

When the successor auditor does not perform sufficient procedures to determine the reasonableness of restatement adjustments, the restatement adjustments should be designated as unaudited in the notes to the financial statements.

When the prior-period financial statements are filed with the SEC, the introductory paragraph of the successor auditor's report on the current-period financial statements should be expanded as explained above. The predecessor auditor's report should be *reprinted*, but in place of a manual signature, a statement similar to the following should be reproduced.

The report that appears below is a copy of the report issued by the company's previous independent auditor, [name of CPA firm]. That firm has discontinued performing auditing and accounting services.

If appropriate, the above statement should be expanded to note that the predecessor firm has filed for protection from creditors under the Bankruptcy Code, and the date of the filing should be disclosed.

Reports on audited financial statements of a nonpublic entity presented with prior-period financial statements compiled or reviewed by a predecessor accountant that has ceased operations When prior-period financial statements of a nonpublic company have been compiled or reviewed by a predecessor accountant that has ceased operations and those financial statements are presented with the current-period audited financial statements, the format of the successor auditor's report depends on whether the prior-period financial statements have been restated.

If prior-period financial statements have not been restated, a separate paragraph, similar to the ones illustrated below, should be added to the successor auditor's report.

[Prior Financial Statements Compiled]

The 19X5 financial statements were compiled by other accountants who have ceased operations, and their report thereon, dated February 12, 19X6, stated they did not audit or review those financial statements and, accordingly, express no opinion or other form of assurance on them.

[Prior Financial Statements Reviewed]

The 19X5 financial statements were reviewed by other accountants who have ceased operations, and their report thereon, dated February 12, 19X6, stated they were not aware of any material modifications that should be made to those statements for them to be in conformity with generally accepted accounting principles. However, a review is substantially less in scope than an audit and does not provide a basis for the expression of an opinion on the financial statements taken as a whole.

If the prior-period reports were other than standard compilation and review reports, the paragraphs illustrated above should be expanded to include the basis for modification.

If the prior-period financial statements have been restated, those statements should be compiled, reviewed, or audited and an appropriate report should be issued.

A successor auditor may believe that financial statements compiled or reviewed by a predecessor auditor that has ceased operations could be materially misstated. Under this circumstance the successor auditor should inform management of the apparent problem and request that management determine whether the financial statements are materially misstated. Management, as part of its investigation, may find it helpful to discuss the matter with the previous engagement partner of the defunct CPA firm. If management concludes that the financial statements are materially misstated, it should convey that information to the individual(s) responsible for concluding the operations of the predecessor firm. Also, the successor auditor should consider whether management action is necessary so that the misstated financial statements will not be relied on in the future. If management does not respond to the problem in a satisfactory manner, the successor auditor should inform the audit committee (or equivalent party) of the matter. If the audit committee does not respond in an appropriate manner, the successor auditor should consider withdrawing from the engagement. Actions contemplated by the auditor should be discussed with legal counsel.

Reports on compiled or reviewed financial statements presented with prior-period financial statements compiled, reviewed, or audited by a predecessor accountant that has ceased operations   When prior-period financial statements of a company have been compiled, reviewed, or audited by a predecessor accountant that has ceased operations and those financial statements are presented with the current-period compiled or reviewed financial statements, the format of the successor accountant's report depends on whether prior-period financial statements have been restated.

If prior-period financial statements have been compiled or reviewed and have not been restated, a separate paragraph, similar to the ones illustrated below, should be added to the successor accountant's report.

[Prior Financial Statements Compiled]

The 19X5 financial statements of X Company were compiled by other accountants who have ceased operations and whose report dated February 12, 19X6, stated that they did not express an opinion or any other form of assurance on those statements.

[Prior Financial Statements Reviewed]

The 19X5 financial statements of X Company were reviewed by other accountants who have ceased operations and whose report dated February 12, 19X6, stated that they were not aware of any material modifications that should be made to those statements in order for them to be in conformity with generally accepted accounting principles.

If prior-period financial statements have been audited and have not been restated, a separate paragraph, similar to the one presented below, should be added to the successor accountant's report.

The financial statements for the year ended December 31, 19X5, were audited by other accountants who have ceased operations, and they expressed an unqualified opinion on them in their report dated February 12, 19X6, but they have not performed any auditing procedures since that date.

If the prior year's auditor's report had been other than unqualified, the above paragraph should be expanded to describe the basis for the report modification.

If the prior-period financial statements have been restated, those financial statements should be compiled, reviewed, or audited and an appropriate report should be issued by the successor accountant.

> **OBSERVATION:** *When the successor accountant believes that prior-period financial statements should be revised but the prede-*

cessor accountant has ceased operations, the successor accountant should suggest that the client notify "the party responsible for winding up the affairs of the predecessor firm" of the matter. If the client refuses to make the communication or the reaction by the client's predecessor accountant is unsatisfactory, the successor accountant should discuss the matter with legal counsel.

OBSERVATION: *Additional guidance for successor auditors who need to work with predecessor auditors is included in the chapter entitled "Pre-Engagement Planning."*

Special Reports

The application of the four reporting standards to special reports is discussed in the chapter entitled "Auditor's Special Reports."

AUDITOR'S SPECIAL REPORTS

CONTENTS

Overview	**12.03**
Special Reports	**12.04**
Reporting on Conformity with a Comprehensive Basis of Accounting Other than GAAP	**12.04**
Adequate Disclosure	**12.07**
Reporting Standards	**12.08**
Reporting on Specified Elements, Accounts, or Items	**12.11**
Reporting Standards	**12.12**
Reporting on Compliance with Aspects of Contractual Agreements or Regulatory Requirements	**12.15**
Reporting Standards	**12.16**
Reporting on Financial Presentations to Comply with Contractual Agreements or Regulatory Provisions	**12.18**
Incomplete Presentations	**12.18**
Presentation Not in Accordance with GAAP or OCBOA	**12.22**
Reporting on Financial Information Presented in Prescribed Forms or Schedules	**12.24**
Modifications to the Standard Auditor's Special Report	**12.25**
Reporting on Financial Statements Prepared on the Liquidation Basis of Accounting	**12.26**
Initial Year Reporting (Single-Year Presentation)	**12.27**
Initial Year Reporting (Comparative-Years Presentation)	**12.27**
Reports on the Application of Accounting Principles	**12.28**
Standards of Performance	**12.30**
Standards of Reporting	**12.31**
Reporting on Financial Statements Prepared for Use in Other Countries	**12.33**
Auditing Standards	**12.34**

General Standards   12.34
Fieldwork Standards   12.35
Auditing Standards of Foreign Countries   12.35
Reporting Standards   12.35
Foreign GAAP / Foreign Use   12.35
Dual Statements (Foreign GAAP / U.S. GAAP)   12.38
Foreign GAAP / General U.S. Distribution   12.39

AUDITOR'S SPECIAL REPORTS

Overview

An *auditor* may be engaged to report on financial statements prepared on a cash basis, on a liquidation basis, or in conformity with accounting principles accepted in another country. Also, an *accountant* may be requested to render an informal opinion concerning the application of accounting principles. The generally accepted auditing standards and/or accountant's responsibilities in connection with these types of reports are discussed in this chapter. These standards include:

- SAS-62 (Special Reports)

- SAS-77 (Amendments to Statements on Auditing Standards No. 22, "Planning and Supervision," No. 59, "The Auditor's Consideration of an Entity's Ability to Continue as a Going Concern," and No. 62, "Special Reports")

- Auditing Interpretation (Reporting on Financial Statements Prepared on a Liquidation Basis of Accounting) (December 1984)

- SAS-51 (Reporting on Financial Statements Prepared for Use in Other Countries)

- SAS-50 (Reports on the Application of Accounting Principles)

SAS-62 provides guidance on auditor's reports in connection with (1) financial statements based on accounting principles other than GAAP, (2) specific items or accounts of a financial statement, (3) contractual or regulatory compliance relating to audited financial statements, (4) financial presentations prepared to comply with contractual agreements or regulatory provisions, and (5) financial information presented in a prescribed form that requires a prescribed form of auditor's report. SAS-62 contains a special report form that is similar to the standard auditor's report (AU 623).

SAS-77 precludes the general distribution of audited financial statements prepared in accordance with financial reporting standards required by a governmental regulatory agency.

An Auditing Interpretation entitled "Reporting on Financial Statements Prepared on a Liquidation Basis of Accounting" (December

1984) provides guidance for reporting on financial statements that are prepared on the *liquidation basis* of accounting (AU 9508.33–.38).

SAS-51 provides guidance to the auditor who is engaged by a U.S. entity to report on financial statements that are based on accounting principles that are generally accepted in another country and that are intended to be used outside the United States. For the purposes of applying the provisions of SAS-51, a U.S. entity is one that is organized or domiciled in the United States (AU 534).

SAS-50 establishes standards relating to an accountant's oral advice or written report concerning an actual or hypothetical situation involving the application of accounting principles. Reports of this nature may be requested by prospective clients, bankers, or lawyers. When rendering oral or written advice to a prospective client concerning the application of accounting principles, the accountant must exercise care because the prospective client may or may not be *shopping* for an opinion (AU 625).

SPECIAL REPORTS

SAS-62 (Special Reports) establishes the generally accepted auditing standards for five broad categories of special reports. The five broad categories are (AU 623.01):

- Reporting on a comprehensive basis of accounting other than GAAP
- Reporting on specified elements or items of a financial statement
- Reporting on compliance with contractual agreements or regulatory requirements related to audited financial statements
- Reporting on financial presentations to comply with contractual agreements or regulatory provisions
- Reporting on financial information presented in prescribed form that requires a prescribed form of auditor's report

Reporting on Conformity with a Comprehensive Basis of Accounting Other than GAAP

Financial statements may be issued by all types of entities or segments of entities, including commercial enterprises, not-for-profit organizations, individuals, estates, and governmental units. SAS-62 defines a *financial statement* as a "presentation of financial data, including accompanying notes, derived from accounting records that are intended to communicate an entity's economic resources or obligations at a point in time or the changes therein for a period of time in conformity with a comprehensive basis of accounting." For reporting purposes, SAS-62 considers a financial statement to consist of a statement of (1) financial position (balance sheet), (2) income or operations, (3) retained earnings, (4) cash flows, (5) changes in owners' equity, (6) assets and liabilities (excludes owners' equity accounts), (7) revenues and expenses, (8) summary of operations, (9) operations by product lines, and (10) cash receipts and disbursements. This broad definition does not restrict financial statements to those that are prepared in accordance with GAAP. Thus, an entity may prepare and issue a financial statement based on a comprehensive basis of accounting other than GAAP (AU 623.02).

When financial statements based on an other comprehensive basis of accounting (OCBOA) are prepared, the accountant should determine whether the financial statements are properly labeled. Care must be taken in titling financial statements so that a reader of the statements will not infer that the financial statements are prepared in accordance with GAAP (AU 623.07).

The earlier definition of a financial statement referred to a presentation of financial data that intends to communicate an entity's economic resources or obligations in accordance with generally accepted accounting principles or a comprehensive basis of accounting other than generally accepted accounting principles. When GAAP-based financial statements are presented, such a statement is referred to as a balance sheet or statement of financial position. When OCBOA-based financial statements are presented, it would be inappropriate to refer to the statement as a balance sheet or statement of financial position. For example, if the financial statements are prepared on a modified cash basis, the title might be "Statement of Assets and Liabilities—Modified Cash Basis." If the financial statements are prepared on a regulatory accounting basis an appropriate name would be "Balance Sheet—Regulatory Accounting Basis" (AU 623.07).

The definitions of a financial statement in Statement on Standards for Accounting and Review Services (SSARS) No. 1 (Compilation and Review of Financial Statements) and SAS-62 refer to presenting financial data related to changes in an entity's economic resources and obligations. When GAAP-based financial statements are presented, they are referred to as an income statement or statement of operations. When OCBOA-based financial statements are presented more appropriate names may be "Statement of Cash Receipts and Disbursements" (for a cash-based financial statement) and "Statement of Revenues and Expenses—Income Tax Basis" (for a tax-based financial statement) (AU 623.07).

A financial statement or presentation should be clearly and accurately titled. If the auditor concludes that a financial statement or presentation is not properly titled, an explanatory paragraph should be added to the auditor's special report, and the opinion on the statement or presentation should be qualified (AU 623.07).

> **OBSERVATION:** *Under SAS-58 (Reports on Audited Financial Statements), if an auditor is requested to report on only one financial statement from a set of financial statements, there is no scope limitation of the audit. Under SAS-58, this type of engagement is classified as a* **limited reporting engagement.**

Under the provisions of SAS-62, a comprehensive basis of accounting other than generally accepted accounting principles is restricted to the following (AU 623.04):

- A basis of accounting that the reporting entity uses to comply with the requirements or financial reporting provisions of a governmental regulatory agency to whose jurisdiction the entity is subject

- A basis of accounting that the reporting entity uses or expects to use to file its income tax return for the period covered by the financial statements

- The cash receipts and disbursements basis of accounting, and modifications of the cash basis having substantial support, such as recording depreciation on fixed assets or accruing income taxes

- A definite set of criteria having substantial support that is applied to all material items appearing in financial statements, such as the price-level basis of accounting

> **OBSERVATION:** *An Auditing Interpretation of SAS-62, "Reporting on Current-Value Financial Statements That Supplement Historical-Cost Financial Statements in a General-Use Presentation of Real Estate Entities" (July 1990), concludes that an engagement to report on current-value financial statements that supplement historical-cost financial statements of a real estate entity may be accepted only if (1) the current-value financial statements are based on measurement and disclosure criteria that are reasonable*

and (2) the current-value financial statements are reliable (competent persons using the same criteria would arrive at similar financial statements that are not materially different from one another) (AU 9623.55–.59).

If an entity reports on a comprehensive basis of accounting not listed above, the concepts established in SAS-69 (The Meaning of "Present Fairly in Conformity with Generally Accepted Accounting Principles" in the Independent Auditor's Report) should be used to determine whether the special-basis financial statements are presented in a manner that results in a material deviation from GAAP. If the deviation(s) from GAAP is considered to be material, reporting standards established by SAS-58 should be observed when preparing the auditor's special report. That is, a qualified or an adverse opinion should be expressed on the financial statements (AU 623.06).

Adequate disclosure Generally accepted auditing standards are applicable to the audit of financial statements prepared in conformity with an other comprehensive basis of accounting. Thus, the third reporting standard (adequate informative disclosures) must be considered by the auditor (AU 623.09).

In determining whether financial statements prepared in conformity with an other comprehensive basis of accounting satisfy the adequate disclosure criterion, the auditor should consider the following concepts established in SAS-69 (AU 411.04):

- The accounting principles selected and applied should have general acceptance.

- The accounting principles should be appropriate in the circumstances.

- The financial statements, including the related notes, should be informative of matters that may affect their use, understanding, and interpretation.

- The information presented in the financial statements should be classified and summarized in a reasonable manner; that is, it should be neither too detailed nor too condensed.

- The financial statements should reflect the underlying events and transactions (in a manner that satisfies the purpose of the financial statements) within a range of acceptable limits; that is, limits that are reasonable and practicable to attain in financial statements.

The notes to the financial statements should include a summary of significant accounting policies to describe the basis of presentation and how the presentation differs from a presentation that conforms with GAAP.

> *OBSERVATION: The summary of significant accounting policies does not have to describe the effects of the differences between an other comprehensive basis of accounting and GAAP in quantitative terms.*

Finally, items that are presented as part of a financial statement prepared in conformity with an other comprehensive basis of accounting and are similar to items that would be presented as part of GAAP-based financial statements should include related disclosures that would be similar to disclosures that would appear in the GAAP-based financial statements. For example, if long-term debt is presented in financial statements prepared on a modified cash basis, information related to the terms, maturity, description, and restrictions of long-term debt must be disclosed (AU 623.10).

> *OBSERVATION: There is no comprehensive list of minimum disclosures for OCBOA-based financial statements. Professional judgment must be used to determine whether the basic concept of adequate disclosure has been achieved in the OCBOA-based financial statements.*

> *OBSERVATION: Another Interpretation of SAS-62, "Evaluation of the Appropriateness of Informative Disclosures in Insurance Enterprises' Financial Statements Prepared on a Statutory Basis" (December 1991) states that the auditor should use the same analysis that is used in the evaluation of GAAP-based financial statements to determine whether financial statements based on accounting standards established by insurance regulators (statutory basis) satisfy the criterion of informative disclosure required by the third standard of reporting. Insurance companies should follow GAAP when preparing general purpose financial statements and appropriate accounting procedures established by each state's insurance department when preparing statutory financial statements (AU 9623.60–.79).*

Reporting standards The title of the special auditor's report should include the word *independent*. In addition, the report should have a manual or printed signature and be dated based on the completion date of fieldwork (AU 623.05).

SAS-62 requires that a four-paragraph format be used in the standard special report. The content of each paragraph is described below (AU 623.05). (See the end of the section on SAS-62 for modifications to the standard auditor's report.)

- Introductory paragraph
  - State that the financial statements identified in the report were audited.
  - State that the financial statements are the responsibility of company's management and that the auditor is responsible for expressing an opinion on the financial statements based on the audit.

- Scope paragraph
  - State that the audit was conducted in accordance with GAAS.
  - State that GAAS require that the auditor plan and perform the audit to obtain reasonable assurance about whether the financial statements are free of material misstatement.
  - State that an audit includes examining, on a test basis, evidence supporting the amounts and disclosures in the financial statements.
  - State that an audit includes assessing the accounting principles used and significant estimates made by management.
  - State that an audit includes evaluating the overall financial statement presentation.
  - State that the auditor believes that his or her audit provides a reasonable basis for the opinion.

- Presentation basis paragraph
  - State the basis of presentation and refer to the note to the financial statements that describes the basis.
  - State that the basis of presentation is a comprehensive basis of accounting other than generally accepted accounting principles.

- Opinion paragraph
  - Express an opinion on whether the financial statements are presented fairly, in all material respects, in conformity with the basis of accounting described.

When the auditor is reporting on financial statements that are prepared in conformity with accounting procedures established by a governmental regulatory agency, an additional paragraph should be included in the standard special auditor's report. The additional paragraph should state that the use of the report is for those within the entity or for filing with the regulatory agency. This additional paragraph should be included even though by law or regulation the report is part of the public record.

> **OBSERVATION:** *When financial statements that are prepared on a regulatory basis of accounting are to be generally distributed, the standard report form, as established by SAS-58, should be modified for departures from generally accepted accounting principles. The standard report may include an additional paragraph that expresses an opinion on whether the financial statements are presented in conformity with the regulatory basis of accounting.*

Presented below is an example of a special auditor's report on financial statements prepared on the cash basis (AU 623.05).

Independent Auditor's Report

We have audited the accompanying statements of assets and liabilities arising from cash transactions of X Company as of December 31, 19X5 and 19X4, and the related statements of revenues collected and expenses paid for the years then ended. These financial statements are the responsibility of the Company's management. Our responsibility is to express an opinion on these financial statements based on our audits.

We conducted our audits in accordance with generally accepted auditing standards. Those standards require that we plan and perform the audit to obtain reasonable assurance about whether the financial statements are free of material misstatement. An audit includes examining, on a test basis, evidence supporting the amounts and disclosures in the financial statements. An audit also includes assessing the accounting principles used and significant estimates made by management, as well as evaluating the overall financial statement presentation. We believe that our audits provide a reasonable basis for our opinion.

As described in Note X, these financial statements were prepared on the basis of cash receipts and disbursements, which is a comprehensive basis of accounting other than generally accepted accounting principles.

In our opinion, the financial statements referred to above present fairly, in all material respects, the assets and liabilities arising from cash transactions of X Company as of December 31, 19X5 and 19X4, and its revenues collected and expenses paid during the years then ended, on the basis of accounting described in Note X.

Reporting on Specified Elements, Accounts, or Items

An auditor may be engaged to report on a specified element(s), account(s), or item(s) of a financial statement. Even though an engagement of this nature is limited in its scope, generally accepted auditing standards must be satisfied (AU 623.11).

> *OBSERVATION: The first reporting standard would not be applicable if the element, account, or item is presented on a basis other than GAAP. The other basis of accounting should not be confused with a comprehensive basis of accounting discussed earlier. For example, the other basis of accounting could be derived from a clause contained in a contract (AU 623.12).*

An engagement to express an opinion on an element, account, or item of a financial statement may be conducted as part of the audit of the financial statements or may be undertaken as a separate engagement. The basis for materiality in the limited-scope audit is the specific element, account, or item being reported on, and for this reason, generally a more detailed audit of the element, account, or item would be conducted (AU 623.13).

> *OBSERVATION: Although the engagement may be limited to reporting on a specified element, account, or item of a financial statement, the scope of the audit includes all related matters and, if appropriate, other related accounts. For example, an engagement to report on accounts receivable requires that the credit sales system and the cash receipts system as part of the entity's internal control structure be considered (AU 623.13).*

> *OBSERVATION: SAS-62 concludes that "if a specified element, account, or item is, or is based on, an entity's net income or stockholders' equity or the equivalent thereof, the auditor should have audited the complete financial statements to express an opinion on the specified element, account, or item" (AU 623.16).*

Reporting standards The specified element, account, or item may be presented in the report or may be presented in a separate document accompanying the report. The title of the special auditor's report should include the word *independent*. In addition, the report should have a manual or printed signature and be dated based on the completion date of fieldwork (AU 623.15).

The following format should be used in the preparation of the standard special auditor's report on a specified element, account, or item of a financial statement (AU 623.15). (See the end of the section on SAS-62 for modifications to the standard auditor's report.)

- Introductory paragraph
  - State that the specified element, account, or item identified in the report was audited.
  - State, if applicable, that the audit was made in conjunction with the audit of the entity's financial statements. (Also disclose the date of the auditor's report and describe any departure from the standard auditor's report on the financial statement if the basis for the departure is considered relevant to the evaluation of the specified element, account, or item.)
  - State that the specified element, account, or item is the responsibility of the company's management and that the auditor is responsible for expressing an opinion on the specified element, account, or item based on the audit.

- Scope paragraph
  - State that the audit was conducted in accordance with GAAS.
  - State that GAAS require that the auditor plan and perform the audit to obtain reasonable assurance about whether the specified element, account, or item is free of material misstatement.
  - State that an audit includes examining, on a test basis, evidence supporting the amounts and disclosures in the presentation of the specified element, account, or item.
  - State that an audit includes assessing the accounting principles used and significant estimates made by management.
  - State that an audit includes evaluating the overall presentation of the specified element, account, or item.
  - State that the auditor believes that the audit provides a reasonable basis for his or her opinion.

- Presentation basis paragraph

  — State the basis on which the specified element, account, or item is presented and, when applicable, any agreement specifying such basis if the presentation is not prepared in conformity with GAAP. (If the basis of presentation is an other comprehensive basis of accounting, state so. Alternatively, the description contained in this paragraph may be incorporated into the introductory paragraph.)

- Opinion paragraph

  — Express an opinion on whether the specified element, account, or item is fairly presented, in all material respects, in conformity with the basis of accounting described.

  — If not presented fairly on the basis of accounting described or if the scope of the engagement has been limited, an explanatory paragraph preceding the opinion paragraph should state all substantive reasons for the above conclusions. The opinion paragraph should include modifying language and a reference to the explanatory paragraph(s).

When the auditor is reporting on a specified element, account, or item to satisfy a contract or agreement, and the information is not presented on a GAAP basis or an other comprehensive basis of accounting, an additional paragraph should be included in the standard special auditor's report. The additional paragraph should state that the distribution of the report is restricted solely to those that are parties to the contract or agreement. When the auditor is reporting on an element, account, or item that is presented on an other comprehensive basis of accounting prescribed by a governmental regulatory agency, an additional paragraph should disclose that the distribution of the report is restricted solely to those within the entity and for filing with the regulatory agency. This additional paragraph should be included even though by law or regulation the report is part of the public record.

An additional paragraph may be added to the standard special auditor's report that describes in more detail the scope of the engagement. *SAS-62 permits an additional paragraph of this nature; however, the additional paragraph must be a separate paragraph and should not be merged into the standard scope paragraph described above* (AU 623.15).

Following is an example of a special auditor's report on accounts receivable (AU 623.18).

Independent Auditor's Report

We have audited the accompanying schedule of accounts receivable of X Company as of December 31, 19X5. This schedule is the responsibility of the Company's management. Our responsibility is to express an opinion on this schedule based on our audit.

We conducted our audit in accordance with generally accepted auditing standards. Those standards require that we plan and perform the audit to obtain reasonable assurance about whether the schedule of accounts receivable is free of material misstatement. An audit includes examining, on a test basis, evidence supporting the amounts and disclosures in the schedule of accounts receivable. An audit also includes assessing the accounting principles used and significant estimates made by management, as well as evaluating the overall schedule presentation. We believe that our audit provides a reasonable basis for our opinion.

In our opinion, the schedule of accounts receivable referred to above presents fairly, in all material respects, the accounts receivable of X Company as of December 31, 19X5, in conformity with generally accepted accounting principles.

SAS-62 concludes that a potential conflict exists when the auditor has expressed an adverse opinion or disclaimed an opinion on the entity's basic financial statements, but has been requested to express an opinion on an element(s), account(s), or item(s) that is part of the basic financial statements. Under this circumstance, an opinion on the element, account, or item can be expressed only when the information being reported on does not constitute a major portion of the financial statement(s). To do otherwise would constitute a piecemeal opinion, which is prohibited by SAS-58. If the auditor decides to express an opinion on an element, account, or item, that report should be presented separately from the report on the entity's basic financial statements (AU 623.14).

> **OBSERVATION:** *The Interpretation of SAS-62 entitled "Auditors' Special Reports on Property and Liability Insurance Companies' Loss Reserves" (May 1981) states that an auditor who has examined the financial statements of a property and liability insurance company may be asked to report on the company's loss and loss adjustment expenses reserves. The latter reporting engagement would be classified as expressing an opinion on one or more specified elements, accounts, or items of a financial statement and, accordingly, SAS-62 guidelines should be observed (AU 9623.40–.46).*

> *OBSERVATION: In some engagements, an auditor may be requested to perform agreed-upon procedures encompassing only a portion of an entity's financial statements. Guidance for this type of service is provided in SAS-75 (Engagements to Apply Agreed-Upon Procedures to Specified Elements, Accounts, or Items of a Financial Statement). SAS-75 is discussed in the chapter entitled "Agreed-Upon Procedures Engagements."*

Reporting on Compliance with Aspects of Contractual Agreements or Regulatory Requirements

Financial statement users, such as banks and regulatory agencies, may request that an entity's auditor specifically state whether a particular contract clause or administrative regulation has been observed by the entity. For example, a loan agreement may require that the entity's working capital be not less than a certain dollar amount. If the entity's financial statements are audited and the clause or regulation is subject to verification, the auditor may issue a negative assurance in an auditor's special report with respect to the contractual clause or regulation (AU 623.19).

> *OBSERVATION: If the regulatory requirement is to be tested to determine compliance with laws and regulations consistent with* **Government Auditing Standards** *(the Yellow Book), the guidance established by SAS-74 (Compliance Auditing Considerations in Audits of Governmental Entities and Recipients of Governmental Financial Assistance) must be observed (AU 801).*

The negative assurance on matters contained in contractual agreements or regulatory requirements must have been related to the audit of the entity's basic financial statements. If an adverse opinion or disclaimer of opinion was expressed on the basic financial statements, a negative assurance on matters contained in contractual agreements or regulatory requirements should not be given (AU 623.19).

> *OBSERVATION: If the matter for which the auditor is providing the assurance has not been subject to audit as part of the audit of the entity's basic financial statements, guidance established in State-*

ment on Standards for Attestation Engagements (SSAE) No. 3 (Compliance Attestation) should be followed.

Reporting standards   The negative assurance on the matter specified in the contractual agreement or regulatory requirement may be expressed in a separate report or added to the auditor's report on the basic financial statements (AU 623.19).

Separate report   The title of the special auditor's report on matters contained in contractual agreements or regulatory requirements should include the word *independent*. Also, the report should have a manual or printed signature and should be dated based on the completion date of fieldwork for the basic financial statements (AU 623.20). (See the end of the section on SAS-62 for modifications to the standard auditor's report.)

The separate report should be formatted in the manner described below.

- Introductory paragraph
    - State that the financial statements were audited in accordance with GAAS, include the date of the auditor's report on the audited financial statements, and, if applicable, disclose any departure from the standard auditor's report on the audited financial statements.

- Limited assurance paragraph
    - Identify the specific covenant or paragraphs of the agreement.

    - Provide a negative assurance on the aspects of the contractual agreement or regulatory requirements insofar as they relate to accounting matters.

    - State that the negative assurance is being given in connection with the audit of the financial statements.

    - State that the audit was not directed primarily toward obtaining knowledge regarding compliance with the contractual agreement or regulatory provision.

- Explanatory paragraph
    - Describe significant interpretations, if any, and their sources, that have been made by the entity's management relating to the contractual agreement or regulatory provision.

- Distribution paragraph
  - State that the distribution of the report is restricted to those within the entity and the parties to the contract or agreement or for filing with the regulatory agency.

The following example illustrates a (separate) auditor's special report expressing a negative assurance on whether certain terms of a debt agreement have been observed (AU 623.21).

Independent Auditor's Report

We have audited, in accordance with generally accepted auditing standards, the balance sheet of X Company as of December 31, 19X5, and the related statements of income, retained earnings, and cash flows for the year then ended, and have issued our report thereon dated February 20, 19X6.

In connection with our audit, nothing came to our attention that caused us to believe that the Company failed to comply with the terms, covenants, provisions, or conditions of the restrictive terms of the loan agreement (dated March 4, 19XO), as explained in Section A of the agreement with First State Bank insofar as they relate to accounting matters. However, our audit was not directed primarily toward obtaining knowledge of such noncompliance.

This report is intended solely for the information and use of the boards of directors and managements of X Company and First State Bank and should not be used for any other purpose.

Report added to standard report The negative assurance on compliance with aspects of contractual agreements or regulatory requirements may be expressed in the auditor's report on the entity's basic financial statements. Under this reporting circumstance, three additional paragraphs, as described below, may need to be added to the standard (three-paragraph) auditor's report after the opinion paragraph (AU 623.21).

- Fourth paragraph
  - Identify the specific covenant or paragraphs of the agreement.
  - Provide a negative assurance on the aspects of the contractual agreement or regulatory requirements insofar as they relate to accounting matters. Note that the negative assur-

ance is being given in connection with the audit of the financial statements.

— State that the audit was not directed primarily toward obtaining knowledge regarding compliance with the contractual agreement or regulatory provisions.

• Fifth paragraph

— Describe significant interpretations, if any, and their sources, that have been made by the entity's management relating to the contractual agreement or regulatory provision.

• Sixth paragraph

— State that the distribution of the report is restricted to those within the entity and the parties to the contract or agreement or for filing with the regulatory agency.

Reporting on Financial Presentations to Comply with Contractual Agreements or Regulatory Provisions

An auditor may be requested to report on *special-purpose* financial statements that have been prepared to satisfy a contractual agreement or governmental regulatory requirements. SAS-62 identifies the following as types of special-purpose financial statement presentations (AU 623.22):

   a. A special-purpose financial presentation prepared in compliance with a contractual agreement or regulatory provision that does not constitute a complete presentation of the entity's assets, liabilities, revenues and expenses, but is otherwise prepared in conformity with GAAP or another comprehensive basis of accounting.

   b. A special-purpose financial presentation (may be a complete set of financial statements or a single financial statement) prepared on a basis of accounting prescribed in an agreement that does not result in a presentation in conformity with GAAP or another comprehensive basis of accounting.

These special-purpose financial presentations are discussed below.

Incomplete presentations   Because of a contractual agreement or regulatory provision, an entity may be required to prepare a financial statement that is incomplete but nonetheless presents financial information that is prepared in accordance with GAAP or an other comprehensive basis of accounting. For example, an entity may be required by contract to present a statement of net assets sold as of a specific date. SAS-62 concludes that these presentations constitute a financial statement even though the presentations are incomplete, and accordingly, an auditor can express an opinion on incomplete financial presentations (AU 623.23).

> *OBSERVATION: An Auditing Interpretation of SAS-62 entitled "Reporting on a Special-Purpose Financial Statement That Results in an Incomplete Presentation But Is Otherwise in Conformity with Generally Accepted Accounting Principles" (May 1995) concludes that an offering memorandum is not considered a contractual agreement as defined by SAS-62. However, an agreement between a client and a third party to prepare financial statements using a special-purpose presentation format is a contractual agreement as defined by SAS-62. Under the latter circumstance, the auditor may agree to the addition of other parties for the receipt of the report, but should obtain written acknowledgment from the additional parties that the financial statements are incomplete (AU 9623.80–.87).*

In conducting an engagement related to incomplete financial presentations, the basis for determining materiality should be the incomplete financial presentation taken as a whole. The presentation should omit only information that is not pertinent to satisfying the contractual agreement or regulatory provision. Information that is presented as part of the incomplete financial presentation and that is similar to information that would be presented as part of GAAP-based financial statements should include related disclosures that would be similar to disclosures that would appear in the GAAP-based financial statements. Finally, the incomplete financial presentation should be titled in a manner that would not suggest that the presentation is a complete financial statement (AU 623.24).

Reporting standards   The title of the special auditor's report should include the word *independent*, and the report should have a manual or printed signature. The report should be dated based on the completion date of fieldwork (AU 623.25).

The format shown below should be used to prepare a special auditor's report on incomplete financial presentations (AU 623.25). (See the end of the section on SAS-62 for modifications to the standard auditor's report.)

- Introductory paragraph
  - State that the financial statements identified in the report were audited.
  - State that the financial statements are the responsibility of the company's management and that the auditor is responsible for expressing an opinion on the financial statements based on the audit.

- Scope paragraph
  - State that the audit was conducted in accordance with GAAS.
  - State that GAAS require that the auditor plan and perform the audit to obtain reasonable assurance about whether the financial statements are free of material misstatement.
  - State that an audit includes examining, on a test basis, evidence supporting the amounts and disclosures in the financial statements.
  - State that an audit includes assessing the accounting principles used and significant estimates made by management.
  - State that an audit includes evaluating the overall financial statement presentation.
  - State that the auditor believes that the audit provides a reasonable basis for his or her opinion.

- Presentation basis paragraph
  - Explain what the presentation is intended to present and refer to the note to the special-purpose financial statements that describes the basis of presentation.
  - If the basis of presentation is in conformity with GAAP, state that the presentation is not intended to be a complete presentation of the entity's assets, liabilities, revenue, and expenses.
  - If the basis of presentation is an other comprehensive basis of accounting, state that the basis of presentation is a comprehensive basis of accounting other than GAAP and that it is not intended to be a complete presentation of the entity's assets, liabilities, revenues, and expenses on the basis described.

- Opinion paragraph
  - Express an opinion on whether the information is fairly presented, in all material respects.

—State that the presentation is intended to present the information in conformity with GAAP or an other comprehensive basis of accounting.

- Distribution paragraph
  —State that the report is restricted to those within the entity, to the parties to the contract or agreement, for filing with a regulatory agency, or to those with whom the entity is negotiating directly. (A distribution paragraph is not necessary when the financial information must be filed with a regulatory agency and is to be included in a document that is distributed to the general public.)

The following example illustrates a report on a statement of assets sold and liabilities transferred to comply with a contractual agreement (AU 623.26).

Independent Auditor's Report

We have audited the accompanying statement of net assets sold of X Company as of July 15, 19X5. This statement of net assets sold is the responsibility of X Company's management. Our responsibility is to express an opinion on the statement of net assets sold based on our audit.

We conducted our audit in accordance with generally accepted auditing standards. Those standards require that we plan and perform the audit to obtain reasonable assurance about whether the statement of net assets sold is free of material misstatement. An audit includes examining, on a test basis, evidence supporting the amounts and disclosures in the statement. An audit also includes assessing the accounting principles used and significant estimates made by management, as well as evaluating the overall presentation of the statement of net assets sold. We believe that our audit provides a reasonable basis for our opinion.

The accompanying statement was prepared to present the net assets of X Company sold to Z Company pursuant to the purchase agreement described in Note 1, and is not intended to be a complete presentation of X Company's assets and liabilities.

In our opinion, the accompanying statement of net assets sold presents fairly, in all material respects, the net assets of X Company as of July 15, 19X5, sold pursuant to the purchase agreement referred to in Note 1, in conformity with generally accepted accounting principles.

This report is intended solely for the information and use of the boards of directors and managements of X Company and Z Company and should not be used for any other purpose.

Presentation not in accordance with GAAP or OCBOA An entity may be required by the terms of a contract to prepare financial statements that are in accordance with neither GAAP nor an other comprehensive basis of accounting. For example, an entity may be required to prepare financial statements that use unacceptable methods to value various accounts and transactions. The auditor may be requested to express an opinion on financial statements of this type but it should be emphasized that this type of engagement is not the same as the engagement described earlier (AU 623.27–.28). (See the section entitled "Reporting on Conformity with a Comprehensive Basis of Accounting Other than GAAP.")

Reporting standards The title of the special auditor's report should include the word *independent*, and the report should have a manual or printed signature. The report should be dated based on the completion date of fieldwork (AU 623.29).

The following format should be used to prepare a special auditor's report on financial statements prepared on a basis of accounting prescribed in an agreement that results in a presentation that is not in conformity with GAAP or OCBOA (AU 623.29).

- Introductory paragraph
  - State that the special-purpose financial statements identified in the report were audited.
  - State that the financial statements are the responsibility of the company's management and that the auditor is responsible for expressing an opinion on the financial statements based on the audit.

- Scope paragraph
  - State that the audit was conducted in accordance with GAAS.
  - State that GAAS require that the auditor plan and perform the audit to obtain reasonable assurance about whether the financial statements are free of material misstatement.
  - State that an audit includes examining, on a test basis, evidence supporting the amounts and disclosures in the financial statements.
  - State that an audit includes assessing the accounting principles used and significant estimates made by management.
  - State that an audit includes evaluating the overall financial statement presentation.

— State that the auditor believes that the audit provides a reasonable basis for his or her opinion.

• Presentation basis paragraph

— Explain what the presentation is intended to present and refer to the note to the special-purpose financial statements that describes the basis of presentation.

— State that the presentation is not intended to be a presentation in conformity with GAAP.

• Explanatory paragraph

— Describe significant interpretations, if any, and their sources, that have been made by the entity's management relating to the contractual agreement.

• Opinion paragraph

— Express an opinion on whether the information is fairly presented, in all material respects, on the basis of accounting specified. If not presented fairly on the basis of accounting described or if the scope of the engagement has been limited, an explanatory paragraph preceding the opinion paragraph should disclose all substantive reasons for the above conclusions. The opinion paragraph should include modifying language and a reference to the explanatory paragraph(s). (See the end of the section on SAS-62 for modifications to the standard auditor's report.)

• Distribution paragraph

— State that the report is restricted to those within the entity, to the parties to the contract or agreement, for filing with a regulatory agency, or to those with whom the entity is negotiating directly.

The following example illustrates a special auditor's report on financial statements prepared pursuant to a loan agreement that results in a presentation not in conformity with GAAP or an OCBOA.

Independent Auditor's Report

We have audited the special-purpose statement of assets and liabilities of X Company as of December 31, 19X5 and 19X4, and the related special-purpose statements of revenues and expenses and cash flows for the years then ended. These financial statements are the responsibility of the Company's management. Our responsibility is to express an opinion on these financial statements based on our audits.

We conducted our audits in accordance with generally accepted auditing standards. Those standards require that we plan and perform the audit to obtain reasonable assurance about whether the financial statements are free of material misstatement. An audit includes examining, on a test basis, evidence supporting the amounts and disclosures in the financial statements. An audit also includes assessing the accounting principles used and significant estimates made by management, as well as evaluating the overall financial statement presentation. We believe that our audits provide a reasonable basis for our opinion.

The accompanying special-purpose financial statements were prepared for the purpose of complying with Section A of a loan agreement between the Company and the First State Bank as discussed in Note 1, and are not intended to be a presentation in conformity with generally accepted accounting principles.

In our opinion, the special-purpose financial statements referred to above present fairly, in all material respects, the assets and liabilities of X Company as of December 31, 19X5 and 19X4, and the revenues, expenses, and cash flows for the years then ended, on the basis of accounting described in Note 1.

This report is intended solely for the information and use of the boards of directors and managements of X Company and the First State Bank and should not be used for any other purpose.

Reporting on Financial Information Presented in Prescribed Forms or Schedules

An entity may be required to file financial information on a form supplied or approved by a governmental agency, institution, or other authority. In addition, an auditor may be engaged to express an opinion on the information in the form, and the wording of the auditor's report may also be part of the prescribed form. For example, a state agency may require certain not-for-profit entities to submit periodic financial reports on prescribed forms. Before signing the prescribed report, the auditor must be careful to protect him- or herself from making inappropriate statements in the report. Under some circumstances, the auditor may be able to sign the prescribed report by modifying the report language in the form. If a significant amount of rewording is necessary, it may be more appropriate for the auditor to attach a separate auditor's report. Guidance for writing a separate report may be found by following the reporting formats on financial statements prepared in accordance with a comprehensive basis of accounting other than generally accepted accounting principles (AU 623.32–.33).

> *OBSERVATION: An Interpretation of SAS-62, "Reports on the Financial Statements Included in Internal Revenue Form 990" (July 1982), states that a special report situation may arise when a charitable organization presents its financial statements in a manner consistent with Internal Revenue Form 990 (Return of Organizations Exempt from Income Tax). These financial statements may be submitted to state and federal regulatory authorities. When the presentation materially departs from GAAP and the financial statements are intended solely for filing with a regulatory agency, a special report following the reporting format established for statements prepared on a comprehensive basis of accounting other than GAAP may be followed. When the presentation materially departs from GAAP and there is public distribution of the report, reporting requirements established by SAS-62 are not applicable. In this situation, SAS-58 must be observed by issuing a qualified or adverse opinion on the financial statements (AU 9623.47–.54).*

Modifications to the standard auditor's special report   When an auditor concludes that an unqualified opinion is not applicable, the special auditor's report should be appropriately modified. If the deficiency is related to accounting principles used to prepare the financial presentation, the modification to the report should include an explanatory paragraph(s) that describes the deficiency, and the opinion paragraph should refer to the explanatory paragraph as the basis for the qualified or adverse opinion. On the other hand, if the deficiency is related to the scope of the audit engagement, an explanatory paragraph(s) should be added to the special auditor's report and the opinion paragraph should refer to the explanatory paragraph as the basis for the qualified opinion or disclaimer of opinion. Under both circumstances (accounting deficiency and scope deficiency), the explanatory paragraph should precede the opinion paragraph (AU 623.31).

In addition to modifications to the special auditor's report arising from accounting and scope deficiencies, the report should be modified under the following circumstances (AU 623.31):

- There is a lack of consistent application of accounting principles.

- Substantial doubt exists about the entity's ability to continue as a going concern.
- Part of the audit was conducted by another auditor.
- The auditor expresses an opinion on the financial presentation that is different from the one expressed in a previous engagement on the same presentation.
- A matter is to be emphasized.

Guidance for modifying the special auditor's report under the circumstances listed above can be found in SAS-58 (AU 508). (See the discussion in the chapter entitled "Auditor's Reports.")

When an entity changes its basis of accounting from GAAP to a comprehensive basis of accounting other than GAAP, in the year of change the matter should not be treated as a consistency violation. Nonetheless, it may be appropriate to include an additional paragraph that discloses that a different basis of accounting was used to prepare financial statements in previous periods or that the entity has also prepared another report that uses generally accepted accounting principles as the basis of accounting (AU 623.31).

In addition, when financial statements are prepared on a tax basis, a change in the tax laws would not constitute a violation of the consistency standard; however, it may be appropriate to disclose the matter in the financial statements.

Reporting on Financial Statements Prepared on the Liquidation Basis of Accounting

The Auditing Interpretation entitled "Reporting on Financial Statements Prepared on a Liquidation Basis of Accounting" (December 1984) provides guidance for reporting on financial statements that are prepared on a liquidation basis. The standard auditor's report is not appropriate when financial statements are prepared on a liquidation basis because the accounting principles used in the going-concern concept are significantly different from the accounting principles based on the concept of liquidation (AU 9508.34).

The Auditing Interpretation discusses the following reporting formats when financial statements are prepared on the liquidation basis of accounting (AU 9508.36–.38):

- Initial year reporting (single-year presentation)
- Initial year reporting (comparative-years presentation)

- Existence of an uncertainty

> **OBSERVATION:** *The auditor may issue an unqualified opinion on financial statements prepared on a liquidation basis provided the basis used is appropriately applied and adequately disclosed.*

Initial Year Reporting (Single-Year Presentation)

When the auditor reports on financial statements for a single year and the year is the year of adoption of the liquidation basis of accounting, the report must include an explanatory paragraph describing the basis of accounting. The opinion paragraph contains a statement that the financial statements are prepared in accordance with generally accepted accounting principles as described in the explanatory paragraph. An example of the explanatory paragraph is presented below (AU 9508.36).

As described in Note 1 to the financial statements, the Board of Directors and stockholders of Omega Company approved a plan of liquidation effective on May 1, 19X5, and the Company commenced liquidation on that date. As a result, the Company has changed its basis of accounting for periods subsequent to April 30, 19X5, from the going-concern basis to a liquidation basis.

Initial Year Reporting (Comparative-Years Presentation)

When financial statements prepared on a liquidation basis are presented on a comparative basis with prior years' financial statements prepared on a going-concern basis, the auditor's report must include an explanatory paragraph describing the liquidation basis of financial reporting. An example of the explanatory paragraph is presented below (AU 9508.36).

As described in Note 1 to the financial statements, the Board of Directors and stockholders of Omega Company approved a plan of liquidation effective on May 1, 19X5, and the company commenced liquidation on that date. As a result, the company has changed its basis of accounting for periods subsequent to April 30, 19X5, from the going-concern basis to a liquidation basis.

In subsequent periods when the auditor reports on the liquidation-based financial statements, the explanatory paragraph describing the financial reporting basis may be included in the auditor's report (AU 9508.37).

Presently it cannot be determined whether the amounts realizable from the disposition of the remaining assets or the amounts that creditors agree to accept in settlement of the obligations due them will differ materially from the amounts shown in the accompanying financial statements.

REPORTS ON THE APPLICATION OF ACCOUNTING PRINCIPLES

Accountants are often requested to give an informal opinion on how a transaction should or could be accounted for or what type of opinion would be appropriate for a particular set of financial statements. Requests of this nature are frequently associated with prospective clients who are "shopping for an opinion." Unfortunately, such requests have resulted in a significant amount of adverse publicity for the accounting profession (AU 625.01).

To provide some guidance in this sensitive area, the Auditing Standards Board, in 1986, issued SAS-50 (Reports on the Application of Accounting Principles). The scope of SAS-50 is not limited to "shopping for opinions," but also includes written reports and oral advice rendered by a reporting accountant in public practice to principals in the transaction, other accountants, and intermediaries. Intermediaries are parties who advise principals and may include such professionals as lawyers and bankers (AU 625.02).

SAS-50 covers the following circumstances, irrespective of whether the request is associated with a proposal to obtain a new client (AU 625.02):

Written Reports

- *Specific Transactions*—Determining the applicability of accounting principles to specified transactions that are either completed or proposed

- *Specific Entity's Financial Statements*—Determining the appropriate opinion that may be expressed on a specified entity's financial statements

- *Hypothetical Transactions*—Determining for an intermediary the applicability of accounting principles to facts or circumstances that are not related to a particular principal

Oral Advice

- *Specific Transactions*—Determining the applicability of accounting principles to specified transactions that are either completed or proposed

- *Specific Entity's Financial Statements*—Determining the appropriate opinion that may be expressed on a specified entity's financial statements

Situations involving oral advice are covered by SAS-50 only when the reporting accountant believes that the advice will constitute an important part in the principal's ultimate decision (AU 625.02).

> **OBSERVATION:** *Clearly, the Auditing Standards Board expanded the scope of SAS-50 to include oral advice so that the reporting accountant could not circumvent professional standards simply by not preparing a written report.*

The standards established in SAS-50 are not applicable to situations in which (AU 625.04):

- A continuing accountant is engaged to report on financial statements.

- An accountant is engaged to assist in litigation involving accounting questions.

- An accountant is engaged to provide expert testimony in litigation involving accounting questions.

- An accountant in public practice gives professional advice to another accountant in public practice.

- An accountant-prepared communication (such as newsletters, articles, and speeches) on an accounting matter is not intended as advice on the applicability of accounting principles to specific transactions or the type of opinion that may be expressed on a specific entity's financial statements.

Standards of performance Although the purpose of reporting on the applicability of accounting principles is different from the purpose of an audit of financial statements, performance standards that are similar to generally accepted auditing standards must be observed. Performance standards include the following (AU 625.05):

- Adequate training and proficiency
- Due professional care
- Engagement planning and supervision of assistants
- Accumulation of sufficient information
- Standards of reporting

The first two performance standards (adequate training and proficiency and due professional care) are similar to the first and third general standards of generally accepted auditing standards, whereas the third standard listed (engagement planning and supervision) is similar to the first fieldwork standard. The last two performance standards (accumulation of sufficient information and reporting standards) are unique to the special engagement described in SAS-50. They are discussed below (AU 625.05).

Accumulation of sufficient information Before the applicability of an accounting principle can be evaluated, the reporting accountant must accumulate sufficient information that provides a reasonable basis for drawing a conclusion with respect to the accounting principle. To make this determination, an adequate understanding of the transactions should be obtained. Once the transactions are understood, the accountant should identify those accounting principles that could be used to account for the transactions. The identification of acceptable accounting principles should be guided by SAS-69 (The Meaning of "Present Fairly in Conformity with Generally Accepted Accounting Principles" in the Independent Auditor's Report). SAS-69 is discussed in the chapter entitled "Generally Accepted Accounting Principles" (AU 625.06).

When the applicability of a specific accounting principle is unclear after the professional literature identified in SAS-69 has been reviewed, it may be appropriate to consult with other experts or perform additional research to identify a precedent or analogous situation that could be used to support the application of the specific accounting principle (AU 625.06).

In addition, the reporting accountant should contact the continuing accountant when the special engagement involves (1) the evaluation of the applicability of accounting principles for specific transactions or the type of opinion to be expressed on a specific entity's financial statements and (2) a request for the service by a principal or an intermediary acting for a principal. The reporting accountant should inform the principal or the intermediary of the importance of communicating with the continuing accountant. SAS-50 lists the following as examples of information that may be obtained from communicating with the continuing accountant (AU 625.07):

- The form and substance of certain transactions

- Management's previous accounting for similar transactions

- Any disagreement(s) between management and the continuing accountant with respect to the transactions or statements in question

- Identification of the continuing accountant's solution to the applicability of accounting principles or the appropriate opinion that should be expressed on the financial statements

The reporting accountant should ask the principal for permission to contact the continuing accountant, and the principal should authorize the continuing accountant to fully respond to any inquiries made by the reporting accountant. With respect to the responsibilities of the continuing accountant, SAS-50 concludes that the continuing accountant's responsibilities are similar to those of a predecessor auditor as described in SAS-7 (Communications Between Predecessor and Successor Auditors).

Standards of reporting   SAS-50 identifies the following as reporting standards that ordinarily should be observed by the reporting accountant when preparing a written report on the applicability of accounting principles (AU 625.08):

- Brief description of the nature of the engagement and a statement that the engagement was performed in accordance with standards established by the AICPA

- Description of transactions, a statement of the relevant facts, circumstances, and assumptions, and a statement about the source of the information (Principals to specific transactions should be identified, and hypothetical transactions should be described using generic references such as Company X and so forth.)

- Statement describing the appropriate accounting principles to be applied or type of opinion that may be rendered on the entity's financial statements, and if appropriate, a description of the reasons for the reporting accountant's conclusion

- Statement that the responsibility for the proper accounting treatment rests with the preparers of the financial statements, who should consult with their continuing accountants

- Statement that any difference in the facts, circumstances, or assumptions presented may change the report

> **OBSERVATION:** *The reporting standards just listed are applicable to written reports prepared by the accountant. As noted earlier, the accountant may provide oral advice on specific transactions or a specific entity's financial statements. SAS-50 provides no reporting standards for oral advice, but footnote 4 of SAS-50 states that the reporting standards for written reports may provide useful guidance for presenting oral advice (AU 625.08).*

The accountant's report should be addressed to the principal or intermediary in the transaction. The accountant's report may be divided into the following four sections: (1) introduction, (2) description of transactions, facts, or circumstances, (3) appropriate accounting principles or opinion to be expressed, and (4) concluding comments. The first and fourth sections will generally contain a single paragraph, which will for the most part have a standard format. The second and third sections will be unique to the specific accounting issue being raised. The following is an example of an accountant's report from SAS-50 that covers the applicability of accounting principles (AU 625.09).

[Introduction]

We have been engaged to report on the appropriate application of generally accepted accounting principles to the specific transactions described below. This report is being issued to Company X for assistance in evaluating accounting principles for the described specific transactions. Our engagement has been conducted in accordance with standards established by the American Institute of Certified Public Accountants.

[Description of Transactions]

The facts, circumstances, and assumptions relevant to the specific transactions as provided to us by the management of Company X are as follows: [Describe transactions being evaluated.]

[Appropriate Accounting Principles]

[Include discussion of accounting principles being evaluated.]

[Concluding Comments]

The ultimate responsibility for the decision on the appropriate application of generally accepted accounting principles for actual transactions rests with the preparers of financial statements, who should consult with their continuing accountants. Our judgment on the appropriate application of generally accepted accounting principles for the described specific transactions is based solely on the facts provided to us as described above; should these facts and circumstances differ, our conclusion may change.

REPORTING ON FINANCIAL STATEMENTS PREPARED FOR USE IN OTHER COUNTRIES

A U.S. practicing auditor may be engaged by a *U.S. entity* to report on financial statements that are intended to be used outside the United States and that are to be prepared in conformity with accounting principles generally accepted in another country. Guidance for reporting on such financial statements is provided by SAS-51 (Reporting on Financial Statements Prepared for Use in Other Countries). For the purposes of SAS-51, a *U.S. entity* is one that is either organized or domiciled in the United States (AU 534.01).

An auditor should have a clear understanding of the purpose and uses of financial statements that are prepared in conformity with accounting principles of another country. The auditor should obtain management's written representations before reporting on such statements. When using the standard report of another country instead of the U.S.-style auditor's standard report, an auditor must determine whether he or she is exposed to any additional legal responsibilities (AU 534.02).

Auditing Standards

Before reporting on financial statements prepared in accordance with accounting principles of another country, the auditor must consider which auditing standards are applicable in the engagement. In some engagements, an auditor may be required to follow both U.S. generally accepted auditing standards and auditing standards established by a foreign country (AU 534.03–.04).

In reporting on financial statements prepared in accordance with accounting principles of another country, an auditor must observe the three general standards and the three fieldwork standards that are part of U.S. generally accepted auditing standards. In this event, the auditor is also required to comply with all related SAS and SAS Interpretations (AU 534.03).

General standards   The first general standard of U.S. GAAS requires that the auditor be adequately trained and proficient as an auditor. Adequate training encompasses the need for an auditor to have a satisfactory understanding of the accounting principles of the foreign country and, if applicable, auditing standards that have been established by the foreign country. An understanding of foreign accounting principles and auditing standards may be obtained by reading professional accounting literature and appropriate foreign statutes. The second part of the first general standard refers to proficiency, which is gained through relevant professional experience. If the auditor does not have the appropriate professional background, it may be necessary to consult with auditors who are proficient in this respect (AU 534.03).

The second general standard requires that an auditor be independent. The concept of independence as established by GAAS is applicable to engagements covered by SAS-51. Thus, guidance as provided by the Code of Professional Conduct, Interpretations, and Rulings on Ethics should be observed by the auditor (AU 543.03).

The final general standard requires that the auditor exercise due professional care in the conduct of an audit engagement, including the preparation of the auditor's report. In addition, engagements to report on financial statements prepared for use in other countries may encompass the following responsibilities (AU 534.05):

- Legal responsibilities beyond those related to generally accepted auditing standards that may arise when the auditor uses the standard report form of another country

- Determination of appropriateness of accounting principles used when accounting principles of a foreign country are not well established

Fieldwork standards   The three fieldwork standards of GAAS must be observed by an auditor who is engaged to report on financial statements that are prepared in accordance with accounting principles of another country. The three fieldwork standards relate to (1) proper planning and supervision, (2) a significant understanding of the internal control structure, and (3) the collection of sufficient competent evidence. Specific audit procedures of a foreign country may vary to some degree from U.S. GAAS. The degree of variance will depend on the accounting principles used in the foreign country. For example, if inflation-adjusted information is part of a foreign country's reporting standards, the auditor should obtain an understanding of the client's internal control structure relating to the development and implementation of price-level adjusted data and should collect evidence to support the valuation of specific accounts and transactions (AU 534.03).

Auditing standards of foreign countries   When the auditor is required to comply with auditing standards of another country, both those standards and U.S. generally accepted auditing standards must be observed during the engagement. Thus, some audit procedures will be employed to comply with U.S. GAAS, whereas other audit procedures will be performed to satisfy auditing standards of the foreign country (AU 534.06).

Reporting Standards

The reporting standards that must be observed in the preparation of the auditor's report on financial statements prepared in accordance with accounting principles of another country are dependent on the purpose of the financial statements. These purposes may be classified as (1) foreign GAAP/foreign use, (2) dual statements (foreign GAAP/U.S. GAAP), and (3) foreign GAAP/general U.S. distribution. Each of these purposes is discussed below (AU 534.07–.08).

Foreign GAAP/foreign use   When financial statements of a U.S. entity that are prepared in accordance with accounting principles of another country are to be used exclusively outside the United States, the auditor may use either the U.S.-style standard auditor's report or the standard auditor's report of the foreign country (AU 534.09).

The following reporting standards should be observed when an auditor decides to use a U.S.-style standard auditor's report for financial statements prepared in accordance with accounting principles of a foreign country (AU 534.09):

- The report must use the word *independent* in the title.

- The report must state that the financial statements were audited.

- The report must refer to the note to the financial statements that discloses the basis of presentation, including the nationality of the accounting principles.

- The report must state that the financial statements are the responsibility of management and that the auditor's responsibility is to express an opinion on them.

- The report must state that the audit was conducted in accordance with U.S. generally accepted auditing standards (and if applicable, the auditing standards of the foreign country).

- The report must state that U.S. standards require the auditor to plan and perform the audit to obtain a reasonable assurance on whether the financial statements are free of material misstatement.

- The report must state that an audit includes (1) examining, on a test basis, evidence supporting the amounts and disclosures in the financial statements, (2) assessing the accounting principles used and significant estimates made by management, and (3) evaluating the overall financial statement presentation.

- The report must state that the auditor believes that the audit provides a reasonable basis for his or her opinion.

- The report must state an opinion on the financial statements with respect to the basis of accounting described. (If the financial statements are not fairly presented, the opinion should be modified appropriately and should refer to a separate paragraph that describes the deficiency.)

- If there is an inconsistent application of the basis of accounting described, the report must contain a separate paragraph that explains the deficiency and the opinion must refer to the note that describes the inconsistency.

The following example illustrates a U.S.-style standard auditor's report (AU 534.10).

We have audited the accompanying balance sheet of X Company as of December 31, 19X5, and the related statements of income, retained earnings, and cash flows for the year then ended, which, as described in Note X, have been prepared on the basis of accounting principles generally accepted in [insert name of foreign country]. These financial statements are the responsibility of the Company's management. Our responsibility is to express an opinion on these financial statements based on our audit.

We conducted our audit in accordance with auditing standards generally accepted in the United States. U.S. standards require that we plan and perform the audit to obtain reasonable assurance about whether the financial statements are free of material misstatement. An audit includes examining, on a test basis, evidence supporting the amounts and disclosures in the financial statements. An audit also includes assessing the accounting principles used and significant estimates made by management, as well as evaluating the overall financial statement presentation. We believe that our audit provides a reasonable basis for our opinion.

In our opinion, the financial statements referred to above present fairly, in all material respects, the financial position of X Company as of December 31, 19X5, and the results of its operations and its cash flows for the year then ended in conformity with accounting principles generally accepted in [insert name of foreign country].

The standard report should be modified when the auditor concludes that the financial statements are not fairly presented in accordance with the basis of accounting described in the note. When the report is modified, a separate paragraph should contain a description of the accounting deficiency. The opinion paragraph should refer to the additional paragraph as the basis of the modification and should contain the appropriate opinion on the financial statements (qualified or adverse) (AU 534.09).

Rather than use the U.S.-style standard auditor's report, the auditor may use the standard auditor's report of the foreign country, provided two conditions are met. First, the standard report of the foreign country must be the same report that would have been issued by auditors of the foreign country under the same circumstances. Second, the auditor must understand the assertions made in the standard auditor's report of the foreign country, and it is appropriate for the auditor to take the responsibility for those assertions.

With respect to the last condition, it must be recognized that the assertions in the standard auditor's report of another country may be different from those in the U.S.-style standard auditor's report. The fundamental assertion in the U.S.-style standard auditor's report is that the financial statements are prepared in accordance with generally accepted accounting principles. On the other hand, a foreign country standard auditor's report may imply or state that the financial statements are prepared in compliance with existing statutory regulations. Thus, before issuing a foreign country's standard auditor's report, the U.S. auditor must fully understand the auditing standards, accounting principles, and laws that are applicable in the foreign country. To gain the appropriate understanding, the U.S. auditor may need to consult with auditors who are familiar with the auditing standards, accounting principles, and laws of the particular foreign country (AU 534.12).

When the U.S. practicing auditor concludes that it is appropriate to issue the foreign country's standard auditor's report, the reporting standards of the foreign country should be observed (AU 534.12).

Dual statements (foreign GAAP/U.S. GAAP)   One set of financial statements may be prepared in accordance with U.S. generally accepted accounting principles and a second set in accordance with accounting principles acceptable in a foreign country, to provide relevant information to users in both countries. For the financial statements presented in accordance with U.S. generally accepted accounting principles, Statements on Auditing Standards issued by the AICPA Auditing Standards Board should be observed in the preparation of the auditor's report. For the financial statements prepared in accordance with accounting principles acceptable in a foreign country and to be used outside of the United States, the U.S.-style standard auditor's report, which was described earlier, may be prepared, or the standard report of another country may be used (AU 534.13).

Some confusion may arise when the same financial statements of a U.S. entity are prepared on two different accounting bases. To reduce the possibility of a misunderstanding, SAS-51 suggests that one or both of the audit reports contain a statement advising the reader of the other audit report, which has been issued on the same financial statements but based on accepted accounting principles of another country. The auditor's report also may refer to the note to the financial statements, if presented, that describes the significant differences between the two bases of accounting. An example of the auditor's reference to such a note is as follows (AU 534.13).

We also have reported separately on the financial statements of Company X for the same period presented in accordance with accounting principles generally accepted in [insert name of foreign country]. The significant differences between the accounting principles accepted in [insert name of foreign country] and those generally accepted in the United States are summarized in Note 1.

Foreign GAAP/general U.S. distribution   Financial statements prepared in accordance with accepted accounting principles of a foreign country may be intended for more than a limited distribution in the United States. When the auditor is asked to report on this type of financial statement, there are two acceptable reporting formats. First, reporting guidance established by SAS-58 (Reports on Audited Financial Statements) should be followed for the U.S.-distributed financial statements. Thus, significant departures from U.S. generally accepted accounting principles, if any, would result in an expression of a qualified opinion or an adverse opinion. The auditor may include an additional paragraph in the standard report to express an opinion on whether the financial statements also are presented in conformity with the accepted accounting principles of another country (AU 534.14).

Second, the auditor may present two reports: (1) either the U.S.-style auditor's report or the foreign country's standard report for foreign distribution (see earlier discussion for a description of these reports) and (2) an audit report based on SAS-58, as described in the previous paragraph for U.S. distribution (AU 534.15).

> **OBSERVATION:** *SAS-51 does not preclude the limited distribution of financial statements to users within the United States who deal directly with the U.S. entity as long as the users can discuss with the U.S. entity the significance of the differences between U.S. accounting principles and the foreign accounting principles that were used to prepare the financial statements.*

PART II
Interim Reviews, Condensed Financials, Filings Under Federal Securities Statutes, and Letters to Underwriters

INTERIM REVIEWS, CONDENSED FINANCIALS, FILINGS UNDER FEDERAL SECURITIES STATUTES, AND LETTERS TO UNDERWRITERS
Public Companies

CONTENTS

Background	13.03
Interim Reviews of Public Companies	13.04
Responsibility and Function of the Accountant	13.05
Pre-Engagement Planning	13.06
Engagement Letter	13.06
Generally Accepted Accounting Principles	13.08
Reporting Accounting Changes—Interim Periods	13.10
Summarized Interim Financial Statements	13.11
Generally Accepted Auditing Standards	13.12
General Standards	13.12
Standards of Fieldwork	13.12
Standards of Reporting	13.13
Planning the Engagement	13.13
Consideration of Internal Control	13.15
Evidence	13.16
Communication with the Audit Committee	13.18
Accountant's Reports	13.19
Modifications to the Standard Review Report	13.21
Subsequent Events	13.24
Responsibilities After the Report Date	13.25
Reports on Interim Financial Information Accompanying Audited Financial Statements	13.25
Filings Under Federal Securities Statutes	13.27
Unaudited Financial Statements	13.30
Document Review of Filings with the SEC	13.30

Letters for Underwriters and Certain Other Requesting
   Parties   **13.31**
Applicability of Statement on Auditing Standards
   No. 72   **13.31**
Required Representation Letter   **13.33**
General Guidance   **13.34**
Scope of Comfort Procedures   **13.35**
Draft of Proposed Comfort Letter   **13.35**
Other Accountants   **13.36**
Shelf Registrations   **13.37**
Comfort Letter Contents   **13.38**
Date   **13.39**
Addressee   **13.39**
Introductory Paragraph   **13.39**
Independence   **13.41**
Compliance with SEC Requirements   **13.41**
Commenting in Comfort Letter on Information Other
   Than Audited Financial Statements   **13.42**
Tables, Statistics, and Other Financial Information   **13.49**
Concluding Paragraph   **13.50**
Disclosure of Subsequently Discovered Matters   **13.50**
Sample Comfort Letter   **13.50**
Reporting on Condensed Financial Statements and
   Selected Financial Data   **13.55**
Condensed Financial Statements   **13.55**
Selected Financial Data   **13.56**

INTERIM REVIEWS, CONDENSED FINANCIALS, FILINGS UNDER FEDERAL SECURITIES STATUTES, AND LETTERS TO UNDERWRITERS
Public Companies

Background

This chapter discusses (1) the review of interim financial information for public companies, (2) the review of interim financial information that is presented or incorporated by reference in a filing under the Securities Act of 1933, (3) guidance to accountants in performing engagements to provide letters to underwriters in conjunction with filings with the Securities and Exchange Commission (SEC) under the Securities Act of 1933, and (4) standards for an auditor's report on condensed financial statements or selected financial data that are derived from audited financial statements. The pronouncements covered in this chapter are:

- Statement on Auditing Standards (SAS) No. 71 (Interim Financial Information)
- Statement on Quality Control Standards (SQCS) No. 2
- Rule 102 (Code of Professional Conduct)
- Rule 201 (Code of Professional Conduct)
- SAS-37 (Filings Under Federal Securities Statutes)
- SAS-72 (Letters for Underwriters and Certain Other Requesting Parties)
- SAS-76 (Amendments to Statement on Auditing Standards No. 72, Letters for Underwriters and Certain Other Requesting Parties)
- SAS-42 (Reporting on Condensed Financial Statements and Selected Financial Data)

SAS-71 creates standards for engagements related to the review of interim financial information issued by public entities (AU 722).

SQCS-2 identifies several elements that a firm must consider when designing a system of quality control (QC 10-1).

Rule 101 of the AICPA Code of Professional Conduct provides guidance when a CPA conducts an engagement that requires that the CPA be independent. Rule 201 identifies broad standards that should be followed by the CPA when professional services are rendered (ET 101; ET 201).

SAS-37 provides guidance to the accountant in reporting on a review of interim financial information that is presented or incorporated by reference in a filing under the Securities Act of 1933. SAS-37 also addresses the appropriate treatment of subsequent events that may occur after an enterprise files with the SEC (AU 711).

SAS-72 provides guidance to accountants in performing engagements to (1) provide letters to underwriters in conjunction with filings with the SEC under the Securities Act of 1933 and (2) provide letters to a requesting party in conjunction with other securities offerings (AU 634).

SAS-76 amends paragraphs 6 and 7 of SAS-72 by providing reporting guidance when an alternative to the comfort letter is provided to certain parties.

SAS-42 establishes the standards for an auditor's report on condensed financial statements or selected financial data that are derived from audited financial statements and that are intended to appear in a client-prepared document. SAS-42 is applicable only to public entities (AU 552).

INTERIM REVIEWS OF PUBLIC COMPANIES

Interim financial information may be issued on a monthly or quarterly basis or at any other interval deemed appropriate by the client or a regulatory authority. SAS-71 (Interim Financial Information) notes that an interim period also includes data or information issued for a twelve-month period ending on a date other than the client's normal year-end date. Interim financial information may be presented alone or may be included in a note to the audited financial statements. SAS-71 was issued to provide guidance for public companies for the review of interim financial information when (1) the information is presented alone as a separate financial statement(s), (2) the information is presented alone as summarized interim financial data, or (3) the information accompanies or is included in a note to the audited financial statements of a public or nonpublic entity. SAS-71 also establishes certain communications that are required when the accountant assists in preparing interim financial information or performs procedures thereon that are less than a review (AU 722.01).

> **OBSERVATION:** *SAS-71 is applicable to interim financial information that is to be reviewed. Interim financial statements may be audited, in which case the auditor would follow the approach discussed in the part of the book entitled "Audited Financial Statements." The special accounting practices and modifications established by Accounting Principles Board (APB) Opinion No. 28 (Interim Financial Reporting) and Financial Accounting Standards Board Interpretation (FIN) No. 18 (Accounting for Income Taxes in Interim Periods) should be followed in the preparation of the interim financial statements, with one exception. APB Opinion No. 28 states that the gross-profit method can be used to determine inventories at the interim date. If the interim financial statements are audited, the inventory would have to be observed by the auditor at or near the date of the interim statements. The special accounting practices for interim financial information are summarized later in this chapter.*

Responsibility and Function of the Accountant

The purpose of an audit is to determine whether the financial statements are presented fairly in accordance with generally accepted accounting principles. A review of interim financial information differs significantly from an audit of financial information because a review does not include the collection of corroborative evidence through the performance of typical substantive audit tests. Basically, the review of interim financial information consists of the performance of certain inquiries and analytical procedures. For these reasons, a review provides limited assurance on the interim financial information (AU 722.09).

SAS-71 states that the purpose of a review is to provide the accountant with a basis for reporting whether material modifications are necessary for the interim financial information to be in conformity with generally accepted accounting principles (GAAP). The accountant acquires the basis for reporting by applying the standards for a review of interim financial information in accordance with SAS-71. The accountant issues a report containing an expression of limited assurance that, on the basis of the review, he or she is not aware of any material modification that should be made to the interim financial information for it to be in conformity with GAAP (AU 722.09).

Pre-Engagement Planning

Rule 201 of the Code of Professional Conduct states, in part, that a professional service engagement must be adequately planned and supervised. The Code defines *professional services* as one or more types of services performed in the practice of public accounting. Thus, Rule 201 is applicable to a review of interim financial information (ET 201).

In most instances, the auditor's review of interim financial information will be a continuation of a professional relationship that has included the audit of the prior period's annual financial statements. For this reason, much of the pre-engagement planning will be an extension of the audit engagement, which was discussed in the part of the book entitled "Audited Financial Statements."

Engagement Letter

SAS-71 states that the auditor should make sure that the client understands the nature of a review engagement and the type of report that the accountant will issue. Ideally, the nature of the engagement should be documented in a separate engagement letter or as part of the audit engagement letter. The letter should include (1) a general description of procedures to be employed by the accountant, (2) an explanation that the engagement will not be conducted in accordance with generally accepted auditing standards, (3) a description of the review report that will be issued by the accountant, and (4) a statement that management is responsible for the financial information (AU 722.07). The following example illustrates an engagement letter for a review of interim financial information.

X Company
Address

Annually, we consider it necessary to confirm our understanding of the terms and objectives of our engagement and the limitations on the services we will provide.

Our objectives will be to perform the following services:

We will review the income statement of X Company for the three-month and six-month periods ending June 30, 19X5, in accordance with standards established by the American Institute of Certified Public Accountants. We will not perform an audit of such interim financial statements, the objective of which is the expression of an opinion regarding the financial statements taken as a whole. Accordingly, we will not express such an opinion on them. Our report on the financial statement for each quarter is presently expected to read as follows:

> We have reviewed the accompanying income statements of X Company as of June 30, 19X5, for the three-month and six-month periods then ended. These financial statements (information) are (is) the responsibility of the company's management.
>
> We conducted our review in accordance with standards established by the American Institute of Certified Public Accountants. A review of interim financial information consists principally of applying analytical procedures to financial data and making inquiries of persons responsible for financial and accounting matters. It is substantially less in scope than an audit conducted in accordance with generally accepted auditing standards, the objective of which is the expression of an opinion regarding the financial statements taken as a whole. Accordingly, we do not express such an opinion.
>
> Based on our review, we are not aware of any material modifications that should be made to the accompanying financial statements (information) for them (it) to be in conformity with generally accepted accounting principles.

Although we will review the financial information, your company's management is responsible for the financial information.

If, for any reason, we are unable to complete our review of your interim financial statements, we will not issue a report on such statements as a result of this engagement.

Our engagement cannot be relied on to disclose all errors, irregularities, or illegal acts, including fraud or defalcations, that may exist. However, we will inform the appropriate level of management of any material errors that come to our attention and any irregularities or illegal acts that come to our attention, unless they are clearly inconsequential.

Fees for the above services at our standard rates, together with any out-of-pocket costs, will be billed as the work progresses. Our invoices are payable on presentation.

We shall be pleased to discuss the services we are to provide you at any time. If you are in agreement with the foregoing, we request that you please sign the copy of this letter in the space provided below and return it to us.

Yours very truly,

[Signature of accountant]

Acknowledged:

X Company

[Officer]

[Date]

Generally Accepted Accounting Principles

In Opinion No. 28, the APB concluded that interim financial statements generally should be based on the accounting principles and practices used by an enterprise in the preparation of its latest annual financial statements. The APB recognized that certain accounting practices should be modified when they are applied to interim financial data.

Each interim period must be viewed as an integral part of the annual period, and accounting principles and reporting practices should be based on those that were used in the preparation of the latest annual reports of the entity, unless there has been a change in an accounting principle.

The accounting and reporting on the results of operations for interim financial statements are discussed in the following paragraphs.

Revenues are recognized as earned using the same methods as those used in the preparation of the company's annual financial statements.

As closely as possible, product costs are determined in a manner similar to the methods used to prepare the company's annual financial statement. The following exceptions apply to the valuation of inventory:

- Companies using the gross-profit method to determine interim inventory costs, or other methods different from those used for annual inventory valuation, should disclose the method used at the interim date and any material difference from the reconciliation with the annual physical inventory.

- A liquidation of a base-period LIFO inventory at an interim date that apparently will be replaced by the end of the annual period should be valued at the expected cost of replacement. Cost of sales for the interim period should include the expected cost of replacement and not the cost of the base-period LIFO inventory.

- Inventory losses from market declines should be included in the interim period in which they occur, and gains in subsequent interim periods should be recognized in such interim periods but should not exceed the losses included in prior interim periods.

- Inventory and product costs computed by the use of a standard cost accounting system should be determined by the same procedures used at the end of a fiscal year. Variances from standard costs that are expected to be eliminated by the end of the fiscal year need not be included in interim-period statements.

Other costs and expenses should be charged or allocated to produce a fair presentation of the results of operation, cash flows, and financial position for all interim periods. The following should apply in accounting for other costs and expenses:

- The general rule in preparing interim-period financial statements is that costs and expenses that clearly benefit more than one period should be properly allocated to the periods affected. This procedure should be consistently applied.

- Companies that have material seasonal revenue variations must avoid the possibility that interim-period financial statements become misleading. Disclosure of material seasonal revenue variations should be made in the interim-period financial statements. It is desirable also to disclose results for a full year, ending at the interim date.

- Unusual and infrequent transactions that are material and are not designated as extraordinary items, such as the effects of a disposal of a segment of a business, should be reported separately in the interim periods in which they occur.

- All other pertinent information, such as accounting changes, contingencies, seasonal results, and purchase or pooling transactions, should be disclosed to provide the necessary information for the proper understanding of the interim financial statements.

Interim reports should not contain arbitrary amounts of costs or expenses. Estimates should be reasonable and should be based on all available information applied consistently from period to period. An effective tax rate is used for income tax provision in interim periods.

Material contingencies and other uncertainties that exist at an interim date must be disclosed in interim reports in the same manner as that required for annual reports. However, contingencies and uncertainties at an interim date should be evaluated in relation to the annual report. The disclosure for such items must be repeated in every interim and annual report until the contingency is resolved or becomes immaterial.

Reporting accounting changes—interim periods The cumulative effect of an accounting change is always included in net income of the first interim period, regardless of in which interim period during the year the accounting change occurs. If the accounting change occurs in other than the first interim period, the current-period and prior-period interim statements should be restated to reflect the newly adopted accounting principle. However, the cumulative effect of the change in an accounting principle is included only in the net income of the first interim period.

When the cumulative effect of a change in an accounting principle cannot be determined, the pro forma amounts cannot be computed. In this event, the cumulative effect and pro forma amounts are omitted. However, the amount of the effect of adopting the new accounting principle and its per share data for each interim period and year-to-date amounts must be disclosed in a footnote to the financial statements, along with the reasons for omitting the cumulative effect and pro forma information.

Publicly traded companies that do not issue separate fourth-quarter reports must disclose in a note to their annual reports any effect of an accounting change made during the fourth quarter. This is similar to other disclosure requirements of publicly traded companies that do not issue fourth-quarter interim reports.

The following disclosure concerning a cumulative-effect type accounting change should be made in interim financial reports:

1. The nature and justification of the change should be made in the interim period in which the new accounting principle is adopted.

2. The effects of the accounting change on income from continuing operations, net income, and related per share data for both, should be made:

— In the interim period in which the change is made

— In each, if any, prior interim period

— In each, if any, restated prior interim period

— In year-to-date and in last-twelve-months-to-date financial reports that include the adoption of a new accounting principle

— In interim financial reports of the fiscal year, subsequent to the interim period in which the accounting change was adopted

3. The pro forma effects of the accounting change on income from continuing operations, net income, and related per share data, should be made:

— For the interim period in which the change is made

— For any interim period of prior fiscal years for which financial information is presented

— In year-to-date and last-twelve-months-to-date financial reports that include the adoption of a new accounting principle

If no interim periods of prior fiscal years are presented, footnote disclosure for the corresponding interim period of the immediate fiscal year in which the accounting change occurred should be made for actual and pro forma income from continuing operations, net income, and related per share data.

Summarized interim financial statements Publicly traded companies reporting summarized financial information at interim dates should include the following minimum information:

1. Gross revenues, provision for income taxes, extraordinary items, effects of accounting changes (principle or practice), and net income

2. Primary and fully diluted earnings-per-share data

3. Material seasonal variations of revenues, costs, or expenses

4. Contingent items and effects of the disposal of a segment of a business

5. Material cash flows

Summarized interim financial statements based on these minimum disclosures *do not* constitute a fair presentation of financial position and results of operations in conformity with GAAP.

In the event that fourth-quarter results are not issued separately, the annual report of a public company should include disclosures for the fourth quarter on the aggregate effect of material year-end adjustments and infrequently occurring items, extraordinary items, and disposal of business segments that occurred in the fourth quarter.

When summarized interim financial information is not presented by a public company, significant changes in liquid assets, working capital, long-term liabilities, and stockholders' equity should be disclosed and disseminated to the public.

Generally Accepted Auditing Standards

SAS-71 notes that the purpose of a review of interim financial information differs significantly from the purpose of an audit of financial statements in accordance with generally accepted auditing standards. As noted earlier, a review of interim financial information does not provide a basis for the auditor to express an opinion on the interim information because all generally accepted auditing standards are not followed. The nonobservance of GAAS is reflected in the scope paragraph of the report on a review of interim financial information (AU 722.09).

General standards Two of the general standards are concerned with technical training and due professional care. Rule 201 of the Code of Professional Conduct is applicable to services performed by a member in the practice of public accounting. This rule specifically states that a member shall (1) undertake only those engagements that he or she or the firm can reasonably expect to complete with professional competence and (2) exercise due professional care in the performance of an engagement. The third general standard of generally accepted auditing standards deals with independence. Once again, the Code of Professional Conduct extends the concept of independence to all other services performed by a member in public practice. Rule 102 states that members shall not subordinate their judgment to others or knowingly misrepresent facts.

Standards of fieldwork The first standard of fieldwork is concerned with planning and supervision. Once again, Rule 201 extends these concepts to the review of interim financial information by requiring that all engagements performed by a member in public practice be adequately planned and supervised. Of course, the planning of a review is different from the planning of an audit engagement. The next standard of fieldwork deals with a client's internal control. SAS-71 requires that the accountant have a sufficient knowledge of the internal controls that relate to the preparation of annual and interim financial information in order to:

- Identify types of potential material misstatements in the interim financial information and consider the likelihood of their occurrence.

- Select the inquiries and analytical procedures that will provide the accountant with a basis for reporting whether material modifications should be made for such information to conform with generally accepted accounting principles.

Finally, the last fieldwork standard is concerned with the collection and evaluation of sufficient competent evidential matter. SAS-71 does not require that evidence be collected to a degree that would allow the auditor to form an opinion on the interim financial information. However, SAS-71 does require that certain review procedures be emphasized, mainly inquiry and analytical procedures, before the accountant's review report can be issued. In addition, Rule 201 of the Code of Professional Conduct requires that sufficient relevant data be obtained to afford a reasonable basis for conclusions drawn by the accountant.

Standards of reporting The first and third standards of reporting deal with accounting principles and adequate disclosure, respectively. Although the accountant does not express an opinion on the reviewed interim financial information, known departures from GAAP or inadequate disclosures would require that the accountant modify the review report. The fourth reporting standard is concerned with the accountant's expression of an opinion on the financial statements taken as a whole. Although SAS-71 does not provide a basis for the expression of an opinion on the interim financial information, it does require that a negative assurance and a disclaimer of opinion be expressed (AU 722.09).

Planning the Engagement

In most instances, the review of interim financial information likely would be an extension of the audit engagement. When the auditor has previously audited the annual financial statements of the client for the immediately preceding year, the audit engagement should provide a basis for the review of subsequent interim financial information. SAS-71 specifically notes that knowledge of the client's internal control includes the five component elements. When the accountant has not audited the preceding year's financial statements, SAS-71 nonetheless requires that a sufficient knowledge of the client's internal control that relate to the preparation of annual and interim financial information be obtained (AU 722.10).

Part of the planning of an engagement for the review of interim financial information should include the evaluation of any new accounting standard and how it might affect the client's interim financial information. For example, the issuance of a pronouncement by the Financial Accounting Standards Board (FASB) that prohibits the capitalization of costs that previously could be deferred should alert the accountant that there may be changes in the interrelationship of accounting information. Moreover, such action by the FASB would require that the accountant ask the client how the new pronouncement affected its accounting system and what specific procedures were adopted to ensure the observance of the new accounting rule. Of course, the accountant should be aware of special accounting principles or practices, if any, that are unique to the client's industry or transactions.

Adequate planning of a review of interim financial information must include consideration of the degree of centralization of the client's accounting function. If the client has multiple locations but the general accounting is performed only at one central location, there would be no need to visit the other locations. When a significant amount of information is processed at multiple locations, however, review procedures must be applied to both the central accounting location and other locations selected by the accountant. In some instances, other locations may be reviewed by other accountants. Under this circumstance, the accountant may be placed in the position of a principal accountant and must evaluate and coordinate the work of the other accountants and decide whether to refer to the work of the other accountants in the interim review report. Relationships and procedures associated with an audit engagement involving a principal auditor and other auditors are discussed in the chapter entitled "Evidence." These guidelines are applicable to a principal accountant in a review of interim financial information.

Planning of the interim review is affected by the very nature of interim financial data. Interim financial information is typically released to interested parties more quickly than is audited information. SAS-71 notes that some review procedures may be performed before the end of the interim period to increase the likelihood that the interim review will be completed on a timely basis. The performance of some review procedures early in the engagement also may identify problems that can be considered earlier in the engagement.

Interim review engagements generally will encompass periods that eventually will be audited. The procedures normally used in the review of interim financial information may be modified because of the use of procedures performed in conjunction with the audit of financial statements. For example, an engagement may include the review of interim data for each of the first three quarters of a year and the audit of the annual financial statements. Preliminary work for the audit engagement may reduce the need for the performance of certain procedures for the second-quarter and third-quarter interim financial statement reviews.

Consideration of Internal Control

SAS-71 requires the accountant to obtain a sufficient knowledge of the client's internal controls that relate to the preparation of annual and interim financial information. However, in most interim review engagements, the accountant would have audited the preceding year's annual financial statements, which would have included an assessment of the client's internal controls. During a subsequent interim review, the client should be asked whether there have been any significant changes in internal control. Any changes should be evaluated by the accountant to determine whether they may affect the client's ability to prepare interim financial information in accordance with generally accepted accounting principles (AU 722.10).

In a first-time engagement of a new client, an accountant who has been engaged to perform a review of interim financial information cannot be expected to understand the client's internal controls. SAS-71 requires that the accountant possess adequate knowledge and understanding of the client's accounting and reporting practices and internal controls (AU 722.10).

With respect to internal control, the accountant's inquiries should be structured to determine whether there have been changes in control since the completion of the preceding audit engagement and to identify control for interim financial reporting that differ from controls used for annual financial reporting. Interim financial reporting procedures may differ from annual reporting procedures because (1) it is usually necessary to use more estimates at the interim date and (2) accounts at an interim date may be affected by forecasts of results for the entire year. These procedures must be evaluated to determine whether they are appropriate for the preparation of interim financial data. If it is concluded that there are reportable conditions in internal controls as it applies to the preparation of interim data, the implications for the engagement should be considered. In some instances, these conditions may be viewed as a restriction on the scope of the engagement, and the accountant may decide not to issue an interim review report or not to permit his or her name to be used in a written communication containing the interim financial information. Senior management and the board of directors or its audit committee should be notified of reportable conditions in internal controls that are used to prepare interim financial data. The accountant may make suggestions to the client for improving the controls (AU 722.10–.11).

Evidence

A review of interim financial information does not include tests of the accounting records or the collection of corroborating evidential matter through the use of audit procedures such as confirmation, observation, inspection, and so on. For the most part, an interim review consists of inquiries and analytical procedures. These procedures are directed toward significant accounting matters that could affect interim financial information. SAS-71 lists the following analytical procedures that would normally be employed (AU 722.13):

- Through inquiries, obtain information about the following:
  - Internal controls for both annual and interim financial information
  - Significant changes in internal controls since the audit or review of the most recent financial statements
- Apply the following analytical procedures to interim financial information:
  - Compare the current-period interim financial information to the previous-period interim financial information.
  - Evaluate the plausibility of relationships among interim financial information and, where relevant, nonfinancial information.
  - Compare recorded amounts (or related ratios) to expectations.

OBSERVATION: When performing analytical procedures for interim financial information, the auditor may find the guidance established in SAS-56 (Analytical Procedures) and SAS-57 (Auditing Accounting Estimates) useful.

- To identify matters that may affect the interim financial information, read the minutes of meetings of (1) stockholders, (2) the board of directors, and (3) committees of the board of directors.

- Considering the information gathered through inquiry and analytical procedures, read the interim financial information to determine whether it conforms to generally accepted accounting principles.

- If appropriate, obtain review reports from other accountants who have been engaged to review the interim financial information of significant affiliates, for example, subsidiaries or other investees.

- Through inquiry of officers and other accounting or financial executives, determine the following:
  - If interim financial information has been prepared in accordance with generally accepted accounting principles
  - Changes in accounting principles or practices
  - Changes in business activities
  - Responses to questions that have arisen from the application of other interim analytical procedures
  - Events that have occurred after the date of the interim financial information but have an effect on the information

- Obtain written representation from the client. See SAS-19 (Client Representations) for guidance on what matters may be contained in the representation letter.

In a review of interim financial information, it is not necessary for the accountant to send audit inquiry letters to a client's attorney unless information comes to the attention of the accountant that leads him or her to believe that the accounting for litigation, claims, or assessments pertaining to unaudited interim information departs from GAAP (AU 722.17).

A review of interim financial information is not necessarily limited to the performance of the procedures described above. Other information that comes to the accountant's attention may provide a basis for additional inquiries. For example, if the accountant becomes aware that the client has significantly changed its product warranties, this change must be discussed with appropriate client personnel to determine its effect on the presentation of the interim data. In addition, the results of inquiries and analytical procedures may suggest to the accountant that the interim financial information may not conform to generally accepted accounting principles. In this case, the accountant should use whatever procedures are deemed appropriate to resolve questions raised (AU 722.17–.18).

> *OBSERVATION: The technique of inquiry and analytical procedures is considered relatively weak with respect to the criteria of obtaining competent evidential matter. However, these analytical procedures are not performed in isolation. The procedures can be performed successfully only if the accountant has (1) a thorough knowledge of the client's accounting and financial reporting practices and (2) a thorough understanding of the client's internal control.*

The analytical procedures applied and the results of these procedures must be adequately documented in the workpapers. SAS-41 (Working Papers) notes that workpapers should aid in the conduct and review of an engagement and should provide adequate support for the conclusions reached by the accountant. SAS-71 does not contain specific suggestions about the content of workpapers for an interim financial information review.

Communication with the audit committee   If the accountant believes that the interim financial information filed or to be filed with the specified regulatory agency is probably materially misstated, the matter should be discussed with the appropriate level of the client's management. If, after being notified, management does not respond in a timely and appropriate manner, the matter should be brought to the attention of the client's audit committee (or equivalent body). The communication with the audit committee may be written or oral; however, if oral communication is used, the communication should be documented in the workpapers (AU 722.20–.21).

If the audit committee does not respond in a timely and appropriate manner, SAS-71 concludes that the accountant should consider the following courses of action (AU 722.22):

- Resign from the interim financial information engagement.
- Resign from the related audit engagement.

When selecting a course of action, the accountant should consider consulting with legal counsel (AU 722.22).

Other matters that should be communicated to the audit committee include the following (AU 722.23–.24):

- Irregularities discovered during the engagement, except those that are clearly inconsequential
- Illegal acts discovered during the engagement, except those that are clearly inconsequential
- Reportable conditions discovered
- Other matters discussed in SAS-61 (Communication with Audit Committees) that may relate to interim financial information

Accountant's Reports

Interim financial information may be presented in a set of separate financial statements, or it may accompany the audited financial statements. The way the accountant reports on the interim financial information depends on the method used to present the information (AU 722.27 and .40).

The accountant cannot allow his or her name to be included in a written communication containing the information unless a review has been performed. The accountant's review report may be addressed to the client, its board of directors, or its stockholders and usually should be dated as of the date of the completion of the review. The standard review report itself should (AU 722.26–.27):

- Include a title that uses the word *independent*.
- Identify the interim information subject to review.
- State that the information is the responsibility of management.
- State that the review was performed in accordance with standards established by the AICPA.

- Describe the nature of review procedures.

- State that the scope of a review is substantially less than that of an audit in accordance with GAAS, the objective of which is an expression of an opinion on the information.

- Disclaim an opinion on the information.

- State that nothing came to the accountant's attention that would suggest that the information needs to be modified in order for it to be in accordance with GAAP (limited assurance).

The date of the auditor's report should be based on the completion date of the engagement, and each page of the interim financial information should be clearly marked "unaudited." Finally, the report should carry the manual or printed signature of the CPA firm (AU 722.27).

The following is an example of a review report that incorporates the requirements listed in the preceding paragraph (AU 722.28).

Independent Accountant's Report

X Company
Stockholders and Board of Directors

We have reviewed the accompanying [describe the statements or information reviewed] of X Company as of June 30, 19X5, and for the three-month and six-month periods then ended. These financial statements [information] are [is] the responsibility of the company's management.

We conducted our review in accordance with standards established by the American Institute of Certified Public Accountants. A review of interim financial information consists principally of applying analytical procedures to financial data and making inquiries of persons responsible for financial and accounting matters. It is substantially less in scope than an audit conducted in accordance with generally accepted auditing standards, the objective of which is the expression of an opinion regarding the financial statements taken as a whole. Accordingly, we do not express such an opinion.

Based on our review, we are not aware of any material modifications that should be made to the accompanying financial statements [information] for them [it] to be in conformity with generally accepted accounting principles.

July 29, 19X5

Signature

When the interim financial information is presented on a comparative basis with that of the corresponding previous period and the accountant has reviewed the previous period, the accountant should report on the prior period (AU 722.28).

Modifications to the standard review report   As with an auditor's report on audited financial statements, circumstances may arise that require the modification of the standard review report. However, because of the nature of a report on the review of interim financial information, the modifications are unique and are summarized below.

Scope modification   An accountant may not be able to perform appropriate procedures for the review of interim financial information. Nonperformance of these procedures may result from an inadequate accounting system, client-imposed restrictions, or reportable conditions in the internal control structure. When the scope of the review is restricted, the accountant should not issue a review report or let his or her name be included in a written communication that contains the interim financial information (AU 722.26).

> *OBSERVATION: SAS-71 does not establish a review report format that would be equivalent to a disclaimer of opinion or a qualified opinion on annual financial statements when the scope of the review has been significantly limited.*

Using the work of another accountant   When an accountant has served as the principal auditor in the audit of a client's annual financial statements, it is likely that the accountant will be in a similar position with respect to reporting on a subsequent interim financial period(s). Under these circumstances, the accountant must decide whether to refer to the work performed by any other accountant. When the principal accountant decides to refer to the work of another accountant, the scope and negative assurance paragraphs should clearly indicate the division of responsibility. The scope paragraph should disclose the magnitude of the portion of the interim financial information reviewed by the other accountant. The magnitude may be described by referring to one or more of the following: total assets, total revenues, or other appropriate criteria, whichever most clearly indicates the portion of the interim financial information reviewed by the other accountant. Dollar amounts or percentages may be used to describe the magnitude of the work performed by the other accountant. Reference to the work of another accountant is not a qualification but rather an indication of the division of responsibility between all the accountants involved in the review (AU 722.13).

> **OBSERVATION:** *When an interim review engagement involves the use of another accountant, guidance established in SAS-1, Section 543 (Part of Audit Performed by Other Independent Auditors), should be followed.*

The following is an example of a review report with reference by the principal accountant to the report of another accountant.

We have reviewed the accompanying [describe statements or information reviewed] of X Company and consolidated subsidiaries as of June 30, 19X5, and for the three-month and six-month periods then ended. These financial statements [information] are [is] the responsibility of the company's management.

We were furnished with the report of other accountants on their review of the interim financial information of Y Subsidiary, whose total assets as of June 30, 19X5, and whose revenues for the three-month and six-month periods then ended, constituted 25%, 10%, and 15%, respectively, of the related consolidated totals.

We conducted our review in accordance with standards established by the American Institute of Certified Public Accountants. A review of interim financial information consists principally of applying analytical procedures to financial data and making inquiries of persons responsible for financial and accounting matters. It is substantially less in scope than an audit conducted in accordance with generally accepted auditing standards, the objective of which is the expression of an opinion regarding the financial statements taken as a whole. Accordingly, we do not express such an opinion.

Based on our review and the report of other accountants, we are not aware of any material modifications that should be made to the accompanying financial statements [information] for them [it] to be in conformity with generally accepted accounting principles.

GAAP modification   During the review, an accountant may discover that the interim financial information is materially affected by a departure from generally accepted accounting principles. When this occurs, an explanatory paragraph should be added to the review report. The explanatory paragraph should describe the nature of the departure from GAAP and, if practical, the effects of the departure on the interim financial information. The last paragraph (limited assurance paragraph) must refer to the departure from GAAP described in the explanatory paragraph (AU 722.31).

When a review report is modified because of a departure from generally accepted accounting principles, paragraphs similar to the ones presented below are added to the first two paragraphs of the standard review report (AU 722.31).

Based on information supplied to us by management, we believe that the company has excluded a net provision for loss or abandonment of certain properties that should be reported as a loss in order to conform with generally accepted accounting principles. This information indicates that if the loss had been recognized at March 31, 19X5, net income and earnings per share would have been decreased by $450,000 and $.17, respectively.

Based on our review, with the exception of the matter described in the preceding paragraph, we are not aware of any material modifications that should be made to the accompanying financial statements [information] for them [it] to be in conformity with generally accepted accounting principles.

Inadequate disclosure modification What constitutes adequate disclosure for interim financial information is not as well defined as disclosures required in annual audited financial statements. In APB Opinion No. 28, the APB adopted the philosophy that users of summarized interim financial data will have read the latest published annual report and that the limited interim data will be evaluated in that context.

When it is concluded that interim financial information does not contain adequate disclosures, the review report should be modified. An explanatory paragraph should be added to the review report in which the nature of the information not disclosed should be described. If practicable, the description should contain all the necessary information to achieve adequate disclosure. The final paragraph of the review report should refer to the explanatory paragraph and a *qualified limited assurance* should be expressed. When a review report is modified because of inadequate disclosures in the interim financial information, paragraphs similar to the ones presented below are added to the first two paragraphs of the standard review report (AU 722.32).

Management has informed us that on April 10, 19X1, the Company issued debentures in the amount of $2,500,000 for the purpose of financing the construction of a new research and development facility. The debentures were placed with a consortium of private investors. The interim financial information failed to disclose this matter, which we believe is required to be disclosed in conformity with generally accepted accounting principles.

On the basis of our review, with the exception of the matter described in the preceding paragraph, we are not aware of any material modifications that should be made to the accompanying financial statements [information] for them [it] to be in conformity with generally accepted accounting principles.

Going-concern modification SAS-71 states that normally substantial doubt about the entity's ability to continue as a going concern would not require the accountant to modify the report, provided the appropriate disclosures were made in the interim financial information. Apparently this position is taken because the accountant is not expressing an opinion on the interim financial information (AU 722.30).

Inconsistency modification A change in the application of accounting principles affecting an interim period will not result in a modification of the standard review report if the inconsistency is appropriately disclosed. If an inconsistency is not appropriately disclosed in the interim financial information, the accountant's report would have to be modified on the basis of inadequate disclosure (AU 722.30).

If the newly adopted accounting principle is not generally accepted, the review report must be modified in the same manner as it would be for a departure from GAAP.

Subsequent events Ordinarily the review report is dated as of the date of completion of the review of interim financial information. However, three circumstances may lead to a departure from this dating practice when a subsequent event occurs after the date of the interim review but before the report is issued. These three circumstances are summarized as follows (AU 722.13):

- The subsequent event results in an adjustment to the interim financial information, and the event is disclosed.
- The subsequent event is disclosed in a note to the supplementary information.

- A subsequent event is not properly accounted for (that is, an adjustment is not made or the event is not disclosed), and the review report is modified because of this departure from GAAP.

When any one of these three circumstances occurs, the accountant must dual-date the interim review report. A dual dating might read: "April 12, 19X5, except for Note B, as to which date is April 22, 19X5." Alternatively, the accountant may use the single date on which the subsequent event was discovered. In the example, that date is April 22. It should be remembered that when the later date is used, the accountant's responsibilities with respect to other subsequent events extend to that date (AU 722.13).

Responsibilities after the report date   An accountant has no responsibility to continue investigating interim financial information after the date of the accountant's report.

Nonetheless, the accountant should not ignore the subsequent discovery of facts that existed at the date of the report and that may have had an effect on the accountant's report. SAS-71 does not provide specific guidance for this circumstance, but recommends that the accountant consider the standards established in SAS-1, Section 561 (Subsequent Discovery of Facts Existing at the Date of the Auditor's Report) (AU 722.34).

Reports on interim financial information accompanying audited financial statements   Certain public companies must disclose selected quarterly financial data in their annual reports or other documents that contain audited financial statements and are filed with the SEC. These disclosures are considered supplementary information and are not a required part of the basic financial statements. Each page of the supplementary information must be clearly marked as unaudited. The accountant should apply the interim review procedures on the supplementary information that were described earlier in this chapter. When the accountant has reviewed the interim financial information, usually no reference is made to the interim review in the auditor's report on the audited financial statements. The reason for no reference to the review or to the interim financial information is that it is considered supplementary information and is not necessary for the annual financial statements to be presented in accordance with generally accepted accounting principles (AU 722.36–.39).

Companies that are not required to disclose the mandated SEC quarterly information may voluntarily choose to disclose this information along with their audited financial statements. Under these circumstances, the auditor must review the supplementary data using the interim review procedures described earlier in this chapter, unless the company indicates that the data have not been reviewed or unless the auditor expands the standard audit report by noting that the supplementary data have not been reviewed (AU 722.37).

The auditor's report on the annual financial statements must be modified if the client does not present the quarterly financial data required by the SEC. Under these circumstances, an additional paragraph is included in the three-paragraph standard audit report and might read as follows (AU 722.41).

The Company has not presented the selected quarterly financial data, specified by item 302(a) of Regulation S-K, which the Securities and Exchange Commission requires as supplementary information to the basic financial statements.

When the quarterly financial information is included but the auditor has not reviewed the information, the additional paragraph to the standard audit report might be worded in the following manner (AU 722.41).

The selected quarterly financial data on page X contain information that we did not audit, and accordingly, we do not express an opinion on that data. We attempted, but were unable, to review the quarterly data in accordance with standards established by the American Institute of Certified Public Accountants, because we believe that the company's system for preparing interim financial information does not provide an adequate basis to enable us to complete such a review.

The inclusion of an additional paragraph when the interim information is not presented or a review of the interim information is not made does not provide the basis for a qualified opinion on the audited financial statements. Therefore, the opinion paragraph contains no reference to the additional paragraph on the selected quarterly financial data (AU 722.40).

In addition, the standard auditor's report should be modified under the following conditions (AU 722.42):

- Interim financial information included in a note to the audited financial statements has been reviewed but has not been clearly marked as "unaudited."
- Quarterly information voluntarily presented has not been reviewed, and the information has not been marked as "not reviewed."
- The interim financial information does not appear to be presented in accordance with generally accepted accounting principles, and the auditor's separate review report, which refers to the departure, is not presented with the information.
- The client notes that a review was made of the interim information but fails to state that a review is substantially less than an audit, and the accountant's separate review report is not presented with the information.

Although these circumstances would lead to an expansion of the auditor's standard report on the annual financial statements, they are not a basis for the expression of a qualified opinion (AU 722.42).

FILINGS UNDER FEDERAL SECURITIES STATUTES

SAS-37 (Filings Under Federal Securities Statutes) provides guidance for the accountant whose report, based on a review of interim financial information, is presented or incorporated by reference in a filing under the Securities Act of 1933. SAS-37 also provides guidance for the auditor and accountant in the area of subsequent events that occur after filings with the SEC (AU 711.04).

SAS-37 states that generally an accountant's responsibility for filings under federal securities statutes is no different from that in any other reporting engagement. However, the Securities Act of 1933 and its related rules and regulations contain specific duties and responsibilities for any expert whose report or valuation is used as part of a registration statement filed with the SEC. An accountant's report on a review of interim financial information is not a *report* under the existing rules of the SEC. If an accountant's report is based on a review of interim financial information, the SEC requires that any reference to such a report in any filing with the SEC contain a statement that the report is not a *report* or part of the registration statement under Sections 7 and 11 of the Securities Act of 1933. Thus, an accountant's report on a review of interim financial information is exempt under Sections 7 and 11 of the Securities Act of 1933. Section

11(a) is one of the most important sections of the Act, in specifying the duties and responsibilities of an auditor or an accountant.

> Section 11(a): If any part of a registration statement that becomes effective contains an untrue statement of a material fact or omits a material fact required in order to make the statement not misleading, any person acquiring such security may either at law or at equity sue:
>
> 1. Every person who signed the registration statement
> 2. Every person who was a director or partner
> 3. Every *accountant*, engineer, or appraiser, or any other expert professional
> 4. Every underwriter with respect to such securities

Although an accountant's report based on a review of interim financial information is exempt from Sections 7 and 11 of the Securities Act of 1933, an auditor's report on an examination of financial statements that is made in accordance with generally accepted accounting standards is not exempt (AU 711.01–.02).

A registration statement is effective on the twentieth day after filing or after filing of the last amendment to the registration statement. The independent auditor's statutory duties and responsibilities for his or her reports, other than those based on an interim review of financial information, do not cease until the effective date of the registration statement. Thus, an auditor must perform certain audit procedures to include the period from the date of the financial statements covered by the report through the effective date of the registration statement. This is called the subsequent-events period. To complete a review of subsequent events, the auditor must arrange for the client to keep him or her informed of the progress of the registration statement. In the subsequent-events period, the auditor should employ the same audit procedures used to identify subsequent events in regular audited statements (AU 711.10).

In addition to the usual audit procedures for the subsequent-events period, the auditor should perform the following additional procedures (AU 711.10):

1. Read thoroughly the entire prospectus and the pertinent parts of the registration statement.
2. Make inquiries of responsible executives of the client regarding any financial and accounting matters of a material nature that may have occurred during the subsequent-events period.

3. Obtain client representation letters covering any subsequent events that have a material effect on the audited financial statements.

A predecessor auditor whose report for a prior period appears in a filing with the SEC is responsible for subsequent events from the date of the financial statements covered in the prior-period report to the effective date of the registration statement that materially relates to the prior-period financial statements. The predecessor auditor should perform the following procedures (AU 711.11):

1. Read carefully the pertinent portions of the prospectus and registration statement.
2. Obtain a representation letter from the current auditor on whether anything of a material nature came to his or her attention during the examination, including subsequent events, for which the predecessor auditor is required to disclose or make an adjustment.
3. If adjustments or disclosures are discovered that affect the prior-period financial statements, the predecessor auditor needs to be satisfied about what procedures are necessary under the circumstances. Thus, the predecessor auditor may need to make inquiries and perform certain audit procedures to be satisfied.

If the client refuses to make adjustments or disclosures for subsequent events as deemed necessary by the auditor, the procedures promulgated for Subsequent Discovery of Facts Existing at the Date of the Auditor's Report should be followed by the auditor. These procedures are discussed in the chapter entitled "Evidence" (AU 711.12).

OBSERVATION: An Auditing Interpretation of SAS-37, "Subsequent-Events Procedures for Shelf Registration Statements Updated After the Original Effective Date" (May 1983), states that an auditor must perform subsequent-events procedures as described in SAS-37 (paragraphs 10 and 11) with respect to filing a single shelf registration statement that permits companies to register a designated amount of securities for continuous or delayed offering when (1) a posteffective amendment to the shelf registration statement is filed pursuant to Item 512(a) of Regulation S-K or (2) a 1934 Act filing that includes or amends audited financial statements is incorporated by reference into the shelf registration statement (AU 9711.01–.11).

> **OBSERVATION:** *Another Interpretation of SAS-37, "Consenting to Be Named as an Expert in an Offering Document in Connection with Securities Offerings Other Than Those Registered Under the Securities Act of 1933" (March 1995), states that the auditor should not consent to be named, or referred to, as an* **expert** *with respect to a securities offering other than those registered under the Securities Act of 1933. Another Interpretation, "Consenting to the Use of an Audit Report in an Offering Document in Securities Offerings Other Than One Registered Under the Securities Act of 1993" (June 1992), states that an auditor may consent to use of his or her audit report in an offering document other than the one registered under the Securities Act of 1933 (AU 9711.12–.17).*

When subsequent events or subsequently discovered facts come to the attention of the auditor, standards established by Section 560 (Subsequent Events) and Section 561 (Subsequent Discovery of Facts Existing at the Date of the Auditor's Report) should be observed.

Unaudited financial statements   If unaudited financial statements or unaudited interim financial statements are presented or incorporated by reference in a filing with the SEC, and if the accountant subsequently determines that such statements are not in conformity with generally accepted accounting principles, the accountant must insist that the client make the appropriate disclosures or revisions. If the client refuses to make the appropriate changes, the accountant should consider withholding consent to the use of the report on the client's audited financial statements, if any, for filings with the SEC. The accountant should also seek the advice of legal counsel (AU 711.13).

Document review of filings with the SEC   Usually, a prospectus contains an expert section that includes the names of the experts whose reports or valuations are included in the registration statement. An important procedure that the auditor or accountant should perform is to read all the pertinent sections of the prospectus, the registration statement, and any other documents filed with the SEC. No document filed with the SEC should imply that the independent auditor actually prepared the financial statements on which the report is based. Financial statements are prepared by, and are direct representations of, the management of an enterprise. The relevant sections of filings made to the SEC should be carefully read by the auditor or accountant to make sure that they contain no indication of responsibility for the financial statement greater than that actually intended (AU 711.08).

LETTERS FOR UNDERWRITERS AND CERTAIN OTHER REQUESTING PARTIES

SAS-72 (Letters for Underwriters and Certain Other Requesting Parties) provides guidance to accountants in performing engagements to provide (1) letters to underwriters in conjunction with filings with the Securities and Exchange Commission (SEC) under the Securities Act of 1933 (the 1933 Act) and (2) letters to a requesting party in conjunction with other securities offerings (AU 634.01).

SAS-72 supersedes SAS-49 (Letters for Underwriters). SAS-49 was issued in 1984, before the issuance of Statements on Standards for Attestation Engagements (Attestation Standards; Financial Forecasts and Projections; and Reporting on Pro Forma Financial Information). Therefore, the guidance and examples pertaining to letters (commonly referred to as "comfort letters") issued to underwriters and certain other parties (referred to hereafter as "requesting parties") had to be revised to reflect the issuance of these standards. Furthermore, since SAS-49 was issued, accountants have been requested to issue comfort letters to parties other than underwriters and in connection with securities offerings other than those registered under the Act. SAS-72 provides guidance on those parties to whom accountants may provide comfort letters (AU 634.02).

> *OBSERVATION: An Auditing Interpretation of SAS-72 entitled "Letters to Directors Relating to Annual Reports on Form 10-K" (April 1981, revised June 1993) concludes that the auditor may perform some services requested by the board of directors relating to the annual reports on Form 10-K (9634.01–.09).*

Applicability of Statement on Auditing Standards No. 72

As part of the registration of securities under the 1933 Act, an accountant is often asked by underwriters of the securities to provide them with a comfort letter. The comfort letter is not a requirement of the 1933 Act and is not included in the registration statement. However, it is requested by underwriters to assist them in discharging their duty of *reasonable investigation* and to help establish their affirmative defense under Section 11 of the 1933 Act (often referred to as "Section 11 investigation" or "due diligence"). Therefore, obtaining the accountant's comfort letter is one of many activities that underwriters undertake to respond to the liability imposed on them under Section 11 of the 1933 Act (AU 634.03).

> **OBSERVATION:** *SAS-72 states that the accountant may address the comfort letter to parties other than a named underwriter only when (1) the requesting party has a statutory due diligence defense under Section 11 of the 1933 Act and (2) legal counsel for the requesting party issues a written legal opinion to the accountant explicitly stating that such party has a statutory due diligence defense under Section 11 of the 1933 Act. If the requesting party cannot provide such a legal opinion letter from its counsel, the accountant should obtain a representation letter, as described below, from the requesting party (AU 634.04).*

SAS-72 states that the accountant may also provide comfort letters to other requesting parties, in addition to underwriters, in the following situations *only if* the representation letter described below is obtained (AU 634.04):

- To a broker-dealer or other financial intermediary in connection with the following types of securities offerings:
  - Foreign offerings (e.g., Regulation S, Eurodollar, and other offshore offerings)
  - Transactions that are exempt from the registration requirements of Section 5 of the 1933 Act, including those pursuant to Regulation A, Regulation D, and Rule 144A
  - Offerings of securities issued or backed by governmental, municipal, banking, tax-exempt, or other entities that are exempt from registration under the 1933 Act
- To a buyer or seller, or both, in connection with acquisition transactions involving an exchange of stock (e.g., Form S-4 or merger proxy situation)

SAS-76 (Amendments to Statement on Auditing Standards No. 72 on Letters for Underwriters) concludes that when a party specifically identified in paragraphs 3 through 5 of SAS-72 (other than an underwriter of a party with a due diligence defense based on Section 11 of the 1933 Act) requests a comfort letter but does not provide the representations established by paragraphs 6 and 7 of SAS-72, the accountant should not provide a comfort letter. However, the accountant may provide an alternative letter that does not include a negative assurance on the financial statements or specified elements, accounts, or items of those statements. In addition, the alternative letter should state the following:

- The accountant had no responsibility for the determination of the procedures enumerated in the letter.

- The enumerated procedures do not constitute an audit of the financial statements.

- The enumerated procedures should not substitute for additional inquiries or procedures that the party may perform as part of considering the proposed offering.

- The letter is solely for the other party's information and should not be used for any other purpose.

- The accountant has no responsibility for updating the letter for events that may occur after the cutoff date.

The guidance established by SAS-72 that applies to performing procedures related to a comfort letter also should apply to the procedures referred to in the alternative letter.

A comfort letter (or alternative letter described above) should be prepared only for parties referred to in paragraphs 3 through 5 of SAS-72. If another party requests a letter, the standards established by SAS-72 and SAS-76 do not apply; however, the accountant may accept an engagement that satisfies the standards established by either SAS-75 (Engagements to Apply Agreed-Upon Procedures to Specified Elements, Accounts, or Items of a Financial Statement) or SSAE-4 (Agreed-Upon Procedures Engagements).

Required representation letter   The required representation letter from the requesting parties identified above should (1) be addressed to the accountant and signed by the requesting party and (2) include a statement that the review process to be applied by the requesting party is substantially consistent with the due diligence review process that would be performed pursuant to the 1933 Act. Following is an example of such a representation letter as illustrated in SAS-72 (AU 634.06).

Dear ABC Accountants:

[Name of financial intermediary], as principal or agent, in the placement of [identify securities] to be issued by [name of issuer], will be reviewing certain information relating to [issuer] that will be included [incorporated by reference] in the document [if appropriate, the document should be identified], which may be delivered to investors and utilized by them as a basis for their investment decision. This review process, applied to the information relating to the issuer, is [will be] substantially consistent with the due diligence review process that we would perform if this placement of securities [or issuance of securities in an acquisition transaction] were being registered pursuant to the Securities Act of 1933 (the Act). We are knowledgeable with respect to the due diligence review process that would be performed if this placement of securities were being registered pursuant to the Act. We hereby request that you deliver to us a "comfort" letter concerning the financial statements of the issuer and certain statistical and other data included in the offering document. We will contact you to identify the procedures we wish you to follow and the form we wish the comfort letter to take.

Very truly yours,

[Name of financial intermediary]

OBSERVATION: If a nonunderwriter requests a comfort letter in connection with a securities offering registered pursuant to the 1933 Act, the second and third sentences of the representation letter should be revised as follows (AU 634.06):

> *This review process, applied to the information relating to the issuer, is substantially consistent with the due diligence review process that an underwriter would perform in connection with this placement of securities. We are knowledgeable with respect to the due diligence review process that an underwriter would perform in connection with a placement of securities registered pursuant to the Securities Act of 1933.*

OBSERVATION: When the requesting party has provided the accountant with a representation letter regarding its due diligence review process as described above, the accountant should make reference to those representations in the comfort letter.

General Guidance

Although SAS-72 provides guidance on comfort letters issued in various types of securities transactions, it generally addresses comfort letters issued in connection with securities offerings registered pursuant to the 1933 Act. Accordingly, guidance provided in SAS-72 with respect to comments made in comfort letters on compliance with SEC rules and regulations (e.g., Regulation S-X or S-K) generally applies when securities offerings are registered pursuant to the 1933 Act (AU 634.11).

Scope of comfort procedures The scope and conclusions in the comfort letter should be guided, wherever possible, by the pertinent sections of the underwriting agreement. Therefore, the accountant should obtain a draft copy of the underwriting agreement and review it at the earliest practicable date (AU 634.12).

In requiring comfort letters from accountants, underwriters are seeking assistance in performing a *reasonable investigation* of data (unaudited financial information and other data) on the authority of an expert. Unfortunately, what constitutes a reasonable investigation of unaudited data sufficient to satisfy an underwriter's purpose has never been authoritatively established. Therefore, it is only the underwriter who can determine the amount of work sufficient to satisfy his or her "due diligence" requirement. Accordingly, accountants are willing to carry out procedures that will aid underwriters in discharging their responsibility for exercising due diligence, but cannot furnish any assurance on whether those procedures are sufficient for the underwriter's purpose (AU 634.12).

To ensure that the accountant's professional responsibility is understood, the accountant should meet with the underwriter and the client and explain the typical procedures (as discussed later in this chapter) employed as a basis for the issuance of a comfort letter. SAS-72 states that the accountant should accompany any such discussion of procedures with a clear statement that the accountant cannot furnish any assurance regarding the sufficiency of the procedures and include a statement to that effect in the comfort letter. Paragraph 4 of the sample comfort letter in this section illustrates this requirement (AU 634.15).

Draft of Proposed Comfort Letter

After receiving a draft of the underwriting agreement or being informed of its contents, the accountant should furnish the underwriter with a draft of the proposed comfort letter that responds to the underwriting agreement. This practice offers the underwriter and the client the opportunity to review the draft letter and discuss with the accountant the procedures expected to be performed. Statements or implications that the accountant will perform procedures that he or she considers necessary in the circumstances should not be made as this may lead to a misunderstanding about the responsibility for the sufficiency of the procedures for the underwriter's purposes (AU 634.16).

To further emphasize the point that the underwriter and not the accountant is responsible for the sufficiency of the comfort procedures, SAS-72 indicates that the accountant may include a legend or a concluding paragraph on the draft letter to the underwriter to address its functions and limitations. The following is an example of such a paragraph as illustrated in SAS-72 (AU 634.16).

This draft is furnished solely for the purpose of indicating the form of letter that we would expect to be able to furnish [name of underwriter] in response to their request, the matters expected to be covered in the letter, and the nature of the procedures that we would expect to carry out with respect to such matters. On the basis of our discussions with [name of underwriter], it is our understanding that the procedures outlined in this draft letter are those they wish us to follow. Unless [name of underwriter] informs us otherwise, we shall assume that there are no additional procedures they wish us to follow. The text of the letter itself will depend, of course, on the results of the procedures, which we would not expect to complete until shortly before the letter is given and in no event before the cutoff date indicated therein.

> **OBSERVATION:** *In the absence of any discussions with the underwriter, the accountant should outline in the draft letter those procedures specified in the underwriting agreement that he or she is willing to perform. In this situation, the second sentence above should be revised as follows (AU 634.16):*
>
> > *In the absence of any discussions with [name of underwriter], we have set out in this draft letter those procedures referred to in the draft underwriting agreement (of which we have been furnished a copy) that we are willing to follow.*

Other Accountants

SAS-72 indicates that comfort letters are sometimes requested from more than one accountant (e.g., in connection with registration statements to be used in the subsequent sale of shares issued in recently effected mergers or from predecessor auditors). The principal accountant should obtain a copy of the draft comfort letter from the other accountant (AU 634.17).

There also may be situations in which a registration statement may include the report of more than one accountant on financial statements included therein. For example, a significant subsidiary or division may be audited by other accountants. In that event, SAS-72 indicates that (AU 634.18):

- The principal accountant should read the comfort letter prepared by the other accountant. Such comfort letter should include statements similar to those contained in the principal accountant's comfort letter, including representations about the accountant's independence.

- The principal accountant should make the following comments in his or her comfort letter: (1) the principal accountant has read the comfort letter prepared by the other accountant, and (2) procedures performed by the principal accountant relate only to the financial statements audited by the principal accountant and the consolidated financial statements.

Shelf registrations A *shelf* registration statement enables an entity to register securities under the 1933 Act and then issue these securities over a period of time. At the effective date of the registration statement, an underwriter or lead underwriter may not have been named, although the accountant may have been asked to issue a comfort letter. Since only the underwriter can determine the appropriate procedures to be performed with respect to the accountant's comfort letter, SAS-72 indicates that the accountant *should not agree to issue a comfort letter to the client, to the counsel for the underwriter group* (when a lead underwriter has not been named), *or to an unspecified party such as "any or all underwriters to be selected."* However, the accountant may issue a *draft* comfort letter to the client or the legal counsel representing the underwriter group, based on the actual procedures performed by the accountant. In this circumstance, the accountant should include a legend or a paragraph in the draft comfort letter addressing the letter's functions and limitations. The following is an example of such a paragraph as illustrated in SAS-72 (AU 634.19).

This draft describes the procedures that we have performed and represents a letter we would be prepared to sign as of the effective date of the registration statement if the managing underwriter had been chosen at that date and had requested such a letter. On the basis of our discussions with [name of client or legal counsel], the procedures set forth are similar to those that experience indicates that underwriters often request in such circumstances. The text of the final letter will depend, of course, on whether the managing underwriter who is selected requests that other procedures be performed to meet his or her needs and whether the managing underwriter requests that any of the procedures be updated to the date of issuance of the signed letter.

Comfort Letter Contents

The contents of comfort letters vary depending on the specific circumstances of the individual engagement. However, a comfort letter typically includes the following (AU 634.22):

1. Date. The comfort letter is usually dated on or shortly before the effective date of the registration statement.

2. Addressee. The comfort letter usually is addressed to the parties to whom the accountant is giving assurance (e.g., the client and the underwriter).

3. Introductory paragraph. This typically refers to the accountant's report on the audited financial statements and related schedules included or incorporated by reference in the registration statement.

4. Independence. The comfort letter typically makes a brief statement regarding the accountant's independence.

5. Compliance with SEC requirements. When the underwriting agreement requests the accountant to comment on compliance with SEC requirements, the accountant should add a paragraph in the comfort letter to that effect.

6. Comments on information other than audited financial statements.

7. Comments on tables, statistics, and other financial data.

8. Concluding paragraph. The comfort letter typically includes a paragraph about its purpose and intended use to avoid misunderstanding by the requesting party.

9. Disclosure of subsequently discovered matters.

Date The comfort letter is ordinarily dated on or shortly before the effective date of the registration statement. Usually, the underwriting agreement specifies the date to which the procedures described in the letter are to relate. This date, which is commonly referred to as the *cutoff date*, is customarily within five business days before the effective date of the registration statement (AU 634.23).

> *OBSERVATION: SAS-72 indicates that the comfort letter should state that the procedures described therein do not cover the intervening period from the cutoff date to the date of the letter (AU 634.23).*

Underwriters also sometimes require that an additional comfort letter be issued and dated at or shortly before the closing date on which the securities are delivered by the entity or selling shareholders to the underwriter in exchange for the proceeds of the offering. SAS-72 does not prohibit the accountant from furnishing both of these letters. However, when both are required, the accountant should carry out the specified procedures as of the cutoff date of each letter (AU 634.24).

Addressee SAS-72 states that the accountant should not address or give the comfort letter to any parties other than the client, the named underwriter, broker-dealer, financial intermediary, or buyer, seller, or both, in connection with acquisition transactions as discussed above (AU 634.25).

Introductory paragraph Although not required, it is customary, and desirable according to SAS-72, for the accountant to include an introductory paragraph in the comfort letter that describes which financial statements are included in the registration statement the accountant has audited. The following is an example of such a paragraph as illustrated in SAS-72 (AU 634.26).

We have audited the [identify the financial statements and financial statement schedules] included [incorporated by reference] in the registration statement (no. 33-00000) on Form X filed by the company under the Securities Act of 1933 (the Act); our reports with respect thereto are also included [incorporated by reference] in that registration statement. The registration statement, as amended as of [date], is herein referred to as the registration statement.

OBSERVATION: Occasionally, underwriters will request that the accountant's opinion on the financial statements contained in the registration statement be repeated in the comfort letter. There does not appear any valid reason to do so, and it should not be done; also, the accountant should not give negative assurance regarding his or her report. Furthermore, the accountant should not give negative assurance with respect to financial statements and schedules that have been audited and are reported on in the registration statement by other accountants (AU 634.28).

Modified introductory paragraph   The introductory paragraph of the accountant's comfort letter should be modified when the accountant's report on audited financial statements and related schedules included in the registration statement contains the following:

- An explanatory paragraph or emphasis-of-matter paragraph
- A qualified opinion on the financial statements

In these instances, the introductory paragraph should be modified to refer to and discuss such matters.

Reference to other reports in the introductory paragraph   The accountant may have previously reported on (AU 634.29):

- Condensed financial statements derived from audited financial statements, in accordance with SAS-42 (Reporting on Condensed Financial Statements and Selected Financial Data)
- Selected financial data, in accordance with SAS-42
- Interim financial information, in accordance with SAS-71 (Interim Financial Information)
- Pro forma financial information, in accordance with Statement on Standards for Attestation Engagements (Reporting on Pro Forma Financial Information; AT 300)
- A financial forecast, in accordance with SSAE-1 (AT 200)

In these situations, the accountant may refer in the introductory paragraph of the comfort letter to the previously issued reports. Accountants *should not repeat their reports* in the comfort letter or otherwise imply that they are reporting as of the date of the comfort letter or that they assume responsibility for the sufficiency of the procedures for the underwriter's purposes (AU 634.29).

Independence   In conjunction with SEC filings, the underwriting agreement customarily requests that the accountant represent in the comfort letter that he or she is independent. A simple statement, such as the one shown below, suffices (AU 634.31).

We are independent certified public accountants with respect to [name of client], within the meaning of the Act and the applicable published rules and regulations thereunder.

In a non-SEC filing, a statement such as the one shown below suffices (AU 634.31).

We are independent certified public accountants with respect to [name of client], under Rule 101 of the AICPA *Code of Professional Conduct* and its interpretations and rulings.

SAS-72 indicates that the accountants for previously nonaffiliated companies recently acquired by the registrant would not be required to have been independent with respect to the company whose shares are being registered. In this situation, the statement regarding independence should be modified, as shown below (AU 634.32).

As of [date of the accountant's most recent report on the financial statements of the client] and during the period covered by the financial statements on which we reported, we were independent certified public accountants with respect to [name of client] within the meaning of the Act and the applicable published rules and regulations thereunder.

Compliance with SEC requirements   Usually, the underwriting agreement requests that the accountant comment on whether the financial statements comply with SEC requirements. The accountant may do so in the comfort letter by adding a paragraph, as shown below (AU 634.33).

In our opinion [include phrase "except as disclosed in the registration statement," if applicable], the [identify the financial statements and financial statement schedules] audited by us and included [incorporated by reference] in the registration statement comply as to form in all material respects with the applicable accounting requirements of the Act and the related published rules and regulations.

If there is a material departure from the pertinent published SEC requirements, the accountant should disclose such departure in the comfort letter. Normally, representatives of the SEC will have agreed to such a departure. An example of wording to be used in the comfort letter when the SEC has agreed to a departure from its published accounting requirements is shown below (AU 634.33).

In our opinion [include phrase "except as disclosed in the registration statement," if applicable], the [identify the financial statements and financial statement schedules] audited by us and included [incorporated by reference] in the registration statement comply as to form in all material respects with the applicable accounting requirements of the Act and the related published rules and regulations; however, as agreed to by representatives of the SEC, separate financial statements and financial statement schedules of ABC Company (an equity investee) as required by rule 3-09 of Regulation S-X have been omitted.

OBSERVATION: SAS-72 states that if departures from pertinent published SEC requirements either are not disclosed in the registration statement or have not been agreed to by representatives of the SEC, the accountant should carefully consider whether to consent to the use of the accountant's report in the registration statement (AU 634.33).

Commenting in comfort letter on information other than audited financial statements   The accountant's comfort letter often refers to information other than audited financial statements. The accountant's comments in the letter generally pertain to (AU 634.35):

- Unaudited condensed interim financial information
- Capsule financial information

- Pro forma financial information
- Financial forecasts
- Changes in capital stock, increases in long-term debt, and decreases in other specified financial statement items

As discussed above, the comfort letter should refer to the agreed-upon procedures with the following exception: when the accountant has been asked to provide negative assurance on interim financial information or capsule financial information, the accountant need not specify the procedures involved in a SAS-71 review. The accountant should make no comments or suggestions that he or she has applied procedures that the accountant considered necessary for the underwriter's purposes. Terms or comments that are subjective and unclear (e.g., *general review, limited review, reconcile, check,* or *test*) should not be used in describing the accountant's work unless the procedures implied by these terms are described in the comfort letter (AU 634.35).

Notwithstanding the above, SAS-72 states that the accountant should not comment in a comfort letter on certain unaudited financial information unless the accountant has obtained knowledge of the client's internal controls as they relate to the preparation of both annual and interim financial information. Such knowledge of internal controls is ordinarily acquired when the accountant audits the entity's financial statements. If the accountant has not acquired such knowledge, the accountant should perform the necessary procedures to obtain that knowledge in order to make the required comments in the comfort letter. This knowledge of internal controls is required when the accountant is requested to comment in a comfort letter on (AU 634.36):

- Unaudited condensed interim financial information
- Capsule financial information
- A financial forecast when historical financial statements provide a basis for one or more significant assumptions for the forecast
- Changes in capital stock, increases in long-term debt, and decreases in selected financial statement items

Unaudited condensed interim financial information　The comfort letter should (1) identify the unaudited condensed interim financial information and (2) state that the accountant has not audited such information in accordance with generally accepted auditing standards and, therefore, does not express an opinion on such information (AU 634.38). (Paragraph 3 of the sample comfort letter at the end of this chapter illustrates this requirement.)

The accountant's comments in the comfort letter regarding unaudited condensed interim financial information should provide negative assurance on whether (AU 634.37):

1. Any material modifications should be made to such information for it to be in conformity with generally accepted accounting principles.

2. Such information complies as to form in all material respects with the applicable accounting requirements of the 1933 Act and the related rules and regulations. (Paragraph 5(a) of the sample comfort letter at the end of this chapter illustrates this requirement.)

The accountant may provide such negative assurance in the comfort letter only when he or she has conducted a review of such information in accordance with SAS-71. In this case, the accountant may (AU 634.37):

1. State in the comfort letter that he or she has performed the procedures identified in SAS-71. (Paragraph 4(a)(i) of the sample comfort letter at the end of this chapter illustrates this requirement.)

2. If the accountant has issued a report on the review of the interim financial information, mention that fact in the comfort letter. In this case, the accountant should attach the review report to the comfort letter unless the review report is already included or incorporated by reference in the registration statement. (See footnote 2 of the sample comfort letter at the end of this chapter.)

If a review in accordance with SAS-71 has not been conducted, the accountant may not provide negative assurance in the comfort letter regarding the interim financial information. The accountant is limited to reporting the procedures performed and results obtained (AU 634.37). (SAS-72, example O in the appendix, illustrates the wording in this case.)

Capsule financial information A registration statement may contain capsule financial information (i.e., unaudited summarized interim information for periods subsequent to the date of the audited financial statements and for the corresponding period of the prior year or the date of the unaudited condensed interim financial information). The accountant may express a negative assurance on whether such capsule financial information conforms with generally accepted accounting principles, and comment on whether the dollar amounts were determined on a basis substantially consistent with corresponding amounts in the audited financial statements, only if both of the following conditions are met (AU 634.39):

1. The capsule financial information meets the minimum reporting requirements established in paragraph 30 of APB Opinion No. 28 (Interim Financial Reporting).

2. The accountant has performed a SAS-71 review of the financial statements underlying the capsule financial information.

If the minimum reporting requirements in (1) above are not met, the accountant may provide only negative assurance on whether the dollar amounts were determined on a basis substantially consistent with corresponding amounts in the audited financial statements, as long as the accountant has performed a SAS-71 review (AU 634.39).

> **OBSERVATION:** *If the accountant determines that a negative assurance cannot be given because the conditions discussed above are not met, the accountant is limited to reporting in the comfort letter the procedures performed and the results obtained (AU 634.39).*

Pro forma financial information   The accountant should not give negative assurance in a comfort letter on (1) pro forma financial information, (2) the application of pro forma adjustments to historical amounts, (3) the compilation of pro forma financial information, or (4) whether the pro forma financial information complies as to form in all material respects with the applicable accounting requirements of rule 11-02 of Regulation S-X, unless one of the following conditions is met (AU 634.42):

1. The accountant has performed an audit of the entity's annual financial statements (or a significant part of a business combination) and has obtained an appropriate level of knowledge of its accounting and financial reporting practices.

2. The accountant has performed a SAS-71 review of the entity's interim financial statements to which the pro forma adjustments were applied.

If the conditions indicated above are not met, the accountant's comments in the comfort letter are limited to the procedures performed and results obtained (AU 634.43). (SAS-72, example O in the appendix, illustrates the wording in this case.)

Financial forecasts In order for the accountant to perform agreed-upon procedures and comment in the comfort letter on a financial forecast, SAS-72 states that the accountant should (AU 634.44):

1. Obtain knowledge of the entity's internal controls as they relate to the preparation of annual and interim financial statements, as discussed earlier.

2. Perform the procedures required for a compilation of a forecast, as prescribed in Appendix B of SSAE-1.

3. Follow the guidance in paragraphs 16 and 17 of SSAE-1 regarding reporting on the compilation of the financial forecast, and attach the report to the comfort letter.

> **OBSERVATION:** *If the forecast is included in the registration statement, the forecast must be accompanied by an indication that the accountant has not examined the forecast and, therefore, does not express an opinion on it. If the accountant has issued a compilation report on the forecast in connection with the comfort letter, the accountant's report need not be included in the registration statement (AU 634.44).*

The accountant may not give negative assurance in the comfort letter on the procedures performed in connection with a financial forecast. Furthermore, the accountant may not give negative assurance on the forecast's compliance with rule 11-03 of Regulation S-X unless the accountant has performed an examination of the forecast in accordance with Financial Forecasts and Projections (AU 634.44). (SAS-72, examples E and O in the appendix, provides illustrations of the accountant's wording in a comfort letter in connection with financial forecasts.)

Subsequent changes The underwriter usually will ask the accountant to comment in the comfort letter on changes in certain financial statement items during a period (commonly referred to as the *change period*) subsequent to that of the latest financial statements included, or incorporated by reference, in the registration statement. These comments usually relate to (1) changes in capital stock, (2) increases in long-term debt, (3) decreases in net current assets, (4) decreases in stockholders' equity, (5) decreases in net sales, and (6) decreases in total and per-share amounts of income before extraordinary items and of net income (AU 634.45).

> **OBSERVATION:** *The accountant should base his or her comments solely on the limited procedures performed with respect to the period between the date of the latest financial statements made available and the cutoff date (i.e., the date to which the procedures described in the comfort letter are to relate). These procedures are usually limited to inquiries of company officials and the reading of minutes, which should be made clear in the comfort letter (AU 634.45). (Paragraph 6 of the sample comfort letter at the end of this chapter illustrates this requirement.)*

The accountant may, on the underwriter's request, provide negative assurance in the comfort letter on subsequent changes in specified financial statement items as of any date that is less than 135 days from the end of the most recent period for which the accountant has performed an audit or a SAS-71 review (AU 634.46). (Paragraphs 5b and 6 of the sample comfort letter at the end of this chapter illustrate appropriate wording for expressing such negative assurance when there have been no subsequent changes. SAS-72, example M in the appendix, provides illustrations of appropriate wording when there have been subsequent changes.)

If the underwriter requests negative assurance with respect to subsequent changes as of any date that is 135 days or more after to the end of the most recent period for which the accountant has performed an audit or a SAS-71 review, the accountant may not provide such negative assurance. In this case, the accountant's comments in the comfort letter are limited to the procedures performed and results obtained (AU 634.47). (SAS-72, example O in the appendix, illustrates the wording in this case.)

> **OBSERVATION:** *The accountant should use in the comfort letter the terms **change, increase,** and **decrease** rather than **adverse change**. When the term **adverse change** is used, it implies that the accountant is making a judgment about the change, which may be misinterpreted by the underwriter (AU 634.48).*

Some subsequent changes may be disclosed in the registration statement and need not be repeated in the comfort letter. Under this circumstance, the accountant should use the phrase "except for changes, increases, or decreases that the registration statement discloses have occurred or may occur" in the comfort letter (AU 634.49). (Paragraph 5b(i) of the sample comfort letter at the end of this chapter illustrates appropriate wording when making such a statement.)

The change period ends on the cutoff date and ordinarily begins (1) immediately after the date of the latest balance sheet in the registration statement, for balance sheet items, and (2) immediately after the latest period for which such items are presented in the registration statement, for income statement items. If the underwriter requests the use of a different change period, the accountant may use the period requested. To avoid any misunderstanding about the change period and the date of the financial statements used in comparison, they both should be identified in the comfort letter in both the draft and final form of the letter (AU 634.50–.52).

When more than one accountant is involved in the audit of the financial statements of the entity, and the principal accountant has obtained a copy of the comfort letter of the other accountant that does not disclose matters that affect the negative assurance given, the principal accountant should make appropriate modifications to the comfort letter commenting on subsequent changes. The modifications consist of an addition to paragraph 4, a substitute for the applicable part of paragraph 5, and an addition to the last sentence of paragraph 6 of the sample comfort letter at the end of this chapter (AU 634.53).

4c. We have read the letter dated [date] of [the other accountants] with regard to [the related company].

5. Nothing came to our attention as a result of the foregoing procedures (which, so far as [the related company] is concerned, consisted solely of reading the letter referred to in 4c), however, that caused us to believe that...

6. On the basis of these inquiries and our reading of the minutes and the letter dated [date] of [the other accountants] with regard to [the related company], as described in 4, nothing came to our attention that caused us to believe that there was any such change, increase, or decrease, except in all instances for changes, increases, or decreases that the registration statement discloses have occurred or may occur.

Tables, statistics, and other financial information The comfort letter may refer to tables, statistics, and other financial information in the registration statement if the accountant has the expertise to make a competent statement. Therefore, comments in the comfort letter regarding such information should be limited to the following categories (AU 634.53–.55):

- Information that is expressed in dollars, or percentages derived from dollar amounts, and that has been obtained from accounting records that are subject to internal controls of the company's accounting system
- Information that has been derived directly from such accounting records by analysis or computation
- Quantitative information that has been obtained from an accounting record if the information is of a type that is subject to the same controls as the dollar amounts

The accountant should not comment in the comfort letter on tables, statistics, and other financial information relating to an unaudited period unless the accountant has obtained a knowledge of the client's internal control (AU 634.55).

The registration statement may include certain financial information to comply with specific requirements of Regulation S-K, such as the following items (AU 634.57):

- Item 301, "Selected Financial Data"
- Item 302, "Supplementary Financial Information"
- Item 402, "Executive Compensation"
- Item 503(d), "Ratio of Earnings to Fixed Charges"

The accountant is limited to providing negative assurance on conformity of the information presented in the registration statement with the disclosure requirements of Regulation S-K. The accountant may provide such negative assurance only if the following conditions are met (AU 634.57):

1. The information presented is derived from the accounting records subject to the internal control structure policies and procedures of the entity's accounting system, or has been derived directly from such accounting records by analysis or computation.
2. The information presented can be evaluated against reasonable criteria that have been established by the SEC.

The accountant should describe in the comfort letter the procedures and related findings with respect to the other financial information. The accountant should use specific, unambiguous references, such as page or paragraph number, in the comfort letter to the other information being commented on. If applicable, the accountant should comment on the acceptability of allocation methods used by the client in the computation of such other financial information. The accountant should not use the phrase "presents fairly" when commenting on tables, statistics, and other financial information, since this phrase relates to presentations of financial statements (AU 634.58–.60). (Appropriate ways of expressing comments on tables, statistics, and other financial information addressing these points are illustrated in SAS-72, examples F, G, and H in the appendix.)

Concluding paragraph   The comfort letter ordinarily concludes with a paragraph describing the purpose and intended use of the letter, including a statement that it is strictly for the use of the addressees and the underwriter (AU 634.61). (Paragraph 7 of the sample comfort letter at the end of this chapter illustrates appropriate wording for a concluding paragraph.)

Disclosure of subsequently discovered matters   When the accountant discovers matters (e.g., decreases or changes in specified items not disclosed in the registration statement) that may require mention in the final comfort letter, the accountant should discuss them with the client so that appropriate consideration is given whether disclosure should be made in the registration statement. The accountant should inform the client that if such disclosure is not made, such matters will be mentioned in the comfort letter. Also, the accountant should recommend that the client promptly inform the underwriter of the matters discovered (AU 634.62).

Sample Comfort Letter

A variety of sample comfort letters is found in the appendix to SAS-72. The following typical comfort letter has been extracted from that appendix (*Example A: Typical Comfort Letter*) (AU 634.64).

This letter assumes the following circumstances: The prospectus (Part I of the registration statement) includes audited consolidated balance sheets as of December 31, 19X5 and 19X4, and audited consolidated statements of income, retained earnings (stockholders' equity), and cash flows for each of the three years in the period ended December 31, 19X5. Part I also includes an unaudited condensed consolidated balance sheet as of March 31, 19X6, and unaudited condensed consolidated statements of income, retained earnings (stockholders' equity), and cash flows for the three-month periods ended March 31, 19X6 and 19X5, reviewed in accordance with SAS-71 but not previously reported on by the accountants. Part II of the registration statement includes audited consolidated financial statement schedules for the three years ended December 31, 19X5. The cutoff date is June 23, 19X6, and the letter is dated June 28, 19X6. The effective date is June 28, 19X6.

Each of the comments in the letter is in response to a requirement of the underwriting agreement. For purposes of this example, the income statement items of the current interim period are to be compared with those of the corresponding period of the preceding year.

June 28, 19X6

[Addressee]

Dear Sirs:

We have audited the consolidated balance sheets of the Blank Company, Inc. (the company) and subsidiaries as of December 31, 19X5 and 19X4, and the consolidated statements of income, retained earnings (stockholders' equity), and cash flows for each of the three years in the period ended December 31, 19X5, and the related financial statement schedules all included in the registration statement (no. 33-00000) on Form S-1 filed by the company under the Securities Act of 1933 (the Act); our reports with respect thereto are also included in that registration statement.[1] The registration statement, as amended on June 28, 19X6, is herein referred to as the registration statement.[2] In connection with the registration statement:

1. We are independent certified public accountants with respect to the company within the meaning of the Act and the applicable published rules and regulations thereunder.

2. In our opinion [include the phrase "except as disclosed in the registration statement," if applicable], the consolidated financial statements and financial statement schedules audited by us and included in the registration statement comply as to form in all material respects with the applicable accounting requirements of the Act and the related published rules and regulations.

3. We have not audited any financial statements of the company as of any date or for any period subsequent to December 31, 19X5; although we have conducted an audit for the year ended December 31, 19X5, the purpose (and therefore the scope) of the audit was to enable us to express our opinion on the consolidated financial statements as of De-

cember 31, 19X5, and for the year then ended, but not on the financial statements for any interim period within that year. Therefore, we are unable to and do not express any opinion on the unaudited condensed consolidated balance sheet as of March 31, 19X6, and the unaudited condensed consolidated statements of income, retained earnings (stockholders' equity), and cash flows for the three-month periods ended March 31, 19X6 and 19X5, included in the registration statement, or on the financial position, results of operations, or cash flows as of any date or for any period subsequent to December 31, 19X5.

4. For purposes of this letter we have read the 19X6 minutes of meetings of the stockholders, the board of directors, and [include other appropriate committees, if any] of the company and its subsidiaries as set forth in the minute books at June 23, 19X6, officials of the company having advised us that the minutes of all such meetings[3] through that date were set forth therein; we have carried out other procedures to June 23, 19X6, as follows (our work did not extend to the period from June 24, 19X6, to June 28, 19X6, inclusive):

   a. With respect to the three-month periods ended March 31, 19X6 and 19X5, we have:

      (i) Performed the procedures specified by the American Institute of Certified Public Accountants for a review of interim financial information as described in SAS No. 71, *Interim Financial Information*, on the unaudited condensed consolidated balance sheet as of March 31, 19X6, and unaudited condensed consolidated statements of income, retained earnings (stockholders' equity), and cash flows for the three-month periods ended March 31, 19X6 and 19X5, included in the registration statement.

      (ii) Inquired of certain officials of the company who have responsibility for financial and accounting matters whether the unaudited condensed consolidated financial statements referred to in a(i) comply as to form in all material respects with the applicable accounting requirements of the Act and the related published rules and regulations.

   b. With respect to the period from April 1, 19X6, to May 31, 19X6, we have:

      (i) Read the unaudited consolidated financial statements[4] of the company and subsidiaries for April and May of both 19X5 and 19X6 furnished us by the company, officials of the company having advised that no such financial statements as of any date or for any period subsequent to May 31, 19X6, were available.

      (ii) Inquired of certain officials of the company who have responsibility for financial and accounting matters whether the unaudited consolidated financial statements referred to in b(i) are stated on a basis substantially consistent with that of the audited consolidated financial statements included in the registration statement.

The foregoing procedures do not constitute an audit conducted in accordance with generally accepted auditing standards. Also, they would not necessarily reveal matters of significance with respect to the comments in the following paragraph. Accordingly, we make no representations regarding the sufficiency of the foregoing procedures for your purposes.

5. Nothing came to our attention as a result of the foregoing procedures, however, that caused us[5] to believe that:

    a.(i) Any material modifications should be made to the unaudited condensed consolidated financial statements described in 4a(i), included in the registration statement, for them to be in conformity with generally accepted accounting principles.[6]

    (ii) The unaudited condensed consolidated financial statements described in 4a(i) do not comply as to form in all material respects with the applicable accounting requirements of the Act and the related published rules and regulations.

    b.(i) At May 31, 19X6, there was any change in the capital stock, increase in long-term debt, or decrease in consolidated net current assets or stockholder's equity of the consolidated companies as compared with amounts shown in the March 31, 19X6, unaudited condensed consolidated balance sheet included in the registration statement, or (ii) for the period from April 1, 19X6, to May 31, 19X6, there were any decreases, as compared to the corresponding period in the preceding year, in consolidated net sales or in the total or per-share amounts of income before extraordinary items or of net income, except in all instances for changes, increases, or decreases that the registration statement discloses have occurred or may occur.

6. As mentioned in 4b, company officials have advised us that no consolidated financial statements as of any date or for any period subsequent to May 31, 19X6, are available; accordingly, the procedures carried out by us with respect to changes in financial statement items after May 31, 19X6, have, of necessity, been even more limited than those with respect to the periods referred to in 4. We have inquired of certain officials of the company who have responsibility for financial and accounting matters whether (a) at June 23, 19X6, there was any change in the capital stock, increase in long-term debt or any decreases in consolidated net current assets or stockholders' equity of the consolidated companies as compared with amounts shown on the March 31, 19X6, unaudited condensed consolidated balance sheet included in the registration statement or (b) for the period from April 1, 19X6, to June 23, 19X6, there were any decreases, as compared with the corresponding period in the preceding year, in consolidated net sales or in the total or per-share amounts of income before extraordinary items or of net income. On the basis of these inquiries and our reading of the minutes as described in 4, nothing came to our attention that caused us to believe

that there was any such change, increase, or decrease, except in all instances for changes, increases, or decreases that the registration statement discloses have occurred or may occur.

7. This letter is solely for the information of the addressees and to assist the underwriters in conducting and documenting their investigation of the affairs of the company in connection with the offering of the securities covered by the registration statement, and it is not to be used, circulated, quoted, or otherwise referred to within or without the underwriting group for any purpose, including but not limited to the registration, purchase, or sale of securities, nor is it to be filed with or referred to in whole or in part in the registration statement or any other document, except that reference may be made to it in the underwriting agreement or in any list of closing documents pertaining to the offering of the securities covered by the registration statement.

---

[1] The example includes financial statements required by SEC regulations to be included in the filing. If additional financial information is covered by the comfort letter, appropriate modifications should be made.

[2] The example assumes that the accountants have not previously reported on the interim financial information. If the accountants have previously reported on the interim financial information, they may refer to that fact in the introductory paragraph of the comfort letter as follows:

> Also, we have reviewed the unaudited condensed consolidated financial statements as of March 31, 19X6 and 19X5, and for the three-month periods then ended, as indicated in our report dated May 15, 19X6, which is included (incorporated by reference) in the registration statement.

The report may be attached to the comfort letter (see paragraph 28 of SAS-72). The accountants may agree to comment in the comfort letter on whether the interim financial information complies as to form in all material respects with the applicable accounting requirements of the published rules and regulations of the SEC.

[3] The accountants should discuss with the secretary those meetings for which minutes have not been approved. The letter should be modified to identify specifically the unapproved minutes of meetings that the accountants have discussed with the secretary.

[4] If the interim financial information is incomplete, a sentence similar to the following should be added: "The financial information for April and May is incomplete in that it omits the statements of cash flows and other disclosures."

[5] If there has been a change in accounting principle during the interim period, a reference to that change should be included therein.

[6] SAS-71 does not require the accountants to modify the report on a review of interim financial information for a lack of consistency in the application of accounting principles provided that the interim financial information appropriately discloses such matters.

REPORTING ON CONDENSED FINANCIAL STATEMENTS AND SELECTED FINANCIAL DATA

SAS-42 (Reporting on Condensed Financial Statements and Selected Financial Data) is applicable to reports on condensed financial statements or selected financial data that are derived from audited financial statements and that appear in a client-prepared document. Specifically, the reporting guidelines established by SAS-42 relate to the following (AU 552.01):

- Condensed financial statements that are derived from *audited* financial statements of a *public* entity that is required to file, at least annually, complete financial statements with a regulatory agency

- Selected financial data that are derived from *audited* financial statements of a *public* or *nonpublic* entity and presented in a document containing *audited* financial statements or incorporated by reference to information filed with a regulatory agency

> **OBSERVATION:** *If the condensed financial information or selected financial data are presented in an auditor-submitted document, SAS-29 (Reporting on Information Accompanying the Basic Financial Statements in Auditor-Submitted Documents) should be followed.*

Condensed Financial Statements

The very nature of condensed financial statements is that they are presented in less detail than conventional financial statements. For this reason, they do not fairly present the financial position or results of operation of an entity. When an auditor is engaged to report on condensed financial statements derived from audited financial statements of a public entity, the following reporting guidelines should be observed in the preparation of the auditor's report (AU 552.03–.05):

- State that the complete financial statements have been audited.

- Disclose the date of the auditor's report on the complete financial statements.

- Describe the type of opinion expressed. If the opinion was other than unqualified, explain the nature of and reason for the modification.

- State whether the condensed information is fairly stated in relation to the audited financial statements from which the information was extracted.

The following example illustrates an auditor's report on condensed financial statements that reflects the reporting guidelines previously described (AU 552.06).

We have audited, in accordance with generally accepted auditing standards, the consolidated balance sheet of B Company and its subsidiaries as of December 31, 19X5, and the related consolidated statements of income, retained earnings, and cash flows for the year then ended (not presented herein); and in our report dated February 12, 19X6, we expressed an unqualified opinion on those consolidated financial statements.

In our opinion, the information set forth in the accompanying condensed consolidated financial statements is fairly stated in all material respects in relation to the consolidated financial statements from which it has been derived.

When the condensed financial statements are presented with financial statements of a subsequent interim period and the auditor's review report on the interim financial statements, the auditor is considered to be *associated* with the condensed financial statements. Under this circumstance, the auditor would add an additional paragraph, similar to the one described above, to the review report to cover the condensed financial statements (AU 552.08).

Selected Financial Data

Selected financial data for a public or nonpublic company may be presented, along with audited financial statements, in a client-prepared document. For example, some reports filed with the SEC must contain selected financial data for a five-year period. The auditor is not required to audit this data, but, as required by SAS-8 (Other Information in Documents Containing Audited Financial Statements), the auditor must read the data for possible material inconsistencies between it and the audited financial statements (AU 552.09).

> *OBSERVATION: SAS-8 is not applicable to filings under the Securities Act of 1933. SAS-37 provides guidance for filings under the Securities Act of 1933.*

Selected financial data are not an integral part of the basic financial statements of a public or nonpublic company and, as noted above, may not be audited. Under certain circumstances, the auditor may be asked or required to examine the supplementary information. In this case, the report should observe the following guidelines (AU 552.09):

- State that the complete financial statements have been audited.

- Describe the type of opinion expressed. If the opinion was other than unqualified, explain the nature of and reason for the modification.

- State whether the selected financial data are fairly stated in relation to the audited financial statements from which the data were derived.

- If appropriate, the report should identify the statements that were audited by another CPA firm, and no opinion should be expressed on the selected data derived from those financial statements.

These reporting requirements may be met by adding an additional paragraph to the standard auditor's report. For example, the following explanatory paragraph is applicable to the audited (comparative) financial statements for 19X4 and 19X5 and the selected financial data from 19X1 through 19X5 (AU 552.10).

We previously audited, in accordance with generally accepted auditing standards, the consolidated balance sheets as of December 31, 19X3, 19X2, and 19X1, and the related consolidated statements of income, retained earnings, and cash flows for the years ended December 31, 19X3, 19X2, and 19X1 (none of which are presented herein); and we expressed unqualified opinions on those consolidated financial statements. In our opinion, the information set forth in the selected financial data for each of the five years in the period ended December 31, 19X5, appearing on pages 18 through 22, is fairly stated in all material respects in relation to the consolidated financial statements from which it has been derived.

The auditor should report only on the data derived from the audited financial statements. For example, if nonaccounting data are presented, such as number of employees, the auditor should specifically identify the data to which the report is applicable (AU 552.09).

> **OBSERVATION:** *An Auditing Interpretation on association with financial statements, "Auditor's Identification with Condensed Financial Data" (November 1979), states that an auditor is not associated with condensed financial data published by a financial reporting service.*
>
> *If financial data are released to the public by a client with the name of the auditor thereon as public information, neither the company nor the auditor can require a financial reporting service company (such as Dun & Bradstreet) to withhold publication of the information (AU 9504.15–.18).*

Part III

Compilation and Review Engagements

COMPILATION AND REVIEW ENGAGEMENTS

CONTENTS

Overview	**14.05**
Responsibility and Function of the Accountant	**14.12**
Pre-Engagement Planning	**14.13**
Evaluation of the Client	**14.13**
Communication with the Predecessor Accountant	**14.14**
Decision to Make Inquiries	**14.15**
Other Inquiries	**14.16**
Revision of Financial Statements	**14.16**
Independence	**14.17**
Engagement Letters	**14.17**
Generally Accepted Accounting Principles	**14.18**
Generally Accepted Auditing Standards	**14.19**
Compilation of Financial Statements	**14.20**
Overview	**14.20**
Compilation Standards	**14.21**
Understanding of a Client	**14.22**
Need for Other Accounting Services	**14.23**
Reading the Financial Statements	**14.24**
Financial Statements That May Be Inaccurate or Incomplete	**14.25**
Additional Procedures	**14.25**
Client Representations	**14.26**
Review of Financial Statements	**14.26**
Overview	**14.26**
Review Standards	**14.27**
Knowledge of Accounting Principles and Practices	**14.28**
Knowledge of Client's Business	**14.28**
Inquiry and Analytical Procedures	**14.29**
Additional Procedures That May Become Necessary	**14.30**

Incomplete Review	**14.31**
Form and Content of Workpapers	**14.31**
Client Representations	**14.32**
Planning the Engagement	**14.32**
Consideration of Internal Control	**14.33**
Compilation and Review Reporting Obligations	**14.34**
Association with Financial Statements	**14.36**
Reference to Accountant's Report	**14.36**
Dating of Accountant's Report	**14.36**
Reporting on a Compilation	**14.37**
Compilation Report Modifications	**14.38**
Substantial Omission of Disclosures	**14.38**
When Accountant Is Not Independent	**14.40**
Departure from GAAP	**14.41**
Inadequate Disclosure	**14.42**
Uncertainty and Going Concern	**14.42**
Inconsistency	**14.43**
Comprehensive Basis of Accounting Other Than GAAP	**14.43**
Emphasis of a Matter	**14.43**
Subsequent Discovery of Facts Existing at Date of Accountant's Report	**14.44**
Supplementary Information	**14.46**
Financial Statements Included in Certain Prescribed Forms	**14.46**
Reporting on a Review	**14.48**
Incomplete Review	**14.49**
Accountant's Independence	**14.50**
Review Report Modifications	**14.50**
Departure from GAAP	**14.50**
Inadequate Disclosure	**14.51**
Uncertainty	**14.52**
Inconsistency	**14.52**
Comprehensive Basis of Accounting Other Than GAAP	**14.52**
Emphasis of a Matter	**14.52**

Inadequacy of Report Modification 14.52
Subsequent Discovery of Facts Existing at Date of
    Accountant's Report 14.53
Supplementary Information 14.53
    Supplementary Information Compiled or Reviewed 14.53
    Supplementary Information Not Compiled or
        Reviewed 14.54
Withdrawing from an Engagement 14.54
Change in Engagement 14.55
Reporting on Comparative Financial Statements 14.56
    All Periods Compiled or Reviewed 14.57
    Current Period Reviewed—Prior Period Compiled 14.58
    Current Period Compiled—Prior Period Reviewed 14.59
    Current or Prior Period Audited—Other Period
        Compiled or Reviewed 14.60
    Changes in Reports of Prior Periods 14.61
    Prior Period, or Periods, Compiled or Reviewed by
        Other Accountants 14.62
        Predecessor Accountant Reissues Unchanged
            Report 14.62
        Predecessor Accountant Issues Changed Report 14.63
        Predecessor Accountant's Report Not Reissued 14.64
        Considerations When the Predecessor Accountant
            Has Ceased Operations 14.65
    Exception to Reporting on the Highest Level of
        Service Rendered 14.66
    Change in Public or Nonpublic Status 14.67
Reports on the Application of Accounting Principles 14.69
Reporting on Personal Financial Statements Contained
    in Written Personal Financial Plans 14.69
Proposed Assembly Service 14.71

COMPILATION AND REVIEW ENGAGEMENTS

Overview

Statements on Standards for Accounting and Review Services (SSARS) cover two different levels of service that an accountant can provide for unaudited financial statements of nonpublic entities. The first level of service is referred to as a compilation. The accountant's report on a compilation includes a statement that an audit or a review was not performed and no opinion or other assurance is expressed on the accompanying financial statements. The second level of service is called a review. The accountant's report on a review includes a statement of limited assurance that the financial statements are in accordance with generally accepted accounting principles (GAAP) or an other comprehensive basis of accounting.

> *OBSERVATION: The material in this chapter provides a discussion of the standards that apply to compilation and review engagements. For a thorough discussion of how to apply these standards and document their application, see* **Miller's Compilations and Reviews** *by Larry P. Bailey, which is also available from Harcourt Brace Professional Publishing.*

Compilation and review services are directed primarily to nonpublic entities, as defined in the pronouncements. However, a review may be performed for a public company that is not required to have audited financial statements (SAS-71 [Interim Financial Information]). In the event a public company decides not to have its financial statements audited and is not required to do so, it may have its interim and annual financial statements reviewed. SSARS-1 (Compilation and Review of Financial Statements) defines a *nonpublic entity* as (1) one whose securities are not traded in a public market or (2) one that has not filed with a regulatory agency for the purpose of selling any of its securities in a public market. A subsidiary, a corporate joint venture, or any other entity controlled by a nonpublic entity is also considered a nonpublic entity. SSARS-1 defines a *financial statement* as a presentation of financial information for the purpose of communicating the resources or obligations of an entity at a specific time or communicating the changes in such resources or obligations during a time period, in accordance with GAAP or an other comprehensive basis of accounting. A financial presentation includes all accompanying notes, but the scope of SSARS-1 does not include financial forecasts, projections, or similar presentations (AR 100.04).

> **OBSERVATION:** *Guidance for services involving financial forecasts or projections for both public and nonpublic companies is discussed in the chapter entitled "Prospective Financial Statements."*

> **OBSERVATION:** *A SSARS Interpretation entitled "Submitting Draft Financial Statements" (September 1990) states that draft financial statements may be submitted to a client if the accountant* **intends** *to compile or review the financial statements* **and** *if each page of the financial statements are identified with "Draft Financial Statements" (or some similar heading) (AR 9100.61–.62).*

A financial presentation may consist of a single financial statement (e.g., a balance sheet, an income statement, a statement of cash flows, a statement of cash receipts and cash disbursements, a statement of assets and liabilities, or a statement of operations by product lines). An accountant may issue a compilation or review report on one financial statement, such as a balance sheet, and not issue a report on other related statements, such as the statement of income or the statement of retained earnings (AR 100.04).

> **OBSERVATION:** *A SSARS Interpretation entitled "Reports on Specified Elements, Accounts, or Items of a Financial Statement" (November 1981) states that SSARS-1 is not applicable to an engagement whereby the accountant reports on presentations of specified elements, accounts, or items of a financial statement because such presentations do not constitute financial statements. The SSARS Interpretation notes that SAS-62 (Special Reports), SAS-75 (Engagements to Apply Agreed-Upon Procedures to Specified Elements, Accounts, or Items of a Financial Statement), and related Interpretations provide guidance when the engagement is*

intended to result in (1) an expression of an opinion on specified elements, accounts, or items of a financial statement or (2) the application of agreed-upon procedures to specified elements, accounts, or items of a financial statement (AR 9100.27–.28).

An *other comprehensive basis of accounting* is defined in SAS-62 as a basis to which at least one of the following applies (AU 623.01):

1. The accounting basis is used to comply with the requirements or financial reporting provisions of a government agency.
2. The accounting basis is used to file income tax returns.
3. The cash receipts and disbursements basis or the modified accrual basis is used.
4. The accounting basis has substantial support, such as price-level accounting.

Both SSARS-1 and SAS-62 identify the following as examples of financial statements (AR 100.04):

- Balance sheet
- Statement of income
- Statement of cash flows
- Statement of changes in owners' equity
- Statement of assets and liabilities (with or without owners' equity accounts)
- Statement of revenue and expenses
- Summary of operations
- Statement of operations by product lines
- Statement of cash receipts and disbursements

SSARS apply to those situations in which the accountant is associated with a financial statement presentation. The standards established by SSARS do not have to be observed when the accountant prepares or assists in the preparation of a client's trial balance. A SSARS Interpretation entitled "Differentiating a Financial Statement Presentation from a Trial Balance" (September 1990) points out that the following factors should be considered in differentiating a financial statement presentation from a trial balance (AR 9100.54–.57):

- Generally, a financial statement requires the grouping of similar accounts or transactions with corresponding subtotals and totals, and the netting of contra accounts, whereas a trial balance presentation is limited to displaying accounts in a debit/credit format.

- Generally, financial statements use titles that relate to financial position, results of operations, or presentation of cash flows, whereas a trial balance presentation uses titles such as "trial balance," "adjusted trial balance," and "listing of general ledger accounts."

- Financial statements are formatted to show a mathematical relationship, such as Assets = Liabilities + Owners' Equity, and Revenues − Expenses = Net income, whereas a trial balance is formatted to show that Debits = Credits.

- The activity statement shows the net results of operations for a period (net income, revenues in excess of expenditures, etc.), whereas a trial balance makes no attempt to disclose results of operations.

- Generally, the statement of financial position shows assets in order of liquidity and liabilities in order of maturity, whereas a trial balance presents accounts in the order in which they appear in the general ledger.

- A set of financial statements demonstrates the articulation of the individual financial statements in that the results of operations are added or subtracted from retained earnings, whereas in a trial balance no such articulation is attempted.

Services provided by CPAs other than compilation, review, or audit services are considered other accounting services. Examples are (1) adjusting and closing books, (2) consulting on financial matters, (3) preparing tax returns, and (4) providing automated bookkeeping or data processing services. Other accounting services may not include the preparation or issuance of financial statements. Other accounting services may be performed prior to or concurrently with an engagement to compile or review financial statements (AR 100.02).

All types of financial statements may be compiled or reviewed and they may be for any type of business organization, including an estate, a trust, or an individual. The financial statements may reflect the operations of not-for-profit organizations, governments, governmental agencies, or other entities that prepare their financial statements using a comprehensive basis of accounting other than GAAP. Whenever the term *GAAP* is used in connection with compilation or review, its meaning also includes an other comprehensive basis of accounting. As mentioned previously, compilation and review standards are not applicable to forecasts, projections, or similar financial presentations, or to financial information included in tax returns (AR 100.04).

> **OBSERVATION:** *When a regulatory body or other user requires or requests that compiled or reviewed financial statements be submitted via computer, the accountant's compilation or review report also must be submitted. There is no need for the accountant to manually sign the electronically transmitted report, and there is no need for the accountant to concurrently or subsequently submit a hard copy of the report to the regulatory body or other user.*

> **OBSERVATION:** *If financial information derived from tax returns is issued separately from the tax return by an accountant, it may be considered a financial statement and is then covered by existing compilation and review standards.*

> **OBSERVATION:** *A SSARS Interpretation entitled "Reporting on Tax Returns" (November 1982) states that an accountant may, at the client's request, compile or review financial information contained in tax returns or Form 5500 (Return of Employee Benefit Plan) (AR 9100.31–.32).*

Services to a nonpublic client could potentially include year-end examination in accordance with GAAS, quarterly reviews (interim), monthly compilations (other than quarter or year end), tax return preparation, and other accounting services. Each of these services is a separate service that may be rendered to a single client. The results accomplished by each service are significantly different from the results accomplished in one of the other services. The performance of one service may overlap that of one or more of the other services, but each service has a different purpose and intended result. The purpose and intended result of each service should be clear to the accountant and documented in the workpapers. Information that the accountant obtains while performing other accounting services may help the accountant complete the compilation or review service. If an engagement to perform accounting services for a client does not include compilation or review services, an accountant may not issue a report on unaudited financial statements of a nonpublic company (AR 100.06).

> **OBSERVATION:** *A SSARS Interpretation entitled "Applicability of Statements on Standards for Accounting and Review Services" to Litigation Services" (May 1991) states that SSARS standards do not apply to financial statements submitted as part of a litigation or regulatory dispute before a "trier of fact" if the (1) accountant is functioning as an expert witness, (2) service involves being a "trier of fact" or acting for one, (3) work performed is to be subject to challenge by each party to the dispute, or (4) work performed is to be used exclusively as part of the dispute and becomes part of the attorney's work (AR 9100.76–.79). (A "trier of fact" means a court, regulatory body, or governmental authority; their agents; a grand jury; or an arbitrator or mediator.)*

The accountant cannot submit financial statements to a nonpublic client or other parties unless those financial statements have been either reviewed or compiled. SSARS-7 (Omnibus Statement on Standards for Accounting and Review Services—1992) defines the *submission* of financial statements as presenting financial statements to the client or others when the accountant has (1) generated the statements either manually or through the use of computer software or (2) materially modified the financial statements directly on the client-prepared statements (AR 100.07).

SSARS-7 specifically states that the following services should not be construed as the submission of financial statements (AR 100.07):

- Reading financial statements prepared by the client.

- Typing or reproducing (without modification) financial statements prepared by the client as an accommodation for the client.

- Proposing correcting journal entries or disclosures (either written or verbal) if the accountant does not **directly** modify the financial statements prepared by the client.

- Preparing monthly standard journal entries.

- Providing the client with financial statement formats that do not include dollar amounts.

- Advising the client about computer software that could be used to prepare the client's financial statements.

- Providing the client with access to computer hardware or software that the client uses to prepare its financial statements.

> **OBSERVATION:** *Before the issuance of SSARS-7 the accountant was prohibited from "merely typing or reproducing" financial statements as an accommodation for a client.*

The pronouncements for unaudited financial statements of a nonpublic entity covered in this chapter are:

- Code of Professional Conduct

- Statement on Quality Control Standards (SQCS) No. 2 (System of Quality Control for a CPA Firm's Accounting and Audit Practice)

- SSARS-1 (Compilation and Review of Financial Statements)

- SSARS-2 (Reporting on Comparative Financial Statements)

- SSARS-3 (Compilation Reports on Financial Statements in Certain Prescribed Forms)

- SSARS-4 (Communications Between Predecessor and Successor Accountants)

- SSARS-6 (Reporting on Personal Financial Statements Included in written Personal Financial Plans)

- SSARS-7 (Omnibus Statement on Standards for Accounting and Review Services—1992)

The AICPA Code of Professional Conduct provides guidelines for accounting practitioners in the conduct of their professional affairs.

SQCS-2 identifies elements a firm must consider when designing a system of quality control (QC 10-1).

SSARS-1 establishes the fundamental guidelines required of a CPA to perform a review or compilation engagement when the CPA's name is associated with the financial statements of a nonpublic entity (AR 100).

SSARS-2 provides requirements for the preparation of reports on comparative financial statements (AR 200).

SSARS-3 provides an alternative reporting format when financial statements are presented in a prescribed form. SSARS-3 applies only to compilation engagements (AR 300).

SSARS-4 provides guidance when the successor CPA decides to communicate with the predecessor CPA (AR 400).

SSARS-6 provides an exemption to the basic requirement that a CPA must issue either a review report or a compilation report when associated with the unaudited financial statements of a nonpublic entity. Under conditions established by SSARS-6, a CPA may issue a single-paragraph report on personal financial statements included in a written personal financial plan (AR 600).

SSARS-7 addresses a number of issues, including the wording of the standard reports for a compilation or review, and removes ambiguities in guidance established in previously issued Statements on Standards for Accounting and Review Services.

RESPONSIBILITY AND FUNCTION OF THE ACCOUNTANT

In a compilation or review engagement, the accountant must comply with the general standards set forth in Rule 201 of the Code of Professional Conduct. The general standards are as follows (AR 100.56):

> A member shall comply with the following standards and with any interpretations thereof by bodies designated by Council.
>
> A. *Professional Competence.* Undertake only those professional services that the member or the member's firm can reasonably expect to be completed with professional competence.
>
> B. *Due Professional Care.* Exercise due professional care in the performance of professional services.
>
> C. *Planning and Supervision.* Adequately plan and supervise the performance of professional services.
>
> D. *Sufficient Relevant Data.* Obtain sufficient relevant data to afford a reasonable basis for conclusions or recommendations in relation to any professional services performed.

OBSERVATION: A SSARS Interpretation entitled "Planning and Supervision" (August 1981) states that Statements on Auditing Standards do not govern a compilation or review engagement of nonpublic entities. However, accountants may still wish to consider a Statement on Auditing Standards (such as SAS-22 [Planning and Supervision]), or other textbooks and articles, when they need guidance on planning and supervising a compilation or review engagement (AR 9100.16–.17).

The degree of responsibility that the accountant takes in a compilation or review must be clearly defined in a written report. An accountant may not issue a report on unaudited financial statements of a nonpublic entity unless he or she has complied with the applicable standards for a compilation or a review. The procedures, standards, and reporting obligations for a compilation or review are quite specific and are discussed in detail later in this chapter (AR 100.06).

It is well established in accounting literature that the accuracy and fairness of financial statements are the responsibility of the management of the entity. Thus, the management of an entity is directly responsible for the design and proper implementation of an effective internal control structure.

PRE-ENGAGEMENT PLANNING

Pre-engagement planning is essential to any type of professional accounting service. One of the general standards of Rule 201 of the Code of Professional Conduct states that a member shall "adequately plan and supervise the performance of professional services" (AR 100.56).

Much has been written and promulgated for pre-engagement planning of an audit. Statements on Auditing Standards are directed to auditing matters only, as are generally accepted auditing standards. However, pre-engagement planning for a compilation or a review is no less important than pre-engagement planning for an audit. Some of the more important items that must be considered during the pre-engagement planning period for a compilation or a review are:

- Evaluation of the client
- Communication, if necessary, with the predecessor accountant
- Related party transactions
- Independence
- Engagement letter

Evaluation of the Client

SQCS-2 states that a firm should establish procedures to determine whether a client should be accepted. The accounting firm must evaluate the integrity of the management of a new or existing client and also determine whether it possesses the competency necessary to properly service the needs of the client (QC 10.07).

> *OBSERVATION: Statements on Quality Control Standards establish procedures for both audit and nonaudit engagements. Thus, Quality Control Standards provide the procedures that should be followed in evaluating a new or existing client for a compilation or review engagement.*

Procedures that may be adopted in evaluating a new or existing client for a compilation or review engagement are:

- Review the client company's financial statements.
- Discuss the company's management with members of the financial community.
- Consider communicating with the predecessor accountant.

The acceptance of a compilation or a review engagement may be documented in the permanent file of the client. Subsequently, the professional relationship between the client and the accounting firm should be evaluated from year to year. This requirement is explicitly mandated by SQCS-2. Therefore, the accounting firm should continue to evaluate the integrity of management and its ability to competently render services to the client.

> *OBSERVATION: SQCS-2 states that an accounting firm, regardless of its size, must have a system of quality control "to provide itself with reasonable assurance of meeting its responsibility to provide professional services that conform with professional standards." Furthermore, the bylaws of the AICPA require that a member of the Institute who is involved in an audit, review, or compilation must be employed by a firm that is enrolled in a practice-monitoring program.*

Communication with the Predecessor Accountant

In December 1981, the AICPA Accounting and Review Services Committee issued SSARS-4, which is entitled "Communications Between

Predecessor and Successor Accountants." SSARS-4 does not require that the successor accountant communicate with the predecessor accountant; however, it identifies circumstances that may cause a successor accountant to decide to communicate with the predecessor accountant. Also, SSARS-4 requires the predecessor accountant to respond promptly and fully to the successor accountant's inquiries. The following definitions are established by SSARS-4 (AR 400.01–.02):

> *Successor accountant*—An accountant who has been invited to make a proposal for an engagement to compile or review financial statements or who has accepted such an engagement.

> *Predecessor accountant*—An accountant who has resigned or who has been notified that his services have been terminated and who, as a minimum, was engaged to compile the financial statements of the entity for the prior year or for a period ended within twelve months of the date of the financial statements to be compiled or reviewed by the successor auditor.

Decision to make inquiries   Although the successor accountant is not required to make inquiries of the predecessor accountant, circumstances surrounding the engagement may suggest that such inquiries be made. SSARS-4 does not attempt to provide general or specific guidelines for defining which circumstances may suggest a need to communicate with the predecessor accountant, but it lists four examples that may lead the successor accountant to contact the predecessor accountant: (1) frequent changes of accountants, (2) limited information about the client and its principals, (3) existing information that raises questions about the client and its principals, or (4) the change of accountants at a date significantly after the end of the accounting period for which the service is to be provided (AR 400.03).

Before the oral or written inquiries are made, the predecessor accountant must obtain the consent of the client so that the predecessor accountant is not put in the position of violating Rule 301 (Confidential Client Information) of the Code of Professional Conduct. If the client refuses to authorize the successor accountant to communicate with the predecessor accountant, the successor accountant should evaluate the basis for such refusal in deciding whether to accept the engagement. The predecessor accountant is expected to respond promptly and fully to the successor accountant's inquiries, except in the case of unusual circumstances. SSARS-4 states that impending litigation with respect to services performed by the predecessor accountant could be an example of an unusual circumstance. If the predecessor accountant refuses to respond to the inquiries, he or she should explain to the successor accountant that responses are limited by circumstances (AR 400.04–.06).

The following items are identified as typical inquiries that may be made by the successor accountant (AR 400.05):

- Information about the management's or owners' integrity

- Disagreements about accounting matters or the performance of procedures

- The degree of cooperation of management or the owners in providing additional or revised information

- The predecessor accountant's explanation of why there was a change of accountants

Other inquiries SSARS-4 notes that a successor accountant may wish to make inquiries of the predecessor accountant as a typical part of the acceptance of any engagement. In other words, circumstances do not suggest that there may be problems with the client's management or its owners. For example, the successor accountant may wish to inquire about the adequacy of underlying financial data or recurring problem areas of the engagement. Again, the predecessor accountant is expected to respond to reasonable requests made by the successor accountant. However, the predecessor accountant must still obtain the client's permission to release information to the successor accountant (AR 400.03–.04).

Responses to inquiries or the availability of workpapers to a successor accountant does not provide a basis for referring to the work of the predecessor accountant in the successor accountant's report. However, the predecessor accountant's report may be used when comparative financial statements are presented. The reporting formats for comparative financial statements when predecessor and successor accountants are involved are discussed in SSARS-2 (Reporting on Comparative Financial Statements) (AR 400.09).

Revision of financial statements During the engagement the accountant may become aware of information that requires the revision of financial statements that were reported on by the predecessor accountant. Under this circumstance, SSARS-7 requires that the successor accountant request that the client communicate the information to the predecessor accountant (AR 400.10).

Independence

SSARS-1 does not require accountants to be independent on compilation engagements. Thus, accountants may issue compilation reports for entities of which they are not independent, provided that the report includes an additional paragraph stating that the accountant is not independent. Accountants must be independent for review engagements, or they may not issue reports on the review. Accountants should be guided by Rule 101 of the Code of Professional Conduct in determining whether they are independent (AR 100.22).

Before a review engagement is accepted, the accounting firm should make inquiries of its staff to determine whether there are any relationships with the client that might impair the firm's independence. For example, a member of the firm's staff in the office performing the engagement may have a relative who is a key employee of the prospective client.

Engagement Letters

The use of engagement letters has long been encouraged. Most CPA firms, large and small, use them for all engagements, including those for write-up or other services. The engagement letter should clearly set forth the nature and limitations, if any, of the engagement. A carefully prepared engagement letter will considerably reduce the possibility of a misunderstanding with a client. Compilation and review standards require accountants to establish an understanding with their clients about the services to be performed. SSARS-1 states a preference that the understanding be in writing and cover at least the following (AR 100.08):

- A description of the specific compilation and/or review services to be performed
- A description of the report expected to be rendered on completion of the engagement and a caveat that if the accountant is unable to complete the compilation or a review, no report will be issued
- An explanation of the limitations of the engagement, including:
  — The engagement cannot be relied on to disclose errors, irregularities, or illegal acts.
  — The accountant will bring to the attention of management any material errors, irregularities, or illegal acts that are

discovered during the engagement, unless they are clearly inconsequential.

- A detailed description of any other accounting services to be performed

If financial statements that omit substantially all disclosures and/or the statement of cash flows are to be compiled, an additional paragraph to the compilation report disclosing such omissions should be included in the engagement letter.

> *OBSERVATION: The engagement letter or other understanding with the client should include a provision that no report will be issued if the accountant is unable to complete the compilation or review. This is an important point, because a number of situations may arise involving a compilation or review that may compel the accountant to consider withdrawing from the engagement and not issuing a report. Withdrawal from a compilation or a review by the accountant is covered later in this chapter.*

At the outset of an engagement the accountant may know that a departure, or departures, from GAAP exists. In this event, it may be appropriate to include in the engagement letter information to the effect that a modified report will be issued reflecting the departure(s) from GAAP, instead of the standard compilation or review report. This procedure should eliminate any misunderstanding about what type of report the client will receive when the engagement is completed.

The engagement letter should represent the understanding and agreement between the accountant and the client, and it may include information on the accountant's fee (AR 100.53).

GENERALLY ACCEPTED ACCOUNTING PRINCIPLES

Generally accepted accounting principles apply to reviews, compilations, and audits. There is no special (limited) set of accounting rules that applies only to reviews and compilations.

> *OBSERVATION: SSARS-7 states that the accounting hierarchies established by SAS-69 (The Meaning of "Present Fairly in Conformity with Generally Accepted Accounting Principles" in the Independent Auditor's Report) applies to reviews and compila-*

tions. *The guidance provided by SAS-69 is discussed in the chapter entitled "Generally Accepted Accounting Principles."*

OBSERVATION: *Disclosure requirements for a compilation or review do not differ from those for an audit. If the client omits the required disclosures, the accountant must modify the accountant's report. As discussed later in this chapter, under certain circumstances, all or substantially all disclosures may be omitted from the compiled financial statements with proper modification to the compilation report.*

OBSERVATION: *A SSARS Interpretation entitled "Special-Purpose Financial Presentations to Comply with Contractual Agreements or Regulatory Provisions" (September 1990) states that an accountant may conduct a review or compilation of special-purpose financial presentations that (1) comply with a contractual agreement or regulatory provision and in so doing are incomplete but are otherwise in accordance with GAAP or OCBOA or (2) are not in accordance with GAAP or OCBOA because the basis of accounting is prescribed by a contractual agreement or regulatory provision. Reports on special-purpose financial presentations should be expanded to explain the purpose of the presentation and to note that the distribution of the accountant's report is restricted (AR 9100.63–.72).*

GENERALLY ACCEPTED AUDITING STANDARDS

Compliance with generally accepted auditing standards is necessary in an audit engagement. GAAS are concerned with the professional qualities and judgment of the independent auditor in the performance of an audit and in the issuance of the audit report. Statements on Auditing Standards are issued as interpretations of GAAS and may also provide guidance to the accountant who performs services in connection with the unaudited financial statements of a public company. Quality Control Standards cover all aspects of auditing or accounting and review services. Thus, they are applicable to compilation or review engagements as well as audit engagements (AR 100.01).

Statements on Standards for Accounting and Review Services are issued to provide guidance to accountants concerning the standards and procedures applicable to the compilation or review of nonpublic entities (AR 100.01).

> **OBSERVATION:** *A review may be performed by an accountant for a public company that is not required to issue audited financial statements (SAS-71) (AR 100.01).*

In a compilation or review engagement, the accountant must first comply with the four general standards of the profession (Rule 201 of the Code of Professional Conduct). These include (1) professional competence, (2) due professional care, (3) planning and supervision, and (4) sufficient relevant data (AR 100.03).

The next set of standards that an accountant must comply with in a compilation or review engagement is the Quality Control Standards of the profession. These standards cover both audit engagements and compilation or review engagements.

The final set of standards that an accountant must comply with are those established by the SSARS series (AR 100.01).

> **OBSERVATION:** *A SSARS Interpretation entitled "Financial Statements Included in SEC Filings" (December 1979) states that an accountant, after considering all relevant facts, may conclude that he or she should rely on Statements on Auditing Standards for guidance, instead of issuing a compilation or review report, where nonpublic companies are required to file unaudited financial statements with the SEC (for example, in issuing common stock to an ESOP or in the sale of limited partnership units) (AR 9100.03–.05).*

COMPILATION OF FINANCIAL STATEMENTS

Overview

A compilation of financial statements is an accounting service in which an accountant prepares, or assists in preparing, financial statements without expressing any assurance that the statements are accurate and complete or are in conformity with GAAP. A compilation engagement may involve compiling and reporting on one financial statement, such as the balance sheet or a statement of income, and not on the other related financial statements, if those statements are not presented. As with audited financial statements, this limited reporting objective is not considered a scope limitation. It may also involve financial statements that omit the statement of cash flows and substantially all disclosures required by GAAP (AR 100.04).

> **OBSERVATION:** *The accountant may actually prepare the financial statements, and the client could rely on the accountant's competence to see that they are appropriate and proper for the industry involved. This situation requires that the financial statements and all significant decisions made in preparing them be reviewed in detail with the client so that the client understands them as much as possible. In this manner, the client should be willing to accept the responsibility that the financial statements are the representations of management and not of the accountant. Compilation engagements may be undertaken for (AR 100.02):*

- *Organizations for which the accountant is also writing up or adjusting the books and/or preparing tax returns*
- *Closely held organizations needing only limited outside credit*
- *Interim periods of a company's fiscal year with quarterly and/ or year-end periods that are reviewed or audited*

As a matter of policy, many large CPA firms have decided not to take compilation engagements unless they also perform other accounting services or audits for such clients.

> **OBSERVATION:** *A problem can arise when an accountant actually prepares all or part of the financial statements in a compilation. In the event litigation occurs, the client may take the position that the financial statements are the representations of the accountant because the accountant actually prepared the statements from the records of the client. If the accountant cannot substantiate that the financial statements are the representations of management, the courts may agree with the client. Thus, the accountant should, in all cases, be able to substantiate through workpapers that the statements are the representations of management. Obviously, the engagement letter should help in substantiating the accountant's arrangement with the client. In addition, conferences with the client should be reduced to written conference reports, and other documentation should be maintained in the accountant's workpapers.*

Compilation Standards

The standards applicable to a compilation are (AR 100.10–.13):

1. The accountant should possess:

    a. An adequate level of knowledge of the accounting principles and practices of the client's industry to enable the accountant to compile financial statements in the appropriate form for the industry

    b. A general understanding of the client's business, including:

       1) Business transactions

       2) Form of accounting records

       3) Stated qualifications of accounting staff

       4) Accounting basis used to prepare statements

       5) Form and content of financial statements

2. On the basis of the accountant's general knowledge of the client's business, the accountant should consider the need to perform other accounting services. (Such services may be limited to consulting on a specific accounting matter or may involve adjusting all or many of the significant accounts in the general ledger.)

3. The accountant should read the compiled financial statements and consider whether they are:

    a. Appropriate in form for the client and the industry in which it operates

    b. Free from obvious material errors

       1) Information taken from the books has been properly organized into financial statements.

       2) No mathematical or clerical errors are included.

       3) Accounting principles have been properly applied and adequate disclosures have been made.

> **OBSERVATION:** *The accountant uses his or her professional skills and specialized knowledge of the client and industry in the reading of the financial statements. This procedure allows the accountant to spot errors and omissions that a less knowledgeable person may not be aware of.*

Understanding of a Client

An understanding of the client can be obtained through (AR 100.11):

1. Experience with the client:

   a. Services in prior years (audits, preparation of tax returns and unaudited financial statements, consulting on various financial matters)

   b. Other accounting services being performed along with the engagement to compile financial statements, such as adjusting the books or preparing a working trial balance

2. Inquiry of responsible client personnel: The inquiries may be limited in that their intent is to obtain information on the broad characteristics of the five areas deemed necessary for adequate understanding. At the same time, however, they should be of sufficient scope that the accountant will understand the client well enough to read the financial statements as a knowledgeable professional and make the following conclusions:

   a. The statements are in the appropriate form for the client and the industry in which it operates.

   b. All necessary disclosures have been made.

   c. Accounting principles apparently have been properly applied.

   d. The relationship of information in the financial statements is not at variance with the accountant's understanding of the client's business transactions.

The level of understanding an accountant should achieve in the course of a compilation is not as deep as is required for a review or an audit. It does not, for example, include a review of the client's internal control structure (AR 100.11).

> **OBSERVATION:** *However, the accountant must have a general understanding of the form of accounting records and the accounting basis used by the client (AR 100.11).*

Need for Other Accounting Services

On the basis of the accountant's understanding of the client, he or she may conclude that other accounting services must be performed. The need for such services may result from discoveries such as (AR 100.12):

- The accounting records are inadequate.

- The accounting or bookkeeping personnel do not possess sufficient abilities or experience.

- The accounting basis used to maintain the books is incorrect.

- The information to be disclosed in the financial statements is not available.

Reading the Financial Statements

After the accountant has obtained the required knowledge of the client and the industry in which the client operates, has completed any other accounting services deemed necessary, and has prepared the financial statements, he or she should then read the financial statements (AR 100.13).

Reading the financial statements is one of the more important procedures in a compilation engagement. The accountant must apply all the knowledge and understanding previously obtained and must effectively use professional expertise. Some of the questions the accountant must answer are (AR 100.13):

- Do the financial statements appear to be in the proper form and complete?

- Do the financial statements appear to be free from obvious material errors?

- Are all necessary disclosures made in reasonable detail?

> **OBSERVATION:** *While it is true that the accountant must develop some broad or general knowledge about accounting principles (as described earlier in this section), the only procedure required by Statements on Standards for Accounting and Review Services that must be applied directly to the assertions contained in the financial statements is the reading of those financial statements.*

Any information that the accountant is aware of, from any source, should be considered for possible indications that the financial statements may be inaccurate, incomplete, or otherwise unsatisfactory (AR 100.13).

Financial Statements That May Be Inaccurate or Incomplete

Compilation standards do not require the accountant to perform any procedures to verify, corroborate, or review information supplied by the entity. However, the accountant may make inquiries or perform other procedures in the course of rendering other accounting services (AR 100.12).

The accountant may discover, through inquiries, completion of other procedures, knowledge from prior engagements, and reading of the financial statements, information that is inaccurate, incomplete, or otherwise unsatisfactory. Compilation standards then require the accountant to obtain additional or revised information. However, the accountant is not required to verify, corroborate, or substantiate any additional or revised information received. If the entity refuses to provide the accountant with the requested additional or revised information, the accountant should withdraw from the compilation engagement. When an accountant is in the above situation, he or she should consider the need for consulting legal counsel (AR 100.12).

> **OBSERVATION:** *Regardless of a disclaimer of any form of assurance on the financial statements, the accountant must still comply with compilation standards. The accountant cannot ignore significant questions that arise or that reasonably could have been expected to be discovered as a result of the services performed. Whatever unresolved information the accountant becomes aware of from any source must be adequately resolved to his or her satisfaction.*

Additional Procedures

When an accountant has reason to suspect that the client's information, records, or statements may be inaccurate or incomplete, he or she must perform *other accounting services* unless the client agrees to correct the deficiencies that are impeding the completion of the accountant's engagement. If a client objects to any procedures the accountant deems necessary, the accountant should consider withdrawing from the engagement. *Additional procedures* are simply extra procedures, not specifically required by applicable compilation or review standards, that an accountant may perform to assure a given set of facts or transactions (AR 100.12).

Additional procedures should not be described in the compilation report. There is no prohibition against the accountant's performing procedures of a review or an audit nature to verify or corroborate any information. However, such additional procedures should not be so expansive that a review, or even an audit, is in substance performed. (9100.46–.49).

> **OBSERVATION:** *A SSARS Interpretation entitled "Additional Procedures" (March 1983) states that when an accountant performs **auditing procedures** such as the confirmation of receivables or the observation of inventories, the nature of the engagement is not changed from a compilation or review engagement to an audit engagement. The accountant is free to perform those additional procedures he or she deems necessary under the circumstances. However, the accountant should be careful that others do not interpret the additional procedures as being part of an audit. For example, if information is confirmed with third parties, the confirmation may state that the information is sought as part of a compilation engagement and not as part of the audit of the client's financial statements (AR 9100.46–.49).*

Client Representations

Compilation standards do not require that client representations be obtained. However, because of the very limited procedures required for a compilation and the possibility of misunderstandings on accounting information, obtaining a client representation letter may sometimes be useful, especially in situations in which the client does not understand that the financial statements are its responsibility.

REVIEW OF FINANCIAL STATEMENTS

Overview

A review is a level of service higher than a compilation because it results in an expression of limited assurance. The limited assurance is contained in a report by the accountant stating that he or she is not aware of any material modifications that should be made to the financial statements in order for them to be in conformity with GAAP. The accountant must perform sufficient inquiry and analytical procedures to give a reasonable basis for that conclusion. These inquiries and analytical procedures are the major difference between a review and a compilation (AR 100.04).

A review is a level of service lower than an audit of financial statements. It does not provide a basis for expressing an opinion under GAAS because many significant auditing procedures are not required by a review. The more prominent auditing procedures *not* required by a review are (AR 100.04):

- An understanding/assessment of internal control
- Tests that the internal controls are as represented and are properly functioning (tests of controls)
- Tests of underlying documentation (substantive testing)
- Observation of inventories
- Confirmation of accounts receivable

Although the accountant is required to obtain an understanding of the client's accounting system, he or she plainly is not obligated to study it for weaknesses in internal control.

A review engagement may involve reporting on all the basic financial statements or on only one financial statement, such as a balance sheet or a statement of income. A review may not include the reporting on financial statements that omit substantially all disclosures required by GAAP, unless such omissions are completely disclosed in the accountant's report. This obviously is not a practical alternative (AR 9100.01–.02).

Review Standards

The standards applicable to a review are (AR 100.24):

1. The accountant should possess:
   a. A level of knowledge of the accounting principles and practices of the industry in which the client operates
   b. An understanding of the client's business:
      1) Organization
      2) Operating characteristics
         a) Types of product or services
         b) Method of production or acquisition of products sold
         c) Method of distributing products or rendering services

         d) Operating locations

         e) Compensation method

      3) Nature of its assets, liabilities, revenues, and expenses

      4) Material transactions with related parties

  2. The accountant should complete inquiry and analytical procedures.

  3. The accountant should obtain a representation letter.

The knowledge and understanding should be of such a level that the accountant's inquiry and analytical procedures will provide a reasonable basis for expressing the limited assurance that is the ultimate goal of a review engagement (AR 100.24).

In addition, during the course of a review, the accountant may consider it necessary to compile the financial statements or to perform other accounting services (AR 100.05).

Knowledge of Accounting Principles and Practices

The level of knowledge of accounting principles should be sufficient enough to provide the accountant with a reasonable basis to express limited assurance that no material modifications are needed to have financial statements conform to GAAP or to an other comprehensive basis of accounting (AR 100.24).

Knowledge of Client's Business

The required level of understanding of a client's business may be obtained by (AR 100.26):

- Previous or current experience rendering to the client services such as audits, preparation of tax returns, compiling financial statements, and consulting on various financial matters

- Inquiry of client personnel

- Previous or current experience with other entities in the same industry as the client

> **OBSERVATION:** *Although organization of the entities in the same industry may differ, it is likely that the operating characteristics and the nature of the assets, liabilities, revenues, and expenses*

of these entities would be similar. Accordingly, an accountant should be able to use experience with entities in a particular industry for a new client.

Inquiry and Analytical Procedures

Inquiries should be directed at persons in the client's organization at sufficiently high levels to obtain reasonable assurance that the responses are proper and adequate. They should be tailor-made for each engagement and should cover all the following (AR 100.27):

- Accounting principles and practices used and the method of applying them

- Procedures for recording, classifying, and summarizing transactions and for accumulating information for disclosure in footnotes

- Actions authorized by stockholders, board of directors, committees of the board, or other management groups

Inquiries also should be directed to officers responsible for financial and accounting matters concerning these questions: (1) Have the financial statements been prepared in conformity with GAAP? (2) Have the accounting principles and practices been consistently applied? (3) Have there been changes in business activities? (4) Have any events occurred subsequent to the date of the financial statements? Further, any questions that have come up in performing the review should be directed to these officers (AR 100.27).

The extent of inquiries is determined by the professional judgment of the accountant. The inquiries must be sufficiently comprehensive to cover all significant amounts and matters. The accountant should consider the following items when determining the extent and type of inquiries:

- Nature and significance of an item

- Probability of misstatement

- Extent to which management's judgment enters into the determination of a particular item

- Knowledge obtained during a previous or the current engagement

- Qualifications of accounting personnel

- Deficiencies in financial data or the accounting system

Analytical procedures to be performed for the purpose of a review should be designed to detect relationships and individual items that appear to be unusual and therefore subject to inquiries addressed to responsible individuals. Additional procedures may involve the following: comparison of current-period financial statements with those for comparable prior period(s) and with budgets or forecast of anticipated results (if available), and the study of financial statements to isolate items that do not conform to their predictable pattern on the basis of prior experience. Examples of some of the elements in financial statements that would be expected to conform to a predictable relationship are (AR 100.27):

- Sales and accounts receivable
- Sales and cost of sales
- Interest expense and debt
- Sales and commissions and freight out
- Depreciation and property (also maintenance and repairs)

Moreover, the accountant should consider adjustments made to the financial statements in previous periods, because they may affect his or her judgment on the results of other analytical procedures. In addition, should similar adjustments be made during the current period?

Review procedures also require that the accountant read the financial statements to determine whether they are in conformity with GAAP (AR 100.27).

Additional Procedures That May Become Necessary

The performance of a review does not provide assurance that the accountant will become aware of all significant matters, nor does it provide assurance that inaccuracies or the omission of necessary disclosures will come to his or her attention. However, any information that the accountant becomes aware of during a review, regardless of its source, that casts doubt on the accuracy or completeness of the financial statements must be resolved. The accountant should perform any additional procedures deemed necessary in order to issue the report with limited assurance. The other procedures may include (AR 100.30):

- Further inquiry of responsible persons
- Other accounting services
- Consultation with the client on matters such as the proper accounting principles to be applied in recording transactions or the proper treatment of transactions for tax purposes

Incomplete Review

There can be no scope limitation on a review. The accountant must be free to perform whatever procedures deemed necessary, and those procedures must be accomplished or the review will be incomplete. An incomplete review will preclude an accountant from issuing a review report. The circumstances may be such that the accountant also will be precluded from issuing a compilation report. Information obtained by an accountant during the performance of an incomplete review cannot be ignored if the engagement is reduced to a compilation. Knowledge of possible inaccuracies or inadequate disclosures, such as inadequate allowance for doubtful accounts or nondisclosure of significant contingencies, must be resolved to the accountant's satisfaction. If some items are not properly adjusted or disclosed, the accountant should consider matters discussed later in the section entitled "Departures from GAAP." In deciding whether or not a review or a compilation report may be issued, matters covered later in the section entitled "Change in Engagement" should be considered (AR 100.36 and .39–.40).

Form and Content of Workpapers

The workpapers should be adequate to support the report issued. They should include (AR 100.31):

1. Descriptions of all inquiries and analytical procedures employed, including any additional procedures deemed necessary, and summaries of the information and conclusions derived from such procedures

2. Unusual matters disclosed by the procedures or brought to the accountant's attention and their subsequent resolution

> *OBSERVATION: Workpapers completed in connection with a review need not be maintained separately from those prepared for other accounting services.*

The accountant may have acquired significant knowledge of the client's affairs, because of past experience with the client or because of other accounting services rendered, to allow for reduction of some of the inquiry procedures. The reasons for such reductions should be clearly set forth in the workpapers (AR 100.29).

Client Representations

Obtaining a client's representation letter is required for each review engagement. Such letters should be signed by the client's chief executive and chief financial officer or by the owners of the entity (AR 100.28).

> **OBSERVATION:** *The accountant must obtain a representation letter for each review engagement that results in the issuance of a review report. For example, if the accountant reviews and reports on monthly interim financial statements, he or she must obtain a representation letter for each of the twelve separate and distinct review engagements.*

PLANNING THE ENGAGEMENT

Planning and supervision of a compilation or a review engagement is required by the general standards of the profession. Unfortunately, no promulgated pronouncements have been issued on this topic. A thorough discussion of planning and supervision is included in *Miller's Compilations and Reviews.*

Probably the best method of planning and supervising a compilation or review engagement is to create a written work program tailored to the specific engagement.

As mentioned previously, no official pronouncements have been issued for supervising a compilation or a review engagement. However, SAS-22 (Planning and Supervision) was issued for audit engagements, and much can be extracted from it and applied to compilation and review engagements. The following discussion is based on SAS-22 (AR 9100.16–.17).

An accountant is required by the general standards of the profession (Rule 201) to adequately plan and supervise a compilation or review engagement. Planning and supervision usually necessitates (1) preparing a written work program, (2) obtaining knowledge of the client's business activities, and (3) dealing with differences that may arise between accountants involved in the engagement. Planning and supervision is a continuous function that lasts throughout the entire engagement, and it may be delegated by the in-charge accountant to other personnel.

More often than not, the accountant with the final responsibility will require assistants to accomplish the objectives of the engagement. Controlling and directing the efforts of the assistants are an integral part of supervising. Assurance must be obtained that the assistants are following the planned procedures.

Both the quality and the quantity of supervision are important. The extent of supervision depends on the qualifications of the assistants and the complexity of the work or subject matter. A supervisor must be kept constantly informed of new developments and significant problems that arise during the engagement. Also, the supervisor usually is charged with the responsibility of evaluating the quality and quantity of work performed by assistants.

A difference between the supervisor and the assistants may arise during the engagement. If the difference is not resolved, it should be appropriately documented in the workpapers of the engagement. In this event, the basis for final resolution of the disagreement should also be documented.

A time and personnel budget should be established and maintained for all but very small engagements. The budget should reflect the estimated time allocated to each item on the work program for the engagement. It should also reflect the type and grade of personnel assigned to the engagement. This budget should be carefully planned to allow the proper time and personnel for each facet of the engagement. More importantly, after the budget is carefully planned, it must be properly supervised to avoid significant variances with the actual results. The client should be informed when actual time on an engagement is significantly exceeding the budgeted time. Clients can become quite upset when faced with a much higher professional fee than was estimated, and the accountant's relationship with the client may suffer irreparable damage. Thus, the planning and supervision of a time and personnel budget, like all other aspects of an engagement, must be carefully planned and executed.

CONSIDERATION OF INTERNAL CONTROL

The objective of a review of financial statements is substantially different from the objective of a compilation of financial statements. In a review, the accountant performs inquiries and analytical procedures to provide a reasonable basis for expressing limited assurance that no material modifications need to be made to the financial statements in order for them to be in conformity with generally accepted accounting principles. In a compilation, the accountant's report includes a statement that he or she did not audit or review the financial statements and does not express any opinion or other form of assurance on them. Thus, a compilation is considered a level of service lower than a review (AR 100.04).

The objective of a review also differs substantially from the objective of an audit of financial statements performed in accordance with generally accepted auditing standards. In an audit, the objective is to provide a reasonable basis for the auditor to express an opinion on the financial statements taken as a whole. The auditor obtains a reasonable basis for expressing an opinion by assessing internal controls, by testing controls, and by performing substantive tests of the accounting records (AR 100.04).

In a compilation of financial statements, the accountant has no basis for expressing any opinion or other form of limited assurance. In a review, the accountant has a limited basis for expressing limited assurance that the financial statements substantially conform to GAAP. In an audit, the auditor is able to form a reasonable basis for expressing an opinion on the financial statements taken as a whole. One reason the auditor can express an opinion is that an assessment of the internal controls over financial reporting is mandatory in an audit of financial statements. However, in a compilation or a review, an assessment of internal controls is not required (AR 100.04).

COMPILATION AND REVIEW
REPORTING OBLIGATIONS

The accountant's report communicates the extent of the responsibility being assumed, or the disclaimer of any responsibility, with respect to financial statements with which the accountant is associated. Compilation and review standards require that an accountant issue a report whenever financial statements of a nonpublic entity have been compiled or reviewed in compliance with standards for such services. Further, an accountant may not issue any report on unaudited financial statements of a nonpublic entity, or may not submit such financial statements to clients or others, unless the accountant has complied with standards for a compilation or a review (AR 100.05–.07).

> *OBSERVATION: A SSARS Interpretation entitled "Submitting Draft Financial Statements" (September 1990) states that the accountant should not submit draft financial statements if the accountant does not plan to complete the compilation or review engagement in a manner consistent with SSARS. When the accountant plans to complete the engagement in accordance with SSARS, draft financial statements may be submitted, but each page of the financial statements should be labeled "Working Draft" or some similar terminology. A draft of the accountant's anticipated report need not accompany the draft financial statements. The Interpretation notes that if the accountant originally intended to complete the engagement and submitted draft financial statements to the client but did not subsequently complete the engagement, it may be appropriate to document in the workpapers the reason for not completing the engagement (AR 9100.61–.62).*

Pencil copies of financial statements prepared solely for internal use of management by the accountant should include an appropriate compilation or review report. Moreover, financial statements or information completed on prescribed forms, such as those requested by regulatory and credit agencies, may not be prepared and issued unless the accountant (auditor) attaches to the prescribed form a compilation, review, or audit report (AR 100.05–.07).

> *OBSERVATION: A SSARS Interpretation entitled "Reporting on the Highest Level of Service" (December 1979) states that if an accountant has both compiled and reviewed a client's financial statements for a review engagement, only the review report should be issued. However, if the accountant had been engaged only to perform a compilation, then the auditor is not obligated to issue the review report, unless the client decides to upgrade the engagement to a review (AR 9100.06–.08).*
>
> *If an accountant is engaged to compile interim-period financial statements and also to review the financial statements for another period that ends on the same date, the accountant may issue both reports (AR 100.06–.12).*

All financial statements prepared under a comprehensive basis of accounting other than GAAP must include adequate disclosure describing the basis of accounting used. If the basis is not disclosed in a footnote or on each page of the financial statements, then it must be disclosed in the accountant's compilation or review report (AR 100.20).

> **OBSERVATION:** *For a complete discussion on "comprehensive basis of accounting other than GAAP," refer to the chapter entitled "Auditor's Special Reports."*

Association with financial statements An accountant's name should not be used in a document that includes a nonpublic client's unaudited financial statements unless the accountant performs a compilation or a review, and prepares an appropriate report to accompany the financial statements. Alternatively, unaudited financial statements that have not been reviewed or compiled may include the name of the accountant if the client indicates the following on the financial statements (AR 100.06):

- The accountant did not compile or review the financial statements.
- The accountant assumes no responsibility for the statements.

This notation may appear on each financial statement or on a separate page as a preface to the financial statements (AR 100.06).

Reference to accountant's report Each page of compiled or reviewed financial statements should be marked (1) "See accountant's compilation report" or (2) "See accountant's review report." If both compilation and review services are involved, the reference might state "See accountant's report" (AR 100.16 and .34).

Dating of accountant's report Reports should be dated at the time substantially all the compilation or review procedures are completed in the field. That date may be prior to the accounting firm's supervisory review of the accountant's work. However, if the quality control review results in significant additional work to be performed at the client's premises, it may be appropriate to change the report date. Dual dating may be used, when necessary, for a compilation or a review report. Dual dating arises when information disclosed in a note to the financial statements is of a date different from the date of the accountant's report. In other words, the accountant's report may refer to one date for most of the financial statement content and to one or more different dates for other specific items in the financial statements. For example, an accountant's report may be dated May 31, 19X1, except for footnote 10, which is dated June 15, 19X1 (AR 100.15 and .33).

If an accountant discovers that his or her name has been used without consent in connection with unaudited financial statements, the accountant should take whatever action is necessary to prevent the further use of his or her name. That may require consulting with legal counsel (AR 100.06).

REPORTING ON A COMPILATION

The accountant's report, which should accompany financial statements that have been compiled, but not reviewed or audited, should state that (AR 100.14):

1. A compilation has been performed.
2. A compilation is limited to presenting information that is the representation of management or owners in the form of financial statements.
3. The accountant has not audited or reviewed the statements and expresses no opinion or any assurance on them.

The compilation report should make no reference to GAAP or to its consistent application. Furthermore, any additional procedures that may have been performed should not be described in the accountant's report (AR 100.14).

> *OBSERVATION: The accountant would refer to GAAP only when the report is modified to disclose any departure from GAAP. The accountant would refer to consistent application of GAAP only when the report is modified to disclose an inconsistency that is not disclosed in a note to the financial statements.*

The following is the recommended form for an accountant's report on a compilation of financial statements (AR 100.17).

We have compiled the accompanying balance sheet of ABC Company as of December 31, 19XX, and the related statements of income, retained earnings, and cash flows for the year then ended, in accordance with Statements on Standards for Accounting and Review Services issued by the American Institute of Certified Public Accountants.

A compilation is limited to presenting in the form of financial statements information that is the representation of management. We have not audited or reviewed the accompanying financial statements and, accordingly, do not express an opinion or any other form of assurance on them.

Compilation Report Modifications

An accountant's report on a compilation of financial statements may have to be modified under some circumstances. The following circumstances may require a modification of the accountant's compilation report:

- Substantial omission of disclosures
- When accountant is not independent
- Departure from GAAP
- Inadequate disclosure
- Uncertainty and going concern
- Inconsistency
- Comprehensive basis of accounting other than GAAP

Substantial omission of disclosures If requested by the client, an accountant may compile financial statements that omit substantially all disclosures required by GAAP. Such disclosures include those often found in the body of the financial statements, such as (AR 100.19):

- Inventories by type (raw materials, work in process, finished goods)
- Property by major classes
- Capital stock authorized, issued, and outstanding

Required disclosures may be omitted only if the accountant believes that the omissions are not intended to mislead any persons who may reasonably be expected to use the financial statements. If the required disclosures are omitted, the accountant's compilation report must clearly indicate the omissions (AR 100.19).

> *OBSERVATION: A SSARS Interpretation entitled "Withdrawal from Compilation or Review Engagement" (August 1981) states that if the accountant concludes that a client's departures from GAAP are intended intentionally to mislead users of the financial*

statements, the accountant should withdraw from the engagement (AR 9100.18–.22).

The accountant must carefully evaluate the reasons for the omission of required disclosures. Management's apparent reasons for the omissions and the intended purpose of the financial statements must be included in the accountant's evaluation.

> **OBSERVATION:** *If the accountant is aware that the compiled financial statements will be used to obtain financing or to sell the business and if there are significant liens on major assets, such as accounts receivable or property, or significant contingent liabilities, which will not be disclosed, the accountant must consider the propriety of issuing a compilation report on financial statements without adequate disclosure of such matters. It also may be necessary to consider the effects of subsequent events, such as the loss of a major customer. Such events may have to be disclosed.*

If the financial statements include some notes and the accountant has concluded that required disclosures may be omitted, the notes should be labeled "Selected information—substantially all disclosures required by generally accepted accounting principles are not included." The compilation report also should be modified by the addition of a third paragraph disclosing the omissions (AR 100.19).

A similar situation arises when the statement of cash flows is omitted from a presentation that includes a balance sheet, a statement of income, and a statement of retained earnings. Under GAAP, a statement of cash flows is a required statement, and reference to such omission must be made in the accountant's compilation report. The following is the recommended third paragraph that should be added to the accountant's compilation report when disclosures and/or a statement of cash flows is omitted (AR 100.21).

Management has elected to omit substantially all the disclosures (and the statement of cash flows) required by generally accepted accounting principles. If the omitted disclosures were included in the financial statements, they might influence the user's conclusions about the Company's financial position, results of operations, and cash flows. Accordingly, these financial statements are not designed for those who are not informed about such matters.

If only the statement of cash flows is omitted, the third paragraph should read:

A statement of cash flows for the year ended December 31, 19XX, has not been presented. Generally accepted accounting principles require that such a statement be presented when financial statements purport to present financial position and results of operations.

> **OBSERVATION:** *A SSARS Interpretation entitled "Reporting on Financial Statements That Previously Did Not Omit Substantially All Disclosures" (November 1980) states that if financial statements that omit substantially all disclosures are compiled from financial statements the accountant had previously audited, the report on the newly issued comparative compiled financial statements should indicate whether the accountant's opinion is qualified, adverse, or disclaimed, and the principal reasons for such opinion. Similarly, if the accountant issued a modified compilation or review report on financial statements that previously did not omit disclosures, the newly issued comparative compilation report should include a discussion of any modifications (AR 9200.01–.04).*

> **OBSERVATION:** *A SSARS Interpretation entitled "Reporting When Management Has Elected to Omit Substantially All Disclosures" (May 1982) encourages the use of the phrase "management has elected to omit substantially all of the disclosures" to make it obvious that it was management's decision, rather than the accountant's decision, to omit the required information. Other phrases may be used if the report clearly indicates that management has made the decision to omit the information. However, the phrase "the financial statements do not include substantially all of the disclosures" should not be used (AR 9100.29–.30).*

When accountant is not independent   An accountant who is not independent with respect to an entity may compile financial statements for such an entity and issue a compilation report thereon. In this circumstance, the accountant adds the following paragraph to the standard compilation report: "We are not independent with respect to Company X" (AR 100.22).

OBSERVATION: *The reason for the lack of independence should* *not* *be included in the accountant's report. Giving a reason could encourage the reader to make her or his own judgment regarding whether the auditor's reason is appropriate (AR 100.22).*

Departure from GAAP During any type of engagement, the accountant may become aware that the financial statements are not in conformity with GAAP, which require adequate disclosure. The acceptability and procedures of omitting substantially all disclosures and/or the statement of cash flows in a compilation of financial statements has been discussed. The omission of substantially all disclosures and/or the statement of cash flows, although such omissions constitute a departure from GAAP, is permitted in a compilation because of the special disclosure provisions. In any other departure from GAAP, however, the accountant should recommend that the financial statements be revised to conform to GAAP. If the client does not agree to revise the financial statements, the accountant must consider whether to modify the compilation report or to withdraw from the engagement and provide no further services to the client regarding the financial statements. In this event, it may be advisable for the accountant to consult with legal counsel (AR 100.39).

If the accountant decides that a modification to the compilation report is adequate to disclose the departure from GAAP, the report should be modified in the following manner (AR 100.40):

- The second paragraph of the standard compilation report should be expanded to include a statement that the accountant has become aware of a departure or departures from GAAP.

- The departure or departures should be described in a separate paragraph.

- The effect of the departure or departures on the financial statements should be disclosed if such effects are known because of determination by management or because of procedures completed by the accountant. If the effects are not known, the accountant is not required to determine them. The accountant must, however, include a statement in the compilation report that the effects of the departure or departures have not been determined.

The following is an example of an accountant's compilation report that has been modified to disclose a departure from GAAP.

We have compiled the accompanying balance sheet of ABC Company as of December 31, 19XX, and the related statements of income, retained earnings, and cash flows for the year then ended, in accordance with Statements on Standards for Accounting and Review Services issued by the American Institute of Certified Public Accountants.

A compilation is limited to presenting in the form of financial statements information that is the representation of management. We have not audited or reviewed the accompanying financial statements and, accordingly, do not express an opinion or any other form of assurance on them. However, we did become aware of a departure from generally accepted accounting principles that is described in the following paragraph.

As disclosed in note X to the financial statements, generally accepted accounting principles require that land and building be stated at cost. Management has informed us that the Company has stated its land and building at appraised value and that, if generally accepted accounting principles had been followed, the land and building accounts and stockholders' equity would have been decreased by $800,000.

> **OBSERVATION:** *Compilation reports should be modified appropriately when the accountant disagrees with management and believes that a material uncertainty can be reasonably estimated and recognized in the financial statements. The nonrecognition of the reasonably estimated amount is a departure from GAAP.*

Inadequate disclosure Generally accepted accounting principles require that adequate disclosure be made of all pertinent information. Thus, inadequate disclosure is a departure from GAAP, and the same modification rules apply (AR 100.39).

Uncertainty and going concern GAAP require that significant uncertainties be disclosed in the financial statements. Thus, an undisclosed uncertainty requires a modification of the accountant's compilation report in the same manner as that of a departure from GAAP.

> **OBSERVATION:** *A SSARS Interpretation entitled "Reporting on Uncertainties" (December 1982) states that SAS-59 (The Auditor's Consideration of an Entity's Ability to Continue as a Going Concern) should be used as a guide when evaluating the disclosure of an uncertainty in compiled or reviewed financial statements. The Interpretation also notes that compiled financial*

statements may omit substantially all of the disclosures required by GAAP, including a disclosure of an uncertainty, no matter how significant the uncertainty may be. However, the phrase "substantial doubt about the entity's ability to continue as a going concern" (as illustrated in SAS-59) should be used only in an audit report and not in a review or compilation report that refers to the going-concern uncertainty (emphasis of a matter) (AR 9100.33–.40).

Inconsistency   A violation of the consistency standard does not require modification of the accountant's standard compilation report if the accounting change is properly accounted for and disclosed in the financial statements. However, the accountant is free to emphasize in a separate paragraph that an accounting change has occurred (AR 100.40).

Comprehensive basis of accounting other than GAAP   A compilation of financial statements may be presented on a comprehensive basis of accounting other than GAAP. The basis of the accounting used must be disclosed in the financial statements. If the basis of accounting other than GAAP is not disclosed in the financial statements, the accountant must modify the compilation report to include the disclosure of the basis of accounting used. The modification of the accountant's report is accomplished in the same manner as that for *substantial omission of disclosures,* which was discussed earlier in this chapter (AR 100.20).

> **OBSERVATION:** *A SSARS Interpretation entitled "Reporting on a Comprehensive Basis of Accounting Other Than Generally Accepted Accounting Principles" (December 1982) states that when compiled financial statements are prepared on a comprehensive basis other than GAAP and omit substantially all disclosures, the following paragraph should be added to the standard compilation report: The financial statements have been prepared on the accounting basis (describe accounting basis), which is a comprehensive basis of accounting other than generally accepted accounting principles (AR 9100.41–.45).*

Emphasis of a Matter

Regardless of the quality and quantity of disclosures for uncertainties, inconsistencies, and other disclosures, the accountant may deem it advisable to emphasize a particular matter in the compilation report (AR 100.40).

Subsequent Discovery of Facts Existing at Date of Accountant's Report

Standards for compilation services do not include any obligation that the accountant perform any procedures after the date of the compilation report. However, the accountant may become aware of information subsequent to the date of the report that may cause doubt about the accuracy or completeness of the information previously received from the client. If the new information is accurate and would have caused the accountant to modify the report or to recommend adjustments to the financial statements, the accountant should look to GAAS for guidance. Under GAAS, this situation is covered by Section 561 (Subsequent Discovery of Facts Existing at the Date of the Auditor's Report) of SAS-1 (Codification of Auditing Standards and Procedures). In applying this guidance, the accountant must keep in mind the different objectives of an audit and a compilation engagement. Because of possible legal implications, the accountant also should consider consulting with legal counsel (AR 9100.13–.15).

The following is a brief review of Section 561 of SAS-1.

Usually, an auditor has no obligation to make continuing inquiries after the date of issuance of the report. However, if an auditor becomes aware (1) of material information that would have affected the report and (2) that persons are currently relying or are likely to rely on the financial statements covered by the report, the auditor should take the following action (AU 561.06):

- The auditor should advise the client to immediately disclose the new information and its impact on the financial statements to persons currently relying or likely to rely on the financial statements.

- The auditor should issue as soon as practical revised financial statements and the new report, describing the reasons for revision.

- If financial statements, accompanied by an auditor's report for a subsequent period are imminent, the auditor may make the necessary disclosures and revisions therein.

- The auditor should advise the client, where applicable, to discuss the new disclosures or revisions with the SEC, stock exchanges, and appropriate regulatory agencies.

- The auditor must be satisfied that appropriate steps have been taken by the client.

If the client refuses to proceed as above, the auditor should notify each member of the board of directors that such refusal has been made and, in the absence of disclosure by the client, that the auditor will take the following steps to prevent further reliance on the report and the financial statements (AU 561.08):

- Notify the client that the report must no longer be associated with the financial statements.
- Notify, if applicable, any regulatory agencies involved that the report should no longer be relied on.
- Notify persons known to be relying or likely to rely on the financial statements that the report should no longer be relied on.

The above notifications should contain the following (AU 561.09):

- A description of the effect that the discovered information would have had on the auditor's report on the financial statements
- Information that is as precise and factual as possible

If the client has refused to cooperate, and as a result the auditor is unable to conduct an adequate investigation of the information, the auditor's disclosure needs to state only that information has come to his or her attention and that if the information is true, the report should no longer be relied on or be associated with the financial statements (AU 561.09).

The auditor should use professional judgment in the circumstances described above, and a consultation with legal counsel may be advisable (AU 561.02).

> **OBSERVATION:** *A SSARS Interpretation entitled "Discovery of Information After the Date of the Accountant's Report" (November 1980) states that if the accountant knows that the financial statements should be revised because of discovery of information after the date of the report, the accountant should follow the general guidance established by SAS-1, Section 561 (AR 9100.13–.15).*

Supplementary Information

In many cases, financial statements reported on by accountants will include supplementary information such as (AR 100.43):

1. Details of balance sheet accounts, such as aging of accounts receivable or inventory by product lines
2. Details of cost of sales and/or operating expenses
3. Sales analysis

Supplementary information that is not part of the client's basic financial statements may be compiled, depending on the requirements of the engagement as specified in the engagement letter or on the understanding with the client. When the client has requested that the supplementary information be compiled, the accountant should clearly indicate in the compilation report that the information has been part of the engagement. Alternatively, the accountant can issued a separate compilation report on the supplementary information.

When the engagement does not include compiling supplementary information, there should be no chance that readers of the financial statements will misunderstand the responsibility of the accountant. Misunderstanding may be avoided by (1) the client clearly stating (positioned as a preamble to the supplementary information) that the supplementary information has not been compiled by the accountant or (2) the accountant adding a separate paragraph stating that the supplementary information has not been compiled (AR 100.43).

Financial Statements Included in Certain Prescribed Forms

In December 1981, the AICPA Accounting and Review Services Committee issued SSARS-3 (Compilation Reports on Financial Statements Included in Certain Prescribed Forms.) The purpose of SSARS-3 is to emphasize that the accountant's reporting responsibility extends to the compilation or review of financial statements included in a prescribed form. Also, the Statement provides an alternative report format when the prescribed form or related instructions call for departures from GAAP (or from a comprehensive basis of accounting other than GAAP). Thus, when a prescribed form is designed with material departures from GAAP, the accountant may (1) issue the standard compilation report with a description of the departures from GAAP or (2) issue the report described in SSARS-3, which makes no reference to the specific departures from GAAP (AR 300.01).

A prescribed form is any "standard form designed or adopted by the body to which it is to be submitted." A form designed or adopted by the client is not considered to be a prescribed form. Prescribed forms include financial statement formats used by industry trade associations, banks, and regulatory authorities (AR 300.02).

> *OBSERVATION:* *A Business Credit Information Package (BCIP) has been developed by the Robert Morris Associates (association of bank lending officers) and the AICPA to be used by nonpublic businesses requesting loans from financial institutions. The BCIP includes, among other documents, a prescribed form for the preparation of financial statements that does not require all GAAP disclosures. This form of financial statement presentation falls within the requirements established by SSARS-3.*

SSARS-3 adopts the basic philosophy that a body that prescribes a form for financial statements has defined the requirements sufficiently to meet its informational needs. Thus, except when an audit report or review report has been requested, the accountant's compilation report need not refer to departures from generally accepted accounting principles (including disclosure). The following report is an example of a compilation report on financial statements included in a prescribed form that specifies measurement principles that do not conform to GAAP (AR 300.03).

We have compiled the accompanying balance sheet of X Company as of December 31, 19X5, and the related statements of income, retained earnings, and cash flows for the year then ended included in the accompanying prescribed form in accordance with Statements on Standards for Accounting and Review Services issued by the American Institute of Certified Public Accountants.

Our compilation was limited to the presentation of information that is the representation of management in the form prescribed by the West Virginia Fine Arts Commission. We have not audited or reviewed the financial statements referred to above and, accordingly, do not express an opinion or any other form of assurance on them.

These financial statements (including related disclosures) are presented in accordance with the requirements of the West Virginia Fine Arts Commission, which differ from generally accepted accounting principles. Accordingly, these financial statements are not designed for those who are not informed about such differences.

OBSERVATION: A SSARS Interpretation entitled "Omission of Disclosures in Financial Statements Included in Certain Prescribed Forms" (May 1982) states that an accountant may, in a compilation report on financial statements included in a prescribed form, refer to the review report previously issued on the financial statements if the difference between the previously reviewed financial statements and the financial statements included in the prescribed form is limited to the omission of disclosures not required by the form. The following sentence might be added to the third paragraph presented above: These financial statements were compiled by us from financial statements for the same period that we previously reviewed, as indicated in our report dated February 12, 19X6 (AR 9300.01–.03).

During the performance of the compilation, the accountant may discover departures from generally accepted accounting principles not sanctioned by the prescribed form or related instructions. Also, the accountant may discover departures from the prescribed format or instructions. In either case, such a departure requires that the accountant modify the compilation report by including a separate paragraph that describes the departure (AR 300.04).

REPORTING ON A REVIEW

The accountant's report on a review of financial statements should contain the following statements (AR 100.32):

1. A review has been performed in accordance with Statements on Standards for Accounting and Review Services issued by the American Institute of Certified Public Accountants.

2. All of the information in the financial statements is the representation of the management or owners of the entity.

3. A review consists principally of inquiries and analytical procedures.

4. A review is substantially less in scope than an audit, and no opinion is expressed.

5. On the basis of a review, the accountant is not aware of any material modifications that should be made to the financial statements in order for them to be in conformity with GAAP, except for those modifications, if any, described in the report.

Any additional procedures that may have been performed should not be described in the accountant's review report, and no reference should be made to GAAP or to its consistent application (AR 100.32).

The following is the recommended form for an accountant's report on a review of financial statements (AR 100.35).

We have reviewed the accompanying balance sheet of ABC, Inc., as of December 31, 19XX, and the related statements of income, retained earnings, and cash flows for the year then ended, in accordance with Statements on Standards for Accounting and Review Services issued by the American Institute of Certified Public Accountants. All information included in these financial statements is the representation of ABC, Inc.

A review consists principally of inquiries of company personnel and analytical procedures applied to financial data. It is substantially less in scope than an examination in accordance with generally accepted auditing standards, the objective of which is the expression of an opinion regarding the financial statements taken as a whole. Accordingly, we do not express such an opinion.

On the basis of our review, we are not aware of any material modifications that should be made to the accompanying financial statements in order for them to be in conformity with generally accepted accounting principles.

Incomplete Review

A review report may not be issued if the review procedures deemed necessary by the accountant have not been completed to his or her satisfaction. In such situations, there is no adequate basis for expressing the limited assurance contemplated by a review. Moreover, the circumstances may be such that the accountant may not issue a compilation report. Information obtained by an accountant during the performance of an incomplete review cannot be ignored if the engagement is reduced to a compilation (AR 100.36).

When determining whether to issue a compilation report where a review is incomplete, the accountant should consider the same points that would be considered when an engagement is changed from a higher service level to a lower service level (AR 100.44–.49).

Review standards require that an accountant perform whatever additional procedures deemed necessary under the circumstances. Additional procedures may include corresponding with the client's legal counsel or confirming balances and transactions. If the client will not agree to such correspondence or will not sign a representation letter, there is a scope limitation, which usually is considered to be of such significance that the accountant should not issue a review report (AR 100.36).

Accountant's Independence

An accountant who is not independent of a client may not issue a review report on the financial statements of that client (AR 100.38).

Rule 101 of the Code of Professional Conduct states, "A member in public practice shall be independent in the performance of professional services as required by standards promulgated by bodies designated by Council." Since no opinion is expressed in a compilation report, the requirement that the accountant be independent does not apply. However, in a review report the accountant is providing negative assurance, and Rule 101 of the Code of Professional Conduct applies (AR 100.38).

Review Report Modifications

An accountant's report on a review of financial statements may have to be modified under some circumstances. The following circumstances may or may not require a modification of the accountant's review report:

1. Departure from GAAP
2. Inadequate disclosure
3. Uncertainty
4. Inconsistency
5. Comprehensive basis of accounting other than GAAP

Departure from GAAP During a review of financial statements, the accountant may become aware of a departure from GAAP. In this case the accountant should recommend that the financial statements be appropriately revised to conform with GAAP. If the client does not agree to revise the financial statements, the accountant must consider whether to modify the review report or to withdraw from the engagement. If the accountant decides to withdraw from the engagement, it may be advisable for him or her to consult with legal counsel (AR 100.39).

If the accountant decides that a modification to the review report is sufficient to disclose the departure from GAAP, the report should read as follows (AR 100.40):

We have reviewed the accompanying balance sheet of ABC, Inc., as of October 31, 19XX, and the related statements of income, retained earnings, and cash flows for the year then ended, in accordance with Statements on Standards for Accounting and Review Services issued by the American Institute of Certified Public Accountants. All information included in these financial statements is the representation of the management of ABC, Inc.

A review consists principally of inquiries of company personnel and analytical procedures applied to financial data. It is substantially less in scope than an examination in accordance with generally accepted auditing standards, the objective of which is the expression of an opinion regarding the financial statements taken as a whole. Accordingly, we do not express such an opinion.

Based on our review, with the exception of the matter described in the following paragraph, we are not aware of any material modifications that should be made to the accompanying financial statements in order for them to be in conformity with generally accepted accounting principles.

As disclosed in note X to the financial statements, generally accepted accounting principles require that inventory cost consist of material, labor, and overhead. Management has informed us that the inventory of finished goods in the accompanying financial statements is stated at material and direct labor cost only. The effects of this departure from generally accepted accounting principles on financial position, results of operations, and cash flows have not been determined by management.

---

*OBSERVATION: A SSARS Interpretation entitled "Omission of Disclosures in Reviewed Financial Statements" (December 1979) states that if the client declines to include **substantially** all the required disclosures in reviewed financial statements, the accountant should not accept an engagement to review the financial statements (AR 9100.01–.02).*

Inadequate disclosure GAAP require that adequate disclosure be made of all pertinent information. Inadequate disclosure in a review of financial information is a departure from GAAP, and the same modification rules for a departure from GAAP apply (AR 100.39).

Uncertainty   GAAP require that significant uncertainties be disclosed appropriately in the financial statements. If the uncertainties are appropriately disclosed in the financial statements, the accountant's review report does not have to be modified. If, however, an uncertainty is not appropriately disclosed in the financial statements, the accountant's review report must be modified in the same manner as that of a departure from GAAP (AR 100.40).

Inconsistency   A violation of the consistency standard does not require modification of the accountant's standard review report if the accounting change is properly accounted for and disclosed in the financial statements. However, the accountant is free to emphasize in a separate paragraph that an accounting change has occurred (AR 100.40).

Comprehensive basis of accounting other than GAAP   A review of financial statements may be presented on a comprehensive basis of accounting other than GAAP. However, the basis of accounting used must be clearly disclosed in the financial statements. If the basis of accounting other than GAAP is not clearly disclosed in the financial statements, the accountant must modify the review report to include disclosure of the basis of accounting that is used.

Emphasis of a Matter

The accountant may conclude that a particular item or matter should be emphasized in a separate paragraph of the review report (AR 100.40).

Inadequacy of Report Modification

The deficiencies in the financial statements, taken as a whole, may be so significant that the accountant concludes that modification of the report would be inadequate. Under these circumstances, the accountant has little choice but to withdraw from the engagement and to consider consulting with legal counsel (AR 100.41).

Subsequent Discovery of Facts Existing at Date of Accountant's Report

Standards for review services do not include any obligation for the accountant to perform any procedures after the date of the review report. However, the accountant may become aware of information subsequent to the date of the report that confirms that the financial statements are inaccurate or incomplete, and the review report should be modified. Under these circumstances, the accountant should refer to Section 561 (Subsequent Discovery of Facts Existing at the Date of the Auditor's Report) of SAS-1 for guidance (AR 100.42).

> *OBSERVATION: A SSARS Interpretation entitled "Discovery of Information After the Date of the Accountant's Report" (November 1980) states that if the accountant knows that the financial statements should be revised because of discovery of information after the date of the report, the accountant should follow the general guidance established by SAS-1, Section 561 (AR 9100.13–.15).*

Supplementary Information

Basic financial statements include descriptions of accounting policies, notes, and additional material specifically identified as part of the basic financial statements. All information that is part of the client's basic financial statements must be either compiled or reviewed according to SSARS (AR 100.43).

Information that is not part of the client's basic financial statements may be reviewed or compiled depending on the requirements of the review engagement as specified in the engagement letter, or based on the understanding with the client (AR 100.43).

Supplementary information compiled or reviewed   When the client has requested that the supplementary information be compiled or reviewed, the accountant should follow the appropriate compilation or review procedures (AR 100.43).

If the supplementary information has been compiled, the accountant's report should clearly state so in the first paragraph of the compilation report. Alternatively, the accountant can issue a separate compilation report on the supplementary information (AR 100.43).

If the supplementary information has been reviewed, the accountant may state so in the review report or issue a separate report on the supplementary information. In either case, the accountant's review report should state the following (AR 100.43):

- That the review was made primarily for the purpose of expressing limited assurance that there are no material modifications that should be made to the financial statements in order for them to be in conformity with GAAP.

- That the other data accompanying the financial statements are presented only for supplementary analysis and have been subjected to the inquiry and analytical procedures applied in the review of the basic financial statements, and the accountant is not aware of any material modifications that should be made to this data.

Supplementary information not compiled or reviewed When the engagement does not include a compilation or review of the supplementary information, the accountant does not have a responsibility to compile or review the information. To reasonably ensure that the role of the accountant is not misunderstood with respect to the supplementary information, the accountant may (1) have the client clearly state (positioned as a preface to the supplementary information) that the supplementary information has not been compiled or reviewed by the accountant or (2) add a separate paragraph stating that the supplementary information has not been compiled or reviewed (AR 100.43).

WITHDRAWING FROM AN ENGAGEMENT

An accountant may decided to withdraw from an engagement before the engagement is completed. Withdrawing from an engagement may expose the accountant to legal liability and for this reason it generally is prudent to consult legal counsel. SSARS-1 specifically states that the accountant should withdraw from an engagement under the following circumstances:

- The accountant is not independent and the client requires reviewed financial statements (AR 100.22).

- The scope of the engagement has substantial limitations (AR 100.36).

- The client has not allowed the accountant to correspond with its legal counsel or has not signed the client representation letter and is requesting a reduction in the level of services offered (either from an audit to a review or from a review to compilation) (AR 100.47).

- The accountant is aware of client-supplied information that is "incorrect, incomplete, or otherwise unsatisfactory," and the client has refused or is unable to provide revised information (AR 100.12 and .29).

- The accountant believes that disclosures were omitted for the purpose of misleading users (AR 100.19).

- The accountant has not (or cannot) obtain sufficient knowledge of the client's business or industry as required for a compilation engagement (AR 100.10).

- The financial statements contain departures from GAAP that cannot be adequately communicated to users in the modified accountant's report (AR 100.41).

CHANGE IN ENGAGEMENT

During, but before the completion of, an engagement, a client may request that the level of service performed by the accountant be changed. If the request for change in services is from a lower level to a higher level, for example, from a review to an audit or from a compilation to a review, no problem arises. A problem does arise, however, when the change is to a level of service lower than that which was being provided. The client may request a change to a lower level of service for many different reasons. Some of the reasons are as follows (AR 100.44–.45):

1. An audit or review may no longer be required or be applicable because of a change in circumstances.

2. The client may have misunderstood the type of service that was being rendered or is not aware of the other levels of service that the accountant can render.

3. A restriction on the scope of the examination may be imposed by the client or by others.

Before agreeing to change to a lower level of service, the accountant carefully must consider the client's reason for the change and all other factors related to the change. Elimination of the requirement for an audit or a review or a misunderstanding of the type of services the accountant can provide ordinarily would be considered a reasonable basis for the accountant to accept a change in the engagement. The accountant should, however, evaluate a restriction on the scope of the examination for the possibility that information affected by the scope restriction may be incorrect, incomplete, or otherwise unsatisfactory. The restriction may preclude an accountant from issuing a review or compilation report because he or she may be unable to satisfy the standards established by Statements on Standards for Accounting and Review Services. Moreover, the accountant may consider the restrictions so severe that a review or compilation report cannot be issued (AR 100.46–.47).

If in an audit engagement the client prohibits the accountant from obtaining information from the client's legal counsel, the accountant ordinarily should not issue a compilation or review report on the financial statements. If in an audit or review engagement the client refuses to provide a client representation letter, the accountant should not issue a review report (when stepping down from an audit) on the financial statements and generally should not issue a compilation report (when stepping down from a review) on the financial statements (AR 100.47).

If in the accountant's judgment a change to a lower level of service is acceptable, the accountant should perform the service in accordance with the standards applicable to the changed engagement. The accountant should make no mention in the report of the original engagement, any procedures accomplished for the original engagement, or any scope limitation that resulted in the changed service (AR 100.49).

REPORTING ON
COMPARATIVE FINANCIAL STATEMENTS

Comparative financial statements are defined as "financial statements of two or more periods presented in columnar form." The *periods* may be other than annual, such as the three months (quarter) ended March 31, 19X9 (current period), compared to the three months ended March 31, 19X8 (prior period). The statements may cover more than two periods; for example, statements for the five years ended May 31, 19XX. However, each type of financial statement (for example, balance sheet, statement of income) for all periods presented must be on the same page in columnar form. The columns may be in vertical or horizontal format (AR 200.07).

When financial statements of more than one period are presented in columnar form, the accountant must report on all periods presented. A reissued report is one that has been issued subsequent to the date of the original report but with its original date. A reissued report should be dual-dated if it is revised for specific events. An updated report is issued by a continuing accountant and bears the same date as the current report. It may or may not contain the same conclusions reached in the original report and should consider information that the accountant becomes aware of during the current engagement (AR 200.02 and .07).

Financial statements that have been compiled, reviewed, or audited and that are accompanied by appropriate reports may not be presented in columnar form with financial statements that are not compiled, reviewed, or audited. In such cases, the accountant should advise the client that the report and his or her name should not be used in connection with such comparative financial statements. In other words, the accountant may not report on client-prepared comparative financial statements containing statements that were not compiled, reviewed, or audited and statements that were compiled, reviewed, or audited. However, the client-prepared statements may be presented on a separate page of a document that includes, on another separate page of the same document, the accountant's compiled, reviewed, or audited financial statements. In this event, each page of the client-prepared statements must bear a comment that the accountant has not compiled, reviewed, or audited the statements and assumes no responsibility for them (AR 200.03).

Substantially all disclosures may be omitted in compiled financial statements. It is inappropriate for an accountant to issue reviewed or audited financial statements that omit substantially all disclosures. Thus, only when all periods are compiled and all periods omit substantially all disclosures, can an accountant report on comparative financial statements that omit substantially all disclosures (AR 200.05).

All Periods Compiled or Reviewed

When periods presented in comparative financial statements are either all compiled or all reviewed, the continuing accountant should update the report on the prior period, or periods, and issue it as part of the report on the current period. An example of a report on all periods compiled is presented below (AR 200.09).

We have compiled the accompanying balance sheets of ABC Company as of March 31, 19X2 and 19X1, and the related statements of income, retained earnings, and cash flows for the years then ended, in accordance with Statements on Standards for Accounting and Review Services issued by the American Institute of Certified Public Accountants.

A compilation is limited to presenting in the form of financial statements information that is the representation of management. We have not audited or reviewed the accompanying financial statements and, accordingly, do not express an opinion or any other form of assurance on them.

An example of a report on all periods reviewed is presented below (AR 200.09).

We have reviewed the accompanying balance sheets of ABC Company as of December 31, 19X2 and 19X1, and the related statements of income, retained earnings, and cash flows for the years then ended, in accordance with Statements on Standards for Accounting and Review Services issued by the American Institute of Certified Public Accountants. All information included in these financial statements is the representation of the management of ABC Company.

A review consists principally of inquiries of company personnel and analytical procedures applied to financial data. It is substantially less in scope than an examination in accordance with generally accepted auditing standards, the objective of which is the expression of an opinion regarding the financial statements taken as a whole. Accordingly, we do not express such an opinion.

Based on our reviews, we are not aware of any material modifications that should be made to the accompanying financial statements in order for them to be in conformity with generally accepted accounting principles.

Current Period Reviewed—Prior Period Compiled

When the accountant performs a level of service in the current period that is higher than that performed in the prior period, he or she should update the report on the prior period, or periods, and issue it as the last paragraph of the report on the current period.

An example of the standard report in this situation follows (AR 200.10).

We have reviewed the accompanying balance sheet of ABC Company as of December 31, 19X2, and the related statements of income, retained earnings, and cash flows for the year then ended, in accordance with Statements on Standards for Accounting and Review Services issued by the American Institute of Certified Public Accountants. All information included in these financial statements is the representation of the management of ABC Company.

A review consists principally of inquiries of company personnel and analytical procedures applied to financial data. It is substantially less in scope than an examination in accordance with generally accepted auditing standards, the objective of which is the expression of an opinion regarding the financial statements taken as a whole. Accordingly, we do not express such an opinion.

Based on our review, we are not aware of any material modifications that should be made to the 19X2 financial statements in order for them to be in conformity with generally accepted accounting principles.

The accompanying 19X1 financial statements of ABC Company were compiled by us. A compilation is limited to presenting in the form of financial statements information that is the representation of management. We have not audited or reviewed the 19X1 financial statements and, accordingly, do not express an opinion or any other form of assurance on them.

Current Period Compiled—Prior Period Reviewed

When the accountant performs a level of service in the current period that is lower than that of the prior period, he or she may report on such comparative financial statements by (1) issuing two separate reports, (2) issuing a compilation report on the current period and adding a last paragraph for the prior period, or (3) issuing a combined compilation and review report (AR 200.11).

If the accountant elects to issue two separate reports, the current period will be covered in a compilation report. The prior period will be covered in a review report bearing its original date (AR 200.11).

If the accountant elects to issue a compilation report with a last paragraph referring to the prior period, certain information must be included. The last paragraph should contain a description of the degree of responsibility the accountant is assuming for the prior period, the date of the accountant's original report, and a statement that the accountant has not performed any procedures in connection with the prior period's review after the date of the prior-period review report. An example of such an additional last paragraph follows (AR 200.12).

The accompanying 19X1 financial statements of ABC, Inc., were previously reviewed by me, and my report dated March 1, 19X2, stated that I was not aware of any material modifications that should be made to those statements in order for them to be in conformity with generally accepted accounting principles. I have not performed any procedures in connection with that review engagement after the date of my report on the 19X1 financial statements.

The combined report should include the current-period compilation report and the reissued review report for the prior period. The combined report should be dated as of the completion of the current-period compilation engagement. The report should also mention that the accountant has not performed any procedures in connection with the prior-period review report after the date of that report (AR 200.11).

Current or Prior Period Audited—Other Period Compiled or Reviewed

When current-period financial statements are audited and included with prior-period compiled or reviewed financial statements, reporting standards are provided by SAS-26 (Association with Financial Statements). When the financial statements are those of a nonpublic entity, the accountant's opinion on the current-year audited financial statements should be expanded to include a final separate paragraph describing the compilation or review of the prior-period financial statements. The separate paragraph may be worded as follows when prior-period financial statements were compiled.

The 19X1 financial statements were compiled by us, and our report thereon, dated January 31, 19X2, stated that we did not audit or review those financial statements and, accordingly, express no opinion or other form of assurance on them.

The separate paragraph may be worded as follows when prior-period financial statements were reviewed.

The 19X1 financial statements were reviewed by us, and our report thereon, dated January 31, 19X2, stated that we were not aware of any material modifications that should be made to those statements for them to be in conformity with generally accepted accounting principles. However, a review is substantially less in scope than an audit and does not provide a basis for the expression of an opinion on the financial statements taken as a whole.

When the prior-period financial statements have been audited, the accountant should issue a compilation or review report on the current-period financial statements and either (1) reissue the audit report for the prior period or (2) add a separate paragraph to the current-period compilation or review report describing the responsibility assumed for the prior-period financial statements. The description paragraph should include the date of the prior-period audit report; a statement that the financial statements were previously examined; the type of opinion expressed and if the opinion was other than unqualified; the substantive reasons for the qualification; and, finally, a statement that no auditing procedures have been performed since the date of the prior-period audit report. An example of this type of paragraph follows (AR 200.29).

The financial statements for the year ended December 31, 19X1, were audited by us (other accountants) and we (they) expressed an unqualified opinion on them in our (their) report dated March 1, 19X2, but we (they) have not performed any auditing procedures since that date.

Changes in Reports of Prior Periods

Before or during the current-period engagement, a continuing accountant may become aware of information that affects the prior-period report. A modification in the prior-period report to disclose a departure from GAAP may no longer be applicable, or a modification may become necessary to disclose a departure from GAAP. In this event, the accountant's report on the prior-period statements should be expanded to include an additional separate paragraph. This separate paragraph should contain (1) the date of the original report, (2) the reasons for the change in the original report, and (3) if applicable, a statement to the effect that the prior-period financial statements have been changed. An example of such an explanatory paragraph follows (AR 200.13–.15).

In my previous review report, dated March 1, 19X2, on the 19X1 financial statements, I referred to a departure from generally accepted accounting principles because the Company carried its land at appraised values. However, as disclosed in note X, the Company has restated its 19X1 financial statements to reflect its land at cost in accordance with generally accepted accounting principles.

If the revised report is reissued (issued separately from the report on the current financial statements), it should be dual-dated. The second date should be the date when substantially all the information that resulted in the revision of the report was obtained. This date may be the same date as that used for the current year's report.

Prior Period, or Periods, Compiled or Reviewed by Other Accountants

Predecessor accountant reissues unchanged report   The successor accountant should consider the provisions of SSARS-4 (Communication Between Predecessor and Successor Accountants) when communicating with the predecessor accountant (auditor) and when determining the types of communications that are appropriate under the circumstances. SSARS-4 indicates that the successor accountant should obtain the permission of the client before communicating with the predecessor accountant (AR 400).

A predecessor accountant is not required to reissue a compilation or review report. The predecessor accountant may, however, reissue the report on prior-period financial statements at the client's request, if the accountant makes satisfactory arrangements with the former client and complies with the following provisions before reissuing the report (AR 200.20–.21):

1. Evaluates whether the prior-period report is still appropriate by considering (a) the form and style of the report presentation, (b) the effects of any subsequent events, and (c) as a result of changes, whether a modification is required or should be deleted

2. Reads the current-period financial statements and accompanying accountant's report

3. Compares the prior-period financial statements to previously issued financial statements and the financial statements of the current period

4. Obtains a letter from the current accountant stating that he or she is (is not) aware of any matter that might have a material effect on the prior-period financial statements

If, as a result of the above procedures, the predecessor accountant becomes aware of information that may affect the prior-period report on the financial statements, he or she should perform (1) procedures similar to those that would have been performed if the accountant had been aware of such information during the prior engagement and (2) any other procedures considered necessary under the circumstances. Because of the seriousness of the situation, the procedures may include discussion with the successor accountant and review of pertinent portions of the current-period workpapers. If the predecessor accountant cannot complete the necessary procedures, he or she should not reissue the report on the prior-period financial statements. Under these circumstances, the predecessor accountant may consider the need to consult with legal counsel regarding appropriate action (AR 200.22).

> **OBSERVATION:** *The situation may be such that the predecessor accountant should consider the guidance provided to an auditor when there is a subsequent discovery of facts existing at the date of the accountant's report (SAS-1).*

After performing the required procedures, if the predecessor accountant is not aware of any information that would require restatement or revision of the prior-period report, the accountant should reissue the report on the former client's request. The reissued report should be dated as it was originally. No reference should be made to any procedures performed, including the representation letter from the current accountant and the report on the current period, which will be issued by the successor accountant (AR 200.23).

Predecessor accountant issues changed report   After following the prescribed procedures, the predecessor accountant may determine that a prior-period report cannot be reissued exactly as it was originally. In this event, the prior-period report and/or financial statements should be appropriately revised, and the report should contain a separate explanatory paragraph. The separate explanatory paragraph should disclose (1) the date of the original report and the date of the revised report, if different, (2) all of the substantive reasons for the change to the original report, and (3) if applicable, a statement to the effect that the financial statements of the prior period have been changed. Before issuing a revised report, the predecessor accountant should obtain a written representation from the former client covering the following (AR 200.22–.23):

1. Complete details on any newly obtained information and its effect on the prior-period financial statements
2. The former client's understanding, if any, of the effects of the new information on the predecessor's report

Predecessor accountant's report not reissued   A predecessor accountant may decide not to reissue the original prior-period report and not to issue any changed report on the prior period. In this event, the successor accountant should either (1) refer to the report of the predecessor accountant in the current report or (2) compile, review, or audit the prior-period financial statements (AR 200.17).

If the predecessor accountant's report is not to be reissued and the successor accountant is not engaged to compile, review, or audit the prior-period financial statements, the successor accountant should expand the report on the current period to include a separate paragraph containing the following information:

1. Without naming the prior-period accountants, a statement that the prior-period financial statements were compiled, reviewed, or audited by other accountants (auditors)
2. The date of the prior-period report
3. A description of the form of disclaimer, limited assurance, or other opinion given in the prior-period report
4. Quotation or description of any modification in the prior-period report and of any matter emphasized in the report

An example of a separate paragraph for a compilation appears below (AR 200.19).

The 19X1 financial statements of ABC Company were compiled by other accountants whose report, dated February 1, 19X2, stated that they did not express an opinion or any other form of assurance on those statements.

An example of a separate paragraph for a review appears below (AR 200.18).

The 19X1 financial statements of ABC Company were reviewed by other accountants whose report, dated March 1, 19X2, stated that they were not aware of any material modifications that should be made to those statements in order for them to be in conformity with generally accepted accounting principles.

Prior-period financial statements may be compiled, reviewed, or audited by the successor accountant even though they have been compiled, reviewed, or audited by the predecessor accountant. This is particularly true in those situations where the client wants to upgrade the services of the prior period. Under these circumstances, the successor accountant (auditor) should consider the guidance provided by SSARS-4 or SAS-7 (Communications Between Predecessor and Successor Auditors). Permission to communicate must be given by the client to both the predecessor and the successor accountants. The predecessor accountant may provide information that may affect the successor accountant's decision to accept the engagement. In addition to specific inquiries to the predecessor accountant, the successor accountant may have an opportunity to review the predecessor accountant's workpapers for the prior period.

Considerations when the predecessor accountant has ceased operations When the accountant presents a compilation or review report with a compilation, review, or audit report of a prior period, and the prior-period report was prepared by a predecessor accountant that has ceased operations, the successor auditor should follow the Notice to Practitioners entitled "Audit, Review, and Compilation Considerations When a Predecessor Accountant Has Ceased Operations," which was issued in February 1991. This Notice is discussed in more detail in the chapter entitled "Auditor's Reports."

> **OBSERVATION:** *The Notice to Practitioners recommends that when the successor accountant believes that prior-period financial statements should be revised but the predecessor accountant has ceased operations, the successor accountant should suggest that the client notify "the party responsible for winding up the affairs of the predecessor firm" of the matter. If the client refuses to make the*

*communication or the reaction by the client's predecessor accoun-
tant is unsatisfactory, the successor accountant should discuss the
matter with legal counsel.*

*A Notice to Practitioners is nonauthoritative guidance prepared
by the AICPA staff in consultation with members of the Auditing
Standards Board and the Accounting and Review Services Committee. Notices generally are published in "The CPA Letter." They
are not approved, disapproved, or otherwise acted on by a senior
technical committee of the AICPA.*

Exception to Reporting on the Highest Level of Service Rendered

SSARS-1 requires that the accountant report on the highest level of
service rendered. For example, when a compilation is performed
followed by a review of the same set of financial statements, the
review report should be issued. An exception occurs, however, when
the prior-period financial statements do not omit substantially all
disclosures required by GAAP and the current-period financial statements do omit these disclosures. In this instance, the current period
must be a compilation engagement because only compiled financial
statements that omit substantially all the disclosures required by
GAAP can be issued by an accountant. It is inappropriate for an
accountant to issue reviewed or audited financial statements that
omit substantially all disclosures. Thus, only when all periods are
compiled and all periods omit substantially all disclosures, can an
accountant report on comparative financial statements that omit
substantially all disclosures. However, a situation may arise where
the accountant issues compiled financial statements that omit substantially all disclosures for the current period and in the prior
period issued a review report. The client wants comparative compiled financial statements that omit substantially all disclosures. In
order for the financial statements to be comparative, the client must
ask the accountant to compile the prior-period statements and omit
substantially all disclosures. Although SSARS-1 requires that the
accountant issue a report on the highest level of service for the prior
period, SSARS-2 provides for an exception. Under SSARS-2, the
accountant can reissue a prior-period report on the basis of a lower
level of service if the following steps are taken (AR 200.29):

1. The accountant must fully comply with all the standards applicable to reporting on compiled financial statements that omit
   substantially all disclosures.

2. A separate paragraph must be included in the accountant's report that discloses (a) the type of previous services rendered by the accountant in the prior period and (b) the date of the accountant's previous report.

An example of the required separate paragraph that is added to the end of the compilation report on the comparative financial statements that omit substantially all disclosures follows (AR 200.30).

We have compiled the accompanying balance sheets of ABC Company as of December 31, 19X2 and 19X1, and the related statements of income, retained earnings, and cash flows for the years then ended, in accordance with Statements on Standards for Accounting and Review Services issued by the American Institute of Certified Public Accountants.

A compilation is limited to presenting in the form of financial statements information that is the representation of management. We have not audited or reviewed the accompanying financial statements and, accordingly, do not express an opinion or any other form of assurance on them.

Management has elected to omit substantially all the disclosures required by generally accepted accounting principles. If the omitted disclosures were included in the financial statements, they might influence the user's conclusions about the company's financial position, results of operations, and cash flows. Accordingly, these financial statements are not designed for those who are not informed about such matters.

The accompanying 19X1 financial statements were compiled by us from financial information that did not omit substantially all of the disclosure required by generally accepted accounting principles and that we previously reviewed, as indicated in our report dated March 1, 19X2.

Change in Public or Nonpublic Status

A company is a public or a nonpublic entity according to its status for the current period. If a company is classified as nonpublic for the current period, compilation or review reports can be issued by an accountant. If a company is classified as public for the current period, however, compilation or review reports usually cannot be issued and standards for public companies (GAAS) must be followed by the accountant (AR 200.31).

A situation may arise where a company is a public entity for the current period and in the prior period was a nonpublic entity. The standards applicable to this situation are those applicable to the current period. Since the company is a public company in the current period, generally accepted auditing standards apply and compilation or review standards do not apply. Thus, a compilation or review report issued for the prior period cannot be reissued or referred to in the audit report for the current period (AR 200.31–.32).

If a company is a nonpublic entity in the current period and its financial statements are compiled or reviewed, and if the company was a public company in the prior period and its financial statements were audited, the rules for "Current Period Compiled or Reviewed and Prior Period Audited" are used. In this event, the accountant should issue a compilation or review report on the current period and either (1) reissue the audit report for the prior period or (2) add a separate paragraph to the current-period compilation or review report describing the responsibility assumed for the prior-period financial statements. The description paragraph should include the date of the prior-period report; a statement that the financial statements were previously examined; the type of opinion expressed, and if the opinion was other than unqualified, the substantive reasons for the qualification; and, finally, a statement that no auditing procedures have been performed since the date of the prior-period audit report. The following is an example of a report where the current period has been compiled and the prior period has been audited (AR 200.28).

We have compiled the accompanying balance sheet of ABC Company as of December 31, 19X2, and the related statements of income, retained earnings, and cash flows for the year then ended, in accordance with Statements on Standards for Accounting and Review Services issued by the American Institute of Certified Public Accountants.

A compilation is limited to presenting in the form of financial statements information that is the representation of management. We have not audited or reviewed the accompanying 19X2 financial statements and, accordingly, do not express an opinion or any other form of assurance on them.

The financial statements for the year ended December 31, 19X1, were audited by us (other accountants) and we (they) expressed an unqualified opinion on them in our (their) report dated March 1, 19X2, but we (they) have not performed any auditing procedures since that date.

If a company is a nonpublic entity in the current period and its financial statements are compiled or reviewed, and if an unaudited disclaimer of opinion was issued in the prior period, the unaudited disclaimer of opinion may not be reissued or referred to in the report on the financial statements for the current period. Under these circumstances, the accountant should comply with the compilation or review standards or should perform an audit on the prior period and report accordingly (AR 200.33).

REPORTS ON THE APPLICATION OF ACCOUNTING PRINCIPLES

Accountants may be asked by entities that are not their clients to give advice on how a transaction should or could be accounted for and what type of opinion or assurance would be appropriate for a particular set of financial statements. In some instances, these requests are made by prospective clients who are "shopping for an opinion." To provide guidance in this area, the Auditing Standards Board issued SAS-50 (Reports on the Application of Accounting Principles). A SSARS Interpretation entitled "Reports on the Application of Accounting Principles" (August 1987) states that standards established by SAS-50 are applicable to requests related to compilations and reviews as well as audit engagements (AU 9400.01-.05).

> **OBSERVATION:** *For a discussion of SAS-55 see the chapter entitled "Auditor's Special Reports."*

REPORTING ON PERSONAL FINANCIAL STATEMENTS CONTAINED IN WRITTEN PERSONAL FINANCIAL PLANS

SSARS-1 states that an accountant associated with unaudited financial statements of a nonpublic entity must either compile or review the financial statements. SSARS-6 (Reporting on Personal Financial Statements Included in Written Personal Financial Plans) provides an exception to this general requirement.

When an accountant prepares a written personal financial plan that includes unaudited *personal* financial statements, the requirements established by SSARS-1 (as amended) do not have to be observed if the following conditions exist (AR 600.01–.03):

- An understanding with the client is reached (preferably in writing) that the financial statements (1) will be used only by the client or the client's advisers to develop personal financial goals and objectives and (2) will not be used to obtain credit or for any purpose other than the establishment of goals and objectives related to the financial plan.

- During the engagement, nothing came to the accountant's attention that would suggest that the personal financial statements would be (1) used to obtain credit or (2) used for any purpose other than the establishment of financial goals and objectives for the client.

> **OBSERVATION:** *A SSARS Interpretation entitled "Submitting a Personal Financial Plan to a Client's Advisers" (May 1991) states that implementing the personal financial plan by the client or the client's advisers (investment adviser, attorney, insurance broker, etc.) is part of "developing a client's personal financial goals and objectives" (AR 9600.01–.03).*

If the accountant concludes that the exemption criteria established by SSARS-6 have been satisfied, a written report should be prepared. The accountant's report should include the following comments (AR 600.04):

- The unaudited financial statements were prepared to facilitate the development of the client's personal financial plan.
- The unaudited financial statements may be incomplete or contain other departures from generally accepted accounting principles and should not be used to obtain credit or for any purpose other than the establishment of the personal financial plan.
- The unaudited financial statements have not been audited, reviewed, or compiled by the accountant.

An example of an accountant's report on personal financial statements included in a written personal financial plan is presented below (AR 600.05).

The accompanying Statement of Financial Condition of [name of client], as of December 31, 19X5, was prepared solely to help you develop your personal financial plan. Accordingly, it may be incomplete or contain other departures from generally accepted accounting principles and should not be used to obtain credit or for any purposes other than developing your financial plan. We have not audited, reviewed, or compiled the statement.

There should be a reference to the accountant's report (such as "See accountant's report") on each personal financial statement (AR 600.06).

> **OBSERVATION:** *SSARS-6 provides an exemption to the requirements established by SSARS-1; however, the accountant is not precluded from observing the standards established by SSARS-1. It should also be noted that when an accountant decides to audit, review, or compile personal financial statements, SOP 82-1 (Accounting and Financial Reporting for Personal Financial Statements) requires that personal financial statements present assets at their estimated current values and liabilities at their estimated current amounts at the date of the financial statements when presented in accordance with GAAP. However, if the personal financial statements are presented at historical cost, instead of current values, the presentation constitutes an other comprehensive basis of accounting.*

> **OBSERVATION:** *For more detailed information on compilations and reviews, please refer to **Miller's Compilations and Reviews**.*

Proposed Assembly Service

The Accounting and Review Services Committee has proposed that a CPA can perform an assembly of financial statements for internal use only. The proposal defines the *assembly* of financial statements as follows:

> Providing various manual or automated bookkeeping or date processing services, the output of which is in the form of financial statements intended for internal use only. The function of assembling financial statements may include preparing a working trial balance, assisting in adjusting the books of account, and consulting on accounting matters. Assembly does not refer to the mere typing or reproduction of client-prepared financial statements.

As part of the engagement, a CPA would be required to reach a written understanding with the client that would cover the following matters:

- Nature and limitations of the engagement
- Confirmation and agreement that the financial statements will be used only for internal purposes
- Agreement that the engagement cannot be relied upon to discover errors, irregularities, or illegal acts

The CPA may not issue a report on the engagement but may prepare a transmittal letter that is limited to the following:

- Identification of the financial statements covered by the letter of transmittal
- Acknowledgment that the financial statements are limited to internal use based on the terms of the engagement letter
- Statements that are of a business advisory nature

> **OBSERVATION:** *The issuance of the Exposure Draft has generated a considerable amount of discussion, and the nature of the action to be taken by the Accounting and Review Services Committee is uncertain.*

PART IV
Prospective Financial Statements

PROSPECTIVE FINANCIAL STATEMENTS

Contents

Overview	**15.03**
Safe Harbor Considerations	**15.06**
Statement Preparation Process	**15.07**
Good Faith	**15.08**
Appropriate Care	**15.08**
Accounting Principles	**15.08**
Best Information	**15.08**
Consistency of Information	**15.08**
Key Factors	**15.09**
Appropriate Assumptions	**15.09**
Assumption Sensitivity	**15.10**
Documentation	**15.10**
Comparison of Results	**15.10**
Review and Approval	**15.10**
Statement Presentation Standards	**15.10**
Internal Use Statements	**15.12**
Partial Presentations	**15.15**
Engagement Procedures	**15.16**
Reporting Standards	**15.16**
Compilation Engagements	**15.16**
Examination Engagements	**15.17**
Reporting on Prospective Financial Statements	**15.18**
Examination Engagement	**15.19**
Independence	**15.20**
Training and Proficiency	**15.20**
Planning and Supervision	**15.20**
Sufficient Evidence for Assumptions	**15.21**

Sufficient Evidence for Preparation and Presentation	**15.23**
Accountant's Report	**15.24**
Departure from Presentation Guidelines	**15.25**
Lack of Reasonable Basis	**15.25**
Scope Limitation	**15.26**
Use of Another Accountant	**15.26**
Emphasis of a Matter	**15.26**
Comparative Information	**15.26**
Larger Engagement	**15.26**
Applying Agreed-Upon Procedures	**15.27**
Compilation Engagement	**15.27**
Training and Proficiency	**15.27**
Due Professional Care	**15.28**
Planning and Supervision	**15.28**
Applicable Procedures	**15.28**
Accountant's Report	**15.30**
Lack of Independence	**15.31**
Departure from AICPA Presentation Guidelines	**15.31**
Emphasis of a Matter	**15.31**
Comparative Information	**15.31**

PROSPECTIVE FINANCIAL STATEMENTS

In October 1985, the Auditing Standards Board (ASB) issued its first Statement on Standards for Accountants' Services on Prospective Financial Information (SSASPFI), entitled "Financial Forecasts and Projections." Subsequently, in early 1986, the Financial Forecasts and Projections Task Force issued an Audit Guide entitled *Guide for Prospective Financial Information* (hereinafter referred to as the PFI Guide). Additional issues related to prospective financial information engagements are addressed in the following publications:

- SOP 92-2 (Questions and Answers on the Term "Reasonably Objective Basis" and Other Issues Affecting Prospective Financial Statements)

The guidance established by SSASPFI and the three Statements of Position have been incorporated into the PFI Guide, and the Guide is the basis for this chapter.

Overview

A prospective financial statement is either a *financial forecast* or a *financial projection* that reflects an entity's expected statement of financial position, results of operations, statement of cash flows, and summaries of significant assumptions and accounting policies. A prospective financial statement is based on expected future economic conditions that represent the best knowledge and belief of the person or persons responsible for the underlying assumptions in the forecast or projection. A prospective financial statement is a financial forecast or projection that covers a period of time that is partially but not completely expired or a period of time wholly in the future. Financial statements that cover an expired period of time are not considered prospective financial statements).

> *OBSERVATION: Pro forma financial statements attempt to reflect the effects of a possible transaction or event on historical*

> *financial statements. Pro forma financial statements are not con-*
> *sidered to be prospective financial statements.*

The person or persons who establish the underlying assumptions for the prospective financial statements are referred to in the PFI Guide as the *responsible party* or *responsible parties.* As a rule, the responsible party for a prospective financial statement is the management of an enterprise, but it may be a prospective buyer or some other outsider. An accountant who is engaged to report on prospective financial statements may assist the responsible party in identifying assumptions and gathering information for the forecast or projection. However, all of the underlying assumptions and the preparation and presentation of the prospective financial statements are the responsibility of the responsible party. Thus, the term *preparation of prospective financial statements* should not be used in the accountant's report or in any other correspondence relating to the engagement.

Under the PFI Guide, an accountant who is engaged to report on prospective financial statements must determine whether such statements are intended for *general use* or for *limited use.* Prospective financial statements that are issued for general use are those that are intended to be used by parties that are not negotiating directly with the responsible party. Since the parties not negotiating directly are generally unable to make direct inquiries about the prospective financial statements, the most useful presentation for them is one that reflects the responsible party's best knowledge and belief of the expected results. Thus, only a financial forecast is appropriate for general use.

Prospective financial statements that are issued for limited use are those that are intended to be used only by the responsible party and those parties negotiating directly with the responsible party. Since the parties are negotiating directly and are able to make direct inquiries of the responsible party, either a financial forecast or a financial projection is appropriate for limited use.

A *financial forecast* reflects an entity's expected statement of financial position, results of operations, and statement of cash flows, *based on the responsible party's assumptions of the conditions that are expected to exist during the forecast period and the course of action that is expected to be taken if the expected conditions materialize. A financial projection* reflects an entity's expected statement of financial position, results of operations, and statement of cash flows, based on the responsible party's assumptions of the conditions that would exist during the projection period *if one or more hypothetical assumptions occur* and the course of action that would be taken if the hypothetical assumptions materialize. Thus, a financial forecast is based on expected future economic conditions and the course of action to be taken if the expected conditions materialize, whereas a financial projection is based on expected future economic conditions that would exist if one or more hypothetical assumptions occur and the course of action that would be taken if the hypothetical assumptions materialize.

A prospective financial statement may be prepared as a single set of estimates or a range of estimates. To facilitate comparisons, prospective financial statements should be presented in the same format as that used for historical financial statements. The following *minimum* presentation standards for prospective financial statements are required by the PFI Guide:

1. Sales or gross revenues

2. Gross profit or cost of sales

3. Unusual or infrequently occurring items

4. Provision for income taxes

5. Discontinued operations or extraordinary items

6. Income from continuing operations

7. Net income

8. Primary and fully diluted earnings per share

9. Significant cash flows

10. Description of what management intends the prospective financial statements to present, a statement that assumptions are based on information about circumstances and conditions existing at the time the prospective information was prepared, and a caveat that the prospective results may not be achieved

11. Summary of significant assumptions

12. Summary of significant accounting policies

> **OBSERVATION:** *A minimum presentation of a prospective financial statement that omits any of the items numbered 1 through 9, above, is generally considered a partial presentation and not suitable for general use. A prospective financial statement that includes all of the items numbered 1 through 9, above, but omits items 10 through 12, is not a partial presentation and is subject to the minimum guidelines of the PFI Guide.*

SAFE HARBOR CONSIDERATIONS

With the passage of the Private Securities Litigation Reform Act of 1995, safe harbor protection was provided under certain circumstances for SEC registrants and their auditors who are associated with so-called "forward-looking information." In May 1996, the AICPA issued a Practice Alert (The Private Securities Litigation Reform Act of 1995) that provided summary information concerning the Act.

The Act provides the following description of what constitutes forward-looking information:

- A statement containing a projection of revenues, income, earnings per share, capital expenditures, dividends, capital structure, or other financial items

- A statement of management's plans and objectives for future operations, including plans and objectives relating to the issuer's products or services

- A statement of future economic performance, including any statement contained in management's discussion and analysis of financial condition or the results of operation included pursuant to SEC rules and regulations

- A report, issued by an outside reviewer who was retained by the issuer, that assesses the issuer's forward-looking statement

- A statement containing a projection or estimate of such other items as may be specified by SEC rules or regulations

Forward-looking information would also include a description of the assumptions upon which the above statements are based. However, in order for the information to be subject to the safe harbor provision of the Act, the information must be (a) identified as forward-looking and (b) accompanied by meaningful and cautionary language referring to factors that could result in a material difference between the information and actual results.

Although the Act does not identify the specific services performed by the auditor that may be subject to the safe harbor provision, the AICPA Practice Alert identified the following services as possible examples:

- *No substantive attention requested by the client*   Under this situation the auditor must comply with the guidance established by

SAS-8 (Other Information in Documents Containing Audited Financial Statements) and SAS-37 (Filing under Federal Securities Statues) if the forward-looking information is included in a document containing the audited financial statements. These standards require that the auditor read the forward-looking information to determine whether the information is materially inconsistent with the audited financial statements.

- *Substantive attention requested by the client (no separate report issued)* Under this situation the consultative role of the auditor should be clearly understood and preferably documented in an engagement letter. However, the Practice Alert warns the auditor of the SEC's position, which is "that accountants who assist in the preparation of a forecast may not be independent from an SEC perspective and may not report on the forecast."

- *Substantive attention requested by the client (separate report issued)* Under this situation the auditor may examine or perform an agreed-upon procedures engagement and should observe the guidance established by Statements on Standards for Attestation Engagement (Financial Forecast and Projections). If the auditor will provide underwriters with a comfort letter that covers forward-looking information, he or she should follow the guidance established by SAS-72 (Letters for Underwriters and Certain Other Requisition Parties).

> **OBSERVATION:** *Auditors who contemplate performing services that may be subject to the safe harbor provision should consult with legal counsel to determine the applicability of and responsibilities mandated by the Act.*

Statement Preparation Process

To enhance the quality of prospective financial statements, the responsible party should adhere to a specific process for preparing a forecast or projection. The process may consist of (1) a formal system for preparing prospective financial statements, (2) performance of a work program that outlines the steps followed in preparing the statements, or (3) documented procedures, methods, and practices used in preparing the statements. No matter which of the three processes is used by the responsible party, the following eleven guidelines should be incorporated into the financial statement preparation process.

Good faith   Good faith should be exercised in the preparation of prospective financial statements because of the subjective nature of the content of such statements. *Good faith* means that assumptions are arrived at in a diligent manner and that there is no attempt to mislead third-party users. The preparation of prospective financial statements should not be based on undue optimism or pessimism.

> *OBSERVATION: The undue optimism/pessimism criterion is not applicable to the preparation of a financial projection since the purpose of the projection dictates the hypothetical assumptions that will be used. However, the undue optimism/pessimism criterion does apply to the future expected economic conditions that would exist if one or more hypothetical assumptions occur.*

Appropriate care   Appropriate diligence, including the adoption of procedures to prevent and detect errors and the use of a specialist, should be used in the preparation of prospective financial statements.

Accounting principles   Future events and transactions should be reflected in the prospective financial statements using the same accounting principles that are expected to be employed if the events or transactions actually occur. If it is expected that accounting principles will be changed, the change should be reported in the prospective financial statements in the same manner as required for historical financial statements using the accounting and reporting standards established by APB Opinion No. 20 (Accounting Changes).

> *OBSERVATION: A financial projection may be prepared in part to show the effects of different accounting principles. In this case, there does not have to be an expectation that the accounting change will actually take place.*

Best information   The prospective financial statements should be based on the best information that is reasonably available at the time. The cost of acquiring information should be justified on the basis of the expected improvement in the quality of the financial statements.

Consistency of information   The information used to prepare prospective financial statements should be consistent with the organization's plans as expressed in budgets, goals, policies, and strategies.

> **OBSERVATION:** *A financial projection does not have to be consistent with an organization's expected future developments; although once an alternative is selected as the basis for the projection, other assumptions should be based on the expected results of the basic hypothetical assumption.*

Key factors   All key factors such as the entity's sales, production, service, and financing activities should be identified and then used as the basis for the construction of the assumption that will lead to the preparation of the prospective financial statements.

Appropriate assumptions   The quality of a prospective financial statement depends on the appropriateness of assumptions. The amount of effort used to develop a particular assumption is a function of the relative effect of the assumption on the prospective financial statement. In general, assumptions should be reasonable and appropriately supported by such items as market surveys, economic indicators, and historical trends.

The PFI Guide provides the following guidance with respect to assumptions made in the preparation of prospective financial statements:

- When a financial forecast includes a hypothetical sale of an entity's real estate investment at the end of the forecast period, the information may be presented either as a note or in a separate statement presented as part of the financial forecast. When the information is included as a note, the standard accountant's report should cover the information in the note. When the information is presented as a separate statement, the accountant's report should be expanded to report on the separate statement.

- When a financial forecast includes a projected sale of an entity's real estate investment at the end of the period, the capitalization rate used to estimate the sales price should be consistent with assumptions used in the forecast, and with the entity's and industry's experience.

The accountant should employ appropriate procedures to determine whether another practitioner's tax opinion provides a suitable basis for tax assumptions used to prepare the financial forecast.

Assumption sensitivity   Particular attention should be paid to assumptions that may significantly affect prospective financial statements when small changes in the assumption occur. Also, increased attention should be directed to those assumptions where a high probability of variation exists.

Documentation   The process by which the prospective financial statements were developed should be documented in a manner that allows a knowledgeable person to trace the prospective financial information to the assumptions on which the information is based.

Comparison of results   Prospective financial statements eventually should be compared to actual financial statements to evaluate, at least in part, the effectiveness of the process used to develop the financial statements. The comparison should include the evaluation of the establishment of key factors and assumptions.

Review and approval   There should be an adequate review and approval of the process used to prepare prospective financial statements, recognizing that the highest level of authority within the responsible party is ultimately responsible for the forecast or projection.

Statement Presentation Standards

Prospective financial statements may be presented only if there is a reasonably objective basis for their preparation. That is, the responsible party must be able to determine that sufficiently objective assumptions can be made for each key factor.

> **OBSERVATION:** *Projected financial statements may be presented even though there is no reasonably objective basis for the hypothetical assumptions; however, the hypothetical assumptions must be consistent with the purpose of the projection.*

Prospective financial statements should be appropriately titled. The title of a financial forecast should include the term *forecast* or *forecasted*. The title of a financial projection should not include the use of the word *forecast* or *forecasted*, but it should adequately describe the nature of the projection. In addition, the date the prospective financial statements were completed should be disclosed, and the responsible party should determine if the assumptions used to prepare the financial statements are still appropriate as of the completion date.

The dollar values presented in a prospective financial statement may be expressed as a single amount or as a range of values. A range of values may be used only when the range is not selected in a biased or misleading manner, and the amounts within the range are expected to occur. When a range is used, it should be made clear that the range does not necessarily represent the best or worst possible alternatives.

When financial forecasts or projections are both presented, each prospective statement should be appropriately titled. Likewise, when prospective and historical financial statements are presented, each should be clearly labeled.

Generally, the prospective financial statements should cover at least one year of normal operations. Although the PFI Guide does not specify a minimum or maximum period of coverage, it implies that "it ordinarily would be difficult to establish that a reasonably objective basis exists for a financial forecast extending beyond three to five years." If it is concluded that the period covered is inadequate to demonstrate long-term results, there should be a description of the possible effects on the financial statements if the period covered were extended.

Significant assumptions must be disclosed as part of the prospective financial statements. Judgment must be used to identify which assumptions are significant, but the PFI Guide concludes that the following assumptions must be disclosed:

- Assumptions for which there is reasonable possibility of the occurrence of a variation that may significantly affect the prospective results

- Assumptions about anticipated conditions that are expected to be significantly different from current conditions, which are not otherwise reasonably apparent

- Other matters deemed important to the prospective information or its interpretation

In addition to the assumptions just listed, projected financial statements should include disclosures about which assumptions are hypothetical. If the hypothetical assumptions are improbable, that fact must be disclosed. The summary of assumptions should be preceded by a statement that includes the following:

- A declaration that the disclosure of assumptions is not all-inclusive
- A declaration that the assumptions made were based on the responsible party's best judgment as of the date the statement was prepared
- A description of the purpose of the prospective financial statements
- A caveat that the results reflected in the statements may not be achieved

In addition to a summary of significant assumptions, the prospective financial statements should include a summary of significant accounting policies. The prospective financial statements should be based on the same accounting policies that are expected to be used to account for future transactions and events in the entity's historical financial statements. When historical and prospective financial statements are prepared on a comprehensive basis of accounting other than generally accepted accounting principles, the prospective financial statements should disclose the basis of accounting and state that the basis differs from generally accepted accounting principles.

After prospective financial statements are issued, it may be necessary to correct or update the statements. A correction will be necessary if an error was made in the preparation of the prospective financial statements. When it is concluded that users are relying on the financial statements, auditing guidelines established in SAS-1, Section 561.06 (Subsequent Discovery of Facts Existing at the Date of the Auditor's Report), may be followed. Updating is necessary to reflect changes in assumptions, actual results, or anticipated events and circumstances. Generally it is not necessary to update prospective financial statements, but if it is decided to do so, revised financial statements should be issued promptly. If the statements cannot be issued promptly, parties using or expected to use the prospective financial statements should be notified not to rely on them.

Internal Use Statements

An accountant may be requested to provide a variety of services with respect to prospective financial statements that are intended to be used only on an internal basis. For example, prospective financial statements that are restricted to internal use may be compiled, examined, or subjected to agreed-upon procedures. Other services also may be performed by the accountant; for example, if requested by the client, the accountant may report on another service performed on prospective financial statements restricted for internal use.

The PFI Guide provides the following guidance on prospective financial statements:

> Whenever an accountant (a) submits, to his client or others, a financial forecast that he has assembled, or assisted in assembling, that is, or reasonably might be, expected to be used by another (third) party or (b) reports on a financial forecast that is, or reasonably might be, expected to be used by another (third) party, he should perform one of the engagements described in the preceding paragraph (that is, a compilation, examination, or an agreed-upon procedures engagement).

Thus, the accountant is not required to issue a report when the accountant is associated with internal prospective financial statements. The accountant should evaluate the client's request to determine whether the prospective financial statements will be used only on an internal basis. In determining the purpose of prospective financial statements, the accountant may rely on either an oral or a written representation made by the responsible party.

When prospective financial statements are to be used exclusively on an internal basis, the accountant may be requested to compile, examine, or perform agreed-upon procedures, or the accountant may be requested to perform a number of "other services" that relate to the generation of prospective financial statements. If the accountant is requested to compile, examine, or perform agreed-upon procedures, professional standards for similar (external) engagements should be followed. When the accountant is requested to perform "other services" (other than a compilation, examination, or the application of agreed-upon procedures), the accountant and the client should come to an understanding about the nature of the engagement. The understanding preferably should be in writing and should state that the prospective financial statements and the accountant's report, if any, should note that the report should not be distributed externally.

Although, as discussed earlier, the accountant is not required to issue a report on internal prospective financial statements, when the statements accompany the accountant's correspondence to the client, the correspondence should note that the prospective financial statements may not be achieved and that they should be used only on an internal basis.

If the accountant decides, on the basis of the client's request, to issue a report on the prospective financial statements restricted to internal use and the type of service rendered is a compilation, examination, or the application of agreed-upon procedures, the reporting format established in the PFI Guide (as discussed later in this chapter) should be followed. If the accountant decides to issue a report based on the performance of another service, the format of the report is flexible but generally would conform to the following guidelines:

- Address the report to the responsible party.
- Identify the prospective financial statements.
- Describe the nature of the service provided and the degree of responsibility taken by the accountant with respect to the statements.
- State that the prospective results may not be achieved.
- Disclose the distribution restriction of statements and report.
- Date the report on the basis of the date of the completion of procedures.
- Describe limitations on the usefulness of the statements (applicable only to financial projections).

The following illustration, extracted from PFI Guide, reports on the assembly of a financial forecast that is restricted to internal use.

We have assembled, from information provided by management, the accompanying forecasted balance sheet and the related forecasted statements of income, retained earnings, and cash flows of XYZ Company as of December 19X5, and for the year then ending. We have not compiled or examined the financial forecast and express no assurance of any kind on it. Further, there usually will be differences between the forecast and actual results, because events and circumstances frequently do not occur as expected, and those differences may be material. In accordance with the terms of our engagement, this report and the accompanying forecast are restricted to internal use and may not be shown to any third party for any purpose.

If the accountant is not independent with respect to the entity reported on, the report should disclose this fact. If the accountant is not independent, the report should contain no form of assurance (reasonable or limited) on the financial statements. In addition, the omission of any disclosures of which the accountant is aware should be described in the report.

When the report is accompanied by the accountant's transmittal letter or similar written communication, the separate communication should state that the results presented in the prospective financial statements may not be achieved and that those financial statements are intended for internal use only.

Partial Presentations

An accountant may assist in the preparation of prospective financial information that is considered to be a *partial presentation*. A partial presentation of prospective financial information lacks one or more of the items discussed earlier in this chapter that are required for a full presentation. Examples of a partial presentation include sales forecasts and projections of financing needs. Generally, the distribution of partial presentations of prospective financial information should be restricted to those parties directly negotiating with the responsible party.

Partial presentations of prospective financial information should be appropriately titled, should reflect the limited nature of the presentation, and should not be described as a financial forecast or projection. In addition, the partial presentation should include the following disclosures:

- Significant accounting policies used to prepare the partial presentation

- If the accounting basis used to prepare the partial presentation is different from the basis that is expected to be used to prepare the historical financial statements that will cover the same period, (1) the basis expected to be used to prepare the historical financial statements and (2) the differences between the two bases (although the differences need not be quantified)

- Summary of significant assumptions on which the partial presentation is based

- Introduction preceding the summary of assumptions that describes (1) the purpose of the partial presentation and (2) limitations of the usefulness of the partial presentation

Engagement procedures   An accountant may compile, examine, or apply agreed-upon procedures to a partial presentation of prospective financial information. If the engagement involves the compilation or examination of a partial presentation, the procedures established for these services in the PFI Guide should generally be observed. In addition, the accountant should include in the scope of the engagement those key factors affecting items that are not part of the partial presentation but are interrelated with elements, accounts, or items that comprise the partial presentation.

In general, the procedures identified in the PFI Guide as applicable to agreed-upon procedures for prospective financial statements should be followed for partial presentations subject to agreed-upon procedures.

Reporting standards   The following reporting standards should be observed in preparing a report based on a compilation, examination, or agreed-upon procedures engagement:

- Identify the period covered by the partial presentation.
- State that forecasted results may not be achieved.
- State that the accountant assumes no responsibility to update the report for events or circumstances that occur after the date of the report.
- Describe any limitations on the usefulness of the partial presentation.

Reports on partial presentations may be modified for the same reasons that reports on prospective financial statements are modified. These modifications are discussed later in this chapter.

Compilation engagements   In addition to the broad reporting standards identified above, a compilation report on a partial presentation of prospective financial information should include the following statements:

- The engagement was performed according to guidelines established by the American Institute of Certified Public Accountants.
- A compilation is limited in its scope and does not provide a basis for expressing an opinion or any other form of assurance on the partial presentation or the assumptions.

The following standard report, extracted from PFI Guide, illustrates a compilation report on a partial presentation of forecasted information.

We have compiled the accompanying forecasted statement of net operating income before debt service, depreciation, and income taxes of AAA Hotel for the year ending December 31, 19X1 (the forecasted statement), in accordance with guidelines established by the American Institute of Certified Public Accountants.

The accompanying forecasted statement presents, to the best of management's knowledge and belief, the net operating income before debt service, depreciation, and income taxes of AAA Hotel for the forecast period. It is not intended to be a forecast of financial position, results of operations, or cash flows. The accompanying forecasted statement and this report were prepared for the ABC Bank for the purpose of negotiating a proposed construction loan to be used to finance expansion of the hotel and should not be used for any other purpose.

A compilation is limited to presenting forecasted information that is the representation of management and does not include evaluation of the support for the assumptions underlying such information. We have not examined the forecasted statement and, accordingly, do not express an opinion or any other form of assurance on the accompanying statement or assumptions. Furthermore, there usually will be differences between forecasted and actual results because events and circumstances frequently do not occur as expected, and those differences may be material. We have no responsibility to update this report for events and circumstances occurring after the date of this report.

Examination engagements   In addition to conforming to the broad reporting standards identified above, an examination report on a partial presentation of prospective financial information should include the following:

- A statement that the engagement was performed according to guidelines established by the American Institute of Certified Public Accountants
- A brief description of the nature of the examination
- The opinion that the partial presentation is presented in conformity with AICPA presentation guidelines and that the underlying assumptions provide a reasonable basis for the forecast (applicable to a financial forecast)

- The opinion that the partial presentation is presented in conformity with AICPA presentation guidelines and that the underlying assumptions provide a reasonable basis for the projection given the hypothetical assumptions (applicable to a financial projection)

The following standard report, extracted from PFI Guide, illustrates an examination report on a partial presentation of forecasted information.

We have examined the accompanying forecasted statement of net operating income before debt service, depreciation, and income taxes of the AAA Hotel for the year ending December 31, 19X1 (the forecasted statement). Our examination was made in accordance with standards established by the American Institute of Certified Public Accountants and, accordingly, included such procedures as we considered necessary to evaluate both the assumptions used by management and the preparation and presentation of the forecasted statement.

The accompanying forecasted statement presents, to the best of management's knowledge and belief, the expected net operating income before debt service, depreciation, and income taxes of AAA Hotel for the forecasted period. It is not intended to be a forecast of financial position, results of operations, or cash flows. The accompanying forecasted statement and this report were prepared for ABC Bank for the purpose of negotiating a proposed construction loan to be used to finance expansion of the hotel and should not be used for any other purpose.

In our opinion, the forecasted statement referred to above is presented in conformity with the guidelines for presentation of forecasted information established by the American Institute of Certified Public Accountants, and the underlying assumptions provide a reasonable basis for management's forecasted statement. However, there usually will be differences between forecasted and actual results because events and circumstances frequently do not occur as expected, and those differences may be material. We have no responsibility to update this report for events and circumstances occurring after the date of this report.

Reporting on Prospective Financial Statements

An accountant may submit to the client, or others, prospective financial statements that he or she has assembled, or assisted in assembling, that are, or reasonably might be, expected to be used by a third party; or an accountant may report on prospective financial statements that are, or reasonably might be, expected to be used by a third party.

Under either of these circumstances, the accountant should examine, compile, or apply agreed-upon procedures to the prospective financial statements.

An accountant may rely on written or oral representations of the responsible party in determining whether the prospective financial statements may be used by a third party, unless information comes to the attention of the accountant that contradicts the representations of the responsible party. The PFI Guide is not applicable to prospective financial statements that are not reasonably expected to be used by a third party, unless the accountant has been engaged to perform an examination, compilation, or the application of agreed-upon procedures.

An examination, compilation, or the application of agreed-upon procedures may be performed by an accountant only when the responsible party has a reasonably objective basis for presenting the prospective financial statements. A client may change an engagement to a lower level of service (for example, from an examination to a compilation) only when the accountant concludes that the change is appropriate.

Examination Engagement

The purpose of an examination of prospective financial statements is to express an opinion on whether the statements are presented in conformity with AICPA guidelines and to determine whether the responsible party's assumptions provide a reasonable basis for the preparation of the prospective financial statements.

> **OBSERVATION:** *For financial projections the accountant must determine whether, given the hypothetical assumptions, the assumptions provide a reasonable basis for the responsible party's presentation.*

Materiality is a highly subjective factor that the accountant must consider in the examination of prospective financial statements in the same manner as in the evaluation of historical financial statements. Because of the higher degree of uncertainty associated with prospective financial statements, prospective financial information cannot be expected to be as precise as historical financial information. Thus, the range or reasonableness for evaluating prospective financial information is broader than the range an auditor would use to evaluate historical financial information.

The following professional standards should be observed by the accountant in an examination of prospective financial statements:

- The accountant should be independent.

- The accountant should have adequate technical training and proficiency to examine a prospective financial statement.

- The examination should be adequately planned, and assistants, if any, should be supervised.

- Sufficient evidence to provide a reasonable basis for the accountant's report must be obtained.

- Reporting standards for the examination of prospective financial statements should be observed in the preparation of the accountant's report.

Independence   An accountant should be independent in the examination of prospective financial statements. For guidance in determining independence, the accountant should refer to the AICPA Code of Professional Conduct, its Rules of Conduct, Interpretations under the Rules and Ethics Rulings, and ethical requirements established by the relevant CPA society or state board of accountancy.

Training and proficiency   The accountant must have an adequate understanding of the AICPA's preparation and presentation guidelines for prospective financial statements. These guidelines (standards) were discussed earlier in the sections entitled "Statement Preparation Process" and "Statement Presentation Standards." In addition, the accountant must be familiar with the accounting principles, practices, and methods that are followed by the industry in which the client operates or plans to operate.

Planning and supervision   To successfully perform an examination of prospective financial statements, the accountant must adequately plan the engagement. Part of the planning of the engagement involves the identification of the attestation risk, which is defined as the probability that the accountant will incorrectly accept (1) the prospective financial statements as being prepared in accordance with AICPA presentation standards or (2) assumptions as providing a reasonable basis for the statement presentation. Attestation risk is a function of the probability that the prospective financial statements contain material errors and the probability that the accountant will not discover the material errors.

OBSERVATION: These elements of risk are referred to as inherent risk, control risk, and detection risk and are discussed in SAS-47 (Audit Risk and Materiality in Conducting an Audit).

A knowledge of a variety of factors, such as an understanding of the entity's operations, industry characteristics, accounting principles, and the responsible party's level of experience with respect to the preparation of prospective financial statements is important in understanding part of the planning process. The accountant may gain adequate knowledge of these and other matters by concentrating on items such as the following:

- The availability and cost of resources needed to operate including raw materials, labor, short-term and long-term financing, and plant and equipment
- The nature and condition of the market in which the entity sells its goods or services, including final consumer markets if the entity sells to intermediate markets
- Factors specific to the industry, including competitive conditions, sensitivity to economic conditions, accounting policies, specific regulatory requirements, and technology
- Patterns of past performance for the entity or comparable entities, including trends in revenue and costs, turnover of assets, uses and capacities of physical facilities, and management policies

An adequate understanding of many of the factors that are prerequisites to planning may be possessed by the accountant if the accountant has examined or reviewed the entity's historical financial statements.

Sufficient evidence for assumptions   Evidence must be collected to determine if assumptions used in the preparation of the prospective financial statements are reasonable. This includes determining whether the responsible party has identified all key factors and has (1) developed appropriate assumptions based on these factors and (2) suitably supported these assumptions.

OBSERVATION: For a financial projection, the accountant must be satisfied that the assumptions provide a reasonable basis for the projection, given the hypothetical assumptions.

Key factors identified by the responsible party should be reviewed to determine whether they are complete and relevant to the preparation of the prospective financial statements. The accountant's understanding of the entity's business operations provides a basis for assessing whether all relevant key factors have been identified. A familiarity with prior financial statements may be helpful in evaluating the responsible party's development of key factors and derived assumptions, although the accountant must be aware that past key factors may no longer be relevant or new factors may affect the prospective financial statements.

Once key factors have been identified, the accountant must be satisfied that the responsible party's assumptions are suitably supported. *Suitably supported* means that a preponderance of the available information supports each significant assumption. The determination of whether there is a preponderance of information is highly subjective and does not suggest that a particular outcome is the only outcome that will actually occur. The accountant's conclusion must be concerned with whether assumptions provide a reasonable basis for the preparation of the prospective financial statements. The following should be considered when determining whether there is suitable support for assumptions:

- Have sufficient pertinent sources of information about the assumptions been considered? Examples of external sources the accountant might consider are government publications, industry publications, economic forecasts, existing or proposed legislation, and reports of changing technology. Examples of internal sources are budgets, labor agreements, patents, royalty agreements and records, sales backlog records, debt agreements, and actions of the board of directors involving entity plans.
- Are the assumptions consistent with the sources from which they are derived?
- Are the assumptions consistent with each other?
- Are the historical financial information and other data used in developing the assumptions sufficiently reliable for that purpose? Reliability can be assessed by inquiry and analytical and other procedures, some of which may have been completed in past examinations or reviews of the historical financial statements. If historical financial statements have been prepared for an expired part of the prospective period, the accountant should consider the historical data in relation to the prospective results for the same period, where applicable. If the prospective financial statements incorporate such historical financial results and that period is significant to the presentation, the accountant

should make a review of the historical information in conformity with the applicable standards for a review.

- Are the historical financial information and other data used in developing the assumptions comparable over the periods specified? Were the effects of any lack of comparability considered in developing the assumptions?

- Are the logical arguments or theory, considered with the data supporting the assumptions, reasonable?

Often an important element of prospective financial statements is the tax assumptions, including financial statements used for tax shelter offerings. The accountant should be satisfied that the tax assumptions are *more likely than not* acceptable for tax purposes. Also, the accountant should be aware of any requirements that may be established by the Treasury Department.

Sufficient evidence for preparation and presentation With respect to the evaluation of the preparation and presentation of prospective financial statements, evidence should be collected by the accountant to satisfy that:

- Suitably supported assumptions are reflected in the statements.

- Computations to convert the assumptions to dollar values are mathematically correct.

- Assumptions are internally consistent.

- Generally accepted accounting principles used in the preparation of the prospective financial statements are the same principles (1) used in the latest historical financial statements and (2) expected to be used in the historical financial statements that will cover the same reporting period as the prospective financial statements (for financial projections the accounting principles should be consistent with the purpose of the presentation).

- Prospective financial statements are presented in accordance with AICPA guidelines.

- Assumptions have been adequately disclosed based on AICPA presentation guidelines.

Written representations should be obtained from the responsible party with respect to the prospective financial statements.

In some engagements, the accountant may not have the skills to adequately evaluate the prospective financial statements, in which case it may be necessary to use the work of a specialist. Guidance for planning and evaluating the work of a specialist can be found in SAS-73 (Using the Work of a Specialist).

The accountant's workpapers should demonstrate that the examination engagement was adequately planned and supervised and that the process used to develop the prospective financial statements was considered in identifying the scope of the engagement. Also, the workpapers should show that sufficient evidence was obtained to support the accountant's report.

Accountant's report   When an accountant examines and reports on an entity's prospective financial statements, he or she must observe the reporting standards by including the following in the report:

- An identification of the prospective financial statements presented
- A statement that the examination of the prospective financial statements was made in accordance with AICPA standards and a brief description of the nature of the examination
- The accountant's opinion that the prospective financial statements are presented in conformity with AICPA presentation guidelines and that the underlying assumptions provide a reasonable basis for the forecast or a reasonable basis for the projection, given the hypothetical assumptions
- A caveat that the prospective results may not be achieved
- A statement that the accountant assumes no responsibility to update the report for events and circumstances occurring after the date of the report

An example of a standard accountant's report for the examination of a financial forecast follows.

We have examined the accompanying forecasted balance sheet and statements of income, retained earnings, and cash flows of X Company as of December 31, 19X5, and the year then ending. Our examination was made in accordance with standards for an examination of a forecast established by the American Institute of Certified Public Accountants and, accordingly, included such procedures as we considered necessary to evaluate both the assumptions used by management and the preparation and presentation of the forecast.

In our opinion, the accompanying forecast is presented in conformity with guidelines for presentation of a forecast established by the American Institute of Certified Public Accountants, and the underlying assumptions provide a reasonable basis for management's forecast. However, there usually will be differences between the forecasted and actual results, because events and circumstances frequently do not occur as expected, and those differences may be material. We have no responsibility to update this report for events and circumstances occurring after the date of this report.

An accountant may encounter a variety of circumstances that may require that the standard accountant's report on prospective financial statements be modified. The following summarizes these modifications.

Departure from presentation guidelines An accountant may conclude that AICPA presentation guidelines have not been followed in the preparation or presentation of the prospective financial statements. When the deviations are considered to be material, either a qualified opinion or an adverse opinion should be expressed. If the accountant decides to modify the opinion, an explanatory paragraph(s) should be included in the report in which the deviations are described. When a qualified opinion is expressed, the opinion paragraph should refer to the explanatory paragraph and use the qualifying language "except for." When an adverse opinion is expressed, the accountant refers to the deviations described in the explanatory paragraph and states that the prospective financial statements are not presented in accordance with AICPA presentation guidelines.

If the presentation deficiency results from the entity's nondisclosure of significant assumptions, the accountant should express an adverse opinion and describe the omitted assumptions. When the following circumstances occur, the accountant should not attempt to examine the prospective financial statements:

- All disclosures of assumptions are omitted.
- Hypothetical assumptions are omitted for a financial projection.
- Description of the limitations of the usefulness of the presentation is omitted for a financial projection.

Lack of reasonable basis An accountant should express an adverse opinion on the prospective financial statements when a significant assumption does (or assumptions do) not provide a reasonable basis for a forecast (or given the hypothetical assumptions, a significant assumption does [or assumptions do] not provide a reasonable basis for a projection).

Scope limitation   A disclaimer of opinion should be expressed when procedures considered necessary by the accountant cannot be performed. The report should describe the nature of the scope limitation in an explanatory paragraph. If the accountant is aware of material departures from the AICPA presentation guidelines for prospective financial statements, the departures should be described in the report, even though a disclaimer of opinion is expressed.

Use of another accountant   When another accountant is involved in the engagement and reports on his or her portion of the examination, the principal accountant must decide whether or not to make reference to the work of the other accountant. The accountant may follow the guidelines for a regular audit engagement (SAS-58 [Reports on Audited Financial Statements]) when determining whether to refer to the work of the other accountant.

Emphasis of a matter   An accountant may emphasize a specific item or event in his or her report and still express an unqualified opinion on the prospective financial statements. The item or event that is emphasized should be described in a separate paragraph of the accountant's report, but the opinion paragraph should make no reference to the item or event emphasized.

Comparative information   Historical financial statements or summarizations of such statements may be included in the document that contains the prospective financial statements or that summarizes the prospective financial information. The accountant's report on the prospective financial statements should include a reference to the historical financial statements, as follows.

The historical financial statements for the year ended December 31, 19X5, and our report thereon are set forth on pages XX through XX of this document.

Larger engagement   The examination of prospective financial statements may be only a part of a larger engagement. For example, a feasibility study may include the examination of prospective financial statements. When an accountant reports on the expanded engagement, the report should be tailored to fit the complete nature of the engagement.

Applying Agreed-Upon Procedures

Agreed-upon procedures engagements for prospective financial statements are discussed in the chapter entitled "Agreed-Upon Procedures Engagements."

Compilation Engagement

The compilation of prospective financial statements does not provide a basis for the accountant to express an opinion on the financial statements. When a compilation report is issued, the accountant gives no assurance that AICPA presentation guidelines have been followed or that assumptions used in the preparation of the statements are reasonable. The accountant should not compile prospective financial statements that exclude a summary of significant assumptions. In addition, a compilation engagement is inappropriate when a financial projection does not identify the hypothetical assumptions that are used or fails to describe the limitation of the usefulness of the presentation.

The following professional standards should be observed by an accountant who compiles prospective financial statements:

- The accountant should have adequate technical training and proficiency to compile the prospective financial statements.
- Due professional care should be exercised.
- The compilation should be adequately planned and assistants, if any, should be properly supervised.
- Applicable compilation procedures should be performed as a basis for the accountant's report.
- Reporting standards for the compilation of prospective financial statements should be observed in the preparation of the accountant's report.

Training and proficiency To perform a compilation of prospective financial statements, the accountant must have an adequate understanding of the preparation and presentation guidelines established by the AICPA for such statements. These standards were discussed earlier (see "Statement Preparation Process" and "Statement Presentation Standards").

Due professional care   Due professional care is achieved by observing the AICPA professional standards for a compilation of prospective financial statements.

Planning and supervision   An important phase of planning a compilation engagement is obtaining an adequate understanding of (1) a general knowledge of the entity's business transactions, (2) the key factors that are likely to have a significant effect on future financial results, and (3) accounting principles used by the entity and within the entity's industry. The accountant may have an understanding of these elements if prior historical financial statements have been audited, reviewed, or compiled by the accountant.

Applicable procedures   A compilation involves (1) assembling (to the extent necessary) the prospective financial statements based on the responsible party's assumptions and (2) performing the required compilation procedures. The PFI Guide requires the accountant to perform the following compilation procedures:

- Establish an understanding with the client, preferably in writing, regarding the services to be performed.

- Inquire about the accounting principles used in the preparation of the prospective financial statements, as follows:

  — For existing entities, compare the accounting principles used to those used in the preparation of previous historical financial statements and inquire whether such principles are the same as those expected to be used in the historical financial statements covering the prospective period.

  — For entities to be formed or for entities formed that have not commenced operations, compare specialized industry accounting principles used, if any, to those typically used in the industry. Inquire whether the accounting principles used for the prospective financial statements are those that are expected to be used when, or if, the entity commences operations.

- Ask how the responsible party identifies the key factors and develops its assumptions.

- List, or obtain a list of, the responsible party's significant assumptions providing the basis for the prospective financial statements. Consider whether there are any obvious omissions in light of the key factors on which the prospective results of the entity appear to depend.

- Consider whether there appear to be any obvious internal inconsistencies in its assumptions.

- Perform, or test the mathematical accuracy of, the computations that translate the assumptions into prospective financial statements.

- Read the prospective financial statements, including the summary of significant assumptions, and consider whether:

  — The statements, including the disclosures of assumptions and accounting policies, appear to be presented in conformity with the AICPA presentation guidelines for prospective financial statements.

  — The statements, including the summary of significant assumptions, appear to be appropriate in relation to the accountant's knowledge of the entity and the industry in which the entity operates.

- If a significant part of the prospective period has expired, inquire about the results of operations or significant portions of the operations (such as sales volume) and significant cash flows. Consider their effects on the prospective financial statements.

- If historical financial statements have been prepared for an expired portion of the period, the accountant should read such statements and consider the results in relation to the prospective financial statements.

- The accountant should confirm his or her understanding of the prospective financial statements (including assumptions) by obtaining written representations from the responsible party.

If, after completing the compilation procedures, the accountant concludes that certain information is incomplete or inappropriate, he or she should request that proper revision be made by the client. If the financial information is not properly revised, the accountant normally would withdraw from the engagement.

Workpapers should serve as a basis for the accountant's report, substantiate that the compilation procedures were performed, and demonstrate that the engagement was adequately planned and properly supervised.

Accountant's report   The following reporting standards should be observed in the preparation of the accountant's report for a compilation engagement:

- The prospective financial statements should be properly identified.

- The report should contain a statement that the accountant has compiled the prospective financial statements in accordance with the standards established by the American Institute of Certified Public Accountants.

- The report should contain a statement that a compilation is limited in scope and does not enable the accountant to express an opinion or any other form of assurance on the prospective financial statements or the related assumptions.

- The report should contain a caveat that the prospective results reflected by the prospective financial statements may not be achieved.

- The report should contain a statement that the accountant assumes no responsibility to update the report for events and circumstances that occur after the date of the report.

The following example illustrates the standard report for the compilation of a financial forecast.

We have compiled the accompanying forecasted balance sheet and statements of income, retained earnings, and cash flows of X Company as of December 31, 19X5, and for the year then ending, in accordance with the standards established by the American Institute of Certified Public Accountants.

A compilation is limited to presenting, in the form of a forecast, information that is the representation of management and does not include evaluation of the support for the assumptions underlying the forecast. We have not examined the forecast and, accordingly, do not express an opinion or any other form of assurance on the accompanying statements or assumptions. Furthermore, there usually will be differences between the forecasted and actual results, because events and circumstances frequently do not occur as expected, and those differences may be material. We have no responsibility to update this report for events and circumstances occurring after the date of the report.

The report on a compilation of prospective financial statements should be dated as of the day on which the compilation procedures are completed by the accountant.

The standard report for a compilation of prospective financial statements may be modified for a number of reasons. Some of these modifications are discussed below.

Lack of independence   An accountant may compile prospective financial statements when he or she is not independent. However, under this circumstance, the following sentence should be added to the last paragraph of the standard report: "We are not independent with respect to X Company."

Departure from AICPA presentation guidelines   An accountant may compile prospective financial statements if presentation departures exist or disclosures, other than those related to significant assumptions, are omitted. However, as mentioned earlier, an accountant cannot issue a compilation report if the entity fails to disclose a summary of the significant assumptions that are used in the prospective financial statements. If the accountant is satisfied that the departures or omissions are not intended to mislead users, a compilation report may be issued, but the report must contain a description of the departures or omissions.

Emphasis of a matter   An item or event may be emphasized in a separate paragraph of a compilation report. However, the emphasized item or event should not represent an assurance that is incompatible with a compilation engagement.

Comparative information   Historical financial statements or a summarization of such statements may be included in the document that contains the compiled prospective financial statements or the summarized information. The accountant's compilation report on the prospective financial statements should include a reference to the historical financial statements.

PART V

Attest Engagements

ATTEST ENGAGEMENTS

CONTENTS

Overview   **16.05**
Citations to Authoritative Pronouncements   **16.06**
Attestation Standards   **16.07**
    Responsibility and Function of the CPA   **16.07**
    Pre-Engagement Planning   **16.08**
       General Standard No. 1—Training and Proficiency   **16.09**
       General Standard No. 2—Knowledge of Assertion   **16.09**
       General Standard No. 3—Reasonable Criteria   **16.10**
       General Standard No. 4—Independence   **16.13**
       General Standard No. 5—Due Care   **16.14**
    Planning the Engagement   **16.14**
       Fieldwork Standard No. 1—Planning and Supervision   **16.14**
          Adequate Planning   **16.14**
          Proper Supervision of Assistants   **16.17**
    Evidence   **16.17**
       Fieldwork Standard No. 2—Sufficient Evidence   **16.17**
          Examination Engagement   **16.18**
          Review Engagement   **16.19**
          Agreed-Upon Procedures   **16.20**
    Accountant's Report   **16.21**
       Reporting Standard No. 1—Character of Engagement   **16.21**
          Examinations and Reviews   **16.21**
          Agreed-Upon Procedures   **16.21**
       Reporting Standard No. 2—Conclusions   **16.22**
          Examination   **16.22**
          Review   **16.23**
          Agreed-Upon Procedures   **16.24**
       Reporting Standard No. 3—Significant Reservations   **16.24**
          Scope Deficiencies   **16.24**
          Presentation Deficiencies   **16.25**

Reports on Matters Relating to Solvency	16.26
Agreed-Upon Procedures Report	16.26
Reporting Standard No. 4—Restricted Distribution	16.26
Workpapers	16.27
Attestation Standards and Consulting Engagements	16.27
Written Assertions	16.28
Criteria	16.28
Evidence	16.28
Reports	16.28
Pro Forma Financial Information	16.28
Accountant's Responsibilities	16.30
Examination Engagements	16.30
Review Engagements	16.30
Audit and Review Procedures	16.31
Reporting on Pro Forma Financial Information	16.33
Examination Engagement Report	16.34
Review Engagement Report	16.35
Report Modifications	16.36
Pooling-of-Interests	16.37
Reporting on Internal Control Over Financial Reporting	16.37
Examination Procedures	16.39
Planning the Engagement	16.40
Understanding Internal Control	16.42
Evaluating the Design	16.42
Testing and Evaluating Operational Effectiveness	16.42
Forming an Opinion	16.44
Separate Report	16.45
Representation Letter	16.46
Report Modifications	16.48
Material Weakness	16.48
Scope Limitation	16.53
Reference to Another Examination Report	16.54
Subsequent Event	16.56

Segment of Internal Control | **16.57**
Assertion Limited to Suitability of Design | **16.57**
Regulatory Control Criteria Not Based on Due Process | **16.59**
Other Information | **16.61**
Material Inconsistency | **16.61**
Material Misstatement of Fact | **16.61**
Written Representations | **16.61**
Other Professional Services and Matters | **16.62**
Audit of Financial Statements | **16.62**
Foreign Corrupt Practices Act | **16.63**
Compliance with Laws and Regulations Engagements | **16.63**
Agreed-Upon Procedures Engagement | **16.63**
Compliance Attestation | **16.64**
Examination Engagement | **16.66**
Risk Assessment | **16.67**
Materiality | **16.69**
Examination Procedures | **16.70**
Agreed-Upon Procedures Engagement | **16.82**

ATTEST ENGAGEMENTS

Overview

Before the promulgation of the standards for attest engagements (or attestation engagements), certain types of auditing and accounting engagements were not specifically addressed by professional standards. For example, there were no professional standards for engagements to report on (1) descriptions of computer software, (2) compliance with statutory, regulatory, and contractual requirements, (3) investment performance statistics, and (4) nonfinancial information supplementary to financial statements. These and other auditing and accounting engagements that are not addressed by other existing professional standards may be covered by the standards for attest engagements (AT 100.01).

An attest engagement is one in which a certified public accountant who is in the practice of public accounting is engaged to issue an opinion about the reliability of another party's written assertion. An assertion is a declaration, or a set of related declarations taken as a whole, that is made by another party. Statement on Standards for Attestation Engagements (SSAE) No. 1, which was issued in March 1986 by the American Institute of Certified Public Accountants (AICPA), contains the following definition of an *attest engagement* (AT 100.01):

> An attest engagement is one in which a practitioner is engaged to issue or does issue a written communication that expresses a conclusion about the reliability of a written assertion that is the responsibility of another party.

Attestation standards apply only to the attest services that are rendered by a certified public accountant who is in the practice of public accounting (hereinafter referred to as a "practitioner").

> ***OBSERVATION:*** *An Interpretation of SSAE-1, "Applicability of Attestation Standards to Litigation Services" (July 1990), concludes that attestation standards apply only to litigation service*

> engagements in which a CPA (1) expresses a written conclusion on a written assertion that is the responsibility of another party, and both the written conclusion and written assertion are of benefit to other parties involved in the proceedings that do not have the opportunity to challenge the assertion, or (2) is specifically hired to perform an attestation service based on the standards established by the Statements on Standards for Attestation Engagements (AT 9100.47–.50).

The attestation standards are issued by the Auditing Standards Board and are covered under Rule 202 (Compliance with Standards) of the Code of Professional Conduct, which is discussed in the chapter entitled "Code of Professional Conduct."

Citations to Authoritative Pronouncements

The authoritative pronouncements covered in this chapter are:

- Statement on Standards for Attestation Engagements (SSAE) No. 1
- SSAE-2 (Reporting on an Entity's Internal Control Over Financial Reporting)
- SSAE-3 (Compliance Attestation)
- SSAE-5 (Amendment to Statement on Standards for Attestation Engagements No. 1, Attestation Standards)
- SSAE-6 (Amendment to Statement on Standards for Attestation Engagements No. 2, Reporting on an Entity's Internal Control Over Financial Reporting)

> **OBSERVATION:** In April 1993, the four original attest standards (Attestation Standards, Attest Services Related to Management Consulting Engagements, Financial Forecasts and Projections, and Reporting on Pro Forma Financial Information) were recodified into SSAE-1. Three of the original standards—Attestation Standards (AT 100), Attest Services Related to Management Consulting Engagements (AT 100), and Reporting on Pro Forma Financial Information (AT 300)—are covered in this chapter. The fourth—Financial Forecasts and Projections (AT 200)—is discussed in the chapter entitled "Prospective Financial Statements." SSAE-2 and SSAE-3 are discussed in this chapter as well.

*SSAE-4 (Agreed-Upon Procedures Engagements) is covered in
the chapter entitled "Agreed-Upon Procedures Engagements."*

SSAE-1 provides broad standards for attestation engagements that involve a written assertion by another party (AT 100; AT 300).

SSAE-2 (as amended by SSAE-6) provides guidance when the auditor is engaged to examine management's assertion about the effectiveness of its internal control (AT 400).

SSAE-3 provides guidance for an engagement in which the auditor either (1) reports on the client's compliance with requirements of specified laws, regulations, rules, contracts, or grants or (2) reports on the effectiveness of the client's internal control over compliance with specified requirements (AT 500).

ATTESTATION STANDARDS

Responsibility and Function of the CPA

If a CPA is engaged to issue, or does issue, a report containing an opinion about the reliability of another party's written assertion, the CPA should examine, review, or apply agreed-upon procedures to the assertion, in accordance with the attestation standards provided in the Statements on Standards for Attestation Engagements (AT 100.03).

In an attest engagement in which an examination is performed, the practitioner issues a report that contains a positive opinion about the written assertion. In an attest engagement in which a review is performed or agreed-upon procedures are applied, the practitioner issues a report that contains a negative assurance about the written assertion. A report on an examination or a review can be made available for general distribution, but a report based on agreed-upon procedures is restricted and cannot be made available for general distribution (AT 100.53, .56, and .59).

An attest engagement may be part of a larger engagement that includes other auditing or consulting services. In this event, the attestation standards should apply only to the attest portion of the engagement, and other standards that are applicable under the circumstances should apply to the other portions of the engagement (AT 100.05).

A practitioner must observe five general standards, two field-work standards, and four reporting standards when performing an attest engagement. The five general standards relate to pre-engagement planning, the two fieldwork standards relate to planning the engagement and collecting evidence, and the four reporting standards relate to the accountant's report (AT 100.06–.52).

In some attest engagements, a practitioner may be required to observe other professional standards in addition to the attestation standards, and in an attest engagement of a governmental unit, governmental standards, laws, and regulations must be followed.

The responsibilities of the CPA with respect to an attest engagement must be carefully evaluated and properly interpreted in the context of the engagement. For example, the following circumstances illustrate the need for properly identifying what constitutes an attest engagement (AT 100.03–.04):

- It may be inferred from the CPA's report that he or she is providing an assurance on a written assertion even though an explicit assurance is not made (for example, when the CPA's report includes enumerated procedures that suggest a basis for making an assurance, but no explicit assurance is made).

- The CPA who has assembled or assisted in assembling an assertion should not claim to be the asserter if the assertion is materially dependent on the actions, plans, or assumptions of some other individual or group. In such a situation, that individual or group is the asserter and the CPA will be viewed as an attester if a conclusion about the reliability of the assertion is expressed.

> **OBSERVATION:** *An Interpretation of SSAE-1, "Defense Industry Questionnaire on Business Ethics and Conduct" (August 1987), states that Statements on Standards for Attestation Engagements apply to an engagement in which a practitioner has been requested to express a written conclusion on a defense contractor's Statement of Responses to the Defense Industry Questionnaire on Business Ethics and Conduct and the additional attached questionnaire and responses (AT 9100.01–.04).*

Pre-Engagement Planning

Pre-engagement planning is an essential element of all professional engagements performed by a CPA. The practitioner must determine whether the attest engagement will include an examination, a review, or the application of agreed-upon procedures. In addition, the practitioner must determine whether to accept or reject the attest engagement. The pre-engagement planning phase of an attest engagement is based on the first five general standards for attest engagements, which are discussed below.

General Standard No. 1 — Training and Proficiency

The first general attestation standard states that "the engagement shall be performed by a practitioner or practitioners having adequate technical training and proficiency in the *attest function.*" Adequate technical training is a combination of an appropriate educational background and extensive practical experience. A CPA with adequate technical training should be competent enough to obtain and evaluate the necessary evidence to determine whether or not another party's written assertions are supportable. Proficiency can be developed only by applying knowledge in an actual attest engagement (AT 100.06–.08).

> **OBSERVATION:** *Unlike the first standard of generally accepted auditing standards, the first general attestation standard does not refer to technical training and proficiency as an auditor. As suggested earlier, the scope of the attestation function described in SSAE-1 goes beyond the boundaries of financial reporting.*

General Standard No. 2 — Knowledge of Assertion

The second general attestation standard concludes that "the engagement shall be performed by a practitioner or practitioners having adequate knowledge in the subject matter of the assertion." Although it can be assumed that a CPA is familiar with financial reporting standards, it cannot be assumed that a CPA is familiar with the procedures and concepts of all attest engagements. Thus, before an attest engagement is accepted by a CPA, he or she should have an adequate understanding of the nature of the written assertion(s). Obviously, a CPA cannot express an opinion on the written assertions unless he or she has a certain level of expertise relating to the nature of the assertions (AT 100.09).

The knowledge required to perform an attest engagement may be obtained through a variety of sources, including formal courses and professional experience. Under some circumstances, a portion of the expertise does not have to be mastered by the CPA but may be obtained through the use of specialists (SAS-73). When a CPA decides to use the work of a specialist, he or she must have a sufficient understanding of the subject matter to explain the objectives of the engagement to the specialist. The CPA also must be able to evaluate the work of the specialist to determine whether the objectives of the engagement have been achieved (AT 100.10).

General Standard No. 3—Reasonable Criteria

Not all engagements provide a basis for attestation. It is concluded in the third general attestation standard that both of the following conditions must be present (AT 100.11):

- The assertion is capable of evaluation against reasonable criteria that either have been established by a recognized body or are stated in the presentation of the assertion in a sufficiently clear and comprehensive manner for a knowledgeable reader to be able to understand them.
- The assertion is capable of reasonably consistent estimation or measurement using such criteria.

The fundamental element in the engagement is the existence of reasonable criteria that provide the basis for the written assertions. In an audit engagement, the reasonable criteria are generally accepted accounting principles, which in turn provide a reasonable basis for the preparation of financial statements. Because of the diversity of attest engagements, there is no single set of reasonable criteria for all such engagements; however, general guidelines for determining whether reasonable criteria exist are identified. SSAE-1 concludes that assertions are assumed to be based on reasonable criteria when the process generates information that is both relevant and reliable (AT 100.12–.15).

> **OBSERVATION:** *The basic concept that information must be both relevant and reliable to be useful is not unique. FASB Concepts Statement No. 1 (Qualitative Characteristics of Accounting Information) extensively discusses relevance and reliability in the*

context of financial reporting. There is a great deal of overlap between the discussion found in the Concepts Statement and that in the Statement on Standards for Attestation Engagements.

Information is relevant if it has the capacity to make a difference in a decision. The decision may be concerned with the (1) prediction of the outcome of events, whether they be past, present, or future, or (2) confirmation or correction of prior expectations. In addition, information must have the following characteristics to be relevant (AT 100.15):

- *Ability to bear upon uncertainty* The assertions are useful in confirming or altering the degree of uncertainty about the result of a decision.

- *Timeliness* The assertions are available to decision makers before they lose their capability to influence decisions.

- *Completeness* The assertions do not omit information that could alter or confirm a decision.

- *Consistency* The assertions are measured and presented in materially the same manner in succeeding time periods or, if material inconsistencies exist, changes are disclosed, justified, and, where practical, reconciled to permit proper interpretations of sequential measurements.

Information is reliable if it represents the event or events it purports to represent (representational faithfulness). In describing these events through assertions, care must be taken to avoid suggesting a degree of certainty or precision that may not be justifiable (absence of unwarranted inference of certainty or precision). One method of dealing with the certainty or precision problem is to express assertions in terms of ranges or probabilities rather than as a single value. For example, an attest engagement involving the processing of certain transactions in conformance with established governmental regulations could be expressed as a 95% probability that the compliance rate is at least 98%. In addition to representational faithfulness and the absence of unwarranted inference of certainty or precision, information should have the following characteristics (AT 100.15):

- *Neutrality* The primary concern is the relevance and reliability of assertions rather than their potential effect on a particular interest.

- *Freedom from bias* The measurements involved in the assertions are equally likely to fall on either side of what they represent (rather than falling more often on one side than the other).

To some extent, reliability and relevance are inconsistent. That is, to increase reliability, it may be necessary to reduce the degree of relevance. The CPA must ultimately use professional judgment to determine whether information exhibits a proper balance between relevance and reliability.

Under limited circumstances, the CPA is not required to determine the reasonableness of criteria on which assertions are made in the written communication. It is assumed that criteria established by a body designated by the AICPA Council under the Code of Professional Conduct are reasonable criteria for assertions. Also, bodies, such as regulatory agencies, that are composed of experts in the field and follow due process provide an acceptable source for reasonable criteria (AT 100.17).

The CPA cannot presume the existence of reasonable criteria that are established by groups, such as industry associations, if they do not follow due process or do not represent the public interest. Such criteria must be critically evaluated by the CPA using the fundamental characteristics of relevance and reliability as the basis for analysis. If it is concluded that the criteria are reasonable, the written communication containing the assertions must include, in a clear and comprehensive manner, a description of the criteria (AT 100.18–.20).

The second condition of the third general standard refers to the need for consistent estimation or measurement of the quantitative or qualitative assertions. In general, knowledgeable individuals using the same or similar measurement or disclosure criteria should arrive at materially similar estimates and measurements. When the assertions are so subjective that there is no basis for forming a conclusion on the assertions, conditions for attestation do not exist. This does not imply that the mere existence of the possibility of materially different estimates or measurements always precludes the attestation function. For example, SSAE-1 notes that the following circumstances could lead to materially different estimates or measurements that do not necessarily prohibit the CPA from attesting to the validity of the assertions contained in the written communication (AT 100.21):

- Estimates and measurements often require the exercise of considerable judgment.
- A slightly different evaluation of the same facts may lead to significantly different assertions.

The materiality concept must be used to determine what is a reasonably consistent estimate or measurement. The acceptable range of materiality varies depending on the nature of the attest engagement. In an engagement in which the CPA is attesting to "hard" data where the estimate or measurement criteria are well defined, the range of acceptable values would be more narrow than in an engagement involving "soft" information. For example, the materiality level would probably be more narrow for an engagement that involves the measurement of the price-level adjusted value of an organization's property, plant, and equipment than for an engagement where the CPA is attesting to the fair value of an organization's property, plant, and equipment (AT 100.19).

The concept of reasonably consistent estimation and measurement is a generalization that does not vary with the type of engagement involved. That is, the engagement, whether it is an examination engagement or a review engagement, must satisfy the concept. An engagement is not more conducive to a review than to an examination. If the characteristics of the engagement suggest that an examination is not appropriate, then it must also be concluded that a review cannot be performed by the CPA (AT 100.17).

General Standard No. 4 — Independence

The fourth general attestation standard requires that a CPA be independent in fact as well as in appearance. Independence in fact is a mental state of mind whereby a CPA is impartial in determining the reliability of assertions made in the written communication. In reaching a conclusion, a CPA favors neither the asserter nor the user of the information. Independence in appearance means that the CPA should avoid situations or relationships that may suggest to an outside party that the CPA is not independent (AT 100.22–.24).

> *OBSERVATION: Although SSAE-1 provides minimal guidance on the observation of the fourth general standard, the CPA should refer to the AICPA Code of Professional Conduct and related Interpretations and Rulings for additional information about independence.*

> *OBSERVATION: Rule 101 of the Code of Professional Conduct provides a general description of independence. In addition, Interpretation 11 of Rule 101 provides guidance for certain attest en-*

gagements. Rule 101 and Interpretation 11 are discussed in the chapter entitled "Code of Professional Conduct."

General Standard No. 5—Due Care

The fifth general attestation standard requires that the CPA exercise due professional care in conducting an attest engagement. Due professional care is achieved by the CPA by observing the two standards of fieldwork and the four reporting standards. When a CPA agrees to perform an attest engagement, it is implied that the practitioner has a level of expertise that is possessed by other CPAs who perform similar services. With the acceptance of the engagement, the CPA is expected to perform the engagement and exercise those skills to a degree expected by a reasonable person. However, this does not imply that the judgment of the CPA is infallible or that he or she can be expected to fill the role of a guarantor of information contained in written reports. If the practitioner is not negligent in the execution of the engagement and conducts himself or herself in an honest manner, the due care standard generally will be satisfied (AT 100.25–.27).

Planning the Engagement

Critical elements of every professional engagement include planning and supervision. The importance of these elements are recognized in the first standard of fieldwork, which states that an attest engagement should be adequately planned, and assistants, if any, should be properly supervised.

Fieldwork Standard No. 1—Planning and Supervision

Adequate planning   Planning allows the practitioner to develop a strategy for conducting an attest engagement. Adequate planning matches the objectives of the attest engagement with the specific procedures that must be performed to achieve the objectives. Each engagement plan is unique because it is based on the specific characteristics of a particular engagement. However, SSAE-1 identifies the following factors that should be part of the planning process of an attest engagement (AT 100.28).

Criteria As identified in the third general attestation standard, assertions contained in the written communication must be based on reasonable criteria. Because the criteria serve as the foundation for the presentation of the assertions, the CPA must be thoroughly familiar with such criteria. The identification of the criteria will assist the practitioner in determining his or her strategy for collecting evidence to support or refute the assertions (AT 100.29–.31).

Risk Attestation risk represents the possibility that the CPA will not discover materially misstated assertions in the written communication. Attestation risk comprises three factors—inherent risk, control risk, and detection risk (AT 100.31).

1. *Inherent risk* Inherent risk is related to the fundamental characteristics of the nature of the attest engagement. Simply, there is more risk associated with attesting to some assertions than other assertions. For example, attest engagements that rely on considerable professional judgment in the application of criteria to develop assertions have a high degree of inherent risk. A CPA cannot change inherent risk but must recognize it as a factor in each attest engagement.

2. *Control risk* Control risk is related to the procedures and processes used by a party to develop assertions made in the written communication. When the design, execution, and monitoring of these procedures and processes are effective, the likelihood of developing information that is materially incorrect is relatively low. The CPA must recognize control risk as a factor in each attest engagement although he or she can make suggestions to strengthen the procedures and processes that could lower the level of control risk for subsequent attest engagements.

   OBSERVATION: The fundamental concepts of internal control for an audit engagement are also applicable to attest engagements. These concepts are discussed in the chapter entitled "Internal Control, Errors, and Irregularities."

3. *Detection risk* Detection risk is the probability that a material misstatement will not be discovered and is a function of the attest procedures employed by the CPA. The more attest procedures employed (sample size) and the more effective the attest procedures (quality of procedures), the less likely it

will be that a material misstatement will go undetected. For this reason, there is an inverse relationship between detection risk, inherent risk, and control risk. In an engagement where there is a high degree of inherent and control risks, the CPA should select a relatively low level of detection risk (probability of not discovering a material misstatement). Although detection risk cannot be quantified on an overall basis for an attest engagement, the CPA can change the level of detection risk through the expansion of the attest sample and the selection of attest procedures, which of course are critical elements in planning an engagement.

Materiality Before attest procedures are designed, the CPA must identify materiality factors for the attest engagement. The materiality levels should be used by the practitioner or assistants during the engagement to focus on those problem areas where there could be materially misstated assertions. If materiality factors are not identified early in the engagement, the practitioner may devote an inordinate amount of time to insignificant elements of the engagement (AT 100.31).

Potential attest problems As part of the planning phase of the engagement, the CPA should anticipate areas that may require the revision or adjustment of data or the extension or modification of attest procedures. By having a broad understanding of the nature of the attest engagement and the procedures and processes used to develop data, the auditor can identify potential problem areas promptly. When these areas are discovered, the nature, extent, and timing of attest procedures should be changed. This does not imply that once planned, an attest strategy cannot be changed by the practitioner. As the attest engagement is executed, the discovery of problems or the absence of anticipated problems will require that the nature, extent, and timing of attest procedures be appropriately changed (AT 100.32).

Nature of report The scope and direction of an attest engagement will be affected by the nature of the CPA's report. As suggested earlier, an examination report, a review report, or an agreed-upon procedures report may be issued. In an examination, the engagement must be planned in a manner that enables the collection of sufficient evidence to express a conclusion on the assertions contained in the written communication. In a review engagement, the overall strategy should be to collect evidence sufficient to allow the practitioner to express a negative assurance on the information. Thus, a higher level of sufficient evidence must be collected in an examination than in a review, and the planning of an engagement should reflect this difference.

Proper supervision of assistants   The second part of the first standard of fieldwork requires that assistants, if any, be properly supervised. The purpose of supervision is to determine whether attest procedures are properly performed and whether the report to be issued by the CPA is justified by the results of applying the attest procedures (AT 100.33).

The actual level of supervision varies in each engagement and is dependent on such factors as the complexity of the engagement and the educational background and proficiency of the assistants. To some extent, supervision and planning overlap. In a properly supervised attest engagement, each assistant should understand the nature and objectives of the engagement before work begins. Subsequently, the supervisor must review the assistants' work on a timely basis and be available to provide professional guidance in resolving conflicts that may arise among assistants. In addition, each assistant should be specifically instructed to bring areas of conflict to the attention of the supervising CPA so that these differences can be evaluated (AT 100.34–.35).

Evidence

The second standard of fieldwork requires that the practitioner obtain sufficient evidence as a reasonable basis for the conclusion expressed in the attest report (AT 100.36).

Fieldwork Standard No. 2 — Sufficient Evidence

There are a variety of attest procedures that may be used to obtain evidential matter. The selection of specific procedures to be employed in a specific attest engagement is based on professional judgment. In addition, SSAE-1 provides the following guidelines (AT 100.37):

- Evidence obtained from independent sources outside an entity provides greater assurance of an assertion's reliability than evidence secured solely from within the entity.

- Information obtained through the practitioner's direct personal knowledge (such as through physical examination, observation, computation, operating tests, or inspection) is more persuasive than information not obtained through the practitioner's personal knowledge.

- Assertions developed under effective internal controls are more reliable than those developed under ineffective internal controls.

The above guidelines are concerned with the quality of the evidential matter that is obtained in an attest engagement, but the practitioner must also be concerned with the quantity of the evidential matter. Here again, professional judgment must ultimately be used to identify what constitutes sufficient evidence in an attest engagement. In addition, SSAE-1 provides that the practitioner should consider the following items in determining the sufficiency of evidential matter (AT 100.42):

- Nature and materiality of the information in the presentation of the assertions taken as a whole
- Likelihood of misstatements
- Knowledge obtained during current and previous engagements
- Practitioner's competence in the subject matter of the assertion
- Extent to which the information is affected by the asserter's judgment
- Inadequacies in the assertions' underlying data

The quality of evidence and the sufficiency of evidence must be determined in the context of the specific type of attest engagement. As described earlier, an attest engagement may be an examination engagement, a review engagement, or an agreed-upon procedures engagement.

Examination engagement Attest procedures must be selected so that the quality and quantity of evidence obtained is sufficient to reduce the attestation risk (probability of not discovering materially misstated assertions) to a low level. Of course the overall attestation risk cannot be qualified, but through the exercise of professional judgment, the CPA must assess inherent risk and control risk and must establish an appropriate level of detection risk. As was discussed earlier, the practitioner has little, if any, influence on the level of inherent risk and control risk that exists in an attest engagement. However, the practitioner can influence the level of detection risk through the selection of attest procedures. The following generalized relationships can be used to establish an acceptable level of detection risk (AT 100.39).

Assessment Risk	Effect on Detection Risk Level
Inherent risk is assessed to be relatively high.	Detection risk should be established at a relatively low level.
Inherent risk is assessed to be relatively low.	Detection risk should be established at a relatively high level.
Control risk is assessed to be relatively high.	Detection risk should be established at a relatively low level.
Control risk is assessed to be relatively low.	Detection risk should be established at a relatively high level.

After considering inherent risk, control risk, and detection risk, a practitioner should attempt to achieve a low level of attestation risk. In an examination engagement, a practitioner can achieve a low level of attestation risk by relying on search and verification procedures, such as physical observation, confirmation, and inspection, in addition to inquiry and analytical procedures (AT 100.39).

Review engagement   The level of assurance provided by the practitioner in a review engagement is not as great as the level of assurance provided in an examination engagement. In a review engagement, a negative assurance is expressed by the practitioner, whereas in an examination engagement, the practitioner expresses a positive assurance on the assertions. For this reason, the level of attestation risk that must be achieved in a review engagement is a moderate level, rather than a low level. On the basis of the interrelationship of inherent risk, control risk, and detection risk, attest procedures that will result in an overall moderate level of attestation risk are selected (AT 100.40).

Generally, in a review engagement, the CPA limits attest procedures to inquiry and analytical procedures, in much the same manner as an accountant would in the conduct of a review of historical financial statements. This is not to suggest that other attest procedures, such as search and verification procedures, are not appropriate under some circumstances. For example, presented below are circumstances that may be encountered in a review engagement and the effects of the circumstances on attest procedures (AT 100.41).

Circumstance	Effects of Circumstance on Attest Procedures Used in a Review Engagement
Inquiry and analytical procedures cannot be performed.	Use other attest procedures to achieve a level of assurance that would have been achieved had the inquiry and analytical procedures been performed.
Inquiry and analytical procedures are considered to be inefficient.	Use other attest procedures that are more efficient to achieve a level of assurance that would have been achieved had the less efficient inquiry and analytical procedures been performed.
Inquiry and analytical procedures are employed but results suggest that assertions may be incorrect or incomplete.	Use additional attest procedures to the extent deemed necessary to remove doubts about the accuracy or completeness of assertions.

Agreed-upon procedures In an agreed-upon procedures engagement, the specified parties are directly involved in the establishment of the nature and scope of the engagement. The practitioner is required to perform only those procedures that have been agreed upon. The procedures may be as limited or extensive as desired by the specified user; however, they must consist of more than a simple reading of the written communication that contains the assertions (AT 100.43–.44). SSAE-4 contains attestation standards for agreed-upon procedures engagements; it is discussed in the chapter entitled "Agreed-Upon Procedures Engagements."

Accountant's Report

Although the nature of attest engagements is varied, there are four reporting standards that must be observed in the preparation of the practitioner's report. These reporting standards are to be followed in the preparation of reports for examination engagements, review engagements, and agreed-upon procedures engagements. A report must be issued for any attest engagement that is accepted by a practitioner. If, after the commencement of an attest engagement, it is decided by the client that no report shall be issued, the practitioner should withdraw from the engagement.

Reporting Standard No. 1—Character of Engagement

The first reporting standard requires that the assertions being reported on and the character of the engagement be clearly referred to in the practitioner's report on the attest engagement (AT 100.45).

Since the asserter is responsible for the assertions, the presentation format of the assertions should clearly emphasize this responsibility. For this reason, the asserter's written communication should either be bound with or accompany the practitioner's report and should not simply be presented as part of the practitioner's attest report (AT 100.46).

Examinations and reviews   When an attest engagement is an examination or a review and the report is to be issued for general distribution, the report should include a description of the nature and scope of the engagement. Also, there should be an explicit reference to the professional standards that were the basis for the attest engagement. For example, if the engagement is conducted in accordance with generally accepted auditing standards, there should be a reference to generally accepted auditing standards in the report. If no authoritative interpretive standards governed the engagement, the practitioner's report should include a statement that the examination or review, whichever is appropriate, was conducted in accordance with "standards established by the American Institute of Certified Public Accountants" (AT 100.47).

Agreed-upon procedures   When an attest engagement is an agreed-upon procedures engagement, the report should include a list of the procedures performed and the findings. Also, the report should refer to the professional standards that were the basis for the attest engagement (AT 100.47–.48). Reporting standards for agreed-upon procedures engagements are discussed in the chapter entitled "Agreed-Upon Procedures Engagements."

Reporting Standard No. 2 — Conclusions

The practitioner's report should state a conclusion about whether the assertions are presented in conformity with the established or stated criteria against which the assertions were measured (AT 100.49).

The nature and scope of the attest engagement should enable the practitioner to draw a conclusion about whether there are material omissions or misstatements in the presentation of the assertions. As noted earlier, the presentation of assertions may be based on either established criteria or stated criteria. Professional judgment must be exercised to identify material deviations from the established or stated criteria. An item is considered material if a user of the information would be influenced by its omission or misstatement. Materiality is expressed in relative (percentages), rather than absolute (dollars), terms (AT 100.50).

The specific wording of the assurance provided by the practitioner in his or her report depends on the nature of the attest engagement as explained below.

Examination   In an examination engagement, the practitioner's report should express a positive conclusion about whether the presentation of assertions is in accordance with the established or stated criteria. Presented below is a practitioner's report that contains an unqualified opinion on the distribution of trust investment and capital transactions to beneficiaries as determined by a trust agreement (AT 100.53–.54).

We have examined the accompanying Distribution of Trust Investment and Capital Transactions of The Porterfield Trust for the year ended December 31, 19X5. Our examination was made in accordance with standards established by the American Institute of Certified Public Accountants and, accordingly, included such procedures as we considered necessary in the circumstances.

In our opinion, the Distribution of Trust Investment and Capital Transactions referred to above presents the distribution of investment and capital transactions of The Porterfield Trust for the year ended December 31, 19X5, in conformity with the measurement criteria as required by the last will and testament executed by John J. Porterfield on June 3, 19X1, and described in Note 1.

The practitioner's report may be expanded by adding paragraphs that emphasize certain matters relating to the attest engagement or the presentation of assertions. This type of report modification does not result in a qualified opinion, and the opinion paragraph of the report should not refer to the emphasized matters. In addition, when the assertions are based on specified criteria agreed to by the asserter and the user, the report should be expanded to encompass the following (AT 100.55):

- A statement of limitations on the use of the report because it is intended solely for specified parties
- An indication, when applicable, that the presentation of assertions differs materially from that which would have been presented if criteria for the presentation of such assertions for general distribution had been followed in its preparation

Circumstances that may lead to the expression of an opinion that is not unqualified are discussed later in this chapter under the section on the third standard of reporting.

Review   When a review engagement is completed, negative assurance is expressed on the written communication that contains the assertions. In addition to negative assurance, the report should state that the scope of a review is narrower than that of an examination and disclaim a positive opinion on the presentation. Presented below is an attest report that expresses a negative assurance on the distribution of trust investment and capital transactions to beneficiaries as determined by a trust agreement (AT 100.57–.58).

We have reviewed the accompanying Distribution of Trust Investment and Capital Transactions of The Porterfield Trust for the year ended December 31, 19X5. Our review was conducted in accordance with standards established by the American Institute of Certified Public Accountants.

A review is substantially less in scope than an examination, the objective of which is the expression of an opinion on the Distribution of Trust Investment and Capital Transactions. Accordingly, we do not express such an opinion.

Based on our review, nothing came to our attention that caused us to believe that the accompanying Distribution of Trust Investment and Capital Transactions is not presented in conformity with the measurement criteria as required by the last will and testament executed by John J. Porterfield on June 3, 19X1, and described in Note 1.

The report may be expanded by adding paragraphs that emphasize certain matters relating to the attest engagement or the presentation of assertions. When the assertions are based on specified criteria agreed to by the asserter and the user, the report should be expanded to encompass the following (AT 100.56):

- A statement of limitations on the use of the report because it is intended solely for specified parties

- An indication, when applicable, that the presentation of assertions differs materially from that which would have been presented if criteria for the presentation of such assertions for general distribution had been followed in its preparation

Other circumstances that may lead to the modification of a review report are discussed later in this chapter under the section on the third standard of reporting.

Agreed-upon procedures   As noted earlier, when an attest engagement is an agreed-upon procedures engagement, the report should include a list of the procedures performed and the findings. The accountant's report should provide no assurance (including negative assurance) on the subject matter of the engagement. Reporting standards for an agreed-upon procedures engagement are discussed in the chapter entitled "Agreed-Upon Procedures Engagements."

Reporting Standard No. 3 — Significant Reservations

The third reporting standard is unique in that it explicitly requires that the attest report include all significant reservations the practitioner has with respect to the engagement and the presentation of assertions. When attestation standards have not been satisfied and the practitioner has significant reservations, an unqualified conclusion should not be expressed in the examination report or the review report. Significant reservations may be categorized as scope deficiencies and presentation deficiencies (AT 100.63–.64).

> *OBSERVATION: Modifications to the accountant's report in an agreed-upon procedures engagement are discussed in the chapter entitled "Agreed-Upon Procedures Engagements."*

Scope deficiencies   The second standard of fieldwork requires that sufficient evidence be obtained to support the practitioner's report.

When significant reservations exist because of the limited scope of the attest engagement, the practitioner should qualify or disclaim any assurance on the presentation of assertions or withdraw from the engagement (AT 100.65).

Scope limitations may arise because all necessary or alternative procedures (examination and review engagements) cannot be performed because of the circumstances surrounding the engagement or because of restrictions imposed by the client. Generally, if the restrictions are imposed by the client, the practitioner should withdraw from the engagement and issue no report or disclaim any assurance on the presentation (AT 100.65).

When the scope limitation is caused by the practitioner's inability to perform attest procedures or express a conclusion on the presentation of assertions, the significance of the restrictions determines whether a qualified conclusion, disclaimer of conclusion, or withdrawal from the engagement is appropriate. Specifically, the actions to be taken by the practitioner depend on the following factors (AT 100.66):

- Nature and magnitude of the scope restrictions

- Significance of restrictions to the presentation of assertions

- The nature of the service being performed (examination or review)

If it is concluded that a qualified conclusion or disclaimer of conclusion should be expressed, the basis for the qualification or disclaimer must be described in the practitioner's report (AT 100.66).

Presentation deficiencies An unqualified conclusion should not be expressed by the practitioner if there are reservations about compliance with established criteria or stated criteria, including the disclosure of information. Deviations from established or stated criteria include the following:

- Measurement of factors affecting the construction of assertions

- Form of presentation that contains the assertions

- Arrangement of material appearing in the presentation of assertions

- Underlying judgments and assumptions that provide the basis for the formulation of assertions

If the practitioner concludes that material presentation deficiencies exist, either a qualified or an adverse conclusion should be expressed. The materiality of the deficiencies, evaluated in the context of each specific engagement, determines whether a qualified or adverse conclusion is more appropriate. The practitioner's report must include a description of the deficiencies that result in the modification of the attest report (AT 100.67–.68).

Reports on matters relating to solvency   According to an Interpretation of SSAE-1 entitled "Responding to Requests for Reports on Matters Relating to Solvency" (February 1988), an accountant should provide *no* level of assurance, through an audit, a review, or an agreed-upon procedures engagement, that an entity *(1) is not insolvent at the time debt is incurred or would not be rendered insolvent thereby, (2) does not have unusually small capital, or (3) has the ability to pay its debt as the debt matures. These and similar situations are referred to as matters relating to solvency* (AT 9100.33–.44).

> **OBSERVATION:** *Although an accountant cannot provide assurance about matters relating to solvency, he or she can provide other services, such as the audit or review of the historical financial statements, the examination or review of pro forma financial information, or the examination or compilation of prospective financial information.*

Agreed-upon procedures report   An accountant may provide professional service to a client or a lender based on agreed-upon procedures. The professional standards that should be observed in agreed-upon procedures engagements are discussed in the chapter entitled "Agreed-Upon Procedures Engagements."

Reporting Standard No. 4—Restricted Distribution

Attest reports may be classified as those available for distribution (examination and review of presentation based on established criteria) and those that are available only for restricted distribution (examination and review of presentations based on agreed-upon criteria and agreed-upon procedures engagement). The fourth standard of reporting requires that reports available only for restricted distribution must clearly state that they are intended only for the use of those parties that participated in determining the agreed-upon criteria or agreed-upon procedures. Also, when a report restricted to specified users is included or combined with an otherwise unrestricted report, all of the reports become restricted (AT 100.69–.70).

Workpapers

The work performed and the conclusions reached by the accountant should be adequately documented in the workpapers. Professional standards regarding workpapers are discussed in SSAE-5, which was an amendment to SSAE-1 (AT 100).

> *OBSERVATION: Workpapers are the property of the accountant, and he or she should establish appropriate procedures to protect the confidentiality of the information. Workpapers should be retained for a period that meets the legal requirements and the needs of the accountant.*

In general, SSAE-5 concludes that workpapers must demonstrate that Fieldwork Standards No.1 (Adequate Planning and Supervision) and No. 2 (Sufficient Evidential Matter) were satisfied. Workpapers may include memorandums, engagement programs, and letters of confirmation and representation; however, the type of workpapers the accountant will prepare will depend on the circumstances of the engagement.

ATTESTATION STANDARDS AND CONSULTING ENGAGEMENTS

A practitioner may accept a consulting service engagement that includes an attest service as described in this chapter. The two separate phases of the single engagement should be performed by observing Statements on Standards for Consulting Services (SSCS) for the consulting phase and Statements on Standards for Attestation Engagements for the attest phase of the engagement. The practitioner should explain to the client the difference between the two services and should obtain the client's agreement that the attest service should be performed in accordance with professional standards. The agreement that an attest service is to be performed should be documented in the consulting engagement letter (AT 100.71–.72).

During the course of a consulting engagement, the practitioner may evaluate a number of written assertions made by other parties. Such assertions may include vendor statements about the capability of computer hardware or software. The evaluation of such assertions is not an attest service unless the practitioner is asked to attest to the reliability of the assertions (AT 100.75).

Written assertions   An attest service may be based on written assertions of another party developed with the assistance of a practitioner as part of a consulting engagement. However, the written assertion must be based on the "actions, plans, or assumptions" of the other party and the other party must be capable of assessing the accuracy of the assertion (AT 100.74).

Criteria   To evaluate the reasonableness of assertions, criteria developed with the assistance of a practitioner may be used. Under this circumstance, criteria must be consistent with SSAE-1 (AT 100.74). (Refer to General Standard No. 3, discussed earlier in this chapter.)

Evidence   The practitioner may use evidential matter obtained as part of a current or prior consulting engagement in the performance of an attest service. The evidential matter must satisfy SSAE requirements. (Refer to Fieldwork Standard No. 2, discussed earlier in this chapter.)

Reports   When a practitioner performs an attest service as part of a consulting engagement, separate reports for each phase of the engagement should be prepared. Reporting standards established by SSAE-1 should be followed to report on the attest service phase of the engagement. Reporting standards established by the consulting standards should be followed to report on the consulting phase of the engagement. When the reports are presented in a single binder, the attest report should be clearly identified as such and presented separately from the consulting report (AT 100.73).

PRO FORMA FINANCIAL INFORMATION

The section of SSAE-1 entitled "Reporting on Pro Forma Financial Information" was issued in September 1988 to provide guidance to accountants who are engaged to report on pro forma financial information. In this type of engagement, the accountant must observe the general standards and fieldwork standards for attest engagements in general, which were discussed earlier in this chapter, in addition to the performance and reporting standards discussed in this section. Engagements to apply agreed-upon procedures to pro forma financial information should be based on the guidance provided for attest engagements in general (AT 300.01).

> **OBSERVATION:** *"Reporting on Pro Forma Financial Information" does not apply to post balance sheet events or transactions that are included in historical financial statements for the purposes of a more meaningful presentation (for example, revision of earnings per share for a stock split or the revision of debt maturities).*

In the event an accountant is not engaged to report on pro forma financial information that is included in the same document as the audited financial statements, the accountant must observe the responsibilities outlined in SAS-8 (Other Information in Documents Containing Audited Financial Statements) and SAS-37 (Filings Under Federal Securities Statutes) (AT 300.02).

Pro forma financial information reflects the effects of applying significant assumptions, such as a proposed transaction, to an enterprise's historical financial statements or information. The more common uses of pro forma financial information include showing the effects of transactions such as a business combination, change in capitalization, change in form of business organization, proposed sale or purchase, or the disposition of a significant segment of a business. When pro forma financial information is presented, the following should be observed (AT 300.04–.06):

- Pro forma financial information should be labeled to distinguish it from historical financial information.

- The transactions or events that are being integrated into the historical financial information should be clearly described.

- The historical financial information that is the basis for the pro forma financial information should be clearly identified.

- The assumptions used by management in constructing the pro forma financial information should be clearly identified.

- Any significant uncertainties related to management's assumptions should be clearly identified.

- A clear indication must be made that the pro forma financial information should be read in conjunction with the related historical financial information.

- It must be clearly indicated that the pro forma financial information is not necessarily indicative of what would have occurred had the transaction taken place at an earlier date.

Accountant's Responsibilities

When an accountant is engaged to examine or review pro forma financial information, the professional responsibilities of the accountant depend on the level of assurance assumed by the accountant in the engagement (AT 300.07).

Examination engagements   SSAE-1 concludes that the purpose of an accountant's examination of pro forma financial information is to provide reasonable assurance about the following (AT 300.10):

- Management's assumptions provide a reasonable basis for presenting the significant effects directly attributable to the underlying transaction or event.
- The related pro forma adjustments give appropriate effect to those assumptions.
- The pro forma amounts reflect the proper application of those adjustments to the historical financial statements.

Review engagements   SSAE-1 concludes that the purpose of an accountant's review of pro forma financial information is to provide *negative* assurance that nothing came to the accountant's attention to cause him or her to believe that (AT 300.10):

- Management's assumptions do not provide a reasonable basis for presenting the significant effects directly attributable to the transaction (or event).
- The related pro forma adjustments do not give appropriate effect to those assumptions.
- The pro forma column does not reflect the appropriate application of those adjustments to the historical financial statements.

An accountant may accept an examination or review engagement if all of the following conditions are met (AT 300.03):

1. The historical financial statements that are the basis for the pro forma financial information must be audited or reviewed.

2. The accountant must have an appropriate level of knowledge of the accounting and reporting practices of the entity.

3. The historical financial statements for the most recent year must be included in the document that contains the pro forma financial information (when the most recent year is not available, the previous year's statements may be used). If the pro forma information is presented for an interim period, the interim historical financial statements (may be a condensed presentation) should be included. (The historical financial statements may be included explicitly or by reference.)

4. The accountant's audit or review report must be included in the document containing the pro forma financial information.

The type of pro forma financial information engagement that can be accepted by an accountant depends on the type of service performed on the related historical financial statements. That is, an audit of the pro forma financial information can be performed only when the historical financial statements have been audited. Only a review of the pro forma financial information can be performed when the historical financial statements have been reviewed only. The rationale for these guidelines is that the level of assurance that can be offered for pro forma financial information can be no higher than the level of assurance made by the accountant with respect to the historical financial statements (AT 300.07).

An accountant generally obtains an appropriate level of knowledge of the accounting and financial reporting practices of the entity by auditing or reviewing the (most recent) historical financial statements that are the basis for the preparation of the pro forma financial information. If another accountant has performed the audit or review of the most recent historical financial statements, the accountant should consider whether it is appropriate to accept the pro forma financial information engagement (AT 300.07).

Audit and Review Procedures

Pro forma financial information simulates the effects of a transaction or event as if the transaction or event *had* occurred on a particular date. For example, a business combination that occurs after the issuance of the annual financial statements may be presented on a pro forma basis in a document.

Since the accountant has audited or reviewed the historical financial statements that are the basis for the pro forma financial information, the audit or review procedures are concerned with management's assumptions and the specific pro forma adjustments. For this reason, the accountant should perform the following procedures for *either* an audit or a review of the pro forma financial information (AT 300.10):

- Understand the transaction or event that is the basis for the pro forma financial information by reviewing relevant contracts, reviewing relevant minutes of meetings of the board of directors, and making inquiries of appropriate management personnel.

- Gain an understanding of each constituent part of the combined entity that enables the accountant to perform the appropriate procedures.

- Discuss the assumptions related to the effects of the transaction or event.

- Determine whether all pro forma adjustments related to the transaction or event have been considered.

- To support the pro forma adjustments, obtain sufficient evidence by reviewing relevant purchase agreements, debt agreements, and legislative actions. (Generally, more evidential matter must be obtained for an examination than for a review engagement.)

- Determine whether management's assumptions are presented in a clear and comprehensive manner.

- Determine whether pro forma adjustments are consistent with each other and with the data used to construct them.

- Recompute pro forma adjustments.

- Determine whether the pro forma adjustments are properly considered in the historical information in order to construct the pro forma financial information.

- Obtain the following written representations from management:

  — Management takes responsibility for the assumptions.

  — Assumptions provide a reasonable basis for presenting the effects of the transaction or event.

  — The pro forma adjustments are based on these assumptions.

— The pro forma financial information reflects the pro forma adjustments.

— Significant effects related to the transaction or event are appropriately disclosed in the pro forma financial information.

• Read the pro forma financial information and determine whether:

— There is a proper description of the transaction or event, pro forma adjustments, significant assumptions, and significant uncertainties.

— There is a proper identification of the sources of the historical financial information that serves as the basis for the pro forma financial information.

Reporting on Pro Forma Financial Information

When preparing either the examination or the review report on pro forma financial information, the accountant should follow the reporting guidelines shown below (AT 300.12):

• Identify the pro forma financial information.

• Refer to the historical financial statements that are the basis for the preparation of the pro forma financial information.

• State whether the historical financial statements were audited or reviewed. (Any modifications to the standard audit or review report also should be disclosed.)

• State that the examination or review was made in accordance with standards established by the American Institute of Certified Public Accountants.

• For a review engagement, state the following:

A review is substantially less in scope than an examination, the objective of which is the expression of an opinion on the pro forma financial information. Accordingly, we do not express such an opinion.

• In a separate paragraph, state the objective and limitations of pro forma financial information.

The accountant's report on pro forma financial information may be presented separately or with the document that contains the accountant's report on the historical financial statements. When the report is presented separately, the report date should be based on the date the engagement procedures were completed. When the report is presented with the report on the historical financial statements, the report should use a dual date similar to the following (AT 300.15).

March 29, 19X2, except for the paragraphs regarding pro forma financial information as to which the date is April 15, 19X2.

In addition, the following reporting guidelines should be followed, depending on whether an examination engagement or a review engagement report is prepared.

Examination engagement report   An examination engagement report on pro forma financial information should state the accountant's opinion on whether (1) management's assumptions provide a reasonable basis for presenting the effects of the transaction or event, (2) these assumptions are appropriately reflected in the pro forma adjustments, and (3) the pro forma adjustments were properly reflected in the historical financial information in order to construct the pro forma financial information (AT 300.16).

Following is an example of a report on the examination of pro forma financial information (AT 300.16).

We have examined the pro forma adjustments reflecting the [transaction or event] described in Note 1 and the application of those adjustments to the historical amounts in the accompanying pro forma condensed balance sheet of X Company as of December 31, 19X5, and the pro forma condensed statement of income for the year then ended. The historical condensed financial statements are derived from the historical financial statements of X Company, which were audited by us, and of Y Company, which were audited by other accountants, appearing elsewhere herein. Such pro forma adjustments are based on management's assumptions described in Note 2. Our examination was made in accordance with standards established by the American Institute of Certified Public Accountants and, accordingly, included such procedures as we considered necessary in the circumstances.

The objective of the pro forma financial information is to show what the significant effects on the historical financial information might have been had the [transaction or event] occurred at an earlier date. However, the pro forma condensed financial statements are not necessarily indicative of the results of operations or related effects on financial position that would have been attained had the above-mentioned [transaction or event] actually occurred earlier.

In our opinion, management's assumptions provide a reasonable basis for presenting the significant effects directly attributable to the [transaction or event] described in Note 1, the related pro forma adjustments give appropriate effect to those assumptions, and the pro forma column reflects the proper application of those adjustments to the historical financial statement amounts in the pro forma condensed balance sheet as of December 31, 19X5, and the pro forma condensed statement of income for the year then ended.

The examination engagement report may be expanded by including additional paragraph(s) to emphasize matters related to the attest engagement.

Review engagement report A review engagement report should include the statements shown below (AT 300.17).

A review is substantially less in scope than an examination, the objective of which is the expression of an opinion of the pro forma financial information. Accordingly, we do not express such an opinion.

In addition, the review engagement report should include a negative assurance that nothing came to the accountant's attention that would suggest that management's assumptions do not provide a reasonable basis for presenting the significant effects of the transaction or event, or that the related pro forma adjustments do not give appropriate effect to those assumptions or that the pro forma column does not reflect the proper application of those adjustments to the historical financial statements (AT 300.17).

The following is an example of a report on the review of pro forma financial information (AT 300.17).

We have reviewed the pro forma adjustments reflecting the [transaction or event] described in Note 1 and the application of those adjustments to the historical amounts in the accompanying pro forma condensed balance sheet of X Company as of March 31, 19X5, and the pro forma condensed statement of income for the three months then ended. These historical condensed financial statements are derived from the historical unaudited financial statements of X Company, which were reviewed by us, and of Y Company, which were reviewed by other accountants, appearing elsewhere herein. Such pro forma adjustments are based on management's assumptions as described in Note 2. Our review was conducted in accordance with standards established by the American Institute of Certified Public Accountants.

A review is substantially less in scope than an examination, the objective of which is the expression of an opinion on management's assumptions, the pro forma adjustments, and the application of those adjustments to historical financial information. Accordingly, we do not express such an opinion.

The objective of this pro forma financial information is to show what the significant effects on the historical information might have been had the [transaction or event] occurred at an earlier date. However, the pro forma condensed financial statements are not necessarily indicative of the results of operations or related effects on financial position that would have been attained had the above-mentioned [transaction or event] actually occurred earlier.

Based on our review, nothing came to our attention that caused us to believe that management's assumptions do not provide a reasonable basis for presenting the significant effects directly attributable to the [transaction or event] described in Note 1, that the related pro forma adjustments do not give appropriate effect to those assumptions, or that the pro forma column does not reflect the proper application of those adjustments to the historical financial statement amounts in the pro forma condensed balance sheets as of March 31, 19X5, and the pro forma condensed statement of income for the three months then ended.

The review engagement report may be expanded by including additional paragraph(s) to emphasize matters related to the engagement.

Report modifications   The accountant may encounter circumstances that could lead to the modification of the accountant's report on pro forma financial information. These circumstances include the following (AT 300.14):

- Restrictions on the scope of the engagement
- Reservations about the propriety of assumptions
- Reservations about the presentation based on management's assumptions
- Uncertainty about management's assumptions

Depending on the nature of the circumstance and the significance of the problem, an accountant may qualify an opinion, express an adverse opinion, disclaim an opinion, or withdraw from an engagement. When the accountant's report is modified, the reason for the modification should be explained in the accountant's report (AT 300.14).

The accountant's report generally should not be modified when there is an uncertainty about whether the transaction or event will actually occur (AT 300.14).

Pooling-of-interests A proposed business combination accounted for as a pooling of interests generally would not require management to establish assumptions. For this reason, a report on a proposed pooling transaction does not have to refer to management's assumptions unless there are assumptions related to adjustments arising from the conformity of accounting principles for the combining entities (AT 300.13).

REPORTING ON INTERNAL CONTROL OVER FINANCIAL REPORTING

The basic concepts of an internal control and its assessment were discussed in the chapter entitled "Internal Control, Errors, and Irregularities." Guidance for reporting on internal control is established in Statement on Standards for Attestation Engagements No. 2 (Reporting on an Entity's Internal Control Structure Over Financial Reporting) (as amended by SSAE-6) and is discussed in this section (AT 400.01).

An auditor may accept an engagement to report on management's assertion about its internal control only if the following conditions are satisfied (AT 400.10):

- Management accepts responsibility for the effectiveness of the internal control.

- Management evaluates the effectiveness of its internal control based on control criteria.

- Sufficient evidential matter is available (or can be developed) to substantiate management's evaluation of its internal control.

- Management presents a written assertion (which is based on the control criteria) about the effectiveness of its internal control.

When an auditor is engaged to examine management's assertion about the effectiveness of its internal control, the general standards, fieldwork standards, and reporting standards established by SSAE-1 (Attestation Standards) should be observed, along with the standards established by SSAE-2 (AT 400.02).

Although the auditor is engaged to report on management's assertion about its internal control, management is responsible for designing and maintaining an effective structure. In addition, management is free to evaluate its internal control without the involvement of the auditor (AT 400.11).

Furthermore, management is responsible for evaluating the effectiveness of its internal control. The evaluation should be based on "control criteria" that are considered essential for the design and implementation of an effective internal control. SSAE-2 states "criteria issued by the AICPA, regulatory agencies, and other bodies composed of experts that follow due process procedures" may be considered reasonable control criteria (AT 400.10).

> *OBSERVATION: A company's management is responsible for defining the components that make up its internal control. Management may accept the five components (control environment, risk assessment, control activities, information and communication, and monitoring) established by the Committee of Sponsoring Organizations of the Treadway Commission (COSO); however, if management selects other components to comprise its internal control, the five components established by COSO may be irrelevant (AT400.12).*

The effectiveness of internal controls can be determined only when appropriate evidence is available to be evaluated (or the evidence can be created) by the auditor. For example, when internal controls are not well documented or supporting documentation is not maintained, the auditor may not be able to form an opinion on management's assertion about the effectiveness of its internal controls (AT 400.10).

Finally, an auditor can examine and report on an internal control only when management presents a written assertion (based on the control criteria referred to in management's report) about the effectiveness of control. Thus, the auditor is not forming an opinion on the effectiveness of the internal control, but rather on management's assertion about the internal control (AT 400.10).

There is no specific language that management must use in its assertion about the effectiveness of its internal control. Management must decide what language is appropriate; however, SSAE-2 provides the following as two examples that could be used (AT 400.04).

Our Company maintained an effective internal control over financial reporting as of September 30, 19X5.

Our Company's internal control over financial reporting is sufficient to meet the stated objectives.

> *OBSERVATION: SSAE-2 concludes that management's assertion about its internal control will generally be as of the date of the balance sheet (AT 400.04).*

Although management decides how to phrase its assertion, SSAE-2 cautions that the assertion should not be so subjective that different auditors would not necessarily agree on the assertion. For example, it may be inappropriate for the auditor to report on management's assertion that its internal control is "extremely strong" (AT 400.04).

Management's assertion on the effectiveness of its internal control may be presented in (1) a separate report that is included with the examination report on management's assertion or (2) a representation letter to the auditor. When the second medium is used, the distribution of the examination report on management's assertion should be restricted to management and others within the organization and, if appropriate, to a regulatory agency. Furthermore, SSAE-2 prohibits the use of the examination report in a general-purpose document unless management presents its written assertion in a separate report about the effectiveness of the internal control (AT 400.03).

Examination Procedures

To express an opinion on management's assertion concerning the effectiveness of its internal control, the auditor must collect sufficient evidence that supports the assertion. The opinion expressed is based on management's assertion, taken as a whole, and is not directed to a specific control policy or procedure or the separate components of internal control (AT 400.15).

The examination approach should consider both the design of the internal control and the operating effectiveness of controls. The design aspect of the audit approach focuses on whether controls are designed in a manner to prevent or detect material misstatements on a timely basis. The evaluation of operating effectiveness focuses on (1) how controls were applied, (2) whether those controls were applied in a consistent manner, and (3) who applied the controls (AT 400.15).

For discussion purposes, SSAE-2 divides an internal control engagement into the following five phases (AT 400.16):

1. Planning the engagement

2. Understanding the internal control

3. Evaluating the design of the structure

4. Testing and evaluating the operating effectiveness of the structure

5. Forming an opinion

Planning the engagement   Proper planning of the engagement requires that the auditor consider a number of factors that may be relevant to forming an opinion on management's assertion on its internal control. SSAE-2 lists the following as some of the factors that may be relevant to planning the engagement (AT 400.17):

- Industry characteristics, such as economic conditions, rate of technological change, extent and nature of governmental regulation, and financial reporting practices

- Understanding of the internal control based on other services that may have been performed by the auditor (such as the audit of the financial statements)

- Characteristics of the client, such as its organizational and financial structure

- Nature and extent of changes in the client's operations or internal control

- Manner by which the client evaluates its internal control

- Preliminary judgments, such as materiality thresholds, inherent risk assessment, and evaluations of other relevant factors that are basic to determining what constitutes a material weakness in the internal control

- Existence of documentation that is relevant to management's assertion about its internal control

- Nature and significance of specific internal controls established to achieve control criteria objectives

- Initial evaluations concerning the effectiveness of the client's internal control

An effective internal audit function can be an important element in management's assessment of the effectiveness of its internal control. The auditor should consider the role of internal auditors in planning the engagement. When making an assessment of the role of the internal audit function, the auditor should rely on the general guidance established in SAS-65 (The Auditor's Consideration of the Internal Audit Function in an Audit of Financial Statements) (AT 400.19).

In addition, the planning of the engagement will be affected by whether the client has multiple locations. If there are multiple locations, the auditor must determine whether the internal control is essentially the same at each location. SSAE-2 states that the following factors should be considered in determining whether it is necessary to understand and test controls at each location (AT 400.18):

- The degree of similarity of operations at each location

- The degree of similarity of internal control features at each location

- The degree to which central records are maintained

- The effectiveness of control environment policies and procedures over each location (especially the ability to exercise direct control over those in authority at each location)

- The nature and magnitude of transactions executed at each location and the amount of assets held at each location

One additional factor that should be considered when planning the engagement is the extent to which the internal control is documented. The selection of methods used to document the structure is a managerial decision based on the size and complexity of the operations, and may include documentation methods such as policy manuals, memoranda, flowcharts, questionnaires, and accounting manuals. These methods should document the relationship between internal controls and the control objectives (AT 400.20).

> *OBSERVATION: Although management is responsible for the documentation of its internal control, the auditor may be engaged to help management document the structure.*

Understanding internal control   The auditor should obtain an understanding of the client's internal control. The understanding is generally obtained in a manner similar to the internal control phase of an audit engagement. That is, the auditor generally makes appropriate inquiries, inspections of documents, and observations of activities (AT 400.21).

> *OBSERVATION: For a thorough discussion of the five components of internal control, see the chapter entitled "Internal Control, Errors, and Irregularities."*

Evaluating the design   The auditor should obtain an understanding of the policies and procedures for each component of an internal control (AT 400.22). The components of the internal control over financial reporting are discussed in the chapter entitled "Internal Control, Errors, and Irregularities."

Testing and evaluating operational effectiveness   After the auditor has evaluated the effectiveness of internal control policies and procedures, those policies and procedures must be tested. The tests should be designed to determine (1) how the policy or procedure was applied, (2) whether the policy or procedure was applied consistently, and (3) who applied the policy or procedure. These determinations can be made by applying a variety of audit procedures, including inquiry, inspection of documents, observation of activities, and reapplication or reperformance of internal control procedures (AT 400.26).

The extent to which examination procedures should be performed is a matter of professional judgment; however, SSAE-2 concludes that sufficient evidence should be collected to limit attestation risk to an "appropriately low level." Generally the nature, timing, and extent of tests of operating effectiveness are based on the preliminary assessment of the client's control environment. Specific factors that the auditor may consider in determining what constitutes sufficient evidential matter include the following (AT 400.27):

- The nature of the policy or procedure
- The significance of a policy or procedure in achieving the objectives of the control criteria
- The nature and extent of tests of operating effectiveness performed by the client

In addition, the appropriate level of sufficient evidential matter should be related to the risk of noncompliance with a control policy or procedure. SSAE-2 notes that assessing the risk may be determined by considering the following (AT 400.27):

- The degree to which the volume or nature of transactions has changed
- Changes in controls employed by the client, if any
- The extent to which the effectiveness of a control relies on another control
- Changes in personnel who are an important part of performing or monitoring a control
- Whether the control is manual or computerized
- The complexity of the control
- Whether more than one control achieves a specific objective

As stated earlier, a client may perform various tests of the operational effectiveness of its internal control. The auditor must decide to what extent, if at all, the work performed by client personnel should be relied on in drawing a conclusion about management's assertion about its internal control. SSAE-2 reiterates a basic professional tenet that it is the auditor's responsibility to obtain sufficient evidence to support management's assertion. If the auditor plans to rely to some degree on the work performed by client personnel, it may be appropriate to corroborate the tests performed internally. Obviously, the auditor would place more reliance on work performed directly by the auditor than on tests performed by the client. Finally, the auditor must make fundamental judgments about the testing process. For example, it would be inappropriate for the client to decide what constitutes sufficient evidence or a material weakness (AT 400.28).

Management's assertion about the effectiveness of its control structure is made as of a specific date; however, the auditor must decide over what period of time the test procedures should be applied. The nature of the control being tested will to some extent determine the period over which it should be tested. For example, some procedures are performed only periodically (e.g., controls over the preparation of interim financial statements and the physical inventory count), while other controls are continuous (e.g., controls over payroll transactions). SSAE-2 concludes that the auditor should apply tests "over a period of time that is adequate to determine whether, as of the date selected by management for its assertion, the controls necessary for achieving the objectives of the control criteria are operating effectively" (AT 400.26–.33).

> **OBSERVATION:** *An auditor may be engaged to express an opinion on management's assertion about its internal control for a period of time. For example, the operating year could be used. If management's assertion is stated to encompass a period of time rather than as of a particular date, the auditor must modify the examination approach accordingly (AT 400.30).*

Management may have changed internal controls before the date of its assertion about the effectiveness of the internal control. There is no need for the auditor to consider the previous controls if the newly adopted controls have been operational long enough for the auditor to assess their effectiveness (AT 400.32).

> **OBSERVATION:** *When management's assertion about its internal control relates to the preparation of interim financial information, the auditor should perform tests of controls related to interim reporting objectives for one or more of the interim periods (AT 400.31).*

Forming an opinion   On the basis of the collection and evaluation of evidence concerning the client's internal control, the auditor forms an opinion concerning management's assertion. The form of the examination report is dependent on the method used by management to communicate its assertion about the effectiveness of its internal control. As noted earlier, the client may present the assertion in a separate report that accompanies the examination report or in a representation letter directed to the auditor (AT 400.33).

Separate Report

When management issues its assertion in a separate report, the examination report on management's assertion should include four paragraphs (introductory, scope, inherent limitations, and opinion) and should satisfy the following reporting standards (AT 400.45):

- The word *independent* should be included in the title of the examination report.

- There should be an identification of management's assertion about its internal control.

- There should be a statement that the examination was performed in accordance with standards established by the AICPA, a brief description of the nature of the examination, and a statement that the auditor believes that the examination provided a reasonable basis for the opinion expressed.

- There should be a description of the inherent limitations of an internal control, along with a warning that the effectiveness of the internal control may be inadequate for future periods.

- There should be an expression of an opinion on management's assertion about the effectiveness of the entity's internal control.

Presented below is an example of a standard report on management's assertion about the effectiveness of its internal control (AT 400.46).

> **OBSERVATION:** *The report presented below assumes that the assertion made in management's report was that "X Company maintained an effective internal control over financial reporting as of December 31, 19X5," and that the assertion was contained in the report prepared by management entitled "Management's Report on Internal Control." The phrase and the name of the report are illustrative only; however, the auditor should be careful to use the same "assertion language" used in the management report and the specific title of the document that contains the assertion. Also, the report presented below refers to the "internal control over financial reporting" as illustrative language and, again, the language should be the same as that used by management in its assertion. Finally, the illustrative examination report refers to "criteria established in*

'Internal Control—Integrated Framework' issued by the Committee of Sponsoring Organizations of the Treadway Commission." Again, the auditor should refer to the criteria used by management to assess the effectiveness of its internal control.

Independent Accountant's Report

We have examined management's assertion that X Company maintained effective internal control over financial reporting as of December 31, 19X5, included in the accompanying Management's Report on Internal Control.

Our examination was made in accordance with standards established by the American Institute of Certified Public Accountants and, accordingly, included obtaining an understanding of internal control over financial reporting, testing and evaluating the design and operating effectiveness of the internal control, and such other procedures as we considered necessary in the circumstances. We believe that our examination provides a reasonable basis for our opinion.

Because of inherent limitations in any internal control, errors or irregularities may occur and not be detected. Also, projections of any evaluation of the internal control over financial reporting to future periods are subject to the risk that the internal control may become inadequate because of changes in conditions, or that the degree of compliance with the policies or procedures may deteriorate.

In our opinion, management's assertion that X Company maintained effective internal control over financial reporting as of December 31, 19X5, is fairly stated, in all material respects, based on criteria established in "Internal Control—Integrated Framework" issued by the Committee of Sponsoring Organizations of the Treadway Commission.

Representation Letter

Management may issue its assertion in a representation letter rather than in a separate report that accompanies the examination report on management's assertion about the effectiveness of its internal control. Under this circumstance the auditor should follow the guidance established for reporting on a separate report, except the introductory paragraph should refer to the representation letter and its date, and a fifth paragraph should be added in which the distribution of the report is limited (AT 400.47–.48).

Presented below is an example of a standard report on management's assertion about the effectiveness of its internal control that was expressed in a representation letter (AT 400.49).

> **OBSERVATION:** *The report presented below assumes that the examination report on management's assertion about its internal control was for the benefit of management and the board of directors. If the report is also for the benefit of a regulatory agency, that agency should be referred to in the last paragraph of the report illustrated below.*

Independent Accountant's Report

We have examined management's assertion, included in its representation letter dated February 2, 19X6, that X Company maintained effective internal control over financial reporting as of December 31, 19X5.

Our examination was made in accordance with standards established by the American Institute of Certified Public Accountants and, accordingly, included obtaining an understanding of internal control over financial reporting, testing and evaluating the design and operating effectiveness of internal control, and such other procedures as we considered necessary in the circumstances. We believe that our examination provides a reasonable basis for our opinion.

Because of inherent limitations in any internal control, errors or irregularities may occur and not be detected. Also, projections of any evaluation of the internal control over financial reporting to future periods are subject to the risk that the internal control may become inadequate because of changes in conditions, or that the degree of compliance with the policies or procedures may deteriorate.

In our opinion, management's assertion that X Company maintained effective internal control over financial reporting as of December 31, 19X5, is fairly stated, in all material respects, based on criteria established in "Internal Control—Integrated Framework" issued by the Committee of Sponsoring Organizations of the Treadway Commission.

This report is intended solely for the information and use of the board of directors and management of X Company and should not be used for any other purpose.

> **OBSERVATION:** *If the report is part of the public record, an additional sentence should be added to the last paragraph that reads, "However, this report is a matter of public record and its distribution is not limited."*

Report Modifications

SSAE-2 concludes that the auditor may modify the standard reports (on both a separate management report and a representation letter) if any of the following circumstances exist (AT 400.50):

- Material weakness
- Scope limitation
- Reference to another examination report
- Subsequent event
- Segment of internal control
- Assertion limited to suitability of design
- Regulatory control criteria not based on due process

Material weakness   SAS-60 (Communication of Internal Control Structure Matters Noted in an Audit) provides the following two definitions for the types of deficiencies that may be discovered when evaluating a client's internal control (AU 325.02 and .15):

> *Reportable condition*—Matters coming to an auditor's attention that represent significant deficiencies in the design or operation of internal control that could adversely affect the entity's ability to record, process, summarize, and report financial data consistent with the assertions of management in the financial statements.

> *Material weakness*—Condition in which the design or operation of one or more of the internal control elements does not reduce to a relatively low level the risk that errors or irregularities in amounts that would be material in relation to the financial statements may occur and not be detected within a timely period by employees in the normal course of performing their assigned functions.

It should be noted that a material weakness is always a reportable condition, but a reportable condition may or may not be severe enough to be considered a material weakness by the management or the auditor (AT 400.36).

Professional judgment must be used to differentiate between a deficiency that is considered a reportable condition and one that is a material weakness; however, SSAE-2 provides the following generalizations that the auditor should consider (AT 400.37):

- The amount of misstatement arising from a deficiency may range from zero to an amount greater than that which appears in an account balance affected by the deficiency.

- The risks of the misstatement of particular amounts within a range will generally not be the same because, for example, the probability of a large misstatement will be less than the probability of a small misstatement.

If there are two or more reportable conditions, the auditor should consider whether the combined effects of the conditions should be considered a material weakness. In making that determination, SSAE-2 notes that the auditor should consider (1) the combined range of misstatements that could arise from the conditions during an accounting period and (2) the joint risk or probability (that is, likelihood of simultaneous occurrence of both events) if the combination of misstatements from the conditions could be material (AT 400.38).

If the auditor discovers a reportable condition(s) that is considered a material weakness, the format of the auditor's report depends on whether management has referred to the weakness in its assertion about the effectiveness of internal control (AT 400.51).

Material weakness referred to in an assertion   When management has referred to the material weakness and its effect on the achievement of the objectives of the control criteria in its assertion, the auditor should modify the opinion paragraph and add an explanatory paragraph (as the fifth paragraph). The explanatory paragraph should describe the material weakness, using essentially the language used by management (in its separate report or representation letter) to describe the weakness and its effect on the entity's internal control. An example of a modified examination report under this circumstance is illustrated below. The illustration assumes that management's assertion is included in a separate report that accompanies the examination report (AT 400.52–.53).

Independent Accountant's Report

We have examined management's assertion that X Company maintained effective internal control over financial reporting as of December 31, 19X5, included in the accompanying Management's Report on Internal Control.

Our examination was made in accordance with standards established by the American Institute of Certified Public Accountants and, accordingly, included obtaining an understanding of internal control over financial reporting, testing and evaluating the design and operating effectiveness of internal control, and such other procedures as we considered necessary in the circumstances. We believe that our examination provides a reasonable basis for our opinion.

Because of inherent limitations in any internal control, errors or irregularities may occur and not be detected. Also, projections of any evaluation of internal control over financial reporting to future periods are subject to the risk that internal control may become inadequate because of changes in conditions, or that the degree of compliance with the policies or procedures may deteriorate.

In our opinion, management's assertion that, except for the effect of the material weakness described in its report, X Company maintained effective internal control over financial reporting as of December 31, 19X5, is fairly stated, in all material respects, based on criteria established in "Internal Control—Integrated Framework" issued by the Committee of Sponsoring Organizations of the Treadway Commission.

As discussed in management's assertion, the following material weakness exists in the design or operation of internal control of X Company in effect at December 31, 19X5. [Describe the client's specific material weakness and its effect on the achievement of the objectives of the control criteria.] A material weakness is a condition that precludes the entity's internal control from providing reasonable assurance that material misstatements in the financial statements will be prevented or detected on a timely basis.

OBSERVATION: When there is a material weakness in management's internal control, management's assertion should not conclude that its internal control is effective.

OBSERVATION: The definition of a material weakness used in the above report is different from the definition established in SSAE-2. As noted in footnote 16 of the pronouncement, one definition should be used in the report (the one used above), while the auditor should use the other definition (reproduced earlier in this section) as the guidance for identifying a material weakness on an operational basis.

OBSERVATION: When a reportable condition is discovered during an examination to report on management's assertion about its internal control, the reportable condition should be communicated to the entity's audit committee (or to individuals with similar responsibility). Also, reportable conditions that are material weaknesses should be identified as such and reported to the audit com-

*mittee. Preferably, the communication should be in writing. The communication of significant matters may be made after the examination is complete or before the examination is complete, if the need for a more timely interim communication is considered appropriate. If no reportable conditions are discovered during the examination, the auditor should **not** prepare a written report stating that reportable conditions were not discovered.*

Disagreements with management When the auditor concludes that a material weakness exists but (1) management refuses to refer to the weakness in its assertion or (2) management describes the weakness but does not modify its assertion that the internal control is effective, the auditor should issue an adverse opinion. The adverse opinion should include standard introductory, scope, and inherent limitations paragraphs, along with an explanatory paragraph. Finally, an opinion paragraph (the last paragraph) should include the auditor's adverse opinion (AT 400.59).

Presented below is an illustration of an adverse opinion on management's assertion concerning its internal control (AT 400.55).

Independent Accountant's Report

We have examined management's assertion that X Company maintained effective internal control over financial reporting as of December 31, 19X5, included in the accompanying Management's Report on Internal Control.

Our examination was made in accordance with standards established by the American Institute of Certified Public Accountants and, accordingly, included obtaining an understanding of internal control over financial reporting, testing and evaluating the design and operating effectiveness of internal control, and such other procedures as we considered necessary in the circumstances. We believe that our examination provides a reasonable basis for our opinion.

Because of inherent limitations in any internal control, errors or irregularities may occur and not be detected. Also, projections of any evaluation of internal control over financial reporting to future periods are subject to the risk that internal control may become inadequate because of changes in conditions, or that the degree of compliance with the policies or procedures may deteriorate.

Our examination disclosed the following condition, which we believe is a material weakness in the design or operation of internal control of X Company in effect at December 31, 19X5. [Describe the client's specific material weakness and its effect on achievement of the objectives of the control criteria.] A material weakness is a condition that precludes the entity's internal control from providing reasonable assurance that material misstatements in the financial statements will be prevented or detected on a timely basis.

In our opinion, because of the effect of the material weakness described above on the achievement of the objectives of the control criteria, management's assertion that X Company maintained effective internal control over financial reporting as of December 31, 19X5, is not fairly stated based on criteria established in "Internal Control—Integrated Framework" issued by the Committee of Sponsoring Organizations of the Treadway Commission.

If the client includes a statement in its separate report or representation letter to the effect that the cost of correcting the weakness would exceed the benefits, the auditor should add the following paragraph to the adverse opinion illustrated above (AT 400.56).

We do not express an opinion or any other form of assurance on management's cost–benefit statement.

> OBSERVATION: *However, if the auditor concludes that the cost-benefit statement is a material misstatement of fact, the guidance discussed later in this chapter (Material Misstatement of Fact) should be followed.*

Assertion includes material weakness and is included in a document containing the auditor's report on the financial statements A document may contain the auditor's report on the financial statements and a report on management's assertion about its internal control that includes a material weakness. Under this circumstance, the auditor should include in his or her examination report that describes the material weakness the following sentence (place in the last paragraph) (AT 400.57).

These conditions were considered in determining the nature, timing, and extent of audit tests applied in our audit of the 19X5 financial statements, and this report does not affect our report dated February 27, 19X6, on these financial statements.

> *OBSERVATION: SSAE-2 notes that the auditor may want to include the above sentence even when the single document does not include the two auditor's reports (AT 400.57).*

Scope limitation When significant examination procedures deemed necessary to achieve the standard of sufficient evidence cannot be performed, the auditor must decide whether the examination report should be qualified or whether a disclaimer of opinion should be expressed (AT 400.58).

An example of an examination report on management's assertion that has been qualified due to a scope limitation, as reproduced in SSAE-2, is illustrated below (AT 400.59).

Independent Accountant's Report

We have examined management's assertion that X Company maintained effective internal control over financial reporting as of December 31, 19X5, included in the accompanying Management's Report on Internal Control.

Except as described below, our examination was made in accordance with standards established by the American Institute of Certified Public Accountants and, accordingly, included obtaining an understanding of internal control over financial reporting, testing and evaluating the design and operating effectiveness of internal control, and such other procedures as we considered necessary in the circumstances. We believe that our examination provides a reasonable basis for our opinion.

Because of inherent limitations in any internal control, errors or irregularities may occur and not be detected. Also, projections of any evaluation of internal control over financial reporting to future periods are subject to the risk that internal control may become inadequate because of changes in conditions, or that the degree of compliance with the policies or procedures may deteriorate.

Our examination disclosed the following material weaknesses in the design or operation of internal control of X Company in effect at December 31, 19X5. A material weakness is a condition that precludes the entity's internal control from providing reasonable assurance that material misstatements in the financial statements will be prevented or detected on a timely basis. Prior to December 23, 19X5, X Company had an inadequate system for recognizing cash receipts, which could have prevented the Company from recording cash receipts on accounts receivable completely and properly. Therefore, cash received could have been diverted for unauthorized use, lost, or otherwise not properly recorded to accounts receivable. Although the Company implemented a new cash receipt system on December 23, 19X5, the system has not been in operation for a sufficient period of time to enable us to obtain sufficient evidence about its operating effectiveness.

In our opinion, except for the effect of matters we may have discovered had we been able to examine evidence about the effectiveness of the new cash receipts system, management's assertion that X Company maintained effective internal control over financial reporting as of December 31, 19X5, is fairly stated, in all material respects, based on criteria established in "Internal Control—Integrated Framework" issued by the Committee of Sponsoring Organizations of the Treadway Commission.

An example of a disclaimer of opinion on management's assertion due to a scope limitation is illustrated below (AT 400.61).

Independent Accountant's Report

We were engaged to examine management's assertion that X Company maintained effective internal control over financial reporting as of December 31, 19X5, included in the accompanying Management's Report on Internal Control.

As part of our examination we planned to visit several retail outlets of X Company; however, management restricted the scope of our examination to the national corporate locations and retail outlets that had been in operation for two years or more.

Since management significantly restricted the scope of our examination as described in the previous paragraph and we were unable to apply other procedures to satisfy ourselves as to management's assertion about the entity's internal control over financial reporting, the scope of our work was not sufficient to enable us to express, and we do not express, an opinion on management's assertion.

OBSERVATION: When scope restrictions are imposed by the client, the practitioner ordinarily disclaims an opinion (AT 400.60).

Reference to another examination report   An auditor may report on management's assertion concerning its internal control if internal control components of the entity are examined by other auditors. Under this circumstance, the auditor must decide whether or not to serve as the principal auditor and, if he or she serves as principal auditor, whether to make reference to the work of the other auditors in the examination report. Specific guidance for making these determinations is discussed in the chapter entitled "Evidence" and is based on AU Section 543 (Part of Audit Performed by Other Independent Auditors). Although the guidance is discussed in the context of an audit of financial statements, SSAE-2 concludes that the general guidance is also applicable to the examination of management's assertion about its internal control (AT 400.62).

The following example illustrates an examination report where reference is made to the work of another auditor (AT 400.63).

Independent Accountant's Report

We have examined management's assertion that X Company maintained an effective internal control over financial reporting as of December 31, 19X5, included in the accompanying Management's Report on Internal Control. We did not examine management's assertion about the effectiveness of internal control over financial reporting of Z Company, a wholly owned subsidiary, whose financial statements reflect total assets and revenues constituting 25% and 20%, respectively, of the related consolidated financial statement amounts as of and for the year ended December 31, 19X5. Management's assertion about the effectiveness of Z Company's internal control over financial reporting was examined by other accountants whose report has been furnished to us, and our opinion, insofar as it relates to management's assertion about the effectiveness of Z Company's internal control over financial reporting, is based solely on the report of the other accountants.

Our examination was made in accordance with standards established by the American Institute of Certified Public Accountants and, accordingly, included obtaining an understanding of internal control over financial reporting, testing and evaluating the design and operating effectiveness of internal control, and such other procedures as we considered necessary in the circumstances. We believe that our examination and the report of the other accountants provide a reasonable basis for our opinion.

Because of inherent limitations in any internal control, errors or irregularities may occur and not be detected. Also, projections of any evaluation of internal control over financial reporting to future periods are subject to the risk that internal control may become inadequate because of changes in conditions, or that the degree of compliance with the policies or procedures may deteriorate.

In our opinion, based on our examination and the report of the other accountants, management's assertion that X Company maintained effective internal control over financial reporting as of December 31, 19X5, is fairly stated, in all material respects, based on criteria established in "Internal Control—Integrated Framework" issued by the Committee of Sponsoring Organizations of the Treadway Commission.

Subsequent event After the date of management's assertion about its internal control but before the date of the examination report, there may have been changes in policies, procedures, or other factors that may have a significant effect on the entity's internal control. SSAE-2 concludes that to determine whether such changes have occurred, the auditor should determine whether the following reports were issued subsequent to the date of the examination report, and, if so, they should be read (AT 400.64).

- Other reports issued by independent auditor(s) that identify reportable conditions or material weaknesses
- Relevant reports issued by internal auditors
- Reports on the client's internal control issued by regulatory agencies
- Information generated through other professional engagements that relate to the effectiveness of the client's internal control structure

> **OBSERVATION:** *As noted later in this section, the client's written representations should include a statement indicating whether there have been changes in the internal control or the occurrence of other factors that might have a significant effect on its internal control.*

When there has been a subsequent event that significantly affects the client's internal control, the auditor should determine if the event has been adequately described in management's assertion. If management has not adequately described the event and its effect on internal control, the auditor should modify the examination report by adding an explanatory paragraph (AT 400.65).

> **OBSERVATION:** *As in an audit of a client's financial statements, the auditor has no responsibility to stay informed of changes in the client's internal control after the date of the examination report. However, should the auditor subsequently become aware of conditions that may have existed as of the date of the examination, the general guidance established for the audit of financial statements (which is established by AU Section 561 and is discussed in the chapter entitled "Evidence") should be followed (AT 400.66).*

Segment of internal control   An auditor may be engaged to report on management's assertion about only a portion of internal control. For example, the assertion may include only the operations of a branch office or controls over cash disbursements. Under such circumstances, the auditor should use the examination procedures established by SSAE-2 (as discussed earlier in this section) and modify the examination report so that it is consistent with management's assertion. An example of an examination report on management's assertion about the effectiveness of a segment of the entity's internal control is illustrated below (AT 400.76).

Independent Accountant's Report

We have examined management's assertion that X Company's Charleston Regional Branch maintained effective internal control over financial reporting as of December 31, 19X5, included in the accompanying Management's Report on Internal Control for the Charleston Regional Branch.

Our examination was made in accordance with standards established by the American Institute of Certified Public Accountants and, accordingly, included obtaining an understanding of internal control over financial reporting, testing and evaluating the design and operating effectiveness of internal control, and such other procedures as we considered necessary in the circumstances. We believe that our examination provides a reasonable basis for our opinion.

Because of inherent limitations in any internal control, errors or irregularities may occur and not be detected. Also, projections of any evaluation of internal control over financial reporting to future periods are subject to the risk that internal control may become inadequate because of changes in conditions, or that the degree of compliance with the policies or procedures may deteriorate.

In our opinion, management's assertion that X Company's Charleston Regional Branch maintained effective internal control over financial reporting as of December 31, 19X5, is fairly stated, in all material respects, based on criteria established in "Internal Control—Integrated Framework" issued by the Committee of Sponsoring Organizations of the Treadway Commission.

Assertion limited to suitability of design   Management may have designed internal control but not put the system into practice. For example, the may have been designed for a newly organized component that has yet to start operations, or the controls may have been designed for a unit that is subject to regulatory approval (for example, approval by a casino regulatory authority) (AT 400.68).

Under this circumstance, management's assertion would encompass only the design and not the operation of internal control. Thus, the examination would focus on evaluating the suitability of the design to achieve control criteria established by due process or by a regulatory authority that does not observe due process (AT 400.68).

Presented below is an example of a examination report issued after the evaluation of management's assertion about the suitability of design of the entity's internal control (AT 400.69).

Independent Accountant's Report

We have examined management's assertion that X Company's internal control over financial reporting is suitably designed to prevent or detect material misstatements in the financial statements on a timely basis as of December 31, 19X5, included in the accompanying Management's Report on the Design of Internal Control.

Our examination was made in accordance with standards established by the American Institute of Certified Public Accountants and, accordingly, included obtaining an understanding of internal control over financial reporting, evaluating the design of internal control, and such other procedures as we considered necessary in the circumstances. We believe that our examination provides a reasonable basis for our opinion.

Because of inherent limitations in any internal control, errors or irregularities may occur and not be detected. Also, projections of any evaluation of internal control over financial reporting to future periods are subject to the risk that internal control may become inadequate because of changes in conditions, or that the degree of compliance with the policies or procedures may deteriorate.

In our opinion, management's assertion that X Company's internal control over financial reporting is suitably designed to prevent or detect material misstatements in the financial statements on a timely basis as of December 31, 19X5, is fairly stated, in all material respects, based on criteria established in "Internal Control—Integrated Framework" issued by the Committee of Sponsoring Organizations of the Treadway Commission.

OBSERVATION: If the control criteria were established by a regulatory authority that did not observed due process, the examination report would include an additional paragraph that would describe the limited distribution of the report illustrated above.

When management's assertion is limited to the design of internal control but the policies and procedures have already been put into operation, the examination report should be modified by adding the following sentence to the scope paragraph (AT 400.69).

We were not engaged to examine and report on the operating effectiveness of X Company's internal control over financial reporting as of December 31, 19X5, and, accordingly, we express no opinion on operating effectiveness.

Regulatory control criteria not based on due process A regulatory agency may develop control criteria that must be followed by entities that are subject to its oversight. When a regulatory agency establishes control criteria, the following two definitions of material weakness are presented by SSAE-2 (AT 400.70–.71):

1. A condition in which the design or operation of one or more of the specific internal control components does not reduce to a relatively low level the risk that errors or irregularities in amounts that would be material in relation to the applicable grant or program might occur and not be detected on a timely basis by employees in the normal course of performing their assigned functions.

2. A condition in which the lack of conformity with the regulatory agency's criteria is material in accordance with any guidelines for determining materiality that are included in such criteria.

If the control criteria are developed through due process, the reporting standards discussed earlier (reporting standards when a separate report or a letter of representation to the auditor is issued by management) should be followed when the auditor prepares an examination report on management's assertion (AT 400.70).

The auditor is not responsible for determining whether the control criteria established by the regulatory agency are comprehensive; however, if the auditor becomes aware of a material weakness, that weakness should be reported whether or not it violates the control criteria established by the regulatory agency (AT 400.73).

Regulatory agency rules may require that management report all conditions (material and immaterial). If the auditor is aware of conditions that have not been reported by management, they should be noted in the examination report issued by the auditor (AT 400.74).

If the control criteria are not the result of due process, the standard examination report should be changed so that there is appropriate reference to the regulatory control criteria and a limited-distribution paragraph should be added. An example of an examination report based on control criteria established by a regulatory agency that did not observe due process is illustrated below (AT 400.72).

Independent Accountant's Report

We have examined management's assertion included in its representation letter dated February 1, 19X6, that X Company's internal control over financial reporting as of December 31, 19X5, is adequate to meet the criteria established by the Casino Commission, as set forth in its audit guide dated September 1981.

Our examination was made in accordance with standards established by the American Institute of Certified Public Accountants and, accordingly, included obtaining an understanding of internal control over financial reporting, testing and evaluating the design and operating effectiveness of internal control, and such other procedures as we considered necessary in the circumstances. We believe that our examination provides a reasonable basis for our opinion.

Because of inherent limitations in any internal control, errors or irregularities may occur and not be detected. Also, projections of any evaluation of internal control over financial reporting to future periods are subject to the risk that internal control may become inadequate because of changes in conditions, or that the degree of compliance with the policies or procedures may deteriorate.

We understand that the Casino Commission considers internal controls over financial reporting that meet the criteria referred to in the first paragraph of this report adequate for its purpose. In our opinion, based on this understanding and on our examination, management's assertion that X Company's internal control over financial reporting is adequate to meet the criteria established by the Casino Commission is fairly stated, in all material respects, based on such criteria.

This report is intended for the information and use of the board of directors and management of X Company and the Casino Commission and should not be used for any other purpose.

OBSERVATION: If the examination report becomes part of the public record, the following sentence should be added to the final paragraph of the examination report: "However, this report is a matter of public record and its distribution is not limited."

Other Information

When other information is included in the document that contains the examination report on management's assertion about internal control, the auditor should read the other information (except for the report of another auditor and information covered by that report) to determine (1) whether there are material inconsistencies between management's report and the other information and (2) whether the other information contains a material misstatement of fact (AT 400.75).

Material inconsistency   If the auditor concludes that there are material inconsistencies, the broad guidance established in SAS-8 (Other Information in Documents Containing Audited Financial Statements) should be observed (AT 400.76).

Material misstatement of fact   If the auditor believes that there may be a material misstatement of fact, the situation should be discussed with the client. As part of the discussion, the auditor should determine whether he or she has the expertise to evaluate the matter. SSAE-2 concludes that if the auditor determines a material misstatement exists, the auditor should propose "that management consult with some other party whose advice might be useful, such as the entity's legal counsel." Finally, if in the opinion of the auditor there is a material misstatement of fact, appropriate action must be considered, including the following (AT 400.77–.78):

- Communicate the matter to the entity's management and audit committee in writing.

- Consult with legal counsel to determine what additional action may be appropriate.

Written Representations

In an engagement to express an opinion on management's assertion concerning its internal control, management should provide the auditor with the following written representations (AT 400.42):

- State that responsibility for establishing and maintaining internal control is that of management.

- State that an evaluation of the effectiveness of internal control based on control criteria (control criteria should be specified) has been performed by management.
- State that management's assertion about the effectiveness of internal control is based on the control criteria.
- State that management has communicated to the auditor all significant deficiencies in the design or operation of internal control that could adversely affect the client's ability to record, process, summarize, and report financial data consistent with the assertions of management in the financial statements, and that management has identified those that it believes to be material weaknesses.
- State that management has described any material irregularities and any other irregularities that involve management or other employees who have a significant role in the client's internal control even though the irregularities are not material.
- State that, subsequent to the date of management's report, there were no events, changes in internal control, or occurrences of other factors that might significantly affect internal control.

> *OBSERVATION: General guidance established in SAS-19 (Client Representations) also should be followed for written representations in an examination to report on management's assertion about its internal control.*

Other Professional Services and Matters

When the auditor conducts an examination directed to management's assertion about its control, the auditor may be involved in a number of other professional engagements for the same client.

Audit of financial statements When the financial statements of an entity are audited, the second standard of fieldwork requires that a sufficient understanding of the client's internal control be obtained in order to plan the engagement and to design the nature, timing, and extent of audit procedures. SAS-55 (Consideration of Internal Control Structure in a Financial Statement Audit) provides guidance for the implementation of the second standard of fieldwork (AT 400.79).

Both the examination of management's assertion about its internal control and the audit of a client's financial statements require an understanding of internal control. However, SSAE-2 concludes that "an auditor's consideration of internal control in a financial statement audit is more limited." When the auditor performs both types of engagements for the same client, the results of an internal control evaluation performed in one engagement may be used in the other engagements. Specifically, the results from evaluating internal control in the assertion engagement may be used in the assessment of internal control in an audit engagement, and, likewise, the results from assessing internal control for an audit engagement may be used in the assertion engagement. However, appropriate professional standards must be satisfied for each engagement (AT 400.81).

Finally, when the examination of management's assertion about its internal control is conducted by one auditor but the audit of the entity's financial statements is performed by another auditor, SSAE-2 notes that the auditor of management's assertion may want to consider the following (AT 400.82):

- Any reportable conditions (including material weaknesses) identified as part of the audit of the financial statements

- Any disagreements between management and the auditor of the financial statements with respect to reportable conditions

Foreign Corrupt Practices Act   SSAE-2 notes that the performance of an examination of management's assertion about its internal control does not indicate that the client is in compliance with the Foreign Corrupt Practices Act of 1977 (AT 400.83).

Compliance with laws and regulations engagement   When the auditor is engaged to determine the effectiveness of internal control as it applies to compliance with laws and regulations, the relevant guidance established by SSAE-1 should be followed. In addition, SAS-74 (Compliance Auditing Considerations in Audits of Governmental Entities and Recipients of Governmental Financial Assistance) provides guidance for reporting on an entity's internal control performed in accordance with Government Auditing Standards (AT 400.01).

Agreed-upon procedures engagement   Agreed-upon procedures engagements are discussed in the chapter entitled "Agreed-Upon Procedures Engagements."

COMPLIANCE ATTESTATION

SSAE-2 provides guidance when an auditor accepts an engagement to report on management's assertion about its internal control that relates to the preparation of financial reports. SSAE-3 provides guidance for an engagement in which the auditor either (1) reports on the client's compliance with requirements of specified laws, regulations, rules, contracts, or grants (referred to as compliance with specified requirements) or (2) reports on the effectiveness of the client's internal control over compliance with specified requirements. However, a report issued under SSAE-3 "does not provide a legal determination on an entity's compliance with specified requirements" (AT 500.01–.03).

When an auditor is engaged to report on compliance with specified requirements, the general, fieldwork, and reporting standards in SSAE-1 should be observed, along with the standards established by SSAE-3. However, the standards established by SSAE-3 do not affect the auditor's responsibilities in the audit of financial statements conducted in accordance with GAAS (AT 500.01–.02).

Although SSAE-3 is concerned with engagements related to compliance with specified requirements, standards established do not apply to the following engagements (AT 500.02):

- Certain audit reports on specified compliance requirements based solely on the audit of financial statements (see paragraphs 19 through 21 of SAS-62 [Special Reports])

- Report on engagements related to (1) *Government Auditing Standards*, (2) the Single Audit Act of 1984, (3) Office of Management and Budget (OMB) Circular A-128 (Audits of State and Local Governments), and (4) OMB Circular A-133 (Audits of Institutions of Higher Education and Other Non-Profit Institutions)

- Program-specific audits performed in accordance with federal audit guides, unless otherwise noted

- Engagements subject to SAS-72 (Letters for Underwriters and Certain Other Requesting Parties)

- Report engagements related to a broker or dealer's internal control as required by Rule 17a-5 of the Securities Exchange Act of 1934

Specifically, the standards established by SSAE-3 apply to the following engagements (AT 500.04):

- Examination of management's written assertion about its compliance with specified requirements
- Performance of agreed-upon procedures with respect to management's written assertion about its compliance with specified requirements
- Performance of agreed-upon procedures with respect to management's written assertion about the effectiveness of its internal control over compliance

Agreed-upon engagements are discussed in the chapter entitled "Agreed-Upon Procedures Engagements."

> **OBSERVATION:** *SSAE-3 provides guidance for the examination of management's assertion about its compliance with specified requirements, but the standard does **not** apply to an **examination** of management's assertion about the effectiveness of its internal control over compliance (AT 500.06).*

> **OBSERVATION:** *SSAE-1 establishes the standard that an attestation engagement cannot be accepted unless management uses reasonable criteria that have either (1) been established by a recognized body or (2) been reproduced in the presentation of management's report (statement of assertion). SSAE-3 concludes that control criteria established by regulatory agencies and other bodies composed of experts that follow due process procedures, including procedures for broad distribution of proposed criteria for public comment, normally should be considered reasonable criteria for this purpose. If a regulatory agency does not observe due process, the control criteria standard can be satisfied, but the distribution of the auditor's report should be limited. Also, SSAE-3 notes that the publication entitled "Internal Control — Integrated Framework" issued by the Committee of Sponsoring Organizations of the Treadway Commission establishes a broad framework for effective internal control; however, that framework is not itself sufficiently detailed to satisfy the control criteria standard. If the auditor concludes that such reasonable criteria exist, the standards established by SSAE-1 must be observed. In addition, SSAE-3 notes that guidance established in SSAE-2 may be helpful in such engagements (AT 500.06).*

> **OBSERVATION:** *It should be noted that the auditor cannot accept an engagement to **review** management's assertion about its*

> compliance with specified requirements or the effectiveness of its internal control. Also, an SSAE-3 engagement can be accepted only when management's assertion is in writing. However, an auditor may accept a consulting engagement in which the auditor makes recommendations for improving internal control over compliance with specified requirements. Statements on Standards for Consulting Services apply to the latter type of engagement (AT 500.07–.08).

Although the auditor can be engaged to report on management's assertion about its compliance with specified requirements or the effectiveness of internal control, management is responsible for designing and maintaining effective internal control. Thus, management must take the initiative to identify which compliance requirements apply to its operations and how those requirements are to be satisfied. Finally, management is responsible for evaluating internal control and constructing an assertion about the (AT 500.09).

Management's construction of an assertion about its compliance with specified requirements may include the use of internal auditors, various other management personnel, as well as the external auditor. If the external auditor is used, the auditor's role is limited to providing management with relevant information. It is the responsibility of management, not the auditor, to evaluate internal control and formulate an assertion. SSAE-3 specifically states that management's assertion cannot be formulated merely on the work performed by the external auditor. Thus, management's approach should generally include such steps as the identification of control objectives, the documentation of the system, the assessment of risk, the evaluation of specific controls, and the formulation of an assertion based on the results of the evaluation (AT 500.14).

Examination Engagement

An auditor may accept an engagement to examine management's assertion about its compliance with specified requirements or the effectiveness of internal control over compliance if all of the following conditions are satisfied (AT 500.09 and 500.11):

- Management accepts responsibility for its compliance with the specified requirements and the effectiveness of the internal control over compliance.

- Management evaluates its compliance with the specified requirements or the effectiveness of the internal control over compliance.

- Management makes a written assertion about its compliance with the specified requirements (when the auditor's report is available for general distribution, the assertion should be made in a representation letter and in a separate management report that will accompany the auditor's report).

- Management's assertion (a) can be evaluated using reasonable criteria (criteria established by a recognized body or criteria clearly stated in a comprehensive manner in management's assertion) and (b) the criteria provides a basis for an assertion that can be estimated or measured reasonably consistently.

- Sufficient evidential matter is available (or can be developed) to support management's evaluation.

Risk assessment   SSAE-3 states the following as the purpose of an examination of management's assertion about its compliance with specified requirements (AT 500.29):

> To express an opinion about whether management's assertion is fairly stated in all material respects based on established criteria or agreed-upon criteria.

Such an engagement should be planned and executed in a manner similar to the audit of financial statements. For this reason, one of the fundamental components of a compliance attestation engagement is the assessment of *attestation risk*, defined as follows (AT 500.31):

> The risk that the practitioner may unknowingly fail to modify appropriately his or her opinion on management's assertion.

When the auditor offers an opinion on management's assertion, there is always a chance that the opinion will be incorrect. Simply stated, it is impossible for the auditor to reduce the attestation risk to zero because, for example, sampling methods must be used, judgments must be made, and management personnel can be involved in collusion to deceive the auditor. To assess attestation risk, the auditor must consider (1) inherent risk, (2) control risk, and (3) detection risk (AT 500.31).

> **OBSERVATION:** *Those who rely on a compliance attestation engagement report must be somewhat sophisticated because of the nature of the engagement. In fact, SSAE-3 notes "it often will be in the best interests of the practitioner and users (including the client) to have an agreed-upon procedures engagement rather than an examination." If the auditor believes it is unlikely that attestation risk can be limited to an appropriately low level, the prudent course would be to conduct an agreed-upon procedures engagement.*

Inherent risk relates to the fundamental characteristics of the entity for which management's assertion is being made. These characteristics provide the background or context in which a particular activity is performed. Not surprisingly, the auditor uses a significant degree of professional judgment in assessing inherent risk.

While there is no comprehensive list of factors that contribute to inherent risk, SSAE-3 notes that some of the factors that may be considered by the auditor can be found in paragraphs 10 through 12 of SAS-53 (The Auditor's Responsibility to Detect and Report Errors and Irregularities). In addition, SSAE-3 lists the following as other factors that should be considered in assessing inherent risk (AT 500.32):

- Level of complexity of specified compliance requirements
- Period of time that the entity has been subject to the specified compliance requirements
- Auditor's prior experience with the entity's compliance with the specified requirements
- Possible ramifications of lack of compliance with the specified requirements

Control risk refers to the probability that material deviations from specified compliance requirements exist. Thus, the design of the client internal control with respect to specified requirements will have an impact on the level of control risk. Control risk, like inherent risk, cannot be changed by the auditor. In general, the stronger the internal control for specified requirements, the more likely it is that material compliance deviations will be prevented or detected by the system on a timely basis. Thus, the auditor must carefully assess control risk at a level that accurately reflects the internal control policies and procedures that have been adopted by the client (AT 500.33). (Of course, the auditor can make recommendations for improving the system, which may affect future engagements.)

As discussed later, the auditor's assessment of the internal control over compliance with specified requirements is based on obtaining an understanding of relevant internal control policies and procedures.

Detection risk is the risk that an auditor's procedures will lead to the conclusion that material deviations from specified requirements do not exist when in fact such deviations do exist. During the planning phase of the engagement, the auditor should consider inherent risk, control risk, and detection risk and select an examination strategy that will result in a low level of attestation risk once the engagement is complete. There is an inverse relationship between the auditor's assessment of inherent and control risks and the level of detection risk. If the inherent risk and control risk are higher, the auditor should establish a lower level of detection risk. The level of detection risk established has a direct effect on the design of the nature, timing, and extent of compliance tests performed (AT 500.34).

Materiality   In a compliance attestation engagement that relates to the client's compliance with specified requirements, the auditor must determine with reasonable assurance whether "management's assertion is fairly stated in all material respects based on established or agreed-upon criteria." Thus, from a broad perspective, the concept of materiality in a compliance attestation engagement is similar to its role in an audit of financial statements. Immaterial deviations (from GAAP or from established or agreed-upon criteria) will generally exist in both types of engagements, but it is unreasonable to direct the focus of the engagements to immaterial items.

Although the concept of materiality applies to both types of engagements, it is probably more difficult to apply the concept in an compliance attestation engagement. First, because the engagement can be directed to a variety of specified requirements, it is very difficult to generalize about the examination approach. Second, the specified requirements may or may not be quantifiable in monetary terms. Third, there has been little, if any, research into what the focal point for determining materiality in a compliance attestation engagement should be. Not surprisingly, SSAE-3 provides little guidance for determining materiality, except to state that the following may affect the determination of materiality (AT 500.35):

- The nature of management's assertion and the compliance requirements, which may or may not be quantifiable in monetary terms
- The nature and frequency of noncompliance identified with appropriate consideration of sampling risk

- Qualitative considerations, including the needs and expectations of the report's users

OBSERVATION: Some compliance attestation engagements may require the auditor to prepare a supplemental report identifying all or certain deviations discovered. Any threshold guidance established for reporting items in the supplemental report should not have an effect on the auditor's determination of a materiality threshold for the primary examination report.

Examination procedures   SSAE-3 specifically states that the following procedures should be performed in a compliance attestation engagement (AT 500.38):

- Obtain an understanding of compliance requirements.
- Plan the examination engagement.
- Consider relevant internal control components.
- Obtain sufficient evidential matter.
- Consider subsequent events.
- Obtain written representations from the client.
- Form and express an opinion.

Obtain an understanding of compliance requirements   Since the scope of SSAE-3 is broad and the standards can be applied to a variety of circumstances, it is difficult to generalize about the auditor's knowledge of compliance requirements. Basically, the auditor must develop an understanding of the specified requirements on which management's assertion is founded. SSAE-3 identifies the following as some of the possible sources of information that can provide the auditor with an adequate understanding (AT 500.39):

- Specific laws, regulations, rules, contracts, and grants on which the specified requirements are based
- Experience developed from previous similar examination engagements
- Information contained in relevant regulatory reports
- Conversations with management personnel concerning the specified requirements

- Conversations with external parties including regulatory authorities and specialist in the area

A professional engagement that deals with management's assertion about its compliance with specified requirements can be executed only when the auditor is comfortable with the specified requirements that are the basis for the examination.

Plan the examination engagement   The second standard of fieldwork for attestation engagements, as established by SSAE-1, states that "the work shall be adequately planned and assistants, if any, shall be properly supervised." That standard must be observed in a compliance attestation engagement.

> **OBSERVATION:** *If the compliance attestation engagement requires the services of a specialist, the auditor should observe the relevant standards established by SAS-73 (Using the Work of a Specialist) (AT 500.42).*

> **OBSERVATION:** *If the auditor is considering the use of the client's internal auditors (or equivalent group) in the compliance attestation engagement, the relevant standards established by SAS-65 (The Auditor's Consideration of the Internal Audit Function in an Audit of Financial Statements) should be observed (AT 500.43).*

In many instances, the operations of the client will encompass two or more locations. As part of the planning of the compliance attestation engagement, the auditor should decide whether the internal control policies and procedures at all or some of the locations should be considered. SSAE-3 states that factors such as the following should be considered when determining the scope of the engagement with respect to the component units (AT 500.41):

- The degree to which the specified requirements apply to each component
- The assessment of materiality in the context of each component's operations
- The degree to which records are processed at each component
- The effectiveness of control environment policies and procedures over each component's operations

- The nature of activities conducted at each component unit
- The similarities of operations among components

Consider relevant internal control components The auditor should obtain an understanding of the relevant internal control policies and procedures related to the entity's ability to comply with the specified requirements. This understanding enables the auditor to properly plan the engagement and to determine the planned assessed level of control risk. At this point, the auditor should have developed insight into the strengths and weaknesses of the internal control by identifying the processing steps and procedures that have that are (1) most likely to enhance the occurrence of material noncompliance and (2) most likely to reduce the likelihood that material noncompliance will occur.

> **OBSERVATION:** *The consideration of the internal control in a compliance attestation engagement is very similar to the consideration of the internal control in an audit of financial statements. In an audit of financial statements, the auditor (1) obtains an understanding of internal control, (2) determines the planned assessed level of control risk, (3) generally performs tests of controls, and (4) designs substantive tests based on the assessed level of control risk. In a compliance attestation engagement, the auditor (1) obtains an understanding of internal control, (2) determines the planned assessed level of control risk, (3) generally performs tests of controls, and (4) designs compliance tests based on the assessed level of control risk. Thus, the only difference is that the auditor performs tests of compliance as the final step in a compliance attestation engagement rather than substantive tests.*

The understanding of internal control may be obtained by performing such procedures as (1) making inquiries of appropriate client personnel, (2) inspecting relevant documents and records, (3) observing the entity's relevant activities and operations, and (4) if applicable, reviewing workpapers from the previous engagement(s). The understanding of internal control includes an analytical phase and a corroborative phase. In the analytical phase, the auditor's responsibility is to gain an understanding of relevant internal control policies and procedures. In the corroborative phase (tests of controls), the auditor must determine the effectiveness of the design of policies and procedures and the operations of the relevant internal control policies and procedures.

OBSERVATION: To assess control risk at a level that is less than the maximum level, the auditor must perform tests of controls. (For a discussion of maximum level of control risk see the chapter entitled "Internal Control, Errors, and Irregularities.")

The evidential matter obtained through these and other examination procedures should provide the auditor with a basis for the design of tests of compliance. SSAE-3 specifically notes that the nature and extent of tests of compliance procedures may be affected by a variety of factors including the following:

- The newness and complexity of the specified requirements
- The auditor's experience with the client's relevant internal control based on previous engagements
- The characteristics of the client
- The assessment as to what constitutes material noncompliance

OBSERVATION: During the engagement, the auditor may discover noncompliance that is considered "significant" but not material. Under this circumstance, guidance established by SAS-60 (Communication of Internal Control Structure Related Matters Noted in an Audit) should be considered.

Obtain sufficient evidential matter The second attestation standard of fieldwork, as established by SSAE-1, must be satisfied in a compliance attestation engagement. That standard reads, "Sufficient evidence shall be obtained to provide a reasonable basis for the conclusion that is expressed in the report." Thus, based on the assessed level of control risk, which is the final phase in the development of an understanding of the client's internal control, the auditor must perform tests of compliance.

OBSERVATION: When obtaining sufficient evidence in the tests of compliance, the auditor should consider the guidance established in paragraphs 36 through 39 of SSAE-1. In addition, if the client is subject to regulatory requirements, the audit approach should include "reviewing reports of significant examinations and related communications between regulatory agencies and the entity and, when appropriate, making inquiries of the regulatory agencies, including inquiries about examinations in progress."

Consider subsequent events   SSAE-3 identifies two types of subsequent events that should be considered by the accountant in the compliance attestation engagement. The first type of subsequent event provides additional information about the entity's compliance during the period covered by management's assertion. In a manner similar to the approach used in an audit of financial statements, the accountant should perform, between the end of the period covered by management's assertion and the date of the report, specific subsequent-event procedures to evaluate the appropriateness of management's assertions. While there is no comprehensive list of those procedures, SSAE-3 list the following as examples of subsequent audit procedures (AT 500.49):

- Review relevant internal audit reports that have been issued during the subsequent period.
- Determine whether relevant reports by external parties have been issued during the subsequent period.
- Consider whether relevant subsequent events have been discovered due to the conduct of other professional engagements for the client.
- Consider reports on the entity's noncompliance issued by regulatory agencies during the subsequent period.

The second type of subsequent events relates to noncompliance events that actually occur between the end of the period covered by management's assertion and the date of the report. While the scope of the engagement focuses on the period covered by management's assertion, the auditor must nonetheless take into consideration subsequent noncompliance events that could have implications for the effectiveness of internal control in operations for the period covered by the auditor's report. SSAE-3 concludes that if the noncompliance is significant, it may be appropriate for the auditor to describe the event in the auditor's report (assuming the event is not adequately disclosed in the report or letter in which management makes its assertion about compliance with specified requirements) (AT 500.51).

Obtain written representations from the client   The auditor should obtain written representations from management concerning an examination to express an opinion on compliance with specified requirements. The representations should be signed by management personnel who are responsible for and knowledgeable of the written representations. The written representations obtained from management should be dated as of the date of the examination report.

SSAE-3 concludes that the following representations should be made by the appropriate management personnel (AT 500.70–.71):

- State that management is responsible for complying with the specified requirements.

- State that management is responsible for establishing and maintaining effective internal control with respect to compliance with specified requirements.

- State that management has evaluated the entity's compliance with specified requirements.

- State management's assertion about the entity's compliance with the specified requirements.

- State that management has informed the auditor of all known noncompliance.

- State that management has made available to the auditor all documentation relevant to the engagement.

- State management's interpretation of any specified requirements that have alternative interpretations.

- State that management has communicated to the auditor all communications from regulatory agencies, internal auditors, and other auditors concerning possible noncompliance, including communications received up to the date of the auditor's report.

- State that management has informed the auditor of any noncompliance that occurred from the date of management's assertion through the date of the auditor's report.

> **OBSERVATION:** *If management refuses to make the appropriate written representations, the auditor must determine whether the scope limitation should result in a qualified opinion or a disclaimer of opinion (AT 500.71).*

Form and express an opinion   Once the auditor has obtained sufficient evidence, an opinion on management's assertion about its compliance with specified requirements is made. If the auditor concludes that management's assertion is "stated fairly in all material respects," the form of the auditor's report depends on whether management's assertion is included in (1) a separate report or (2) a representation letter directed to the auditor (AT 500.53).

When management issues its assertion in a separate report, the examination report on management's assertion should include three paragraphs (introductory, scope, and opinion) and should satisfy the following reporting standards (AT 500.54):

- The word *independent* should be included in the title of the examination report.

- Management's assertion about its compliance with the specified requirements and the period covered by the assertion should be identified.

- A statement concerning the responsibilities of management and the auditor should be included.

- A statement that the examination was performed in accordance with standards established by the AICPA, a brief description of the nature of the examination, and a statement that the auditor believes that the examination provided a reasonable basis for the opinion expressed should be included.

- A statement that the auditor's examination did not make a legal determination with respect to compliance with specified requirements should be included.

- An opinion on management's assertion about its compliance with specified requirements should be expressed.

- The report should be dated based on the completion date of the examination.

> **OBSERVATION:** *Management's assertion may be as of a point in time (for example, December 31, 19X5) rather than for a specific period (for example, for the year ended December 31, 19X5). The wording of the examination report should be appropriately changed when the management assertion is for a point in time.*

Presented below is an example of a standard report on management's assertion about its compliance with specified requirements when the assertion is included in a separate report (AT 500.55).

Independent Accountant's Report

We have examined management's assertion about X Company's compliance with adult education and training grant requirements established by the

State of New Jersey under Regulation SAXX-95 during the year ended December 31, 19X5, included in the accompanying Management's Report on Compliance with Regulation SAXX-95. Management is responsible for X Company's compliance with those requirements. Our responsibility is to express an opinion on management's assertion about the Company's compliance based on our examination.

Our examination was made in accordance with standards established by the American Institute of Certified Public Accountants and, accordingly, included examining, on a test basis, evidence about X Company's compliance with those requirements and performing such other procedures as considered necessary in the circumstances. We believe that our examination provides a reasonable basis for our opinion. Our examination does not provide a legal determination of X Company's compliance with specified requirements.

In our opinion, management's assertion that X Company complied with the aforementioned requirements for the year ended December 31, 19X5, is fairly stated, in all material respects.

OBSERVATION: The auditor is not precluded from adding a paragraph to the report to restrict its use.

OBSERVATION: If the compliance requirements have been agreed to by the auditor and management, the examination report should include a paragraph that restricts the distribution of the report to specified parties (AT 500.58).

When management issues its assertion in a representation letter directed to the auditor, the examination report on management's assertion should include four paragraphs (introductory, scope, opinion, and limited distribution).

Presented below is an example of a standard report on management's assertion about its compliance with specified requirements when the assertion is included in a representation letter directed to the auditor (AT 500.57).

We have examined management's assertion, included in its representation letter dated December 31, 19X5, that X Company complied with adult education and training grant requirements established by the State of New Jersey under Regulation SAXX-95 during the year ended December 31, 19X5. As discussed in that representation letter, management is responsible for X Company's compliance with those requirements. Our responsibility is to express an opinion on management's assertion about the Company's compliance based on our examination.

Our examination was made in accordance with standards established by the American Institute of Certified Public Accountants and, accordingly, included examining, on a test basis, evidence about X Company's compliance with those requirements and performing such other procedures as considered necessary in the circumstances. We believe that our examination provides a reasonable basis for our opinion. Our examination does not provide a legal determination of X Company's compliance with specified requirements.

In our opinion, management's assertion that X Company complied with the aforementioned requirements for the year ended December 31, 19X5, is fairly stated, in all material respects.

This report is intended solely for the information of the audit committee, management, and New Jersey Department of Community Services.

OBSERVATION: If the report is part of the public record, an additional sentence should be added to the last paragraph that reads, "However, this report is a matter of public record and its distribution is not limited."

In some instances it may be necessary to interpret the specified requirements established by laws, regulations, rules, contracts, or grants. If the examination report (on either the separate management report or the representation letter) is based on significant interpretations, the auditor may add an additional paragraph to the report explaining the nature of the interpretation and its source (AT 500.59).

SSAE-3 notes that it may be necessary to modify the examination report for the following reasons (AT 500.61):

- A material noncompliance with specified requirements exists.
- A material uncertainty exists.
- The scope of the engagement has been restricted.
- There is a reference to the work of another auditor.

Material noncompliance with specified requirements exists During the examination, a noncompliance may be discovered that the auditor believes has a material effect on the entity's compliance with the specified requirements. Under this circumstance, the examination report should be modified; however, the nature of the modification depends on whether management's assertion includes a description of the noncompliance (AT 500.62).

When management's assertion includes a description of the noncompliance and appropriately modifies the assertion to reflect the noncompliance, the examination report should be changed by (1) referring in the opinion paragraph to management's reference to the noncompliance and (2) adding an explanatory paragraph to the examination report. An example of such a report is illustrated below (AT 500.63–.64).

Independent Accountant's Report

We have examined management's assertion about X Company's compliance with adult education and training grant requirements established by the State of New Jersey under Regulation SAXX-95 during the year ended December 31, 19X5, included in the accompanying Management's Report on Compliance with Regulation SAXX-95. Management is responsible for X Company's compliance with those requirements. Our responsibility is to express an opinion on management's assertion about the Company's compliance based on our examination.

Our examination was made in accordance with standards established by the American Institute of Certified Public Accountants and, accordingly, included examining, on a test basis, evidence about X Company's compliance with those requirements and performing such other procedures as considered necessary in the circumstances. We believe that our examination provides a reasonable basis for our opinion. Our examination does not provide a legal determination of X Company's compliance with specified requirements.

In our opinion, management's assertion that, except for the noncompliance with certain residential requirements established by the grant, X Company complied with the aforementioned requirements for the year ended December 31, 19X5, is fairly stated, in all material respects.

As discussed in management's assertion, a material noncompliance occurred at X Company during the year ended December 31, 19X5. The noncompliance event occurred when some adults were admitted to the program who had not substantiated their residency in the county covered by the state grant.

When management's assertion does not include a description of the noncompliance or does not appropriately modify the assertion to reflect the noncompliance, the examination report should be qualified or an adverse opinion should be expressed depending on the "significance of the noncompliance to the entity and the pervasiveness of the noncompliance." An example of a qualified opinion is illustrated below (AT 500.65–.66).

Independent Accountant's Report

We have examined management's assertion about X Company's compliance with adult education and training grant requirements established by the State of New Jersey under Regulation SAXX-95 during the year ended December 31, 19X5, included in the accompanying Management's Report on Compliance with Regulation SAXX-95. Management is responsible for X Company's compliance with those requirements. Our responsibility is to express an opinion on management's assertion about the Company's compliance based on our examination.

Our examination was made in accordance with standards established by the American Institute of Certified Public Accountants and, accordingly, included examining, on a test basis, evidence about X Company's compliance with those requirements and performing such other procedures as considered necessary in the circumstances. We believe that our examination provides a reasonable basis for our opinion. Our examination does not provide a legal determination of X Company's compliance with specified requirements.

Our examination disclosed a material noncompliance that occurred at X Company during the year ended December 31, 19X5. The noncompliance event occurred when some adults were admitted to the program who had not substantiated their residency in the county covered by the state grant.

In our opinion, except for the material noncompliance described in the third paragraph, management's assertion that X Company complied with the aforementioned requirements for the year ended December 31, 19X5, is fairly stated, in all material respects.

> **OBSERVATION:** *The above report differs from the report that covers a management assertion that is properly modified due to a material noncompliance. In the latter circumstance the explanatory paragraph is placed as the last paragraph, and there is no reference to that paragraph in the opinion paragraph.*

An example of an adverse opinion that arises because management has not disclosed a material noncompliance or has not appropriately modified its assertion is illustrated below (AT 500.67).

Independent Accountant's Report

We have examined management's assertion about X Company's compliance with adult education and training grant requirements established by the State of New Jersey under Regulation SAXX-95 during the year ended December 31, 19X5, included in the accompanying Management's Report on Compliance with Regulation SAXX-95. Management is responsible for X Company's compliance with those requirements. Our responsibility is to express an opinion on management's assertion about the Company's compliance based on our examination.

Our examination was made in accordance with standards established by the American Institute of Certified Public Accountants and, accordingly, included examining, on a test basis, evidence about X Company's compliance with those requirements and performing such other procedures as considered necessary in the circumstances. We believe that our examination provides a reasonable basis for our opinion. Our examination does not provide a legal determination of X Company's compliance with specified requirements.

Our examination disclosed a material noncompliance that occurred at X Company during the year ended December 31, 19X5. The noncompliance event occurred when some adults were admitted to the program who had not substantiated their residency in the county covered by the state grant.

In our opinion, because of the material noncompliance described in the third paragraph, management's assertion that X Company complied with the aforementioned requirements for the year ended December 31, 19X5, is not fairly stated.

When a report on management's assertion describes a material noncompliance and that report is included in the document that includes the auditor's report on the client's financial statements, the sentence shown below should be added to report on management's assertion (AT 500.68).

These conditions were considered in determining the nature, timing, and extent of audit tests applied in our audit of the 19X5 financial statements, and this report does not affect our report dated February 18, 19X5, on those financial statements.

OBSERVATION: SSAE-3 notes that the auditor may include the above sentence when the two reports are not presented in the same document.

Material uncertainty exists Although specified requirements may have been established, there may be some disagreement with regulatory authorities or other parties as to what constitutes acceptable compliance. When a material uncertainty exists, the type of modification of the examination report depends on whether the uncertainty is reflected in management's assertion (AT 500.69).

When management's assertion includes a description of the uncertainty, an explanatory paragraph (placed as the last paragraph) that describes the uncertainty should be added to the standard examination report. When management's assertion does not include a description of the uncertainty, an explanatory paragraph (placed as the paragraph before the opinion paragraph) should be added to the examination report, and a qualified or adverse opinion should be expressed (AT 500.69).

Scope of the engagement has been restricted SSAE-3 states that the guidance established in paragraphs 63 through 66 (Scope Limitations) in SSAE-2 should be followed when the auditor encounters a scope limitation in an examination of management's assertion about its compliance with specified requirements (AT 500.61).

Reference to the work of another auditor SSAE-3 states that the guidance established in paragraphs 67 and 68 (Opinion Based in Part on the Report of Another Practitioner) in SSAE-2 should be followed when the auditor refers to the report of another auditor as part of the basis of the opinion expressed on management's assertion about its compliance with specified requirements (AT 500.61).

Agreed-Upon Procedures Engagements

Agreed-upon procedures are discussed in the chapter entitled "Agreed-Upon Procedures Engagements."

PART VI

Agreed-Upon Procedures Engagements

AGREED-UPON PROCEDURES ENGAGEMENTS

Contents

Overview	**17.03**
Statement on Auditing Standards No. 75	**17.04**
Definition and Presentation of Specified Elements, Accounts, or Items	**17.05**
Pre-Engagement Conditions	**17.06**
Sufficiency of Procedures	**17.07**
Engagement Letter	**17.08**
Additional Specified Users	**17.08**
Engagement Procedures	**17.09**
Internal Control	**17.10**
Use of a Specialist	**17.10**
Use of Internal Auditors and Other Similar Personnel	**17.10**
Reporting Standards	**17.11**
Other Matters	**17.14**
Explanatory Language	**17.14**
Restrictions on the Performance of Procedures	**17.14**
Written Representations	**17.15**
Knowledge of Matters Outside Agreed-Upon Procedures	**17.15**
Change to an AUP Engagement	**17.15**
Combined or Included Reports	**17.16**
Working Papers	**17.17**
Statement on Standards for Attestation Engagements No. 4	**17.17**
Description and Presentation of an Assertion	**17.18**
Pre-Engagement Conditions	**17.20**
Sufficiency of Procedures	**17.20**
Engagement Letter	**17.20**
Additional Specified Users	**17.21**

Engagement Procedures   **17.21**
    Use of a Specialist   **17.22**
    Use of Internal Auditors   **17.22**
    Reporting Standards   **17.22**
    Other Matters   **17.24**
Compliance Attestation   **17.24**
    Obtain an Understanding of the Compliance
        Requirements   **17.25**
    Perform Certain Procedures as Part of the Planning
        Phase   **17.26**
    Obtain Written Representations from the Client   **17.26**
    Express the Findings Made by the Auditor   **17.26**
    Other Information Included in Client-Prepared
        Documents   **17.27**
Financial Forecasts and Projections   **17.28**
Internal Control Reports   **17.28**

AGREED-UPON PROCEDURES ENGAGEMENTS

Overview

The scope of an engagement may be limited to the performance of agreed-upon procedures for specified elements, accounts, or items of a financial statement. When an accountant accepts an agreed-upon procedures (AUP) engagement related to specified elements, accounts, or items of a financial statement, the standards established by Statement on Auditing Standards (SAS) No. 75 (Engagements to Apply Agreed-Upon Procedures to Specified Elements, Accounts, or Items of a Financial Statement) or Statement on Standards for Attestation Engagements (SSAE) No. 4 (Agreed-Upon Procedures Engagements) must be observed. The standards established by SSAE-4 apply to AUP engagements in which the subject matter of the engagement is a written assertion.

The pronouncements covered in this chapter are:

- SAS-75 (Engagements to Apply Agreed-Upon Procedures to Specified Elements, Accounts, or Items of a Financial Statement)

- SSAE-4 (Agreed-Upon Procedures Engagements)

- SSAE-3 (Compliance Attestation)

- SSAE-1 (Codification of Statements on Standards for Attestation Engagements)

SAS-75 establishes standards for AUP engagements that apply to specified elements, accounts, or items of a financial statement.

SSAE-4 establishes standards for an AUP engagement related to a written assertion or matters that are not elements, accounts, or items of a financial statement. In this type of engagement, the accountant issues a report on the assertion based on procedures agreed to by the accountant and specified users. Specified users assume the responsibility for the sufficiency of the agreed-upon procedures.

SSAE-3 establishes standards for AUP engagements to perform procedures directed to management's assertion about its compliance with specified requirements (AT 300).

SSAE-1, in part, establishes broad standards for AUP engagements to perform procedures directed to management's assertion about its internal control (AT 100).

STATEMENT ON AUDITING STANDARDS NO. 75

The standards established by SAS-75 should be observed for AUP engagements related to specified elements, accounts, or items of a financial statement; however, SAS-75 specifically excludes the following engagements:

- Situations in which an accountant reports on an engagement to apply agreed-upon procedures to other than specified elements, accounts, or items of a financial statement pursuant to SSAE-4

- Situations in which an accountant reports on specified compliance requirements based solely on an audit of financial statements, as addressed in paragraphs 19 through 21 of SAS-62 (Special Reports)

- Engagements for which the objective is to report in accordance with SAS-74 (Compliance Auditing Considerations in Audits of Governmental Entities and Recipients of Governmental Financial Assistance)

- Circumstances covered by paragraph 58 of SAS-70 (Reports on the Processing of Transactions by Service Organizations), when the service auditor is requested to apply substantive procedures to user transactions for assets at the service organization and he or she makes specific reference in the service auditor's report to having carried out designated procedures (However, SAS-75 would apply when the service auditor provides a separate report on the performance of applying agreed-upon procedures to specified elements, accounts, or items of a financial statement.)

- Engagements covered by SAS-72 (Letters for Underwriters and Certain Other Requesting Parties)

> **OBSERVATION:** *When an auditor is requested to perform agreed-upon procedures for an assertion and report the results as part of a*

letter to an underwriter, the guidance established by SAS-72 (Letter for Underwriters and Certain Other Requesting Parties) should be followed. In addition, when a letter based on guidance established by SAS-72 has been issued, the auditor is precluded from issuing an agreed-upon procedures report directed to the underwriter or other requesting parties in connection with the offering or placement of securities if the comments contained in the agreed-upon report violate preclusions established by SAS-72.

> **OBSERVATION:** *An Attestation Interpretation entitled "Responding to Requests for Reports on Matters Relating to Solvency" (May 1988) prohibits the accountant from accepting an AUP engagement related to providing any assurance on matters relating to solvency, including the financial presentation of matters relating to solvency (AT 9100.33–.44).*

In an AUP engagement, the accountant does not perform an audit and offers no form of assurance on the fair presentation of the information that is the basis for the engagement. However, the accountant should observe the three general standards (adequate training and proficiency, independence, and due care) and the first standard of fieldwork (planning and supervision) of generally accepted auditing standards. SAS-75 states that the "interpretative guidance" relating to the third standard of fieldwork (sufficient competent evidential matter) should be observed. Reporting standards for AUP engagements are established by SAS-75 and are discussed later in this chapter.

Definition and Presentation of Specified Elements, Accounts, or Items

Specified elements, accounts, or items are not financial statements but rather are part of a financial statement. The basis of the engagement could be a specific line item account (cash), part of a note to the financial statements (long-term debt payment schedule), information derived from data contained in the financial statements (acid test ratio), or detail support for a line item included in the financial statements (schedule of accounts payable). The basis of this information can be generally accepted accounting principles; another comprehensive basis of accounting, as defined in SAS-62; and special-purpose financial presentations to comply with contractual agreements or regulatory provisions, as defined in SAS-62.

While an AUP engagement is concerned with specified elements, accounts, or items in a financial statement, the specific procedures of the engagement are directed to the assertions (both explicit and implicit) related to the specified elements, accounts, or items. SAS-75 specifically states that "in an engagement to apply agreed-upon procedures, it is the subject matter underlying the assertions to which the accountant's procedures are applied (referred to in this Statement as *specific subject matter*)." For example, the line item inventory that appears on the balance sheet may represent that inventories are valued at a particular amount but the specific subject matter would include such items as cost factors applied to specific inventory quantities and the mathematical process used to determine the inventory amount. Once the agreed-upon procedures have been applied to the specific subject matter, the accountant can formulate the findings of the AUP engagement.

> **OBSERVATION:** *SAS-31 (Evidential Matter) provides a discussion of explicit and implicit assertions that are related to financial statements.*

The specified element, account, or item may be presented in the following manner:

- As a schedule or statement
- As part of the accountant's report with proper identification of the specified element, account, or item and the point in time or period covered
- Identified in accounting records (such as a general ledger account or account in a computer printout)

Pre-Engagement Conditions

Before an AUP engagement is accepted, SAS-75 requires that the following conditions be satisfied:

- The accountant must be independent.
- The accountant and the specified users must agree on the agreed-upon procedures (including materiality limits, where

applicable), and the basis of accounting must be clear to the accountant and the specified users.

- The specified users must take responsibility for the sufficiency of the agreed-upon procedures.
- The application of the agreed-upon procedures must be expected to generate reasonably consistent findings.
- The specific subject matter of the engagement must be subject to reasonably consistent estimation or measurement.
- Evidential matter related to the specific subject matter must be expected to exist and to provide a reasonable basis for the accountant's finding.
- The accountant's report must be restricted to use by the specified users. (However, the accountant may accept an engagement in which the report will be a matter of public record.)

> **OBSERVATION:** *AUP engagements are not based on the concept of materiality. In other words, an accountant must report all errors (no matter how small) discovered while performing agreed-upon procedures. However, as noted above, the accountant and specified user may agree to a definition of materiality and thus report only those errors that exceed the materiality limit.*

Sufficiency of procedures   Specified users (not the accountant) assume the risk for the sufficiency of the agreed-upon procedures (nature, timing, and extent of procedures) based on their perceived needs. The accountant assumes the risk (1) for misapplication of the procedures that may lead to inappropriate findings and (2) that appropriate findings may not be reported or may be incorrectly reported. The accountant has no responsibility to determine whether the agreed-upon procedures would be appropriate for another form of engagement such as an audit or review.

To determine if the specified users agree with and assume responsibility for the procedures, the accountant should communicate directly with the specified users and obtain an "affirmative acknowledgment." When the accountant is unable to communicate directly with the specified users, an alternative approach is to perform one or more of the following:

- Compare the written requirements established by specified users with the proposed agreed-upon procedures.

- Discuss the agreed-upon procedures with appropriate representatives of specified users.

- Review relevant contracts with, or correspondence from, specified users.

If specified users do not agree to the procedures and/or accept responsibility for their sufficiency, the accountant should *not* issue a AUP engagement report.

Engagement letter   The terms of the AUP engagement should be clearly understood by the accountant and ideally should be expressed in an engagement letter that includes such matters as the following:

- Nature of the engagement, including the specified elements, accounts, or items (including the basis of accounting); the party responsible for their preparation; specified users; and restrictions on the distribution of the report

- Request for acknowledgment from specified users' of their responsibility for the sufficiency of the agreed-upon procedures

- Reference to AICPA standards that will govern the engagement

- List of agreed-upon procedures

- Disclaimer that is expected to be part of the accountant's report

- If applicable, description of assistance to be provided to the accountant and/or any specialists

- If applicable, the role of specialists

- If applicable, the definition of materiality for the engagement

The engagement letter should be addressed to the client, and, in some circumstances, to all specified users.

Additional specified users   After the completion of the AUP engagement, the accountant may be requested to add another party as a specified user. When determining whether the request should be honored, the accountant should consider the identity of the prospective specified user (nonparticipant party) and how that party intends to use the AUP report. If the accountant agrees to the addition of another specified user, acknowledgment should be received from

the additional party that the party agrees with the procedures specified in the original arrangement and also accepts responsibility for
the sufficiency of the agreed-upon procedures.

Also, the accountant may be requested to add another party as a
specified user after the AUP report has been issued. Under this
circumstance, the accountant may reissue the original report or provide some other form of written communication that acknowledges
the addition of the new specified user. (Again, the prospective specified user must acknowledge agreement with the procedures and
assume responsibility for the sufficiency of the agreed-upon procedures.) When the accountant agrees to reissue the report, the original
date of the AUP report should be used. SAS-75 notes that "if the
accountant provides written acknowledgment that the nonparticipant party has been added as a specified user, such written acknowledgment originally should state that no procedures have been performed subsequent to the date of the report."

Engagement Procedures

The standards do not specify a list of minimum procedures that the
accountant must perform in an AUP engagement; however, the
mere reading of the information cannot the basis for the engagement. During the course of the engagement, the originally agreed-
upon procedures may be modified. SAS-75 emphasizes that the
scope of an AUP engagement is flexible and procedures may be
changed as long as specified users agreed to the changes and accept
responsibility for the sufficiency of the procedures. However, the
accountant should not agree to perform procedures that are beyond
his or her expertise.

The procedures agreed to should not be so general as to be subject
to various interpretations. For example, the terms *test* and *check*
should be avoided unless they are defined as part of the AUP engagement. Likewise, evaluating the competency of another individual or acquiring an understanding of a particular activity are too
subjective to be considered agreed-upon procedures. On the other
hand, procedures such as the confirmation of specified information
and the inspection of documents for specified characteristics are
within the scope of an AUP engagement.

The procedures agreed to and the evidence derived from the
performance of the procedures are the basis for expressing the findings in the accountant's report. For example, an agreed-upon procedure could be the confirmation of all accounts receivable greater than

$1,000, and the accountant's finding could be expressed as, "65% of the number of accounts selected were confirmed by customers."

Internal control   An accountant may perform agreed-upon procedures on specified elements, accounts, or items of a financial statement, and agreed-upon procedures on part of the client's internal control over financial reporting. For example, the accountant may perform agreed-upon procedures on accounts receivable and on control procedures related to cash receipts from customers. SAS-75 concludes that separate AUP reports should not be issued under this circumstance, but rather the accountant's report on specified elements, accounts, or items of a financial statement should express a disclaimer of opinion on the effectiveness of internal control over financial reporting (or any part thereof). Furthermore, the accountant is prohibited from providing negative assurance on the portion of internal control that was subjected to the agreed-upon procedures.

Use of a specialist   The accountant may use the work of a specialist (an expert in a field other than accounting or auditing who does not work for the accounting firm) to assist in the execution of an AUP engagement. The role of the specialist should be agreed to by the accountant and specified users. The role of the specialist should be described in the accountant's AUP report.

The application of procedures to the work product of a specialist does not involve the work of a specialist in an AUP engagement; however, the application of procedures to the work product may be described as part of the agreed-upon procedures. Simply reading the specialist's report is not an appropriate basis for an AUP engagement and subsequent AUP report.

Use of internal auditors and other similar personnel   The accountant is responsible for the performance of the agreed-upon procedures (except for work performed by a specialist as described above). This requirement does not prohibit internal auditors (and other entity personnel) from preparing schedules and analyses that the accountant may use in the engagement. In addition, *internal auditors* may perform (and report on) the same or similar procedures as those performed by the accountant in the AUP engagement.

While the internal auditors can perform procedures similar to those performed by the accountant, SAS-75 requires that the accountant, not the internal auditors, perform the agreed-upon procedures. However, the accountant (as part of the agreed-upon procedures) may agree to apply procedures to the internal auditors' work product. Simply reading the internal auditors' report is not an appropriate basis for an AUP engagement. The accountant should *not* refer to the work of internal auditors in the accountant's report, which would imply responsibility or a degree of responsibility (or shared responsibility) for the work performed by internal auditors.

Reporting Standards

Based on the performance of the agreed-upon procedures, the accountant should formulate the findings to be expressed in the accountant's report. The findings must be based on the evidence gathered during the performance of the agreed-upon procedures and must be expressed in a way that is not vague or beyond the scope of the agreed-upon procedures. All findings should be reported, unless agreed-on materiality limits indicate otherwise.

SAS-75 prohibits the accountant from expressing negative assurance on the specified elements, accounts, or items. For example, it would be inappropriate to state in the report that "nothing came to our attention that caused us to believe that cash is not fairly stated in accordance with generally accepted accounting principles." The prohibition of negative assurance applies to a broad conclusion (such as a statement about cash) as well as to a more narrow conclusion (such as a statement about dates that appear on customer invoices).

The following guidance should be observed in preparing the accountant's report for an AUP engagement on specified elements, accounts, or items of a financial statement:

- Use the word *independent* in the report title.

- Identify the entity; the nature of the engagement; the specified elements, accounts, or items of the financial statements; and the basis of accounting (unless clearly evident).

- Identify specified users.

- State that the procedures were agreed to by specified users.

- Refer to the standards established by the AICPA as the basis for the engagement.

- State that specified users are responsible for the sufficiency of the procedures and disclaim any responsibility for the sufficiency of the procedures.

- List the procedures performed (or reference thereto), and describe the findings.
- If applicable, describe the agreed-upon materiality limits.
- State that the accountant was not engaged to perform an audit of the specified elements, accounts, or items included in the financial statements; disclaim an opinion on the specified elements, accounts, or items; and state that had additional procedures been performed, other matters may have been identified and reported.
- Disclaim an opinion on the specified elements, accounts, or items included in the financial statements, and state that had additional procedures been performed, other matters may have come to the accountant's attention that would have been reported.
- If applicable (when the accountant had performed procedures related to the entity's internal control), disclaim an opinion on the effectiveness of internal control over financial reporting (or any part of that structure).
- State that the use of the report is restricted to the specified users. (If the report is a matter of public record, state that fact and note that the distribution is not limited.)
- If applicable, note specific reservations or restrictions (explanatory language, restrictions on the performance of procedures, no receipt of a representation letter, and knowledge of matters outside agreed-upon procedures) identified in SAS-75. (These are discussed later in this chapter.)
- If applicable, describe the role of any specialists in the engagement.

An example of a AUP engagement report on specified elements, accounts, or items of a financial statement is presented below.

Independent Accountant's Report on Applying Agreed-Upon Procedures

We have performed the procedures enumerated below, which were agreed to by the Board of Directors of X Company, solely to assist you with respect to the evaluation of inventory and property, plant, and equipment of Y Company as part of the proposed acquisition of Y Company by X Company. This engagement to apply agreed-upon procedures was performed in accordance with standards established by the American Institute of Certified Public Accountants. The sufficiency of the procedures is solely the responsibility of the specified users of the report. Consequently, we make no representation regarding the sufficiency of the procedures described below either for the purpose for which this report has been requested or for any other purpose.

The agreed-upon procedures that were performed and the related findings are as follows:

Inventory

1. We obtained the inventory summarization as of December 31, 19X5, and traced 20% of the quantities listed on the summarization to the inventory tags used by Y Company during its physical count on December 31, 19X5.

   We found no differences between the quantities on the inventory summarization and the quantities on the inventory tags.

2. For 1 out of 10 line items on the inventory summarization, we traced the inventory cost per unit listed to vendor invoices for purchases made during the last quarter of 19X5.

   We found no differences between the cost listed on the inventory summarization and vendor invoices for purchases made during the last quarter of 19X5.

3. We added the inventory summarization and compared the total with the total unaudited balance ($2,000,000) in the general ledger account as of December 31, 19X5.

   We found no difference between the total inventory amount we computed and the balance in the general ledger account.

4. For all inventory line items on the inventory summarization that exceeded $10,000, we recomputed their extended value by multiplying the number of units by the cost per unit.

   We found no errors as the result of this procedure.

Property, Plant, and Equipment

1. We obtained a computer printout of assets classified as property, plant, and equipment having an unaudited balance of $3,500,000 as of December 31, 19X5, which we added and traced to the appropriate general ledger accounts.

   We found no differences between the amounts per the computer printout and the appropriate general ledger account balances.

2. We physically inspected approximately 30% of the assets (based on the original cost of the asset as shown on the computer printout) listed on the computer printout and traced the property identification number, which appeared on each, to the appropriate ledger card contained in the computerized plant ledger.

   We found no differences between the identification number that appeared on each asset and the corresponding number included in the plant ledger cards.

We were not engaged to and did not perform an audit, the objective of which would be the expression of an opinion on the specified elements, accounts, or items. Accordingly, we do not express such an opinion. Had we been engaged to perform additional procedures, other matters might have come to our attention that would have been reported to you.

This report is intended solely for the use of the Board of Directors of X Company and should not be used by those who have not agreed to the procedures and taken responsibility for the sufficiency of the procedures for their purposes.

The accountant's report should be dated based on the completion of the agreed-upon procedures.

Other Matters

SAS-75 provides guidance for (1) explanatory language in the accountant's report, (2) restrictions on the performance of procedures, (3) written representations, (4) knowledge of matters outside agreed-upon procedures, (5) a change to an AUP engagement, (6) combined or included reports, and (7) workpapers.

Explanatory language   SAS-75 states that the accountant's report in an AUP engagement on specified elements, accounts, or items of a financial statement may include explanatory language for conditions such as the following:

- Description of stipulated facts, assumptions, or interpretations (and their sources) used in applying the agreed-upon procedures
- Description of the condition of records, data, or controls that were subjected to the agreed-upon procedures
- Statement that the accountant has no responsibility to update the report
- Explanation of sampling risk

Restrictions on the performance of procedures   When circumstances preclude the accountant from performing an agreed-upon procedure(s), the modification to the engagement should be agreed to by the specified users. If the specified users do not or cannot agree (for instance, a regulatory agency) to the modification, the accountant should consider withdrawing from the engagement or describing the restriction in the accountant's report.

Written representations While SAS-75 does not require the accountant to obtain a representation letter, it suggests that such a letter may be useful to document the representations related to the AUP engagement. Examples of representations that may be provided to the accountant include the following:

- The responsible party has disclosed to the accountant all known matters contradicting the specified elements, accounts, or items of a financial statement.
- The responsible party has disclosed to the accountant all communications from regulatory agencies affecting the specified elements, accounts, or items of a financial statement.

If the accountant determines that a representation letter should be obtained but the responsible parties refuse the request, the accountant should take one of the following actions:

- Disclose in the accountant's report the lack of obtaining written representations.
- Withdraw from the engagement.
- Change the AUP engagement to another type of engagement.

Knowledge of matters outside agreed-upon procedures The accountant has no obligation to perform procedures other than those agreed to by the parties of the engagement. However, if the accountant, through means other than the performance of the agreed-upon procedures, becomes aware of matters that contradict the basis of accounting used to present the specified elements, accounts, or items, the contradiction generally should be disclosed in the accountant's report.

Change to an AUP engagement When the accountant is performing an engagement other than an AUP engagement, the accountant may be requested to change the other engagement to an AUP engagement. In determining whether to agree to the change in engagements, the accountant should consider the following:

- The chance that procedures performed as part of the original engagement may not be appropriate to the AUP engagement
- The reason for the requested change and its implications (such as the possible implications of restrictions imposed on the original engagement or matters that the accountant may have to report on in the original engagement)
- The amount of effort needed to complete the original engagement
- If applicable, the implications of changing from a general-distribution to a restricted-use accountant's report

The following conditions generally would constitute an acceptable reason to change from one engagement to an AUP engagement:

- A change in circumstances that results in different client requirements
- A misunderstanding of the original engagement
- A misunderstanding of the availability of alternative services provided by the accountant
- A restriction on the original engagement (which may be imposed by circumstances or the client)

When the accountant concludes that it is appropriate to change from the original engagement to an AUP engagement, the standards established by SAS-75 must be observed and the accountant's report should not refer to the original engagement.

Combined or included reports An accountant may perform an AUP engagement along with other services or other separate engagements. Such services or separate engagements could include audits, reviews, compilations, engagements based on Statements on Standards for Attestation Engagements, or nonattest engagements. However, for each service or separate engagement the accountant must satisfy the appropriate standards established by the AICPA. SAS-75 concludes that the AUP report may be *combined or included* with reports resulting from other engagements if "the types of services can be clearly distinguished." When the reports are combined or included, *all* of the combined or included reports distributed are subject to the restricted-use standard established for AUP engagements for specified elements, accounts, and items of a financial statement.

Workpapers   The accountant should prepare and maintain work-papers that are appropriate for the AUP engagement. While the specific workpapers to be created depend on the circumstances of the particular engagement, at a minimum they should demonstrate that (1) the engagement was adequately planned and supervised and (2) evidence was collected to provide a reasonable basis to support findings expressed in the accountant's report.

STATEMENT ON STANDARDS
FOR ATTESTATION ENGAGEMENTS NO. 4

The standards established by SSAE-4 (as amended by SSAE-6) should be observed for AUP engagements that are based on written assertions; however, SSAE-4 specifically excludes the following engagements:

- Situations in which an auditor reports on the application of agreed-upon procedures to one or more specified elements, accounts, or items of a financial statement, pursuant to SAS-75

- Situations in which an auditor reports on specified compliance requirements based solely on an audit of financial statements, as addressed in paragraphs 19 through 21 of SAS-62

- Engagements for which the objective is to report in accordance with SAS-74, unless the terms of the engagement specify that the engagement be performed pursuant to Statements on Standards for Attestation Engagements

- Circumstances covered by paragraph 58 of SAS-70, when the service auditor is requested to apply substantive procedures to user transactions or assets at the service organization and he or she makes specific reference in his or her service auditor's report to having carried out designated procedures (However, SSAE-4 applies when the service auditor provides a separate report on the performance of agreed-upon procedures in an attestation engagement.)

- Engagements covered by SAS-72

- Engagements for which there is no written assurance (In such a situation, a practitioner may provide certain nonattest services involving advice or recommendation to a client. A practitioner engaged to provide such nonattest services should refer to the guidance in the Statement on Standards for Consulting Services [Consulting Services: Definitions and Standards] or other applicable professional standards.)

- Certain professional services that would not be considered as falling under SSAE-4 as described in paragraph 2 of SSAE-1

In an AUP engagement related to a written assertion, the accountant issues a report on the assertion based on procedures agreed to by the accountant and specified users. Specified users assume responsibility for the sufficiency of the agreed-upon procedures. The accountant does not perform an examination or review and expresses no opinion (neither reasonable assurance nor negative assurance) on the assertion.

The general standards, standards of fieldwork, and standards of reporting established in SSAE-1 (as interpreted by SSAE-4) apply to AUP engagements that are subject to the standards established by SSAE-4.

> **OBSERVATION:** *Rule 101 of the Code of Professional Conduct provides a general description of independence. In addition, Interpretation 11 of Rule 101 provides guidance for certain attest engagements. Rule 101 and Interpretation 11 are discussed in the chapter entitled "Code of Professional Conduct."*

Description and Presentation of an Assertion

SSAE-4 provides the following definitions:

Assertion—Any declaration (or set of related declarations taken as a whole) by a party responsible for it.

Subject matter of an assertion—Any attribute, or subset of attributes, referred to or contained in an assertion and may in and of itself constitute an assertion.

The third general standard established by SSAE-1 states that the practitioner should perform an engagement only if he or she has reason to believe that the following two conditions exists:

1. The assertion is capable of evaluation against reasonable criteria that either have been established by a recognized body or are stated in the presentation of the assertion in a sufficiently

clear and comprehensive manner for a knowledgeable reader to be able to understand them.

2. The assertion is capable of reasonably consistent estimation or measurement using such criteria.

The agreed-upon procedures are applied to the specific subject matter and not to the assertion. For example, while the declaration that an entity maintained effective internal control over financial reporting based on established criteria as of a specific date is an assertion, the agreed-upon procedures would be applied to the entity's internal control components that comprise internal control. The specific criteria by which the specific subject matter must be measurable can be enumerated or referred to in the accountant's report.

Other examples of written assertions illustrated in SSAE-4 include the following:

- A narrative description about an entity's compliance with requirements of specified laws, regulations, rules, contracts, or grants during a specified period (this example also is discussed in SSAE-3)

- A representation by management that all investment securities owned by an entity during a specified period were traded on one or more of the markets specified in the entity's investment policy

- A statement that the documentation of employee evaluations included in personnel files are dated within the time frame set forth in the entity's personnel policy

- A schedule of statistical production data prepared in accordance with the policies of an identified entity for a specified period

An assertion should be written and presented in a representation letter or some other form of written communication from the responsible party.

In some circumstances, the specific wording of the assertion may not have been finalized before an engagement is accepted or before all procedures are executed by the accountant (even though the general nature of the assertion is known). That circumstance is acceptable; however, SSAE-4 requires that the written assertion be communicated to the accountant before the accountant's report is issued.

Pre-Engagement Conditions

Before an AUP engagement based on a written assertion is accepted, SSAE-4 requires that the following conditions be satisfied:

- The written assertion must be provided to the accountant before the accountant's report is issued.
- Criteria that are the basis for the accountant's findings must be agreed to by the accountant and the specified users.
- The application of the agreed-upon procedures must be expected to generate reasonably consistent findings based on the agreed-upon criteria.

In addition, the pre-engagement conditions discussed in the earlier section on SAS-75 also apply to an AUP engagement based on a written assertion.

> **OBSERVATION:** *When the AUP engagement relates to prospective financial information, a summary of significant assumptions must be included with the prospective financial statements.*

> **OBSERVATION:** *When the AUP engagement is based on the standards established by SSAE-3, management must evaluate its compliance with specified requirements or the effectiveness of its internal control over compliance.*

Sufficiency of procedures Specified users assume the risk for the sufficiency of the agreed-upon procedures. The SAS-75 guidance on sufficiency of procedures, discussed earlier in this chapter, also applies to AUP engagements that relate to a written assertion.

Engagement letter The terms of the engagement should be clearly understood by the accountant and ideally should be expressed in an engagement letter. The SAS-75 guidance for the preparation of an engagement letter, discussed earlier in this chapter, applies to AUP engagements that relate to written assertions except that there should be identification of, or reference to, the assertion (rather than identification of the specified elements, accounts, or items of the financial statements).

Additional specified users After the completion of the AUP engagement, the accountant may be requested to add another party as a specified user. Under this circumstance, the SAS-75 guidance, discussed earlier in this chapter, should be observed for AUP engagements that relate to a written assertion.

Engagement Procedures

Specified users, not the accountant, are responsible for the nature, timing, and extent of agreed-upon procedures; however, the accountant must have an adequate knowledge of the specific subject matter to which the agreed-upon procedures will be applied. General guidance for the performance of an AUP engagement that involves a written assertion is similar to the SAS-75 guidance discussed earlier.

SSAE-4 provides the following examples of appropriate agreed-upon procedures:

- Executing a sampling application after agreeing on relevant parameters.
- Inspecting specified documents evidencing certain types of transactions or detailed attributes thereof.
- Confirming specific information with third parties.
- Comparing documents, schedules, or analyses with certain specified attributes.
- Performing specific procedures on work performed by others (including the work of internal auditors).
- Performing mathematical computations.

On the other hand, SSAE-4 concludes that the following would be inappropriate procedures in an AUP engagement related to a written assertion:

- Merely reading the work performed by others solely to describe their findings.
- Evaluating the competency or objectivity of another party.
- Obtaining an understanding about a particular subject.
- Interpreting documents outside the scope of the practitioner's professional expertise.

Use of a specialist   The accountant may use the work of a specialist. The SAS-75 guidance discussed earlier applies to the work of a specialist in an AUP engagement that involves a written assertion.

Use of internal auditors   The accountant may use the work of internal auditor. The SAS-75 guidance discussed earlier applies to the work of internal auditors in an AUP engagement that involves a written assertion.

Reporting Standards

Based on the performance of the agreed-upon procedures, the accountant should formulate the findings to be expressed in the accountant's report. SSAE-4 prohibits the accountant from expressing negative assurance on the assertion. For example, it would be inappropriate to state in the report that "nothing came to our attention that caused us to believe that the assertion is not fairly stated in accordance with" the established or stated criteria.

The following guidance should be observed in preparing the accountant's report on an AUP engagement involving a written assertion:

- Use the word *independent* in the report title.

- Identify the specified users and the character of the engagement, and refer to the assertion.

- State that the procedures were agreed to by specified users.

- Refer to the standards established by the AICPA as the basis for the engagement.

- State the specified users are responsible for the sufficiency of the procedures, and disclaim any responsibility for the sufficiency of the procedures.

- List the procedures performed (or reference thereto) and findings.

- If applicable, describe the agreed-upon materiality limits.

- State that the accountant was not engaged to perform an examination on the assertion.

- Disclaim an opinion on the assertion, and state that had additional procedures been performed, other matters may have come to the accountant's attention that would have been reported.

- State that the use of the report is restricted to the specified users. (If the report is a matter of public record, state that fact and note that the distribution is not limited.)

- If applicable, note specific reservations or restrictions (explanatory language, restrictions on the performance of procedures, no receipt of a representation letter, and knowledge of matters outside agreed-upon procedures) identified in SSAE-4.

- If applicable, describe the role of any specialists in the engagement.

OBSERVATION: If the engagement involves prospective financial information, the reporting guidance established by SSAE-1 (AT 200) for AUP engagements also must be observed.

Presented below is an illustration an accountant's report on a written assertion reproduced from SSAE-4.

Independent Accountant's Report on Applying Agreed-Upon Procedures

We have performed the procedures below, which were agreed to by the Audit Committees and Managements of ABC Inc. and XYZ Fund, solely to assist you in evaluating the accompanying Statement of Investment Performance Statistics of XYZ Fund (prepared in accordance with the criteria specified therein) for the year ended December 31, 19X1. This agreed-upon procedures engagement was performed in accordance with standards established by the American Institute of Certified Public Accountants. The sufficiency of these procedures is solely the responsibility of the specified users of the report. Consequently, we make no representation regarding the sufficiency of the procedures described below either for the purpose for which this report has been requested or for any other purpose.

[Include paragraphs to enumerate procedures and findings.]

We were not engaged to and did not perform an examination, the objective of which would be the expression of an opinion on the accompanying Statement of Investment Performance Statistics of XYZ Fund. Accordingly, we do not express such an opinion. Had we been engaged to perform additional procedures, other matters might have come to our attention that would have been reported to you.

This report is intended solely for the use of the audit committees and managements of ABC Inc. and XYZ Fund, and should not be used by those who have not agreed to the procedures and taken responsibility for the sufficiency of the procedures for their purposes.

The accountant's report should be dated based on the completion of the agreed-upon procedures.

Other Matters

SSAE-4 provides guidance similar to that of SAS-75 (see the earlier discussion) for (1) explanatory language in the accountant's report, (2) restrictions on the performance of procedures, (3) written representations, (4) knowledge of matters outside agreed-upon procedures, (5) a change to an AUP engagement, (6) combined or included reports, and (7) working papers.

COMPLIANCE ATTESTATION

An auditor may accept an engagement to perform agreed-upon procedures directed to management's assertion about (1) its compliance with specified requirements and/or (2) the effectiveness of its internal control over compliance if the standards established by SSAE-4 and all of the following standards are followed (AT 500.09):

- Management accepts responsibility for its compliance with specified requirements and the effectiveness of internal control as it relates to the compliance with the specified requirements.

- Management evaluates (1) its compliance with the specified requirements and/or (2) the effectiveness of internal control as it relates to the compliance with specified requirements (depending on the nature of the engagement).

When determining whether management's assertion can be subjected to agreed-upon (by the auditor and the client or a specified user) procedures, the auditor should consider the scope of the assertion. Also, the auditor should consider whether reasonable criteria have been established on which management's assertion is based.

The specific procedures to be performed in an agreed-upon procedures engagement are based on an agreement between the auditor and the specified user (which may or may not be the client). For this reason, there is no minimum list of specific procedures to be performed. SSAE-3 notes that the agreed-upon procedures "may be as limited or extensive as specified users desire." However, simply reading the assertion is *not* sufficient (AT 500.16).

Under all circumstances the following conditions must be satisfied:

- The specified user must agree to the specified procedures.

- The specified user must take responsibility for the sufficiency of the agreed-upon procedures.

If the auditor is unable to discuss the nature of management's assertion and the agreed-upon procedures with the specified user, procedures such as the following should be performed (AT 500.17):

- The auditor may compare the written requirements established by the specified user with the agreed-upon procedures.

- The auditor may discuss the agreed-upon procedures with legal counsel or other appropriate parties representing the specified user.

- The auditor may review contracts or correspondence from the specified user that are relevant to the engagement.

- The auditor may send the specified user an anticipated report on management's assertion or a copy of the engagement letter and instruct the specified user to concur with the agreement.

Obtain an understanding of the compliance requirements   Since the scope of SSAE-3 is broad and the standards can apply to a variety of agreed-upon procedures engagements, it is difficult to comment about the auditor's knowledge about compliance requirements. In general, the auditor must develop an understanding of the specified compliance requirements on which management's assertion is based. SSAE-3 identified the following as some of the possible sources of information that can provide the auditor with an adequate understanding (AT 500.19):

- Specific laws, regulations, rules, contacts, and grants on which the specified requirements are based

- Information from prior engagements and relevant regulatory reports
- Conversations with management personnel concerning the specified compliance requirements
- Conversations with external parties including regulatory authorities and specialists in the area

Perform certain procedures as part of the planning phase   In an agreed-upon procedures engagement, the auditor must satisfy the first attestation standard of fieldwork, which states, "The work shall be adequately planned and assistants, if any, shall be properly supervised." SSAE-3 notes that in an agreed-upon procedures engagement, the planning concepts discussed in paragraphs 28 through 32 of SSAE-1 should be satisfied. These concepts relate to (1) developing an overall strategy, (2) identifying relevant planning factors (such as consideration of the criteria used as the basis for the assertion, risk, materiality, potential engagement problems, and the nature of the report), and (3) the nature, timing, and extent of procedures.

Obtain written representations from the client   The auditor should obtain written representations from management concerning an agreed-upon procedures engagement. The representations should be signed by management personnel who are responsible for and knowledgeable of the written representations. The written representations should be dated as of the date of the examination report.

Express the findings made by the auditor   Once the auditor has performed the agreed-upon procedures, the findings should be expressed in an engagement report. In an agreed-upon procedures engagement, the auditor is not expressing an opinion on management's assertion about its compliance with specified requirements or the effectiveness of internal control with respect to compliance with those requirements. Thus, the engagement report should be formatted so that the agreed-upon procedures are presented along with the findings. Negative assurance should not be expressed in the engagement report (AT 500.23).

The engagement report on management's assertion should satisfy the reporting standards established by SSAE-4 and all of the following standards (AT 500.23):

- State that procedures, agreed to by the specified user, were performed to assist the user in evaluating management's assertion about compliance with specified requirements and / or the effectiveness of its internal control over compliance.

- Identify management's assertion about its compliance with the specified requirements and / or the effectiveness of its internal control over compliance and the period covered by the assertion.

The agreed-upon procedures listed in the engagement report should be sufficiently specific and descriptive so that the reader has a clear understanding of the scope of the engagement.

Generally, the report will be addressed to the entity. In addition, the date referred to in the report, which is related to management's assertion, could be for a period of time (usually applicable to an assertion concerning compliance with specified requirements) or as of a point in time (usually applicable to an assertion concerning the internal control over compliance).

In some instances, it may be necessary to interpret the specified requirements established by laws, regulations, rules, contracts, or grants. If the engagement report is based on significant interpretation, the auditor may add an additional paragraph to the report explaining the nature of the interpretations and their sources (AT 500.25).

If the auditor has been engaged to report on management's assertion about its compliance with specified requirements and the effectiveness of its internal control over compliance, a separate report can be prepared for each of the engagements or a single report can be prepared for both engagements (AT 500.27).

Other Information Included in Client-Prepared Documents

Management's assertion about its compliance with specified requirements and the effectiveness of its internal control over compliance may be included in a client-prepared document that includes other information. The auditor should read the other information to determine whether it is materially inconsistent with the information appearing in management's report or whether the other information contains a material misstatement of fact. The auditor is not required to corroborate any of the other information.

If the auditor discovers a material inconsistency or a material misstatement of fact, the guidance established by paragraphs 81 through 83 of SSAE-2 should be observed (AT 500.72–.73).

FINANCIAL FORECASTS AND PROJECTIONS

An accountant may be engaged to apply certain agreed-upon procedures to prospective financial statements. The performance of the agreed-upon procedures does not constitute an examination of the statements, and the accountant has no basis for expressing an opinion on the prospective financial statements. Because an engagement to apply agreed-upon procedures is a limited-scope engagement, it should be accepted by the accountant only when prospective financial statements include a summary of significant assumptions (AT 200.50d).

When an accountant is engaged to apply agreed-upon procedures to prospective financial statements, the standards established by SSAE-4 should be observed. In addition to the elements that should be included in the accountant's report, as described in SSAE-4, the report on prospective financial statements should also include the following:

- A caveat that the prospective results reflected in the prospective financial statements may not be achieved.

- A statement that the accountant assumes no responsibly to update his or her report for events and circumstances that occur after the date of the report.

> *OBSERVATION: When an auditor is requested to perform agreed-upon procedures for a forecast and report the results as part of a letter to an underwriter, the guidance established by SAS-72 should be followed.*

INTERNAL CONTROL REPORTS

When the auditor is engaged to perform agreed-upon procedures relating to management's assertion about its internal control, the relevant guidance established by SSAE-1 should be followed. In an agreed-upon procedures engagement, the auditor should not provide negative assurance about whether management's assertion is fairly stated (AT 400.05).

PART VII

Specialized Industry
Accounting and Auditing Practices

AUDITS OF CONSTRUCTION CONTRACTORS

CONTENTS

Overview	18.03
Specialized Accounting Practices	18.03
Percentage-of-Completion Method	18.03
Applicability of Percentage-of-Completion Method	18.05
Completed Contract Method	18.05
Applicability of Completed Contract Method	18.06
The Profit Center	18.07
Combining Contracts	18.07
Segmenting a Contract	18.08
Construction Joint Ventures	18.08
Affiliated Entities	18.09
Tax Accounting Methods	18.10
Revised Estimates	18.10
Financial Statement Presentation and Disclosures	18.11
Specialized Industry Practices	18.12
Estimation and Bidding	18.12
Evaluation and Project Administration	18.13
Controls at the Job Site	18.13
Billing Procedures	18.13
Contract Costs	18.14
Contract Revenues	18.14
Construction Equipment	18.14
Internal Audit Staff	18.14
Specialized Audit Procedures	18.15
Job-Site Procedures	18.15
Accounts Receivable	18.15
Liabilities	18.17

Contract Costs Incurred	**18.18**
Estimated Contract Costs	**18.18**
Acceptability of Income Recognition Methods	**18.19**
Percentage-of-Completion Method	**18.21**
Completed Contract Method	**18.21**
Combined or Segmented Contracts	**18.21**
Backlog Information	**18.22**
Representation Letter	**18.22**
Reports	**18.22**
Special Reports	**18.23**

AUDITS OF CONSTRUCTION CONTRACTORS

Overview

The specialized accounting and auditing practices for construction contractors appear in the AICPA Audit and Accounting Guide entitled *Construction Contractors* (hereinafter referred to as the Construction Contractors Guide). Specialized accounting practices also appear in Statement of Position (SOP) 81-1 (Accounting for Performance of Construction-Type and Certain Production-Type Contracts).

The Construction Contractors Guide and SOP 81-1 were issued concurrently in 1981 and supersede the previous AICPA Audit and Accounting Guide issued in 1965.

In the case of construction-type contracts, revenue must be recognized using the percentage-of-completion method or, if certain conditions exist, using the completed contract method. The completed contract method may result in an irregular recognition of income and a distorted balance sheet and, therefore, its use should be limited. The percentage-of-completion method is preferable when the estimated cost to complete the contract and the extent of progress made on the contract are reasonably determinable. Users of contractors' financial statements, such as surety companies, prefer the percentage-of-completion method and generally question the use of other methods.

SPECIALIZED ACCOUNTING PRACTICES

Percentage-of-Completion Method

Revenues are generally recognized when (1) the earning process is complete or virtually complete and (2) an exchange has occurred.

Accounting for long-term construction contracts on the percentage-of-completion method is an exception to the basic realization principle. This exception is allowed because usually the ultimate proceeds from the contract are available, and a better matching of periodic income results.

The principal advantages of the percentage-of-completion method are the reflection of the status of the uncompleted contracts and the periodic recognition of income currently rather than irregularly as contracts are completed. Further, revenues and costs are matched under the *normal operating cycle concept.*

The principal disadvantage of the percentage-of-completion method is the necessity of relying on estimates of the ultimate costs.

The percentage-of-completion method recognizes income as work progresses on the contract.

The recommended method for recognizing income is to determine the percentage of estimated total income either (1) that incurred costs to date bear to total estimated costs based on the most recent construction information (cost to cost method) or (2) that may be indicated by such other measure of progress toward completion appropriate to the work performed.

During the early stages of a contract, all or a portion of items such as material and subcontract costs may be excluded if it appears that the results would produce a more meaningful allocation of periodic income.

When current estimates of the total contract costs indicate a loss, a provision for the loss on the entire contract should be made. However, when a loss is indicated on a total contract that is part of a related group of contracts, the group may be treated as a unit in determining the necessity of providing for losses.

Under the cost-to-cost method, gross profit or loss is recognized in each period using the following formula:

$$\frac{\text{total costs to date}}{\text{estimated total costs}} \times \frac{\text{total estimated gross profit or loss}}{} - \frac{\text{gross profit recognized in prior periods}}{} = \frac{\text{realized gross profit}}{}$$

Billings in excess of costs and estimated earnings, or overbillings, are recognized as a current liability. *Costs and estimated earnings in excess of billings,* or underbillings, are recognized as a current asset. The auditor should view underbillings with a skeptical eye.

Applicability of percentage-of-completion method   The basic philosophy adopted by SOP 81-1 is that a construction-type contract should be viewed as a *continuous* sale that occurs as work on the contract progresses. Consistent with this philosophy, the Statement of Position concludes that in most circumstances a construction-type contract should be accounted for by using the percentage-of-completion accounting method. Thus, the percentage-of-completion method is preferable when the contractor can make reasonably dependable estimates with respect to contract revenues and costs and the degree to which the project is completed. The percentage-of-completion method should be used when all of the following conditions exist:

- The contract specifies enforceable rights with respect to goods or services to be provided or received, the consideration involved, and the manner and terms of settlement.

- It is expected that the buyer will be able to perform in accordance with the terms of the contract.

- It is expected that the contractor will be able to perform in accordance with the terms of the contract.

Significantly, SOP 81-1 notes that it is presumed that a client with a significant amount of contracting has the ability to make reasonably dependable estimates. In fact, the Statement of Position states that such a client would overcome this presumption only if persuasive evidence to the contrary can be offered.

Completed Contract Method

The completed contract method recognizes income only on completion or substantial completion of the contract. A contract is regarded as substantially complete if the remaining costs are insignificant.

Billings to date on uncompleted contracts are recognized as the current liability *progress billings*. Costs to date on uncompleted contracts are recognized as the prepaid expense *construction in progress*.

In some cases, it is preferable to allocate general and administrative expenses to contract costs and not to period income. In years when no contracts are completed, a better matching of costs and revenues is achieved by carrying general expense as a charge to the contract. If a contractor has many jobs, however, it is more appropriate to charge these expenses to current periods.

In all cases, although income is not recognized until completion of the contract, a provision for an expected loss must be recognized when it becomes evident that a loss on the total contract is apparent.

The primary advantage of the completed contract method is that it is based on final results rather than on estimates. The primary disadvantage of the completed contract method is that it does not reflect current performance when the period of the contract extends over more than one accounting period.

The following are important points to remember in accounting for contracts under the completed contract method:

1. Charge applicable overhead and direct costs to a construction in progress account (an asset).

2. Credit billing and/or cash received to a progress billings account (a liability).

3. At completion of the contract, gross profit or loss is recognized as follows: Contract price less total costs equals gross profit or loss.

4. At interim balance sheet dates, the excess of either the construction in progress account or the progress billings account over the other is classified as a current asset or a current liability. It is a current asset or a current liability because of the normal operating cycle concept.

5. An expected loss on the total contract is calculated by:

   a. Adding estimated costs to complete to the recorded costs to date to arrive at total contract costs

   b. Adding to progress billings any additional revenue expected to arrive at total contract revenue

   c. Subtracting b from a to arrive at total estimated loss on the contract

Losses should be recognized in full in the year they are discovered.

Applicability of completed contract method SOP 81-1 concludes that the use of the completed contract method may result in an irregular pattern of income. For this reason, the percentage-of-completion method is the preferable accounting method in most circumstances. However, the completed contract method can be used under the following circumstances:

- There is no material difference on the financial statements between the use of the completed contract method and the percentage-of-completion method. (This probably would be true for construction-type contracts that are short in duration.)

- Estimates of revenue and costs are not reasonably determinable.

- Estimates of revenues and expenses are subject to inherent hazards because of contract conditions or external factors that make estimates doubtful.

Where the above conditions exist and it is apparent that no loss on the contract will occur, the percentage-of-completion method based on a zero profit margin, rather than the completed contract method, should be used. The percentage-of-completion method based on a zero profit margin simply means that equal amounts of revenues and expenses are reflected on the income statement.

If no material differences exist between the use of the two methods, percentage-of-completion is preferable. Use of this exception to justify the completed contract method requires that percentage-of-completion be calculated. Therefore, reasonably dependable estimates can be made.

When a contractor cannot make reasonably dependable estimates, more serious problems may exist that are not solved by using the completed contract method.

The Profit Center

It is assumed that each individual contract is a profit center. Each contract is also accounted for separately to determine the degree of completion and estimates of revenue and expenses. However, SOP 81-1 does state that in some circumstances contracts can be combined or a segment of a contract can be segregated to form a profit center.

Combining contracts   In some instances, a series of contracts may be so related that they actually represent, and should be accounted for as, a single contract from a practical point of view. If this is true, the revenue and profit earned should be reported as the series of contracts are performed, using a single estimated gross margin percentage. In order for a series of contracts to be treated as a profit center, all the following conditions must be met:

- Contracts are negotiated in the same economic conditions and at approximately the same time with a single overall profit objective. In essence, the series of contracts represents a single project.

- Construction activity on the contracts is interrelated with substantial common costs that cannot be reasonably allocated to each contract.

- The contracts are under the same project management, are at the same location or in the same general area, and represent concurrent or continuous production. In essence, the contracts are with a single customer.

Production-type contracts that do not meet the above guidelines may nonetheless be combined into groupings, such as production lots, when (1) the contracts are for identical items produced concurrently or sequentially for one or more customer and (2) the units-of-delivery method, which is a variation of the percentage-of-completion method, is being used to account for revenue.

Segmenting a contract In some instances, a single contract or combination of contracts, as previously described, may include elements or phases that can be treated as a profit center. To be accounted for as a profit center with different rates of profitability, the single contract or combination of contracts must have been negotiated separately with the same customer, and each contract is to be performed without regard to the other contracts. Moreover, segmenting of a contract(s) can occur only if (1) separate proposals are submitted on the components and the entire project, (2) the customers can accept the proposal on either basis, and (3) the total amount of the proposals on the separate contracts approximates the amount of the entire project.

Construction Joint Ventures

Two or more businesses may form a construction joint venture. The joint venture itself may take the form of a corporation, general or limited partnership, or undivided interests. Accounting Principles Board (APB) Opinion No. 18 (The Equity Method of Accounting for Investments in Common Stock) states that the equity method should be used to account for an investment in a corporate joint venture where the venturer has a noncontrolling interest. If the venturer has a controlling interest in the joint venture, the venture is analogous to a parent/subsidiary relationship. These general guidelines are applicable to general and limited partnerships and undivided interests, and the appropriate accounting method depends on whether the venturer has a controlling interest.

In addition to the presentation of the basic financial statements, the venturer should consider disclosing the following:

- Name, percentage of ownership, and important provisions of each venture agreement

- Separate or combined summary financial statements of the venturers of the joint venture that are not fully consolidated

- Nature of intercompany transactions, including the basis of billings and charges

- Liabilities and contingent liabilities related to the venture agreement

Affiliated Entities

The Construction Contractors Guide notes that nonaccounting considerations, such as taxation and risk, result in several affiliated entities that are really a single economic unit. When this occurs, it is preferable for the group of affiliated entities to present consolidated or combined financial statements. When combined financial statements are presented, the normal disclosures should be expanded to include (1) a statement that the combined financial statements do not reflect a single legal entity, (2) a list of names and year ends of the entities that make up the combination, and (3) a description of the relationships among the entities.

If it is concluded that separate entities constitute an affiliated group, thus requiring the presentation of consolidated or combined financial statements, it may be necessary to present separate financial statements for one or more of the entities. For example, a financial institution may be considering making a loan directly to one of the combining or consolidated entities. In all likelihood, the entities are involved in reciprocal transactions with one another, which means the transactions are classified as related party transactions. For this reason, guidelines established by SAS-45 (Omnibus Statement on Auditing Standards—1983) must be followed. Also, the following disclosures must be made in the entity's separate financial statements:

- Nature of the relationships

- Description of the related party transactions for the period

- Dollar volume of transactions and the effects of changing methods of valuing the transactions when compared to the preceding period

- Terms, manner of settlement, and amounts due to or from related parties

In a note to the single entity's financial statements, the condensed consolidated or combined financial statements of the affiliated group also should be presented.

Tax Accounting Methods

Revenue recognition for income tax purposes generally is determined by a contractor's annual revenues. Normally, a contractor will use different methods of accounting to account for construction-type contracts on a tax basis and for those on a financial reporting basis. When the results of applying the different methods are material, interperiod tax allocation rules as described in Financial Accounting Standards Board Statement (FAS) No. 109 (Accounting for Income Taxes) must be followed.

Revised Estimates

Invariably, estimates are revised during the construction period. Estimates of revenue and costs may change at any time because of many factors. Revisions resulting from changes in estimates are accounted for as changes in accounting estimates. The two methods usually used to account for changes in estimates are (1) the cumulative catch-up method and (2) the reallocation method.

Under the cumulative catch-up method, the effect of revised estimates is recognized in the period of revision. In other words, the entire effect of any revised estimates is recognized in the current period.

Under the reallocation method, the effects of any revision are spread prospectively over the current period and any remaining subsequent periods. In other words, the effect of any revision is recognized ratably in the period of revision and any remaining periods.

SOP 81-1 requires that the cumulative catch-up method be used to account for the effects of any revised estimates.

Financial Statement Presentation and Disclosures

The Construction Contractors Guide reaffirms the balance sheet classification guidelines established by Accounting Research Bulletin (ARB) No. 43 (Restatement and Revision of Accounting Research Bulletins). Specifically, the Bulletin states that current assets are "cash and other resources commonly identified as those which are reasonably expected to be realized in cash or sold or consumed during the operating cycle of the business." Therefore, accounts receivable (including retentions), unbilled receivables, cost in excess of billings, and other deferred contract costs should be classified as current assets. Likewise, accounts payable, accrued contract costs, billings in excess of cost, and deferred income tax credits are classified as current liabilities. In other words, a classified (current and noncurrent) balance sheet is used for construction contractors.

The following items should be disclosed as significant accounting policies (APB Opinion No. 22 [Disclosure of Accounting Policies]):

- Method of reporting affiliated entities

- When the normal operating cycle exceeds one year, the length of the contracts

- Method of recognizing revenue

- When the percentage-of-completion method is used, the method of determining the percentage of completion

- When the completed contract method is used, the reason for using the method

- Method of accounting for joint ventures

- Deferred costs and the policy for determining deferrals

- Total amount of contract costs represented by unapproved change orders, claims, or similar items

- Amount of progress payments netted against contract costs

SPECIALIZED INDUSTRY PRACTICES

In the audit of construction contractors, the auditor must pay particular attention to the specialized accounting practices established by SOP 81-1. Because of the nature of the accounting practices, the auditor will be required to use a considerable amount of judgment to evaluate the many estimates that must be made by the contractor. For this reason, the auditor must thoroughly understand the contractor's internal control structure, operating characteristics, and the nature of the construction projects.

These factors should provide a foundation for the evaluation of the profitability of contracts or profit centers. Evaluation of contracts or profit centers encompasses the review of estimated costs, stage of completion, and gross profit recognized during an accounting period.

Although the audit approach described in the above paragraph is no different from the audit of a commercial enterprise, the Construction Contractors Guide emphasizes the greater amount of subjectivity involved in the audit of the construction contractor. This statement not withstanding, the audit approach requires the auditor to (1) understand the contractor's internal control structure, (2) perform tests of controls, and (3) perform substantive tests of revenues, costs, gross profit or loss, and related receivables and payables.

Because of the unique nature of a client involved with construction-type contracts, the client's internal control structure should have certain characteristics to enhance the likelihood that its financial statements will be prepared in accordance with generally accepted accounting principles. The following sections summarize control features discussed in the Construction Contractors Guide.

Estimation and Bidding

The very existence of the contractor is in no small part dependent on its ability to estimate costs as a basis for bidding on a project. From an accounting perspective, poor controls in this area can result in the overestimation of gross profit at various stages of a project or in the nonrecognition of a loss until the final stages of a project.

Estimating the future cost of a project can be a complicated task, and its complexity depends on the nature of the project. Many individuals and departments should be involved in the process, and cooperation among all the parties is important. Some of the features of an adequate cost estimation and bidding function are listed as follows:

- External evidence of job progress, such as progress reports prepared by project engineers should be examined.
- External evidence of contracts, such as signed contracts, should be examined.
- All cost elements should be consistent with contract specifications, plans, and drawings.
- Cost factors used should be reliable and current (or projections should be based on inflation factors).
- For extended contracts, escalation clauses should be used.
- Final contract estimates should be verified for clerical accuracy.
- Final contract estimates should be reviewed for completeness and reasonableness by someone independent of the preparation of the original cost estimates.

Evaluation and Project Administration

Once a project is started, its progress must be monitored to identify problems as early as possible. Therefore, the accounting system should provide management with detailed actual costs and expected future costs needed to complete the project. These costs should be compared to budgeted costs or costs used in the original estimate.

Controls at the Job Site

When administrative duties are performed at a job site, management should establish procedures to enhance the likelihood that transactions are properly authorized and executed. For example, management should consider performing a surprise audit of the distribution of payroll. In addition, controls should be instituted so that appropriate levels of personnel authorize the purchase of material at the job site. Only properly supported vouchers should be paid. Finally, appropriate controls should be established to protect and properly record assets such as equipment, material, and supplies.

Billing Procedures

The construction contract itself will specify how the contractor is to bill the customer. Those responsible for the billing function should be aware of the billing features for each contract and should receive appropriate data on the progress of the contract to allow for the timely billing of customers. Often, this information is received independently.

Contract Costs

To monitor the progress of a contract, management must have an adequately designed cost accounting system. As suggested earlier, detailed actual costs should be compared with estimated costs. The auditor should consider tests of job costs.

Contract Revenues

The accounting system must supply information to enable the contractor to recognize revenue consistent with the accounting method being used. If the percentage-of-completion method is used, the accounting system must accumulate sufficient information to determine the degree to which the contract is complete. If the completed contract method is used, information must be adequate to determine when the contract is substantially complete.

Construction Equipment

The accounting system should be designed so that each contract or job site is held responsible for the physical safeguarding of major pieces of construction equipment. The records should also enable management to allocate costs associated with equipment to the appropriate contract. Periodically, construction equipment should be inventoried and compared to accounting records. For smaller pieces of equipment, controls should be instituted at each project site to minimize losses.

Internal Audit Staff

Many of the control features discussed in this section can be implemented or enhanced by the use of an internal audit staff. The internal audit staff may perform operational as well as financial audits. For example, the internal audit staff may witness a payroll distribution or take an inventory of equipment at a particular job site.

SPECIALIZED AUDIT PROCEDURES

The auditor generally performs tests of controls on the internal control features discussed in the prior section of this chapter. The results of these tests determine the extent to which the auditor should rely on the client's internal controls. Once the tests of controls are complete, the auditor determines the nature, timing, and extent of audit procedures to be used in the examination of the contractor's financial statements. Some of the unique audit procedures used during the review of a contractor's financial statements are summarized as follows.

Job-Site Procedures

An auditor should consider visiting a job site for a number of reasons. An inspection of a job site is similar to a plant tour because it allows the auditor to better understand the contractor's method of operations. Accounting functions that require the auditor to review the internal controls employed at the site may be performed at the job site. A job-site visit should be used to determine the status of a job and to discuss the progress of the contract with project personnel.

A visit to a job site may be made during the accounting period or at the end of the period. However, the auditor should consider visiting a job site at or near the end of the accounting period if the contract is significant, if internal control procedures are weak, or if other factors suggest that there are potential problems with the contract. The auditor also may consider independent expert appraisal as an alternative procedure.

Accounts Receivable

A construction contractor's receivables should be confirmed. The auditor should use positive confirmations in a format similar to the one shown in Exhibit 10.09 of the Construction Contractors Guide. The confirmation request should ask the contractor's customer to confirm the amount due and other information, such as the original contract price, total billings, and total payments.

A contractor's accounts receivable may include unbilled receivables. Unbilled receivables may arise because of a clerical delay in billing for work that has been performed. Since the customer is not aware of the unbilled amount, it would not be possible to confirm the amount. To substantiate unbilled receivables, alternative audit procedures should be used. Such procedures include the review of subsequent cash collections and the inspection of documentation to support the unbilled receivable.

The construction contract may allow the customer to hold back part of the amount that has been billed until the contract is completed or other commitments are met. Retentions should be confirmed with the customer. The auditor also should determine whether it appears that the retentions will be collected.

The original terms of a contract may change because of unapproved change orders and claims. A change order may be initiated by the contractor or customer because of changes in the design of the work, in materials, or in other similar factors. A claim represents an amount in excess of the original contract price caused by such factors as errors in the original project specifications or delays caused by the customer. In many cases the auditor will not be able to confirm amounts related to change orders or claims because of disputes between the contractor and the customer. Under these circumstances, the auditor must evaluate the likelihood that the disputed amount will eventually be collected. The evaluation should include a review of the original contract and a discussion with appropriate client personnel. The opinion of legal counsel may be obtained, especially in the case of a claim. Finally, cost data to support the unapproved change order or claim should be tested and evaluated. Material disputed items recorded as revenue are required to be disclosed under SOP 81-1.

For some contracts, subsequent modifications instituted by the contractor's customer may change the scope of the contract. The Construction Contractors Guide notes that this occurs frequently in large cost-plus contracts. The difficult audit problem arises when the final scope of the contract is not definite and it is uncertain whether certain costs are actually unreimbursable contract costs. These costs should be carefully evaluated by the auditor to make reasonably certain that they will be paid by the customer.

When reviewing accounts receivable, the auditor must be on guard to identify problems that might arise from guarantees, cancellations, or postponements. A construction contract may guarantee that the completed project will perform in a certain manner. The auditor should carefully read the project contract and discuss potential problems with appropriate client personnel. On the other hand, the contract may allow a contract to be canceled under certain conditions. Again, the auditor should be aware of these terms and should discuss the progress of each significant contract with the client. If a project has been canceled, the auditor must determine the collectibility of amounts due from the contractor's customer. Finally, if a contract has been postponed, the auditor should consider the reason for the postponement and the party that is responsible. The reason for the postponement may have implications as to the eventual recoverability of costs.

In addition to the substantiation of receivables through the confirmation process, the collectibility of receivables must be determined. The ability of the contractor's customers to meet their obligations should be evaluated. This evaluation may include the auditor's review of (1) a customer's financial statements, (2) the financial agreement between the customer and its source of finance, or (3) other factors that may suggest that the customer will not or cannot meet its obligation.

Liabilities

A contractor's accounts payable should include amounts due to suppliers and subcontractors. The terms of each contract will determine how much is due to a subcontractor. The auditor must be cautious to differentiate between the amount that is billable under the contract terms and the amount that represents work actually completed by the contractor. Although the amount billable represents an account payable, only actual work performed should be used as a basis in determining the degree to which the contract is complete. The amounts due to suppliers and subcontractors may be confirmed. When a confirmation is sent, the following items should be confirmed:

- Contract price and approved change orders

- Total billings and payments to date

- Amount outstanding at the balance sheet date, including the amount of retentions

- Estimated date of completion

- Pending claims

In addition, standard cutoff procedures should be used to make sure the contractor included all transactions in the appropriate accounting period.

Contract Costs Incurred

Accumulating costs for each contract is a vital element of a contractor's cost accounting system. Appropriate audit procedures must be adopted to determine that all costs have been assigned to the proper contract. For example, direct charges for material used may be substantiated by inspecting vendor invoices and material requisitions. Indirect costs and overhead costs allocated to the contract should also be tested. The nature, extent, and timing of procedures used by the auditor depend on the results of the study and the evaluation of the contractor's internal control structure.

Estimated Contract Costs

Perhaps the most difficult phase of the audit of a contractor is the evaluation of future contract costs estimated by the client. These estimates are a basis for recognizing periodic revenue when the percentage-of-completion contract method is used. These estimates are also used for both the percentage-of-completion method and the completed contract method to determine whether a contract will result in a loss. To review the contractor's cost estimates, the auditor should consider reviewing the following reports and analyses:

- Schedules of contracts for a three- to five-year historical period, with original estimated gross profit and actual completed gross profit for each contract

- Summarizations about the results of internal audit investigations or other reports concerned with bidding procedures, project management, contract costs, and claims

- Reports comparing costs to date and estimated costs to original estimates, with explanations of variances and with detailed cost components used in original bid and actual costing

- Industry averages for gross profit

- Progress reports prepared by project engineers

- Summarizations that evaluate disputes and disagreements between contractor and customer, or between the contractor and suppliers and subcontractors

- Reports by independent architects or engineers

- Correspondence from the contractor's attorney concerning claims or other disputes

- Schedules of subcontracts by project, including total subcontract amount and related paid and unpaid amounts

- Reports of bid spread for each contract (dollar amount between contractor and second bidder)

- Contract agreements and correspondence

Using these sources of information, if available, and the results of other audit procedures used during the engagement, the auditor must determine whether the estimates are reasonable. As noted earlier in this chapter, for complex projects it may be necessary to use the work of a specialist to determine whether cost estimates are reasonable. When a specialist is used, guidelines established by SAS-73 (Using the Work of a Specialist) should be followed.

Acceptability of Income Recognition Methods

SOP 81-1 establishes criteria for determining which income recognition method should be used on the basis of the characteristics of the contractor and the specific contract. The following income recognition methods may be employed by a contractor:

- Percentage-of-completion method

- Percentage-of-completion method with a zero profit basis

- Completed contract method based on immateriality justification

- Completed contract method

The auditor must gather evidence to support (or refute) the contractor's adoption of a specific income recognition method. The following summarizes the income recognition method criteria established by SOP 81-1 and the related audit procedures suggested by the Construction Contractors Guide.

Criteria for Determining the Appropriate Income Recognition Method (SOP 81-1)	Audit Procedures to Be Employed to Test the Appropriateness of the Income Recognition Method (Construction Contractors Guide)
Percentage-of-Completion Method:	
• Reasonably dependable estimates can be made with respect to the extent of progress, contract revenues, and contract costs.	• Review an appropriate number of contracts on a test basis.
• The contract is specific with respect to the rights or obligations of each party.	• For the sample contracts selected, obtain and evaluate documentation supporting contract costs, revenues, and extent of progress.
• The contractor is expected to perform in accordance with the contract.	• Consider consulting with independent engineers or architects.
• The contractor's customer is expected to perform in accordance with the contract.	• Review an appropriate number of completed contracts to determine the quality of estimates made by the contractor.
Percentage-of-Completion/ Zero Profit Base Method:	
• A reasonable estimate of profit or range of profit cannot be made.	• Review an appropriate number of zero profit base contracts.
• No loss is expected when the contract is completed.	• For the sample contracts selected, evaluate management's justification for the adoption of this income recognition method.
	• Consider consulting with independent engineers or architects.
Completed Contract Method/ Immaterial Circumstances:	
• There are no material differences on the financial statements between the use of the completed contract method and the percentage-of-completion method (probably for short-term contracts).	• Review the nature and probable length of contracts accounted for by the completed contract method.
	• Determine the volume of contracts for the period.
	• Determine whether there would have been a material effect on the financial statements if the percentage-of-completion method rather than the completed contract method had been used.

Criteria for Determining the Appropriate Income Recognition Method (SOP 81-1)	Audit Procedures to Be Employed to Test the Appropriateness of the Income Recognition Method (Construction Contractors Guide)
Completed Contract Method:	
• Reasonably dependable estimates cannot be made regarding the extent of progress, contract revenues, and contract costs.	• Review an appropriate number of contracts on a test basis. • Consider consulting with independent engineers or architects.

Percentage-of-completion method   Once the auditor has determined the appropriateness of using the percentage-of-completion method, other audit objectives must be achieved. The audit of costs accumulated for a specific contract was discussed in an earlier section. The auditor also must be satisfied that the basis for determining the measure of progress for a project is a reasonable measure of determining the degree to which the contract is complete. Measurement bases may include such factors as cost incurred, labor hours worked, or machine hours. The Construction Contractors Guide notes that job-site visits may be useful in determining the degree to which the contract is completed. In some instances, the auditor may want to use the work of a specialist to estimate the measure of progress achieved.

Completed contract method   When the completed contract method is used, the auditor is concerned with costs accumulated to date and the possibility that a loss may have to be recognized for a particular contract. These audit objectives are achieved using the audit procedures discussed in the prior paragraph. In addition, the auditor must determine when a contract is substantially complete. As suggested in SOP 81-1, a contract is substantially complete when remaining costs and potential risks are insignificant. Factors to be considered to measure potential costs or risks include the delivery of the product, acceptance by the customer, and compliance with contract specifications.

Combined or Segmented Contracts

SOP 81-1 notes that under certain circumstances contracts may be combined or segmented for revenue recognition purposes. The auditor should adopt appropriate audit procedures to determine whether the requirements established by SOP 81-1 are being followed.

Backlog Information

The Construction Contractors Guide encourages contractors to present backlog information. When data on signed contracts that are not expected to be canceled are presented, the Guide concludes that this information is within the scope of an examination of the contractor's financial statements and should therefore be reviewed and evaluated. On the other hand, when backlog information consists of letters of interest, it is beyond the scope of the examination. The auditor should compare subcontract backlog to contract backlog as a test of uncompleted job cost. The auditor also should consider disclosing the subcontract backlog.

Representation Letter

General guidelines for the content of client representation letters are established by SAS-19 (Client Representations). In addition to the items discussed in SAS-19, a representation letter from a contractor should include the following:

- A detailed schedule of contract estimates used in financial statements
- Appropriateness of the income recognition method
- Contract loss provisions
- Unapproved change orders and claims
- Contract postponements and cancellations
- Related party transactions

Reports

Reporting requirements applicable to other commercial and industrial engagements are equally applicable to a construction contractor engagement.

Special Reports

A contractor may be required to file reports with governmental agencies in order to bid on contracts. The agencies may mandate the audit report format. Under these circumstances, the auditor should be guided by reporting requirements established by SAS-62 (Special Reports). The agency-mandated report format may be worded differently from the standard audit report. In some instances, the prescribed report may be made acceptable by including additional phrases. In other situations, the prescribed report may have to be completely revised.

AUDITS OF CREDIT UNIONS

Contents

Overview	19.03
Specialized Accounting Principles	19.05
Cash	19.05
Investments in Securities	19.05
Loans and Allowance for Losses	19.07
Loan Participations	19.09
Savings Accounts and Deposits	19.09
Borrowed Funds	19.10
Notes Payable	19.10
Promissory Notes	19.10
Federal Funds Payable	19.10
Treasury Tax and Loan Notes	19.10
Reverse Repurchase Agreements	19.10
Equity	19.11
Income Statement	19.11
Disclosures for Certain Debt Securities	19.12
Specialized Industry Practices	19.13
Specialized Audit Procedures	19.14
Credit Risk	19.15
Interest Rate Risk	19.15
Liquidity Risk	19.15
Cash	19.16
Investments in Securities	19.17
Loans	19.18
Collateralized Loans	19.19
Line-of-Credit Loans	19.19
Credit Card Loans	19.19
Mortgage Loans	19.19
Loan Participation	19.20

Allowance for Losses   **19.20**
Savings Accounts   **19.22**
Borrowed Funds   **19.23**
Equity   **19.24**
Income Statement   **19.24**
Examination by Regulatory Agencies   **19.25**
Reports   **19.25**
Special Reports   **19.27**

AUDITS OF CREDIT UNIONS

Overview

Credit unions serve a unique financial role in the savings and lending industry. They are cooperative financial institutions, owned and controlled by their members. Because they are financial institutions, they must be chartered by a federal or state agency and must comply with various laws and regulations established by the level of government under which they are chartered. Federally chartered credit unions are subject to the provisions of the Federal Credit Union Act of 1934 and are regulated by the National Credit Union Administration (NCUA), which administers a depositor insurance program called the National Credit Union Share Insurance Fund (NCUSIF). State chartered credit unions are regulated by similar legislation established at the state level and may obtain depositor insurance coverage through the NCUSIF.

The NCUA issues a number of publications that provide background information for auditors who are engaged to provide professional services for a credit union. Some of the publications that may be useful to the auditor include the following:

- Accounting Manual for Federal Credit Unions
- Credit Manual for Federal Credit Unions
- Supervisory Committee Manual for Federal Credit Unions
- National Credit Union Administration Rules and Regulations
- The Federal Credit Union Act
- Federal Credit Union Handbook
- Annual Report of the National Credit Union Administration

To provide more specific guidance for auditors, in 1986 the AICPA issued an Audit and Accounting Guide entitled *Audits of Credit Unions* (hereinafter referred to as the Credit Union Guide). Statement of Position (SOP) 90-5 (Inquiries of Representatives of Financial Institution Regulatory Agencies) and SOP 90-11 (Disclosure of Certain Information by Financial Institutions About Debt Securities Held as Assets) were issued in 1990 and amended the Credit Union Guide. Subsequently, the Credit Union Guide was revised to incorporate relevant guidance from the following:

- SOP 92-3 (Accounting for Foreclosed Assets)

- SOP 90-3 (Definition of the Term *Substantially the Same* for Holders of Debt Instruments, as Used in Certain Audit Guides and a Statement of Position)

> **OBSERVATION:** *AICPA Practice Bulletin 7 (Criteria for Determining Whether Collateral for a Loan Has Been in-Substance Foreclosed) and AICPA Practice Bulletin 10 (Amendment to Practice Bulletin 7) have been superseded by Financial Accounting Standards Board Statement (FAS) No. 114 (Accounting by Creditors for Impairment of a Loan).*

The Credit Union Guide differentiates between an *examination* and an *audit*. An examination refers to an examination conducted by a supervisory authority such as the NCUSIF, whereas an audit is defined as an examination made by a CPA in accordance with generally accepted auditing standards for the purpose of expressing an opinion on the financial statements of a credit union. A supervisory committee, which is similar to an audit committee, must be elected or appointed by the members of a credit union. Under the provisions of the Federal Credit Union Act of 1934 (Section 115), the following requirement is established with respect to an audit:

> The supervisory committee shall make or cause to be made an annual audit and shall submit a report of that auditor to the board of directors and a summary of the report to the members at the next annual meeting of the credit union; shall make or cause to be made such supplemental audits as it deems necessary or as may be ordered by the Board, and submit reports of the supplementary audits to the board of directors.

The audit approach for a credit union is similar to the approach used for other business enterprises. The Credit Union Guide discusses the unique aspects of audits of credit unions and identifies accounting principles and methods that should be observed in the preparation of their financial statements.

SPECIALIZED ACCOUNTING PRINCIPLES

Generally accepted accounting principles as established by the Financial Accounting Standards Board and its predecessors (Accounting Principles Board and the Committee on Accounting Procedure) must be followed in the preparation of a credit union's financial statements. The Credit Union Guide also establishes specialized accounting principles and methods for the credit union industry. SAS-69 (The Meaning of "Present Fairly in Conformity with Generally Accepted Accounting Principles" in the Independent Auditor's Report) identifies AICPA Audit and Accounting Guides as a source that should be considered in determining what constitutes generally accepted accounting principles.

Cash

The amount reported as cash for a credit union may include petty cash, cash working funds, funds in vaults, and funds in automated teller machines. These amounts may be combined with other cash items, such as deposits with other financial institutions and funds in transit, and presented under a single cash caption if all elements of the balance are subject to immediate use with no restrictions.

Investments in Securities

Excess funds are invested in various securities to maximize the return on invested capital and still provide a degree of liquidity required by the credit union's operations. In a manner similar to other regulated financial institutions, a credit union is restricted in the types of investments it can make. The Credit Union Guide notes that in general the following investments can be held by a credit union:

- Investments in corporate central credit unions
- U.S. Treasury obligations, such as Treasury bills, notes, and bonds

- Obligations and instruments of any agency of the United States
- Mortgage-backed securities issued or fully guaranteed by an agency of the United States
- Common trust or mutual investment funds approved by appropriate regulatory authorities
- Investment in the Central Liquidity Facility
- Investment deposits in any federally insured financial institution
- Investment in or loans to other credit unions
- Other investments, as outlined in Section 107 of the Federal Credit Union Act or similar state statutes

Investments should be recorded as purchases and sales as of the trade date (date the transaction is executed); however, the settlement date may be used when the use of the settlement date does not result in material differences in the credit union's financial statements.

Investments held by a credit union are subject to the accounting and reporting standards established by FAS-115 (Accounting for Certain Investments in Debt and Equity Securities). FAS-115 applies to investments in (1) equity securities that have readily determinable fair values and (2) all debt securities. Such investments should be classified as (1) debt securities expected to be held to maturity, (2) debt and equity securities that are considered trading securities, and (3) debt and equity securities that are available for sale. Debt securities expected to be held to maturity should be reported at amortized cost. Those securities classified as trading securities should be reported at fair value, and unrealized holding gains and losses should be reported on the income statement. Securities held for sale should also be reported at fair value; however, the related unrealized holding gains and losses should be reported as a component of equity.

Certain investments are prohibited by the NCUA. The Credit Union Guide identifies the following as unauthorized investments:

- Standby commitments to purchase or sell a security
- Adjusted trading or short sales
- Futures and other options contracts, except purchased put options related to loans held for sale
- Common stocks, except for those issued by credit union service organizations
- Corporate debt obligations
- Equity participations in commercial real estate projects

In addition, credit unions are prohibited from participating in "wash" sales, whereby the credit union is obligated to repurchase the same or "substantially the same" securities.

> OBSERVATION: *To determine what is considered "substantially the same" security, the guidance established in SOP 90-3 should be observed.*

Credit unions are subject to a number of disclosure requirements including those established by FAS-107 (Disclosures About Fair Value of Financial Instruments), FAS-105 (Disclosure of Information About Financial Instruments with Off-Balance-Sheet Risk and Financial Instruments with Concentrations of Credit Risk), and SOP 90-11.

> OBSERVATION: *The Emerging Issues Task Force of the FASB, which was formed in 1984, issues consensuses related to rather narrow accounting issues. Many of the consensuses are concerned with business transactions entered into by financial institutions, including credit unions. Auditors of credit unions should be aware of these pronouncements since they are a source (Level C) of generally accepted accounting principles as defined in SAS-69.*

Loans and Allowance for Losses

A major purpose of a credit union is to provide loans to its members. These loans may include collateralized consumer loans, unsecured consumer loans, real estate mortgages, and other loans such as business and education loans. Loans should be reported on a net realizable basis after taking into account an estimation of an allowance for uncollectible loans.

The effective interest method should be used to compute periodic interest income on loans. The calculation may be based on either a 360- or a 365-day assumption, but once an assumption is selected it should be applied consistently from period to period. Once a loan is determined to be delinquent due to nonpayment by a debtor, the credit union should not continue to accrue interest income on the outstanding balance. Specific guidelines for identifying delinquent loans (nonaccrual status) have been established by governmental supervisory agencies.

An adequate allowance for uncollectible loans applicable to all types of loans, including direct financing leases, should be recorded by a credit union. The allowance amount is an estimate based on the characteristics of the loan portfolios. When a loan is determined to be uncollectible, it should be written off by a charge to the allowance accounts. The provision for loan losses should be classified as an operating expense. Activity of the allowance account should be summarized in notes to the financial statements. The summary may include the amount of the provision for loan losses, loans charged off, and recoveries for the period.

Classifying a loan in the nonaccrual status does not necessarily mean that the account should be written off; nonetheless, the loan should be reexamined to determine whether it is likely to be collected. When interest is no longer accrued on a loan, any amounts received from the debtor should be carefully evaluated to determine whether the amount represents a reduction of the principal outstanding or a receipt of interest income. When the ultimate collectible of the nonaccrual status loan is in doubt, amounts received from the debtor should be treated as a reduction of the principal portion of the loan rather than as interest income.

When loans held by a credit union are considered impaired, the guidance established by FAS-114 should be followed. Impaired loans should be reported at their "expected future cash flows discounted at the loan's effective interest rate, except that as a practical expedient, a creditor may measure impairment based on a loan's observable market price, or the fair value of the collateral if the loan is collateral dependent." The standards established by FAS-114 should be followed when the terms of a loan are restructured (troubled debt). Other troubled debt restructuring should be accounted for in a manner consistent with the standards provided by FAS-15 (Accounting by Debtors and Creditors for Troubled Debt Restructurings).

When a financial institution takes possession of collateral, the accounting for the foreclosed assets depends on whether the assets are held for sale or held for the production of income. Foreclosed assets should be accounted for in a manner consistent with the standards established by FAS-114.

The Credit Union Guide concludes that the following information should be disclosed with respect to loans in the entity's summary of significant accounting policies:

- The basis of accounting for loans held in the portfolio
- The method used to recognize loan losses
- The method for recognizing interest income on loans, including the policy for discounting accrual of interest on nonperforming loans; the treatment of loan fees and costs, including

the method of amortizing net deferred fees or costs; and the policy for discontinuing the amortization of deferred loan fees on nonperforming loans

Loan Participations

Loans held by credit unions may be sold to external parties either individually or as part of a loan participation arrangement. Generally, a gain or loss should be recognized at the time the loans are sold. The gain or loss is measured by the difference between the carrying value of the loans and their selling price. When it is anticipated that a loan or group of loans will be sold at a loss after the end of the fiscal year, the loss should be provided for in the year-end financial statements even though the sale has not taken place.

A credit union that sells its loans may continue to service the loans by collecting the periodic payments from debtors, handling escrow transactions, and preparing reports for the parties that purchased the loans. A fee is paid to the credit union for servicing the loans, and when the servicing fee approximates the current rate for such services, the fee should be recognized as income by the credit union as the services are performed. On the other hand, when the servicing fee is significantly different from the current rate, FAS-65 (Accounting for Certain Mortgage Banking Activities) requires that the selling price of the loans be adjusted. The adjustment, either a deferred charge or a credit, should be amortized as part of servicing fee income over the life of the loans. If the servicing fee is insufficient to cover the expected future cost of servicing the loans, a loss should be recognized at the date the loans are sold.

Loan participations may be sold at a price equal to the carrying value of the loans, but the credit union may guarantee the purchasers of the loans an interest rate that is different from the interest rates stated in the individual loans. Under this circumstance, a premium or discount must be recognized based on the present value of the difference between the guaranteed interest amounts and the stated interest amounts. As required by APB Opinion No. 21 (Interest on Receivables and Payables), the discount or premium should be amortized over the life of the loans using the effective interest method.

Savings Accounts and Deposits

Resources of a credit union are to a great extent derived from interest-bearing deposits made by its members. These deposits include savings accounts, such as passbook and money market accounts, and certificates, such as minimum deposit and money market certificates. Although these funds are provided by members of the credit union, they do not represent equity contributions but rather must be classified as liabilities. The various types of savings accounts and deposits should be disclosed in a note to the financial statements. The related interest paid and accrued on savings accounts and deposits is often referred to as dividends paid to members of the credit union, but for financial reporting purposes the amounts must be classified as interest expense.

Borrowed Funds

In addition to deposits made by its members, a credit union may obtain resources by borrowing funds from various external parties. The extent of such borrowing is generally limited by regulatory authorities. Those liabilities that are unique to credit unions are summarized below.

Notes payable   Funds may be borrowed from other financial institutions, the Central Liquidity Facility (established by the NCUA), and the Federal Reserve System.

Promissory notes   Notes may be sold to nonmembers (and members) and represent a special type of interest-bearing time deposit.

Federal funds payable   A credit union may borrow (or loan) funds for a one-day period from (or to) a Federal Reserve Bank.

Treasury tax and loan notes   A credit union may elect to retain amounts due to the U.S. Treasury Department. Amounts due may include payments of federal taxes and payments for U.S. obligations. When these funds are retained by a credit union, they represent an interest-bearing liability and are substantiated by an open-end note held at the Federal Reserve Bank.

Reverse repurchase agreements   When a credit union enters into a reverse repurchase agreement, it involves the selling of certificates and a commitment to repurchase identical certificates at a set price within a specified period of time. Generally a reverse repurchase agreement represents a liability collateralized by the related certificates.

Amounts representing borrowed funds should be shown as a liability, and a related note to the financial statements should disclose the following:

- Due dates and interest rates
- Pledged collateral or compensating balance agreements
- Restrictive loan agreement covenants
- Five-year maturity schedule as established by FAS-47 (Disclosure of Long-Term Obligations)

Equity

A credit union does not issue capital stock; it is a cooperative organization in which each member is entitled to one vote irrespective of the amount of deposits made to the credit union by the member. For this reason, the equity of a credit union is generally composed of retained earnings and occasionally donated equity.

> **OBSERVATION:** *For regulatory purposes, members' shares are considered equity; however, generally accepted accounting principles require that they be classified as liabilities.*

Retained earnings include a regular reserve that is mandated by regulatory authorities and serves as a restriction on the disposition of a credit union's retained earnings. In addition, a credit union may appropriate retained earnings for a specific purpose such as the construction of new facilities. Retained earnings should be shown as a single item in the balance sheet, and any significant restrictions on retained earnings should be described in notes to the financial statements. When a substantial portion of retained earnings is restricted, the retained earnings amount on the face of the balance sheet should be described as *substantially restricted*.

Assets donated to a credit union should be recorded at their estimated fair market values, and an equal amount should be recognized as donated capital.

Income Statement

Revenues and expenses of a credit union are recognized on the accrual method, and revenues usually are reported on a functional basis (loan income, investment income, etc.) while expenses are grouped into natural classifications (payroll, depreciation, etc.). Loan losses should be disclosed, if material.

The Credit Union Guide notes that a credit union's income statement may be presented in either of the following two formats:

- *Net interest format*   Interest (dividends) on savings and interest on borrowed funds are separately disclosed and subtracted from income (from loans and investments) to arrive at net interest income. Other expense and income items are then subtracted from or added to net interest income to arrive at net income.

- *Gross income and expense format*   All income items are grouped and all expense items are grouped. Total expense is deducted from total income to arrive at net income.

Disclosures for Certain Debt Securities

SOP 90-11 establishes specific disclosure requirements for debt securities (including redeemable preferred stock) held as assets and accounted for at cost or the lower of cost or market. For these securities, the following disclosures must be made:

- Description of accounting policies for investments in debt securities (including the basis for classification)

- Amortized cost, estimated market values, and gross unrealized gains or gross unrealized losses for each pertinent category (investments in U.S. governmental debt, corporate debt, mortgage-backed debt, etc.)

- Amortized cost and estimated market values for debt securities due (for the most recent balance sheet)

  — In 1 year or sooner

  — After 1 year through 5 years

  — After 5 years through 10 years

  — After 10 years

- Proceeds from sales of debt securities and gross realized gains and gross realized losses on those sales (for each operating statement presented)

SPECIALIZED INDUSTRY PRACTICES

The auditor should evaluate a credit union's internal control to determine the nature, timing, and extent of substantive audit procedures. There are several internal control procedures unique to the industry that are important in determining the strength of the internal control system. Those identified in the Credit Union Guide include the following:

- The daily reconciliations of all loan, deposit, and related interest trial balances with the general ledger
- The daily balancing of tellers' and vault cash
- The tellers' proof function
- The establishment of dual controls over certain assets and records, such as vault, cash, consigned items, dormant account information, and investment records

> **OBSERVATION:** *The Credit Union Guide states that Section 5140, "Internal Controls," of the NCUA's Accounting Manual for Federal Credit Unions may be helpful in the auditor's assessment of a credit union's internal control.*

When a credit union uses external parties to process its data, guidance established in SAS-70 (Reports on the Processing of Transactions by Service Organizations) should be followed by the auditor.

Although the auditor is concerned with the accounting system's ability to produce financial statements that are prepared in accordance with generally accepted accounting principles, he or she must also be aware of the degree of compliance with regulations issued by the supervising governmental agency. These regulations may address such issues as the acceptability of investments held by the credit union, interest rate controls, and liquidity reserves. Noncompliance with supervisory regulation may have a direct effect on the financial statements or may result in penalties assessed against the credit union. The auditor should be aware of the regulatory environment in which the credit union operates and should review reports on the credit union issued by the supervisory agency.

As in any other audit engagement, the auditor should follow the guidelines established by SAS-54 (Illegal Acts by Clients) in assessing the possibility that illegal acts may have been committed. While the auditor is not held responsible for the detection of illegal acts perpetrated by management, the auditor should be aware of the possibility that such illegal acts may have occurred.

When material violations of regulations or laws occur, the effects should be reflected or disclosed in the financial statements. If the effects of the material violations are not adequately described in the financial statements, the auditor should express a qualified or adverse opinion. If the effects of the violations cannot be reasonably estimated, the auditor should consider whether a qualified opinion or disclaimer of opinion should be expressed.

SPECIALIZED AUDIT PROCEDURES

In determining the scope of the audit and the nature, timing, and extent of specific audit procedures, the auditor should take into consideration inherent risk, control risk, and detection risk. SAS-47 (Audit Risk and Materiality in Conducting an Audit) defines these three risks as follows:

> *Inherent risk*—Inherent risk is the susceptibility of an account balance or class of transactions to an error that could be material, when aggregated with error in other balances or classes, assuming that there were no related internal controls.

> *Control risk*—Control risk is the risk that error that could occur in an account balance or class of transactions and that could be material, when aggregated with error in other balances or classes, will not be prevented or detected on a timely basis by the internal control structure.

> *Detection risk*—Detection risk is the risk that an auditor's procedures will lead him to conclude that error in an account balance or class of transactions that could be material, when aggregated with error in other balances or classes, does not exist when in fact such error does exist.

For a particular engagement, inherent risk and control risk are given and cannot be influenced by the auditor. The level of detection risk is established by the auditor based on the auditor's assessment of the existing levels of inherent and control risks. When, for example, the levels of inherent and control risks are relatively high, the auditor would be unwilling to establish a relatively high level of detection risk. The level of detection risk, in part, determines the nature, timing, and extent of audit procedures for an engagement.

In assessing the level of inherent risk, the auditor should be aware of risk factors that are unique to the credit union industry. The Credit Union Guide discusses credit risk, interest rate risk, and liquidity risk.

Credit risk   Risk associated with the general credit rating of those that owe money to the credit union should be evaluated by the auditor to gain insight into the adequacy of the allowance for loan losses. Factors that should be considered with respect to credit risk are described below:

- Improper procedures for credit extension
- Economic changes in the overall economy and the economy of the area in which the credit union operates
- Changes affecting the organization for which the members of the credit union work
- Undue loan concentration
- Reduction of the credit rating of debtors

Interest rate risk   A credit union is exposed to interest rate risk because funds may be invested on an intermediate or long-term basis, while interest rates paid depositors may be based on short-term interest rates. If interest rates rise significantly, there may be a shortfall between interest income and interest payments. The interest rate risk is an inherent risk of the credit union industry and has a significant effect on the level of profitability.

Liquidity risk   The liquidity risk exists because a credit union may invest funds on a long-term basis to an extent that it misjudges the need for funds to meet operational needs. When the interest rate risk and liquidity risk are combined, the auditor must be aware that under certain circumstances it may be necessary to consider the writedown of long-term investments as of the end of the fiscal year. Specifically, if interest rates rise and the credit union is liquid, it may be necessary to sell long-term investments at a loss in order to service short-term commitments. In this case, the auditor must consider whether the loss should be provided for at the end of the credit union's fiscal year even though the investments have not been sold as of that date. Under extreme circumstances, the liquidity problem and the investment position may be so severe that the question of going concern as described in SAS-59 (The Auditor's Consideration of an Entity's Ability to Continue as a Going Concern) should be evaluated.

The inherent characteristics of the credit union industry should be taken into consideration when the auditor asks for written representations from the client. In addition to the typical representations described in SAS-19 (Client Representations), the Credit Union Guide concludes that representations such as the following should be requested:

- All contingent assets and liabilities, including loans charged off, have been adequately disclosed in the financial statements.

- Adequate provision has been made for any losses, costs, or expenses that may be incurred on securities, loans, or leases as of the statement of financial condition date.

- Liabilities are adequate for interest on deposits and borrowed funds.

- Permanent declines in value of securities and other investments have been properly reported in the financial statements.

- Commitments to purchase or sell securities have been adequately disclosed in the financial statements.

The audit of a credit union must adhere to generally accepted auditing standards. In general, the same audit procedures that are used to examine the financial statements of other commercial enterprises are used in a credit union audit engagement. Described below are audit procedures that are unique to the credit union industry or are especially significant in such an audit.

Cash

Typically a credit union will process a significant number of cash transactions, such as savings deposits and withdrawals. Cash transactions are supported by various documents such as savings deposit and withdrawal slips, checks, and journal vouchers. The auditor should review and test the tellers' proof sheets, mail receipts, and the propriety of authorized accounts and signatures. In addition, bank reconciliations and interbank transfers should be tested. Generally the auditor should simultaneously count cash, confirm account balances, control undeposited receipts, and reconcile cash subsidiary ledgers to the cash control accounts. Consigned items such as money orders and savings bonds should be confirmed directly with the appropriate party.

Investments in Securities

The nature, timing, and extent of audit procedures for investments in securities should be determined based on the auditor's assessment and test of the credit union's internal control.

Investments owned by a credit union should be substantiated by inspecting the securities or confirming those securities held by other parties. The auditor should consider whether these substantiation procedures should be coordinated with the examination of other negotiable items such as cash and consigned items.

As noted earlier, investments held by a credit union should be classified as (1) held-for-trading purposes, (2) held-for-sale, or (3) held-for-investment assets. The auditor should evaluate how the credit union determines how investments are classified to decide whether the approach is consistent with appropriate accounting standards and regulatory investment directives. Investments accounted for at amortized cost should be subject to recomputation by the auditor, and those presented at market value should be substantiated by reference to appropriate financial publications.

Guidance for applying analytical procedures as substantive tests is found in SAS-56 (Analytical Procedures). The Credit Union Guide lists the following analytical procedures that may be considered by the auditor:

- Compare current-year investment income with expected and prior-year income.

- Review changes in the mix between different investment types in the portfolio.

- Assess the reasonableness of accrued interest receivable on investments.

- Assess the reasonableness of average yields through the period computed.

- Compare current-year activity in the trading, investment, and held-for-sale accounts with expectations and the credit union's investment policy.

- For transactions accounted for as hedges, assess the degree of correlation between financial instruments and the items they are hedging to determine whether the correlation requirement for hedge accounting has been met.

The Credit Union Guide lists the following as other audit procedures to be considered by the auditor:

- Compare investment totals in the credit union's reconciliations with the investment subsidiary ledger and the general ledger control accounts (significant discrepancies and any large or unusual reconciling items should be investigated).
- Read the minutes of meetings of the investment committee and board of directors, and test whether transactions have been properly authorized.
- Consider evidence of impairment to the carrying amount of investments and inquire of management and brokers regarding the reflection of such impairments in the market values.
- Determine that only approved brokers are used.
- Review for property changes in the valuation allowance account (for investments held for sale) during the period.
- Test gains and losses on sales of securities.
- Obtain from management appropriate representations regarding its intent with respect to the trading and investment portfolios.

Credit unions may enter into agreements to buy or sell securities including repurchase agreements and reverse repurchase agreements. The commitments should be confirmed.

> **OBSERVATION:** *Additional guidance for the audit of repurchase agreements and reverse repurchase agreements may be found in the AICPA's publication entitled "Report of the Special Task Force on Audits of Repurchase Securities Transactions."*

Loans

The auditor should reconcile the loan control ledger accounts with the details in subsidiary ledgers. A sample of loans outstanding during the period should be substantiated by inspecting appropriate documentation such as credit rating information, loan applications, executed notes, and approvals of loans. In addition, a sample of loans should be confirmed directly with debtors. Loans made to credit union officials, employees, and organizations affiliated with officials or employees should be substantiated and reviewed for appropriate approval. Information maintained by the credit union to satisfy potential conflict of interest regulations established by federal or state agencies may be used to identify related or affiliated parties.

In addition to the procedures described above, audit procedures related to specific types of loans are summarized below.

Collateralized loans The auditor should substantiate the existence and value of collateral for loans. Documentation to support the current value of collateral should be reviewed and, if appropriate, the adequacy of insurance coverage should be evaluated. Controls over collateral should be reviewed, especially if the collateral is negotiable. Loan guarantees should be confirmed directly with the guarantor, and the auditor should determine whether the guarantor is in a financial position to perform if the guarantee clause is executed.

Line-of-credit loans Members of a credit union may be granted line-of-credit loans, which generally require members to complete a loan application only once, except for periodic updating. The requirements for updating should be reviewed. The credit-limit policies should be evaluated to determine whether they are based on the earning power of the individual credit union member. Also, policies employed to grant loans in excess of a credit limit should be reviewed. When collateral is involved, the auditor should determine that the pledge agreement is consistent with policies established by the credit union.

Credit card loans The credit union's credit card internal control should be evaluated to determine the extent to which controls can be relied on by the auditor. When the credit union assumes the responsibility for the collection of receivables arising from credit card transactions, the resulting receivables should be examined in the same manner as any other receivable held by a commercial enterprise.

Mortgage loans Generally, the auditor would concentrate on reviewing documentation to support mortgages that have arisen during the current fiscal year. Escrow transactions should be tested, and consideration should be given to the possibility of confirming escrow amounts when the loan is confirmed with the mortgagee. The auditor should also review procedures employed by the credit union for the following purposes:

- Adequacy of insurance coverage over mortgaged property
- Periodic payment of real estate taxes
- Evaluation of condition of mortgaged property

Loan participation   The balance of collateral, if any, should be confirmed with the managing credit union. In addition, details of the participation loan arrangement should be confirmed with participating purchasers. When loans have been sold as part of a participation agreement, the auditor must be careful to confirm the total amount of the loan (including amounts sold to other participating credit unions) with the borrower.

> *OBSERVATION: A credit union may use another organization to process some of its transactions. Under this circumstance, the auditor should refer to SAS-70.*

> *OBSERVATION: When loans are confirmed, the standards established by SAS-67 (The Confirmation Process) should be followed.*

Allowance for Losses

The allowance for loan losses is evaluated to determine whether the amount established by the credit union is reasonable. As suggested earlier, a credit union may engage in a variety of loan activities, including secured and unsecured consumer loans and real estate loans. To some extent the audit approach for evaluating the adequacy of the allowance account is dependent on the types of loans made by the credit union. For this reason, loans can be categorized as (1) relatively small loans with similar characteristics and (2) relatively large loans.

The audit approach for relatively small loans with similar characteristics is broad. Because this type of loan portfolio is generally composed of numerous small loans, the auditor is not as concerned with sampling and examining individual accounts. Typically, factors that would be used to determine the adequacy of the allowance for this type of portfolio are as follows:

- History of loan losses
- Recent trend of delinquent loans
- Loans to parties that belong to a group or industry that is economically unstable

These factors should be evaluated in the context of the current economic environment and should not simply result in the application of a historical average to the current loan balance in the portfolio.

Alternatively, when a portfolio of loans is made up of relatively large balances, for example when the credit union holds mortgages, the emphasis changes from a broad approach to the evaluation of specific loans. For this type of loan portfolio, the following factors should be considered by the auditor:

- Loans with excessive renewals or extensions
- Loans secured by property that does not have a ready market or property that is susceptible to a loss in realizable value
- Lack of current financial data relative to the debtor or guarantor
- Debtors or guarantors that are having financial difficulties
- Loans that are not adequately documented

Governmental supervisory agencies and the management of the credit union may prepare various reports on the quality of outstanding loans. The auditor may take into consideration their efforts in determining the scope of the examination of the allowance for losses; however, the auditor must be cautious when the work of a governmental agency is used. Governmental agencies may apply arbitrary formulas in evaluating the adequacy of the allowance account. For example, the NCUA defines two such formulas as follows:

Experience method—Under this method, the amount needed in the allowance for loan losses is based on the credit union's loss experience and its average loan balances for the current year plus the five preceding calendar years and the average maturity of all loans outstanding.

Adjustment method—The credit union will perform a review of all loans delinquent two months or more and loan-derived assets to determine its best feasible estimate of potential losses that will be sustained in collection and as to the adequacy of the Allowance for Loan Losses account. The estimate should be based on the best judgment of the credit union officials taking all pertinent factors into consideration, including loan delinquency status, collection experience of the credit union, unusual economic conditions that may affect collectibility, availability of endorsers, pledged shares and/or other collateral or security, insured FHA or educational loan coverage, and the general credit reputation of the borrowers.

These two formulas as well as other arbitrary formulas may or may not result in a fair presentation of the credit union's portfolio of loans. The auditor, using professional judgment, must be satisfied that the allowance account balance is reasonable after taking into consideration all relevant factors.

The Credit Union Guide lists the following as possible ways of identifying problem loans:

- Various internally generated listings, such as "watch list" loans, past-due loans, loans on nonaccrual and restructured status, loans to insiders (including directors and officers), and over-drafts

- Management reports of total loan amounts by borrower, to assist in identifying significant exposures and concentrations

- Loan documentation and compliance exception reports

In addition, regulatory examination reports may provide insight into assessing the adequacy of the credit union's allowance for loan losses. The Credit Union Guide notes that refusal by management to allow the auditor access to such reports is a scope limitation and may preclude the auditor from issuing an opinion on the financial statements.

Savings Accounts

A credit union will typically offer a variety of savings accounts to its members including passbook accounts, money market accounts, and certificates of deposit. Although the internal controls may vary somewhat depending on the nature of the savings account, the Credit Union Guide lists the following as some of the procedures that the auditor should consider:

- Reviewing the control over the origination of and access to signature cards

- Testing the daily deposit and withdrawal slips in relation to receipts and disbursement totals

- Comparing the withdrawal slips to the applicable subsidiary record and signature cards

- Reviewing the control over the origination of and access to mailing address files

- Reviewing the control over mail receipts

- Testing accounts for compliance with the credit union's policy regarding early withdrawal penalty interest recognition

- Reviewing dormant accounts and transactions relative to deceased members' accounts, particularly savings insurance claims

- Testing compliance with Internal Revenue Service Form 1099 reporting

- Testing compliance with state escheat laws

- Testing service charge income in accordance with board policy

- Testing transactions and restrictions on savings accounts pledged as collateral for loans

The evaluation of internal controls, including the performance of tests of controls, should be used to establish the scope of substantive tests with respect to savings accounts. Initially, a trial balance of savings accounts should be obtained from the client, footed, and agreed to the general ledger accounts. A representative sample should be selected from the trial balance of savings accounts for confirmation. If the credit union is not federally insured, the evaluation of the credit union's savings accounts should be guided by SAS-39 (Audit Sampling), which concludes that either a statistical or a nonstatistical sampling method may be used. When a nonrandom selection method is used as part of a nonstatistical sampling approach, each savings account must have a chance of selection, but the probability of selection need not be the same for all accounts. On the other hand, if the credit union is federally insured, regulations established by NCUA require that either (1) all accounts be confirmed or (2) a random statistical sampling method be used to evaluate the accuracy of the accounts.

Accounts that are designated as *no mail* status and accounts selected for confirmation but returned by the postal system should be substantiated by using alternative auditing procedures. When alternative auditing procedures cannot be performed, the auditor must evaluate the effects of the scope limitation on the audit report.

Borrowed Funds

Liabilities of a credit union may include such debts as notes, mortgages, federal funds payable, and reverse repurchase agreements. The minutes of the board of directors meetings should be read to determine that loans have been properly authorized. Loan agreements should be read, and restrictions that should be disclosed in the financial statements should be noted. The basic features of the debt instrument should be confirmed directly with the creditor. In addition, lines of credit and compensating balance agreements should be confirmed.

Equity

Equity accounts should be reviewed to determine whether reserve requirements established by federal or state regulatory agencies have been observed. When reserve requirements have been violated, they should be discussed with the management of the credit union or other appropriate parties, and the auditor should consider whether the matter should be discussed with appropriate regulatory authorities. The auditor should consider the consequences of a reserve deficiency, which may include restrictions on the payment of dividends, or perhaps the liquidation of the credit union. When an uncertainty question arises as to the continued existence of the credit union, the auditor should refer to SAS-59.

Income Statement

Nominal accounts are generally examined at the same time that related balance sheet accounts are audited. For example, the examination of borrowed funds should include the substantiation of interest expense and accrued interest. Substantiation tests of nominal accounts should include the direct tests of details of transactions and balances as well as analytical review procedures. For example, the Credit Union Guide notes that material fluctuations of income and expenses should be investigated and that overall tests of income from loans and interest expenses should be made.

> *OBSERVATION: SAS-56 provides general guidance for the performance of analytical procedures but explicitly states that no specific procedures are required by the Statement. As explained above, the Credit Union Guide identifies specific analytical procedures that should be employed as part of the examination of the financial statements of a credit union.*

With respect to payroll expense, the auditor should be aware that, by law, certain officials of a credit union cannot receive compensation.

The Internal Revenue Code exempts credit unions from the provisions of the federal income tax. In addition, the Federal Credit Union Act exempts federal credit unions from federal, state, and local income taxes. For these reasons, there generally should be no provision for income taxes; however, unrelated business income may be subject to taxation. Unrelated business income is income not related to the credit union's usual business operations.

Examination by Regulatory Agencies

A credit union may be examined by various federal and state governmental agencies. Reports issued by the governmental agencies should be reviewed by the auditor. Specifically, the Credit Union Guide requires the auditor to do the following:

- Request that the client allow access to all examination reports and related correspondence.
- Review significant reports and related correspondence for examinations through the date of the auditor's report.
- Communicate directly with the examiners (with the approval of the client) for examinations not completed or not reported on.

If the client will not allow the auditor to perform the procedures described above, generally an opinion should not be expressed on the financial statements. If the examiners will not communicate with the auditors, the scope limitation should be evaluated to determine whether an unqualified opinion can be expressed.

Finally, the Credit Union Guide concludes that the auditor should consider attending as an observer (with the permission of the client) the exit conference between the client and the examiner.

Reports

The purpose of an audit of the financial statements of a credit union is to determine whether the financial statements are prepared in accordance with generally accepted accounting principles. The same reporting responsibilities and reporting guidelines applicable to the audit of a commercial enterprise are also applicable to the audit of a credit union. If, at the conclusion of the engagement, the auditor believes that the financial statements are fairly stated, the standard audit report should be issued. Deficiencies discovered during the engagement, such as scope deficiencies and deviations from generally accepted accounting principles, may lead to a modification of the standard audit report as described in SAS-58 (Reports on Audited Financial Statements).

In addition, the following pronouncements establish reporting guidelines that should be considered by the auditor:

- SAS-8 (Other Information in Documents Containing Audited Financial Statements) The auditor should read other information in documents that contain audited financial statements to determine whether (1) there are material inconsistencies between the audited financial statements and the other information and (2) there are material misstatements of fact in the other information.

- SAS-29 (Reporting on Information Accompanying the Basic Financial Statements in Auditor-Submitted Documents) The auditor should clearly describe the character of the examination and the degree of responsibility, if any, taken by the auditor with respect to information accompanying but presented outside of the basic financial statements in auditor-submitted documents.

- SAS-42 (Reporting on Condensed Financial Statements and Selected Financial Data) The auditor should clearly describe the character of the examination and the degree of responsibility, if any, taken by the auditor with respect to the presentation of condensed financial statements and selected financial data derived from audited financial statements.

- SAS-52 (Omnibus Statement on Auditing Standards—1987) The auditor should make inquiries and perform analytic procedures to determine whether supplementary information required by the FASB has been presented.

The reporting guidelines established by these pronouncements should be followed without modification in the preparation of the auditor's report on the financial statements of a credit union.

Special Reports

When financial statements are prepared in accordance with reporting provisions of a governmental regulatory agency, and those provisions result in material deviations from generally accepted accounting principles, the distribution of the financial statements determines how the auditor should report. When the financial statements are intended solely for the regulatory agency, the auditor may report on the financial statements as being prepared on a comprehensive basis of accounting other than generally accepted accounting principles and follow the reporting format established by SAS-62 (Special Reports). Presented below is an example of an auditor's report of financial statements based on accounting standards established by the National Credit Union Administration.

We have audited the accompanying statements of financial condition–regulatory basis of X Credit Union as of December 31, 19X5 and 19X4, and the related statements of income–regulatory basis, members equity–regulatory basis, and cash flows–regulatory basis for the years then ended. These financial statements are the responsibility of the credit union's management. Our responsibility is to express an opinion on these financial statements based on our audits.

We conducted our audits in accordance with generally accepted auditing standards. Those standards require that we plan and perform the audit to obtain reasonable assurance about whether the financial statements are free of material misstatement. An audit includes examining, on a test basis, evidence supporting the amounts and disclosures in the financial statements. An audit also includes assessing the accounting principles used and significant estimates made by management, as well as evaluating the overall financial statement presentation. We believe that our audits provide a reasonable basis for our opinion.

As described in Note X, these financial statements were prepared in conformity with the accounting principles prescribed or permitted by the National Credit Union Administration, which is a comprehensive basis for accounting other than generally accepted accounting principles.

In our opinion, the financial statements referred to above present fairly, in all material respects, the financial position of X Credit Union as of December 31, 19X5 and 19X4, and the results of its operations and its cash flows for the years then ended, on the basis of accounting described in Note X.

This report is intended solely for the information and use for the board of directors and management of X Credit Union and for filing with the National Credit Union Administration, and should not be used for any other purpose.

When the distribution of the financial statements is not restricted, the auditor must report in accordance with reporting standards established by SAS-58, which means that either a qualified or an adverse opinion must be expressed. Presented below is an example of an auditor's report qualified because of a deviation from generally accepted accounting principles when the deviation is consistent with principles established by a regulatory authority.

We have audited the accompanying statements of financial condition of X Credit Union as of December 31, 19X5 and 19X4, and the related statements of income, members equity, and cash flows for the years then ended. These financial statements are the responsibility of the credit union's management. Our responsibility is to express an opinion on these financial statements based on our audits.

We conducted our audits in accordance with generally accepted auditing standards. Those standards require that we plan and perform the audit to obtain reasonable assurance about whether the financial statements are free of material misstatement. An audit includes examining, on a test basis, evidence supporting the amounts and disclosures in the financial statements. An audit also includes assessing the accounting principles used and significant estimates made by management, as well as evaluating the overall financial statement presentation. We believe that our audits provide a reasonable basis for our opinion.

The credit union has reported members' shares as equity in the accompanying statements of financial condition that, in our opinion, should be reported as liabilities in order to conform with generally accepted accounting principles. If these shares were properly reported, liabilities would increase and equity would decrease by $1,400,000 and $1,100,000 as of December 31, 19X5 and 19X4, respectively.

In our opinion, except for the effects of reporting members' shares as equity as discussed in the preceding paragraph, the financial statements referred to above present fairly, in all material respects, the financial position of X Credit Union as of December 31, 19X5 and 19X4, and the results of its operations and its cash flows for the years then ended in conformity with generally accepted accounting principles.

The auditor may be requested to report on a credit union's system of internal controls. For this type of engagement, the reporting standards established by Statement on Standards for Attestation Engagements (SSAE) No. 2 (Reporting on an Entity's Internal Control Structure Over Financial Reporting), SSAE-3 (Compliance Attestation), and SSAE-4 (Agreed-Upon Procedures Engagements) should be followed.

AUDITS OF EMPLOYEE BENEFIT PLANS

Contents

Overview	20.03
Background	20.03
PWBA Reviews	20.04
Specialized Accounting Principles	20.05
Defined Benefit Pension Plans	20.05
Statement of Net Assets Available	20.06
Statement of Changes in Net Assets	20.07
Accumulated Plan Benefits	20.07
Changes in Accumulated Plan Benefits	20.08
Other Financial Statement Disclosures	20.09
Defined Contribution Pension Plans	20.10
Statement of Net Assets Available	20.11
Statement of Changes in Net Assets	20.11
Additional Disclosures	20.11
Employee Health and Welfare Benefit Plans	20.12
Statement of Net Assets Available	20.14
Statement of Changes in Net Assets	20.14
Information Regarding Benefit Obligations	20.14
Information Regarding Changes in Benefit Obligations	20.15
Additional Disclosures	20.16
Other Accounting Issues and Developments	20.18
401(h) Plans	20.18
Defined Contribution Pension Plan Disclosures	20.19
Derivative Disclosures	20.19
Fair Value Disclosures	20.19
Specialized Industry Practices	20.20
Planning the Engagement	20.20
Internal Control	20.21

Specialized Audit Procedures	20.22
Investments	20.22
Trusteed Assets	20.22
Assets Held by Insurance Companies	20.24
Other Investments	20.25
Contributions and Receivables	20.26
Benefit Payments	20.27
Participants' Data	20.27
Plan Obligations	20.29
Defined Benefit Plan	20.29
Defined Contribution Plan	20.29
Health and Welfare Benefit Plan	20.30
Party-in-Interest Transactions	20.31
Other Audit Factors	20.33
Reports	20.34
Scope Limitation	20.35
Valuation of Investments Not in Accordance with GAAP	20.36
Other Auditors Used	20.36
Omission of Required Information in the Supplemental Schedules Required by ERISA	20.36
Trust Established Under a Plan	20.37
Special Reports	20.38

AUDITS OF EMPLOYEE BENEFIT PLANS

Overview

The specialized accounting and auditing practices for employee benefit plans appear in the following publications:

- Financial Accounting Standards Board Statement (FAS) No. 35 (Accounting and Reporting by Defined Benefit Pension Plans)
- FAS-110 (Reporting by Defined Benefit Pension Plans of Investment Contracts)
- SOP 94-4 (Reporting of Investment Contracts Held by Health and Welfare Benefit Plans and Defined Contribution Plans)
- Employee Retirement Income Security Act of 1974 (ERISA)
- Industry Audit Guide, *Audits of Employee Benefit Plans*, Third Edition (hereinafter referred to as the Benefit Plans Guide)

The latest edition of the Benefit Plans Guide supersedes the previous editions. This latest edition was issued to reflect new auditing standards established by the American Institute of Certified Public Accountants and new pronouncements adopted by the Department of Labor (DOL).

Background

Employee benefit plans include defined benefit pension plans, defined contribution pension plans, and employee health and welfare benefit plans. Under a defined benefit pension plan, an employee is promised pension payments based on such factors as number of years employed and level of compensation. In a defined contribution plan, future pension payments are based on contributions made by the employer and/or employee and investment income earned on the contributions. Health and welfare benefit plans include a variety of plans that may cover medical and dental expenses, accidental death payments, disability and unemployment payments, and certain other benefits.

FAS-35 provides accounting and reporting standards for defined benefit pension plans only. The Benefit Plans Guide provides for specialized accounting rules for defined contribution plans and employee health and welfare plans. Specialized accounting practices established in the Benefit Plans Guide were established to be consistent, where appropriate, with accounting rules promulgated in FAS-35.

Generally accepted accounting principles and generally accepted auditing standards are applicable to engagements in which the auditor reports on the financial statements of employee benefit plans. In some instances, employee benefit plans subject to ERISA are required to file reports with the DOL that contain financial statements prepared in accordance with generally accepted accounting principles or an other comprehensive basis of accounting. In addition, DOL regulations may allow an employee benefit plan administrator to limit the scope of the audit examination with respect to certain investment-related information certified as to both completeness and accuracy by certain eligible financial institutions that are examined periodically by a state or federal agency. The Benefit Plans Guide is equally applicable to engagements where the scope is not limited and where the scope is limited in a manner just described.

PWBA reviews   The Department of Labor's Pension and Welfare Benefits Administration (PWBA) performs periodic quality control reviews of ERISA audits, and, based on the results of these reviews, may refer deficient performances to the AICPA's Professional Ethics Division or the appropriate state licensing board for disciplinary action. Deficiencies discovered by past DOL quality control reviews, including the recently completed DOL review of approximately 270 randomly selected 1992 employee benefit plan audits, include the following:

- Inadequate or no audit program or planning.

- Inadequate or no documentation of the audit work performed.

- Inadequate or no documentation of the auditor's understanding of the internal control structure.

- Auditor's report was not filed.

- Auditor's report did not conform to the standards established by SAS-58 (Reports on Audited Financial Statements).

- Auditor reported on the trust's instead of the plan's financial statements.
- Auditor's report was not signed.
- The scope of the auditor's report did not cover the required Form 5500 supplemental schedules.
- Limited-scope auditor's report was filed even though plan did not qualify for such a report.
- Statement of net assets was not presented on a comparative basis.
- Required disclosures were omitted or incomplete.
- Required supplemental schedules were omitted or incomplete.

SPECIALIZED ACCOUNTING PRINCIPLES

Defined Benefit Pension Plans

FAS-35 provides guidance for the accounting and reporting by defined benefit pension plans. In general, the objective of FAS-35 was to provide information to determine a plan's present and future ability to pay benefits as they become due. The financial statements should contain information about (1) the resources of the pension plan, (2) the accumulated plan benefits of participants, (3) the transactions affecting the plan's resources and benefits, and (4) other additional information, as necessary to provide clarity to the financial statement presentation.

FAS-35 requires that the annual financial statements of defined benefit pension plans include:

- A statement of net assets available for benefits
- A statement of changes in net assets available for benefits
- Information on the actuarial present value of accumulated plan benefits
- Information on the year-to-year changes in the actuarial present value of accumulated plan benefits (if significant)

All financial statements and information should be prepared and presented for the same fiscal or calendar period.

Statement of net assets available   For the most part, investments are to be presented at their fair values. In some instances, it may be necessary to use a specialist to estimate the fair value of an investment. FAS-35 defines *fair value* as the amount that could reasonably be expected to be received in a current sale between a willing buyer and a willing seller, neither under compulsion to buy or sell. Plan investments include debt or equity securities, real estate, and other types of investments held to provide benefits for the plan's participants.

Contributions receivable from employees, employers, state or federal grants, and other sources should be reported on the accrual basis pursuant to actual legal or contractual obligations or formal commitments.

For the purposes of presenting contracts with insurance companies in the statement of net assets available for benefits, FAS-35 requires that all pension plans, including those not subject to ERISA, value such contracts in the same manner as that required by item 13 of the Federal Government's Form 5500 or 5500C (Annual Return/ Report of Employee Benefit Plan). Form 5500 is for employee benefit plans with 100 or more participants, and Form 5500C is for employee benefit plans with fewer than 100 participants.

The instructions for item 13 of Form 5500 and 5500C affect two aspects of FAS-35: (1) allocated insurance contracts are not included in the financial statements that are required by FAS-35, except for some footnote disclosure, and (2) unallocated insurance contracts (other than pooled separate accounts) must be broken down into (a) unallocated separate accounts and (b) unallocated other accounts. These accounts should be valued at current value. Forms 5500 and 5500C define current value as the fair market value where available and otherwise as the fair value determined in good faith by a trustee or a named fiduciary pursuant to the terms of the plan, assuming an orderly liquidation at the time of such determination.

> **OBSERVATION:** *The financial information required by Forms 5500 and 5500C must be submitted at current values—which is basically what is required by FAS-35. In addition, many of the financial disclosures required by FAS-35 also appear on Forms 5500 and 5500C. Thus, it may be advisable to prepare these forms before preparing the financial statements required by FAS-35.*

Assets that are used in the actual operation of a pension plan should be reported on the financial statements at amortized cost. Thus, buildings, leasehold improvements, furniture, equipment, and fixtures that are used in the everyday operation of a pension plan should be presented at historical cost less accumulated depreciation or amortization.

FAS-110 requires that insurance contracts held by defined benefit pension plans be presented at fair value (investment contracts) or contract value (insurance contracts) based on the standards contained therein.

Statement of changes in net assets Significant changes in net assets available for benefits should be identified in reasonable detail in the statement of changes in net assets available for benefits. The minimum disclosures required by FAS-35, which should appear in the statement of changes in net assets available for benefits or in its related notes, are as follows:

- Investment income, other than from realized or unrealized gains or losses on investments, should be separately disclosed in reasonable detail.

- Realized and unrealized gains or losses on investments presented at quoted market values should be reported separately from those of investments presented at estimated fair value.

- Contributions from employers, participants, and others, should be reported separately. Cash and noncash contributions from employers should be disclosed. Noncash contributions should be recorded at their fair value on the date of receipt and, if significant, they should be fully described in the financial statements or footnotes thereto.

- Direct benefit payments to participants should be reported separately.

- Purchases of insurance contracts that are excluded from the plan's assets should be separately reported. Dividend income on insurance contracts that are excluded from the plan's assets may be netted against the purchase of such contracts. The dividend income policy on insurance contracts should be disclosed in a footnote to the financial statements.

- Expenses of administrating the plan should be reported separately.

Accumulated plan benefits FAS-35 requires that certain specified information regarding the actuarial present value of accumulated plan benefits of participants be disclosed as part and within the financial statements. The present value of the accumulated plan benefits must be determined as at the plan benefit information date. Thus, if the plan benefit information date is the beginning of the year, the present value of the accumulated plan benefits must be determined as at the beginning of the year.

In addition, financial statements as at the beginning of the year must also be included in the presentation. On the other hand, if the plan benefit information is dated as at the end of the year, the present value of the accumulated plan benefits must be determined as at the same date, and financial statements as at the end of the year must also be included in the presentation. FAS-35 states a preference for the use of end-of-year benefit information.

FAS-35 requires that the total actuarial present value of accumulated plan benefits be broken down and presented in at least three categories: (1) vested benefits of participants currently receiving payments, (2) vested benefits of other participants, and (3) non-vested benefits. Vested benefits of participants currently receiving payments should include benefits due and payable as of the benefit information date. Disclosure of the accumulated contributions of present employees, including interest, if any, as of the benefit information date, should be made in a footnote to the financial statements. In addition, the rate of interest, if any, should be disclosed.

Changes in accumulated plan benefits   Certain factors that cause changes in the actuarial present value of accumulated plan benefits between the current and prior benefit information dates, if significant either individually or in the aggregation, should be identified in the financial statements or the footnotes thereto. Significant changes that are caused by individual factors should be separately identified. The minimum disclosure required by FAS-35 includes the effects of the following factors, if significant:

- Plan amendments
- Changes in the nature of the plan, such as a merger with another plan, or a spinoff of a plan
- Changes in actuarial assumptions

Other factors that result in changes in the actuarial present value of accumulated plan benefits, if significant, may also be identified in the financial statements. Other factors that may cause significant changes in the actuarial present value of accumulated plan benefits are factors that affect (1) the amount of accumulated benefits, (2) the discount period, and (3) the amount of benefits paid. Actuarial gains and losses may be separately disclosed, or included with the effect of additional accumulated benefits.

Other financial statement disclosures   In addition to the financial statements and footnote disclosures mentioned previously, FAS-35 requires two specific additional footnote disclosures and several other disclosures if they are applicable. The two required footnote disclosures must appear in the footnote disclosures of the pension plan's "significant accounting policies," which is usually the first footnote disclosure (APB Opinion No. 22 [Disclosure of Accounting Policies]). They are as follows:

1.   The significant assumptions and method used to determine fair value of investments and the value of reported insurance contracts must be adequately described.

2.   The significant assumptions and method used to determine the actuarial present value of accumulated plan benefits must be adequately described. In addition, any significant changes in assumptions or methods that occur during the reporting period must be described.

A number of additional financial statement disclosures also must be made, if applicable. They are as follows:

- The important provisions of the pension plan agreement should be described briefly. However, if this information is made generally available from sources other than the financial statements, reference to such sources may be made in the financial statements instead of providing the brief description.

- Significant amendments to the pension plan that are adopted on or before the latest benefit information date should be described. In the event that significant plan amendments are adopted between the latest benefit information date and the end of the plan's year, disclosure should be made to the effect that the present value of accumulated plan benefits do not include the effects of those amendments.

- The order of priority for plan participants' claims to the assets of the plan upon termination of the plan should be described. In addition, any benefits guaranteed by the Pension Benefit Guaranty Corporation (PBGC) should be described. Also, the applicability of any PBGC guaranty to any recent plan amendment should be described.

- Significant plan administration costs that are being absorbed by the employer should be disclosed.

- The policy for funding the pension plan and any changes in policy during the plan year should be described. The method for determining participants' contributions, if any, should be described and plans subject to ERISA's minimum funding standards must disclose whether these requirements have been met. The status of minimum funding waivers should be disclosed, if applicable.

- The pension plan's policy concerning purchased insurance contracts that are excluded from the pension plan's assets should be disclosed, as applicable.

- Disclosure should be made of whether a favorable "determination letter" has been obtained for federal income tax purposes.

- Disclosure should be made of any plan investments that represent 5% or more of the net assets available for benefits.

- Disclosure should be made of any party-in-interest transactions between the plan and (1) the employer, (2) the sponsor, or (3) the employee organization.

- Disclosure should be made of unusual or infrequent events and the effects of such events that occur subsequent to the latest benefit information date, but before the issuance of the financial statements, which may significantly affect the plan's present and future ability to pay benefits. If the effects of such events are not reasonably determinable, all substantive reasons should be disclosed.

Defined Contribution Pension Plans

The Benefit Plans Guide provides guidance for the accounting and reporting by defined contribution pension plans. A plan's financial statements should provide information about (1) the plan's resources, (2) the stewardship responsibility with respect to the resources, (3) current transactions and events concerning the plan's resources, and (4) other factors necessary for the understanding of the information.

A defined contribution pension plan's financial statements should include the following:

- A statement of net assets available for plan benefits
- A statement of changes in net assets available for plan benefits

Under GAAP, defined contribution plans, including both health and welfare and pension plans, should report fully benefit-responsive contracts at contract value with certain supplemental disclosures.

Certain events relating to fully benefit-responsive contracts should be handled pursuant to FAS-5 (Accounting for Contingencies).

Under GAAP, the accrual basis of accounting should be used to prepare a plan's financial statements.

Statement of net assets available   A plan's investments should be stated at their fair values. Fair value is the expected current sales price established between a willing buyer and a willing seller, other than in a forced or liquidation sale. The following methods may be used to measure fair value:

- Market quotations
- Selling prices of similar assets
- Discounted values of expected cash flows

Amounts due from employers, employees, and other sources such as those due from state or federal agencies should be reported on the accrual basis. A receivable from an employer should be established when there is evidence of a formal commitment, such as a resolution adopted by a company's board of directors approving the contribution of a specified amount.

Statement of changes in net assets   Significant changes in net assets available for benefits should be identified in reasonable detail in the statement of changes in net assets available for benefits. The Benefit Plans Guide requires the following minimum disclosures:

- For each significant class of investments, the net appreciation or depreciation on a fair value basis
- Investment income not included above
- Cash and noncash contributions from employers (the nature of noncash contributions should be disclosed)
- Contributions from participants
- Contributions from other identifiable sources
- Amounts paid to participants
- Acquisitions of purchase contracts from insurance companies not included in the plan's assets
- Administrative expenses

Additional disclosures   Descriptions of methods and significant assumptions used to determine the fair value of investments and reported value of contracts with insurance companies should be disclosed. In addition, the following disclosures should be made, when applicable:

- A description of the plan agreement
- The amount of unallocated assets and their bases when that basis is different from the recorded amount
- The basis for determining contributions by employers and participants
- Explanation of when purchase contracts with insurance companies are not part of the plan's assets
- Description and effects of plan amendments
- Federal income tax status if a favorable letter of determination has not been obtained or maintained
- Description of investments that represent at least 5% of net assets
- Description of significant related party transactions
- For participant-direct investment programs, separate disclosure for amounts related to nonparticipant-directed and participant-directed investments by type of fund either on the face of the financial statements, or in the related disclosures, or by separate financial statements for each program
- For plans that assign units to participants, total number of units and the net asset value per unit
- Amounts allocated to withdrawal accounts that represent a component of net assets available for benefits
- Description of pledged investments and debt guarantees by others
- Unusual or infrequent events occurring after the financial statement date that affect the usefulness of the financial statements

Employee Health and Welfare Benefit Plans

The Benefit Plans Guide provide guidance for the accounting and reporting by employee health and welfare benefit plans. The objective of financial reporting by defined benefit health and welfare plans is the same as that of defined benefit pension plans; both types of plans provide a determinable benefit. Accordingly, the primary objective of the financial statements of a defined benefit health and welfare plan is to provide financial information that is useful in assessing the plan's present and future ability to pay its benefit obligations when due. To accomplish that objective, a plan's financial statements should provide information about (1) plan resources and the manner in which the stewardship responsibility for those resources has been discharged, (2) benefit obligations, (3) the results of transactions and events that affect the information about those resources and obligations, and (4) other factors necessary for users to understand the information provided.

The objective of financial reporting by a defined contribution health and welfare plan is to provide financial information that is useful in assessing the plan's present and future ability to pay its benefits when due. To accomplish that objective, a plan's financial statements should provide information about (1) plan resources and the manner in which the stewardship responsibility for those resources has been discharged, (2) the results of transactions and events that affect the information about those resources, and (3) other factors necessary for users to understand the information provided.

An employee health and welfare benefit plan's financial statements should include the following:

- A statement of net assets available for plan benefits
- A statement of changes in net assets available for plan benefits
- Information regarding the plan's benefit obligations, as applicable
- Information regarding the effects, if significant, of certain factors affecting the year-to-year change in the plan's benefit obligations, as applicable

SOP 94-4 requires that defined benefit health and welfare benefit plans should report investment contracts at fair value and insurance contracts in the same manner as required by ERISA annual reporting requirements.

Defined contribution plans, including both health and welfare and pension plans, should report fully benefit-responsive contracts at contract value with certain supplemental disclosures. Certain events relating to fully benefit-responsive contracts should be handled pursuant to FAS-5 (Accounting for Contingencies).

Under GAAP, the accrual basis of accounting should be used to prepare an employee health and welfare benefit plan's financial statements.

Statement of net assets available   Plan investments should be presented at their fair values. The measurement methods used to value the investments of a defined contribution pension plan should be used to value the investments of an employee health and welfare benefit plan. Amounts due from others should be reported on the accrual basis. Assets that are used in the actual operation of the employee health and welfare benefit plan should be reported at amortized cost on the financial statements.

As stated earlier, contracts with insurance companies should be measured in accordance with SOP 94-4. Contributions receivable from employers, participants, and others should be reported when due.

Group insurance premiums due but not paid should be shown as a liability on the plan's statement of net assets. Additional premiums that may be payable based on the experience of the insured plan should be described.

Deposits with insurance companies should be disclosed as assets until it is probable that the insurance company will apply the deposits to premiums due. If a reasonable estimate can be made of refunds due from insurance companies based on an experience rate adjustment, an accrual should be made. When a reasonable estimate cannot be made, this fact should be disclosed in the financial statements.

A self-insured plan should present as liabilities claims reported to the plan but not paid and claims incurred but not yet reported to the plan. In addition, estimated liabilities for death benefits should be based on projections made by the plan's actuary.

It may be necessary to report as a liability accumulated eligibility credits earned by some participants when the participants' benefits continue during periods of unemployment and the employer contributions to the plan do not provide for such benefits.

Statement of changes in net assets   The minimum disclosures required by the Benefit Plans Guide with respect to an employee health and welfare benefit plan are similar to the disclosures required for a defined contribution pension plan discussed earlier.

Information regarding benefit obligations   Benefit obligations for health and welfare benefit plans should include the actuarial present value, as applicable, of the following:

- Claims payable and currently due for active and retired participants
- Premiums due under insurance arrangements

- Claims incurred but not reported to the plan for active participants
- Accumulated eligibility credits for active participants
- Postretirement benefits for:
  - Retired participants, including their beneficiaries and covered dependents
  - Active or terminated participants who are fully eligible to receive benefits
  - Active participants not yet fully eligible to receive benefits

Benefits expected to be earned for future service by active participants (for example, vacation benefits) during the term of their employment should not be included. Benefit obligations should be reported as of the end of the plan year. The effect of plan amendments should be included in the computation of the expected and accumulated postretirement benefit obligations once they have been contractually agreed to, even if some provisions take effect only in future periods. For example, if a plan amendment grants a different benefit level for employees retiring after a future date, that increased or reduced benefit level should be included in current-period measurements of employees expected to retire after that date.

As noted previously, information regarding benefit obligations may be presented either in a separate statement or with other information on another financial statement. However, all the information must be located in one place.

Information regarding changes in benefit obligations   Information regarding changes in the benefit obligations within a plan period should be presented to identify significant factors affecting year-to-year changes in benefit obligations. Like the benefit obligation information, the changes should be presented within the body of the financial statements. Providing such information in the following three categories generally will be sufficient: (1) claims payable and premiums due to insurance companies, (2) incurred-but-not-reported (IBNR) and eligibility credits, and (3) postretirement benefit obligations.

Minimum disclosure regarding changes in benefit obligations should include the significant effects of (1) plan amendments, (2) changes in the nature of the plan (mergers or spinoffs), and (3) changes in actuarial assumptions (health care cost-trend rate or interest rate). Changes in actuarial assumptions are to be considered as changes in accounting estimates and, therefore, previously reported amounts should not be restated. The significant effects of other factors also may be identified. These include, for example, benefits accumulated, the effects of the time value of money (for interest), and benefits paid. If presented, benefits paid should not include benefit payments made by an insurance company pursuant to a contract that is excluded from plan assets. However, amounts paid by the plan to an insurance company pursuant to such a contract (including purchases of annuities with amounts allocated from existing investments with the insurance company) should be included in benefits paid. If only the minimum disclosure is presented, presentation in a statement format will necessitate an additional unidentified "other" category to reconcile the initial and ultimate amounts.

Additional disclosures   The plan's financial statements also should disclose other information. Separate disclosures may be made to the extent the plan provides both health and other welfare benefits. The disclosures should include, when applicable:

- A brief, general description of the plan agreement, including, but not limited to, participants covered, vesting, and benefit provisions. If a plan agreement or a description thereof providing this information is otherwise published or made available, the description in the financial statement disclosures may be omitted, provided that a reference to the other source is made.

- A description of significant plan amendments adopted during the period, as well as significant changes in the nature of the plan (for example, a plan spinoff or merger with another plan) and changes in actuarial assumptions.

- The funding policy and any changes in the policy made during the plan year. If the benefit obligations exceed the net assets of the plan, the method of funding this deficit, as provided for in the plan agreement or collective bargaining agreement, also should be disclosed. For a contributory plan, the disclosure should state the method of determining participants' contributions.

- The federal income tax status of the plan. There is no determination letter program for health and welfare plans; however, a 501(c)(9) VEBA trust must obtain a determination letter to be exempt from taxation.

- The policy regarding the purchase of contracts with insurance companies that are excluded from plan assets. Consideration should be given to disclosing the type and extent of insurance coverage, as well as the extent to which risk is transferred (for example, coverage period and claims reported or claims incurred).

- Identification of investments that represent 5% or more of total plan assets. Consideration should be given to disclosing provisions of insurance contracts included as plan assets that could cause an impairment of the asset value upon liquidation or other occurrence (for example, surrender charges and market value adjustments).

- The amounts and types of securities of the employer and related parties included in plan assets, and the approximate amount of future annual benefits of plan participants covered by insurance contracts issued by the employer and related parties.

- Significant real estate or other transactions in which the plan and any of the following parties are jointly involved: the sponsor, the plan administrator, employers, or employee organizations.

- Unusual or infrequent events or transactions occurring after the financial statement date, but before issuance of the financial statements, that might significantly affect the usefulness of the financial statements in an assessment of the plan's present and future ability to pay benefits. For example, a plan amendment adopted after the latest financial statement date that significantly increases future benefits attributable to an employee's service rendered before that date, a significant change in the market value of a significant portion of the plan's assets, or the emergence of a catastrophic claim should be disclosed. If reasonably determinable, the effects of such events or transactions should be disclosed. If such effects are not reasonably determinable, the reasons why they are not quantifiable should be disclosed.

- Material lease commitments, other commitments, or contingent liabilities.

- The assumed health care cost-trend rate(s) used to measure the expected cost of benefits covered by the plan for the next year, a general description of the direction and pattern of change in the assumed trend rates thereafter, the ultimate trend rate(s), and when that rate is expected to be achieved.

- For health and welfare benefit plans providing postretirement health care benefits, the effect of a one-percentage-point increase in the assumed health care cost-trend rates for each future year on the postretirement benefit obligation.

- Any modification of the existing cost-sharing provisions that are encompassed by the substantive plan(s) and the existence and nature of any commitment to increase monetary benefits provided by the plan and their effect on the plan's financial statements.

- Termination provisions of the plan and priorities for distribution of assets, if applicable.

- Restrictions, if any, on plan assets (for example, legal restrictions on multiple trusts).

The above list does not include information that, in accordance with ERISA requirements, must be disclosed in the schedules filed as part of a plan's annual report. If ERISA requires certain information to be disclosed in the schedules, that information must be disclosed in the schedules, not in the footnotes to the financial statements. Disclosure of the information in the footnotes and not in the schedules is not acceptable to the DOL.

> **OBSERVATION:** *The FASB's Emerging Issues Task Force (EITF) attempts to respond quickly to emerging accounting problems. Many, if not a majority, of the issues addressed by the EITF since its inception in 1984 focus on financial instruments and transactions. Auditors of employee benefit plans should be aware of the consensuses reached by the EITF.*

Other Accounting Issues and Developments

401(h) plans   A number of employers have amended defined benefit pension plans that they sponsor to provide for the payment of certain health benefits for retirees, their spouses, and dependents in addition to the normal retirement benefits. The IRC permits defined benefit pension plan sponsors to fund (subject to certain restrictions and limitations) all or a portion of their postretirement medical obligations through a 401(h) account in their defined benefit pension plans. Contributions to a 401(h) account may be used only to pay health benefits. Auditors should be aware that the assets set aside in a 401(h) account are *not* assets available to pay pension benefits, and should not be characterized as such in the plan's financial statements.

Defined contribution pension plan disclosures   In September 1994, the AICPA's Employee Benefit Plans Committee issued Practice Bulletin 12 (Reporting Separate Investment Fund Option Information of Defined Contribution Pension Plans), which clarifies the related reporting requirements established by paragraph 3.23k of *Audits of Employee Benefit Plans*. Practice Bulletin 12 is effective for plan years beginning after December 15, 1993.

Derivatives disclosures   In October 1994, the FASB issued Statement No. 119 (Disclosure About Derivative Financial Instruments and Fair Value of Financial Instruments). FAS-119 requires disclosures about derivative financial instruments—futures, forward, swap, and option contracts, and other financial instruments with similar characteristics.

More specifically, the Statement requires disclosures about amounts, nature, and terms of derivative financial instruments that are not subject to FAS-105 (Disclosure of Information About Financial Instruments with Off-Balance-Sheet Risk and Financial Instruments with Concentrations of Credit Risk), because they do not result in off-balance-sheet risk of accounting loss. It requires that a distinction be made between financial instruments held or issued for trading purposes (including dealing and other trading activities measured at fair value with gains and losses recognized in earnings) and financial instruments held or issued for purposes other than trading. Employee benefit plans that engage in such activities are required to provide those disclosures in their financial statements.

FAS-119 is effective for financial statements issued for fiscal years ending after December 15, 1994, except for entities with less than $150 million in total assets. For those entities, the Statement is effective for financial instruments issued for fiscal years ending after December 15, 1995.

In December 1994, the FASB issued a Special Report, *Illustrations of Financial Instrument Disclosures*, which illustrates the disclosure requirements set out in FAS-119, FAS-105, and FAS-107 (Disclosures About Fair Value of Financial Instruments). It was prepared to assist financial statement preparers, auditors, and others in understanding and implementing FAS-119 in the context of those other disclosure Statements.

Fair value disclosures   FAS-107, as amended by FAS-119, requires all entities to disclose, within the body of the financial statements or in the accompanying notes, the fair value of financial instruments, both assets and liabilities recognized and not recognized in the statement of financial position, for which it is practicable to estimate fair value. The disclosures should distinguish between financial instruments held or issued for trading purposes, including dealing and other trading activities measured at fair value with gains and losses recognized in earnings, and financial instruments held or issued for purposes other than trading. An entity also should disclose the method(s) and significant assumptions used to estimate the fair value of financial instruments. Auditors should be aware that, generally, financial instruments of an employee benefit plan other than insurance contracts as defined in FAS-110, are included in the scope of FAS-107 and are subject to the disclosure requirements of paragraphs 10–14 of that Statement.

SPECIALIZED INDUSTRY PRACTICES

As noted earlier, generally accepted auditing standards are applicable to audits of employee benefit plans. However, because of some unique characteristics of the plan and specialized accounting practices, certain specialized auditing practices must be applied.

Planning the Engagement

The auditor should first determine the scope of the engagement. On the basis of regulations established under ERISA, the engagement may be considered a full-scope audit or a limited-scope audit. In a full-scope engagement, the audit is conducted in accordance with GAAS. Under a limited-scope engagement, information prepared or certified as to both completeness and accuracy by certain parties (financial institutions or regulated insurance carriers) does not have to be substantiated by the auditor.

To identify the significant characteristics of the engagement, information about the employee benefit plan should be gathered during the planning phase. The following procedures should be considered in this phase of the audit:

- Determine the scope of the engagement and the types of reports to be issued or services to be rendered through discussions with trustees and other parties.
- Determine the type and number of plans to be audited.

- Determine whether this will be a full-scope audit or an ERISA limited-scope audit.
- Based on the discussions described above, prepare an engagement letter.
- Read the plan's instrument, including amendments.
- Determine whether the plan is self-insured, insured, or split-funded (if the plan is insured or split-funded, determine the type of insurance contract).
- Read the prior-year annual report and other reports filed with regulatory agencies.
- Determine the role of third-party service providers, (e.g., TPAs, trustee, custodian, investment advisors), specialists, consultants, internal auditors, and other independent auditors. If these parties have issued reports, review the reports.

In addition, the auditor should inquire about the following matters:

- The accounting basis of the financial statements (GAAP or an other comprehensive basis of accounting allowed by ERISA or the DOL)
- The location of investment assets held by outside custodians
- The nature of the plan's accounting records and other data maintained by the plan's sponsor or other parties
- The frequency of financial statement preparation
- The maintenance of procedures for identifying reportable transactions as defined by ERISA and applicable DOL regulations
- The maintenance of a list of *parties in interest* as defined by ERISA Sec. 3(14)
- Identification of employers participating in the plan

Internal Control

The basic concepts established in SAS-55 (Consideration of the Internal Control Structure in a Financial Statement Audit) should be used to obtain an understanding of and test an employee benefit plan's internal control structure.

A plan's internal control may encompass procedures established by another party such as a bank, insurance company, or the plan's sponsors. The auditor should consider these controls during the analysis of internal controls. The auditor may either evaluate these internal controls personally or, if appropriate, read the third-party auditor's internal control report. Guidance established by SAS-70 (Reports on the Processing of Transactions by Service Organizations) should be followed when the auditor relies on internal control assessments by the service auditor.

In analyzing the plan's internal controls, particular attention should be paid to controls related to investments, contributions received and related receivables, benefits paid, participants' data and plan obligations, administrative expenses, and reporting.

Guidance established in SAS-60 (Communication of Internal Control Structure Related Matters Noted in an Audit) should be used to identify reportable conditions.

SPECIALIZED AUDIT PROCEDURES

The typical audit procedures performed in the examination of a commercial enterprise are usually employed in the examination of the financial statements of an employee benefit plan. In addition, special attention should be directed to certain accounts and transactions because of their significance and unique nature. The degree to which the accounts or transactions are tested depends on the evaluation of the plan's internal control structure.

Investments

An employee benefit plan may hold a variety of investments including capital stock, bonds, notes, real estate investments, and mortgages. The Benefit Plans Guide classifies investments as (1) trusteed assets, (2) assets held by insurance companies, and (3) other investments.

Trusteed assets Usually the plan's investment activities are administered by a trustee or investment adviser. The trustee agreement may allow the trustee to make investment decisions (discretionary trust) or execute transactions based on directives received from another party such as the plan administrator (directed trust). In addition, the trustee may be responsible for the custody of the investments.

Typically the following audit procedures should be performed for investment assets:

- Obtain an understanding of the plan's investment strategy and that strategy's effect on the investment portfolio.

- Obtain an analysis of activity in the investment accounts on both a cost and a fair value basis.

- Substantiate ownership (and possible restrictions) through physical inspection of documents or confirmation with trustee.

- If ownership is substantiated by confirmation, obtain information concerning the trustee's responsibility and financial capabilities by:

  — Reading the trust instrument.

  — Determining whether trustee has insurance covering assets held.

  — Reviewing trustee's recent financial statements.

- To identify pledges, liens, etc., review minutes and agreements.

- Select investment transactions and (1) verify authorization, (2) inspect documentation supporting the purchase or sale, (3) compare purchase price or sales price to published market quotations, and (4) recompute realized gain or loss on sales transactions.

- Substantiate status of securities in transit through confirmation with plan's broker.

- Test the accrual of investment income.

- Test fair value of investments and net change during the period.

- Determine whether restrictions imposed by the plan's instrument have been violated.

- Inquire about whether investment activity has violated applicable laws or agency regulations.

- Evaluate the procedures used to determine fair value.

- Review documentation supporting estimates of fair value.

- Inquire about whether the plan's board of trustees, administrative committee, or other designated party agrees with the estimate of fair value.

In addition, the Benefit Plans Guide suggests that the auditor refer to SAS-73 (Using the Work of a Specialist) when a specialist is used to determine estimated fair value.

When the employee benefit plan is administered through a discretionary trust, accounting records reflecting transactions executed by the trust department will not be maintained by the plan. In this circumstance the plan's auditor may obtain the trust department's special independent auditor's report on the department's internal controls. The special-report engagement should follow the guidelines established by SAS-70. If the special report was not prepared or cannot be obtained, the plan's auditor should apply audit procedures at the trust department.

When the plan's assets held by a bank are part of a common or commingled fund, the following procedures should be applied:

- Confirm the plan's units of participation (investment units) with the trustee.

- Review authorization for investment transactions in units of participation.

- Determine the reasonableness of information recorded by the participating plan by reviewing current financial statements of the common or commingled trust fund.

If the trust fund's current financial statements are audited, the plan's auditor should read the report to determine if conditions exist that may have an effect on the carrying value of the units of participation as recorded by the employee benefit plan. When the trust fund's financial statements are unaudited, the plan's auditor should consider performing audit procedures at the bank to substantiate income and unit values reported by the bank.

Assets held by insurance companies An employee benefit plan may enter into a variety of contracts with an insurance company. Payments made to an insurance company may represent contributions allocated to purchase insurance or annuities for the individual participants (allocated contracts). Allocated contracts are excluded from the plan's assets. On the other hand, contributions may represent unallocated funds to be used to meet benefit payments as they become payable. Unallocated contracts are included in the plan's assets.

The deposit administration (DA) type of group annuity contract and the immediate participation guarantee (IPG) contract are two types of unallocated funding contracts.

DA contracts with insurance companies involve contributions that are not used to purchase annuities for individual participants on a current basis. Under this type of contract the insurance company will guarantee a minimum stipulated interest rate on the funds. Amounts in excess of the guaranteed interest rate may be earned by the fund but these amounts are determined solely at the discretion of the insurance company. IPG contracts are similar to DA contracts except no minimum stipulated interest rate is guaranteed on the fund. The interest rate is based on the actual earnings of the fund.

The following audit procedures should be applied to insurance contracts:

- Read the contract with the insurance company.
- Confirm the following items with the insurance company:
  - Payments made during the year
  - Interest, dividends, refunds, and other changes during the year
  - The contract value of the funds in the general account
  - Fees charged by the insurance company
  - Fund transfers made during the year
  - Annuity purchases or benefits paid from unallocated plan assets
- Evaluate reasonableness of interest credited for DA contracts.
- Evaluate reasonableness of interest credited for IPG contracts. (If the calculation is unreasonable and inquiries of the insurance company are unsatisfactory, the plan's auditor may consider having the insurer's independent auditor perform an agreed-upon procedures engagement as described in SAS-75 [Engagements to Apply Agreed-Upon Procedures to Specified Elements, Accounts, or Items of a Financial Statement].)
- Determine that annuity purchases were consistent with rates established by the contract.
- Determine that expenses paid to the insurance company were consistent with provisions in the contract.
- Review the insurance company's financial statements.

Other investments An employee benefit plan may hold real estate investments or invest in loans and mortgages. The Benefit Plans Guide suggests the following audit procedures for these investments:

Real Estate Investments

- Substantiate cost of investment.
- Substantiate ownership of property.
- Evaluate reasonableness of property's estimated fair value.
- Test investment income and expenses related to investment.
- Inquire as to whether investment has violated applicable laws or agency regulations.

Investments in Loans and Mortgages

- Inspect documentation supporting investment.
- Select loans and mortgages for confirmation with debtor.
- Evaluate reasonableness of investment's estimated fair value.
- Test interest income recognized during the period.
- Inquire as to whether investment has violated applicable laws or agency regulations.

Contributions and Receivables

Contributions received or receivable by the plan are determined by the plan instrument or in some instances by standards established by ERISA. The following procedures should be employed to audit employer and employee contributions:

- Identify all participating employers by referring to appropriate plan documents.
- Obtain a list of contributions received or receivable from participating employers.
- Test mathematical accuracy of contribution reports and consistency with requirements established by plan documents.
- Reconcile contributions received per the reports described above with cash receipts records and bank statements.
- Trace postings from contribution reports to accounting records and vice versa.
- Confirm amounts received and receivable.
- Determine that accruals for contributions are made in accordance with generally accepted accounting principles.
- Evaluate the plan's allowance for doubtful accounts.

In addition, the following procedures should be performed, depending on the nature of the employee benefit plan:

Defined Benefit Pension Plan

- Review the plan's actuary report to determine if it is consistent with employer contributions.
- Determine that the amount contributed is sufficient to meet the requirements of the funding standard account. (ERISA requires that plans subject to the minimum funding standards maintain a memorandum account called the funding standard account, which is not included in the plan's financial statements.)
- Review the results of audit procedures applied to the participants' data (which is discussed later in this chapter).

Defined Contribution Plan

- Determine that the plan's contribution requirements are being observed.
- Compare recorded amounts of contributions to amounts approved by the board of directors.
- Review the results of audit procedures applied to the participants' data (which is discussed later in this chapter).

Benefit Payments

To determine whether benefits paid are made in accordance with the plan's provisions, selected payments should be reviewed for proper approval. The employee's status should be reviewed to determine whether he or she was eligible to receive the payment. The amount of the payment made should be recomputed to determine whether the amount is consistent with the plan's instrument. The payment should be traced to cash disbursement records or the trustee's report.

Procedures to determine the eligibility of participants or beneficiaries should be reviewed.

Participants' Data

Participants' data must be reviewed by the auditor to determine whether (1) employees have been properly included in eligibility records and (2) reliable information has been supplied to the plan administrator and, if appropriate, the plan actuary. Audit procedures that may be used are listed below.

- Read plan instruments describing the nature of benefits and determine what information is relevant to the audit of the plan's financial statements.
- Test payroll summarizations and participants' data schedules.
- For selected pay periods, test payroll data by:
  — Tracing data per payroll journal to participants' earnings records.
  — Substantiating hours worked by hourly employee.
  — Substantiating pay rates.
  — Recomputing earnings.
  — Reviewing personnel files for hiring authorization, pay rate, and similar relevant payroll information.
- Determine consistency of data maintained by the plan administrator and the employer's payroll information.
- For multiemployer plans, compare employer's contribution reports with the participants' earnings records.

In addition to the audit procedures described above, the following procedures should be applied depending on the type of employee benefit plan:

Defined Benefit Plan

- Determine if the actuary's findings support the related representations in the financial statements and make appropriate tests of accounting data provided by the client to the actuary (SAS-73).
- Trace information substantiated during tests of participant data to data supplied to the actuary by the plan administrator.
- Test basic data used by actuary (either in a report or in a separate confirmation letter received from actuary) against data supplied to the actuary by the plan administrator.

Defined Contribution Plan

- Test covered compensation of individual participants.
- Test contributions made by participants.
- Test application of criteria used to determine eligibility and vesting.

Health and Welfare Benefit Plan

- Test accuracy of payroll data.
- Test accuracy of demographic data, such as sex and date of birth.
- Test claims history as maintained by the plan administrator.
- Determine if the actuary's findings support the related representations in the financial statements and make appropriate tests of accounting data provided by the client to the actuary (SAS-73), if applicable.
- Trace information substantiated during tests of participant data to data supplied to the actuary by the plan administrator, if applicable.
- Test basic data used by actuary (either in a report or in a separate confirmation letter received from actuary) against data supplied to the actuary by the plan administrator, if applicable.

Plan Obligations

The type of employee benefit plan determines the audit approach with respect to a plan's obligations.

Defined benefit plan   For a defined benefit plan, the auditor must determine whether the actuarial present value of accumulated plan benefits, components of those benefits, and amount of changes in the actuarial present value of accumulated plan benefits are consistent with the requirements established in FAS-35. Since these data are based on actuarial computations, the auditor should follow guidelines established in SAS-73. In addition, the auditor should instruct the plan administrator to send a letter to the plan's actuary asking the actuary to (1) provide the auditor with a copy of the actuarial report, Schedule B of Form 5500, or comparable information or (2) confirm with the auditor that the actuarial information has already been obtained from the plan in connection with the audit.

Defined contribution plan   For a defined contribution plan the auditor must perform procedures designed to determine whether (1) net assets are properly allocated to the individual participants' accounts and (2) total net assets reconcile with the sum of the participants' accounts. To achieve these audit objectives, the following procedures may be performed:

- Review plan documents to determine an understanding of how allocations are to be made.

- Test allocation of (1) income or loss, (2) appreciation or depreciation in value of investments, (3) administrative expenses, and (4) forfeited amounts.

- Test allocation of employer contributions.

- For plans that involve employee contributions, test allocation to specific accounts and types of investments.

- Reconcile total net assets to the sum of individual accounts.

Health and welfare benefit plan   A health and welfare benefit plan may be either self-insured or insured through an insurance company. For a self-insured plan, obligations for claims reported but not paid, claims incurred but unreported, accumulated eligibility credits, and accumulated postretirement benefit obligations must be shown as an obligation in the plan's statement of accumulated plan benefits, as applicable. The auditor should obtain a list of unpaid reported claims and review supporting documentation for selected claims. In addition, the auditor should test the reasonableness of all other accrued benefit obligation amounts.

For insured plans the auditor should test premium payments made to the insurance company by performing the following procedures:

- Recompute monthly premiums due based on the insurance contract terms and eligibility records.

- Compare participants in eligibility records to those listed in the premium computation.

- Evaluate fluctuations in monthly premiums.

- Confirm directly with the insurance company (1) premiums paid, (2) premiums payable, and (3) other liabilities and assets of the plan.

If the employee benefit plan requires an actuarial estimation of the plan's accrued obligations, the following information should be confirmed with the actuary:

- Scope of plan
- Factors used to make actuarial calculations
- Number of participants and beneficiaries who are active, terminated with vested benefits, or retired under the plan

- Present value of accumulated obligations by category
- Dates of (1) valuation and (2) data used
- Summary of assumptions used, changes in assumptions, and effects of changes in assumptions
- Effects of plan amendments
- Sponsor's intention to terminate plan
- Unpaid actuarial fees

Party-in-Interest Transactions

ERISA prohibits certain transactions between the plan and a "party in interest" as defined under Section 3(14) of ERISA. Party-in-interest transactions (in effect, related party transactions) include transactions with the following:

- Fiduciaries or plan employees
- Any person who provides services to the plan
- An employer whose employees are covered by the plan
- An employee organization whose members are covered by the plan
- A person who owns 50% or more of such an employer or employee association
- Certain relatives of parties listed above

As part of the engagement, the auditor should be aware of possible transactions that should be disclosed according to standards established by FAS-57 (Related Party Disclosures) and the Department of Labor. However, in a manner consistent with standards applicable to other audit engagements, the auditor does not guarantee that the engagement will discover all party-in-interest transactions.

To identify party-in-interest relationships, the auditor should consider performing the following procedures:

- Review and evaluate procedures for identifying, accounting for, and reporting party-in-interest transactions.
- Obtain a list of all parties in interest and inquire whether transactions with such parties have occurred during the year.

- Review regulatory filings that identify parties in interest.
- Refer to prior-year workpapers to identify parties in interest. In a noncontinuing engagement, communicate with the predecessor auditor.
- Inquire about whether governmental investigations have identified prohibited transactions with parties in interest.

To determine whether material prohibited transactions have occurred with known parties in interest, and to identify transactions that may be likely to involve unknown parties in interest, the auditor should consider the following procedures:

- Communicate names of parties in interest to audit personnel.
- Review minutes for the board and other key committees in order to identify transactions discussed or approved.
- Review communications with regulatory agencies for possible identification of party-in-interest transactions.
- Review conflict-of-interest statements prepared by plan officials.
- Review the extent and nature of transactions with vendors, creditors, etc., to identify relationships not previously disclosed.
- Consider whether unrecorded transactions are occurring (for example, a major stockholder of the plan's sponsor performs accounting services for no charge).
- Review unusual transactions (especially ones occurring near the end of the year).
- Review confirmations of compensating balances to determine whether balances are being maintained by or for a party in interest.
- Review invoices from legal counsel for possible identification of party-in-interest transactions.
- Review receivable/payable confirmations for possible indications of guarantees.

If a material party-in-interest transaction is discovered, the auditor should use appropriate procedures to determine that the transaction is properly accounted for and reported in the financial statements and the applicable supplemental schedule.

If a particular party-in-interest transaction is prohibited by ERISA, the auditor should follow the guidance established in SAS-54 (Illegal

Acts by Clients). Importantly, if the auditor becomes aware of a prohibited transaction during the course of his or her examination, the auditor must assure that it is properly reported in the applicable supplemental schedule, irrespective of quantitative materiality, or otherwise modify the auditor's report on the supplemental schedule.

Other Audit Factors

The tax status of the employee benefit plan should be investigated by reviewing the IRS tax determination letter and making informed inquiries regarding applicable design and operating requirements under the Internal Revenue Code. These inquiries generally should be made or reviewed by a qualified specialist.

The auditor should make inquiries about whether prohibited transactions (as defined by ERISA) have occurred that may give rise to receivables from the plan administrator or other parties or which may require disclosure in the applicable supplemental schedule.

A representation letter should be obtained from the plan trustee, administrator, or administrative agent. In addition to the items listed in SAS-19 (Client Representations), the letter should include the following representations:

- Amendments to the plan instrument
- Omissions from the participants' data
- Acceptability of methods and assumptions used by the actuary
- Changes in actuarial assumptions and methods
- Qualification of the plan under the appropriate section of the Internal Revenue Code
- Compliance with fidelity bonding required by ERISA
- Transactions with parties in interest as defined in ERISA Sec. 3(14)
- Defaulted or uncollectible investments
- Reportable transactions as defined in ERISA Sec. 103(b)(3)(H)
- Possible termination of the plan

A legal representation letter generally should be obtained, and a subsequent-events review should be conducted. In addition, the auditor should read information in Form 5500 filed with the IRS and observe the standards established in SAS-8 (Other Information in Documents Containing Audited Financial Statements).

Reports

The four reporting standards of generally accepted auditing standards are applicable to employee benefit plan engagements. Thus, as shown below, the standard audit report for these engagements is very similar to the auditor's report for other engagements.

We have audited the accompanying statements of net assets available for benefits and of accumulated plan benefits of Interstate Pension Plan as of December 31, 19X5, and the related statements of changes in net assets available for benefits and of changes in accumulated plan benefits for the year then ended. These financial statements are the responsibility of the Plan's management. Our responsibility is to express an opinion on these financial statements based on our audit.

We conducted our audit in accordance with generally accepted auditing standards. Those standards require that we plan and perform the audit to obtain reasonable assurance about whether the financial statements are free of material misstatement. An audit includes examining, on a test basis, evidence supporting the amounts and disclosures in the financial statements. An audit also includes assessing the accounting principles used and significant estimates made by management, as well as evaluating the overall financial statement presentation. We believe that our audit provides a reasonable basis for our opinion.

In our opinion, the financial statements referred to above present fairly, in all material respects, the financial status of the Plan as of December 31, 19X5, and the changes in its financial status for the year then ended in conformity with generally accepted accounting principles.

The financial statements may contain information required by ERISA and related DOL regulations. If the additional information is audited, the following paragraph may be added.

Our audit was made for the purpose of forming an opinion on the basic financial statements taken as a whole. The supplemental schedules of [identify] are presented for purposes of complying with the Department of Labor's Rules and Regulations for Reporting and Disclosure under the Employee Retirement Income Security Act of 1974 and are not a required part of the basic financial statements. The supplemental schedules have been subjected to the auditing procedures applied in the examination of the basic financial statements and, in our opinion, are fairly stated in all material respects in relation to the basic financial statements taken as a whole.

If the information is not audited, it should be marked as such or should be referenced to the auditor's disclaimer of opinion. The last sentence of the opinion paragraph should read as follows.

The supplemental schedules have not been subjected to the auditing procedures applied in the audit of the basic financial statements, and, accordingly, we express no opinion on them.

Additional guidance can be found in SAS-29 (Reporting on Information Accompanying the Basic Financial Statements in Auditor-Submitted Documents).

The standard report described above may be modified for the following reasons as described in the Benefit Plans Guide:

- Scope limitation
- Valuation of investments not in accordance with GAAP
- Other auditors used
- Trust established under a plan

Scope limitation   As noted earlier, DOL regulations allow the plan administrator to limit the scope of the audit with respect to certain "certified" information prepared by banks or insurance carriers that are subject to periodic reviews by state or federal agencies.

If the auditor considers the restriction to be significant with respect to the financial statements taken as a whole, a disclaimer of opinion may be expressed. In the disclaimer of opinion report, the scope paragraph would refer to an explanation paragraph in which the basis for the scope limitation would be explained. The opinion paragraph may read as follows.

Because of the significance of the information that we did not audit, we are unable to, and do not, express an opinion on the accompanying financial statements and schedules taken as a whole. The form and content of the information included in the financial statements and schedules, other than that derived from the information certified by the trustee, have been audited by us and, in our opinion, are presented in compliance with the Department of Labor's Rules and Regulations for Reporting and Disclosure under the Employee Retirement Income Security Act of 1974.

Valuation of investments not in accordance with GAAP   The auditor may conclude that nonreadily marketable investments are not properly reported at their fair value. Under this circumstance, the auditor may express a qualified or adverse opinion on the financial statements taken as a whole. The report would include an explanatory paragraph(s) describing the valuation deficiency. The paragraph expressing the qualified or adverse opinion would refer to the explanatory paragraph(s). An example of a qualified opinion paragraph is presented below.

In our opinion, except for the effect on the financial statements of the procedures used by the Plan to determine the valuation of investments, as described in the preceding paragraph, the financial statements referred to above present fairly in all material respects the financial status of the Interstate Pension Plan as of December 31, 19X5, and the changes in its financial status for the year then ended in conformity with generally accepted accounting principles.

Other auditors used   Generally, the plan auditor would serve as the principal auditor even though other auditors may issue reports covering a significant portion of the plan's assets or internal control structure. Since there can be no meaningful way to indicate the division of responsibility for each auditor, the Benefit Plans Guide concludes that the plan auditor should ordinarily not refer to the work performed by other auditors.

Omission of required information in the supplemental schedules required by ERISA   The auditor may conclude that certain information required by ERISA has been inappropriately omitted from the applicable supplemental schedule(s). An example of a qualified opinion paragraph is shown below.

Our audits were performed for the purpose of forming an opinion on the financial statements taken as a whole. The supplemental schedules of [identify] are presented for the purpose of additional analysis and are not a required part of the basic financial statements, but are supplementary information required by the Department of Labor's Rules and Regulations of Reporting and Disclosure under the Employee Retirement Income Security Act of 1974. The supplemental schedules have been subjected to the auditing procedures applied in the audits of the basic financial statements and, in our opinion, are fairly stated in all material respects in relation to the basic financial statements taken as a whole.

The schedule of assets held for investment purposes that accompanies the Plan's financial statements does not disclose the historical cost of certain plan assets held by the Plan trustee [or custodian]. Disclosure of this information is required by the Department of Labor's Rules and Regulations for Reporting and Disclosure under the Employee Retirement Income Security Act of 1974.

Trust established under a plan   A trust may be established as part of an employee benefit plan. Accounting standards and government regulations identify the plan itself, not the trust, as the accounting entity. However, the plan administrator may engage an auditor to report on the trust's financial statements. The provisions of the Benefit Plans Guide are applicable to a trust engagement.

An audit report on the trust's financial statements would consist of a standard introductory paragraph, standard scope paragraph, and standard opinion paragraph. In addition, the following paragraph should be included in the audit report.

The accompanying financial statements are those of the Interstate Pension Trust Fund, which is established under the Interstate Pension Plan; the financial statements do not purport to present the financial status of the Interstate Pension Plan. The financial statements do not contain certain information on accumulated plan benefits and other disclosures necessary for a fair presentation of the financial status of the Interstate Pension Plan in conformity with generally accepted accounting principles. Furthermore, these financial statements do not purport to satisfy the Department of Labor's Rules and Regulations for Reporting and Disclosure under the Employee Retirement Income Security Act of 1974, which relates to the financial statements of employee benefit plans.

The opinion paragraph should not refer to the paragraph presented above.

Special Reports

Accounting principles or governmental regulations do not prohibit financial statements of an employee benefit plan from being prepared on a basis of accounting other than generally accepted accounting principles. For example, a plan's financial statements could be prepared on a modified cash basis where investments are presented on a fair value basis. When financial statements are prepared on a basis other than GAAP, guidelines established by SAS-62 (Special Reports) must be observed.

AUDITS OF HEALTH CARE PROVIDERS

CONTENTS

Overview	**21.03**
Background	**21.04**
Specialized Accounting Principles	**21.05**
Cash and Cash Equivalents	**21.05**
Investments	**21.05**
Receivables	**21.06**
Advance Fees	**21.07**
Costs of Acquiring Initial Continuing Care Contracts	**21.07**
Property and Equipment, Supplies, and Other Assets	**21.07**
Current and Long-Term Obligations	**21.08**
Commitments and Contingencies	**21.09**
Obligation Related to Future Services for Continuing Care Retirement Communities	**21.11**
Revenue, Expenses, Gains, and Losses	**21.11**
Reporting Entity and Related Organizations	**21.12**
Specialized Industry Procedures	**21.13**
Investments	**21.13**
Receivables	**21.14**
Property and Equipment, Supplies, and Other Assets	**21.14**
Current and Long-Term Obligations	**21.14**
Commitments and Contingencies	**21.14**
Revenue, Expenses, Gains, and Losses	**21.15**
Reporting Entity and Related Organizations	**21.15**
Specialized Audit Procedures	**21.15**
Investments	**21.15**
Receivables	**21.16**
Property and Equipment, Supplies, and Other Assets	**21.17**
Current and Long-Term Obligations	**21.18**
Commitments and Contingencies	**21.18**

Revenue, Expenses, Gains, and Losses   **21.19**
Related Organizations   **21.20**
Reports   **21.21**
Receipt of Federal Awards by Not-for-Profit
    Organizations   **21.21**

AUDITS OF HEALTH CARE PROVIDERS

Overview

The specialized accounting principles and auditing procedures for health care providers appear in the AICPA Audit and Accounting Guide entitled *Audits of Providers of Health Care Services* (hereinafter referred to as the Health Care Guide), SOP 89-5 (Financial Accounting and Reporting by Providers of Prepaid Health Care Services), and SOP 90-8 (Financial Accounting and Reporting by Continuing Care Retirement Communities). The Health Care Guide supersedes the previous Audit and Accounting Guide entitled *Hospital Audit Guide* and the following publications:

- Statement of Position (SOP) (unnumbered) (Clarification of Accounting, Auditing, and Reporting Practices Relating to Hospital Malpractice Loss Contingencies [1978])

- SOP 78-1 (Accounting by Hospitals for Certain Marketable Equity Securities)

- SOP 81-2 (Reporting Practices Concerning Hospital-Related Organizations)

- SOP 85-1 (Financial Reporting by Not-for-Profit Health Care Entities for Tax-Exempt Debt and Certain Funds Whose Use Is Limited)

- SOP 87-1 (Accounting for Asserted and Unasserted Medical Malpractice Claims of Health Care Providers and Related Issues)

The AICPA released an Exposure Draft of a proposed new Audit and Accounting Guide entitled *Health Care Organizations* on April 14, 1995. The new Guide will supersede *Audits of Providers of Health Care Services* as well as incorporate SOP 89-5 and SOP 90-8.

Background

Health care providers covered by the Health Care Guide include the following entities:

- Clinics, medical group practices, individual practice associations, individual practitioners, and other ambulatory care organizations
- Continuing care retirement communities
- Health maintenance organizations and similar prepaid health care plans
- Home health agencies
- Hospitals
- Nursing homes that provide skilled, intermediate, and less intensive levels of health care
- Drug and alcohol rehabilitation centers

The financial statements for a health care provider should include (1) a balance sheet, (2) a statement of operations, (3) a statement of changes in equity (or net assets), (4) a statement of cash flows, and (5) notes to the financial statements. The balance sheet should reflect the assets, liabilities, and net assets of the organization. Assets and liabilities should be classified as current or noncurrent. Not-for-profit organizations are required under Financial Accounting Standards Board (FASB) Statement No. 117 (Financial Statements of Not-for-Profit Organizations) to provide information about the liquidity of assets or liabilities on the balance sheet. In addition, they must classify net assets into three broad groups: unrestricted net assets, temporarily restricted net assets, and permanently restricted net assets. The statement of cash flows summarizes all of the financing and investing activities of the health care provider and reflects the amount of cash generated from or used in operations for the period. The statement of changes in equity (or net assets) should include a reconciliation of the beginning and ending equity or net asset balances. The statement of operations should show the results of operations for the period, and reflect the principal sources of support and revenue. The statement of operations may be combined with the statement of changes in equity balances.

The statement of operations for not-for-profit organizations reports all changes in unrestricted net assets for the period.

SPECIALIZED ACCOUNTING PRINCIPLES

As a general rule, financial statements of health care providers are prepared in accordance with the generally accepted accounting principles used by commercial enterprises. The discussion that follows summarizes accounting methods and financial reporting circumstances unique to the health care industry.

Cash and Cash Equivalents

Health care organizations may hold assets owned by others under agency relationships. The organization incurs a liability for the assets. Agency funds are included in unrestricted net assets.

Investments

In November 1995 the FASB issued FAS-124 (Accounting for Certain Investments Held by Not-for-Profit Organizations), which eliminated some of the financial accounting and reporting inconsistencies established by AICPA Guides and Statements of Position. FAS-124 applies to all investments in equity securities that have a "readily determinable fair value" and to all investments in debt securities; however, it does not apply to investments accounted for under the equity method or to investments in consolidated subsidiaries.

FAS-124 requires that investments in marketable equity securities and investments in debt securities be reported at fair value on a not-for-profit organization's statement of financial position. In addition, FAS-117 (Financial Statements of Not-for-Profit Organizations) requires that gains and losses related to these investments be reported in the organization's statement of activities as increases or decreases in unrestricted net assets, unless the changes are temporarily or permanently restricted. Investment income should be reported as increases in unrestricted net assets unless its use is limited by restrictions imposed by donors, in which case the income should be reported as an increase to either temporarily restricted net assets or permanently restricted net assets, depending on the nature of the restriction.

Gains and investment income that are subject to donor-imposed restrictions may be reported as increases in unrestricted net assets if the donor-imposed restrictions are satisfied during the same period in which the gain or investment income is recorded and if a similar policy applies to the reporting of contributions received by the organization.

Gains and losses that are related to donor-restricted contributions and must be invested in perpetuity or invested for a specified period of time should be reported as changes in unrestricted net assets, with one exception: If the gains or losses related to the donor-restricted assets are temporarily or permanently restricted explicitly by the donor or by a law that specifically extends the restriction to the gains or losses, such gains or losses should be reported as changes in restricted assets. On the other hand, FAS-124 points out that "if a donor allows the organization to choose suitable investments, the gains are not permanently restricted unless the donor or the law requires that an amount be retained permanently."

Receivables

Receivables and the related revenue arising from health care services should be recognized on the accrual basis and recorded at the provider's full established rates. Contractual adjustments based on differences between normal charges and amounts paid by third-party payers, and discounts granted to certain individuals should be recorded on an accrual basis and deducted from gross revenue in order to measure net service revenue. However, services provided on a charitable basis in conformity with established policies by the health care provider should not be recognized as revenue.

Receivables as of the date of the balance sheet should be reported on a net realizable basis with appropriate allowances for bad debts, contractual adjustments, and discounts.

When rates charged by the health care provider are established on a retrospective basis, an estimate should be made as of the balance sheet date for any additional amounts due from or due to the third party based on services provided under the retrospective arrangement. Any differences between the estimate and the final adjustment under the retrospective arrangement should be recognized as an adjustment to revenue in the year in which the final settlement is made, unless the final adjustment satisfies the criteria established by FAS-16 (Prior Period Adjustments). In this case, the adjustment is treated as a prior-period adjustment.

Loss contingencies, such as those arising under state Medicare waivers, should be accounted for using FAS-5 (Accounting for Contingencies).

To transfer part of the risk of providing health care services for a fixed fee, some health care providers obtain stop-loss insurance. Under stop-loss insurance arrangements, an insurance company agrees to pay health care costs in excess of a stated amount. The premium paid for a stop-loss insurance policy should be reported as an operating cost, and reimbursements under the policy should be reported as a reduction to operating costs.

Advance Fees

Financial accounting standards for advance fees received by a continuing care retirement community are established by SOP 90-8.[1] Refundable advance fees expected to be returned to current residents based on the terms of the existing contracts should be estimated and reported as a liability. The residual portion of the advancement should be reported as deferred revenue and recognized as revenue based on the lesser of the estimated remaining lives of residents or contract term. Portions of advance fees that are refundable only on death or withdrawal, and only on the condition that a new entrance fee is received for the same unit, should be accounted for as deferred revenue and amortized over the useful life of the facility. Nonrefundable advance fees should be recognized as revenue over the estimated lives of residents or the term of the contract, whichever is shorter.

Costs of Acquiring Initial Continuing Care Contracts

The costs incurred to acquire initial continuing care contracts should be capitalized and amortized over the average expected remaining lives of residents or the contract term, whichever is shorter. The capitalized costs should include only those costs incurred through the date of substantial occupancy, but in no case should costs incurred one year after the date that construction of the facility was completed be capitalized.

Property and Equipment, Supplies, and Other Assets

Property and equipment and related depreciation should be accounted for and reported in a manner similar to methods used by

---

[1] SOP 90-8 will be superseded by the new Health Care Guide.

a business enterprise. Not-for-profit organizations should follow FAS-93 (Recognition of Depreciation by Not-for-Profit Organizations), and depreciation and amortization of property and equipment should be recorded in conformity with GAAP.

Supplies and other assets should be accounted for and reported using generally accepted accounting principles for business enterprises.

Current and Long-Term Obligations

In general, standards applicable to the accounting and reporting of debt for other business enterprises are equally applicable to the preparation of financial statements for health care providers. However, because of the unique nature of health care providers, specialized accounting and reporting standards should be considered.

Some health care providers are involved in continuing care retirement contracts, in which health care is provided for life (or for a specified period of time) to a patient. The fee for providing this service may include an advance fee and/or a periodic fee. In addition, the advance fee may be fully or partially refundable. If the estimated future costs of providing continuing care is expected to exceed the advance fees and the periodic fees, a liability should be established for the difference. An entity that operates continuing care retirement communities should make the following financial statement disclosures:

- A description of the continuing care retirement contract and the nature of related contracts
- The statutory escrow or similar requirement
- Refund policies for refundable fees
- Interest rate used to discount the liability to provide future services

Generally, health care facilities owned by state and local governments and other not-for-profit health care entities are not subject to the provisions of the Internal Revenue Code. If the health care entity is involved in unrelated business activities, those activities may be subject to income taxation. If the entity is subject to unrelated business income tax, the accounting system should be appropriately designed to measure such activities, including the allocation of indirect costs. To determine whether a health care facility must make a provision for income taxes, the relevant sections of the Internal Revenue Code should be consulted.

Due to the tax-exempt status of governmental entities, funds may be borrowed at one interest rate and invested at a higher rate. Under the Internal Revenue Code, a governmental health care provider must determine whether it is subject to arbitrage rebate payments and therefore should reflect a liability in its financial statements.

Commitments and Contingencies

A health care provider may encounter a variety of commitments and contingencies. Some of these commitments and contingencies, such as lease arrangements, purchase commitments, and pension plans, are accounted for in the same manner used by a business enterprise. Other commitments and contingencies are unique to the health care industry, and accounting guidance is provided in the Health Care Guide.[2] In general, commitments and contingencies should be accounted for and reported in the financial statements based on the standards established by FAS-5.

Uninsured asserted and unasserted malpractice claims should be accrued when it is *probable* that a liability has arisen and a reasonable estimate of the claims can be made. Asserted claims and unasserted claims based on reported incidents should be evaluated on an individual basis or on a group basis using relevant industry experience. The accrual for unpaid claims should be classified as either a current or a noncurrent liability on the basis of the expected date of payment. If a reasonable estimate of losses arising from malpractice claims cannot be made, disclosures consistent with those established by FAS-5 should be made in the financial statements. Also, the entity should describe its medical malpractice insurance coverage and the basis for any accrual made under the coverage. Finally, if the accrual for malpractice claims is computed on a discounted basis, the amount of claims discounted and the interest rate(s) used in the discounting should be disclosed.

A health care provider is responsible for claims that are not reported to the insurance company during the term of a *claims-made* policy. The health care provider should evaluate the probability of making payments under a claims-made policy and accrue any estimated payments to satisfy the requirements established by FAS-5.

---

[2] SOP 89-5 will be superseded by the new Health Care Guide.

Health care providers may obtain insurance coverage that is retrospective, in that the total insurance premium is based on payments made under the policy. The health care provider should use the standards established by FAS-5 to determine whether an amount in excess of the minimum insurance premium should be recognized as a loss contingency; however, the amount of the total expense (premium plus the accrual) should not exceed the maximum insurance premium payable under the contract. If the retrospective insurance coverage is based on the experience of a group of health care providers, the initial premium should be amortized over the life of the contract and a provision should be made for an additional premium or a refund based on the experience of the group.

A health care provider may obtain medical malpractice coverage through a captive insurance company. Standards established by FAS-94 (Consolidation of All Majority-Owned Subsidiaries) should be followed to determine whether the financial statements of the captive insurance company should be consolidated with the financial statements of the health care provider. When the ownership percentage in the multiprovider captive insurance company is 50% or less, standards established by APB Opinion No. 18 should be observed. If a health care provider is insured through an unconsolidated multiprovider captive insurance company under a retrospective policy, claims should be accounted for in a manner similar to the approach described earlier for an entity that has a retrospective insurance policy directly with an unrelated insurance company. Likewise, if a health care provider is insured through an unconsolidated multiprovider captive insurance company under a retrospective policy based on the experience of a group of health care entities, claims should be accounted for in a manner similar to the approach described earlier for an entity that has a retrospective insurance policy (based on the experience of the group) directly with an unrelated insurance company.

Generally, a trust fund established to account for malpractice claims should be included in the financial statements of the health care provider. Assets of the trust fund equal to the amount expected to be used to pay claims should be classified as a current asset. Under the following conditions it may be impossible to include a trust fund in the health care provider's financial statements:

- The trust fund exists for a group of health care providers.
- The trust fund is administered as a common municipality risk-financing internal service fund.
- Legal, regulatory or indenture restrictions prohibit the inclusion of the trust fund's financial statements.

If the trust fund cannot be included in the financial statements of the health care provider, the degree of risk assumed by the health care provider determines how malpractice claims should be reported. If the health care provider does not transfer the risk to the trust fund, claims should be evaluated on the basis of the standards established by FAS-5. If the risk has been transferred to the trust fund, the accounting for malpractice claims is based on the type (such as claims-made or retrospectively rated) of insurance coverage obtained.

Obligation Related to Future Services for Continuing Care Retirement Communities

For continuing care retirement communities, if the estimated cost of providing future services to current residents exceeds anticipated revenues from those residents, a liability should be recognized. The estimated cost of the future services should include the present value of net cash outflows, depreciation of facilities related to the contracts, and the unamortized costs of acquiring the related continuing care contracts (if greater than unamortized deferred revenue).

Revenue, Expenses, Gains, and Losses

In general, revenue should be recorded when the health service is provided to the patient or resident. Patient service revenue includes various fees arising from services such as room, board, nursing, radiology, and physicians' care. Residential service revenue includes fees related to maintenance or rental fees and amortization of advanced fees. Other revenues, gains, or losses include revenues arising from providing other services to patients and residents (such as TV rentals) and sales and services to nonpatients (such as revenues from cafeteria operations and educational programs).

Not-for-profit health care organizations should refer to FAS-116 (Accounting for Contributions Received and Contributions Made) for guidance on recording contributions and support received.

Expenses should be recognized in a manner similar to recognition methods used by business enterprises. Not-for-profit organizations report expenses as decreases in unrestricted net assets.

FAS-116 requires that, generally, contributions received should be recorded as revenues or gains in the period they are received and should be measured at fair value. However, when services are contributed they should be recorded at fair value only if one of the following conditions is satisfied:

- The contributed service creates or enhances nonfinancial assets.

- The contributed service requires a specialized skill and the person who contributes the service possesses the required skill.

The fair value of contributed services should be reported in the financial statements, and the nature of those services should be described. Contributed services that do not meet one of the above conditions should not be recorded, but if practical, the fair value of the (unrecorded) contributed services should be disclosed in the financial statements.

Reporting Entity and Related Organizations

Health care providers may have a direct or indirect relationship with various separate organizations such as foundations and auxiliaries. Standards established by FAS-94, APB Opinion No. 18, and Accounting Research Bulletin (ARB) No. 51 (Consolidated Financial Statements) should be used to determine how, if at all, the activities of these separate organizations should be reflected in the financial statements of a health care provider.

If the criteria established in ARB-51 and FAS-94 are satisfied, the financial statements of the separate organizations should be consolidated or combined with the health care provider's financial statements. If the criteria established in ARB-51 and FAS-94 are not satisfied, but the health care provider controls and is the sole beneficiary of the separate organization's activities, the following information should be disclosed in the health care provider's financial statements:

- Summaries of the assets, liabilities, results of operations, and changes in fund balances of the separate organization

- Description of the relationship between the health care provider and the separate organization

If the financial statements of the separate organization are not consolidated or combined with the statements of the health care provider, or the disclosures described above are not made but the separate organization holds material amounts of assets that have been designated for the benefit of the health care provider, the existence and the nature of the relationship between the two entities should be disclosed.

Finally, if there have been material transactions between the health care provider and a separate organization (irrespective of how the relationship between the two parties is presented in the provider's financial statements), the following disclosures should be made:

- Description of the transactions, their amounts, and other information that may provide insight into understanding the effect of the transactions on the provider's financial statements

- Dollar values of transactions and the effects of any changes in the terms of the transactions when compared to the previous period

- Amounts due from and due to the separate organization and the terms and manner of settlement of those amounts

In addition to adequately disclosing relationships and transactions with separate organizations, the financial statements should disclose the nature and effect of transactions with other related parties (such as medical staff and management) in accordance with FAS-57 (Related Party Disclosures).

SPECIALIZED INDUSTRY PROCEDURES

As in all audits, an adequate understanding of the internal control structure of a health care provider must be obtained to satisfy the second standard of fieldwork. A summary of internal control policies and procedures unique to the health care industry is provided below.

Investments

Internal control procedures for investments generally are similar to those of other organizations. Additional procedures should be in place to assure marketable securities are fairly stated, properly classified, described, and disclosed.

Receivables

Internal control procedures should be designed to ensure that charges are generated automatically when services are performed and that cash receipts from patients and third-party payers are properly recorded. Receipts and settlements from third-party payers should be reviewed and recalculated to determine if they are consistent with reimbursement and rate-setting methods applicable to the health care provider and are properly reported.

Appropriate procedures should be employed to make a reasonable estimate of allowances for uncollectibles, contractual adjustments and other adjustments, and the identification of writeoffs of receivables on a timely basis.

Property and Equipment, Supplies, and Other Assets

The internal control structure should include procedures that enable the health care provider to identify donated property and equipment, and to value the donations at market value. In addition, some health care providers should establish procedures to regularly monitor compliance with health care planning agencies related to additions to property and equipment.

Current and Long-Term Obligations

Internal control procedures should be designed to ensure that providers monitor compliance with restrictive debt covenants. The health care provider should establish internal control procedures to stay abreast of tax regulations that relate to its tax status and the evaluation of activities that may have an effect on its tax status.

Commitments and Contingencies

A health care provider should design a risk management system that identifies and monitors malpractice incidents on a timely basis. Appropriate expertise (internal, external, or both) should be used to evaluate malpractice claims to satisfy generally accepted accounting principles. In addition, insurance coverage should be reviewed periodically to determine whether coverage is adequate and appropriate and whether insurance providers are financially sound.

Revenue, Expenses, Gains, and Losses

Internal control procedures should enable the health care provider to accurately and promptly bill for services rendered. Appropriate documentation, verification of billed rates, and review of reports for internal consistency should be part of the internal control procedures. In addition, proper cutoff procedures should be employed to determine that revenue has been recognized in the period in which the service was performed, and that related contractual and other adjustments and estimates of bad debts are recognized in the appropriate period.

Internal control procedures should be designed to properly classify operating expenses and to record them in the appropriate period.

Reporting Entity and Related Organizations

The health care provider should adopt internal control procedures so that relationships with other related organizations are evaluated to determine how those relationships should be reflected in the financial statements. In addition, related party transactions should be approved by the governing board of the health care provider, and adequate documentation and records should be maintained to adequately disclose such transactions in the financial statements.

SPECIALIZED AUDIT PROCEDURES

The Health Care Guide contains certain audit procedures that specifically apply to health care providers. Common audit procedures not necessarily covered in the Health Care Guide are generally applicable to health care provider engagements. These latter audit procedures are applied to health care providers in the same manner as they are to any other organization. The following summarizes specialized audit procedures identified in the Health Care Guide.

Investments

Audit procedures such as the following should be used to substantiate the existence and valuation of investments:

- Verify existence through confirmation.
- Test the valuation of securities not intended to be held to maturity by comparing recorded values with fair market values.

If a health care provider has investment pools, substantive procedures include reviewing financial statements for proper disclosure of pooled investments.

Receivables

To test financial statement assertions related to the existence of receivables, procedures such as the following are suggested by the Health Care Guide:

- Review and test subsequent receipts.
- Compare billing data to medical records.
- Trace receipts to patient accounts and to accounts receivable records.
- Review peer review organization and insurance company reviews of receivables.
- Review policies established for charitable cases for reasonableness and test the application of policies to specific accounts.

In addition to the procedures described above, the auditor should consider confirming receivable balances; however, patients often may be unsure of the amount they owe or third-party payers will not confirm specific amounts due. If the auditor believes that it is impracticable to confirm receivables, alternative procedures such as the following may be used to determine the existence of receivables:

- Perform analytical procedures on subsequent receipts.
- Review third-party contracts.
- Compare billings to documentation in medical records.
- Review the results of third-party payer audits and peer review reports.
- Confirm interim payments with third-party payers.

To test the valuation assertions related to receivables, audit procedures similar to the following may be performed:

- Review and test the method used to determine the allowance for uncollectibles.
- Substantiate that receivables are properly classified as self-payment or third-party payer.
- Test Medicare logs for accuracy and completeness.
- Test aged trial balance and evaluate factors used to determine allowance provision.
- Review pledges and receivables for collectibility.
- Substantiate that accounts were billed at the proper rate according to diagnosis-related group (DRG) classification.
- Confirm third-party payer rates and test rates for propriety.

The Health Care Guide identifies the following as procedures that could be used to test estimated third-party settlements:

- Substantiate arrangements with third-party payers through confirmation or review of correspondence.
- Test cost reimbursements reports and other settlement reports to establish consistency with agreements.
- Review audit reports of third-party payers from previous years to determine whether adjustments were properly reported in the financial statements and to identify current situations that might lead to adjustments applicable to the current financial statements.
- Obtain representation from management concerning provisions for estimated retroactive adjustments by third-party payers.
- Review financial statements for proper description of tentative nature of third-party settlement amounts.

Property and Equipment, Supplies, and Other Assets

Specialized auditing procedures that may be used to substantiate the accounting for property and equipment include the following:

- Review documentation that supports valuation of the fair market value of donated property and equipment.

- Determine that property held for nonoperating purposes is reported separately.

- Review documentation that justifies the acquisition of property and equipment that is subject to purchase authorization by health care planning agencies.

- Review a summary of property and equipment.

Current and Long-Term Obligations

For tax-exempt debt, review the debt instruments for presence of any restrictive debt covenants and test compliance. The tax status and tax obligation, if any, arising from the operations of the health care provider may be tested using the following procedures:

- Determine if the not-for-profit entity has obtained tax-exempt status.

- Determine if a tax report has been filed on a timely basis.

- Review prior-year tax returns.

- Read minutes for evidence of unrelated business income activities.

- Recalculate any income tax arising from unrelated business activities.

- Review financial statements for proper disclosure of tax-exempt status of the health care provider.

Commitments and Contingencies

The insurance coverage of a health care provider should be carefully evaluated to determine to what degree the risk of loss has been transferred to an insurance provider. Once the nature of risk transferal and the details of insurance coverage are understood, the auditor should evaluate the financial viability of the insurance provider. Other procedures identified in the Health Care Guide that should be considered by the auditor include the following:

- Test the accuracy and completeness of the incident reporting and monitoring system.

- Send letters of inquiry to insurance providers and legal counsel as required by SAS-12 (Inquiry of a Client's Lawyer Concerning Litigation, Claims, and Assessments).

- Review and test the method used to estimate incidents incurred but not reported.

- Review prior estimates and historical loss experience.

- Determine whether additional premiums based on retrospectively rated policies are reported as a liability.

- Determine whether uncertainties related to malpractice claims are disclosed in the auditor's report.

- Review the financial statements to determine the propriety of disclosures related to malpractice insurance.

Revenue, Expenses, Gains, and Losses

Revenues from providing patient services or resident services may be tested by using audit procedures such as the following:

- Perform a walk-through of the system.

- Apply analytical procedures to revenues budgeted, earned during the current period, and earned during the previous period.

- Substantiate the accuracy of revenue earned on the basis of DRG assignments.

- Determine that revenues are reported net of contractual adjustments and other adjustments and are computed in accordance with appropriate contracts and established policies.

- Test contractural adjustments and bad debts.

- Test third-party payments by comparing prior-year estimates with prior-year settlements.

Expenses of a health care provider may be substantiated by comparing current expenses with prior-period and/or budget and obtain explanations for large or unusual variances.

Related Organizations

To determine whether the reporting entity is properly defined for the health care provider, the following procedures should be considered:

- Identify related parties through review of articles of incorporation, shareholder lists, and other documents.

- Obtain written representation from management that all investees, affiliates, and related entities have been properly accounted for and reflected in the financial statements.

- Review transactions with related entities and parties to determine whether they have been properly accounted for and disclosed.

To audit the treatment of related party transactions, procedures such as the following should be performed:

- Review the documentation for related party transactions and evaluate their economic substance.

- Determine whether related party transactions are recorded consistently with their economic substance.

- Evaluate the collectibility of receivables and advances arising from related party transactions.

- Determine whether significant related party transactions have been identified by referring to previous transactions and relationships, minutes of directors' and other meetings, unusual transactions, discussions with client personnel, and responses to conflict-of-interest questionnaires.

- Determine that related party transactions and related balances are properly presented in the financial statements.

> **OBSERVATION:** *Health care providers that receive federal funds may be subject to auditing standards and procedures established by* **Government Auditing Standards** *(the Yellow Book) and standards established by the Office of Management and Budget. Audit guidance for these circumstances are discussed in SOP 92-9 (Audits of Not-for-Profit Organizations Receiving Federal Awards).*

Reports

Standards established by SAS-58 (Reports on Audited Financial Statements) should be observed in preparing the auditor's report on the financial statements of health care providers. If a health care provider is required to prepare financial statements in accordance with a comprehensive basis of accounting other than generally accepted accounting principles, the standards established by SAS-62 (Special Reports) should be followed.

Receipt of Federal Awards by Not-for-Profit Organizations

Not-for-profit organizations that receive federal awards may be subject to regulations established by Office of Management and Budget (OMB) Circular A-133 (Audits of Institutions of Higher Education and Other Nonprofit Institutions). In 1992, the AICPA issued SOP 92-9 (Audits of Not-for-Profit Organizations Receiving Federal Awards) in order to provide guidance to auditors who are engaged to perform audits in accordance with regulations established by the OMB. Although SOP 92-9 does not establish new audit guidance, it does compile relevant guidance established by a variety of promulgations, including SAS-68 (Compliance Auditing Applicable to Governmental Entities and Other Recipients of Governmental Financial Assistance), OMB Circular A-133, and SOP 92-7 (Audits of State and Local Governmental Entities Receiving Federal Financial Assistance).

SOP 92-9 describes an auditor's general responsibility in an audit of federal awards and specifically addresses the following:

- Describes the applicability of OMB Circular A-133
- Summarizes the differences between Circular A-133 and OMB Circular A-128 (Audits of State and Local Governments)
- Describes the auditor's responsibility for considering the internal control and for performing tests of compliance with certain laws and regulations
- Describes the auditor's responsibility for reporting and provides examples of the reports required by Circular A-133

AUDITS OF NOT-FOR-PROFIT ORGANIZATIONS

CONTENTS

Overview	**22.03**
Specialized Accounting Practices	**22.03**
Accrual Basis and Fund Accounting	**22.04**
Financial Statements	**22.04**
Reporting Related Entities	**22.06**
Contributions and Other Revenues	**22.08**
Investments	**22.09**
Annuity and Life Income Funds	**22.10**
Expense Classification and Other Accounting Issues	**22.11**
Specialized Industry Practices	**22.12**
Expenses	**22.13**
Fund-Raising Costs	**22.13**
Revenue	**22.14**
Service Fees	**22.14**
Sales of Products	**22.14**
Investment Transactions	**22.14**
Third-Party Reimbursements	**22.14**
Support and Capital Additions	**22.15**
Cash Contributions	**22.15**
Donated or Contributed Services	**22.15**
Securities and Nonmonetary Items	**22.16**
Future Interests and Interest-Free Loans	**22.16**
Net Assets	**22.16**
Financial Statements	**22.16**
Specialized Audit Procedures	**22.17**
Expenses	**22.17**

Revenue	22.18
Support and Capital Additions	22.19
Contributions and Grants	22.19
Donated or Contributed Services	22.19
Securities and Nonmonetary Items	22.19
Future Interests and Interest-Free Loans	22.20
Assets	22.20
Liabilities	22.21
Net Assets	22.21
Affiliated Organizations	22.22
Reports	22.22
Special Reports	22.22
Basis Other than GAAP	22.22
Component Financial Statements	22.23
Special-Purpose Financial Presentation	22.24
Receipt of Federal Awards by Not-for-Profit Organizations	22.25

AUDITS OF
NOT-FOR-PROFIT ORGANIZATIONS

Overview

Since 1981, the AICPA has issued Audit and Accounting Guides that provide guidance for engagements involving the following specific kinds of not-for-profit entities: colleges and universities, voluntary health and welfare organizations, and other not-for-profit organizations not covered by these other Guides. In June 1993, the Financial Accounting Standards Board (FASB) issued Statement No. 117 (Financial Statements of Not-for-Profit Organizations) (FAS-117). This Statement is effective for annual financial statements issued for fiscal years beginning after December 15, 1994, except for organizations with less than $5 million in total assets and less than $1 million in annual expenses. For these organizations, FAS-117 is effective for fiscal years beginning after December 15, 1995. Earlier application is encouraged. The accounting guidance presented in this chapter reflects FAS-117.

> **OBSERVATION:** *The AICPA has issued an Exposure Draft of an Audit and Accounting Guide that will cover not-for-profit organizations, including colleges and universities and voluntary health and welfare organizations. This Audit and Accounting Guide will standardize some of the diverse accounting practices now used by the various types of not-for-profit organizations.*

SPECIALIZED ACCOUNTING PRACTICES

Financial information prepared for internal use may be reported in any manner that management or the governing board of an institution deems appropriate under the circumstances. Not-for-profit organizations may still use fund accounting for their internal records, even though fund accounting will not be used for financial reporting. Financial statements prepared for persons outside the management or the governing board of the not-for-profit organization must comply with the provisions of FAS-117.

Accrual Basis and Fund Accounting

The actual books and records of a not-for-profit organization need not necessarily be kept on the accrual basis of accounting. However, financial statements that purport to be in conformity with generally accepted accounting principles (GAAP) must be prepared and reported on the accrual basis. In other words, to be in conformity with GAAP, financial statements for not-for-profit organizations generally should be presented on the accrual basis, but the underlying books need not be kept on the accrual basis.

Cash-basis financial statements ordinarily should be considered special-purpose reports and reported on as such by the independent auditor. However, if cash-basis financial statements are not materially different than the same statements would be if they were presented on the accrual basis, the independent auditor may conclude that they are presented in conformity with GAAP.

Financial Statements

The basic financial statements for a not-for-profit organization should include a statement of financial position, a statement of activities, a statement of cash flows, and all necessary related footnotes. In addition, voluntary health and welfare organizations (and other not-for-profit organizations that choose to) present a statement of functional expenses.

The statement of financial position should reflect the assets, liabilities, and net assets of the not-for-profit organization. Information about the liquidity of a not-for-profit organization should be provided by one or more of the following: (1) sequencing assets in the statement of position according to the nearness of their conversion to cash and sequencing liabilities according to the nearness of their maturity and resulting use of cash; (2) classifying assets and liabilities in the statement of position as current or noncurrent; and/or (3) disclosing in the footnotes relevant information about maturity.

The statement of financial position reports the amounts for each of three classes of net assets—permanently restricted net assets, temporarily restricted net assets, and unrestricted net assets. FAS-117 defines these classifications as follows:

Permanently Restricted Net Assets—The part of the net assets of a not-for-profit organization resulting (a) from contributions and other inflows of assets whose use by the organization is limited by donor-imposed stipulations that neither expire by passage of time nor can be fulfilled or otherwise removed by actions of the organization, (b) from other asset enhancements and diminishments subject to the same kinds of stipulations, and (c) from reclassifications from (or to) other classes of net assets as a consequence of donor-imposed stipulations.

Temporarily Restricted Net Assets—The part of the net assets of a not-for-profit organization resulting (a) from contributions and other inflows of assets whose use by the organization is limited by donor-imposed stipulations that either expire by passage of time or can be fulfilled and removed by actions of the organization pursuant to those stipulations, (b) from other asset enhancements and diminishments subject to the same kinds of stipulations, and (c) from reclassifications to (or from) other classes of net assets as a consequence of donor-imposed stipulations, their expiration by passage of time, or their fulfillment and removal by actions of the organization pursuant to those stipulations.

Unrestricted Net Assets—The part of net assets of a not-for-profit organization that is neither permanently restricted nor temporarily restricted by donor-imposed stipulations.

The statement of activities reports the amount of change in permanently restricted net assets, temporarily restricted net assets, and unrestricted net assets.

Information about revenues, expenses, and gains and losses, as well as reclassifications, is provided by aggregating items that possess similar characteristics into reasonably homogenous groups. Revenues and expenses should be reported at their gross amounts rather than their net amounts. Further classification of revenues, expenses, and gains and losses into categories such as operating and nonoperating, recurring and nonrecurring, or expendable and nonexpendable is permitted.

The statement of activities (or notes to the financial statements) should provide information about expenses reported by their functional classification, such as major classes of program services and supporting activities. Voluntary health and welfare organizations are required to continue reporting functional expense information and information about expenses in their natural classifications, such as salaries, rent, utilities, depreciation, etc., in a matrix format in a separate financial statement, or in another reasonable presentation. FAS-117 encourages, but does not require, not-for-profit organizations other than voluntary health and welfare organizations to provide information about expenses in their natural classifications.

The statement of cash flows summarizes all the financing and investing activities of the not-for-profit organization and reflects the amount of cash generated from or used in operations for the period. (Originally, not-for-profit organizations were specifically excluded from the statement of cash flows standard, which was set forth in FAS-95 [Statement of Cash Flows]. FAS-117 removed this exclusion.)

Comparative financial statements for not-for-profit organizations are desirable, but are not required by FAS-117.

The concept of fund accounting for financial reporting purposes has been eliminated by FAS-117. However, not-for-profit organizations may continue to use the fund accounting concept in their own internal accounting records if they so desire. The requirements of FAS-117 apply to nongovernmental colleges and universities, which eliminates many of the financial reporting differences between nongovernmental colleges and universities and other not-for-profit organizations. Governmental colleges and universities should not adopt FAS-117. The Governmental Accounting Standards Board (GASB) is in the process of revising the reporting model for governmental colleges and universities.

Reporting Related Entities

In September 1994, the AICPA issued Statement of Position (SOP) 94-3 (Reporting of Related Entities by Not-for-Profit Organizations). This SOP is effective for financial statements issued for fiscal years beginning after December 15, 1994, except for not-for-profit organizations that have less than $5 million in total assets and less than $1 million in annual expenses. For those organizations, the effective date is for fiscal years beginning after December 15, 1995. Earlier application is permitted (and encouraged when FAS-117 has been implemented early).

SOP 94-3 addresses the reporting for a not-for-profit organization's investments in for-profit entities and in financially related not-for-profit organizations. SOP 94-3 provides the following guidance:

Investment in For-Profit Entities

- A reporting not-for-profit organization should consolidate a for-profit entity in which it has a controlling financial interest through direct or indirect ownership of a majority voting interest if the guidance in Accounting Research Bulletin (ARB) No. 51 (Consolidated Financial Statements), as amended by FAS-94 (Consolidation of All Majority-Owned Subsidiaries), requires consolidation.

- A reporting not-for-profit organization should use the equity method in conformity with Accounting Principles Board (APB) Opinion No. 18 (The Equity Method of Accounting for Investments in Common Stock) to report investments in common stock of a for-profit entity if the guidance in the opinion requires the use of the equity method.

- Not-for-profit organizations that choose to report investment portfolios at market value in conformity with the current AICPA Audit Guides may do so instead of reporting those investments by the equity method, which otherwise would be required by SOP 94-3.

Financially Interrelated Not-for-Profit Organizations

- A not-for-profit organization should consolidate another not-for-profit organization in which it has a controlling financial interest through direct or indirect ownership of a majority voting interest, unless control is likely to be temporary or does not rest with the majority owner.

- A not-for-profit organization should consolidate another not-for-profit organization if the reporting not-for profit organization has both control of the other not-for-profit organization, as evidenced by either majority ownership or a majority voting interest in the board of the other not-for-profit organization, and an economic interest in the other not-for-profit organization, unless control is likely to be temporary or does not rest with the majority owner.

- A not-for-profit organization may exercise control of another not-for-profit organization in which it has an economic interest by means other than majority ownership or a majority voting interest in the board of the other not-for-profit organization. In such circumstances, the not-for-profit organization is permitted, but not required, to consolidate the other not-for-profit organization, unless control is likely to be temporary.

- If either (but not both) control or an economic interest exists, the financial statement disclosures required by FAS-57 (Related Party Disclosures) should be made.

Loosely affiliated local entities need not be combined with a parent or national entity whose resources are substantially collected and expended in the local area. However, local affiliates and affiliates of entities that do not meet the criteria for combined financial statements should be fully disclosed in the separate financial statements of all affiliated entities.

Contributions and Other Revenues

Before the issuance of FAS-117, the statement of activities for not-for-profit organizations was sometimes called the "statement of support, revenue, expenses, capital additions, and changes in fund balances."

Revenues for a not-for-profit entity may come from dues, services, grants, tuition and fees, ticket sales, or investment income. However, revenues usually do not produce enough funds to cover operating costs. Not-for-profit organizations also usually seek support from individuals, corporations, foundations, governmental units, and others. Thus, support funds are different from revenues and should be appropriately segregated in the statement of activities. Revenue and support funds may be permanently or temporarily restricted or unrestricted depending on the donor and the nature of the restrictions, if any, imposed, or because of any legal restrictions.

FAS-116 (Accounting for Contributions Received and Contributions Made) requires that contributions received generally be measured at fair value and recorded as revenues or gains in the period they are received. Contributions received must be classified as those that increase permanently or temporarily restricted assets or unrestricted assets. When services are contributed they should be recorded at fair value only if one of the following conditions is satisfied:

1. The contributed service creates or enhances nonfinancial assets.

2. The contributed service requires a specialized skill and the person who contributes the service possesses that skill.

The fair value of contributed services should be reported in the financial statements and the nature of those services should be described. Contributed services that do not meet one of the above conditions should not be recorded, but if practical, the fair value of the (unrecorded) contributed services should be disclosed in the financial statements.

Investments

In November 1995 the FASB issued FAS-124 (Accounting for Certain Investments Held by Not-for-Profit Organizations), which eliminated some of the financial accounting and reporting inconsistencies established by AICPA Guides and Statements of Position. FAS-124 applies to all investments in equity securities that have a "readily determinable fair value" and to all investments in debt securities; however, it does not apply to investments accounted for under the equity method or to investments in consolidated subsidiaries.

FAS-124 requires that investments in marketable equity securities and investments in debt securities be reported at fair value on a not-for-profit organization's statement of financial position. In addition, FAS-117 (Financial Statements of Not-for-Profit Organizations) requires that gains and losses related to these investments be reported in the organization's statement of activities as increases or decreases in unrestricted net assets, unless the changes are temporarily or permanently restricted. Investment income should be reported as increases in unrestricted net assets unless its use is limited by restrictions imposed by donors, in which case the income should be reported as an increase to either temporarily restricted net assets or permanently restricted net assets, depending on the nature of the restriction.

Gains and investment income that are subject to donor-imposed restrictions may be reported as increases in unrestricted net assets if the donor-imposed restrictions are satisfied during the same period in which the gain or investment income is recorded and if a similar policy applies to the reporting of contributions received by the organization.

Gains and losses that are related to donor-restricted contributions and must be invested in perpetuity or invested for a specified period of time should be reported as changes in unrestricted net assets, with one exception: If the gains or losses related to the donor-restricted assets are temporarily or permanently restricted explicitly by the donor or by a law that specifically extends the restriction to the gains or losses, such gains or losses should be reported as changes in restricted assets. On the other hand, FAS-124 points out that "if a donor allows the organization to choose suitable investments, the gains are not permanently restricted unless the donor or the law requires that an amount be retained permanently."

Annuity and Life Income Funds

As a general rule, an annuity issued by a college or university is controlled by a regulatory agency. An annuity usually is an agreement whereby the educational institution receives certain resources and agrees to pay a stipulated amount periodically to one or more beneficiaries. The resources (assets) are either income producing or invested to produce income. The income produced is then used to make the periodic payments to the beneficiaries. At a specified time, the periodic payments cease and the resources become the property of the institution.

Although *Audits of Colleges and Universities* describes two different methods for accounting for and reporting annuity funds, only one is considered acceptable for the purposes of GAAP. The acceptable method is called the *actuarial method.* Under this method, the actuarial value of the periodic payments that must be made to the beneficiaries is determined and recorded as a liability. The opening journal entry for an annuity fund under the actuarial method is as follows:

Resources (Assets)	XX,XXX	
Annuity Payable		X,XXX
Net Assets		XX,XXX

The annuity payable is a liability account that is reduced for each periodic payment made. However, the annuity payable account must be recomputed periodically and adjusted for actuarial gains or losses, particularly those caused by changes in the life expectancy of the beneficiaries.

The valuation methods for reporting investments held in annuity funds are the same as those for other investments, including endowments.

The other method for accounting and reporting annuity funds appears in a manual entitled *College and University Business Administration* (1974) published by the National Association of College and University Business Officers. This method does not provide for a liability in the amount of the present value of the annuity payable and is not considered acceptable for the purposes of GAAP.

Life income and annuity agreements are quite similar. Under each type of agreement, the institution receives resources (assets), the institution makes periodic payments to designated beneficiaries, and after the last periodic payment is made, the resources are transferred to the institution in accordance with the stipulations contained in the agreement. The difference between the two types of agreements is the periodic payment. In an annuity agreement, the amount of periodic payment may be whatever is agreed upon; in a life income agreement, the periodic payment consists only of the income actually earned on the resources.

Many colleges and universities maintain *pooled life income funds,* which must be carefully planned and executed to ensure a tax-exempt status.

The valuation methods for reporting investments held in life income funds are the same as those for other investments.

At the termination of the life income agreement, the periodic payments of income cease and the resources become the property of the institution.

Expense Classification and Other Accounting Issues

The costs of providing services or activities should be reported by functional classification in the statement of activities or footnotes to the financial statements. This information should include a break-down of these expenses by major classes of program services and supporting activities. Voluntary health and welfare organizations should report functional classification information and information about expenses by natural classifications, such as salaries, rent, utilities, etc.

Not-for-profit entities should record purchased fixed assets at cost and donated fixed assets at fair value at the date of receipt. In addition, the amount of any assets pledged as collateral and the basis for their valuation should be disclosed in the financial statements.

FAS-93 (Recognition of Depreciation by Not-for-Profit Organizations) requires the recognition of depreciation expense for not-for-profit organizations, except in the case of certain individual works of art or historical treasures.

Depreciation expense should be systematic and rational and should allocate the cost of a fixed asset over its estimated useful life. The amount of depreciation expense for historical cost assets and other than historical cost assets should be separately disclosed in the financial statements.

Assets that are not exhaustible and structures used primarily as houses of worship need not be depreciated.

Not-for-profit organizations do not need to recognize contributions of works of art, historical treasures, and similar assets if the donated items are added to collections that meet the following criteria (set forth in FAS-116):

- The collections are held for public exhibition, education, or research, in futherance of public service rather than financial gain.
- The collections are protected and kept unencumbered.
- The collections are subject to an organizational policy that requires the proceeds from sales of collection items to be used to acquire items for the collection.

FAS-116 encourages entities either to capitalize retroactively collections acquired in previous periods (at their cost or fair value at the date of acquisition, current cost, or current market value, whichever is deemed more practical) or to capitalize collections on a prospective basis.

SPECIALIZED INDUSTRY PRACTICES

Generally accepted auditing standards are applicable to a not-for-profit organization engagement. Therefore, the engagement must include an evaluation of the client's internal control structure. The purpose of the evaluation of the system of internal controls is the same for a not-for-profit organization engagement as it is for a commercial engagement. However, a not-for-profit organization's internal control structure may be weakened because of (1) a volunteer governing board, (2) a small or inexperienced staff, (3) a mixture of volunteers and organizational employees responsible for the conduct of the organization's affairs, and (4) a budget approved by the governing board, which serves as the primary instrument of authorization and the focus of a significant degree of attention in contrast to the financial statements. All these factors may affect the degree to which the auditor will rely on the client's internal control structure.

> **OBSERVATION:** *For a comprehensive discussion of the consideration of internal control structure, please refer to* **Part I: Audited Financial Statements.** *Not-for-profit engagements must meet all the professional standards discussed in* **Audited Financial Statements.** *For example, SAS-60 (Communication of Internal Control Structure Related Matters Noted in an Audit) requires the auditor to inform the client of the existence of reportable conditions. Thus, if conditions that weaken the internal control structure exist, the auditor is obligated to inform "senior management and the governing board or its audit committee" that reportable conditions exist.*

Expenses

The auditor should evaluate the not-for-profit organization's internal controls over expenses to determine whether the expenses are incurred consistent with management's authorization. All expenses should be properly supported, classified, and recorded in the appropriate accounting period. Because of the significance of payroll costs for many not-for-profit organizations, the auditor should pay particular attention to the payroll accounting system. Expense control features for a not-for-profit organization are similar to those that should be used by a commercial enterprise. Some specific control features are summarized below:

- A well-defined organizational chart
- Comparison of actual expenses to budgeted amounts and an investigation of significant variances
- Approval of disbursements
- Review of the distribution of expenses

Expenses may include grants made by the not-for-profit organization to other organizations. Grant payments should be approved, processed, and reviewed in a manner similar to that used for the payment of any other expense.

> *OBSERVATION:* The auditor should be aware of any federal award programs in order to determine whether an audit in accordance with Office of Management and Budget Circular A-133 (Audits of Institutions of Higher Education and Other Not-Profit Organizations) is required.

Fund-raising costs   A difficult allocation problem arises when fund-raising activities are conducted jointly with other activities. The allocation of joint costs for fund raising and informational materials and activities was addressed in SOP 87-2 (Accounting for Joint Costs of Informational Materials and Activities for Not-for-Profit Organizations That Include a Fund-Raising Appeal).

SOP 87-2 establishes the basic standard that, unless it can be otherwise demonstrated, all joint costs of informational materials and services that include a fund-raising appeal should be reported as fund-raising expense. When it can be demonstrated that a program or management and general expense has been incurred, the joint costs should be allocated among fund-raising expense, program expense, and management and general expense.

> **OBSERVATION:** *The AICPA is considering revisions to the guidance established by SOP 87-2.*

Revenue

The following four sources of revenue may be found in a not-for-profit organization.

Service fees   Revenue from service fees includes tuition, membership dues, and admission fees. Internal control features include the use of budget estimates as a basis for variance analysis; controls and accountability over used and unused tickets; segregation of the cash receipts function and the membership, enrollment, or admission activities; and controls over onetime fees such as membership fees.

Sales of products   A not-for-profit organization may sell books, magazines, souvenirs, and other items. Internal control procedures in this area should be similar to procedures used by commercial enterprises and should include inventory control procedures.

Investment transactions   Revenue may be received on a recurring basis and may include rents, royalties, dividends, and interest. Moreover, investments may be sold at a gain or loss, or the fair value of investments may change, resulting in unrealized gains or losses. The not-for-profit organization should adopt internal control procedures to reasonably assure that investments and related transactions are properly recorded and reported in accordance with generally accepted accounting principles.

Third-party reimbursements   Certain costs for some not-for-profit organizations may be reimbursed by a third party. Basically, the auditor should determine whether amounts due from third parties have been properly accrued. The following internal controls apply to third-party reimbursements:

- Regular review of third-party reimbursement agreements to determine if the terms are consistent with services rendered

- Timely preparation of reimbursement reports
- Adequate procedures to ensure that reimbursable costs are billed and collected from the third party

Support and Capital Additions

In addition to revenue, a not-for-profit organization may receive nonreciprocal resources, referred to as *support*. Capital additions also may be received for endowment, plant, or loan purposes. Support and capital additions may be acquired through direct solicitation, special events, grants or allotments by federated fund-raising associations, or the contributions may be unsolicited. All these contributions may give rise to the receipt of cash. Gifts, grants, or bequests also may be in the form of cash, services, securities and other nonmonetary items, and future interests or interest-free loans.

Cash contributions Adequate internal controls over cash receipts include the adoption of procedures used for incoming mail for a profit-oriented organization. Third-party control mechanisms also may be employed, such as the use of an outside depository agency that receives the contributions to the organization through the mail and allows for subsequent testing to determine if the receipts were recorded. When direct-solicitation campaigns are employed, the following procedures should be used:

- Solicitors should be properly supervised.
- Solicitation materials and identifications should be controlled and given only to authorized solicitors.
- As quickly as practical, control totals and cash reports should be established over collections. Copies of reports should be sent to the organization's accounting department.
- The number of people who have access to cash and the amount each person has under his or her control should be kept to a minimum.

Donated or contributed services Services contributed to an organization should be recorded simultaneously as support and as an expense. The audit objective is to determine whether the transaction has been properly recorded and valued in accordance with FAS-116. The not-for-profit organization should establish policies identifying the services that should be recorded. Work performed should be documented and approved by an appropriate official. Methods used to value services should be reviewed and approved.

Securities and nonmonetary items   A not-for-profit organization may receive securities, materials, facilities, and other nonmonetary items. There should be a separation of duties between those responsible for reviewing and those responsible for recording the items. Procedures should include the physical inspection of items donated. In addition, methods used to value items received should be reviewed and approved by the governing board.

Future interests and interest-free loans   Internal control features should include procedures necessary to adequately identify gifts in the form of future interests and interest-free loans. Restrictions and other characteristics of the gifts should be adequately documented. To ensure the proper recording of income earned from the gifts, control procedures also should be adopted.

Net Assets

The net assets of a not-for-profit organization are similar to the stockholders' equity section of a corporation. Net assets should be classified into three amounts—permanently restricted net assets, temporarily restricted net assets, and unrestricted net assets. The not-for-profit organization's internal controls should provide for the recording of permanent and temporary restrictions imposed by donors. There should be a periodic review to determine whether donor-imposed restrictions are being followed, as well as controls to ensure the proper transfer of assets and liabilities among classifications of net assets.

Financial Statements

FAS-117 requires that all not-for-profit organizations have a statement of financial position as of the end of the reporting period, a statement of activities, and a statement of cash flows for the reporting periods. In addition, FAS-117 requires voluntary health and welfare organizations (and encourages other not-for-profit organizations) to present a statement of functional expenses. FAS-117 also requires the financial statements to include the appropriate notes.

SPECIALIZED AUDIT PROCEDURES

During a not-for-profit engagement, sufficient competent evidential matter must be collected by the auditor to support an opinion on the not-for-profit organization's financial statements. Most of the audit procedures used in a commercial-client engagement are equally applicable to a not-for-profit client engagement. The unique applications of audit procedures for a not-for-profit client are summarized below.

Expenses

A not-for-profit organization may report its expenses on an object basis (natural classification, such as salaries expense) in addition to a functional basis (program classification). Voluntary health and welfare organizations are required to present information about expenses in their natural classifications in addition to their program classifications. When the expenses are reported on a functional basis, the following procedures should be used:

- Determine if the classification scheme adequately reflects the major activities of the not-for-profit organization.
- Determine the appropriateness of procedures used to allocate expenses to programs.
- Test the allocation of expenses to programs and determine if the allocation procedures are being consistently followed.
- Determine if classifications for the current accounting period are consistent with those used in the prior period.

If the expenditures include grants paid to another organization, the auditor should read the grant agreement and determine if the grant expenses were properly recorded. Other grant procedures, such as those used to determine the grantee's accountability and procedures for canceling grants and obtaining refunds, should be reviewed. Where appropriate, the documentation to support the tax status of the grantee should be reviewed.

Although a not-for-profit organization generally will be exempt from income taxes, it may have to collect and/or pay a variety of other taxes, for example, excise, payroll, and property taxes. In addition, it may be liable for taxes on its unrelated business income, if any. The auditor should identify which taxes must be paid by the not-for-profit organization. For those taxes for which the organization is exempt, the exemption status and related documentation should be reviewed. The results of recent examinations made by tax authorities, such as the IRS, should be reviewed. The auditor must determine whether the organization complies with the provisions of the appropriate sections of the Internal Revenue Code.

Revenue

As noted earlier, revenue for a not-for-profit organization usually is generated by four major sources. These sources and the related audit procedures listed in the AICPA Audit and Accounting Guide *Audits of Certain Nonprofit Organizations* are summarized below.

Source of Revenue	Audit Procedures
Service fees	Compare recorded revenue with independently prepared statistical reports (analytical review).
	If internal control is inadequate, select cash receipts transactions from a source independent of the accounting function and confirm receipts directly with member, patron, etc.
Sale of products	No special audit procedures suggested.
Investment transactions	No special audit procedures suggested.
Third-party reimbursements	Read significant third-party reimbursement agreements.
	Test reimbursement reports to determine if they were prepared in accordance with reimbursement contracts.
	Test the allocation of indirect costs to the programs administered by the not-for-profit organization for which costs will be reimbursed.
	Review status of audits conducted by or for a third party.

When the not-for-profit organization's funding depends significantly on third-party agreements, the auditor should determine whether the financial statements disclose the nature of the reimbursement arrangements.

Support and Capital Additions

Audit procedures for support and capital additions are summarized below.

Contributions and grants Audit procedures should be employed to determine that all contributions have been properly recorded in accordance with FAS-116. The following procedures are suggested by *Audits of Certain Nonprofit Organizations*:

- If available, select names from an independently prepared list of donors, and through direct communication with the donor, confirm whether a contribution was made.
- Use information directly received from a donor or grantor to determine if the gift was appropriately recorded.
- Identify possible grantors or donors by referring to minutes of the meetings of the governing board. Determine whether this information is consistent with contribution receipts.
- For direct-contact solicitations, test cash receipts recapitulation schedules.
- Use substantive analytical procedures to test appropriateness of contributions by geographical locations, etc.
- Confirm amounts received (or receivable) from funding agencies and the remaining balance of grants or contracts.

Donated or contributed services The auditor should determine the reasonableness of the organization's policies with respect to recording donated or contributed services. A list of donated services performed should be obtained. Documentation supporting the donated or contributed services should be reviewed. Valuations assigned to the services should be reviewed for reasonableness.

Securities and nonmonetary items The client should prepare a list of assets received during the accounting period. The existence of an item may be determined by physically inspecting the item or reviewing documentation to support the receipt of the item. Also, a confirmation may be sent directly to the donor. The auditor may elect to use a specialist to determine the value of an asset donated to the not-for-profit organization. If securities are involved, the auditor may confirm the valuation by referring to recent security quotations.

Future interests and interest-free loans   Initially, the auditor should read the agreement that was the basis of the gift and determine whether governmental regulations are being observed with respect to the gift. Payments made to beneficiaries should be tested to determine if the payments are consistent with the terms of the agreement. The auditor should consider confirming payments directly with the beneficiary. For interest-free loans, the auditor should determine that imputed interest has been properly calculated and recorded.

Assets

A not-for-profit organization may have unique assets, such as restricted resources, investment pools, grants and pledges receivable, and collections of art and similar items. Audit procedures applicable to the assets are summarized below.

Asset	Audit Procedures
Restricted resources	Read the appropriate grantor agreement (consider obtaining the advice of a lawyer).
	Determine if the organization has complied with the restrictions imposed by the agreement.
	Determine if the resources are properly classified in the financial statements.
Investment pools	Determine if appropriate controls exist over the allocation of participating funds.
	Test the allocation computations.
	Determine if proper controls exist over investment selection, transactions, and valuations.

Asset	Audit Procedures
Grants and pledges receivable	Determine if the grants and pledges receivable are properly reflected in the financial statements.
	Apply appropriate procedures to ascertain the existence of the receivable, including the mailing of confirmations.
	Evaluate the allowance for uncollectible items.
Collections of art and similar items	Evaluate procedures for recording accessions and de-accessions.
	Determine if the valuation is appropriate and is properly reflected in the financial statements.
	Evaluate procedures for physically controlling the collection.
	Consider observing any collections recorded in the financial statements.

Liabilities

A not-for-profit organization may have unique liabilities, such as tax-deferred annuities. Under Internal Revenue Code Section 501(c)(3), a not-for-profit organization may adopt employee tax-deferred annuity plans. The auditor should determine if the plan is in compliance with the Employee Retirement Income Security Act of 1974. The auditor also should review the client's calculations and read the actuary's report.

Net Assets

The auditor should determine whether net assets are properly classified in the financial statements as permanently restricted net assets, temporarily restricted net assets, and unrestricted net assets and whether adequate disclosures are provided in the notes to the financial statements.

Affiliated Organizations

The auditor should determine whether the not-for-profit entity is affiliated with other organizations. If affiliation does exist, the auditor must determine whether it is necessary to combine the financial statements of the affiliate in order to report in accordance with generally accepted accounting principles. When the auditor concludes that combined financial statements are not required, he or she should determine whether notes to the financial statements adequately describe the affiliations.

Reports

Reporting standards established by Statements on Auditing Standards should be followed when preparing an auditor's report on the financial statements of a not-for-profit organization. The guidance of SAS-58 (Reports on Audited Financial Statements) applies to auditors' reports on the financial statements of not-for-profit organizations.

It may be necessary to modify the auditor's report. For example, the scope of the audit may be restricted, which could result in the issuance of a qualified opinion on the not-for-profit organization's financial statements. Other circumstances that may lead to a modification of the auditor's report are discussed and illustrated elsewhere in this book.

Special Reports

A not-for-profit organization engagement may require the auditor to issue a special report on the entity's financial statements. Special reporting circumstances may arise under the following conditions:

- Financial statements are prepared in accordance with a comprehensive basis of accounting other than generally accepted accounting principles.
- Financial statements are for a component of a not-for-profit organization.
- Special-purpose financial presentations are prepared.

Basis other than GAAP Guidance for the preparation of special reports on financial statements has been established by SAS-62 (Special Reports). One category of special reports discussed in SAS-62 is concerned with a comprehensive set of accounting rules other than generally accepted accounting principles. The statement specifically lists the following as examples of comprehensive bases:

- Accounting rules established by a governmental regulatory agency to which the client is required to report
- Tax rules used or expected to be used by the client in the preparation of its income tax returns (not applicable to most not-for-profit organizations)
- The cash method or the modified cash method that has substantial support
- A definite set of accounting rules applicable to all material items on the financial statements and that has substantial support

When an auditor expresses an opinion on a not-for-profit organization's financial statements prepared in accordance with one of the four comprehensive bases of accounting described above, a four-paragraph report should be prepared. The introductory and scope paragraphs are similar to the standard report paragraphs. The special reporting criteria are described in the third paragraph by explaining the basis of presentation. A note to the financial statements should describe the differences between the special criteria and GAAP, although the monetary difference need not be disclosed. The third paragraph explicitly refers to the note. Finally, the report must state that the financial statements are not intended to be presented in accordance with GAAP.

The auditor should state, in the opinion paragraph, that the financial statements are presented in accordance with the special accounting criteria. If the auditor concludes that the financial statements are not prepared in accordance with the comprehensive basis of accounting other than GAAP, a qualified or adverse opinion should be issued and the deviation should be described in the explanatory paragraph.

> **OBSERVATION:** *For a more detailed discussion on auditor's reports, see the chapters entitled "Auditor's Reports" and "Auditor's Special Reports."*

Component financial statements   If the net assets and activities of a not-for-profit organization can be clearly distinguished, an auditor can report on the financial statements of a component of the organization. A branch, operation, or fund could qualify as a component.

The component's financial statements should clearly describe what component(s) of the not-for-profit organization is (are) included. If the auditor has not audited the not-for-profit organization, he or she should follow the following procedures:

- Ensure that transactions related to the component unit are not duplicated in the records of other parts of the organization.
- Review transactions with other components.
- Test the allocation of common costs among components.
- Obtain from the not-for-profit organization a written representation that all material transactions or other matters have been properly disclosed.

Presented below is an example of an auditor's report on the financial statements of a component unit of a not-for-profit organization.

We have audited the accompanying statement of financial position of the Washington Branch Office of the XYZ Trade Association as of June 30, 19X5, and the related statements of activities and cash flows for the year then ended. These financial statements are the responsibility of the Association's management. Our responsibility is to express an opinion on these financial statements based on our audit.

We conducted our audit in accordance with generally accepted auditing standards. Those standards require that we plan and perform the audit to obtain reasonable assurance about whether the financial statements are free of material misstatement. An audit includes examining, on a test basis, evidence supporting the amounts and disclosures in the financial statements. An audit also includes assessing the accounting principles used and significant estimates made by management, as well as evaluating the overall financial statement presentation. We believe that our audit provides a reasonable basis for our opinion.

In our opinion, the financial statements referred to above present fairly, in all material respects, the financial position of the Washington Branch Office of XYZ Trade Association as of June 30, 19X5, and the changes in its net assets and its cash flows for the year then ended in conformity with generally accepted accounting principles.

Special-purpose financial presentation   An auditor may be engaged to express an opinion on a special-purpose financial presentation, for example, the statement of allowable expenses of an individual grant. For such an engagement, materiality is determined by referring to the financial presentation as a whole. The auditor's report on the financial presentation should:

- State whether the financial information conforms with generally accepted accounting principles.
- Clearly state what the financial presentation is intended to represent.

The auditor also should determine whether the title of the financial presentation is appropriate.

Presented below is an example of an auditor's report on a special-purpose financial presentation.

We have audited the accompanying statement of grant revenues and allowable expenses of the XYZ Not-for-Profit Organization for the year ended March 31, 19X5, pursuant to grant no. 78743, described in Note X, between XYZ Not-for-Profit Organization and Grantor, dated January 1, 19X4. The financial statement is the responsibility of the Organization's management. Our responsibility is to express an opinion on the financial statement based on our audit.

We conducted our audit in accordance with generally accepted auditing standards. Those standards require that we plan and perform the audit to obtain reasonable assurance about whether the financial statement is free of material misstatement. An audit includes examining, on a test basis, evidence supporting the amounts and disclosures in the financial statement. An audit also includes assessing the accounting principles used and significant estimates made by management, as well as evaluating the overall financial statement presentation. We believe that our audit provides a reasonable basis for our opinion.

In our opinion, the financial statement referred to above presents fairly, in all material respects, the grant revenues and allowable expenses of XYZ Not-for-Profit Organization for the year ended March 31, 19X5, pursuant to the grant referred to above in conformity with generally accepted accounting principles.

Receipt of Federal Awards by Not-for-Profit Organizations

Not-for-profit organizations that receive federal awards may be subject to regulations established by Office of Management and Budget

(OMB) Circular A-133 (Audits of Institutions of Higher Education and Other Nonprofit Institutions). In 1992, the AICPA issued SOP 92-9 (Audits of Not-for-Profit Organizations Receiving Federal Awards) in order to provide guidance to auditors who are engaged to perform audits in accordance with regulations established by the OMB. Although SOP 92-9 does not establish new audit guidance, it does compile relevant guidance established by a variety of promulgations, including SAS-68 (Compliance Auditing Applicable to Governmental Entities and Other Recipients of Governmental Financial Assistance), OMB Circular A-133, and SOP 92-7 (Audits of State and Local Governmental Entities Receiving Federal Financial Assistance).

SOP 92-9 describes an auditor's general responsibility in an audit of federal awards and specifically addresses the following:

- Describes the applicability of OMB Circular A-133
- Summarizes the differences between Circular A-133 and OMB Circular A-128 (Audits of State and Local Governments)
- Describes the auditor's responsibility for considering the internal control and for performing tests of compliance with certain laws and regulations
- Describes the auditor's responsibility for reporting and provides examples of the reports required by Circular A-133

AUDITS OF STATE AND LOCAL GOVERNMENTAL UNITS

Contents

Overview	23.03
Background	23.04
General Fund	23.05
Special Revenue Fund	23.05
Debt Service Fund	23.06
Capital Projects Fund	23.06
Agency Fund	23.06
Trust Fund	23.06
Pension Trust Fund	23.07
Internal Service Fund	23.07
Enterprise Fund	23.07
General Fixed Assets Account Group	23.08
General Long-Term Debt Account Group	23.08
Reporting Entity	23.08
Scope of Audit	23.09
Specialized Accounting Practices	23.09
Exhibit I: Public-Sector Accounting Hierarchy	23.11
Basis of Accounting and Measurement Focus	23.13
Revenues	23.14
Capital Expenditures	23.14
Expenditures	23.15
Encumbrances	23.15
Debt	23.15
Proprietary Funds and Nonexpendable Trust Funds	23.16
Specialized Auditing Practices	23.16
Planning the Engagement	23.16
Understanding the Scope of the Engagement	23.16
Consideration of Internal Control	23.17
The Budget	23.18
Errors, Irregularities, and Illegal Acts	23.19

Compliance   23.19
   Audits of Governmental Entities   23.19
   Audits of Entities That Receive Governmental
      Support   23.21
   Tests of Controls   23.22
   Tests of Controls with Laws and Regulations   23.22
   Substantive Tests   23.22
Specialized Audit Procedures   23.23
   Cash and Investments   23.23
   Receivables and Related Transactions   23.25
   Expenditures and Related Liabilities   23.27
   Capital Expenditures   23.27
   Debt and Debt Service   23.28
   Interfund Transactions   23.29
   Fund Balances   23.29
   Proprietary Fund Types   23.30
   Fiduciary Funds   23.30
   State Governments   23.31
      Defining the Reporting Entity   23.31
      Revenue Sharing   23.31
      Lotteries   23.31
      Medicaid   23.31
      Income Taxes   23.32
      Independence   23.32
      Joint Audits   23.32
      Aid to Local Governments   23.32
      Pass-Through Grant Programs   23.32
      Escheat Property   23.33
   Concluding the Audit   23.33
      Letter of Audit Inquiry   23.33
      Management Representation Letter   23.33
      Related Party Transactions   23.34
      Going-Concern Consideration   23.34
   Reports   23.35
      Standard Report   23.35
      Audit Report Modifications   23.39
   Special Reports   23.40
   Additional Reports That May Be Required   23.40
Receipt of Federal Awards by Not-for-Profit Organizations   23.41

AUDITS OF STATE AND LOCAL GOVERNMENTAL UNITS

Overview

Guidance for the audit of governmental units was first established with the issuance of *Audits of State and Local Governmental Units* (hereinafter referred to as the Governmental Audit Guide) in 1974. The Governmental Audit Guide has been revised several times, most recently in 1994. The 1974 and 1978 editions of the Governmental Audit Guide provided authoritative support for governmental accounting principles as well as governmental auditing procedures.

The 1994 edition of the Governmental Audit Guide was the first guide reviewed by the Governmental Accounting Standards Board (GASB) in accordance with the accounting hierarchy established under Statement on Auditing Standards (SAS) No. 69 (The Meaning of "Present Fairly in Conformity with Generally Accepted Accounting Principles" in the Independent Auditor's Report) and GASB Statement No. 20 (Accounting and Financial Reporting for Proprietary Funds and Other Governmental Entities That Use Proprietary Fund Accounting). All accounting principles contained in the Guide are in conformance with GASB pronouncements or cover areas GASB has not yet addressed.

The 1994 Guide also incorporates and supersedes the previous AICPA Statement of Position (SOP) 92-7 (Audits of State and Local Governmental Entities Receiving Federal Financial Assistance).

In July 1995, the AICPA modified its 1994 Guide to incorporate the 1994 revision of *Government Auditing Standards*. The new Guide is now amended as "with conforming changes as of May 1, 1995."

> *OBSERVATION: This chapter discusses the audit of a state or local governmental entity's financial statements using generally accepted auditing standards. Governmental financial statements also may be audited using generally accepted governmental auditing standards developed by the General Accounting Office (GAO). The latter standards are codified in the GAO's **Government Auditing***

> *Standards,* commonly referred to as the *"Yellow Book."* In addi-
> tion, state and local governmental auditing agencies may establish
> auditing standards or procedures that must be followed in the audit
> of a governmental entity under its jurisdiction.

Background

It is estimated that there are more than 80,000 governmental units in
the United States. Governmental units are usually organized by the
citizens of a locality to provide certain services to the general public.
Although profit is the goal of most commercial enterprises, governmental units are not usually organized to make a profit. Instead,
governmental units are established to operate a government for the
benefit of the citizens of a particular area. The operation of a government is controlled and regulated by legal provisions in statutes,
charters, appropriations, administrative regulations, and constitu-
tions. Therefore, the revenues and expenditures of a governmental
unit are usually authorized in some manner. Public officials become
stewards of public funds and must account for the revenues and
expenditures in accordance with the underlying authorizations or
legal provisions that created the revenue and authorized the expenditures. Therefore, the principal purpose of financial statements for
governmental units is to report on the stewardship of the public
officials with respect to their handling of public funds.

Governmental units provide services to the citizens of a particular
community. The services provided may (1) produce no profit, (2)
produce enough profit to break even, or (3) occasionally produce a
profit in the same manner as a commercial enterprise. Recurring
operations geared to providing services without producing any profit
include fire and police protection, sanitary services, education, welfare, and other similar services. These types of services are controlled by a legal budget, and fund accounting is used to account for
the budgeted funds.

Governmental operations that break even or produce a profit are
accounted for in the same manner as a commercial enterprise. Thus,
these governmental operations generally are accounted for by the
accrual method of accounting. Examples of these types of governmental operations are motor pools, central purchasing, airport and
other transportation authorities, utilities, and other similar operations.

Private enterprises receive their resources in exchange for other
resources, obligations to repay, or the rights of ownership. Governmental units, in contrast, frequently receive their resources in

exchange for obligations to expend or care for these resources for specified purposes. To account for the resources received (revenues) and their restrictions and use for appropriate purposes, the government uses the concept of *fund accounting*. A fund is a separate and distinct accounting entity pertaining to a specific activity, purpose, or objective. In fund accounting, the fund balance account is similar in concept to stockholders' equity accounts on the balance sheet of a commercial enterprise in that the fund balance represents the difference between the assets and the liabilities of the fund. When a governmental unit undertakes activities in a self-supporting manner similar to a commercial enterprise—for example, a water utility—the fund for these activities is accounted for on the same basis as a commercial enterprise.

The financial activities of a governmental unit are controlled by laws that dictate how revenues will be raised and the manner in which they should be disbursed. Each activity of a governmental unit should have a separate fund for accountability. Very simply, *a fund is accounted for separately and has its own complete set of books, including subsidiary ledgers.* Usually, a fund is established by a legal requirement or an executive order; abolition of a fund must come from the same or a higher source of authority.

The beginning of a fund is a budget that, when adopted by the appropriate legal body, gives sanction to the proposed expenditures and indicates the sources of estimated revenue. The budget then becomes the basis for opening the accounts in the fund, and, in effect, the budget is incorporated into the fund accounting system. The estimates of revenue or authorized appropriations are reflected in the fund accounts and are called *budgetary accounts.* The actual results of transactions that occur in the fund accounts are called *proprietary accounts.* Commitments made against authorized appropriations are called *encumbrances. Subsidiary ledgers* are used to record the detail of budgetary accounts, encumbrances, and other general ledger accounts that require supporting detail.

In addition to funds, a governmental unit uses two account groups: the general fixed assets account group and the general long-term debt account group. The following is a review of the funds and account groups generally used in governmental accounting.

General fund   A general fund accounts for all transactions not required to be included in any other fund. It accounts for the general activities of government.

Special revenue fund   The special revenue fund is used to account for revenues that are legally restricted for specific purposes and are required to be accounted for in a special revenue fund. Revenue sources that are not required to be accounted for in a special revenue fund may be accounted for in the general fund.

Debt service fund   The debt service fund accounts for the cash accumulated for the purpose of paying interest and principal on long-term debt. The cash needed by the debt service fund is usually obtained by transfers from other funds, particularly the general fund. Budgetary accounts are used in the debt service fund, and the modified accrual basis of accounting is used. It is important to remember that under the modified accrual basis, interest on long-term debt is recorded only when the interest is due. No accruals for interest are made.

Capital projects fund   The capital projects fund accounts for capital projects other than those accounted for by the enterprise fund. The revenue from either appropriations or the sale of bonds and the disbursements of cash for the construction of capital projects are accounted for in this fund.

> **OBSERVATION:** *Special assessment transactions were addressed in GASB-6 (Accounting and Financial Reporting for Special Assessments). Before the issuance of GASB-6, special assessment transactions were accounted for in special assessment funds. GASB-6 prohibits the use of special assessment funds for financial reporting purposes. Special assessment transactions must be recorded in the remaining four governmental funds (general fund, special revenue funds, capital projects funds, and debt service funds) or in enterprise funds.*

Agency fund   An agency fund is used primarily as a clearing account for the collection of cash that is subsequently (usually a short period of time) disbursed to the authorized recipient, which may be another fund or some individual or firm outside of the government. Sometimes an agency fund will charge a collection fee that is deducted from the amount subsequently disbursed.

Trust fund   A trust fund usually is more complex and has a longer period of existence than an agency fund. Gifts of public appropriations are put in a trust fund for a specific purpose, and may be either expendable or nonexpendable. An expendable trust fund is one in which both principal and income may be expended. A nonexpendable trust fund usually has a restriction on expending the principal or income or, in some cases, both. Obviously, in a nonexpendable trust fund, it is important to segregate the principal (corpus) from the income.

Pension trust fund Pension trust funds must be established for single-employer or multiple-agent-employer pension plans in which the employer has a fiduciary responsibility for the assets, benefits, and disbursements of the plan. In November 1994, the GASB issued three Statements that directly affect pension trust funds:

- Statement 25 (Financial Reporting for Defined Benefit Pension Plans and Note Disclosures for Defined Contribution Plans)
- Statement 26 (Financial Reporting for Postemployment Health Care Plans Administered by Defined Benefit Pension Plans)
- Statement 27 (Accounting for Pensions by State and Local Governmental Employers)

Internal service fund Internal service funds are established to account for internal services provided by various departments in a government for use by other departments, other governments, or not-for-profit organizations. Usually, the objective of an internal service fund is to break even, and sometimes the general fund will cover any losses and receive any profits. Some of the activities accounted for in internal service funds are central garages, printing facilities, motor pools, heating plants, and central governmental purchasing. This type of fund generally is established by a nonrepayable appropriation from the general fund, a sale of bonds, or a repayable advance from the general fund. Internal service funds are intended to be self-supporting, and a balance sheet, statement of operations, and analysis of changes in retained earnings are prepared on an accrual basis. Also, it is preferable to classify the balance sheet into current assets and current liabilities. Fixed assets that will be replaced by the fund are depreciated. Budgetary accounts are optional, since conventional accounting principles are used and it is not necessary to make disbursements through the process of appropriations and encumbrances.

The government should prepare, on a regular basis, a full set of financial statements for its internal service funds.

Enterprise fund Enterprise funds are used to account for services provided to the public. These funds usually are established for utility plants (electric, water, sewer, etc.), airports, public transportation, hospitals, golf courses, and a multitude of other services a local government can perform for the public.

Enterprise funds must be accounted for in the same manner as a privately owned commercial business and must use, whenever possible, those accounting and reporting principles recommended for private businesses.

A separate enterprise fund should be set up for each activity, although similar activities may be accounted for in one fund. Charges to governmental units must be made on the same basis as those to the general public. Fixed assets and long-term debt of an enterprise fund are not reported in the governmental unit account groups, but rather are presented on the balance sheet of the enterprise fund.

A full set of financial statements should be prepared on a regular basis for an enterprise fund.

General fixed assets account group   Long-lived assets that are not accounted for in a specific fund are recorded and accounted for in the general fixed assets account group. Generally, such assets are recorded at cost and are not depreciated.

General long-term debt account group   The general long-term debt account group is similar to the general fixed assets account group, except that it accounts for all long-term debt that is not recorded in any other fund.

In fund accounting, an entry made in one fund frequently will affect one or more other funds, necessitating journal entries to the affected funds. For example, when an internal service fund bills a government department for its services, the billed department must record the charges in its own fund accounts. If the general fund makes an advance to an enterprise fund, the enterprise fund also must record the advance. Frequently, interfund transactions do not involve cash, as is the case in the general fixed assets account group and general long-term debt account group, which never record cash. Regardless, the journal entry on the other fund affected must be recorded.

Reporting Entity

While the activities of a governmental unit are accounted for in various funds, the scope of the governmental "financial reporting entity" may be much broader than the accountability established by an individual fund. To provide guidance about which funds, public authorities, agencies, and other operating public units should be included in the financial statements of the governmental reporting entity, the GASB issued GASB-14 (The Financial Reporting Entity). According to GASB-14, the financial reporting entity should be built around the concept of financial accountability. If a primary government is financially accountable for another entity, that entity's financial statements should be included in the financial statements for the reporting entity. Based on the guidance provided in GASB-14, a governmental financial reporting entity consists of the following:

- The primary government
- Organizations for which the primary government is financially accountable
- Other organizations that, because of the nature and significance of their relationship with the primary government, may not be excluded from the financial reporting entity

For the most part, the financial information of component units should not be blended with similar financial information of the primary government. Instead, component unit information should be presented in a discrete column in the combined financial statements of the financial reporting entity. The discrete presentation method is used to distinguish the financial position and operations of the primary government from those of its component units. The blending method may be used only when the component unit's activities are so interrelated with those of the primary government that it is simply an extension of the latter.

Scope of Audit

The purpose of the Governmental Audit Guide is to provide guidance for an audit of a state or local government performed to determine whether (1) financial statements are presented in accordance with generally accepted accounting principles and (2) applicable compliance provisions that have a direct and material effect on the financial statements.

SPECIALIZED ACCOUNTING PRACTICES

After considerable debate, the GASB was created in 1984 to establish accounting and reporting standards for state and local governments.

In 1992, SAS-69 established the public-sector accounting hierarchy. The hierarchy is presented in Exhibit I.

The hierarchy has five levels and each level is subordinate to the level(s) directly above it. For example, if an accounting issue is addressed both in Level B and Level C, the guidance established in Level B must be followed since it is the highest source of accounting principles for the particular accounting issue.

Shortly after its inception, the GASB issued GASB-1 (Authoritative Status of NCGA Pronouncements and AICPA Industry Audit Guide), which identified the following pronouncements as constituting generally accepted accounting principles for state and local governments:

- NCGA-1 (Governmental Accounting and Financial Reporting Principles)

- NCGA-2 (Grant, Entitlement, and Shared Revenue Accounting by State and Local Governments)*

- NCGA-3 (Defining the Governmental Reporting Entity)

- NCGA-4 (Accounting and Financial Reporting Principles for Claims and Judgments and Compensated Absences)

- NCGA-5 (Accounting and Financial Reporting Principles for Lease Agreements of State and Local Governments)

- NCGA-6 (Pension Accounting and Financial Reporting: Public Employee Retirement Systems and State and Local Government Employers)

- NCGA-7 (Financial Reporting for Component Units within the Governmental Reporting Entity)*

- NCGA Interpretation No. 2 (Segment Information for Enterprise Funds)

- NCGA Interpretation No. 3 (Revenue Recognition—Property Taxes)

- NCGA Interpretation No. 5 (Authoritative Status of Governmental Accounting, Auditing, and Financial Reporting)

---

* Subsequently superseded by GASB promulgations.

EXHIBIT I
PUBLIC-SECTOR ACCOUNTING HIERARCHY

Authoritative GAAP

Level A
- GASB Statements
- GASB Interpretations
- FASB pronouncements made applicable by a GASB Statement or GASB Interpretation
- AICPA pronouncements made applicable by a GASB Statement or GASB Interpretation

Level B
- GASB Technical Bulletins
- AICPA Industry Audit and Accounting Guides made applicable by the AICPA
- AICPA Statements of Position made applicable by the AICPA

Level C
- AICPA Practice Bulletins made applicable by the AICPA
- GASB Emerging Issues Task Force consensus positions (if created)

Level D
- GASB Implementation Guides (Qs and As)
- Practices widely recognized and prevalent in state and local governments

Other Accounting Literature

- GASB Concepts Statements
- Sources identified in Levels A through D in the private-sector accounting hierarchy that have *not* been made applicable by the action of the GASB
- APB Statements
- FASB Concepts Statements
- AICPA Issues Papers
- International Accounting Standards of the International Accounting Standards Committee
- Pronouncements of other professional associations or regulatory agencies
- AICPA Technical Practice Aids
- Accounting textbooks
- Handbooks
- Articles

- NCGA Interpretation No. 6 (Notes to the Financial Statements Disclosure)

- NCGA Interpretation No. 7 (Clarification as to the Application of the Criteria in NCGA Statement 3, "Defining the Governmental Reporting Entity")*

- NCGA Interpretation No. 8 (Certain Pension Matters)

- NCGA Interpretation No. 9 (Certain Fund Classifications and Balance Sheet Accounts)

- NCGA Interpretation No. 10 (State and Local Government Budgetary Reporting)

- NCGA Interpretation No. 11 (Claim and Judgment Transactions for Governmental Funds)

- Industry Audit Guide entitled *Audits of State and Local Governmental Units* (1974 edition only)

- SOP 75-3 (Accrual of Revenues and Expenditures by State and Local Governmental Units)

- SOP 77-2 (Accounting for Interfund Transfers of State and Local Governmental Units)

- SOP 78-7 (Financial Accounting and Reporting by Hospitals)

- SOP 80-2 (Accounting and Financial Reporting by Governmental Units)

The GASB may establish generally accepted accounting principles for state and local governments by issuing GASB Statements and GASB Interpretations. Statements address major governmental accounting issues, whereas Interpretations are concerned with more narrow issues. Both types of pronouncements follow a due process and are voted on by members of the GASB. In addition, the GASB staff may issue GASB Technical Bulletins. Technical Bulletins follow a somewhat abbreviated due process, and they are not directly voted on by members of the GASB. Generally, Technical Bulletins are issued under the following circumstances:

---

* Subsequently superseded by GASB promulgations.

- The guidance is not expected to cause a major change in accounting practice for a significant number of entities.

- The administrative cost involved in implementing the guidance is not expected to be significant to most affected entities.

- The guidance does not conflict with a broad fundamental principle or create a novel accounting practice.

Each Technical Bulletin is published with a legend that reads, "The GASB has reviewed this Technical Bulletin and a majority of its members do not object to its issuance."

A detailed discussion of governmental generally accepted accounting principles can be found in the *Miller Governmental GAAP Guide*.

Basis of accounting and measurement focus Generally accepted accounting principles for state and local governments are significantly influenced by the basis of accounting and measurement focus adopted for the governmental accounting model.

An entity's accounting basis determines when transactions and economic events are reflected in its financial statements. Generally, accounting transactions and events may be recorded on a cash basis, an accrual basis, or a modified accrual basis. For example, goods may be purchased on one date, consumed on another date, and paid for on still a third date. The accounting basis determines when the economic consequences of transactions and events are reflected in financial statements. The modified accrual basis is used to account for the transactions of a governmental unit.

The second critical element in the establishment of generally accepted accounting principles is the selection of a measurement focus. The measurement focus identifies what transactions and events should be recorded and is concerned with the inflow and outflow of resources that affect an entity. The balance sheet should reflect those resources that are available to meet current obligations and to be used in the delivery of goods and services in subsequent periods. The activity statement for the period should summarize those resources received and those consumed during the current period. Although there are a number of measurement focuses, governmental accounting is concerned with the flow of current financial resources.

The flow of current financial resources applied on a modified accrual basis is a narrow interpretation of what constitutes assets and liabilities of a fund. Revenues, and the resulting assets, are accrued at the end of the year only if the revenues are earned and the receivables are expected to be collected in time to pay for liabilities in existence at the end of the period. On the other hand, expenditures and the related liabilities are accrued when they are expected to be paid from revenues recognized during the current period.

Revenues For governmental funds, revenues should be accrued only when they are both measurable and available (modified accrual basis). *Measurable* means that the revenue is subject to reasonable estimation, and *available* means that the revenue must be realized in time to pay current expenditures of the governmental fund. Presented below is a summary of revenue recognition methods for various taxes and charges.

Revenue Source	Revenue Source Recognition Method
Property taxes	Subject to accrual if expected payments will be received within 60 days of the close of the fiscal year.
Taxpayer-assessed revenue (income taxes, sales taxes, gross receipts taxes, etc.)	Subject to accrual when the measurable and available criteria have been satisfied.
Grants	Recognized when qualifying expenditures are incurred.
Entitlements and shared revenues	Cash basis. However, accrual basis may be used when measurable and available criteria can be satisfied.
Miscellaneous revenues (fines, fees, etc.)	Cash basis.
Special assessments	Subject to accrual when special assessment installment becomes available (balance of special assessments is recorded as deferred revenue).

Capital expenditures Purchases or the construction of capital assets are recorded as expenditures in the governmental fund authorized to execute the capital transaction. The capital asset is not recorded as an asset of the governmental fund but rather is presented as part of the governmental unit's general fixed assets account group. Depreciation is not recognized in the governmental fund's activity statement; however, depreciation may be (but is not required to be) recognized in the account group by reducing both the carrying value of the capital asset and the investment source of the capital asset. There is no requirement to capitalize expenditures for infrastructure capital assets such as bridges, roads, and sewer systems.

Expenditures   NCGA-1 defines *expenditures* as reductions in net financial resources of a fund and concludes that most expenditures should be recorded when the related liability is incurred. An expenditure is recorded when the related liability is expected to be paid from current expendable financial resources. For example, a governmental unit may incur a loss contingency but if the actual payment of the liability is not expected to occur for several months or years, the liability would be recorded as part of the unit's general long-term debt account group rather than as part of a fund's (current) liabilities.

Encumbrances   Executory contracts that are outstanding at the end of the year represent commitments of the governmental fund, but they are not accounted for as current expenditures or outstanding liabilities. For example, a purchase order for goods may have been sent to a vendor, but as of the balance sheet date the goods have not been received. A liability does not exist until title to the goods passes, but the encumbrance system provides control over the executory contract and similar transactions.

Debt   The accounting for the proceeds of debt depends on whether the debt is short-term or long-term. For short-term debt, the governmental fund responsible for the debt records a liability since current financial resources will be used to service the debt. When the debt is long-term, the governmental fund records the proceeds as a financing source, which is reported on its activity statement. The long-term liability is recorded in the general long-term debt account group.

NCGA-1 emphasizes that general long-term debt includes more than liabilities created through a loan arrangement or agreement. Liabilities related to certain lease agreements, pension plans, compensated absences, and other liabilities that are long-term in nature must be included in the general long-term debt account group.

Interest on general obligation long-term debt is not accrued as an expenditure. The expenditure is recorded for the maturing principal and interest when they are due and payable. Although this approach employs a cash method rather than a modified accrual basis, it prevents an inconsistency between budgetary financial statements and historical financial statements prepared on a GAAP basis.

Proprietary funds and nonexpendable trust funds Generally accepted accounting principles applicable to commercial enterprises should be used by proprietary funds, pension trust funds, and nonexpendable trust funds.

SPECIALIZED AUDITING PRACTICES

Statements on Auditing Standards and their Interpretations should be followed in the examination of a governmental unit's financial statements. If a state or local government has adopted specific audit procedures, these procedures, in addition to the SAS and SAS Interpretations, should be observed. When the auditor is requested to audit financial statements or information related to federal programs, the auditor must be aware of specified audit objectives and procedures related to this type of examination.

The basic audit approach in the examination of a state or local government's financial statements is similar to an audit of the financial statements of a commercial enterprise. The major phases of the examination may be identified as (1) planning, (2) review of internal controls, (3) tests of controls, and (4) substantive tests.

Planning the Engagement

To execute a successful audit of a governmental entity, the auditor should plan the engagement using the guidance established by SAS-22 (Planning and Supervision). Some the elements of planning that are unique to the audit of a governmental entity are summarized below.

Understanding the scope of the engagement From a financial perspective, a governmental entity usually is composed of a variety of funds, component units, and other relationships that define the scope of the engagement. The auditor, in consultation with the client, should determine whether the scope of the engagement is narrow (perhaps the audit of an individual fund) or broad (perhaps the audit of the reporting entity as defined by GASB-14). In addition, the auditor and the client must determine whether the audit is to be performed in accordance only with GAAS, in accordance with GAAS *and* generally accepted government auditing standards, or in accordance with Office of Management and Budget (OMB) Circular A-128 (Audits of State and Local Governments). The Governmental Audit Guide notes that the following additional sources should be considered to determine whether specialized audit standards or procedures apply to component units of the governmental entity:

- *Audits of Providers of Health Care Services*
- *Audits of Colleges and Universities*
- *Audits of Certain Nonprofit Organizations*
- *Audits of Employee Benefit Plans*

The understanding of the scope of the engagement includes the clear determination of the roles of the principal auditor and other auditor, if any. In making that determination, the auditor should follow the guidance established by SAS-1, Section 543 (Part of Audit Performed by Other Independent Auditors).

Consideration of Internal Control

The auditor must observe the guidance established by SAS-55 (Consideration of the Internal Control Structure in a Financial Statement Audit) when performing a governmental audit in accordance with GAAS. The approach described in SAS-55 is discussed in the chapter entitled "Internal Control, Errors, and Irregularities" and is equally applicable to the financial statements audit of a state or local government. The Governmental Audit Guide concludes that the following factors, unique to a governmental environment, may have an effect on the auditor's assessment of control risk:

- There may be enhanced control over expenditures because of the budget and appropriations process used by governmental entities.
- There may be a level of control over the recognition of liabilities because of the use of an encumbrance system.
- There may be a higher level of control over personnel hirings and terminations because of strict governmental regulations and civil service constraints.

- There may be a greater degree of control over certain acquisitions because of detail procedures related to a governmental entity's procurement and contracting system.

- There may be additional scrutiny of control procedures because of the involvement of grantor agencies (other governmental entities that provide resources to the state or local governmental entity).

> *OBSERVATION: Additional audit procedures and reporting standards must be observed when an examination is being performed to satisfy governmental auditing standards (the Yellow Book) and when OMB Circular A-128 applies. The single audit is discussed in detail in **Miller's Single Audits**.*

The Budget

Generally, state and local governments adopt a (legal) budget for various funds, including the general fund and special revenue funds. The adoption of a budget provides a basis for the eventual authorization of expenditures. For this reason, the auditor should understand the budgetary process used by the governmental entity to determine whether the process has been completed in compliance with relevant laws and regulations.

In addition to providing the initial basis for the expenditure of funds (and the levying of taxes), the budgetary process is the basis for preparing the governmental financial statement entitled Combined Statement of Revenues, Expenditures, and Changes in Fund Balances—Budget and Actual. This financial statement is included in the scope of the auditor's report and therefore must be subjected to auditing procedures similar to the audit of any other required financial statement.

Once a budget is established, it will provide a basis for the required disclosures in the financial statements. That is, if expenditures exceed appropriations, that circumstance must be disclosed in the financial statements. The level of budgetary control (comparison of expenditures and appropriations) may occur at various levels in an entity, including the fund level, program function level (for example, public safety), department level (for example, maintenance department), character level (for example, capital outlays), or object level (for example, personnel costs). Thus, depending on the level of budgetary control established by the governmental entity, the auditor should adopt appropriate procedures to determine whether the government has complied with budgetary laws and regulations.

The budgetary process includes an encumbrances system in which commitments related to contracts not yet performed are used to control expenditures for the year and to enhance cash management. Encumbrance systems vary among governmental entities because of the differing budgetary laws and regulations. The auditor should obtain an understanding of the encumbrance system and use appropriate procedures to determine whether encumbrances are accounted for and appropriately reported in the entity's financial statements.

Errors, Irregularities, and Illegal Acts

Professional standards established in SAS-53 (The Auditor's Responsibility to Detect and Report Errors and Irregularities) and SAS-54 (Illegal Acts by Clients) are applicable to the audit of governmental entities. Essentially, an audit should be designed to discover errors, irregularities, and illegal acts that may arise from violations of laws and regulations, and that have a direct and material effect on the entity's financial statements. The assurance that such discoveries will be made by the auditor is not absolute but rather a *reasonable assurance*.

Compliance

Audits of governmental entities   As in every engagement, the auditor should consider all significant and relevant factors when planning and conducting an audit. Because of the nature of a governmental entity, an auditor should be aware of (1) laws and regulations that have a direct and material effect on the financial statements and (2) risk factors that are unique to a governmental reporting entity.

A governmental entity is subject to a variety of laws and regulations that are not applicable to a commercial enterprise. For example, financial reporting requirements that must be observed by a governmental entity may be established by a law or regulation. More specifically, some governmental entities are required to establish separate funds to account for activities specified by a statute.

SAS-74 (Compliance Auditing Considerations in Audits of Governmental Entities and Recipients of Governmental Financial Assistance) concludes that an auditor should obtain an understanding of laws and regulations that could have a *possible direct and material effect* on the financial statements. This requirement should be viewed in the context that the auditor is not a lawyer and that the management of the governmental entity is responsible for the preparation of the financial statements. Thus, the audit approach should include an assessment of management's identification of laws and regulations that may affect the financial statements. To achieve these audit objectives (understanding and assessment), the auditor may adopt the following procedures:

- Using prior-year audits, identify relevant laws and regulations.

- Discuss relevant laws and regulations with appropriate officials, including entity's legal counsel and chief financial officer.

- Obtain written representations that (1) management is responsible for complying with laws and regulations that may have a direct and material effect on the financial statements and (2) management has identified and disclosed to the auditors all such laws and regulations.

- Review the relevant portions of any directly related agreements, such as those related to grants and loans.

- Review minutes of the entity's legislative body to identify laws and regulations that may be of concern to the auditor.

- Contact relevant oversight units, such as the state auditor, to determine which laws and regulations (including statutes and uniform reporting requirements) apply to the reporting entity.

- Contact program administrators of governmental entities that provided grants to the reporting entity for identification of terms of grants.

- Review compliance requirements compiled by state societies of CPAs or associations of governments.

- Review information about compliance requirements, such as the information included in OMB's *Compliance Supplement for Single Audits of State and Local Governments* and *Compliance Supplement for Audits of Institutions of Higher Learning and Other Non-Profit Institutions*; the *Catalog of Federal Domestic Assistance*, issued by the Government Printing Office; and state and local policies and procedures.

An integral part of an audit is the assessment of audit risk at the financial statement level and at the account balance or transaction class level. With respect to the audit of a governmental entity, consideration must be given to the effect on audit risk of the possibility of violations of laws and regulations. Similarly, the auditor must consider a governmental entity's internal control structure in assessing control risk from the perspective that laws and regulations may be violated in such a manner that the financial statements of the entity would be materially affected. While SAS-74 does not attempt to construct a comprehensive audit program with respect to the consideration of a governmental entity's internal control structure, and its observance of laws and regulations, there are several factors that would be relevant to the auditor's investigation:

- Management's awareness or lack of awareness of applicable laws and regulations

- Entity policy regarding such matters as acceptable operating practice and codes of conduct

- Assignment of responsibility and delegation of authority to deal with such matters as organizational goals and objectives, operating functions, and regulatory requirements

In conducting compliance audit requirements described in SAS-74, the auditor should follow all applicable Statements on Auditing Standards, including SAS-41 (Working Papers), SAS-55, and SAS-60.

Audits of entities that receive governmental support A governmental entity may provide a variety of financial support to other governmental entities, not-for-profit organizations, and commercial enterprises. The recipient of the financial support may be subject to laws and regulations that, if violated, may have a direct and material effect on the recipient entity's financial statements. SAS-74 notes that laws and regulations of this nature may involve the following restrictions and requirements:

- General requirements that involve national policy and apply to all or most federal financial assistance programs; and

- Specific requirements that apply to a particular federal program and generally arise from statutory requirements and regulations.

Both of these requirements are contained in the OMB *Compliance Supplements* discussed earlier.

The auditor of an entity that receives financial aid from a governmental entity and that is subject to laws and regulations that may have a direct and material effect on its financial statements should follow the guidelines discussed earlier (see section entitled "Audits of Governmental Entities").

Tests of Controls

In an audit engagement, it may be possible to assess control risk related to some (or all) assertions embodied in the financial statements at a level less than the maximum. Control risk can be assessed at a lower level only if (1) specific internal control structure policies and procedures related to specific assertions can be identified and (2) tests of controls are performed. Tests of controls are used to determine the effectiveness of the design of policies and procedures, and operations of policies and procedures.

As in other audit engagements, the auditor should consider whether it is both efficient and effective to perform tests of controls during the audit of a governmental entity. The performance of tests of controls is more thoroughly described in the chapter entitled "Internal Control, Errors, and Irregularities."

Tests of Controls with Laws and Regulations

When an auditor has been contracted to perform an audit in accordance with *Government Auditing Standards,* procedures should be adopted to determine whether the entity has complied with applicable laws and regulations. To achieve this objective the auditor should execute the audit in a manner that satisfies the requirements established by SAS-53.

Substantive Tests

An auditor performs substantive tests to determine whether financial statements are presented in accordance with generally accepted accounting principles. In addition, as suggested above, substantive tests are performed to determine whether laws and regulations that govern the financial activities of the governmental unit are being followed. Substantive tests are discussed in the following section of this chapter.

SPECIALIZED AUDIT PROCEDURES

To a large extent, substantive tests (tests of balances, tests of transactions, and analytical review) for a governmental audit are similar to substantive tests used in the examination of a commercial enterprise. Summarized below are the unique features of substantive tests performed in the governmental audit environment.

Cash and Investments

Cash collections for a governmental unit may be made at a number of locations within the unit. Each significant collection point's internal controls should be evaluated to determine whether controls are adequate. If controls are inadequate, the auditor must consider whether extended cash audit procedures should be used.

Once collected, cash may be restricted to a particular fund or to a specific activity. In addition, idle cash may be invested; however, the types of investments that can be made often are limited by governmental regulations. Audit procedures should be employed to substantiate whether imposed restrictions for cash received and investments made have been followed.

State laws or other regulations may require the deposits with financial institutions to be collateralized. For example, the bank or other financial institution that holds the governmental deposit may be required to pledge securities that are equal to the amount of the unsecured deposit. The auditor must be aware of collateralization requirements and determine whether the financial institution has observed the requirements.

To facilitate administrative procedures and maximize returns on assets, cash and investments for various funds and related agencies often are pooled. Because the assets and related earnings must be identified with specific funds, audit procedures should be used to determine whether pooled transactions, including earnings and gains and losses from investment dispositions, have been properly allocated to each fund. In addition, investments must be evaluated to identify writedowns that may be required because of permanent declines in their values or liquidity requirements that will require the unit to sell investments at amounts below costs.

Governments that engage in securities lending practices will need to follow the accounting and disclosure requirements contained in GASB-28 (Accounting and Financial Reporting for Securities Lending Transactions).

Governments that engage in the purchase of derivative-type securities will need to follow the additional disclosure requirements contained in GASB Technical Bulletin (GASB:TB) 94-1 (Disclosures about Derivatives and Similar Debt and Investments Transactions).

> **OBSERVATION:** *In addition to the substantiation of cash and investments, the auditor should collect sufficient competent evidence to support disclosures required by GASB-3 (Deposits with Financial Institutions, Investments [Including Repurchase Agreements], and Reverse Repurchase Agreements) and GASB:TB 87-1 (Applying Paragraph 68 of GASB Statement 3).*

> **OBSERVATION:** *The GASB and its predecessor have provided limited guidance for the accounting and reporting of investments made by governmental entities. For those responsible for the preparation of governmental financial statements, questions such as the following were difficult to address: Should investments in debt securities that are purchased at a discount or premium be reported at cost, at amortized cost, at market value, or at the lower of amortized cost or market value? If discounts or premiums on debt instruments are subject to amortization, which method—straight-line or effective interest method—should be used? Should the accounting methods be different for debt investments, for debt instruments that are purchased at par, and for those that are made with no stated interest rate, such as deep discount or zero-coupon investments? Should investments in equity securities be reported at cost, at market value, or at the lower of cost or market value? In March 1996, the GASB decided to address these and other questions related to investments by issuing an Exposure Draft entitled "Accounting and Financial Reporting for Certain Investments and for External Investment Pools." The Exposure Draft defines investment as "a security or other asset acquired primarily for the purpose of obtaining income or profit." The proposed standard would apply to (a) all investments held by governmental external investment pools and (b) most investments in securities held by all other governmental entities (except external investment pools, de-*

*fined benefit pension plans, and Internal Revenue Code Section
457 deferred compensation plans) and would require that investments be presented at fair value.*

Receivables and Related Transactions

Receivables may arise from the recognition of revenue or an interfund transfer. Revenue is recorded when it is both measurable and
available to pay current expenditures of the governmental fund.
Interfund transfers should be recognized simultaneously in the two
funds affected by the interfund transaction.

The auditor should subject receivables to confirmation or substantiation through alternative audit procedures such as review of
subsequent cash collections or vouching. In addition, the auditor
should follow the audit procedures listed below for receivables and
related transactions, if applicable:

Property Tax Receivables and Revenues

- Compare assessed value of property for current and prior year
  and evaluate explanations for significant changes.

- Compare ratio of taxes collected to tax assessment for current
  and prior year.

- Test computation of assessments.

- Reconcile beginning and ending balance of receivables.

- Recompute tax levy.

- If legally required, determine whether list of delinquent and
  uncollectible receivables was properly filed.

- Determine if tax sales (of property) were executed in a legal
  manner.

- Compare current and prior years' proceeds from tax sales.

- Determine whether tax rolls include all properties.

- Summarize tax revenue and compare to budgeted amounts
  and prior-year amounts.

- Review abatements, exonerations, and refunds for appropriate
  approval.

Other Receivables and Revenues from Sales, Income, and Other Taxes

- Compare revenues for current year (actual and budget) with prior year's actual.

- Evaluate allocation of indirect cost to grant programs.

- Determine whether grant expenditures are consistent with grant program requirements.

- Determine whether revenue recognition methods have been consistently applied.

- Evaluate accrual of tax refunds.

- Review grant records for noncompliance and questionable costs.

- Review supporting documentation for compliance with matching fund grants.

Interfund Receivables and Transfers

- Vouch interfund transactions for approval.

- Determine whether interfund advances are current or noncurrent.

- Determine whether interfund borrowings have occurred through allocation of pooled cash and investments.

- Evaluate classification of interfund transactions and need for reserving or designating part of the fund balance because of the transaction.

- If an internal service fund has an operating deficit in retained earnings, consider the need for an audit adjustment to reflect full cost of the service provided.

- Determine where permanent transfers are accounted for as equity transfers.

- Consider whether a deficit/surplus in an internal service fund is in compliance with GASB-10 (Accounting and Financial Reporting for Risk Financing and Related Insurance Issues).

> **OBSERVATION:** *The confirmation process can be used as part of the audit of a number of governmental accounts and transactions, and other information. SAS-67 (The Confirmation Process) provides broad guidance for the use of confirmations in an audit engagement; it is discussed in the chapter entitled "Evidence."*

Expenditures and Related Liabilities

The operating expenditures and related liabilities of a government are audited in much the same manner as those of a commercial enterprise, except that, for a government, the auditor must understand the unique characteristics of the governmental control environment. For example, when auditing payroll expenditures, the auditor must consider civil service requirements, union contracts, and budget authorization.

The Government Audit Guide notes that the following unique characteristics should be considered in the audit of expenditures and related liabilities:

- Determine if expenditures are in accordance with the approved budget.

- Determine if encumbrances are properly identified, supported, classified, and recorded.

- Determine if expenditures comply with applicable laws and regulations.

- Determine if expenditures arising from grant programs comply with the grant requirements.

Capital Expenditures

Capital expenditures generally are recorded in a governmental entity's general fund, special revenue funds, and capital projects funds. These expenditures are audited in much the same way as similar expenditures for commercial enterprises. The Governmental Audit Guide notes that the following objectives are unique to the audit of the capital expenditures of a governmental entity:

- Determine if capital assets are substantiated by appropriate titles.

- Determine if capital expenditures, including those arising from lease transactions, are recorded.

- Determine if all relevant transactions (acquisitions, dispositions, and trade-ins) have been properly recorded.

- Determine if capital expenditures comply with budgetary authorization and legal and contractual requirements.

- Determine if special assessments for capital assets have been properly authorized and correctly billed to affected owners on a timely basis.
- Determine if capital expenditures have been properly reflected in the entity's general fixed assets account group.
- Determine if depreciation (which is optional) has been properly computed and reported in the general fixed assets account group.
- Determine if transfers of capital assets between governmental funds and proprietary funds are recorded correctly.

Debt and Debt Service

Governmental units may issue short-term debt, which is recorded directly in the financial statements of the fund responsible for the liquidation of the obligation, or long-term debt, which is reported as part of the entity's general long-term debt account group. Because of the constraints generally imposed on a governmental entity's ability to borrow funds, the auditor should understand its borrowing authority. When the auditor considers it necessary to confirm debt transactions, aspects of the transactions that may be confirmed include legal compliance of the borrowing, existence of restrictions, and compliance with appropriate covenants with the debt trustee. In addition, the auditor should consider performing the following audit procedures:

- Determine whether all debt for which the governmental entity is obligated is properly authorized and reported in the financial statements.
- Determine, where applicable, whether there is appropriate intent and adequate resources to pay general obligation debt from proprietary funds.
- Determine whether lease agreements create capital leases.
- Determine the existence of debt issued by other entities that may be guaranteed by the governmental entity.
- Determine whether sinking fund calculations are reasonable.
- Determine whether loan and similar agreements create pledged assets or restrictive covenants.
- Determine whether the governmental entity is in violation of any loan restrictions or covenants.

- Determine whether interest earned and unexpended debt proceeds are expended in compliance with applicable laws and bond covenants.
- Determine whether arbitrage rebate liabilities are computed correctly.
- Determine whether debt limit calculations are computed correctly.

Interfund Transactions

A governmental entity may be involved in a number of interfund transactions including reimbursements among funds, operating transfers, loans, and residual equity transfers. The Governmental Audit Guide concludes that the following objectives may be used to substantiate interfund transactions:

- Determine if all interfund transfers have been properly identified and classified.
- Determine if all interfund transfers have been properly authorized.

Fund Balances

A governmental fund's net equity is reported as the fund balance and may be composed of reserved amounts, designated amounts, and unreserved amounts. To substantiate that these amounts are properly reflected in the entity's financial statements, the auditor should consider the following audit objectives:

- Adequate documentation of all reserved fund balances
- Adequate presentation of reserve for encumbrances (if appropriate)
- Appropriate documentation for designated fund balances
- Determination that charges or credits were not made to reserved and designated fund balances during the period
- Proper disposition of amounts in reserved and designated fund balances when the need for their presentation is no longer required

Proprietary Fund Types

Accounting and reporting standards applicable to commercial enterprises must be used, for the most part, by proprietary funds (enterprise funds, internal service funds, and nonexpendable trust funds). However, with the issuance of GASB-20 proprietary funds must follow one of the following two approaches when determining whether FASB Statements should be observed during the preparation of their financial statements:

- *Alternative 1*   Implement (1) all GASB Statements and (2) FASB Statements and Interpretations, Accounting Principles Board (APB) Opinions, and Accounting Research Bulletins (ARBs) issued on or before November 30, 1989, except those that conflict with a GASB pronouncement.
- *Alternative 2*   Implement (1) all GASB pronouncements and (2) all FASB Statements and Interpretations, APB Opinions, and ARBs, no matter when issued, except those that conflict with a GASB pronouncement.

The auditor may have to consider the following audit problems when auditing a proprietary fund:

- When a proprietary fund is affected by rate-setting rules, the auditor should consider whether applicable regulations have been observed and whether customers have been billed according to the rates allowed.
- When restrictions or compliance requirements apply to grants received by a proprietary fund, the auditor should consider whether there should be an accrual based on noncompliance by the fund.

Fiduciary Funds

Governmental units use fiduciary funds to exercise custodial control over assets that are not assets of the entity. Fiduciary funds include expendable trust funds, nonexpendable trust funds, pension trust funds, and agency funds. The unique focus of the audit of a fiduciary fund is to determine whether the fund's assets are being used in a manner consistent with the fiduciary agreement and applicable laws and regulations.

State Governments

In general, the audit approach for the examination of the financial statements of a state government is the same as that used to examine the financial statements of a local government. However, because of the size and complexities of some state governments, there may be additional procedures that should be considered by the auditor.

Defining the reporting entity Because a number of agencies, special districts, and authorities may be created by a state government, the auditor must be satisfied that established criteria (GASB-14) have been properly used to determine whether financial statements of component units should be incorporated into the state government's financial statements (reporting entity).

Revenue sharing Various revenues, grants, or entitlements may be made available by the state to local governments. The computation of the resources to be distributed to specific localities may be based on a formula or specific criteria. Audit procedures should be employed to determine if allocations are properly computed and, if appropriate, year-end accruals for subsequent payments are reflected in the state government's financial statements.

In addition, a state government may function as an agent to facilitate the distribution of federal funds to local governments. The auditor must determine whether the state government has complied with federal regulations in releasing funds to the various localities.

Lotteries Generally, state lotteries are accounted for in an enterprise fund, and special attention should be directed to the recognition of liabilities arising from lottery participation. When the state purchases an annuity contract to satisfy the future payout requirements, no liability should be recognized, although it may be necessary to disclose the item as a contingent liability. If the state is directly responsible for the future payments, a liability equal to the present value of all required payouts must be recorded. For games in progress at year-end (lottery tickets have been sold but no winner has been identified), an estimated accrual should be recorded, again at present value.

Medicaid State governments make payments to health care providers such as hospitals and nursing homes based on reimbursement provisions and guidelines established by the state. At the end of the year, based on reports submitted by the health care provider, the state government may have a receivable from (overpayment) or payable to the provider. Audit procedures must be employed to determine the reasonableness of the year-end accrual.

Income taxes   Because the filing date for income tax returns differs from the state government's year-end date, it is necessary to estimate the total amount of income taxes receivable or payable to the taxpayers as a group. The auditor must review the estimate for reasonableness.

Independence   The primary government's external auditor must be independent of the primary government and each component unit included in the reporting entity. Also, a component unit's external auditor must be independent of the component unit and the primary government.

> **OBSERVATION:** *Additional guidance for determining independence can be found in Rule 101 of the Code of Professional Conduct and Interpretation 101-10. This guidance is discussed in the chapter entitled "Code of Professional Conduct."*

Joint audits   When a joint audit is conducted (the audit is conducted by both the external auditor and the governmental auditor), the external auditor must determine whether the governmental audit agency is independent and satisfies appropriate professional standards. To meet those standards, the Governmental Audit Guide notes that the governmental audit agency must be "objective, professionally competent, and its work should have been peer reviewed by a recognized professional organization."

Aid to local governments   States and local governments are involved in a variety of resource allocation programs, which include shared revenues, grants, and aid based on predetermined formulas. The auditor should understand the basis for these programs and make appropriate tests to determine whether accruals (both receivables and payables) are properly reflected in the financial statements.

Pass-through grant programs   State governments participate in various pass-through grant programs, and the nature of the programs and the responsibilities of the states should be understood by the auditor. In addition, the auditor should be aware of the accounting and reporting standards established by GASB-24 (Accounting and Financial Reporting for Certain Grants and Other Financial Assistance). The auditor should employ appropriate procedures to determine whether accruals, referrals, and disallowed costs under the programs are properly reflected in the financial statements.

Escheat property   Under certain conditions, privately owned property may become the property of a state government. For example, if an individual dies without a will or heirs, the probate assets may become the property of the state. Accounting and reporting standards established by GASB-21 (Accounting for Escheat Property) should be observed by the state government. The auditor should employ appropriate procedures to determine whether escheat property, any estimated related liability, and revenue arising from the escheatment are property reflected in the financial statements.

Concluding the Audit

The auditor concludes an audit of a governmental entity in much the same way that a commercial enterprise audit is concluded. Some of the unique aspects of this phase of the audit in the context of a governmental audit are summarized below.

Letter of audit inquiry   As required by SAS-12 (Inquiry of a Client's Lawyer Concerning Litigation, Claims, and Assessments), a letter of audit inquiry should be sent to the governmental unit's chief legal officer (for example, the City Attorney) or independent legal counsel.

> **OBSERVATION:** *If the governmental entity's attorney is unable to provide the auditor with an appropriate response to the letter of audit inquiry, the Governmental Audit Guide notes that "the auditor should plan early in the engagement to take the appropriate steps and discuss with the client the qualification that may be necessary when expressing an opinion."*

Management representation letter   The auditor should obtain a representation letter from the governmental unit as required by SAS-19 (Client Representations). In addition to the typical coverage of a representation letter prepared by a commercial enterprise, the governmental unit's letter should include the following representations or acknowledgments:

- Management's responsibility for complying with applicable laws and regulations
- Management's identification and disclosure of all laws and regulations that have a direct and material effect on its financial statements
- Proper identification of the financial statements to be audited
- Scope of the financial statements including all component units and joint ventures
- Proper classification of funds and account groups
- Proper approval of fund reserves and designations
- Compliance with relevant laws and regulations
- Compliance with tax or debt limits
- Appropriate presentation of GASB-required supplementary information
- Identification of all federal assistance programs
- Compliance with grant-imposed restrictions

Related party transactions   The complexity of many governmental entities provides an environment in which a variety of related party transactions may occur. Accounting and reporting standards established by FAS-57 (Related Party Disclosures) must be observed in the preparation of a governmental entity's financial statements. The Governmental Audit Guide notes that related party audit procedures are applied throughout an engagement, especially as part of planning. At the conclusion of the engagement, the auditor should determine whether related parties that should be disclosed in the financial statements have been identified.

Going-concern consideration   There always has been a debate in the public sector about whether a governmental entity with the power to assess and levy taxes and other charges is exposed to the going-concern standard. That, of course, is a constitutional question that the Governmental Audit Guide correctly avoids answering. Nonetheless, the Guide implies that a prudent auditor should be alert for the possibility. Some of the circumstances that may challenge the going-concern assumption include the following:

- Significant pension plan commitments coupled with a decreasing tax base

- Significant investment losses
- Losses to infrastructure assets due to major natural disasters
- Recurring deficits financed through short-term borrowing

If the going-concern assumption arises, the auditor should consider modifying the auditor's report.

Reports

When an auditor is engaged to examine a governmental unit's financial statements, the purpose of the audit is to express an opinion on whether the statements are presented in accordance with generally accepted accounting principles. The auditor's report on the financial statements must satisfy the four reporting standards of generally accepted auditing standards and related Statements on Auditing Standards. The Governmental Audit Guide discusses the application of reporting standards in the context of a governmental audit engagement.

Standard report A governmental reporting entity's basic financial statements are referred to as general purpose financial statements and include the following:

- Combined balance sheet—all fund types and account groups
- Combined statement of revenues, expenditures, and changes in fund balances—all governmental fund types
- Combined statement of revenues, expenditures, and changes in fund balances—budget and actual, general and special revenue fund types (and all other governmental funds that legally adopt an annual budget)
- Combined statement of revenues, expenses, and changes in retained earnings (or equity)—all proprietary fund types
- Combined statement of cash flows—all proprietary fund types
- Notes to the financial statements

The following is an example of an auditor's report on a governmental unit's general purpose financial statements.

We have audited the accompanying general purpose financial statements of the City of Centerville, N.J., as of and for the year ended June 30, 19X5, as listed in the table of contents. These financial statements are the responsibility of the entity's management. Our responsibility is to express an opinion on these financial statements based on our audit.

We conducted our audit in accordance with generally accepted auditing standards. These standards require that we plan and perform the audit to obtain reasonable assurance about whether the financial statements are free of material misstatement. An audit includes examining, on a test basis, evidence supporting the amounts and disclosures in the financial statements. An audit also includes assessing the accounting principles used and significant estimates made by management, as well as evaluating the overall financial statement presentation. We believe that our audit provides a reasonable basis for our opinion.

In our opinion, the financial statements referred to above present fairly, in all material respects, the financial position of the City of Centerville, N.J., at June 30, 19X5, and the results of its operations and the cash flows of its proprietary fund types for the year then ended, in conformity with generally accepted accounting principles.

When the auditor is reporting on a component unit's financial statements, the standard report as shown above should refer to the "financial statements" rather than to the "general purpose financial statements."

> *OBSERVATION: Usually a state or local government presents total-all-funds information for a prior period instead of information by individual funds to save space or avoid presenting a cumbersome financial statement. The auditor is not required to report on prior-period financial statements if only summarized comparative information for the prior period is presented.*

In those situations where a material portion of the reporting entity's financial statements is examined by another auditor, the principal auditor must decide whether to refer to the work of the other auditor. When the principal auditor decides to refer to the other auditor's work, the following sentences should be added to the standard scope paragraph:

We did not examine the financial statements of [refer to the fund or component unit], which represent X percent and XX percent, respectively, of the assets and revenues of the [identify fund type]. Those financial statements were audited by other auditors whose report thereon has been furnished to us and our opinion expressed herein, insofar as it relates to the amounts included for [identify fund or component unit], is based solely on the report of the other auditors.

In addition, the opinion paragraph should refer to the principal auditor's examination and the other auditor's report as the basis for expressing an overall opinion on the reporting entity's financial statements.

The governmental unit's financial report, in addition to the general purpose financial statements, may include combining financial statements, statements of individual funds and account groups, and supporting schedules. When the auditor is requested to examine the general purpose financial statements and the additional financial statements and schedules, the standard auditor's report would appear as follows:

We have audited the accompanying general purpose financial statements of the City of Centerville, N.J., and the combining, individual fund, and individual account group financial statements of the City of Centerville as of and for the year ended June 30, 19X5, as listed in the table of contents. These financial statements are the responsibility of the entity's management. Our responsibility is to express an opinion on these financial statements based on our audit.

We conducted our audit in accordance with generally accepted auditing standards. Those standards require that we plan and perform the audit to obtain reasonable assurance about whether the financial statements are free of material misstatement. An audit includes examining, on a test basis, evidence supporting the amounts and disclosures in the financial statements. An audit also includes assessing the accounting principles used and significant estimates made by management, as well as evaluating the overall financial statement presentation. We believe that our audit provides a reasonable basis for our opinion.

In our opinion, the general purpose financial statements referred to above present fairly, in all material respects, the financial position of the City of Centerville, N.J., as of June 30, 19X5, and the results of its operations and the cash flows of its proprietary fund types for the year then ended in conformity with generally accepted accounting principles. Also, in our opinion, the combining, individual fund, and individual account group financial statements referred to above present fairly, in all material respects, the financial position of each of the individual funds and account groups of the City of Centerville, N.J., as of June 30, 19X5, and the results of operations of such funds and the cash flows of individual proprietary funds for the year then ended in conformity with generally accepted accounting principles.

Our audit was made for the purpose of forming an opinion on the general purpose financial statements taken as a whole and on the combining, individual fund, and individual account group financial statements. The accompanying financial information listed as supporting schedules in the table of contents is presented for purposes of additional analysis and is not a required part of the financial statements of the City of Centerville, N.J. Such information has been subjected to the auditing procedures applied in the audit of the general purpose, combining, individual fund, and individual account group financial statements and, in our opinion, is fairly stated in all material respects in relation to the financial statements of each of the respective individual funds and account groups, taken as a whole.

When the auditor is engaged to examine only the general purpose financial statements, but also submits combining, individual fund, and individual account group financial statements, SAS-29 (Reporting on Information Accompanying the Basic Financial Statements in Auditor-Submitted Documents) applies, and the standard three-paragraph auditor's report as illustrated earlier is expanded by adding the following paragraph.

Our audit was made for the purpose of forming an opinion on the general purpose financial statements taken as a whole. The combining, individual fund, and individual account group financial statements and schedules listed in the table of contents are presented for purposes of additional analysis and are not a required part of the general purpose financial statements of the City of Centerville, N.J. Such information has been subjected to the auditing procedures applied in the audit of the general purpose financial statements and, in our opinion, is fairly stated in all material respects in relation to the general purpose financial statements taken as a whole.

The scope of the audit engagement may be limited to a single fund. Under this circumstance, the auditor's report should contain a middle paragraph explaining that the financial statements present only the specific fund and do not present fairly the financial position and results of operations of the state or local government. In the opinion paragraph, an unqualified opinion may be expressed on the specific fund's financial statements.

Audit report modifications   The auditor's report on the financial statements of a governmental unit may have to be modified for a number of reasons, including deviations from generally accepted accounting principles and limitations of the audit scope.

A governmental unit's financial statements may be incomplete for a number of reasons, including the following: (1) one or more component units are omitted, (2) a fund type or account group is omitted, or (3) a fund is omitted from a fund type. These omissions are in violation of generally accepted accounting principles and must be evaluated to determine whether a qualified or adverse opinion should be expressed. An explanatory paragraph should describe the significance of the omitted financial statements, and the opinion paragraph should refer to the explanatory paragraph as the basis for the qualified or adverse opinion.

On the other hand, the governmental unit's financial statements may include the financial statements of component units that have not been audited. This scope limitation may lead to the expression of a qualified opinion or disclaimer of opinion on the reporting entity's financial statements, depending on the materiality of the unaudited financial statements. An example of a qualified opinion is presented below.

We have audited the accompanying general purpose financial statements of the City of Centerville, N.J., as of and for the year ended June 30, 19X5, as listed in the table of contents. These financial statements are the responsibility of the entity's management. Our responsibility is to express an opinion on these financial statements based on our audit.

Except as explained in the following paragraph, we conducted our audit in accordance with generally accepted auditing standards. Those standards require that we plan and perform the audit to obtain reasonable assurance about whether the financial statements are free of material misstatement. An audit includes examining, on a test basis, evidence supporting the amounts and disclosures in the financial statements. An audit also includes assessing the accounting principles used and significant estimates made by management, as well as evaluating the overall financial statement presentation. We believe that our audit provides a reasonable basis for our opinion.

The general purpose financial statements referred to above include the financial statements of the Centerville Parking Authority, which are unaudited. Those financial statements are included in the Enterprise Fund type and represent 20% and 25% of the assets and revenues, respectively, of that fund type.

In our opinion, except for the effects on the financial statements of such adjustments, if any, as might have been determined to be necessary had we audited the financial statements of the Centerville Parking Authority referred to above, the general purpose financial statements referred to above present fairly, in all material respects, the financial position of the City of Centerville, N.J., as of June 30, 19X5, and the results of its operations and the cash flows of the City of Centerville, N.J., as of June 30, 19X5, and the results of its operations and the cash flows of its proprietary fund types for the year then ended in conformity with generally accepted accounting principles.

Although there is disagreement about whether a governmental unit faces the same going-concern considerations that a commercial enterprise does, a state or local governmental unit faces a number of uncertainties that must be evaluated by the auditor. These uncertainties include the possibility of default on outstanding debt, inability to meet other obligations such as those arising from pension plans, and continued funding of operations at current levels. These uncertainties may lead to a modified report (addition of a fourth paragraph describing the uncertainty) or a disclaimer of opinion on the reporting entity's financial statements.

Special Reports

The auditor may be engaged to examine financial statements of a governmental unit that are prepared in conformity with a comprehensive basis of accounting other than generally accepted accounting principles. SAS-62 (Special Reports) prescribes reporting standards for this type of engagement.

Additional Reports That May Be Required

In the event that the auditor is required to audit the government entity in accordance with *Government Auditing Standards*, two additional reports will be required: (1) a separate report on the auditor's work on internal controls as they relate to the audit of the financial statements and (2) a separate report on the auditor's work on compliance with laws, regulations, contracts, and grant agreements as they relate to the audit of the financial statements.

Additionally, the auditor is required to indicate in the auditor's report that the audit was conducted in accordance with *Government Auditing Standards, and* that the two additional reports were issued.

An auditor conducting an audit in accordance with OMB Circular A-128 must issue several additional reports on compliance with federal laws and regulations, and on the internal controls as they relate to the applicable compliance requirements of federal programs.

Receipt of Federal Awards by Not-for-Profit Organizations

Not-for-profit organizations that receive federal awards may be subject to regulations established by Office of Management and Budget (OMB) Circular A-133 (Audits of Institutions of Higher Education and Other Nonprofit Institutions). In 1992, the AICPA issued SOP 92-9 (Audits of Not-for-Profit Organizations Receiving Federal Awards) in order to provide guidance to auditors who are engaged to perform audits in accordance with regulations established by the OMB. Although SOP 92-9 does not establish new audit guidance, it does compile relevant guidance established by a variety of promulgations, including SAS-68 (Compliance Auditing Applicable to Governmental Entities and Other Recipients of Governmental Financial Assistance), OMB Circular A-133, and SOP 92-7 (Audits of State and Local Governmental Entities Receiving Federal Financial Assistance).

SOP 92-9 describes an auditor's general responsibility in an audit of federal awards and specifically addresses the following:

- Describes the applicability of OMB Circular A-133
- Summarizes the differences between Circular A-133 and OMB Circular A-128 (Audits of State and Local Governments)
- Describes the auditor's responsibility for considering the internal control and for performing tests of compliance with certain laws and regulations
- Describes the auditor's responsibility for reporting and provides examples of the reports required by Circular A-133

> *OBSERVATION: More information on the additional reports the auditor may be required to issue can be found in* **Miller's Single Audits**.

PART VIII

Code of Professional Conduct

CODE OF PROFESSIONAL CONDUCT

Contents

Overview	**24.03**
Principles	**24.04**
Rules	**24.05**
Rule 101—Independence	**24.05**
Interpretations	**24.08**
Rule 102—Integrity and Objectivity	**24.20**
Interpretations	**24.20**
Rule 201—General Standards	**24.22**
Interpretations	**24.23**
Rule 202—Compliance with Standards	**24.24**
Interpretations	**24.25**
Rule 203—Accounting Principles	**24.26**
Interpretations	**24.27**
Rule 301—Confidential Client Information	**24.28**
Interpretations	**24.29**
Rule 302—Contingent Fees	**24.30**
Interpretations	**24.32**
Rule 501—Acts Discreditable	**24.33**
Interpretations	**24.34**
Rule 502—Advertising and Other Forms of Solicitation8	**24.35**
Interpretations	**24.35**
Rule 503—Commissions and Referral Fees	**24.36**
Interpretations	**24.38**
Rule 504—Incompatible Occupations (Withdrawn)	**24.38**
Rule 505—Form of Organization and Name	**24.38**
Interpretations	**24.40**
Rulings on Ethics	**24.40**
Rulings on Independence, Integrity, and Objectivity (Rules 101 and 102)	**24.41**

Rulings on General and Technical Standards
(Rules 201, 202, and 203)   **24.53**
Rulings on Responsibilities to Clients
(Rules 301 and 302)   **24.54**
Rulings on Other Responsibilities and Practices
(Rules 501, 502, 503, and 505)   **24.57**

CODE OF PROFESSIONAL CONDUCT

Overview

The Code of Professional Conduct provides guidelines for accounting practitioners in the conduct of their professional affairs. A member of the AICPA must observe all the Rules of Conduct unless an exception applies. The need to observe the Rules of Conduct also extends to individuals who carry out tasks on behalf of an AICPA member. A member may be held responsible for a violation of the rules committed by fellow partners, shareholders, or any other person associated with him or her and engaged in the practice of public accounting. The bylaws of the AICPA, through the efforts of the Professional Ethics Division and the Trial Board, provide the basis for determining whether a member has violated the Rules of Conduct. If, after due process, a member is found guilty of a violation, he or she may be admonished, suspended, or expelled.

A member of the AICPA also must be aware of Interpretations of the AICPA Rules of Conduct. After exposure to state societies and state boards of accountancy, Interpretations of the AICPA Rules of Conduct are published, modified, or deleted by the Executive Committee of the Professional Ethics Division. Interpretations are not intended to limit the scope or application of the Rules of Conduct. A member of the AICPA who departs from the guidelines provided in the Interpretations has the burden of justifying such departure in any AICPA disciplinary hearings. In this chapter, Interpretations are either discussed as part of the analysis of a particular Rule of Conduct or summarized after the analysis of the Rule of Conduct.

> **OBSERVATION:** *This chapter discusses the Code of Professional Conduct as established by the AICPA. An AICPA member also should be familiar with rules of conduct and due process procedures, if applicable, established by the appropriate state board of accountancy, state society of CPAs, the Securities and Exchange Commission, and other relevant government agencies.*

The Code of Professional Conduct includes two sections: Principles and Rules.

PRINCIPLES

The Principles of the Code of Professional Conduct, which provide the conceptual framework for the Code, include the following six articles (ET 52.01–57.03).

I — Responsibilities	In carrying out their responsibilities as professionals, members should exercise sensitive professional and moral judgments in all their activities.
II — The Public Interest	Members should accept the obligation to act in a way that will serve the public interest, honor the public trust, and demonstrate commitment to professionalism.
III — Integrity	To maintain and broaden public confidence, members should perform all professional responsibilities with the highest sense of integrity.
IV — Objectivity and Independence	A member should maintain objectivity and be free of conflicts of interest in discharging professional responsibilities. A member in public practice should be independent in fact and appearance when providing auditing and other attestation services.
V — Due Care	A member should observe the profession's technical and ethical standards, strive continually to improve competence and the quality of services, and discharge professional responsibility to the best of the member's ability.
VI — Scope and Nature of Services	A member in public practice should observe the Principles of the Code of Professional Conduct in determining the scope and nature of services to be provided.

These articles establish the basis for characterizing the responsibilities the CPA has to clients, colleagues, and the public at large. The fundamental theme of the six articles is *to be committed to honorable behavior, even at the sacrifice of personal advantage* (ET 51.02).

RULES

The Rules of the Code of Professional Conduct are more specific than the six broad articles that comprise the Principles. The bylaws of the AICPA state that members of the AICPA must observe the Rules.

The following definitions are used in the Rules of the Code of Professional Conduct (ET 92.09–.10):

> *Practice of public accounting*—The practice of public accounting consists of the performance for a client, by a member or a member's firm, while holding out as CPA(s), of the professional services of accounting, tax, personal financial planning, litigation support services, and those professional services for which standards are promulgated by bodies designated by Council, such as Statements of Financial Accounting Standards, Statements on Auditing Standards, Statements on Standards for Accounting and Review Services, Statement on Standards for Consulting Services, Statements of Governmental Accounting Standards, Statements on Standards for Attestation Engagements, and Statement on Standards for Accountants' Services on Prospective Financial Information.
>
> However, a member or a member's firm, while holding out as CPA(s), is not considered to be in the practice of public accounting if the member or the member's firm does not perform, for any client, any of the professional services described in the preceding paragraph.
>
> *Professional services*—Professional services include all services performed by a member while holding out as a CPA.

Rule 101—Independence

> A member in public practice shall be independent in the performance of professional services as required by standards promulgated by bodies designated by Council.

Independence is a highly subjective term because it concerns an individual's ability to act with integrity and objectivity. Integrity relates to an auditor's honesty, while objectivity is the ability to be neutral during the conduct of the engagement and the preparation of the auditor's report. Two facets of independence are independence in fact and independence in appearance. The second general standard of generally accepted auditing standards requires that an auditor be independent in mental attitude in all matters relating to the engagement. In essence, the second standard embraces the concept of independence in fact. However, independence in fact is impossible to measure, since it is a mental attitude; the Code of Professional Conduct takes a more pragmatic approach to the concept of independence (ET 101.01).

Rule 101 is applicable to professional services provided by a CPA that require independence. Engagements that require that a CPA be independent include the following:

- Professional services subject to Statements on Auditing Standards
    - Audits of financial statements prepared in accordance with GAAP
    - Audits of financial statements prepared in accordance with a comprehensive basis of accounting other than GAAP (SAS-62 [Special Reports])
    - Reports expressing an opinion on one or more specified elements, accounts, or items of a financial statement (SAS-62)
    - Reports on compliance with aspects of contractual agreements or regulatory requirements related to audited financial statements (SAS-62)
    - Reports on information accompanying the basic financial statements in auditor-submitted documents (SAS-29 [Reporting on Information Accompanying the Basic Financial Statements in Auditor-Submitted Documents])
    - Reports on internal accounting control (SSAE-2 [Reporting on an Entity's Internal Control Structure Over Financial Reporting])
    - Reports on applying agreed-upon procedures to specified elements, accounts, or items of a financial statement (SAS-35 [Special Reports—Applying Agreed-Upon Procedures to Specified Elements, Accounts, or Items of a Financial Statement])
    - Reports on reviews of interim financial information (SAS-71 [Interim Financial Information])

- — Reports on condensed financial statements and selected financial data (SAS-42 [Reporting on Condensed Financial Statements and Selected Financial Data])

- — Special-purpose reports on internal accounting control at service organizations (SAS-70 [Reports on the Processing of Transactions by Service Organizations])

- — Reports on financial statements prepared for use in other countries (SAS-51 [Reporting on Financial Statements Prepared for Use in Other Countries])

- • Professional services subject to Statements on Standards for Accounting and Review Services

  - — Reviews of financial statements prepared by nonpublic entities

  - — Compilations of financial statements prepared by nonpublic entities

    OBSERVATION: A CPA may conduct a compilation engagement when he or she is not independent, but the compilation report must be modified to disclose the lack of independence.

- • Professional services subject to Statements on Standards for Accountants' Services on Prospective Financial Information

  - — Examinations, compilations, or applications of agreed-upon procedures to financial forecasts and projects

    OBSERVATION: Statements on Standards for Accountants' Services on Prospective Financial Information have been codified as Statements on Standards for Attestation Engagements.

- • Professional services subject to Statements on Standards for Attestation Engagements

  - — Examinations, reviews, or applications of agreed-upon procedures to engagements where the accountant expresses a written conclusion about the reliability of a written assertion that is the responsibility of another party

Interpretations

Summarized below are the Interpretations of Rule 101 issued by the AICPA.

Interpretation 101-1 (Interpretation of Rule 101) Whereas Rule 101 establishes the broad principle that a CPA must be independent (independence in fact), this Interpretation provides more specific guidelines concerning the types of relationships that a CPA should avoid. Independence is considered to be impaired under the following circumstances (ET 101.02):

A. During the period of a professional engagement or at the time of expressing an opinion, a member or a member's firm:

1. Had or was committed to acquire any direct or material indirect financial interest in the enterprise.

2. Was a trustee of any trust or executor or administrator of any estate if such trust or estate had or was committed to acquire any direct or material indirect financial interest in the enterprise.

3. Had any joint, closely held business investment with the enterprise or with any officer, director, or principal stockholders thereof that was material in relation to the member's net worth or to the net worth of the member's firm.

4. Had any loan to or from the enterprise or any officer, director, or principal stockholder of the enterprise, except for those allowed under Interpretation 101-5.

B. During the period covered by the financial statements, during the period of the professional engagement, or at the time of expressing an opinion, a member or a member's firm:

1. Was connected with the enterprise as a promoter, underwriter, or voting trustee, as a director or officer, or in any capacity equivalent to that of a member of management or of an employee.

2. Was a trustee for any pension or profit-sharing trust of the enterprise.

The above examples are not intended to be all-inclusive.

Part (A) of the Interpretation lists certain financial relationships with a client that must be avoided to prevent losing the appearance of independence, if not independence in fact. On the other hand, the rule recognizes that some financial relationships are reasonable and are not prohibited. For example, an indirect immaterial interest in the client is not prohibited. An example of an indirect immaterial financial interest would be an investment in a mutual fund that has an investment in the client's common stock.

Part (B) of the Interpretation prohibits relationships in which the auditor becomes or has been an employee or a member of management during the period covered by the financial statements.

Interpretation 101-2 (Former Practitioners and Firm Independence)
The term *a member or a member's firm* does not include a former practitioner as described in Rule 101 if the following conditions exist (ET 101.04):

- Payments for the former practitioner's interest in the firm do not call into doubt the ability of the firm to continue as a going concern.

- Amounts due should be fixed and based on a reasonable payment schedule and payable over a reasonable period of time, and unpaid amounts may carry a reasonable rate of interest.

- The former practitioner does not participate in or associate with the firm's activities except in an advisory capacity during a reasonable transition period.

- The former practitioner's name should not be used in a manner that would suggest the appearance of participation or association with the firm.

- The former practitioner may have an office in the firm's suite and other office amenities such as secretarial support, if the former practitioner does not have a position of significant influence with a client.

Interpretation 101-3 (Accounting Services) A member may audit a client and perform other accounting services if (1) none of the relationships with the client impair the member's integrity and objectivity; (2) the client accepts the responsibility for the financial statements as the client's own; (3) the CPA does not function as an employee or part of management; and (4) the audit engagement is conducted in accordance with generally accepted auditing standards (ET 101.05).

Interpretation 101-4 (Honorary Directorships and Trusteeships of Not-for-Profit Organizations) A member may lend the prestige of his or her name to a charitable, civic, or similar organization by accepting appointment as an honorary director or trustee and still be considered independent with respect to the organization when the following conditions exist (ET 101.06):

- The position is honorary and restricted to the use of his or her name.
- The position is identified as honorary on all letterheads and in materials externally circulated.
- The member does not vote or otherwise participate in board or management functions.

Interpretation 101-5 (Loans from Financial Institution Clients and Related Terminology)   As stated in Interpretation 101-1, loans between a CPA and an enterprise, or any officer, director, or principal stockholder of the enterprise, would impair independence; however, Interpretation 101-5 concludes that certain loans of this nature would not impair independence. Specifically, loans that are not considered impairments of independence are (1) grandfathered loans and (2) other permitted loans (ET 101.07).

Grandfathered loans   The following loans from financial institutions do not impair independence:

- Home mortgages
- Loans that are secured (the collateral must at least be equal to the amount of the loan as of January 1, 1992, and for all subsequent dates)
- Loans considered immaterial to the CPA's net worth

The above loans must have been made under normal lending conditions established by a financial institution and must meet one of the following conditions:

- Exist as of January 1, 1992
- Be obtained from a financial institution before that institution becomes an engagement client that requires independence
- Be obtained from a financial institution for which independence was not required that was sold to a financial institution for which independence was required
- Be obtained from a financial institution for which independence was required but was made to the individual before that individual became a member of the CPA firm

Loans that are considered grandfathered must be and remain current, and the terms of such loans must not be renegotiated after the latest of the dates expressed or implied in the four circumstances listed above.

> **OBSERVATION:** *Independence will be considered impaired for the types of loans described above made after January 1, 1992, if, at the date of the loan, the lending entity is a client requiring independence.*

Other permitted loans   The following personal loans from a financial institution requiring independence, if made under the normal lending practices, will not impair independence:

- Loans or leases for automobiles when collateralized by the automobile
- Loans based on the surrender value of an insurance policy
- Loans fully collateralized by cash deposits held at the same financial institution
- Cash advances from checking accounts and credit cards with total unpaid current balances of $5,000 or less

Personal loans must remain current at all times in order for them not to be considered impairments of independence.

Interpretation 101-5 established the following definitions related to loans from financial institution clients:

> *Financial institution*—An organization whose normal operations include making loans to the general public.

> *Loan*—A financial transaction that includes such characteristics as repayment terms and an interest rate; a loan would encompass a guarantee of a loan, a letter of credit, and a line of credit.

> **OBSERVATION:** *Members of a CPA firm who collectively have more than a 50% ownership interest in a limited partnership are considered to have loans from financial institutions that have made loans directly to the limited partnership.*

> *Normal lending procedures*—Procedures, terms, and requirements that would be the basis for making similar loans to other par-

ties; factors such as the following should be considered in determining normal lending procedures:

- Amount of loan in relation to collateral pledged and credit standing of the member
- Repayment terms
- Interest rate (including *points*)
- Closing costs
- Availability of the loan to the public

Interpretation 101-6 (The Effect of Actual or Threatened Litigation on Independence) Litigation or threatened litigation (when it is probable a claim will be filed) between the client and the auditor that is related to audit work for the client may impair independence. Litigation brought by security holders against the client, its officers, directors, underwriters, and auditors would not impair the auditor's independence with respect to the client. Litigation brought by creditors or companies providing insurance coverage against the auditor would not affect the auditor's independence (ET 101.08).

Interpretation 101-7 Deleted.

Interpretation 101-8 (Effect on Independence of Financial Interests in Nonclients Having Investor or Investee Relationships with a Member's Client) Financial interests in a nonclient that has a relationship(s) with the client should be considered to determine whether independence is impaired. In evaluating a relationship between a client and a nonclient, Interpretation 101-8 establishes the following definitions (ET 101.10):

> *Client*—The person or entity with whose financial statements the member or the member's firm is associated.

> *Investor*—A parent, general partner, or natural person or corporation that has the ability to exercise significant influence. (Note: *Significant influence* is defined in APB Opinion No. 18 [The Equity Method of Accounting for Investments in Common Stock].)

> *Investee*—A subsidiary or an entity over which an investor has the ability to exercise significant influence.

When a client investor has a *material* interest in a nonclient investee, a direct financial interest or a material indirect financial interest by the CPA in the nonclient investee would impair independence. On the other hand, when a investor client has an *immaterial* interest in a nonclient investee, only a material interest (indirect or direct) by the CPA in the nonclient investee would impair independence.

When a nonclient investor has a *material* interest in a client investee, a direct or material indirect financial interest by the CPA in the nonclient investor would impair independence. However, when a nonclient investor has an *immaterial* interest in a client investee, independence is impaired only when the CPA can exercise significant influence over the nonclient investor.

Generally, when a brother–sister common control relationship exists, an *immaterial* financial interest by the CPA in the nonclient investee (either the brother entity or the sister entity) would not impair independence with respect to the client investee, assuming that the CPA cannot exercise significant influence over the nonclient investor. For example, assume that Parent Company (nonclient investor) owns Brother Company and Sister Company, and a CPA has an immaterial financial interest in Sister Company (nonclient investee) and audits the financial statements of Brother Company (client investee). The relationship with Sister Company does not impair independence with respect to Brother Company, assuming that the CPA cannot exercise significant influence over Parent Company through its interest in Sister Company. When a brother–sister common control relationship exists, a *material* financial interest by the CPA in the nonclient investee (Sister Company) would impair independence with respect to the client investee (Brother Company) because the CPA could be influenced by the nonclient investor (Parent Company).

Generally, when a joint venture relationship exists, an *immaterial* financial interest by the CPA in the nonclient investor would not impair independence with respect to the client investor, assuming that the CPA could not exercise significant influence over the nonclient investor. For example, assume that Alpha Company (nonclient investor) and Beta Company (client investor) form Omega Company (the joint venture). An immaterial financial interest in Alpha Company would not impair independence with respect to Beta Company, assuming the CPA could not exercise significant influence over Alpha Company.

Other relationships with nonclient entities could exist that may impair independence. The CPA is responsible for making "reasonable" inquiries about whether such relationships exist, and if they do, each relationship should be evaluated to determine whether the financial interest might suggest to a reasonable observer that the relationship impairs independence. On the other hand, if the CPA "does not and could not reasonably be expected" to be aware of financial interests in nonclients described in Interpretation 101-8, independence is not considered to be impaired.

Interpretation 101-9 (The Meaning of Certain Independence Terminology and the Effect of Family Relationships on Independence) Rule 101 requires that a member be independent under certain circumstances, but the scope of the terms *member* (from Rule 101) and *member's firm* (from Interpretation 101-1) is very broad. The terms *member* and *a member or a member's firm* encompass the following (ET 101.11):

1. All of the firm's proprietors, partners, and shareholders, depending on the legal form of the practice and the form allowed by the AICPA Council.

2. All individuals who participate in an engagement, including all contractors hired by the member except specialists covered by SAS-73 (Using the Work of a Specialist). (Individuals who perform strictly clerical operations, such as typing and photocopying, would not be included in this group.)

3. All individuals in managerial positions in an office that participates in a significant part of the engagement.

4. Any entity whose operating, financial, or accounting policies can be controlled (as defined in FAS-94 [Consolidation of All Majority-Owned Subsidiaries]) by an individual described in categories (1), (2), or (3) or two or more of these individuals acting together.

The term *member's firm* also includes those who perform services for the client and function in a capacity described in Interpretation 101-1-B.

Managerial positions There is no all-encompassing definition of what constitutes a managerial position, but Interpretation 101-9 notes that making such a determination is dependent on the responsibilities of the individual and *how the individual is held out to clients and third parties.* Responsibilities that would suggest that an individual is a member of management include managing the firm, planning and supervising engagements, determining when an engagement is complete, and maintaining client relations. Individuals receiving a significant portion of compensation based on a profit-sharing arrangement may also be members of management.

Significant influence Interpretation 101-9 suggests that a person or entity can exercise significant influence over another entity under the following circumstances:

- The person or entity is a promoter, underwriter, voting trustee, general partner, or director (other than an honorary director) of the other entity.

- The person or entity is in a policy-making position with respect to the other entity.

- The person or entity has a relationship with the other entity that would satisfy the standards established by APB Opinion No. 18 (including Interpretations) with respect to the definition of *exercise significant influence over the operating, financial, or accounting policies of another entity.*

The above list is illustrative only, and the relationships between the two parties must be evaluated to determine what constitutes significant influence.

Office participation The accountant must exercise professional judgment when determining whether an office participates in a significant portion of an engagement. Certainly the office that has primary responsibility for an engagement that involves two or more offices constitutes significant participation. Other factors that might be considered include the relative number of hours worked and the importance of the work performed by a particular office.

Spouses and dependent persons Dependent and nondependent spouses and other dependents (whether or not related) are part of the definition of a member and a member's firm except when the spouse or other dependent cannot "significantly influence" a client's operating, financial, or accounting policies. However, when a spouse or dependent person (irrespective of whether that person can exercise significant influence) is in an audit-sensitive position, the member should not participate in the engagement. Interpretation 101-9 states that audit-sensitive positions include cashier, internal auditor, accounting supervisor, purchasing agent, inventory warehouse supervisor, and other activities normally considered to be an element of, or subject to, significant internal accounting controls. This list is not exhaustive.

Nondependent close relatives   Close relatives are nondependent children, stepchildren, brothers, sisters, grandparents, parents-in-law, and their respective spouses. Brothers and sisters of the member's spouse are not considered close relatives. Generally, the terms *member* and *member's firm* do not include nondependent close relatives of the individuals described in categories (1) through (3) (see earlier discussion). However, Interpretation 101-9 does note that independence would be impaired by a relationship with a nondependent close relative under the following circumstances:

- An individual participating in an engagement has a close relative who has a material financial interest in a client (during the period of the engagement or at the time an opinion is expressed), and the individual is aware of the interest.

- During the period covered by the engagement, during the engagement, or at the time an opinion is expressed:

  — An individual participating in an engagement has a close relative who can exercise significant influence over the client or is in an audit-sensitive position.

  — An owner of the CPA firm located in an office that participates in a significant portion of the engagement has a close relative who can exercise significant influence over the operating, financial, or accounting policies of the client.

Other considerations   Interpretation 101-9 concludes that it is impossible to list all relationships and circumstances that could lead to an impairment of independence. Thus, the accountant should carefully assess all situations involving relatives, dependent persons, nondependent close relatives, and others to determine whether a reasonable person aware of the pertinent facts would conclude that the accountant's independence has been impaired because of the relationship.

Interpretation 101-10 (The Effect on Independence of Relationships with Entities Included in the Governmental Financial Statements)   Governmental GAAP require that a governmental unit's (primary government) financial report include the financial statements of a component unit when the primary government exercises oversight responsibility over the component unit.

GASB-14 (The Financial Reporting Entity), which provides guidance for determining what constitutes a governmental financial reporting entity, focuses on the concept of financial accountability. The guidance established by GASB-14 is rather broad and not only has implications for the scope of the financial statements but also affects the concept of auditor independence. For this reason, a governmental entity and the auditor who is engaged to audit, review, or compile its financial statements (or a portion of the entity's financial statements) must be aware of relationships that may impair independence and thus place the auditor in violation of the AICPA's Code of Professional Conduct.

As required by GASB-14, the reporting entity includes the financial statements of the primary government (including blended component units) and discretely presented component units and note disclosures for certain entities (such as related organizations and joint ventures). Interpretation 101-10 provides the following guidelines for determining an auditor's independence with respect to the *governmental reporting entity* as defined by GASB-14:

- *Auditor of reporting entity* The auditor expressing an opinion on the reporting entity's general purpose financial statements must be independent of the primary government and its component units (both blended and discretely presented); however, the auditor need not be independent of a related organization if (a) financial accountability is not present and (b) required disclosures relative to the related organization do not include financial information.

- *Auditor of a material portion of the reporting entity* The auditor of a material fund type, fund, account group, component unit (but not the primary government), or entity that should be disclosed in the notes to the financial statements must be independent with respect to all of these entities (including the primary government); however, the auditor need not be independent of other accounting entities and account groups of the reporting entity if (a) financial accountability is not present or (b) significant influence cannot be exerted between the audited organization and the other accounting entities. (The audited organization is the governmental unit for which the professional service is being performed.)

- *Auditor of an immaterial portion of the reporting entity* The auditor of one or more fund types, funds, account groups, component units (but not the primary government), or entities that should be disclosed in the notes to the financial statements that are immaterial (both individually and in the aggregate) in relationship to the general purpose financial statements must be independent with respect to the portion of the entity being audited and should not be associated with the primary government in a way described in Interpretation 101-B (as discussed earlier in this chapter).

> OBSERVATION: *When the audited entities (fund types, funds, account groups, component units, or entities that should be disclosed in a note) in the aggregate are material, the auditor must also be independent with respect to the primary government.*

Interpretation 101-11 (Independence and the Performance of Professional Services under the Statements on Standards for Attestation Engagements and Statement on Auditing Standards No. 75, Engagements to Apply Agreed-upon Procedures to Specified Elements, Accounts, or Items of a Financial Statement) The following definitions are applicable to evaluating independence for SSAEs and SAS-75 (ET101.13):

Assertion—Any declaration, or a set of related declarations taken as a whole, by a party responsible for it.

Subject matter of an engagement—Any attribute or subset of attributes referred to or contained in an assertion that may in and of itself constitute an assertion.

Responsible party—The person(s) or entity responsible for an assertion or the subject matter of an assertion; or a specified element, account, or item of a financial statement that is the specific subject matter of the engagement.

Engagement—An engagement in which a member or a member's firm is engaged to issue or does issue a written communication that expresses a conclusion about the reliability of a written assertion. Also can be an engagement in which a member is engaged to issue or does issue a report of findings based on specific procedures performed on the specific subject matter of specified elements, accounts, or items of a financial statement.

Engagement team—Owners, partners, shareholders, and full-time or part-time professional employees of a firm who participate in the acceptance or the performance of an engagement.

The engagement team also may include individuals who provide consultation or supervisory services for the engagement.

Firm—Any organization permitted by state law or regulation to engage in the practice of public accounting, whose characteristics conform to resolutions of the AICPA Council, (*ET appendix B*) of which an individual on the engagement team includes an owner, a partner, a shareholder, or an employee, but does not include owners, partners, shareholders, or employees as individuals.

Interpretation 101-11 applies to the SSAEs and to SAS-75 only if "the report issued states that its use is to be restricted to identified parties and the member reasonably expects that the report will be restricted to those parties." Under the Interpretation, independence is impaired during the engagement or at the time the written communication is issued when the following conditions exist:

- A member of the engagement team (or the member's spouse or dependent) or the firm has a relationship with the responsible party that is restricted by Interpretation 101-1. (However, Interpretation 101-6 does not apply "unless the litigation relates to the engagement or is material to the firm or to the financial statements of the responsible party.")

- A member of the engagement team has a nondependent close relative who has (a) a position of significant influence with the responsible party or (b) a material interest in the responsible party. (*Nondependent close relative* and *position of significant influence* are defined in Interpretation 101-9.)

- An owner of the firm works in an office that participates in a significant portion of the engagement, or the spouse or dependent of that owner has (a) a position of significant influence with the responsible party or (b) a material interest in the responsible party.

- A firm, a member of the engagement team (or the member's spouse or dependent), or an owner of the firm who participates in a significant portion of the engagement will (a) contribute to the "subject matter of an engagement" or (b) financially gain from the outcome of the engagement.

- A member of the engagement team knows (or could reasonably be expected to know) that an owner who works in an office of the firm (a) contributed to the "subject matter of an engagement" or (b) has a position of significant influence with the responsible party.

Interpretation 101-12 (Independence and Cooperative Agreements with Clients) Independence is impaired when a member's firm and a client of the firm jointly engage in business activity (cooperative arrangements) when the arrangement is material to the member's firm or to the client. However, joint participation with a client generally would not be considered a cooperative arrangement if the following conditions exist:

- The participation by each party (the member's firm and the client) is governed by a *separate* agreement or understanding.
- The member's firm is not responsible for the activities of the client, and the client is not responsible for the activities of the member's firm.
- Neither the member's firm nor the client has the authority to act as the agent/representative of the other.

Relationships that are considered inappropriate under Interpretation 101-12 include a joint venture to market a service and the "bundling" of services offered by the two participants whereby there is reference to both parties.

Rule 102—Integrity and Objectivity

> In the performance of any professional service, a member shall maintain objectivity and integrity, shall be free of conflicts of interest, and shall not knowingly misrepresent facts or subordinate his or her judgment to others.

Rule 102 is very broad and could be described as an element of flexibility in the Code. The Code of Professional Conduct could not possibly prescribe every action that is to be avoided. Thus, Rule 102 could cover a variety of misconduct (ET 102.01).

Interpretations

Summarized below are the Interpretations of Rule 102 issued by the AICPA.

Interpretation 102-1 (Knowing Misrepresentations in the Preparation of Financial Statements or Records)   A misrepresentation of facts occurs when a member knowingly makes or allows or directs another to make false and misleading entries in an entity's financial statements or records. This is a violation of Rule 102 (ET 102.02).

Interpretation 102-2 (Conflicts of Interest)   A conflict of interest may arise when a member performs a professional service for a client or employer and has a "significant relationship" with another party. For example, the firm may provide investment advice for a client but may have a relationship with a financial product that is sold to the client. This situation is not prohibited if the client is informed of the relationship. In making the disclosure to the client the member should make sure that Rule 301 (Confidential Client Information) is not violated. The disclosure and consent option is available only for conflicts of interest. Impairments of *independence* cannot be so eliminated (ET 102.03).

Interpretation 102-3 (Obligations of a Member to His or Her Employer's External Accountant)   When a member who is not in public practice communicates with his or her employer's external accountant, the member "must be candid and not knowingly misrepresent facts or knowingly fail to disclose material facts." This guidance applies, for example, to written representations requested by the employer's external accountant (ET 102.04).

Interpretation 102-4 (Subordination of Judgment by a Member)   During the performance of a professional service (all services performed by a member while holding out as a CPA), a member should not subordinate his or her judgment to the position taken by a supervisor. Specifically, if there is a disagreement about the preparation of financial statements or the recording of a transaction, the member should observe the following guidelines (ET 102.05):

- Determine whether the position taken by the supervisor is consistent with an acceptable alternative accounting principle. If the principle is generally acceptable, the member does not need to take additional action.

- If the member determines that the alternative accounting principle is not acceptable, the member should communicate the disagreement to an "appropriate higher level(s) of management with the organization." This higher level could include the supervisor's supervisor, members of senior management, or the audit committee.

- If, after the appropriate higher level(s) of management was informed of the disagreement, appropriate action was not taken, the member should consider whether to continue as an employee and whether there is any responsibility to notify appropriate regulatory agencies or the employer's current or former external accountant. Consultation with legal counsel may be appropriate before communicating with external parties.

- The member should be aware of obligations established under Interpretation 102-3.

> **OBSERVATION:** *In an audit engagement, guidance established by SAS-22 (Planning and Supervision) with respect to the subordination of judgment should be observed.*

Interpretation 102-5 (Applicability of Rule 102 to Members Performing Educational Services) A member may be involved in educational services such as teaching full time or part time at a college or university, or writing books, monographs, and articles. Rule 102 applies to educational services.

Interpretation 102-6 (Professional Services Involving Client Advocacy) When a member is engaged to serve as an advocate for a client—for example, in a tax or consulting engagement or to support the client's position on financial reporting issues—the engagement is subject to the standards established by the Code of Professional Conduct and must be conducted to satisfy Rule 201, Rule 202, Rule 203, and Rule 102. If the engagement requires the member to maintain independence, Rule 101 must be satisfied. Interpretation 102-6 notes that some engagements involving client advocacy should be carefully evaluated to determine whether the risk of the loss of the firm's integrity is unacceptably high.

Rule 201—General Standards

A member shall comply with the following standards and with any interpretations thereof by bodies designated by Council.

A. *Professional Competence.* Undertake only those professional services that the member or the member's firm can reasonably expect to be completed with professional competence.

B. *Due Professional Care.* Exercise due professional care in the performance of professional services.

C. *Planning and Supervision.* Adequately plan and supervise the performance of professional services.

D. *Sufficient Relevant Data.* Obtain sufficient relevant data to afford a reasonable basis for conclusions or recommendations in relation to any professional services performed.

In general, these standards are applicable to all professional services rendered by an accounting firm. For example, an accountant who performs a consulting services engagement must properly plan and supervise the job (ET 201.01).

Rule 201 requires that a firm have a certain level of expertise before an audit, tax, or consulting engagement is accepted. This does not suggest that an accounting firm must have complete knowledge in an area before the engagement is accepted—a lack of competence is not apparent just because an accounting firm accepts a client knowing that additional research may be necessary to complete the job.

Interpretations

Summarized below are the Interpretations of Rule 201 issued by the AICPA.

Interpretation 201-1 (Competence) *Competence* includes technical qualifications, ability to supervise and evaluate work performed, knowledge of professional standards and techniques, and ability to exercise sound judgment. A member may have knowledge to complete the engagement before the engagement is accepted, or may acquire some of the knowledge through research or consultation during the engagement (ET 201.02).

Interpretation 201-2 Deleted.

Interpretation 201-3 Deleted.

Interpretation 201-4 Deleted.

Rule 202—Compliance with Standards

> A member who performs auditing, review, compilation, management consulting, tax, or other professional services shall comply with standards promulgated by bodies designated by Council.

Rule 202 requires members to observe technical standards promulgated by bodies designated by the AICPA Council. To date, the bodies designated by the Council are the Auditing Standards Board (ASB), Accounting and Review Services Committee (ARSC), and Management Consulting Services Executive Committee (MCSEC) (ET 202.01 and Appendix A).

The authority of the ASB is derived from the following two resolutions passed by the Council:

1. That the AICPA Auditing Standards Board is hereby designated as the body authorized under Rules 201 and 202 to promulgate auditing and attest standards and procedures.

2. That the Auditing Standards Board shall establish under Statements on Auditing Standards the responsibilities of members with respect to standards for disclosure of financial information outside financial statements in published financial reports containing financial statements.

Under this authority, the ASB issues Statements on Auditing Standards and Statements on Standards for Attestation Engagements.

The authority of the ARSC is derived from the following resolution passed by the Council.

> That the AICPA Accounting and Review Services Committee is hereby designated to promulgate standards under Rules 201 and 202 with respect to unaudited financial statements or other unaudited financial information of an entity that is not required to file financial statements with a regulatory agency in connection with the sale or trading of its securities in a public market.

Under this authority, the ARSC issues Statements on Standards for Accounting and Review Services.

The authority of MCSEC is derived from the following resolutions passed by the Council.

> That the AICPA Management Consulting Services Executive Committee is hereby designated to promulgate standards under Rules 201 and 202 with respect to the offering of management consulting services, provided, however, that such standards do not deal with the broad question of what, if any, services should be proscribed.

Under this authority, the MCSEC issues Statements on Standards for Consulting Services.

The AICPA Council has not given the Federal Tax Division (of the AICPA) the authority described in Rule 202. Each pronouncement in the Statements on Responsibilities in Tax Practice carries the notation that each Statement's authority depends on its general acceptance. However, a practitioner must observe the standards and rules established by the U.S. Treasury Department. Finally, it should be remembered that while the Statements on Responsibilities on Tax Practice are not incorporated in Rule 202, a practitioner must still observe the general standards established by Rule 201 of the Code of Professional Conduct.

All boards and committees that have the authority to promulgate standards under Rules 201 and 202 must follow due process by exposing proposed standards to the general membership of the AICPA and to other boards and committees that may be affected by the proposed standards.

> **OBSERVATION:** *The Code of Professional Conduct does not refer to Audit and Accounting Guides that may be issued by a committee or task force established by the AICPA. Although each Audit Guide contains a preamble that states that a Guide does not have the authority of a pronouncement by the ASB, it does note that a member may be called upon to justify departures from the Guide if the member's work is challenged.*

Interpretations

The AICPA has issued no Interpretations of Rule 202.

Rule 203—Accounting Principles

> A member shall not (1) express an opinion or state affirma-tively that the financial statements or other financial data of any entity are presented in conformity with generally accepted accounting principles or (2) state that he or she is not aware of any material modifications that should be made to such statements or data in order for them to be in confor-mity with generally accepted accounting principles, if such statements or data contain any departure from an accounting principle promulgated by bodies designated by Council to establish such principles that has a material effect on the statements or data taken as a whole. If, however, the state-ments or data contain such a departure and the member can demonstrate that due to unusual circumstances the financial statements or data would otherwise have been misleading, the member can comply with the rule by describing the de-parture, its approximate effects, if practicable, and the rea-sons why compliance with the principle would result in a misleading statement.

In 1973, the AICPA's Council designated the Financial Accounting Standards Board (FASB) as the body to establish accounting prin-ciples. Before this date, the Accounting Principles Board (APB) (1959–1973) and the Committee on Accounting Procedure (up to 1959) had the authority to promulgate accounting rules. Thus, the rule is appli-cable to FASB Statements and Interpretations, APB Opinions, and Accounting Research Bulletins issued by the Committee on Ac-counting Procedure, unless these pronouncements have been super-seded by later promulgations (ET 203.02).

In 1984, the AICPA Council designated the Governmental Ac-counting Standards Board (GASB) as the body to establish account-ing principles for financial statements prepared by state and local governments.

Rule 203 also provides flexibility in the application of accounting principles. Once an accounting rule is written there is a definite loss in flexibility, which is, of course, one of the important purposes of promulgation. However, a single rule may not be applicable to every reporting circumstance. In other words, the observance of the writ-ten rule could result in misleading financial statements. The auditor must use professional judgment to determine if literal adherence to the pronouncement will result in meaningless information. Obviously, in the vast majority of audits the written rule will be observed. In fact, most auditors are probably very reluctant to accept the responsibility of a departure from promulgated generally accepted accounting principles.

When the auditor concludes that a written accounting rule should not be followed, the auditor's standard report must be expanded to include an explanatory paragraph. The explanatory paragraph would describe the nature of the departure; however, the opinion expressed would be an unqualified opinion and no reference to the explanatory paragraph would be made in the opinion paragraph.

There are numerous examples of financial statements not prepared in accordance with generally accepted accounting principles. SAS-62 (Special Reports) deals, in part, with financial statements prepared in accordance with a comprehensive basis of accounting other than GAAP. However, under this circumstance, the auditor's report must be changed to note the unique accounting basis and to explicitly state that the financial statements are not prepared in accordance with GAAP. Other aspects of SAS-62 are described in the part of the book entitled "Audited Financial Statements."

Interpretations

Summarized below are the Interpretations of Rule 203 issued by the AICPA.

Interpretation 203-1 (Departures from Established Accounting Principles) New legislation or the evolution of a new form of business transaction may justify a departure from promulgated principles; however, the degree of materiality or the existence of conflicting industrial practices would not be a basis for departure (ET 203.02).

Interpretation 203-2 (Status of FASB and GASB Interpretations) The Professional Ethics Division will evaluate FASB Statements, APB Opinions, and Accounting Research Bulletins in the context of any relevant FASB Interpretation issued when determining a departure from a promulgated principle. GASB Interpretations will be considered when determining the departure from a promulgated governmental accounting standard (ET 203.03).

Interpretation 203-3 Deleted.

Interpretation 203-4 (Responsibility of Employees for Preparation of Financial Statements in Conformity with GAAP) Rule 203 applies to all members (including those not in public practice) and is not limited to references to GAAP in the auditor's report. Thus, a nonpracticing member who makes a representation that financial statements or other financial data are presented in conformity with GAAP in a letter to the external auditors, regulatory authorities, and creditors would be in violation of Rule 203 if the information does not conform to GAAP (ET 203.05).

Rule 301—Confidential Client Information

A member in public practice shall not disclose any confidential client information without the specific consent of the client.

This rule shall not be construed (1) to relieve a member of his or her professional obligations under rules 202 and 203, (2) to affect in any way the member's obligation to comply with a validly issued and enforceable subpoena or summons, or to prohibit a member's compliance with applicable laws and government regulations, (3) to prohibit review of a member's professional practice under AICPA or state CPA society or Board of Accountancy authorization, or (4) to preclude a member from initiating a complaint with, or responding to any inquiry made by, the professional ethics division or trial board of the Institute or a duly constituted investigative or disciplinary body of a state CPA society or Board of Accountancy.

Members of any of the bodies identified in (4) above and members involved with professional practice reviews identified in (3) above shall not use to their own advantage or disclose any member's confidential client information that comes to their attention in carrying out those activities. This prohibition shall not restrict members' exchange of information in connection with the investigative or disciplinary proceedings described in (4) above or the professional practice reviews described in (3) above.

An auditor should have access to a variety of information held by the client if the engagement is to be successful. The client will grant the auditor access to sensitive files and reports only if it can expect the auditor to hold the information in confidence. The purpose of Rule 301 is to encourage a free flow of information from the client to the CPA; however, the rule makes it clear that the principle of confidentiality is not absolute. The confidentiality concept does not allow the client to omit information that is required by generally accepted accounting principles. SAS-32 (Adequacy of Disclosure in Financial Statements) reinforces this position by stating that if a client omits information that is required by GAAP, a qualified or adverse opinion must be expressed. On the other hand, SAS-32 does note that an auditor ordinarily should not make available information that is not required to be disclosed to comply with GAAP (ET 301.01).

Rule 301 recognizes the confidentiality of client information, but makes it clear that the information does not constitute privileged communication. In most states, and all federal courts, the CPA can be forced to testify in a case involving the client. Thus, the rule recognizes that an auditor must respond to a subpoena or summons.

In recent years, the concept of peer review has been accepted by the profession. Rule 301 allows a peer or quality review of a CPA's professional practice as part of an AICPA or state society of CPAs program.

Finally, Rule 301 states that it is not a violation of confidentiality when a member initiates a complaint with or responds to inquiries from a recognized investigative or disciplinary body such as the AICPA's Professional Ethics Division or Trial Board.

Interpretations

Summarized below are the Interpretations of Rule 301 issued by the AICPA.

Interpretation 301-1 Deleted.

Interpretation 301-2 Deleted.

Interpretation 301-3 (Confidential Information and the Purchase, Sale, or Merger of a Practice) A member's professional practice may be reviewed by another CPA as part of a possible purchase, sale, or merger of all or part of the member's practice. The member should take appropriate steps to reasonably ensure the confidentiality of client information reviewed by the other CPA. This may, for example, include a written agreement between the two CPAs recognizing the confidential nature of client information. The CPA reviewing the confidential information should not use the information in a manner unrelated to the purchase or merger (ET 301.04).

Rule 302—Contingent Fees

A member in public practice shall not:

1. Perform for a contingent fee any professional services for, or receive such a fee from, a client for whom the member or the member's firm performs:

    (a) an audit or review of a financial statement; or

    (b) a compilation of a financial statement when the member expects, or reasonably might expect, that a third party will use the financial statement and the member's compilation report does not disclose a lack of independence; or

    (c) an examination of prospective financial information; or

2. Prepare an original or amended tax return or claim for a tax refund for a contingent fee for any client.

The prohibition in (1) above applies during the period in which the member or the member's firm is engaged to perform any of the services listed above and the period covered by any historical financial statements involved in any such listed services.

Except as stated in the next sentence, a contingent fee is a fee established for the performance of any service pursuant to an arrangement in which no fee will be charged unless a specified finding or result is attained, or in which the amount of the fee is otherwise dependent upon the finding or result of such service. Solely for the purposes of this rule, fees are not regarded as being contingent if fixed by courts or other public authorities, or, in tax matters, if determined based on the results of judicial proceedings or the findings of governmental agencies.

A member's fees may vary depending, for example, on the complexity of services rendered.

The accounting profession has had a long-standing tradition that a contingent fee would infringe on the CPA's ability to be independent. A contingent fee is based on an arrangement whereby the client is not required to pay the CPA unless a specified finding or result is attained. For example, a contingent fee arrangement would exist if the auditor's fee is dependent on the net proceeds of a public stock offering. Engagement fees should be determined by such factors as the number of hours required to perform the engagement, the type of personnel needed for the engagement, and the complexity of the engagement (ET 302.01).

Fees are not considered to be contingent if they are determined (1) by courts or other public authorities or (2) by judicial proceedings or governmental agencies in the case of tax matters.

Before 1991, Rule 302 prohibited contingent fees for all professional engagements (with the exception of certain fees fixed by the judicial or quasi-judicial process). In 1985, the Federal Trade Commission (FTC) challenged the position of the profession concerning contingent fees on the basis of restraint of trade. After prolonged negotiations between the AICPA and the FTC, Rule 302 (as reproduced above) was issued to modify the existing prohibition against contingent fees.

Rule 302 prohibits contingent fees for all additional professional services when the CPA has performed an attestation engagement, which includes audits, reviews, and examinations of prospective financial information. Also, the CPA may not perform any services for a client on a contingent fee basis when the CPA has performed a compilation engagement if the compilation report is expected to be used by a third party and does not disclose that the CPA is not independent with respect to the client.

The period of prohibition includes the date covered by the financial statements and the period during which the attestation service (and compilation service, as described above) is performed. For example, if the CPA is auditing a client's financial statements for the year ended December 31, 19X5, and the date of the auditor's report is March 12, 19X6, no services could be performed on a contingent fee basis by the auditor for the period from January 1, 19X5, through March 12, 19X6.

Rule 302 also prohibits the CPA from charging a contingent fee to prepare an original or amended tax return or claim for a refund. While independence is not an issue in performing tax services, the AICPA takes the position that it would be unprofessional to charge a fee, for example, based on the amount of refund that may be claimed on the tax return.

Interpretations

Summarized below are the Interpretations of Rule 302 issued by the AICPA.

Interpretation 302-1 (Contingent Fees in Tax Matters)   The first Interpretation of Rule 302 was issued to define the following two phrases used in the Rule (ET 302.02):

> Preparation of an original or amended tax return or claim for tax refund includes giving advice on events which have occurred at the time the advice is given if such advice is directly relevant to determining the existence, character, or amount of a schedule, entry, or other portion of a return or claim for refund.
>
> A fee is considered determined based on the findings of governmental agencies if the member can demonstrate a reasonable expectation, at the time of a fee arrangement, of substantive consideration by an agency with respect to the member's client. Such an expectation is deemed not reasonable in the case of preparation of original tax returns.

In addition to defining certain phrases, Interpretation 302-1 identifies the following circumstances under which the CPA may charge a contingent fee:

- Representing a client in an examination of the client's income tax return.

- Filing an amended income tax return for a client whereby a tax refund is claimed based on an issue (1) that is the subject of a test case (not involving the client) or (2) for which the taxing authority is developing a position.

- Filing an amended income tax return (or refund claim) for the client whereby the claimed refund is greater than the threshold for review by the Joint Committee on Internal Revenue Taxation or state taxing authority.

- Requesting an overpayment refund charged to the client's account, or deposits for taxes improperly accounted for by the taxing authority whereby the authority has established procedures for the substantive review of such refund requests.

- Requesting on the behalf of a client consideration for reduction in the assessed value of property under a taxing authority's established review process.

- Representing a client in an attempt to obtain a private letter ruling or influencing the drafting of tax laws or regulations.

Finally, Interpretation 302-1 notes that a contingent fee may not be charged for an engagement involving the amendment of an income tax return that is based on the obvious omission of a deduction.

> *OBSERVATION: Rule 401 (Encroachment) and Rule 402 (Offers of Employment) were revoked in 1979 and 1977, respectively, and there are currently no rules in the 400 series under the revised Code of Professional Conduct.*

Rule 501—Acts Discreditable

A member shall not commit an act discreditable to the profession.

Rule 501 is very broad. It is basic to ethical conduct, and only through its observance can the profession expect to win the confidence of the public. What constitutes a discreditable act is highly judgmental. There has been no attempt to be specific about what constitutes a discreditable act; however, the AICPA bylaws (Section 7.3) state that the following actions will lead to membership suspension or termination, without the need for a disciplinary hearing (ET 501.01):

- If a member commits a crime punishable by imprisonment for more than one year.

- If a member willfully fails to file an income tax return that he or she, as an individual taxpayer, is required by law to file.

- If a member files a false or fraudulent income tax return on his or her behalf, or on a client's behalf.

- If a member willfully aids in the preparation and presentation of a false and fraudulent income tax return of a client.

- If a member's certificate as a certified public accountant, or license or permit to practice as such, is revoked by a governmental authority as a disciplinary measure.

Interpretations

Summarized below are the Interpretations of Rule 501 issued by the AICPA.

Interpretation 501-1 (Retention of Client Records) Retaining client records after their return has been requested violates Rule 501. The conclusion is valid even though a state may allow a lien on client records held by the auditor. On the other hand, a member does not have to surrender workpapers to the client, since they are the property of the auditor (ET 501.02).

An auditor's workpapers may include information that would cause the client's accounting records to otherwise be incomplete. Examples include adjusting entries, consolidating entries, and information normally included in journals and ledgers. When an engagement has been completed, information of this type included in the workpapers should be made available to the client on request; however, the auditor may stipulate that the engagement fee must be paid before the information is provided. Once the auditor has provided the information, subsequent requests for the auditor to provide the information again need not be honored.

Interpretation 501-2 (Discrimination in Employment Practices) Discrimination based on race, color, religion, sex, age, or national origin is a violation of Rule 501 (ET 501.03).

Interpretation 501-3 (Failure to Follow Standards and/or Procedures or Other Requirements in Governmental Audits) When an engagement involving the audit of government grants, governmental units, or other recipients of government funds is accepted and the auditor agrees to follow specified government audit standards guides, procedures, statutes, rules, and regulations in addition to generally accepted auditing standards, a failure to do so is a violation of Rule 501 unless the reason for not following the requirements is stated in the audit report (ET 501.04).

Interpretation 501-4 (Negligence in the Preparation of Financial Statements or Records) A discreditable act occurs when a member, through negligence, makes or allows or directs another to make false and misleading entries in the entity's financial statements or records (ET 501.05).

Interpretation 501-5 (Failure to Follow Requirements of Governmental Bodies, Commissions, or Other Regulatory Agencies in

Performing Attest or Similar Services) When a member performs an attest or similar service as part of the reporting requirements to governmental bodies, commissions, or other regulatory agencies, audit standards, guides, and rules and regulations established by those regulatory entities must be observed. If those guidelines are not observed, the member is guilty of an act discreditable to the profession unless (1) the member states in the report that such guidelines were not followed and gives the reason for not following the guidelines and (2) the member, if required, follows any other disclosure requirements established by the regulatory entity (ET 501.06).

Interpretation 501-6 (Solicitation or Disclosure of CPA Examination Questions and Answers) A discreditable act occurs when a member solicits or knowingly discloses questions or answers to the CPA Examination without written authorization from the AICPA (ET 501.07).

Rule 502—Advertising and Other Forms of Solicitation

> A member in public practice shall not seek to obtain clients by advertising or other forms of solicitation in a manner that is false, misleading, or deceptive. Solicitation by the use of coercion, overreaching, or harassing conduct is prohibited.

Before 1978, Rule 502 expressly prohibited advertising. Currently, a member is not prohibited from advertising or soliciting clients. The change in Rule 502 resulted from legal action taken by the Justice Department against a number of professional groups. In 1977, the U.S. Supreme Court ruled that the American Bar Association could not prohibit advertising by its members. The AICPA, after extensive debate, revised Rule 502 (ET 502.01).

Interpretations

Summarized below are the Interpretations of Rule 502 issued by the AICPA.

Interpretation 502-1 Deleted.

Interpretation 502-2 (False, Misleading, or Deceptive Acts in Advertising or Solicitation)   Advertising or other forms of solicitation that are false, misleading, or deceptive are not in the public interest and are prohibited. Such activities include those that (ET 502.03):

- Imply false or unjustified expectations of favorable results

- Imply the ability to influence any court, tribunal, regulatory agency, or similar body or official

- Contain a representation that specific professional services in current or future periods will be performed for a stated fee, estimated fee, or fee range when it was likely at the time of the representation that such fees would be substantially increased and the prospective client was not advised of that likelihood

- Contain any other representations that would be likely to cause a reasonable person to misunderstand or be deceived

Interpretation 502-3   Deleted.

Interpretation 502-4   Deleted.

Interpretation 502-5 (Engagements Obtained Through Efforts of Third Parties)   A firm may accept engagements for clients or customers of third parties who have obtained these clients or customers through advertising and solicitation. However, the firm must determine that all promotional efforts on the part of third parties did not violate the Rules of Conduct (ET 502.06).

Rule 503—Commissions and Referral Fees

A. Prohibited Commissions

A member in public practice shall not for a commission recommend or refer to a client any product or service, or for a commission recommend or refer any product or service to be supplied by a client, or receive a commission, when the member or the member's firm also performs for that client:

(a)   an audit or review of a financial statement; or

(b) a compilation of a financial statement when the member expects, or reasonably might expect, that a third party will use the financial statement and the member's compilation report does not disclose a lack of independence; or

(c) an examination of prospective financial information.

This prohibition applies during the period in which the member is engaged to perform any of the services listed above and the period covered by any historical financial statements involved in such listed services.

B. Disclosure of Permitted Commissions

A member in public practice who is not prohibited by this rule from performing services for or receiving a commission and who is paid or expects to be paid a commission shall disclose that fact to any person or entity to whom the member recommends or refers a product or service to which the commission relates.

C. Referral Fees

Any member who accepts a referral fee for recommending or referring any service of a CPA to any person or entity or who pays a referral fee to obtain a client shall disclose such acceptance or payment to the client.

A CPA cannot receive a commission for recommending a client's product or services if the CPA audits or reviews that client's financial statements or examines that client's prospective financial information. In addition, no commissions can be received when the CPA compiles a client's financial statements if the CPA believes that a third party will rely on the statements, unless any lack of independence is disclosed in the compilation report (ET 503.01).

When a CPA receives a commission (and is not in violation of part A of Rule 503), the party related to the earning of the commission should be told that the CPA has received or will receive a commission.

If a CPA pays a referral fee to obtain a client, the client should be informed of the fee.

> **OBSERVATION:** *Rule 503 was amended on the basis of an agreement between the AICPA and the Federal Trade Commission.*

> *Some state societies of CPAs and state boards of accountancy have decided not to enforce Rule 503. They take the position that commissions and fees should not be received or paid by the CPA for the referral of services. Each member should refer to the position taken by his or her particular state organization.*

Interpretations

The only Interpretation of Rule 503 (Interpretation 503-1) has been withdrawn.

Rule 504—Incompatible Occupations (Withdrawn)

Before the revision of the Code, Rule 504 stated that a member who is engaged in the practice of public accounting shall not concurrently engage in any business or occupation that would create a conflict of interest in rendering professional services. The concept of incompatible occupations now is covered by Rule 101 (Independence).

Rule 505—Form of Organization and Name

> A member may practice public accounting only in a form of organization permitted by state law or regulation whose characteristics conform to resolutions of Council.
>
> A member shall not practice public accounting under a firm name that is misleading. Names of one or more past owners may be included in the firm name of a successor organization. Also, an owner surviving the death or withdrawal of all other owners may continue to practice under a name which includes the name of past owners for up to two years after becoming a sole practitioner.
>
> A firm may not designate itself as "Members of the American Institute of Certified Public Accountants" unless all of its owners are members of the Institute.

An accounting firm may be organized as a sole proprietorship, as a partnership, as a limited liability partnership, or in another form permitted by state law. Before a firm was allowed to incorporate, it was often argued that it was not in the best interests of the profession because incorporation would lead to limited liability and a loss of personal contact between the accountant and the client (ET 505.01).

Over the past several decades, the character of the practice of accounting has broadened to include a variety of activities that are beyond the scope of accounting. These activities include, among others, environmental auditing, executive recruitment, and the design of sophisticated computer systems that are not part of the client's accounting system. With the expansion of the types of services provided by accounting firms, there is an obvious need to recruit personnel who do not have an accounting/auditing background. For many accounting firms, these nontraditional professionals are increasingly important to their growth and development. However, because of the rules adopted by the AICPA, a nontraditional professional, no matter how competent or important to the firm, could not be an owner of the firm.

In 1994, after considerable debate within the profession, the AICPA passed a resolution that allows a CPA firm to be owned by non-CPAs if the form of ownership is sanctioned by the particular state and if the following guidelines are observed (ET Appendix B):

- Two-thirds of the ownership (as measured by financial interest and voting rights) must be held by CPAs.

- A non-CPA owner must be actively engaged in providing services to clients of the firm, and that participation must be the principal occupation of the non-CPA.

- A CPA must be ultimately responsible for all services provided by the firm that involve financial statement attestation, compilation services, and "other engagements governed by Statements on Auditing Standards or Statements on Standards for Accounting and Review Services."

- A non-CPA who becomes an owner after the adoption of the AICPA resolution must have a baccalaureate degree (after 2010, the individual must have completed 150 semester hours of education).

- A non-CPA may not hold him- or herself out as a CPA, but may be referred to as a(n) principal, owner, officer, member, shareholder, or other title allowed by state law.

- A non-CPA owner must observe the AICPA Code of Professional Conduct.

- A non-CPA owner must complete the same number of CPE units as CPAs.

While the resolution allows for accounting firm ownership by non-CPAs, those individuals are not eligible for membership in the AICPA.

> **OBSERVATION:** *Each state is responsible for determining what forms of ownership may be used to practice public accounting; however, the AICPA notes that a practitioner can practice only in a business organization form that conforms to resolutions of the AICPA Council.*

Interpretations

Summarized below are the Interpretations of Rule 505 issued by the AICPA.

Interpretation 505-1 (Investment in Accounting Organization)   A member may invest in a corporation that performs accounting services; however, if the state does not allow the practice of public accounting in a corporate form, the member must function only as an investor and the investment cannot enable the member to significantly influence the corporation (ET 505.02).

Interpretation 505-2 (Application of Rules of Conduct to Members Who Operate a Separate Business)   A member who practices as a public accountant and participates in a separate business that performs public accounting services (that is, any of the professional services of accounting, tax, personal financial planning, litigation support services, and other services for which standards are promulgated by bodies designated by the AICPA Council) is considered a practicing public accountant with respect to the separate business and must observe the Code of Professional Conduct. A member who does not otherwise practice as a public accountant but participates in a separate business that performs for clients professional services included in the definition of the practice of public accounting, and holds himself or herself out as a CPA, must observe the Code of Professional Conduct with respect to the separate business (ET 505.03).

RULINGS ON ETHICS

After exposure to state societies and state boards of accountancy, Rulings on Ethics are formalized and issued by the Executive Committee of the AICPA. These rulings set forth the application of the Rules of Conduct and Interpretations to a particular set of circumstances. AICPA members who depart from such rulings may be required to justify their departures.

> **OBSERVATION:** *Publication of a ruling in the Journal of Accountancy constitutes notice to AICPA members that the ruling is effective. The publication date of the Journal of Accountancy is considered the effective date of the ruling unless a later date is specifically indicated.*

Rulings on Independence, Integrity, and Objectivity (Rules 101 and 102)

1—**Acceptance of a Gift**. The acceptance of more than a token gift from a client may impair independence (ET 191.001–.002).

2—**Association Membership**. Being a member of a trade association that is a client does not impair independence if the CPA does not serve as a member of the trade association's management (ET 191.003–.004).

3—**Member as Signer or Cosigner of Checks**. Cosigning checks, even in an emergency situation, would impair independence (ET 191.005–.006).

4—**Payroll Preparation Services**. Performing payroll preparation, processing checks through the CPA firm's single bank account, and cosigning the checks along with an officer of the client would impair independence (ET 191.007–.008).

5—Deleted.

6—**Member's Spouse as Accountant of Client**. Independence is not necessarily impaired when the spouse of a member is the audit client's bookkeeper, as long as the spouse's role conforms with Interpretation 101-3 (ET 191.011–.012).

7—**Member Providing Contract Services**. Supervising client office personnel, approving vouchers for payment, and preparing reports would impair independence (ET 191.013–.014).

8—**Member Providing Advisory Services.** Independence is not impaired when a member provides extensive accounting and management consulting services for a client—such as attending board meetings; interpreting financial statements, forecasts, and other analyses; counseling on potential expansion plans; and counseling on negotiations with banks—provided Interpretation 101-3 is observed (ET 191.015–.016).

9—**Member as Representative of Creditor's Committee.** Performing such tasks as (1) cosigning checks, (2) cosigning purchase orders in excess of established minimum amounts, and (3) general supervision for a creditor's committee in control of a debtor company would impair independence with respect to the debtor company (ET 191.017–.018).

10—**Member as Legislator.** Independence is impaired when a member of a firm is an elected legislator in a municipal body and the municipality is an audit client, even if the city manager is an elected official (ET 191.019–.020).

11—**Member as Executor or Trustee.** Serving as an executor and trustee of the estate of an individual who owns the majority of the stock of a closely held corporation would impair independence (ET 191.021–.022).

12—**Member as Trustee.** Serving as a trustee of a tax-exempt charitable foundation would impair independence with respect to the foundation and the estate that made the foundation its sole beneficiary (ET 191.023–.024).

13—Deleted.

14—**Member on Board of Directors of Federated Fund-Raising Organization.** Independence is not impaired with respect to a charity that receives funds from a federated fund-raising organization (such as the United Way) when a member is a director or officer of the local unit of the federated fund-raising organization if the latter organization does not exercise managerial control over the charity (ET 191.027–.028).

15—Deleted.

16—**Member on Board of Directors of Nonprofit Social Club.** Serving on the board of directors of a nonprofit social club would impair independence with respect to the social club (ET 191.031–.032).

17—**Member of Social Club.** Independence is not impaired when a member belongs to a social club (such as a country club) in which he or she must acquire a pro rata share of equity or debt securities as long as the member does not take part in the management of the club (ET 191.033–.034).

18—Deleted.

19—**Member on Deferred Compensation Committee.** Serving on a client's committee that administers the client's deferred compensation program would impair independence (ET 191.037–.038).

20—**Member Serving on Governmental Advisory Unit.** Independence is not impaired with respect to a county when a member serves on a citizens' committee that is studying possible changes in the form of the county, and he or she also is a member of a committee appointed to make a study of the financial status of the state in which the county is located (ET 191.039–.040).

21—**Member as Director and Auditor of the Entity's Profit Sharing Trust.** Serving as a director of an enterprise and auditor of the enterprise's profit-sharing and retirement trust would impair independence with respect to the trust (ET 191.041–.042).

22–27—Deleted.

28—**Cash Account with Brokerage Client.** Superseded by Ethics Ruling No. 59.

29—**Member as Bondholder.** Investing in the bonds of a municipal authority by a member of a CPA firm would impair independence with respect to the municipal authority because the investment represents a direct financial interest (ET 191.057–.058).

30—Deleted.

31—**Financial Interest in a Cooperative, Condominium Association, Planned Unit Development, Homeowners Association, Timeshare Development, or Other Common Interest Realty Association.** Independence is impaired when a partner of a firm owns a unit in a cooperative, condominium association, planned unit development, homeowners association, timeshare development, or other common interest realty association (ET 191.061–.062).

32—Deleted.

33—**Member as a Participant in Employee Benefit Plan.** Joining a client employee benefit plan would impair independence (ET 191.065–.066).

34—Deleted.

35—**Stockholder in Mutual Funds.** Independence is not impaired when a member owns shares in a regulated mutual investment fund and that fund owns shares of stock in clients of the firm, as long as the mutual fund's portfolio is not heavily invested in a client's securities (ET 191.069–.070).

36—**Participant in Investment Club.** Having an interest in an investment club would impair independence for any client in which the club invests because the member's investment represents a direct financial interest (ET 191.071–.072).

37—Deleted.

38—**Member as Co-Fiduciary with Client Bank.** Independence is not impaired with respect to a bank or its trust department when a member serves with a client bank in a co-fiduciary capacity to an estate or trust, provided the assets in the estate or trust were not material in relation to the total assets of the bank and/or trust department (ET 191.075–.076).

39—**Member as Officially Appointed Stock Transfer Agent or Registrar.** Serving as an officially appointed stock transfer agent and/or registrar for a client would impair independence (ET 191.077–.078).

40—Deleted.

41—**Member as Auditor of Insurance Company.** Independence is not impaired with respect to a mutual insurance company when a retirement plan for the CPA firm's employees is funded with a mutual insurance company that manages contributions made by the firm in a pooled separate account (ET 191.081–.082).

42–43—Deleted.

44—**Past Due Billings.** Superseded by Ethics Ruling No. 52.

45—Deleted.

46—**Member as General Counsel.** Superseded by Ethics Ruling No. 51.

47—Deleted.

48—**Faculty Member as Auditor of a Student Fund.** Auditing a university's student senate fund by a member who is part of the school's full- or part-time faculty, when (1) the university acts as a collection agent for student fees and remits them to the student senate and (2) a member of the administration must sign student senate checks, would impair independence (ET 191.095–.096).

49—**Investor and Investee Companies.** Superseded by Interpretation 101-8.

50—Deleted.

51—**Member Providing Legal Services.** Serving as general counsel for a client would impair the independence of a CPA who is also an attorney (ET 191.101–.102).

52—**Unpaid Fees.** Independence is impaired when a member has an amount due from a client as of the date of issuing a current report if at that date fees are unpaid from previous engagements that represent work performed more than one year before the date of the current report. The ruling does not apply to clients in bankruptcy (ET 191.103–.104).

53—Deleted.

54—**Member Providing Appraisal, Valuation, or Actuarial Services.** Independence is not impaired when a CPA firm provides appraisal, valuation, or actuarial services that affect the client's financial statements, provided all significant matters of judgment involved are determined or approved by the client and the client is in a position to have an informed judgment on the results (ET 191.107–.108).

55—**Independence During Systems Implementation.** Independence is not impaired when a CPA firm performs a nonrecurring engagement involving the implementation of an information system in which the firm will, only during the period of conversion, arrange interviews for client's hiring of new personnel and instruct and oversee the training of current personnel, provided the client makes all significant management decisions related to the project (ET 191.109–.110).

56—**Executive Search.** Recruiting and hiring a controller and a cost accountant for a client's new operation in another locality would impair independence (ET 191.111–.112).

57—Deleted.

58—**Member as Lessor.** Renting space in a building owned by a member to a client would impair independence when the relationship created by the lessor/lessee transaction is deemed to create a material indirect interest in the client (ET 191.115–.116).

59—Deleted.

60—**Employee Benefit Plans—Member's Relationships with Participating Employer(s).** Independence is not impaired when a member audits the financial statements of an employee benefit plan that has a participating employer if the member has no financial interest in the employer or other relationship with the employer that would result in the member having significant influence over the employer (ET 191.119–.120). (Note: When a member audits an employee benefit plan, Department of Labor regulations must be observed.)

61—**Participation of Member's Spouse in Client's Stock Ownership Plans (Including an ESOP).** When the spouse of a member is employed by a client and the spouse participates in an employee stock ownership plan, independence is lost if (1) the right of possession occurs or (2) the interest is material to the member's net worth (ET 191.121–.122).

62–63—Deleted.

64—**Member on Board of Organization for Which Client Raises Funds.** A member may not audit a fund-raising foundation whose only purpose is to raise funds for an agency for which the member serves on its board of directors. A member may audit such a foundation if the member's position with the agency is honorary and restricted to the use of the member's name (ET 191.128–.129).

65—**Use of the CPA Designation by Member Not in Public Practice.** A member who is not in public practice may use the CPA designation on a business card and in connection with his or her employer's financial statements and correspondence provided the designation is not used in a manner that implies the member is independent of the employer. In these situations, it is advisable to clearly indicate the employee's title (ET 191.130–.131).

66—**Member's Retirement or Savings Plan Has Financial Interest in Client.** Independence is impaired when a member's retirement or savings plan, in which the member has a financial interest, has a financial interest in the client (ET 191.132–.133).

67—**Servicing of Loan.** The mere servicing of a member's loan by a client financial institution would not impair the member's independence (ET 191.134–.135).

68—**Blind Trust.** Placing a direct financial interest in a client in a blind trust is still an impairment of independence with respect to the client (ET 191.136–.137).

69—**Investment with a General Partner.** Independence is impaired with respect to a limited partnership when a member has a material interest in another limited partnership if both limited partnerships are controlled by a general partner that is a private, closely held entity (ET 191.138–.139). (See FAS-94 [Consolidation of All Majority-Owned Subsidiaries] for the definition of *control.*)

70—**Member's Depository Relationship with Client Financial Institution.** Checking accounts, savings accounts, certificates of deposit, and money market accounts held by the auditor in a client-financial institution would not impair independence if (1) the amounts are fully insured by a deposit insurance agency or (2) uninsured amounts are not material to the member or the member's firm (ET 191.140–.141).

71—**Use of Nonindependent CPA Firm on an Engagement.** A firm that uses members of another firm would be considered in violation of Rule 101 if the other firm is not independent of the firm's client (ET 191.142–.143).

72—**Member on Advisory Board of Client.** A member's service on a client's advisory board would impair independence unless (1) the role of the board is exclusively advisory, (2) the board has no authority and there is no appearance to make management decisions, and (3) the board is distinct (with minimal or no common membership) from those having authority to make management decisions (including the board of directors or its equivalent) (ET 191.144–.145).

73—**Meaning of the Period of a Professional Engagement.** The "period of professional engagement" starts at the date professional services are performed and ends at the date that the member (or client) notifies the client (or member) that the professional relationship is terminated (ET 191.146–.147).

74—**Audits, Reviews, or Compilations and a Lack of Independence.** A member cannot issue an audit opinion or a review report if the member is not considered independent with respect to the client; however, a compilation report can be issued. In the latter case, the compilation report should state that the member is not independent, but the reason for the lack of independence should not be disclosed in the compilation report (ET 191.148–.149).

75—**Member Joining Client Credit Union.** Independence would not be considered impaired with respect to a credit union when a member's partners and employees are members of the credit union if (1) membership in the credit union is based on criteria other than the fact the member or the member's partners and employees perform professional services for the credit union, (2) the influence of the member or the member's partners and employees does not have a significant influence on the credit union's operating, financial, or accounting policies, (3) loans to the member or the member's partners and employees reflect normal lending standards, and (4) deposits with the credit union meet the guidelines established by Ethics Ruling No. 70 (ET 191.150–.151).

76—Deleted.

77—**Individual Considering or Accepting Employment with the Client.** When an individual involved in an engagement has sought or been offered a position with a client, that individual should remove himself or herself from the engagement so as not to give the appearance that integrity or objectivity has been impaired. If, after the completion of an engagement, a member discovers that an individual was considering a position with a client, the member should consider what additional procedures should be performed in order to ensure that the standards of objectivity and integrity were observed during the engagement (ET 191.154–.155).

78—Deleted.

79—**Member's Investment in a Partnership That Invests in Member's Client.** Independence would be impaired when a member is a general partner (with direct financial interest) in a partnership that invests in a client of the member's firm; however, when the member is a limited partner (with indirect financial interest), independence is impaired only if the interest in the client is material to the member (ET 191.158–.159).

80—**The Meaning of a Joint Closely Held Business Investment.** A joint closely held business investment, as referred to in Interpretation 101-1, is a business investment subject to control by a member, the client, its officers, directors, or principal stockholders, individually or collectively (ET 191.160–.161). (See FAS-94 [Consolidation of All Majority-Owned Subsidiaries] for a definition of *control*.)

81—**Member's Investment in a Limited Partnership.** When a member is a limited partner and a member's client is a general partner in the same limited partnership, (1) independence with respect to the limited partnership is impaired because there is a direct financial interest; (2) independence with respect to the client is impaired only when both the member's and the client's interests in the limited partnership are material; and (3) independence with respect to a subsidiary of the limited partnership would be impaired only when the interest in the subsidiary (indirect interest) is material to the member (ET 191.162–.163). (See Ethics Ruling No. 80 when a member or a client, either separately or collectively, can control the limited partnership.)

82—**Campaign Treasurer.** When a member serves as the campaign treasurer of the campaign organization of a candidate for mayor, the member is independent with respect to the political party and the municipality but is not independent with respect to the campaign organization (ET 191.164–.165).

83–84—Deleted.

85—**Bank Director.** A member in public practice may serve as a bank director; however, if the member has clients that are also customers of the bank the member should consider complications arising from Rule 301 (Confidential Client Information) and Interpretation 102-2 (Conflicts of Interest) (ET 191.170–.171).

86—**Partially Secured Loans.** When a member has a loan that is partially secured by real estate from a financial institution, the loan is considered to be grandfathered under Interpretation 101-5, if "at all times after the member is required to be independent with respect to the client, the portion of the loan that exceeds the value of the collateral is not material to the member's net worth" (ET 191.172–.173).

87—**Loan Commitment or Line of Credit.** In applying the "grandfathered loans" provisions of Interpretation 101-5, the date of the loan commitment or line of credit may be used rather than the closing date of the transaction if the loan meets the requirements of the Interpretation as of the loan date commitment or the date the line of credit was extended (ET 191.174–.175).

88—**Loans to Partnership in Which Members Are Limited Partners.** A loan to a limited partnership by a financial institution in which members' (who are limited partners) combined interest exceeds 50% of the limited partnership is considered a loan to those members and should be ascribed to each limited partner on the basis of individual legal liability for applying the "grandfathered loans" provision of Interpretation 101-5 (ET 191.176–.177).

89—**Loans to Partnership in Which Members Are General Partners.** A loan to partnership by a financial institution in which a member is a general partner is considered a loan to the member and should be ascribed to the partner on the basis of individual legal liability (usually 100% of the loan) for applying the "grandfathered loan" provision of Interpretation 101-5 (ET 191.178–.179).

90—**Credit Card Balances and Cash Advances.** Independence would not be impaired under Interpretation 101-1.A.4 and Interpretation 101-5 when a member has credit cards and cash advances from a client financial institution, assuming the aggregate outstanding balance is decreased to $5,000 or less on a current basis (ET 191.180–.181).

91—**Member Leasing Property from a Client.** Independence would not be impaired if a member (lessee) leases property from a client and at the time of the transaction the lease would not be considered a capital lease as defined by FAS-13 (Accounting for Leases) and the lease is made under normal leasing arrangements. Independence would be impaired if the lease is considered a capital lease unless the lease transaction is in compliance with Interpretation 101-1.A.4 and Interpretation 101-5 (ET 191.182–.183).

92—**Joint Interest in Vacation Home.** When a member has a joint investment in a vacation home with an officer, director, or principal stockholder of a client that uses services that require independence, the relationship is a "joint closely held business investment" under Interpretation 101-1.A.3 (ET 191.184–.185).

93—**Service on Board of Directors of Federal Fund-Raising Organization.** When a member is a director or officer of a local United Way (or similar organization) that operates as a federated fund-raising entity and dispenses funds to clients of the member, a conflict of interest does not arise if any significant relationship is disclosed and consent is obtained from appropriate parties (ET 191.186–.187).

94—**Indemnification Clause in Engagement Letters.** Independence is not impaired when a client agrees to include in an engagement letter a clause stating the client will not hold the member liable for any damages arising from misrepresentations knowingly made by management (ET 191.188–.189).

95—**Agreement with Attest Client to Use ADR Techniques.** Independence is not impaired when a member and a client enter into a predispute agreement to use alternative dispute resolution (ADR) techniques (rather than litigation) to settle future disagreements (ET 191.190–.191).

96—**Commencement of ADR Proceeding.** Independence is generally not impaired when an ADR proceeding is begun; however, if the proceeding is similar to the litigation process, the member and the client are in a position of having "material adverse interests" and the guidance established by Interpretation 101-6 should be observed (ET 191.192–.193).

97—**Performance of Certain Extended Audit Services.** Independence is not impaired when a member performs internal audit activities or extends the audit service when the client does not maintain an internal audit function, if the member does not assume the role of performing managerial functions or making managerial decisions (ET 191.194–.195).

98—**Member's Loan from a Nonclient Subsidiary or Parent of an Attest Client.** Independence is impaired with respect to a client when a nonclient subsidiary (of the client) makes a loan to the member (assuming the loan is not grandfathered or permitted under Interpretation 101-5); however, independence is not impaired with respect to a client when a nonclient parent (of the client) makes a loan to the member (assuming the subsidiary is not material to the parent) (ET 191.196–.197).

99—**Member Providing Services for Company Executives.** A member who has been requested by a company to perform personal financial planning or tax services for its executives should consider the possibility that recommendations made to the executives may be detrimental to the company. For this reason, the member should accept the engagement only if the standards established by Rule 102 can be satisfied. If the engagement is accepted, the member also must satisfy the standards established by Rule 301 as it applies to both clients (the company and the executives) (ET 191.198–.199).

100—**Actions Permitted When Independence Is Impaired.** A member may re-sign or consent to the use of his or her report if it was initially issued when the member was independent, if the member has subsequently lost independence with respect to the client, and if no "post-audit" work was performed during the period of independence impairment. Post-audit work does not include "inquiries of successor auditors, reading of subsequent financial statements, or such procedures as may be necessary to assess the effect of subsequently discovered facts on the financial statements covered by the member's previously issued report" (ET 191.200–.201).

101—**Client Advocacy and Expert Witness Services.** A member is not considered an advocate of a client (as discussed in Interpretation 102-6) when the member serves as an expert witness for the client (ET 199.202–.203).

102—**Member's Indemnification of a Client.** Independence is impaired when a member agrees to "indemnify the client for damages, losses, or costs arising from lawsuits, claims or settlements that relate, directly or indirectly, to client acts" (ET 191.204-.205).

Rulings on General and Technical Standards (Rules 201, 202, and 203)

1–6—Deleted.

7—**Non-CPA Partner.** Transferred to ET 591.379–.380 as Ethics Ruling No. 190 under Section 591.

8—**Subcontractor Selection for Management Consulting Service Engagements.** The following selection procedures should be followed when a member has been engaged to design and program a computer system and the member has decided to retain a programming company as a subcontractor: (1) obtain evaluations of the programming company from business, finance, and personal references, (2) evaluate the subcontractor's professional reputation and recognition, (3) read materials written by the subcontractor, and (4) read personal evaluations written by the practitioner (ET 291.015–.016).

9—**Supervision of Technical Specialist on Management Consulting Service Engagements.** A member who employs a specialist in designing a computer system must be able to supervise and evaluate the work of the specialist. Although the member should be capable of defining the tasks and evaluating the completed work, he or she does not have to be capable of performing each of the specialist's tasks (ET 291.017–.018).

10—**Preparation and Transmittal of Financial Statements by a Member in Public Practice.** A member in public practice who prepares financial statements for another entity in which he or she is a stockholder, a partner, a director, or an employee and who transmits those financial statements to a third party should describe to that party, preferably in writing, his or her relationship with the reporting entity and specifically should not imply that an independent relationship exists (ET 219.019–.020).(If the member states that the financial statements are prepared in accordance with GAAP, the member is subject to Rule 203.)

11—**Applicability of Rule 203 to Members Performing Litigation Support Service.** Rule 203 applies to members who perform litigation support services (ET 219.021–.022).

Rulings on Responsibilities to Clients (Rules 301 and 302)

1—**Computer Processing of Clients' Returns.** A member may use an outside service bureau for processing a client's tax return, provided all necessary precautions are taken to prevent the release of confidential information (ET 391.001–.002).

2—**Distribution of Client Information to Trade Associations.** A member's firm may release to a trade association profit and loss percentages taken from the reports of the accountant's clients and requested by the association, provided the firm has the client's permission to release the data (ET 391.003–.004).

3—**Information to Successor Accountant about Tax Return Irregularities.** When a member has withdrawn from an engagement because of the discovery of irregularities in a client's tax return, the member, once contacted by the successor accountant, should, at a minimum, suggest that the successor accountant ask the client to permit the member to discuss all matters freely with the successor accountant. Because of the legal implications, the member should obtain legal advice regarding his or her status and obligation in the matter (ET 391.005–.006).

4—Deleted.

5—**Records Retention Agency.** A member may use a records retention agency to store workpapers, etc.; however, responsibility for the confidentiality of the material is retained by the member (ET 391.009–.010).

6—**Revealing Client Information to Competitors.** A member may be employed by a municipality to determine whether a business that is subject to a personal property tax has declared the proper amount. The member will examine the business's records. In such an engagement all parties concerned must realize that Rule 301 prohibits members and their employees from disclosing confidential information (ET 391.011–.012).

7—**Revealing Names of Clients.** A member may disclose the name of a client, whether the client is public or private, without the client's permission unless such disclosure would imply something about the client that would be considered confidential information (ET 391.013–.014).

8–13—Deleted.

14—**Use of Confidential Information on Management Consulting Service Engagements.** When using pertinent information that will come from an outside nonclient source and must remain confidential, the terms of the engagement with the client should specify that the confidences of the nonclient sources will not be divulged even when they might affect the outcome of the engagement (ET 391.027–.028). (Note: This ruling rests not on Rule 301 since that rule is not applicable to nonclient confidentiality, but rather on Rule 501, which is concerned with discreditable acts.)

15—**Earlier Similar Management Consulting Service Study with Negative Outcome.** A member conducting a feasibility study of a newly developed electronic ticketing system for the industry should state his or her reservations about the system when they are based on a similar study done for another client, provided the details of the other engagement are not disclosed. However, if the circumstances of the other engagement are such that the origin of the information is clear and the information is sensitive, the engagement should not be accepted without clearance from the first client (ET 391.029–.030).

16—**Disclosure of Confidential Client Information.** When a member has prepared a joint tax return for A and B (a married couple), the member has dealt exclusively with A, and as part of a divorce process B requests the member to release certain tax information, release of such information is not in violation of Rule 301, even if A requests that the member not release the information (ET 391.031–.032).

17—**Definition of the Receipt of a Contingent Fee or a Commission.** In determining whether a fee or commission has been *received*, the receipt occurs when the related service has been completed and the fee or commission determined (ET 391.033–.034). (The actual date the fee or commission is paid is irrelevant.)

18—**Bank Director.** A member in public practice may serve as a bank director; however, if the member has clients that are also customers of the bank, the member should consider complications arising from Rule 301 (Confidential Client Information) and Interpretation 102-2 (Conflicts of Interest). In view of Rule 301 and Interpretation 102-2, it generally is not desirable for a member in public practice to serve as a bank director where the member's clients are likely to engage in significant transactions (ET 391.035–.036).

19—**Receipt of Contingent Fees or Commissions by a Member's Spouse.** A member's spouse may provide a service to a member's attest client for a contingent fee or may receive or pay a commission to that client if the spouse's activities are separate from those of the member and the member's participation in the spouse's activities is not significant (ET 391.037–.038). (The relationship should also be evaluated for possible conflict of interest as described under Rule 102.)

20—**Disclosure of Confidential Client Information to Professional Liability Insurance Carrier.** A member does not violate confidentiality when information concerning a client is given to the firm's insurance provider in order to prepare for an actual or potential claim (ET 391.039–.040).

21—**Member Providing Services for Company Executives.** See Ruling No. 99 on Independence, Integrity, and Objectivity (Rules 101 and 102) (ET 391.041–.042).

Rulings on Other Responsibilities and Practices (Rules 501, 502, 503, and 505)

1—**Retention of Records**. Superseded by Interpretation 501-1.

2—**Fees: Collection of Notes Issued in Payment**. It is acceptable for a member to make arrangements with a bank to collect notes issued by a client in payment of fees due. The client was advised of the arrangement (ET 591.003–.004).

3—**Employment by a Non-CPA Firm**. A member must comply with all the Rules of Conduct when employed by a public accounting firm made up of one or more non-CPA practitioners. If the member is a partner of the firm, he or she will be held responsible for all actions taken by persons associated with the member as established by the Rules of Conduct (ET 591.005–.006).

4–32—Deleted.

33—**Course Instructor**. In advertising a course taught by a member, the instructor's background, such as degrees obtained, professional affiliations, and the name of his or her firm would be of value to prospective students (ET 591.065–.066).

34–37—Deleted.

38—**CPA Title, Controller of Bank**. A bank that employs a CPA who is not in public practice may identify the member as a CPA on bank stationery and in paid advertisements listing the officers and directors of the bank (ET 591.075–.076).

39–44—Deleted.

45—**CPA Title on Agency Letterhead**. Superseded.

46–62—Deleted.

63—**Directory Listing, White Pages**. Superseded.

64–77—Deleted.

78—**Letterhead: Lawyer—CPA**. A member who is also admitted to the Bar may simultaneously practice accounting and law and may be represented on letterhead as both an attorney and a CPA. However, the member should consult the rules of the relevant Bar Association (ET 591.155–.156).

79–81—Deleted.

82—**Newsletter.** A newsletter on financial management may be issued by a publishing company for a fee and subscriptions may be solicited by direct mail or other forms of advertising prominently featuring the member's name, provided (1) the member prepared or supervised the preparation of the newsletter and (2) Rule 502 is not violated with respect to promotion about the member or the member's writings (ET 591.163–.164).

83–90—Deleted.

91–92—**Press Release on Change in Staff.** Superseded.

93–107—Deleted.

108—**Member Interviewed by the Press.** When interviewed by a member of the media, a member may not release information for publication that the member could not publish. All Rules of Conduct also must be observed (ET 591.215–.216).

109–115—Deleted.

116—**Bank Director.** Superseded.

117—**Consumer Credit Company Director.** A member in public practice may serve as a director or officer of a consumer credit company that purchases installment sales contracts from retailers and receives payments from consumers, provided the member does not audit the company and does not involve himself in matters that might constitute a conflict of interest (ET 591.233–.234).

118–133—Deleted.

134—**Association of Accountants Not Partners.** Members should not use a letterhead showing the names of two accountants when, in fact, a partnership does not exist (ET 591.267–.268).

135—**Association of Firms Not Partners.** Using the title *Smith, Jones & Associates* by three CPA firms that form an association—not a partnership—is not allowed (ET 591.269–.270). (Note: Each firm may use its own name and refer to the other two firms as correspondents.)

136—**Audit with Former Partner.** When a partnership of one CPA and one non-CPA has been dissolved and one account is to be retained and serviced jointly by the two, the report should be presented on plain paper and signed separately by both accountants, with a notation after each name to indicate that one is a CPA and one is an accountant (ET 591.271–.272).

137—**Nonproprietary Partners.** Using the designation *nonproprietary partner* for someone who is not a partner of a firm is prohibited (ET 591.273–.274).

138—**Partner Having Separate Proprietorship.** A member may be a partner in a firm of public accountants who are not CPAs, and also may practice on his or her own as a CPA, provided clients and other interested parties are advised of the two roles (ET 591.275–.276).

139—**Partnership with Non-CPA.** A member may form a partnership for the practice of public accounting with a non-CPA; however, all partners must comply with the Code of Professional Conduct, and the firm cannot hold itself out as a partnership of CPAs (ET 591.277–.278).

140—**Political Election.** Members of a firm may continue to practice under the name of the managing partner after the managing partner is elected to a high public office and withdraws from the firm, provided the managing partner's name is followed by the designation *and Company* (ET 591.279–.280).

141—**Responsibility for Non-CPA Partner.** A member who has formed a partnership with a noncertified public accountant is ethically responsible for all acts of the partnership (ET 591.281–.282).

142–143—Deleted.

144—**Title: Partnership Roster.** An established firm may use the same name in different states, even though the roster of partners may be different in some states (ET 591.287–.288).

145—**Firm Name of Merged Partnerships**. A newly merged firm may use the name of a partner who retired from one of the two firms prior to the merger (ET 591.289–.290).

146—**Membership Designation**. A firm that is a partnership of CPAs and noncertified public accountants may, on its letterhead, designate appropriate partners as "Members of the American Institute of Certified Public Accountants" (ET 591.291–.292).

147–157—Deleted.

158—**Operation of Separate Data Processing Business by a Public Practitioner**. The rules of conduct apply to a member who participates in a separate business that provides data processing services to the public and who also practices public accounting (ET 591.315–.316).

159–161—Deleted.

162—**CPA Designation on Professional Organization Letterhead**. Superseded.

163–167—Deleted.

168—**Audit Guides Issued by Governmental Agencies**. Superseded by Interpretation 501-3.

169–174—Deleted.

175—**Bank Director**. Superseded by Ethics Ruling No. 85 under Rule 102 and Ethics Ruling No. 18 under Rule 301.

176—**Newsletters and Publications Prepared by Others**. A member may permit a newsletter, tax booklet, or similar publications to be imprinted with the firm's name, even though the firm did not prepare the publication, assuming that the firm has a reasonable basis to believe that the information contained in the publication is not false, misleading, or deceptive (ET 591.351–.352).

177—**Data Processing: Billing Services**. Performing centralized billing services in a separate company for local doctors is a type of service performed by public accountants. Therefore, a member in public practice must operate the company in conformance with the Code of Professional Conduct (ET 591.353–.354).

178—Deleted.

179—**Practice of Public Accounting Under Name of Association or Group.** CPA firms that are members of an association or group whereby joint advertising, training, and the like will occur, may not practice under the name of the association or group. Each CPA firm should practice only in its own name, but may indicate the association or group name elsewhere on the firm's stationery. Also, each firm may list on its stationery the names of the other firms in the association or group (ET 591.357–.358).

180–181—Deleted.

182—**Termination of Engagement Prior to Completion.** When an engagement to prepare a tax return is terminated by the client or the member, the member is not required to furnish the client a tax return or supporting details; however, the member must return or furnish copies of material given to the member by the client (ET 591.363–.364).

183—**Use of the AICPA Accredited Personal Financial Specialist Designation.** A firm may use the designation "Accredited Personal Financial Specialists" (APFS) in its letterhead if all partners or shareholders have obtained the designation; however, an individual member with the designation may use it after his or her name (ET 591.365–.366).

184—**Definition of the Receipt of a Contingent Fee or Commission.** See Ethics Ruling No. 17 under Rule 302 (ET 591.367–.368).

185—**Sale of Products to Clients.** When a member *purchases* a product (takes title to the product) and resells that product to a client, the profit on the sale is not considered a commission (ET 591.369–.370).

186—**Billing for Subcontractor's Services.** When a member contracts a computer hardware maintenance servicer to provide support for a client's computer operations, Rule 503 is not violated if the member bills the client a fee for the service that is higher than the fee billed by the computer servicer to the member (ET 591.371–.372).

187—**Receipt of Contingent Fees or Commissions by Member's Spouse.** See Ethics Ruling No. 19 under Rule 302 (ET 591.373–.374).

188—**Referral of Products of Others**. The guidance established by Rule 503 applies when a member refers computer products of a wholesaler to a client through a distributor or agent and receives payments from the wholesaler for products sold under the arrangement. For example, the Code of Professional Conduct would be violated if the member performs services for the client listed in Rule 503; however, no violation occurs if the listed services are not performed by the member (ET 591.375–.376). (See Rule 503 for additional guidance.)

189—**Requests for Client Records and Other Information**. A member may be involved with individuals associated with a client entity who are parties to an internal dispute (partnership v. general partner, company v. majority shareholder) and there may be requests by the parties to supply information under Interpretation 501-1. The member will have satisfied professional standards by supplying information to the "individual who has been previously designated or held out as the client's representative" on one occasion (ET 591.377–.378).

190—**Non-CPA Partner**. A member who is in partnership with non-CPAs may sign reports with the firm name, then below sign his own name with the CPA designation, only if it is clear that the partnership is not being held out as composed entirely of CPAs (ET 591.379–.380).

Continuing Professional Education

MILLER

GAAS GUIDE
CPE PROGRAM

Module 1—*Audited Financial Statements*

Module 2—*Specialized Industry Accounting
and Auditing Practices*

Module 3—*Interim Reviews, Unaudited
and Prospective Financial Statements, Attest
Engagements, and Agreed-Upon Procedures
Engagements*

HARCOURT BRACE PROFESSIONAL PUBLISHING

A Division of
Harcourt Brace & Company
SAN DIEGO   NEW YORK   LONDON

INTRODUCTION

Thank you for choosing this self-study CPE course from Harcourt Brace Professional Publishing. Our goal is to provide you with the most clear, most concise, and most up-to-date accounting and auditing information to help further your professional development, as well as the most convenient method to help you satisfy your continuing professional education obligations.

This CPE program is intended to be used in conjunction with your *1997 GAAS Guide*. This course has the following characteristics:

Prerequisites: None

Recommended CPE credits: 10 hours per module

Level of Knowledge: Basic

Field of Study: Accounting and Auditing

The complete, three-module *1997 GAAS Guide* Self-Study CPE Program is designed to provide 30 hours of CPE credit if all tests are submitted for grading and earn a passing score. You may complete any or all of the three modules that make up the CPE Program.

Credit hours are recommended in accordance with the Statement on Standards for Formal Continuing Professional Education (CPE) Programs, published by the AICPA. CPE requirements vary from state to state. Your state board is the final authority for the number of credit hours allowed for a particular program, as well as the classification of courses, under its specific licensing requirement. Contact your state board of accountancy for information concerning your state's requirements for the number of CPE credit hours you must earn and the acceptable fields of study.

To receive credit, complete the course according to the instructions on page **25.04**. The modules cost $59.00 each. Payment options are shown on the answer sheets.

Each CPE test is graded within two weeks of its receipt. A passing score is 70 percent or above. Participants who pass the test will receive a Certificate of Completion to acknowledge their achievement. The self-study CPE Program offered in conjunction with the *1997 GAAS Guide* will expire on December 31, 1998. Participants may submit completed tests for the program until that date.

Instructions for Taking This Course

Each module consists of chapter learning objectives, reading assignments, review questions and suggested solutions, and an examination. Complete each step listed below for each module you want to submit for grading:

1. Review the chapter learning objectives.

2. Read the assigned material in the *GAAS Guide.*

3. Complete the review questions, and compare your answers to the suggested solutions.

4. After completing all assigned chapters in the module, take the examination, writing each answer on the appropriate line on the answer sheet.

5. When you have completed the examination, remove the answer sheet, place it in a stamped envelope, and send it to the following address:

   GAAS Guide CPE Coordinator
   Harcourt Brace Professional Publishing
   525 B Street, Suite 1900
   San Diego, CA 92101-4495

Be sure to indicate your method of payment on the answer sheet.

Module 1—Audited Financial Statements

Responsibility and Function of the Independent Auditor

After completing this section, you should be able to:

- Understand the three general standards that apply to all auditors.
- Understand the five components of a quality-control system that apply to accounting and audit organizations.
- Discuss the administration of a quality-control process.

Read Chapter 2, "Responsibility and Function of the Independent Auditor," of the *1997 GAAS Guide*.

Answer question 1 on page **25.08**.

Generally Accepted Accounting Principles

After completing this section, you should be able to:

- Understand the basic or pervasive principles that constitute generally accepted accounting principles.
- Understand the sources of the detailed accounting principles.
- Understand the authoritative support for GAAP and the GAAP hierarchy.

Read Chapter 3, "Generally Accepted Accounting Principles," of the *1997 GAAS Guide*.

Answer question 2 on page **25.08**.

Generally Accepted Auditing Standards

After completing this section, you should be able to:

- Discuss the three general standards.
- Discuss the three fieldwork standards.
- Discuss the four reporting standards.

Read Chapter 4, "Generally Accepted Auditing Standards," of the *1997 GAAS Guide*.

Answer question 3 on page **25.08**.

Pre-Engagement Planning

After completing this section, you should be able to:

- Perform a new client evaluation.
- Understand the requirements for communication with the predecessor auditor.
- Understand the criteria for independence.
- Understand the steps for accepting a client.

Read Chapter 5, "Pre-Engagement Planning," of the *1997 GAAS Guide*.

Answer question 4 on page **25.08**.

Planning the Engagement

After completing this section, you should be able to:

- Understand the nature, timing, and extent of planning procedures.
- Understand the nature of engagement supervision.
- Perform the required planning and analytical procedures.

Read Chapter 6, "Planning the Engagement," of the *1997 GAAS Guide*.

Answer question 5 on page **25.08**.

Internal Control, Errors, and Irregularities

After completing this section, you should be able to:

- Understand the implications of the Committee of Sponsoring Organizations of the Treadway Commission (COSO) Report.
- Understand the three elements of internal control.
- Understand the requirements for documenting internal controls.
- Understand how to perform the tests of controls, if applicable.
- Evaluate the planned level of control risk.
- Understand how to design substantive tests based on the assessed level of control risk.
- Identify reportable conditions and material weaknesses.
- Understand the nature of errors and irregularities.

- Understand the nature of illegal acts.
- Understand the role of the internal audit function.
- Understand the nature of service organizations and internal controls.

Read Chapter 7, "Internal Control, Errors, and Irregularities," of the *1997 GAAS Guide*.

Answer questions 6–12 on pages **25.08–25.09**.

Evidence

After completing this section, you should be able to:

- Understand the characteristics of evidence, including its sufficiency and competency.
- Understand the nature of sampling.
- Understand the nature of materiality and audit risk.

Read Chapter 8, "Evidence," of the *1997 GAAS Guide*.

Answer review questions 13–15 on page **25.09**.

Sampling Techniques and Procedures

After completing this section, you should be able to:

- Understand the relationship between audit risk and sampling.
- Understand sampling in tests of controls.
- Understand sampling in substantive tests.

Read Chapter 9, "Sampling Techniques and Procedures," of the *1997 GAAS Guide*.

Answer review questions 16–17 on page **25.09**.

Completing the Audit

After completing this section, you should be able to:

- Identify the audit procedures necessary for completing the audit.
- Evaluate the audit findings.
- Understand post-audit responsibilities.

Read Chapter 10, "Completing the Audit," of the *1997 GAAS Guide*.

Answer review questions 18–19 on page **25.09**.

Auditor's Reports

After completing this section, you should be able to:

- Understand the types of reports that an auditor may issue if necessary.
- Understand how an auditor modifies the report for accounting conditions.
- Understand how an auditor modifies the report for accounting changes.
- Understand how an auditor modifies the report for scope conditions.
- Understand how an auditor handles other conditions that may arise.
- Describe types of special reports that an auditor may issue.

Read Chapters 11 and 12, "Auditor's Reports," and "Auditor's Special Reports" in the *1997 GAAS Guide*.

Answer review questions 20–25 on page **25.09**.

REVIEW QUESTIONS

1. What are the five components of a quality-control system that are described in Statement on Quality Control Standards No. 2?

2. What are the components of the four levels of the private-sector accounting hierarchy?

3. What are the four reporting standards of GAAS?

4. What is the primary objective of the communication process between a successor auditor and a predecessor auditor prior to the successor auditor's acceptance of an engagement?

5. What matters should an auditor consider when evaluating the effects of an entity's use of computer processing?

6. List the five components of internal controls contained in SAS-78.

7. What factors should an auditor consider when evaluating a client's internal controls?

8. Describe the monitoring component of internal controls.

9. What must be achieved for an auditor to understand a client's internal controls well enough to plan an audit engagement?

10. What are the five financial statement assertions listed in SAS-31?

11. Describe the methods that may be used for documenting the auditor's understanding of internal controls.

12. Define *reportable conditions* as contained in SAS-60.

13. What are the three component risks of audit risk?

14. In addition to confirmation, what procedures are required to be performed on inventories held in public warehouses that are significant in relation to the current assets and total assets of an entity?

15. Explain why detection risk always exists in an audit conducted under GAAS.

16. What are the two principle categories of statistical sampling plans, and under what circumstances should they be used?

17. Discuss the documentation requirements for sampling when the auditor is using substantive tests.

18. Describe how an auditor could use analytical procedures for the required overall review of the audit.

19. What effect would a client's refusal to sign the management representation letter have on an auditor's report?

20. When there are departures from GAAP, an auditor may issue an unqualified, a qualified, or an adverse report. Describe the circumstances that would lead to the issuance of each of the above three types of reports.

21. Discuss the procedures that an auditor must follow when a client adopts an alternative accounting procedure to prevent the financial statements from being misleading.

22. What types of special reports are covered by SAS-62?

23. Describe the circumstances in which an auditor would *not* make any reference to the consistent application of accounting principles in the auditor's report.

24. Describe the three classifications of loss contingencies.

25. Describe the circumstances that would cause an auditor to include an explanatory paragraph in the audit report relating to required supplementary information.

SUGGESTED SOLUTIONS

1. The five components of a quality-control system that are described in Statement on Quality Control Standards No. 2 are as follows:

a. Independence, integrity, and objectivity

b. Personnel management

c. Acceptance and continuance of clients and engagements

d. Engagement performance

e. Monitoring

2. The four levels of authoritative GAAP in the GAAP hierarchy for the private sector are made up of the following:

Level A

FASB Statements and Interpretations

APB Opinions

AICPA Accounting Research Bulletins

Level B

FASB Technical Bulletins

AICPA Industry Audit and Accounting Guides

AICPA Statements of Position

Level C

FASB Emerging Issues Task Force Consensus Positions

AICPA Practice Bulletins

Level D

AICPA Accounting Interpretations

Implementation Guides published by FASB

Practices widely recognized and prevalent generally or in industry

3. The four reporting standards of GAAS are as follows:

a. The report shall state whether the financial statements are presented in accordance with generally accepted accounting principles.

b. The report shall identify those circumstances in which such principles have not been consistently observed in the current period in relation to the preceding period.

c. Informative disclosures in the financial statements are to be regarded as reasonably adequate unless otherwise stated in the report.

d. The report shall contain either an expression of opinion regarding the financial statements taken as a whole, or an assertion to the effect that an opinion cannot be expressed. When an overall opinion cannot be expressed, the reasons should be stated. In all cases where an auditor's name is associated with financial statements, the report should contain a clear-cut indication of the character of the auditor's work, if any, and the degree of responsibility the auditor is taking.

4. The primary objective of the communication process is for a successor auditor to make various inquiries of the predecessor auditor in order to determine if a prospective client should be accepted.

5. An auditor should consider the following matters when evaluating the effects of an entity's use of computer processing:

   a. The degree to which computers are used to process accounting information that could materially affect the financial statements

   b. The organization of an entity's computer processing facilities

   c. The availability of evidential matter, such as input documents, transactions files, and master files, and the length of time that the information is accessible to the auditor

   d. The availability of computer-generated information that may be used in substantive testing, especially for analytical purposes

   e. The use of computer-assisted audit techniques to increase efficiency, or as the only alternative way to obtain essential evidential matter

6. The five elements of internal controls contained in SAS-78 are:

   a. Control environment

   b. Risk assessment

   c. Control activities

   d. Information and communication

   e. Monitoring

7. The auditor should consider the following factors when evaluating a client's internal controls:

   a. The organization and ownership characteristics of the client

   b. The nature of the client's business

   c. The diversity and complexity of the client's activities

   d. The data-processing methods used by the client to transmit, process, maintain, and access information

   e. The legal and regulatory environment in which the client operates

8. The monitoring component of internal controls refers to management's need to assess the controls (from both a design and an operational perspective) on a timely basis and to make modifications to the controls when appropriate.

9. For an auditor's understanding of internal controls to be sufficient to plan an audit engagement, the auditor should achieve the following:

    a. Identify misstatements that could occur in the financial statements.

    b. Identify factors that affect the degree of risk for misstatements in financial statements.

    c. Identify factors relevant to the design of substantive tests.

10. The five financial statement assertions listed in SAS-31 are:

    a. *Existence or occurrence*—The auditor should determine whether assets or liabilities of the entity exist at a given date and whether recorded transactions have occurred during a given period.

    b. *Completeness*—The auditor should determine whether all transactions and accounts that should be presented in the financial statements are also included.

    c. *Rights and obligations*—The auditor should determine whether assets are the rights of the entity and whether liabilities are the obligations of the entity at a given date.

    d. *Valuation or allocation*—The auditor should determine whether assets, liabilities, revenue, and expense components have been included in the financial statements at appropriate amounts.

    e. *Presentation and disclosure*—The auditor should determine whether particular components of the financial statements are properly classified, described, and disclosed.

11. The following methods may be used for documenting internal controls:

    a. Flowcharts

    b. Internal control questionnaires

    c. Narrative descriptions

12. SAS-60 defines *reportable conditions* as:

    Matters coming to the auditor's attention that, in his or her judgment, should be communicated to the audit committee because they represent significant deficiencies in the design or operation of the internal control structure, which could adversely affect the organization's ability to record, process, summarize, and report financial data consistent with the assertions of management in the financial statements.

13. The three components of audit risk are:

    a. Inherent risk

    b. Control risk

    c. Detection risk

14. The following additional procedures are required by GAAS when inventories in public warehouses are significant to current and total assets:

a. Discuss with the client (owner of the goods) the client's control procedures in investigating the warehouse manager, including tests of related evidential matter.

b. Observe the warehouse manager's or client's count of goods whenever practical and reasonable.

c. If warehouse receipts have been pledged as collateral, confirm details with the lenders to the extent deemed necessary by the auditor.

d. Obtain an independent auditor's report on the warehouse manager's control procedures relevant to the custody of goods.

15. Detection risk exists because not all items that make up an account balance or a transaction class are examined by the auditor (sampling misstatement) and audit procedures may not be properly applied (nonsampling misstatement).

16. The two types of statistical sampling plans are:

a. *Attribute sampling*—Used when the auditor is concerned about the number of exceptions or errors in the test work. This form of sampling is best used in the tests of controls.

b. *Variable sampling*—Used when the auditor is concerned about the amount of error, rather than the number of errors. This form of sampling is best used in substantive tests.

17. Documentation should address the following matters when sampling is used in substantive tests:

a. Description of audit procedures and objectives tested

b. Definition of population and sampling unit

c. Definition of a misstatement

d. Basis for establishment of risk of incorrect acceptance, incorrect rejection, tolerable misstatement, and expected misstatement

e. Audit sampling technique used

f. Method of sampling selection

g. Description of sampling procedures performed and list of misstatements discovered

h. Evaluation of sample and summary of overall conclusions

18. The auditor could use the following approach for analytical procedures as part of the overall review of the audit:

a. Evaluate the adequacy of the data collected in response to unusual or unexpected balances identified as a part of the preliminary analysis.

b. Identify any other unusual or unexpected balances not previously identified.

19. The refusal of a client to sign the management letter should result in a scope limitation to the auditor's report, and a qualified opinion, or a disclaimer of opinion should be expressed.

20. An unqualified opinion could be issued if the departure is not significant to the fair presentation of the financial statements. A qualified opinion could be issued if the departure affects the fairness of the financial statements but overall the statements can be relied on. An adverse opinion should be issued whenever the departure is so significant that the financial statements cannot be relied on.

21. Assuming the auditor agrees with the client's assessment, the auditor would include an explanatory paragraph in his or her opinion explaining the circumstances. The explanatory opinion would not be referred to in the opinion paragraphs, and the other paragraphs would not be modified.

22. The categories of special reports for which SAS-62 establishes generally accepted accounting principles are:

    a. Reporting on a comprehensive basis of accounting other than GAAP

    b. Reporting on specified elements or items of a financial statement

    c. Reporting on compliance with contractual agreements or regulatory requirements related to audited financial statements

    d. Reporting on financial presentations to comply with contractual agreements or regulatory provisions

    e. Reporting on financial information presented in a prescribed format that requires an auditor's report in a prescribed format

23. The auditor would not make any reference to the consistency of the application of accounting principles under the following conditions:

    a. There have been no changes in the application of accounting principles in the preparation of the current year's financial statements.

    b. There have been changes in the application of accounting principles in the preparation of the current year's financial statements, but the effects of the changes are considered immaterial.

24. The three classifications of loss contingencies are:

    a. *Probable*—The chance of the future event or events occurring is likely.

    b. *Reasonably possible*—The chance of the future event or events occurring is more than remote but less than likely.

    c. *Remote*—The chance of the future event or events occurring is slight.

25. An explanatory paragraph applicable to required supplementary information should not be added to the standard auditor's report *except* in the following circumstances:

a. Required supplementary information is omitted.

b. Measurement or presentation of the required supplementary information deviates from the guidelines established by the FASB or GASB.

c. The auditor is unable to apply the limited procedures to the required supplementary information.

d. The auditor has substantial doubt about whether the required supplementary information conforms to established guidelines.

Examination for CPE Credit

1. *True or false:* An auditor who is not independent must disclaim an opinion on the financial statements even if all other generally accepted auditing standards have been followed.

2. *Multiple choice:* Which of the following has the authority to issue pronouncements on quality-control standards for AICPA member firms?
   a. Securities and Exchange Commission.
   b. Auditing Standards Board.
   c. Financial Accounting Standards Board.
   d. State boards of accountancy.

3. *True or false:* Accounting Research Bulletins are no longer considered an authoritative source of GAAP.

4. *True or false:* Not-for-profit organizations should follow the public-sector accounting hierarchy.

5. *Multiple choice:* Which of the following has the lowest level of authority in the private-sector accounting hierarchy?
   a. AICPA Practice Bulletins.
   b. FASB Interpretations.
   c. APB Opinions.
   d. AICPA Statements of Position.

6. *True or false:* The consistency principle does *not* prohibit a company from changing accounting principles.

7. *True or false:* An engagement to issue an opinion on financial statements is considered an attestation engagement.

8. *Multiple choice:* Statements on Auditing Standards are issued by which of the following?
   a. Financial Accounting Standards Board.
   b. Securities and Exchange Commission.
   c. American Institute of Certified Public Accountants.
   d. Accounting Research Board.

9. *True or false:* An auditor's acceptance of a client on the basis that the auditor will require additional training or knowledge before completing the engagement does *not* represent a lack of competence under Rule 201.

10. *True or false:* SQCS-2 requires that the independent auditor periodically evaluate management's integrity and that he or she determine the firm's ability to service its clients.

11. *True or false:* SAS-7 requires that a successor auditor communicate with a predecessor auditor (if any) to determine whether there are factors that should be considered in determining whether to accept the client.

12. *True or false:* Assistants performing work on an audit should *not* be permitted to document their positions if they disagree with how a particular audit question was resolved, provided they made their view known to the engagement supervisors.

13. *Multiple choice:* The policies and procedures that help ensure that management's directives are being carried out are referred to as:

    a. The control environment.

    b. Monitoring.

    c. Control activities.

    d. Risk assessment.

14. *Multiple choice:* The probability that an auditor will *not* detect a material error that exists in the financial statements is known as:

    a. Inherent risk.

    b. Control risk.

    c. Financial statement risk.

    d. Audit risk.

15. *True or false:* If an auditor desires a lower level of detection risk, the quality and/or quantity of audit evidence he or she collects through substantive tests should increase.

16. *True or false:* When an auditor discovers no reportable conditions during an engagement, he or she should prepare a report to the audit committee (or its equivalent) stating that there were no reportable conditions found.

17. *Multiple choice:* Unintentional misstatements in the financial statements are referred to as:

    a. Errors.

    b. Irregularities.

    c. Illegal acts.

    d. Fraud.

18. *True or false:* If an auditor does not plan to assess control risk at below the maximum level, he or she does not need to gain an understanding of the five components of internal controls.

19. *True or false:* The identification of a material weakness in an entity's internal controls would preclude an auditor from issuing an opinion on the entity's financial statements.

20. *True or false:* SAS-65 concludes that the evaluation of significant accounting estimates should not be made by internal auditors but that they should be made by the auditor of the financial statements.

21. *Multiple choice:* The financial-statement assertion that an asset or a liability exists at the balance-sheet date is known as:
    a. Rights and obligations.
    b. Existence or occurrence.
    c. Completeness.
    d. Presentation and disclosure.

22. *True or false:* Tests of controls are primarily performed to determine the validity and propriety of transactions and balances and are usually concerned with dollar values rather than with error rates.

23. *True or false:* SAS-67 requires confirmation of accounts receivable even if confirmation is not necessary to reduce audit risk to an acceptable low level.

24. *True or false:* A principal auditor relies on and refers to an audit performed by another auditor. If the other auditor's opinion is qualified, the principal auditor must always qualify his or her opinion on the financial statements.

25. *True or false:* FAS-57's definition of *related parties* includes management and the immediate families of an entity.

26. *True or false:* SAS-59 concludes that the projection of the going-concern concept is limited to a reasonable period of time, which is defined as five years beyond the date of the audited financial statements.

27. *True or false:* SAS-77 precludes the auditor from using language in the audit report that suggests that an entity's ability to continue as a going concern is conditional on future events.

28. *Multiple choice:* The failure of an auditor to identify an error on a document that he or she examined is an example of:
    a. Sampling risk.
    b. Nonsampling risk.
    c. Inherent risk.
    d. Control risk.

29. *Multiple choice:* Nonstatistical sampling, which consists of selecting sample units without any conscious bias, is known as:
    a. Judgmental sampling.
    b. Random sampling.
    c. Sequential sampling.
    d. Haphazard sampling.

30. *True or false:* Sampling risk can be quantified when either statistical or nonstatistical sampling is used.

31. *True or false:* Management's representation letter should be dated as of the balance-sheet date being reported on.

32. *True or false:* SAS-56 requires that analytical procedures be used as a part of the overall review of the audit.

33. *True or false:* The auditor should not issue an unqualified opinion on financial statements if management refuses to sign a representation letter.

34. *True or false:* In evaluating audit findings, an auditor should consider both known and likely misstatements.

35. *True or false:* An accountant is considered associated with financial statements that he or she has prepared, regardless of whether the accountant's name appears on the financial statements.

36. *True or false:* When financial statements contain a departure from GAAP that is so pervasive that it affects the fair presentation of the overall financial statements, an auditor should issue a disclaimer of opinion.

37. *True or false:* With the issuance of SAS-79, there is no longer a requirement to modify an audit report when material uncertainties exist.

38. *True or false:* When an adverse opinion is issued on financial statements, the auditor may issue an unqualified opinion on items in the financial statements that are fairly presented in accordance with GAAP.

39. *True or false:* When financial statements that are prepared on a regulatory basis of accounting are to be generally distributed, the standard auditor's report should be modified for departures from GAAP.

40. *True or false:* Under SAS-62, the cash receipts and disbursements basis of accounting is considered a comprehensive basis of accounting other than GAAP.

1997 *GAAS Guide* CPE Program
Module 1—Audited Financial Statements

Please record your CPE answers in the space provided on the left and return this page for scoring.
Simply place the completed answer sheet in a stamped envelope and mail it to:

GAAS Guide CPE Coordinator
Harcourt Brace Professional Publishing
525 B Street, Suite 1900
San Diego, California, 92101-4495

NAME _____

FIRM NAME _____

ADDRESS _____

PHONE ( ) _____

CPA LICENSE # _____

ISBN (MODULE 1): 0-15-606477-4

TO ORDER: Call Toll-Free 1-800-831-7799

METHOD OF PAYMENT

☐ **Payment enclosed ($59.00 per Module).**
(Make checks payable to Harcourt Brace & Company.)

Please add appropriate sales tax.
Be sure to sign your order below.

Charge my:
☐ MasterCard ☐ Visa ☐ American Express

Account number _____

Expiration date _____
Please sign below for all credit card orders.

☐ **Bill me.** *Be sure to sign your order below.*

Signature _____

See the reverse side of this page for the CPE evaluation.

MODULE 1 CPE ANSWERS

1. _____		21. _____	
2. _____		22. _____	
3. _____		23. _____	
4. _____		24. _____	
5. _____		25. _____	
6. _____		26. _____	
7. _____		27. _____	
8. _____		28. _____	
9. _____		29. _____	
10. _____		30. _____	
11. _____		31. _____	
12. _____		32. _____	
13. _____		33. _____	
14. _____		34. _____	
15. _____		35. _____	
16. _____		36. _____	
17. _____		37. _____	
18. _____		38. _____	
19. _____		39. _____	
20. _____		40. _____	

GAAS Guide CPE Evaluation

1. Were you informed in advance of the:
a. Objectives of the course? y n
b. Experience level needed to complete the course? y n
c. Program content? y n
d. Nature and extent of preparation necessary? y n
e. Teaching method? y n
f. Number of CPE credit hours? y n

c. Program content? y n
d. Nature and extent of advance preparation necessary? y n
e. Teaching method? y n
f. Number of CPE credit hours? y n

2. Do you agree with the publisher's assessment of:
a. Objectives of the course? y n
b. Experience level needed to complete the course? y n

3. Was the material relevant? y n

4. Was the presentation of the material effective? y n

5. Did the program increase your professional competence? y n

6. Was the program content timely and effective? y n

Please make any other comments that you feel would improve this course. We appreciate the time you take to complete this questionnaire. Be assured that all of your comments will be considered carefully.

_____

_____

_____

_____

_____

Module 2—Specialized Industry Accounting and Auditing Practices

Audits of Construction Contractors

After completing this section, you should be able to:

- Understand the specialized accounting practices for construction contractors.
- Understand the specialized industry practices for construction contractors.
- Understand the specialized audit procedures for construction contractors.
- Understand the acceptability of income recognition methods.

Read Chapter 18, "Audits of Construction Contractors," of the *1997 GAAS Guide.*

Answer questions 1–4 on page **25.25**.

Audits of Credit Unions

After completing this section, you should be able to:

- Understand the specialized accounting practices for credit unions.
- Understand the specialized audit procedures for credit unions.

Read Chapter 19, "Audits of Credit Unions," of the *1997 GAAS Guide.*

Answer questions 5–8 on page **25.25**.

Audits of Employee Benefit Plans

After completing this section, you should be able to:

- Understand the specialized accounting practices for employee benefit plans.
- Understand the specialized audit procedures for employee benefit plans.

Read Chapter 20, "Audits of Employee Benefit Plans," of the *1997 GAAS Guide.*

Answer questions 9–12 on page **25.25.**

Audits of Health Care Providers

After completing this section, you should be able to:

- Understand the specialized accounting practices for health care providers.
- Understand the specialized industry practices of health care providers.
- Understand the specialized audit procedures for health care providers.

Read Chapter 21, "Audits of Health Care Providers," of the *1997 GAAS Guide.*

Answer questions 13–16 on pages **25.25–25.26.**

Audits of Not-For-Profit Organizations

After completing this section, you should be able to:

- Understand the specialized accounting practices of not-for-profit organizations.
- Understand the specialized industry practices of not-for-profit organizations.
- Understand the specialized audit procedures of not-for-profit organizations.

Read Chapter 22, "Audits of Not-For-Profit Organizations," of the *1997 GAAS Guide.*

Answer questions 17–21 on page **25.26.**

Audits of State and Local Governmental Units

After completing this section, you should be able to:

- Understand the background of state and local governmental units.
- Understand the specialized accounting practices for state and local governmental units.
- Understand the specialized audit procedures for state and local governmental units.

Read Chapter 23, "Audits of State and Local Governmental Units," of the *1997 GAAS Guide.*

Answer questions 22–25 on page **25.26.**

REVIEW QUESTIONS

1. Discuss the two primary authoritative sources of accounting and audit practices of construction contractors.

2. Discuss the completed contract method of accounting.

3. What items should be added to a standard representation letter from a construction contractor?

4. Discuss why an auditor should consider visiting the job site for construction contractors.

5. What is the difference between an *examination* and an *audit* of a credit union?

6. Discuss the information that must be disclosed with respect to loans in a credit union's summary of significant accounting policies.

7. What are the disclosure requirements for a credit union related to reverse repurchase agreements?

8. What audit procedures should be considered for collateralized loans of a credit union?

9. What are the primary sources of specialized accounting and auditing practices for employee benefit plans?

10. What does FAS-35 require annual financial statements of defined benefit pension plans to include?

11. Discuss the difference between when Form 5500 and Form 5500C are used.

12. Discuss the applicability of FAS-107 (Disclosures About Fair Value of Financial Instruments) to employee benefit plans.

13. What proposed pronouncement may take effect soon relating to the accounting and auditing for health care providers?

14. Discuss the disclosures that are required when the criteria of ARB-51 and FAS-94 are not met as they relate to consolidating related health care provider organizations.

15. Discuss the audit procedures that should be used to verify the existence of accounts receivable for a health care provider.

16. Discuss the audit procedures that an auditor should consider when testing estimated third-party settlements for a health care provider.

17. What are the primary requirements of FAS-124 (Accounting for Certain Investments Held by Not-for-Profit Organizations)?

18. Discuss the criteria that must be met for a not-for-profit organization not to be required to capitalize historical treasures.

19. Discuss the types of controls that should be used in a direct-solicitation campaign by a not-for-profit organization.

20. What factors would suggest that internal controls in a not-for-profit organization might be weak?

21. What are the three classifications of net assets for not-for-profit organizations?

22. Discuss the auditor's responsibility as it relates to compliance with laws and regulations in the audit of a governmental unit.

23. Discuss the basis of accounting for grant revenues that are restricted to reimbursement of certain expenditures.

24. What are the two methods of reporting component units in the financial statements of a primary government?

25. Discuss the concept of the accrual of revenue in a general fund.

SUGGESTED SOLUTIONS

1. The two primary authoritative sources of accounting and auditing practices for construction contractors are the AICPA Audit and Accounting Guide entitled *Audits of Construction Contractors* and SOP 81-1 (Accounting for Performance of Construction-Type and Certain Production-Type Contracts).

2. The completed contract method recognizes income only on completion or substantial completion of the contract. A contract is regarded as substantially complete if the remaining costs are insignificant. Billings to date on uncompleted contracts are recognized as the current liability progress billings. Costs to date on uncompleted contracts are recognized as the prepaid expense construction in progress.

3. The following items should be added to the standard representation letter received as part of an audit of a construction contractor:
   a. A detailed schedule of contract estimates used in financial statements
   b. Appropriateness of the income recognition method

    c. Contract loss provisions

    d. Unapproved change orders and claims

    e. Contract postponements and cancellations

    f. Related party transactions

4. The auditor should consider visiting the job site for the following reasons:

    a. A job-site visit is similar to a plant tour of a manufacturing audit client, in that it allows the auditor to better understand the contractor's method of operations.

    b. Accounting functions that require the auditor to review the internal controls employed at the site may be performed at the job site.

    c. Job-site visits allow the auditor to determine the status of a job and to discuss the progress of the contract with the project personnel.

5. An *examination* of a credit union is conducted by a supervisory authority, such as the National Credit Union Share Insurance Fund. An *audit* is conducted by a CPA in accordance with generally accepted auditing standards for purposes of expressing an opinion on the financial statements of the credit union.

6. A credit union's notes should disclose the following information about its loans:

    a. The basis of accounting used for loans held in the portfolio

    b. The method used to recognize loan losses

    c. The method for recognizing interest income on loans, including the policy for discounting accrual of interest on nonperforming loans; the treatment of loan fees and costs, including the method of amortizing net deferred fees or costs; and the policy for discontinuing the amortization of loan fees on nonperforming loans

7. The disclosure requirements for reverse repurchase agreements of a credit union should include the following:

    a. Due dates and interest rates

    b. Pledged collateral and compensating balance agreements

    c. Restrictive loan agreement covenants

    d. Five-year maturity schedule as established by FAS-47

8. Audit procedures for collateralized loans of a credit union that should be considered are as follows:

    a. Substantiate the existence and value of collateral for loans.

    b. Review the documentation to support the current value of collateral and, if appropriate, evaluate the adequacy of insurance coverage.

    c. Review controls over collateral, especially if the collateral is negotiable.

    d. Confirm loan guarantees directly with the guarantor, and determine whether the guarantor is in a financial position to perform if the guarantee clause is executed.

9. The sources of specialized accounting and auditing practices for employee benefit plans are:

    a. FAS-35 (Accounting and Reporting by Defined Benefit Pension Plans)

    b. FAS-110 (Reporting by Defined Benefit Pension Plans of Investment Contracts)

    c. Employee Retirement Income Security Act of 1974 (ERISA)

    d. Industry Audit Guide, *Audits of Employee Benefit Plans*, Third Edition

10. FAS-35 requires the financial statements of defined benefit pension plans to include:

    a. A statement of net assets available for benefits

    b. A statement of changes in net assets available for benefits

    c. Information on the actuarial present value of accumulated plan benefits

    d. Information on the year-to-year changes in the actuarial present value of accumulated plan benefits (if significant)

11. Form 5500 is used for pension plans that have more than 100 participants, and Form 5500C is used for plans with less than 100 participants.

12. In general, the financial instruments of employee benefit plans, other than insurance contracts as defined by FAS-110, are included in the scope of FAS-107 (as amended by FAS-119) and the instruments are subject to the disclosure requirements of paragraphs 10–14 of the Statement.

13. The AICPA has an Exposure Draft outstanding for a new Audit and Accounting Guide entitled *Health Care Organizations* that will supersede *Audits of Providers of Health Care Services* as well as incorporate SOP 89-5 and SOP 90-8.

14. The following disclosures are required of a health care provider when the criteria of ARB-51 and FAS-94 are not met:

    a. Summaries of the assets, liabilities, results of operations, and changes in fund balances of the separate organizations

    b. Description of the relationship between the health care provider and the separate organization

15. The auditor should confirm the accounts receivable for a health care provider. If the auditor deems confirmation to be impractical, the following alternative procedures may be used:

    a. Perform analytical procedures on subsequent receipts.

    b. Review third-party contracts.

    c. Compare billings to documentation in medical records.

    d. Review the results of third-party payer audits and peer review reports.

    e. Confirm interim payments with third-party payers.

16. The Health Care Audit and Accounting Guide identifies the following procedures that an auditor should consider when testing estimated third-party settlements:

    a. Substantiate arrangements with third-party payers through confirmation or review of correspondence.

    b. Test cost reimbursements reports and other settlement reports to establish consistency with agreements.

    c. Review audit reports of third-party payers from previous years to determine whether adjustments were properly reported in the financial statements and to identify current situations that might lead to adjustments applicable to the current financial statements.

    d. Obtain representation from management concerning provisions for estimated retroactive adjustments by third-party payers.

    e. Review financial statements for proper description of tentative nature of third-party settlement amounts.

17. FAS-124 requires that equity investments with readily determinable market values and all debt securities be recorded at fair value. Gains and losses on investments are recorded as increases and decreases in unrestricted net assets, unless the gains and losses are temporarily or permanently restricted.

18. The following three criteria must be met in order for historical treasures not to be capitalized:

    a. The collections are held for public exhibition, education, or research.

    b. The collections are protected and kept unencumbered.

    c. The collections are subject to an organizational policy that requires the proceeds from sales of collection items to be used to acquire items for the collection.

19. The following control procedures should be employed in a direct-solicitation campaign:

    a. Solicitors should be properly supervised.

    b. Solicitation materials and identifications should be controlled and given only to authorized solicitors.

    c. As quickly as practical, control totals and cash reports should be established over collections. Copies of cash reports should be sent to the accounting department.

    d. The number of people who have access to cash and the amount each person has under his or her control should be kept to a minimum.

20. Internal controls for not-for-profit organizations may be weakened by the following factors:

    a. Volunteer governing board

    b. Small or inexperienced staff

    c. Mixture of volunteers and organizational employees responsible for the conduct of the organization's affairs

21. The three classifications of net assets for not-for-profit organizations are:

    a. Unrestricted

    b. Temporarily restricted

    c. Permanently restricted

22. The auditor's responsibilities are to identify any law or regulation that would have a direct and material effect on the financial statements, if not complied with, and to test for compliance.

23. Grant revenues are recognized only when the appropriate costs allowed under the grant agreement have been incurred.

24. The two methods of reporting component units in the financial statements of a primary government are discrete presentation and blending.

25. General fund revenues are accrued if they meet the criteria of being measurable and available. If they do not meet these criteria, they are reported when the cash is collected.

Examination for CPE Credit

1. *True or false:* The percentage-of-completion method of accounting is the preferable method for long-term construction contracts.

2. *True or false:* An expected loss on a long-term construction contract should be recognized proportionately in the remaining years of the contract.

3. *Multiple choice:* Collections received by a contractor while working under a contract that is being accounted for using the completed-contract method should be reported as:

   a. A separate component of stockholder's equity.

   b. Revenue.

   c. A liability.

   d. A prepaid expense.

4. *True or false:* When estimates are made that will be used in a long-term construction contract using the percentage-of-completion method, the cumulative catch-up method should be used to account for the effects of the revised estimates.

5. *True or false:* When using the completed-contract method in accounting for a long-term construction contract, an auditor should charge applicable overhead costs and direct costs to a construction progress account, which is an asset account.

6. *True or false:* Generally, it is assumed that each long-term construction contract is accounted for separately to determine the degree of completion and estimates of revenues and expenses for each contract.

7. *True or false:* Once a credit union determines that a loan is delinquent due to nonpayment by a debtor, the credit union should *not* continue to accrue interest income on the outstanding balance.

8. *True or false:* Credit unions are not subject to the disclosure requirements of FAS-107 (Disclosures About Fair Values of Financial Instruments).

9. *Multiple choice:* The risk that a credit union may invest funds on a long-term basis to the extent that it misjudges the needs for funds to meet its operational needs is referred to as:

   a. Credit risk.

   b. Interest rate risk.

    c. Liquidity risk.

    d. Inherent risk.

10. *Multiple choice:* A credit union may have investments classified as:

    a. Held-for-trading purposes.

    b. Held for sale.

    c. Held-for-investment assets.

    d. All of the above.

    e. Only b and c.

11. *True or false:* Because of the nature of a credit union's accounts, the Credit Union Guide prohibits the use of analytical procedures, such as substantive tests, during an audit of a credit union.

12. *True or false:* A credit union that sells loans to third parties through a loan participation agreement should generally recognize any gain or loss at the time of the sale.

13. *True or false:* Debt securities held by an employee benefit plan for investment should be valued on the statement of net assets available for benefits at amortized cost.

14. *True or false:* The present value of accumulated plan benefits of a defined benefit pension plan should always be presented as of the date of the statement of net assets available for benefits.

15. *Multiple choice:* Which of the following methods are acceptable for measuring the fair value of investments of a defined contribution pension plan?

    a. Market quotations

    b. Selling prices of similar assets

    c. Discounted values of expected cash flows

    d. All of the above

    e. Only a and b

16. *True or false:* The disclosure requirements of FAS-119 (Disclosure About Derivative Financial Instruments and Fair Value of Financial Instruments) are not applicable to employee benefit plans.

17. *True or false:* One objective of reviewing a defined benefit plan's participant data is to ensure that reliable information has been supplied to the plan's actuary.

18. *True or false:* Assets (such as furniture, equipment, and buildings) used in the operation of a pension plan should be reported in the financial statements of the pension plan at cost less accumulated depreciation.

19. *True or false:* If a continuing care retirement community's estimated cost of providing future services to its current residents exceeds anticipated revenues from those residents, the community should recognize a liability for the difference.

20. *True or false:* Foundations and auxiliaries with direct or indirect relationships to a health care provider would never meet the criteria for consolidation with a health care provider's financial statements.

21. *True or false:* Health care providers that are not-for-profit organizations would be included in the scope of FAS-117 (Financial Statements of Not-for-Profit Organizations).

22. *True or false:* The costs incurred to acquire initial continuing care contracts should be capitalized by health care providers and amortized over the average expected remaining lives of residents or the contract term, whichever one is shorter.

23. *True or false:* Generally, a trust fund established to account for malpractice claims should be included in the financial statements of a health care provider.

24. *True or false:* Valuation of receivables from third-party payers is an important issue in the audit of a health care provider.

25. *True or false:* All not-for-profit organizations are required by FAS-117 to provide information about expenses in their natural classification.

26. *Multiple choice:* Contributions with donor-imposed restrictions should be recorded by not-for-profit organizations as an increase in:
    a. Unrestricted net assets.
    b. Temporarily restricted net assets.
    c. Permanently restricted net assets.
    d. None of the above.

27. *True or false:* A not-for-profit organization should not consolidate the financial statements of any for-profit organizations in which it has a controlling interest.

28. *True or false:* Not-for-profit organizations should not record the value of contributed services that they receive.

29. *Multiple choice:* FAS-124 requires that investments in debt securities be recorded at:
    a. Historical cost.
    b. Amortized cost.
    c. Fair value.
    d. Lower of cost or market value.

30. *True or false:* Not-for-profit organizations are required to record depreciation on their fixed assets.

31. *True or false:* Under FAS-117, a statement of cash flows is a required financial statement for not-for-profit organizations.

32. *True or false:* Voluntary health and welfare organizations must report information on expenses in both their functional and their natural classifications.

33. *True or false:* If a primary government is financially accountable for another entity, that entity's financial statements generally are included in the financial statements of the reporting entity.

34. *Multiple choice:* Which of the following pronouncements has the highest level of authority in the public-sector accounting hierarchy?

    a. GASB Interpretations.

    b. GASB Technical Bulletins.

    c. AICPA Statements of Position.

    d. GASB Implementation Guides.

35. *Multiple choice:* If revenues are legally restricted for specific purposes and are required to be accounted for as a separate fund, a government would ordinarily account for them in the:

    a. General fund.

    b. Special revenue fund.

    c. Capital projects fund.

    d. Enterprise fund.

36. *True or false:* Internal service funds are established to account for services provided to the general public.

37. *True or false:* Governmental funds use the flow of current financial resources measurement focus.

38. *True or false:* Generally, the assets recorded by a government in the general fixed asset account group are not depreciated.

39. *Multiple choice:* A government has issued a purchase order to a vendor for goods that have not been received by the balance sheet date. Which of the following would have been recorded by the government?

    a. Expenditure

    b. Encumbrance

    c. Deferred charge

    d. Inventory

40. *True or false:* A government should record taxpayer-assessed revenues on a cash basis.

1997 GAAS Guide CPE Program
Module 2—Specialized Industry Accounting and Auditing Practices

Please record your CPE answers in the space provided on the left and return this page for scoring. Simply place the completed answer sheet in a stamped envelope and mail it to:

GAAS Guide CPE Coordinator
Harcourt Brace Professional Publishing
525 B Street, Suite 1900
San Diego, California, 92101-4495

METHOD OF PAYMENT

☐ **Payment enclosed ($59.00 per Module).**
(Make checks payable to Harcourt Brace & Company.)
Please add appropriate sales tax.
Be sure to sign your order below.

Charge my:
☐ MasterCard ☐ Visa ☐ American Express

Account number _____

Expiration date _____
Please sign below for all credit card orders.

☐ **Bill me.** *Be sure to sign your order below.*

NAME _____

FIRM NAME _____

ADDRESS _____

PHONE ( ) _____

CPA LICENSE # _____

ISBN (MODULE 2): 0-15-606483-9

TO ORDER: Call Toll-Free 1-800-831-7799

Signature _____

See the reverse side of this page for the CPE evaluation.

MODULE 2 CPE ANSWERS

1. _____	21. _____
2. _____	22. _____
3. _____	23. _____
4. _____	24. _____
5. _____	25. _____
6. _____	26. _____
7. _____	27. _____
8. _____	28. _____
9. _____	29. _____
10. _____	30. _____
11. _____	31. _____
12. _____	32. _____
13. _____	33. _____
14. _____	34. _____
15. _____	35. _____
16. _____	36. _____
17. _____	37. _____
18. _____	38. _____
19. _____	39. _____
20. _____	40. _____

GAAS Guide CPE Evaluation

1. Were you informed in advance of the:
   a. Objectives of the course? Y N
   b. Experience level needed to complete the course? Y N
   c. Program content? Y N
   d. Nature and extent of preparation necessary? Y N
   e. Teaching method? Y N
   f. Number of CPE credit hours? Y N

   c. Program content? Y N
   d. Nature and extent of advance preparation necessary? Y N
   e. Teaching method? Y N
   f. Number of CPE credit hours? Y N

2. Do you agree with the publisher's assessment of:
   a. Objectives of the course? Y N
   b. Experience level needed to complete the course? Y N

3. Was the material relevant? Y N

4. Was the presentation of the material effective? Y N

5. Did the program increase your professional competence? Y N

6. Was the program content timely and effective? Y N

Please make any other comments that you feel would improve this course. We appreciate the time you take to complete this questionnaire. Be assured that all of your comments will be considered carefully.

_____

_____

_____

_____

_____

Module 3—Interim Reviews, Unaudited and Prospective Financial Statements, Attest Engagements, and Agreed-Upon Procedures Engagements

Interim Reviews, Condensed Financials, Filings Under Federal Securities Statutes, and Letters to Underwriters

After completing this section, you should be able to:

- Understand the nature of interim reviews of public companies.
- Understand the accountant's reports that are issued in an interim review.
- Understand the requirements for filings under federal securities statutes.
- Understand the reporting requirements for condensed financial statements and selected financial data.

Read Chapter 13, "Interim Reviews, Condensed Financials, Filings Under Federal Securities Statutes, and Letters to Underwriters," of the *1997 GAAS Guide*.

Answer questions 1–6 on page **25.39**.

Compilation and Review Engagements

After completing this section, you should be able to:

- Understand the difference between compilation engagements and review engagements.
- Understand the auditor's responsibility for compilation and review engagements.
- Understand the contents of a compilation report.
- Understand the contents of a review report.

Read Chapter 14, "Compilation and Review Engagements," of the *1997 GAAS Guide*.

Answer questions 7–13 on page **25.39**.

Prospective Financial Statements

After completing this section, you should be able to:

- Understand the standards established for examination engagements.
- Understand the standards established for agreed-upon procedures engagements.
- Understand the standards established for compilation engagements.

Read Chapter 15, "Prospective Financial Statements," of the *1997 GAAS Guide*.

Answer questions 14–18 on page **25.39**.

Attest Engagements

After completing this section, you should be able to:

- Understand the attestation standards.
- Understand the pro forma financial information standards.

Read Chapter 16, "Attest Engagements," of the *1997 GAAS Guide*.

Answer questions 19–21 on pages **25.39–25.40**.

Agreed-Upon Procedures Engagements

After completing this section, you should be able to:

- Understand the requirements of SAS-75.
- Understand the requirements of SSAE-4.

Read Chapter 17, "Agreed-Upon Procedures Engagements," of the *1997 GAAS Guide*.

Answer questions 22–24 on page **25.40**.

Code of Professional Conduct

After completing this section, you should be able to:

- Understand the key rules contained in the AICPA Code of Professional Conduct.

Read Chapter 24, "Code of Professional Conduct," of the *1997 GAAS Guide*.

Answer question 25 on page **25.40**.

REVIEW QUESTIONS

1. Discuss the minimum information that is required to be presented when publicly traded companies report summarized financial information at interim dates.

2. Discuss the types of modifications that can be made to the standard review report.

3. Under what circumstances would a subsequent event affect the dating of an auditor's report?

4. Discuss the additional procedures an auditor should perform for subsequent events for federal registration statements.

5. What limitations does SAS-72 impose on to whom a comfort letter may be addressed?

6. Discuss the applicability of SAS-42 to condensed financial statements.

7. Discuss the key difference between a *compilation* engagement and a *review* engagement.

8. What are the basic workpaper requirements for a review engagement?

9. Discuss some of the topics that are recommended for inclusion in an engagement letter for a compilation or review engagement.

10. Summarize the compilation standards.

11. Summarize the review standards.

12. Briefly discuss the contents of the accountant's compilation report.

13. Briefly discuss the contents of the accountant's review report.

14. What are the minimum presentation standards for prospective financial statements?

15. What are the minimum assumptions that must be disclosed for prospective financial statements?

16. What professional standards should an accountant observe in an examination of prospective financial statements?

17. Discuss the reporting standards that must be observed by an accountant who examines and reports on an entity's prospective financial statements.

18. What constitutes forward-looking information under the Private Securities Litigation Reform Act of 1995?

19. What is the definition of *attest engagement*?

20. What are the general standards for attest engagements?

21. Discuss the types of engagements to which SSAE-3 applies.

22. Distinguish between the applicability of SAS-75 and the applicability of SSAE-4 for agreed-upon procedures engagements.

23. What are some examples of client representations that could be obtained by an auditor performing an agreed-upon procedures engagement under SAS-75?

24. What conditions generally would constitute an acceptable reason to change an engagement to an agreed-upon procedures engagement?

25. Describe the events that will result in an automatic membership suspension or termination from the AICPA.

SUGGESTED SOLUTIONS

1. The following information is required to be presented when publicly trading companies report summarized financial information at interim dates:

    a. Gross revenues, provisions for income taxes, extraordinary items, effects of accounting changes, and net income

    b. Primary and fully diluted earnings-per-share data

    c. Material seasonal variations of revenues, costs, or expenses

    d. Contingent items and effects of the disposal of a segment of a business

    e. Material cash flows

2. The types of modifications to the standard review report that may arise are:

    a. Scope modification

    b. Modifying to incorporate the work of another accountant

    c. GAAP modification

    d. Inadequate disclosure modification

3. The following are circumstances that may affect the dating of the auditor's report:

    a. A subsequent event results in an adjustment to the interim financial information, and the event is disclosed.

    b. A subsequent event is disclosed in a note to the supplementary information.

    c. A subsequent event is not properly accounted for, and the review report is modified because of this departure from GAAP.

4. The additional procedures for subsequent events for federal registration statements are as follows:

   a. Read the entire prospectus and the pertinent parts of the registration statement thoroughly.

   b. Make inquiries of responsible executives of the client regarding any financial and accounting matters of a material nature that may have occurred during the subsequent-events period.

   c. Obtain client representation letters covering any subsequent events that have a material effect on the audited financial statements.

5. SAS-42 states that, in connection with acquisition transactions, the accountant should not address or give a comfort letter to any parties other than the client, the named underwriter, the broker-dealer, the financial intermediary, or the buyer and/or the seller.

6. SAS-42 is applicable to condensed financial statements and selected financial data only under the following two circumstances:

   a. Condensed financial statements are derived from audited financial statements of a public entity that is required to file, at least annually, complete financial statements with a regulatory agency.

   b. Selected financial data are derived from audited financial statements of a public or nonpublic entity and are presented in a document containing audited financial statements or are incorporated by reference into information filed with a regulatory agency.

7. A report for a compilation engagement includes a statement that an audit or a review was not performed and no opinion or other assurance is expressed on the accompanying financial statements. A review engagement report includes a statement of limited assurance that the financial statements are presented in accordance with generally accepted accounting principles or an other comprehensive basis of accounting.

8. The workpapers for a review engagement should support the report issued. They should include:

   a. Descriptions of all inquiries and analytical procedures employed, including any additional procedures deemed necessary, and summaries of the information and conclusions derived from such procedures

   b. Unusual matters disclosed by the procedures or brought to the accountant's attention, and their subsequent resolution

9. The following items are recommended for inclusion in the engagement letter for compilation or review engagements:

   a. A description of the specific compilation and/or review service to be performed

    b. A description of the report expected to be rendered on completion of the engagement and a caveat that if the accountant is unable to complete the compilation or a review, no report will be issued

    c. An explanation of the limitations of the engagement

    d. A detailed description of any other accounting services to be performed

10. The compilation standards are as follows:

    a. The accountant must possess an adequate level of knowledge of the accounting principles applicable to the client's industry and a general understanding of the client's business.

    b. The accountant should consider the need to perform other accounting services.

    c. The accountant should read the compiled financial statements and consider if they are appropriate in form and free from obvious material errors.

11. The review standards are as follows:

    a. The accountant must possess an adequate level of knowledge of the accounting principles applicable to the client's industry and a general understanding of the client's business.

    b. The accountant should complete inquiries and analytical procedures.

    c. The accountant should obtain a representation letter.

12. A compilation report should state that:

    a. A compilation has been performed.

    b. A compilation is limited to presenting information that is the representation of management or owners in the form of financial statements.

    c. The accountant has not audited or reviewed the statements and expresses no opinion or any assurance on them.

13. A review report should state that:

    a. A review has been performed in accordance with Statements on Standards for Accounting and Review Services, which is issued by the AICPA.

    b. All of the information in the financial statements is the representation of the management or owners of the entity.

    c. A review consists principally of inquiries and analytical procedures.

    d. A review is substantially less in scope than an audit, and no opinion is expressed.

    e. On the basis of a review, the accountant is not aware of any material modifications that should be made to the financial statements in order for them to be in conformity with GAAP, except for those modifications, if any, described in the report.

14. The following are the minimum presentation standards for prospective financial statements:

   a. Sales or gross revenues

   b. Gross profit or cost of sales

   c. Unusual or infrequently occurring items

   d. Provision for income taxes

   e. Discontinued operations

   f. Income from continuing operations

   g. Net income

   h. Primary and fully diluted earnings per share

   i. Significant cash flows

   j. Description of what management intends the prospective financial statements to present, a statement that assumptions are based on information about circumstances and conditions existing at the time the prospective information was prepared, and a caveat that the prospective results may not be achieved

   k. Summary of significant assumptions

   l. Summary of significant accounting policies

15. The following items are minimum disclosures for prospective financial statements:

   a. Assumptions for which there is reasonable possibility of the occurrence of a variation that may significantly affect the prospective results

   b. Assumptions about anticipated conditions that are expected to be significantly different from current conditions, which are not otherwise reasonably apparent

   c. Other matters deemed important to the prospective information or its interpretation

16. The following are minimum professional standards that should be observed in an examination of prospective financial statements:

   a. The accountant should be independent.

   b. The accountant should have adequate technical training and proficiency to examine a prospective financial statement.

   c. The examination should be adequately planned, and assistants, if any, should be supervised.

   d. Sufficient evidence to provide a reasonable basis for the accountant's report should be obtained.

e. Reporting standards for the examination of prospective financial statements should be observed in the preparation of the accountant's report.

17. The following reporting standards must be observed when an accountant examines and reports on an entity's prospective financial statements:

a. The report should identify the prospective financial statements presented.

b. The report should state that the examination of the prospective financial statements was made in accordance with AICPA standards and should include a brief description of the nature of the examination.

c. The report should include the accountant's opinion that the prospective financial statements are presented in conformity with AICPA presentation guidelines and that the underlying assumptions provide a reasonable basis for the forecast or a reasonable basis for the projection, given the hypothetical assumptions.

d. The report should include a caveat that the prospective results may not be achieved.

e. The report should state that the accountant assumes no responsibility for updating the report for events and circumstances occurring after the date of the report.

18. The following is considered forward-looking information under the Private Securities Litigation Reform Act of 1995:

a. A statement containing a projection of revenues, income, earnings per share, capital expenditures, dividends, capital structure, or other financial items

b. A statement of management's plans and objectives for future operations, including plans and objectives relating to the issuer's products or services

c. A statement of future economic performance, including any statement contained in management's discussion and analysis of financial condition or the results of operation included pursuant to SEC rules and regulations

d. A report, issued by an outside reviewer who was retained by the issuer, that assesses the issuer's forward-looking statement

e. A statement containing a projection or estimate of such other items as may be specified by SEC rules or regulations

19. An *attest engagement* is defined as follows:

An engagement in which a CPA who is in the practice of public accounting issues an opinion about the reliability of another party's written assertion. An assertion is a declaration, or a set of declarations taken as a whole, that is made by another party.

20. The general standards for attest engagements are:
    a. Training and proficiency
    b. Knowledge of assertion
    c. Reasonable criteria
    d. Independence

21. SSAE-3 applies to the following types of engagements:
    a. Examination of management's written assertion about its compliance with specified requirements
    b. Performance of agreed-upon procedures with respect to management's written assertions about its compliance with specified requirements
    c. Performance of agreed-upon procedures with respect to management's written assertions about the effectiveness of its internal control over compliance

22. SAS-75 establishes standards for agreed-upon procedures engagements that apply to specified elements, accounts, or items of a financial statement. SSAE-4 establishes standards for agreed-upon procedures engagements related to a written assertion or matters that are not elements, accounts, or items of a financial statement.

23. Examples of additional representations that could be obtained by an auditor performing an agreed-upon procedures engagement under SAS-75 are:
    a. Representation that the responsible party has disclosed to the accountant all known matters contradicting the specified elements, accounts, or items of a financial statement
    b. Representation that the responsible party has disclosed to the accountant all communications from regulatory agencies affecting the specified elements, accounts, or items of a financial statement

24. The conditions that generally would constitute acceptable reasons to change from one engagement to an agreed-upon procedures engagement are:
    a. A change in circumstances that results in different client requirements
    b. A misunderstanding of the original engagement
    c. A misunderstanding of the availability of alternative services provided by an accountant
    d. A restriction on the original engagement (which may be imposed by circumstances or the client)

25. The following events will result in an automatic membership suspension or termination from the AICPA:

a. A member commits a crime punishable by imprisonment for more than one year.

b. A member willfully fails to file an income tax return that he or she, as an individual taxpayer, is required by law to file.

c. A member files a false or fraudulent income tax return on his or her behalf, or on a client's behalf.

d. A member willfully aids in the preparation and presentation of a false and fraudulent income tax return for a client.

e. A member's certificate as a certified public accountant, or license or permit to practice as such, is revoked by a governmental authority as a disciplinary measure.

Examination for CPE Credit

1. *True or false:* The cumulative effect of an accounting change should be included in the net income of the first interim period, regardless of which interim period the accounting change occurs in during the year.

2. *True or false:* SAS-71 requires that an auditor obtain a written engagement letter when performing a review of interim financial statements.

3. *True or false:* An accountant performing a review of interim financial statements should not make references to any review report issued by other accountants.

4. *Multiple choice:* The date that relates to the procedures described in a comfort letter is referred to as the:
   a. Cut-off date.
   b. Effective date.
   c. Registration filing date.
   d. Closing date.

5. *True or false:* An auditor should always disclaim an opinion on condensed financial statements.

6. *True or false:* When a standard cost system is utilized, variances from standard costs that are expected to be eliminated by the end of the fiscal year need not be included in interim period statements.

7. *True or false:* When an auditor has not audited the preceding year's financial statements, the auditor is precluded from reviewing interim financial information in the current year.

8. *True or false:* An accountant may apply the compilation and review standards to report on financial statements prepared on another comprehensive basis of accounting.

9. *True or false:* An accountant cannot submit unaudited financial statements to a nonpublic client or other parties unless the financial statements have been either compiled or reviewed.

10. *Multiple choice:* An accountant that is not independent may perform which (if any) of the following engagements?
    a. Compilation
    b. Review
    c. Both a and b
    d. Neither a nor b

11. *True or false:* An accountant's compilation report should state that he or she is not aware of any departures from generally accepted accounting principles in the financial statements.

12. *True or false:* An accountant must always issue a compilation or review report when he or she includes unaudited personal financial statements in a written personal financial plan.

13. *True or false:* An accountant may issue a compilation or review report on a single financial statement, such as a balance sheet.

14. *True or false:* A compilation or review report is not required when, as an accommodation to the client, an accountant types or reproduces (without modification) financial statements prepared by the client.

15. *True or false:* Compilation standards do not require the accountant to perform any procedures to verify, corroborate, or review information supplied by the entity.

16. *True or false:* An accountant should indicate in a report on prospective financial statements that he or she prepared the statements.

17. *True or false:* In order for information to be subject to the safe-harbor provisions of the Private Securities Litigation Reform Act of 1995, the information must be identified as forward looking.

18. *True or false:* The title of a financial projection should include the word *forecast.*

19. *True or false:* An accountant should not be associated with a partial presentation of prospective financial information.

20. *True or false:* An accountant should be independent in an examination of prospective financial statements.

21. *True or false:* A prospective financial statement may be either a financial forecast or a financial projection.

22. *True or false:* A prospective financial statement may be prepared as either a single set of estimates or a range of estimates.

23. *True or false:* An auditor who is not requested by an SEC registrant to give substantive attention to forward-looking information must comply with the requirements of SAS-8 when the forward-looking information is included in a document containing the audited financial statements.

24. *Multiple choice:* The risk that the CPA will not discover materially misstated assertions in the written communication is referred to as:

   a. Inherent risk.

   b. Control risk.

   c. Detection risk.

   d. Attestation risk.

25. *True or false:* An accountant may be engaged to perform a review of pro forma financial information.

26. *True or false:* A CPA is *not* required to obtain a representation letter when performing an audit of pro forma financial information.

27. *True or false:* A CPA may *not* accept an attest engagement to report on management's assertions regarding an entity's internal controls.

28. *Multiple choice:* In which of the following attestation engagements would the CPA *not* make his or her report available for general distribution?

   a. Examination

   b. Review

   c. Agreed-upon procedures

   d. None of the above

29. *True or false:* If it is to provide the basis of an attestation engagement, an assertion must be capable of being evaluated using reasonable criteria.

30. *True or false:* A CPA must be independent to perform attestation engagements.

31. *True or false:* SSAE-4 generally applies to agreed-upon procedures engagements that apply to specified elements, accounts, or items of a financial statement.

32. *True or false:* SAS-75 prohibits the accountant from expressing negative assurance on the specified elements, accounts, or items to which agreed-upon procedures have been applied.

33. *True or false:* SAS-75 requires that the accountant obtain a representation letter from management when performing agreed-upon procedures engagements.

34. *True or false:* An engagement to report on specified compliance requirements based solely on an audit of financial statements would not be included in the scope of SSAE-4.

35. *True or false:* A statement that the documentation of employee evaluations included in personnel files is dated within the time frame set forth in an entity's personnel policy is an example of an assertion that would be included in the scope of SSAE-4.

36. *True or false:* When an accountant is engaged to apply agreed-upon procedures to prospective financial statements, the standards established by SSAE-4 should be observed.

37. *True or false:* An AICPA member in public practice may not prepare a tax refund claim based on a contingent fee.

38. *True or false:* An AICPA member convicted of a crime punishable by imprisonment for more than one year may have his or her AICPA membership suspended or terminated without a disciplinary hearing.

39. *True or false:* Discrimination in employment practices based on race, color, religion, sex, age, or national origin has been interpreted as a violation of Rule 501 of the AICPA Code of Professional Conduct.

40. *True or false:* An AICPA member is not prohibited from advertising or soliciting clients.

1997 GAAS *Guide* CPE Program

Module 3—Interim Reviews, Unaudited and Prospective Financial Statements, Attest Engagements, and Agreed-Upon Procedures Engagements

Please record your CPE answers in the space provided on the left and return this page for scoring. Simply place the completed answer sheet in a stamped envelope and mail it to:

GAAS Guide CPE Coordinator
Harcourt Brace Professional Publishing
525 B Street, Suite 1900
San Diego, California, 92101-4495

METHOD OF PAYMENT

☐ **Payment enclosed ($59.00 per Module).**
(Make checks payable to Harcourt Brace & Company.)

Please add appropriate sales tax.
Be sure to sign your order below.

Charge my:
☐ MasterCard ☐ Visa ☐ American Express

Account number _____

Expiration date _____
Please sign below for all credit card orders.

☐ **Bill me.** *Be sure to sign your order below.*

NAME _____

FIRM NAME _____

ADDRESS _____

PHONE ( ) _____

CPA LICENSE # _____

ISBN (MODULE 3): **0-15-606489-8**

TO ORDER: Call Toll-Free **1-800-831-7799**

Signature _____

See the reverse side of this page for the CPE evaluation.

MODULE 3 CPE ANSWERS	
1. _____	21. _____
2. _____	22. _____
3. _____	23. _____
4. _____	24. _____
5. _____	25. _____
6. _____	26. _____
7. _____	27. _____
8. _____	28. _____
9. _____	29. _____
10. _____	30. _____
11. _____	31. _____
12. _____	32. _____
13. _____	33. _____
14. _____	34. _____
15. _____	35. _____
16. _____	36. _____
17. _____	37. _____
18. _____	38. _____
19. _____	39. _____
20. _____	40. _____

GAAS Guide CPE Evaluation

1. Were you informed in advance of the:
a. Objectives of the course? Y N
b. Experience level needed to complete the course? Y N
c. Program content? Y N
d. Nature and extent of preparation necessary? Y N
e. Teaching method? Y N
f. Number of CPE credit hours? Y N

c. Program content? Y N
d. Nature and extent of advance preparation necessary? Y N
e. Teaching method? Y N
f. Number of CPE credit hours? Y N

2. Do you agree with the publisher's assessment of:
a. Objectives of the course? Y N
b. Experience level needed to complete the course? Y N

3. Was the material relevant? Y N

4. Was the presentation of the material effective? Y N

5. Did the program increase your professional competence? Y N

6. Was the program content timely and effective? Y N

Please make any other comments that you feel would improve this course. We appreciate the time you take to complete this questionnaire. Be assured that all of your comments will be considered carefully.

_____

_____

_____

_____

_____

_____

INDEX

A

Acceptable principle, changing to, and
  auditor's report **11.21**
Acceptance, incorrect, risk of (substantive
  tests) **9.05–9.06**
Acceptance of client **5.09–5.11**
Accounting and Review Services Committee
  (ARSC), authority of **24.24**
*Accounting by Creditors for Impairment of a
  Loan. See* FAS-114
*Accounting by Debtors and Creditors for Troubled
  Debt Restructuring. See* FAS-15
Accounting changes
  acceptable principle, changing to **11.21–
    11.22**
  Accounting Changes. See APB Opinion No.
    20
  consistency **3.18–3.19, 11.17–11.19**
  error, correction of **3.20, 11.22**
  estimate
    change in **11.25**
    change in principle inseparable from
      11.25–11.26
  FIFO to LIFO **11.19**
  financial statement format **11.19–11.20**
  future material effect of **11.28**
  inappropriate treatment of **11.23–11.24**
  interim periods, reporting **13.10–13.11**
    cumulative effect type, disclosure of
      13.10–13.11
  lack of consistency, report **11.17–11.18**
  pooling of interest **11.26–11.27**
  reasonable justification for, lack of
    11.24–11.25
  reporting entity, change in **11.26**
  reporting on **11.09–11.11, 11.17–11.28**
  segment information **11.20–11.21**
  statement of cash flows **11.19–11.20**
  transactions or events, substantially
    different **11.27**
  unacceptable principle, changing
    to **11.21–11.22**

Accounting estimates. *See* Estimates
Accounting for Contingencies. See FAS-5
Accounting hierarchy
  private-sector **3.13–3.14, 3.15**
  public-sector **3.13–3.14, 3.16**
Accounting Manual for Federal Credit Unions
  19.03
Accounting principles. *See also* Generally
  accepted accounting principles (GAAP)
  application of, reporting on **12.28–12.33**
  Code of Professional Conduct **24.26–
    24.28**
  information, accumulation of sufficient
    12.30–12.31
  oral advice **12.29**
  SAS-50 **12.28**
  standards of performance **12.30–12.31**
  standards of reporting **12.31–12.33**
  written reports **12.29**
Accounting Principles Board (APB)
  opinions of **3.11.** *See also specific APB
    opinions*
Accounting Research Bulletins (ARB) **3.11.**
  See also specific ARBs
Accounting services and independence
  24.09
Accounting Standards Executive Committee
  3.12
Accounting system
  computerization of **6.04–6.06**
  design of, and accounting information
    processing methods **6.04–6.06**
Accounting Trends and Techniques **3.14**
Accounts
  budgetary **24.05**
  completeness of **7.17**
  unconfirmed **8.34–8.35**
Accounts payable. *See* Liabilities
Accounts receivable
  confirmation of **8.35–8.36**

Accounts receivable, *cont.*
  construction contractors   **18.15–18.17**
  definition   **8.35**
  SAS-67   **8.35–8.36**
Accrual basis of accounting, not-for-profit
  organizations   **22.04**
Accumulated depreciation. *See* Depreciation
AcSEC   **3.12**
Acts discreditable   **24.33–24.35**
  discrimination   **24.34**
  failure to follow regulations   **24.34–24.35**
  failure to follow standards   **24.34**
  negligence   **24.34**
  retention of client records   **24.34**
Solicitation or Disclosure   **24.35**
Actuarial method, and annuity funds   **22.10**
Actuary use of, benefit plans   **20.28, 20.30**
Adequacy of Disclosure in Financial Statements.
  See SAS-32
Adjustments. *See* Prior-period adjustments
Advance fees, for health care provid-
  ers   **21.07**
Adverse change   **13.47**
Adverse opinion
  departure from GAAP   **11.11**
Advertising, and Code of Professional
  Conduct   **24.35–24.36**
  deceptive/false   **24.36**
Third-Party Engagements   **24.36**
Advocacy of client   **24.22**
Affiliated organizations   **22.22**
Agency fund   **23.06**
Agreed-upon procedures engagement
  assertions, management's   **17.18–17.19**
    about compliance   **17.24–17.25**
    about internal control   **17.28**
    definition of   **17.18**
    examples of   **17.19**
    presentation of   **17.19**
  attest engagements   **16.20, 16.21–16.22,
    16.24, 16.26.** *See also* SSAE-3
  change to   **17.15–17.16**
  compliance attestation   **17.24–17.27**
    client-prepared documents   **17.27**
    findings   **17.26–17.27**
    management's assertions   **17.24–
      17.25**
    management's requirements   **17.27**
    planning   **17.26**
    procedures   **17.25–17.26**
    representations from client   **17.26**
  engagement letter   **17.08, 17.20**

explanatory language   **17.14**
forecasts, financial   **17.28**
internal auditors, use of   **17.10–17.11,
  17.22**
internal control reports   **16.63, 17.10,
  17.28**
  reporting on   **16.63**
  pre-engagement conditions   **17.06–17.09,
    17.20–17.21**
  procedures   **17.07–17.08, 17.09–17.11,
    17.20, 17.21–17.22**
  compliance attestation   **17.24–17.26**
  restrictions on   **17.14–17.15**
projections, financial   **17.28**
prospective financial statements   **15.27**
reporting standards   **17.11–17.14, 17.22–
  17.24**
  combined reports   **17.16**
  compliance attestation   **17.27**
  forecasts   **17.28**
  included reports   **17.16**
  projections   **17.28**
  responsibility to update report   **17.14**
representation letter   **17.15**
representations from client   **17.15**
restrictions of performance of procedures   **17.14–17.15**
sampling risk, explanation of   **17.14**
SAS-75   **17.04–17.17**
  exclusions from   **17.04–17.05**
solvency, matters relating to   **17.05**
specialists, use of   **17.10, 17.21**
specific subject matter   **17.18**
specified elements, accounts, or
  items   **17.05–17.06**
    definition   **17.05–17.06**
    presentation of   **17.06**
specified users   **17.08–17.09, 17.20**
  responsibilities of   **17.18**
SSAE-4   **17.17–17.24, 17.28**
  exclusions from   **17.17–17.18**
workpapers   **17.17**
AICPA. *See* American Institute of Certified
  Public Accountants
All-inclusiveness, v. current operating
  performance   **3.07–3.08**
Allocation   **7.17**
  systematic and rational   **3.08**
Allowances for loan losses
  adequacy of   **19.21**
  credit unions   **19.07, 19.20–19.22**
American Institute of Certified Public
  Accountants (AICPA)
    Accounting Research Bulletins
    (ARBs)   **3.11**

Accounting Standards Executive Committee **3.12**

audit and accounting guides. *See* Audit and accounting guides

Auditing Standards Board (ASB) **4.04**

Code of Professional Conduct. *See* Code of Professional Conduct

committees. *See specific committees* and GAAS **4.04**

National Automated Accounting Research System **3.17**

Practice Bulletin 7 **19.04**

Practice Bulletin 10 **19.04**

Practice Bulletin 12 **20.19**

Analytical procedures. *See also* SAS-56

applicability of **8.62**

application of **8.59–8.60**

auditor's expectations **8.59–8.60**

data, quality of **8.62–8.63**

deviations, significant **8.63–8.64**

evidence from **8.59–8.64**

materiality thresholds **8.63**

overall review **8.61**

planning **8.60–8.61**

planning the engagement **6.08**

review of interim financial information **13.16–13.18**

SAS-56 **8.59–8.60**

significant deviations **8.63–8.64**

sources of **8.59**

substantive tests **8.61–8.63**

Annuity

funds, for colleges and universities **22.10–22.11**

not-for-profit organizations **22.10–22.11**

APB. *See* Accounting Principles Board

APB Opinion No. 15 **8.53**

APB Opinion No. 18 **8.39–8.42, 18.08–18.09, 21.12**

APB Opinion No. 20 **3.18–3.19, 11.19, 11.20, 11.23, 15.08, 22.07**

APB Opinion No. 21 **8.42, 19.09**

APB Opinion No. 22 **18.11, 20.09**

APB Opinion No. 28 **11.19, 13.05, 13.08, 13.23, 13.45**

ARB. *See* Accounting Research Bulletins

ARB-43 **3.11, 18.11**

ARB-51 **21.12, 22.07**

ARSC. *See* Accounting and Review Services Committee

ASB. *See* Auditing Standards Board

Assertions, management's **17.18–17.19**

about compliance **17.24–17.25**

about internal control **17.28**

definition of **4.13, 17.18**

examples of **17.19**

presentation of **17.19**

Assessments. *See also* Special assessments

procedures to identify **10.05–10.09**

Assets

employee benefit plans **20.22–20.26**

existence or occurrence of **7.16**

health care providers **21.07–21.08, 21.14, 21.17–21.18**

held by insurance companies **20.24–20.25**

not-for-profit organizations **22.05, 22.16, 22.20–22.21**

offsetting of **3.10**

as rights of entity **7.17**

trusteed **20.22–20.24**

Associating cause and effect **3.08**

Association with Financial Statements. See SAS-26

Assumptions

and prospective financial statements **15.09–15.10, 15.21–15.23**

nondisclosure of significant, for prospective financial statements **15.25**

suitable support for, criteria **15.21–15.23**

summary of significant **17.28**

for tax shelters **15.23**

Attest engagement. *See also* Pro forma financial information; SSAE-1; SSAE-2; SSAE-3; SSAE-5

agreed-upon procedures engagement **16.20, 16.21–16.22, 16.24, 16.26**

assertions, defined **24.18**

basis for **16.10**

compliance attestation **16.64–16.82**. *See also* Compliance attestation

agreed-upon procedures **16.82**

examination **16.66–16.82**

definition of **16.05, 25.17**

evidence **16.17–16.20**

examination engagement **16.18–16.19, 16.21–16.23, 16.30**

and independence **24.18–24.20**

internal control over financial reporting **16.37–16.63**. *See also* Internal control

examination **16.39–16.44**

report modifications **16.48–16.60**

Attest engagement, *cont.*
    representation letter **16.46–16.47**
    separate report **16.45–16.46**
    written representations **16.61–16.62**
    planning the engagement **16.14–16.17**
        criteria **16.15**
        engagement risk **16.15–16.16**
        materiality **16.16**
        potential attest problems **16.16**
        report, nature of **16.16**
        risk **16.15–16.16**
    pre-engagement planning **16.08–16.14**
        due care **16.14**
        independence **16.13**
        knowledge of assertion **16.09–16.10**
        reasonable criteria **16.10–16.13**
        training and proficiency **16.09**
    pro forma financial information **16.28–16.37**
        accountant's responsibilities **16.30–16.31**
        audit and review procedures **16.31–16.33**
        reporting on **16.33–16.37**
    relevant information, characteristics of **16.10–16.13**
        materiality **16.12–16.13**
        reasonableness of criteria **16.13**
        reasonably consistent estimation and measurement, concept of **16.12**
        reliability **16.11**
    reporting on **16.21–16.27**
        agreed-upon procedures engagement **16.21–16.22, 16.24, 16.26**
        distribution **16.26–16.27**
        examination engagements **16.22–16.23**
        internal control structure over financial reporting **16.37–16.63**
        presentation deficiencies **16.25–16.26**
        restricted distribution **16.26–16.27**
        review engagement **16.21–16.22**
        scope deficiencies **16.24–16.25**
        solvency, matters relating to **16.26**
    responsibility and function of the CPA **16.07–16.08**
        identifying an attest engagement **16.08**
        written assertion, positive opinion about **16.07**
    review engagement **16.19–16.20, 16.21–16.22, 16.23–16.24, 16.30–16.31**

risk
    control risk **16.15**
    detection risk **16.15–16.16**
    inherent risk **16.15**
    and prospective financial statements **15.20–15.21**
    solvency **16.26**
    standards. *See* Attestation standards
    team, definition of **24.18–24.19**
Attest function **1.03**
Attestation. *See* Attest engagement
Attestation Interpretations
    (August 1987) **16.08**
    (February 1988) **16.26**
    (May 1988) **17.05**
    (July 1990) **16.05–16.06**
Attestation standards **4.13–4.15, 16.07–16.27**
    criteria **16.28**
    evidence **16.17–16.20, 16.28**
    fieldwork standards **4.14, 16.14–16.20**
    general standards **4.14, 16.09–16.14**
    reporting standards **4.14–4.15, 16.21–16.27**
    reports **16.28**
    written assertions **16.28**
Attorney
    client privilege **10.07**
    Inquiry of a Client's, Concerning Litigation, Claims, and Assessment. See SAS-12
    and letter of audit inquiry **10.05–10.10**
Attribute sampling **9.04–9.05**
Audit
    accuracy and effectiveness of **9.06**
    characteristics of **7.43–7.44**
    completion **10.03–10.27**
    definition of **1.03, 19.04**
    due professional care in **4.07–4.08**
    efficiency of **9.06**
    findings **10.15–10.17**
    initial design of **6.06–6.07**
    planning. *See also* Planning
        checklist for **6.08–6.10**
        engagement **6.03–6.10, 7.42–7.44**
        professional skepticism and **7.44–7.45**
    purpose of **2.03**
    reports. *See* Reporting
    risk. *See* Audit risk; Risk
    withdrawal from **7.46**
Audit and accounting guides
    Audits of Certain Nonprofit Organizations **22.03, 22.19, 23.17**

Audits of Colleges and Universities **22.03, 22.10, 23.17**
Audits of Construction Contractors **18.03**
Audits of Credit Unions **19.03**
Audits of Employee Benefit Plans **20.03, 23.17**
Audits of Providers of Health Care Services **21.03, 23.17**
Audits of State and Local Governmental Units **23.03, 23.17**
Audits of Voluntary Health and Welfare Organizations **22.03**
Consideration of the Internal Control Structure in a Financial Statement Audit **7.05**
Guide for Prospective Financial Information **15.03–15.31**
Audit committee
  of board of directors **7.09**
  communicating (with) **10.24–10.27**
    errors and irregularities to **7.45**
    illegal acts to **7.50–7.52**
    in review of interim financial information **13.17–13.18**
  composition **10.24**
  SAS-61 **10.24–10.25**
Audit objectives, and balance sheet assertions **8.10**
Audit procedures
  analytical procedures. *See* Analytical procedures; SAS-56
  claims, litigation, and assessments **10.05–10.10**
  completing the audit **10.03–10.27**
  construction contractors **18.15–18.23**
  credit unions **19.14–19.28**
  dual-purpose tests **8.77**
  employee benefit plans **20.22–20.38**
  evaluating findings **10.15–10.17**
  governmental units **23.16–23.41**
  health care providers **21.15–21.21**
  illegal acts **7.49–7.50**
  not-for-profit organizations **22.17–22.26**
  oil and gas reserve information **10.19–10.21**
  omitted **10.23–10.24**
  other information **10.21**
  planning **6.06–6.07, 6.08**
    nature, timing, and extent of **6.06–6.07**
  post-audit **10.21–10.24**
  reasonableness **8.76–8.77**
  related parties **8.64–8.69**

  representation letters **8.76, 10.12–10.15**
  required supplementary information **10.17–10.21**
  subsequent events **8.76, 10.10–10.12**
  using the work of another auditor **8.55–8.59.** *See also* SAS-73
Audit risk **8.11–8.12, 8.17–8.22.** *See also* Risk
  assessing **7.77, 8.21–8.22**
  and auditor's quality of performance **8.11–8.12**
  classifications of **9.05–9.06**
  and materiality **8.17–8.18**
  nonsampling **8.11–8.12**
  sampling **8.11–8.12, 9.05–9.06**
  SAS-47 **8.05, 8.06, 8.19-8.22**
  and timing of substantive tests **8.14–8.17**
Audit Risk and Materiality in Conducting an Audit. See SAS-47
Audit sampling. *See* Sampling; SAS-39
Auditing Interpretations **4.04**
  (February 1974) **11.19**
  (January 1975) **11.19**
  (July 1975) **8.38**
  (March 1977) **10.07, 10.08**
  (October 1978) **7.74**
  (March 1979) **10.14**
  (April 1979) **8.56, 8.58, 8.64**
  (October 1979) **11.17**
  (November 1979) **11.45, 13.58**
  (July 1980) **8.41**
  (March 1981) **10.14, 11.30**
  (May 1981) **12.14**
  (December 1981) **8.57**
  (July 1982) **12.25**
  (May 1983) **13.29**
  (June 1983) **10.09, 10.13**
  (December 1984) **8.74, 12.03–12.04**
  (January 1985) **9.03**
  (May 1985) **5.06**
  (February 1986) **6.07**
  (April 1986) **8.09**
  (May 1986) **8.66**
  (September 1986) **5.05**
  (January 1989) **11.07**
  (February 1989) **7.36, 10.23**
  (February 1990) **10.08**
  (July 1990) **12.06**
  (December 1991) **12.08**
  (June 1992) **13.30**
  (February 1993) **8.46, 11.45**
  (June 1993) **13.31**

Auditing Interpretations, *cont.*
  (August 1993) **10.25**
  (May 1994) **7.39**
  (July 1994) **8.24–8.27**
  (March 1995) **13.30**
  (April 1995) **5.06**
  (May 1995) **12.19**
  of Auditing Standards Board **4.04**
Auditing responsibilities, after the report date **8.75**
Auditing standards. *See also* Generally accepted auditing standards (GAAS); *Government Auditing Standards*
  defined **4.03**
Auditing Standards Board (ASB) **4.04**
  authority of **24.24**
Auditor
  appointment of **6.04**
  due professional care **2.05–2.06, 4.07–4.08**
  as expert **2.04**
  independence of **2.05, 2.07, 4.07, 5.09**
  independent
    appointment of **6.04**
    role of **2.03–2.06**
  mental attitude of **7.44–7.45**
  other auditor, using the work of **8.55–8.56**
  predecessor
    ceased operations **5.07–5.09, 11.56–11.62**
    communication with **5.04–5.06**
    reporting by **11.54–11.56**
  proficiency of **2.04–2.05, 4.05–4.07**
  report by **7.46**
  responsibility and function
    general standards **2.04–2.06**
    post-audit **10.22–10.24**
    quality control standards **2.06–2.08**
    with respect to fraud **7.75–7.76**
    risk assessment **7.77**
    role **2.03–2.06**
  responsibility for information outside the financial statements. *See* SAS-8; SAS-29
  of service organization
    role of user auditor **7.58–7.61**
    evaluating service auditor **7.61–7.62**
    role of service auditor **7.62–7.66**
  training of **2.05, 4.05–4.07**
  v. accountant **12.03**
  withdrawal from engagement **7.46**

Auditor-submitted documents **10.21, 11.48–11.51**
  financial statements, consolidated or combined **11.49–11.50**
  required supplementary information **11.51**
  SAS-29 **10.21, 11.48**
Auditor's reports. *See* Reporting
AUP. *See* Agreed-upon procedures engagement
Authoritative Status of NCGA Pronouncements and AICPA Industry Audit Guide. See GASB-1
Authoritative support for GAAP **3.13–3.17**

B

Balance sheet
  date, events subsequent to **8.76**
  fair value **11.46–11.47**
Basic financial statements. *See* Financial statements
Basis of accounting **23.13–23.14**
  other than GAAP (OCBOA) **12.04–12.11**
    liquidation basis **12.04, 12.26–12.27**
    not-for-profit financial statements **22.04**
Benefit plans. *See* Employee benefit plans
Bequests. *See* Contributions; Support
Block sampling **9.11**
Board of directors
  audit committee of **7.09**
  control environment and **7.08–7.11**
Borrowed funds
  for credit unions **19.10–19.11, 19.23–19.24**
Bribery **7.72–7.74**
Budgets
  governmental units **23.18–23.19**

C

Capital additions, for not-for-profit organizations **22.15–22.16, 22.19–22.20**
Capital changes **3.10**
Capital expenditures **23.14–23.15, 23.27–23.28**
Capital projects fund **23.06**
Capsule financial information **13.44–13.45**
Cash
  credit unions **19.05, 19.16**
  governmental units **23.23–23.25**
  health care providers **21.05**

Cash basis. *See* Basis of accounting
Cash contributions
    to not-for-profit organizations **22.15**
Cash equivalents
    health care providers **21.05**
Cause and effect, associating **3.08**
Central Liquidity Facility **19.06, 19.10**
Certain not-for-profit organizations. *See* Not-for-profit organizations
Certified public accountant (CPA). *See* Auditor
Changes. *See* Accounting changes
Charitable organizations. *See* Not-for-profit organizations
Claims
    procedures to identify **10.05–10.10**
Client
    acceptance of **5.03–5.04, 5.09–5.11**
    advocacy **24.22**
    continuation of **5.11–5.12**
    definition of **24.12**
    engagement letter **5.10–5.11**
    evaluation of **5.03–5.04**
        continuing audits and **5.11–5.12**
    loans from **24.10–24.12**
    prospective, evaluation of **5.03–5.04**
    representations of **8.76**. *See also* Representation letters
        agreed-upon procedures engagements **17.15, 17.26**
        Client Representations. *See* SAS-19
Client-prepared documents **10.21**. *See also* SAS-8
Code of Professional Conduct **4.05, 24.03–24.62**
    accounting principles (Rule 203) **24.26–24.28**
    acts discreditable (Rule 501) **24.33–24.35**
    advertising and other forms of solicitation (Rule 502) **24.35–24.36**
    commissions and referral fees (Rule 503) **24.36–24.38**
    compliance with standards (Rule 202) **24.24–24.25**
    confidential client information (Rule 301) **24.28–24.30**
    contingent fees (Rule 302) **24.30–24.33**
    definitions used in **24.05**
    form of organization and name **24.38–24.40**
    general standards (Rule 201) **24.22–24.23**
    incompatible occupation (Rule 504/ withdrawn) **24.38**

    independence (Rule 101) **24.05–24.20**
        interpretations **24.08–24.20**
        types of engagements that require **24.06–24.07**
    integrity and objectivity (Rule 102) **24.20–24.22**
    principles of **24.04**
    Rule 101 **24.05–24.20**
    Rule 102 **24.20–24.22**
    Rule 201 **5.04, 13.12–13.13, 24.22–24.23**
    Rule 202 **16.06, 24.24–24.25**
    Rule 203 **4.11, 24.26–25.28**
    Rule 301 **5.04, 24.28–24.30**
    Rule 302 **24.30–24.33**
    Rule 501 **24.33–24.35**
    Rule 502 **24.36–24.38**
    Rule 503 **24.40–24.62**
    Rule 505 **24.38–24.40**
    rulings on ethics **24.40–24.62**
    rulings on general and technical standards (Rules 201, 202, & 203) **24.53–24.54**
    rulings on independence, integrity, and objectivity (Rules 101 & 102) **24.40–24.53**
    rulings on other responsibilities and practices (Rules 501, 502, 503, & 505) **24.56–24.62**
    rulings on responsibilities to clients (Rules 301 & 302) **24.54–24.56**
Collateralized loans
    credit unions **19.19**
Collections **22.11–22.12**
College and University Business Administration (1974) **22.10**
Colleges and universities. *See also* Not-for-profit organizations
    actuarial method **22.10**
    annuity **22.10–22.11**
    Audits of Colleges and Universities **22.03, 22.10**
    FAS-117 **22.06**
    governmental **22.06**
    investments **22.10**
    life income funds **22.10–22.11**
    pooled life income funds **22.11**
    valuation of investments **22.10–22.11**
Combined financial statements. *See* Financial statements, consolidated
Comfort letter. *See* Underwriters, letters for
Commissions, and Code of Professional Conduct **24.36–24.38**

Commitments
  health care providers   21.09–21.11, 21.14, 21.18–21.19
Committee of Sponsoring Organizations (COSO)   7.06, 16.38, 16.46
Communication of Internal Control Structure Related Matters Noted in an Audit. See SAS-60
Communication with Audit Committees. See SAS-61
Communication with predecessor auditor   5.04–5.09
  predecessor auditor has ceased operations   5.07–5.09
  SAS-7   5.04–5.09, 6.03–6.04
Communications Between Predecessor and Successor Accountants. See SSARS-4
Comparability. *See* Consistency
Comparative financial statements
  different opinions on the comparative financial statements, example of report   11.53–11.54
  predecessor auditor, reporting by   11.54–11.62
  reporting on   11.51–11.62
  SAS-58   11.51
  for unaudited financial statements of nonpublic companies
    all periods compiled or reviewed   14.57–14.58
    change in public or nonpublic status   14.67–14.69
    changes in reports of prior periods   14.61–14.62
    current or prior period audited, other period compiled or reviewed   14.60–14.61
    current period compiled, prior period reviewed   14.59–14.60
    current period reviewed, prior period compiled   14.58–14.59
    exception to reporting on the highest level of service rendered   14.66–14.67
    prior period, or periods, compiled or reviewed by other accountants   14.62–14.66
  updated opinion differs from previous opinion   11.53–11.54
Comparative-years presentation   12.27–12.28
Competence   24.22, 24.23
Compilation and Review of Financial Statements. See SSARS-1
Compilation engagement. *See also* SSARS-1
  applicability of   14.07

client representations   14.26
compilation standards   14.21–14.22
definition of   14.20
emphasis of a matter   14.43–14.44
financial statements in prescribed forms   14.46–14.48
inaccurate or incomplete financial statements   14.25
internal control structure, consideration of   14.33–14.34
knowledge of accounting principles and practices   14.21–14.23
level of service   14.26
other accounting services, need for   14.23–14.24
partial presentations   15.16–15.17
prospective financial information   15.16–15.17, 15.27–15.31
  applicable procedures   15.28–15.30
  due professional care   15.28
  limitations of   15.27
  planning and supervision   15.28
  report on   15.30–15.31
  training and proficiency   15.27–15.28
reporting obligations   14.34–14.37
reporting on   14.37–14.39
  disclosure, inadequate   14.42
  disclosures, substantial omission of   14.38–14.40
  GAAP, departure from   14.41–14.42
  going concern   14.42–14.43
  inconsistency   14.43
  independence   14.40–14.41
  uncertainty   14.42–14.43
subsequent discovery   14.44–14.45
supplementary information   14.46
types of clients   14.21
understanding of a client   14.22–14.23
Compilation Reports on Financial Statements in Certain Prescribed Forms. See SSARS-3
Completed contract method of income recognition   18.05–18.07, 18.21
Completing the audit
  analytical procedures, overall   10.05
  communication with audit committees   10.24–10.27
  evaluating audit findings   10.15–10.17
  identifying litigation, claims, and assessments   10.05–10.10
  post-audit responsibilities   10.22–10.24
  representation letter   10.12–10.15
    appropriateness of report   10.22–10.23

continuing inquiries **10.22–10.23**
omitted procedures **10.23–10.24**
required supplementary information **10.17–10.21**
responsibilities for information included
with the financial statements **10.17–
10.21**
responsibilities for information outside
the financial statements **10.21**
subsequent events, identifying **10.10–
10.12**
Compliance
attestation. *See also* SSAE-3
agreed-upon procedures engagement **17.24–17.27**
client-prepared documents **17.27**
findings **17.26–17.27**
management's assertions **17.27**
management's requirements **17.27**
planning **17.26**
procedures **17.25–17.26**
representations from client **17.26**
auditing. *See* SAS-74
with contracts or regulations
reporting on **12.15–12.18**
financial presentation **12.18–12.24**
examination engagement **16.66–16.67**
with SEC, reporting on in comfort
letter **13.41–13.42**
with standards, Code of Professional
Conduct **24.24–24.25**
Component financial statements, not-for-
profit organizations **22.23–22.24**
Component units. *See also* Reporting entity
financial statement presentation **23.09**
Computer processing
computerized accounting systems
engagement planning **6.05–6.06**
significant accounting applications
and **6.05**
specialists **6.06**
Condensed financial statements
nature **13.55–13.56**
reporting on **13.55–13.58**
SAS-42 **13.55–13.58**
selected financial data **13.56–13.58**
Confidential client information
and Code of Professional Conduct **24.28–24.30**
exemptions **24.28–24.29**
Confirmations
accounts receivable **8.35–8.36**
SAS-67 **8.35–8.36**

characteristics of respondents **8.32**
construction contractors **18.15–18.16**
design of **8.29–8.32**
evaluating responses **8.34–8.35**
by facsimile **8.33**
negative **8.30–8.31**
oral **8.33**
positive **8.30–8.31**
procedures, performance of **8.32–8.33**
process **8.28–8.35**
The Confirmation Process. See SAS-67
request, design of **8.29–8.32**
unconfirmed balances **8.34–8.35**
Conflicts of interest **24.21**
Conservatism **3.06**
*Consideration of Fraud in a Financial Statement
Audit* **7.75–7.80**
*Consideration of the Internal Control Structure in
a Financial Statement Audit* **7.05**
Consistency **3.07, 3.18–3.19**
lack of, and standard auditor's report **11.17–11.19**
reporting standards and **4.11**
Consolidated financial statements. *See* ARB-
51; Financial statements, consolidated
*Consolidation of all Majority-Owned Subsidiaries.
See* FAS-94
Construction contractors
accounting for **18.03–18.11**
completed contract method **18.05–
18.07, 18.21**
percentage-of-completion
method **18.03–18.04, 18.21**
accounts receivable **18.15–18.17**
affiliated entities **18.09–18.10**
auditing **18.15–18.23**
backlog information **18.22**
bidding **18.12–18.13**
billing procedures **18.13–18.14**
Construction Contractors Guide **18.03**
costs **18.14, 18.18–18.19**
disclosures **18.11**
equipment **18.14**
estimates **18.10–18.11, 18.12–18.13**
financial statements **18.11**
joint ventures **18.08–18.09**
income recognition **18.19–18.21**
industry practices **18.12–18.15**
internal audit staff **18.14–18.15**
internal control **18.13**
job site controls **18.13**
liabilities **18.17–18.18**

Construction contractors, *cont.*
  profit center   18.07–18.08
  project administration   18.13
  reporting on   18.22–18.23
  representation letter   18.22
  revenue   18.14
  tax accounting methods   18.10
Construction-type contracts, accounting for.
  See SOP 81-1
Consulting standards   16.27–16.28
Contingencies
  classifications of   11.35–11.36
  FAS-5   10.06, 10.09, 11.35–11.36
  health care providers   21.09–21.11, 21.14,
    21.18–21.19
  litigation, claims, and assessments   10.06
  reporting standards for   11.36–11.37
Contingent fees, and Code of Professional
  Conduct   24.30–24.33
Continuation of client   5.11–5.12
Continuing care. *See* Health care providers
  retirement communities. *See* SOP 90-8
Continuity. *See* Going concern
Contracts
  compliance with, reporting on   12.15–
    12.18
  construction contractors   18.03–18.23
    combining   18.21–18.22
    segmenting   18.11
  continuing care   21.07, 21.11
  employee benefit plans   20.24
  financial presentation to comply
    with   12.18–12.24
  insurance   20.24
  noncompliance with, reporting on   16.05
Contributed services. *See* Donated services
  and materials
Contributions
  employee benefit plans   20.26–20.27
  not-for-profit organizations   22.08–22.09,
    22.15–22.16
Control activities   7.11–7.12. *See also*
  SAS-55
Control environment   7.08–7.11. *See also*
  SAS-55
  board of directors   7.09
  human resource policies and prac-
    tices   7.10–7.11
  management philosophy and operating
    style   7.09
  organizational structure   7.09–7.10
Control risk   8.20
  assessment   7.30–7.31

  in attestation engagements   16.15
  defined   7.23
  documenting assessed level   7.29–7.30
  evaluate the planned level   7.27–7.29
  risk of assessing too high/low   9.05, 9.12
  substantive tests based on   7.30–7.31
  and tests of controls   7.25–7.27
Controls. *See also* Internal control
  and sampling   8.12–8.13
  tests of. *See* Tests, of controls
Cooperative agreements with clients   24.20
Corruption   7.72–7.74
COSO. *See* Committee of Sponsoring
  Organizations
Cost method, long-term investments   8.41–
  8.42
Costs. *See also* Expense recognition principles;
  specific types of costs
  construction contractors   18.14, 18.18–
    18.19
  deferred   3.05
Country clubs. *See* Not-for-profit organizations
CPA. *See* Auditor
Credit card loans, credit unions   19.19
Credit risk   19.15
Credit unions
  accounting for   19.05–19.12
  auditing   19.14–19.28
  borrowed funds   19.10–19.11, 19.23–19.24
  cash   19.05, 19.16
  credit cards   19.19
  Credit Union Guide   19.03–19.04
  debt securities   19.12
  deposits   19.09–19.10
  disclosures   19.12
  equity   19.11, 19.24
  examination v. audit   19.04
  federal, accounting manual   19.03, 19.13
  federal funds   19.10
  financial statements   19.05–19.12
  going concern   19.15
  income statement   19.11–19.12, 19.24–
    19.25
  industry practices   19.13–19.14
  internal control   19.13–19.14
  investments   19.05–19.07, 19.17–19.18
  lines of credit   19.19
  loans   19.07–19.09, 19.18–19.20
  losses   19.07–19.09, 19.20–19.22
  mortgages   19.19
  notes payable   19.10

promissory notes **19.10**
regulations on **19.03, 19.25**
reporting on **19.25–19.28**
representation letter **19.16**
reverse repurchase agreements **19.10–19.11**
risk **19.14–19.16**
    audit **19.14**
    credit **19.15**
    interest rate **19.15**
    liquidity **19.15**
savings accounts **19.09–19.10, 19.22–19.23**
securities **19.05–19.07, 19.12, 19.17–19.18**
taxes **19.10**
CUBA. *See College and University Business Administration*
Cumulative-effect type accounting change, disclosure of **13.10–13.11**
Current obligations. *See* Obligations
Current-value financial statements **12.06–12.07**

D

Data processing. *See* Computer processing
Debt, governmental units **23.15–23.16, 23.28–23.29**
Debt securities
    Accounting for Certain Investments in Debt and Equity Securities. See FAS-115
    credit unions **19.12**
Debt service fund **23.06**
Deferred revenue. *See* Revenue
Deferred support. *See* Support
Defined benefit pension plan. *See* Employee benefit plans
Defined contribution pension plan. *See* Employee benefit plans
Deposits
    credit unions **19.09–19.10**
Deposits with Financial Institutions, Investments (Including Repurchase Agreements), and Reverse Repurchase Agreements. See GASB-3
Depreciation
    not-for-profit organizations **22.11–22.12**
Detection risk **7.30, 8.20–8.21, 19.14**
    attestation engagement **16.15–16.16**
    SAS-47 definition **8.20**
    SAS-55 definition **7.24**
Detective controls **9.08**
Deviation rate **9.17–9.18**
Deviations
    analytical procedures **8.63–8.64**

expected rate, in a population **9.14**
maximum tolerable rate of **9.12–9.14**
qualitative aspects of **9.20**
rate, calculation of **9.17–9.18**
Director, honorary, and independence **24.09–24.10**
Disclaimer of opinion
    due to limited access **10.13–10.14**
    going concern **8.74**
Disclosure assertion **7.17**
Disclosure of Information About Financial Instruments with Off-Balance-Sheet Risk and Financial Instruments with Concentrations of Credit Risk. See FAS-105
Disclosures **3.10–3.11**
    adequacy of. *See* SAS-32
    basis of accounting other than GAAP **12.07–12.08**
    construction contractors **18.11**
    credit unions **19.12**
    debt securities **19.12**. *See also* SOP 90-11
    employee benefit plans **20.09–20.10, 20.11–20.12, 20.16–20.18, 20.19**
    fair value **8.46, 11.45–11.48**. *See also* FAS-107
    FAS-57 **8.68**
    going concern **8.74**
    minimum, for publicly traded companies **13.27**
    related party transactions **8.68–8.69**
    reporting standards and **4.12**
    SAS-59 **8.73**
Discreditable acts and Code of Professional Conduct **24.33–24.35**
    discrimination **24.34**
    failure to follow regulations **24.34–24.35**
    failure to follow standards **24.34**
    negligence **24.34**
    retaining client records **24.34**
Discrimination **24.34**
Doctors. *See* Health care providers
Donated services and materials
    not-for-profit organizations **22.15–22.16, 22.18**
Dual-dating **13.25**
Dual-purpose tests **8.76–8.77**
Due professional care **2.05–2.06, 4.07–4.08, 24.23**
    attestation engagements **16.14**

E

Earned revenue. *See* Revenue

Earning process **3.05**
Earnings per share. *See* APB Opinion No. 15
Educational services **24.22**
Emphasis of a matter in auditor's reports **11.39–11.40, 12.25–12.26**
Employee benefit plans
   accounting for **20.05–20.20**
   assets held by insurance companies **20.24–20.25**
   auditing **20.22–20.38**
   Audits of Employee Benefit Plans **20.03**
   benefit payments **20.27**
   Benefit Plans Guide **20.03**
   contributions **20.26–20.27**
   defined benefit pension plan **20.03–20.04**
      accounting for **20.05–20.10**
      accumulated plan benefits **20.07–20.08**
      contributions, auditing **20.27**
      disclosures **20.09–20.10**
      FAS–35 requirements **20.05–20.10**
      financial statements **20.06–20.09**
      obligations, auditing **20.29**
      participants' data, auditing **20.28**
      receivables, auditing **20.27**
   defined contribution pension plan **20.03–20.04**
      accounting for **20.10–20.12**
      contributions, auditing **20.27**
      disclosures **20.11–20.12, 20.19**
      financial statements **20.10–20.12**
      obligations, auditing **20.29–20.30**
      participants' data, auditing **20.28**
      receivables, auditing **20.27**
   employee health and welfare plan **20.03–20.04**
      accounting for **20.12–20.18**
      disclosures **20.16–20.18**
      financial statements **20.13–20.16**
      obligations, auditing **20.30**
      participants' data, auditing **20.29**
   ERISA **20.03**
      audits under **20.04–20.05**
         PWBA/DOL reviews of **20.04–20.05**
      reports **20.34–20.35**
      supplemental schedules **20.36–20.37**
   fair value disclosures **20.19–20.20**
   FAS-35 **20.05–20.10**
   financial statements
      defined benefit pension plan **20.06–20.09**

defined contribution pension plan **20.11–20.12**
employee health and welfare plan **20.14–20.18**
401(h) plans **20.18–20.19**
industry practices **20.20–20.22**
insurance companies, contracts with **20.27**
internal control **20.21–20.22**
investments **20.22–20.26**
   valuation **20.06**
obligations **20.29–20.30**
participants' data **20.27–20.29**
party-in-interest transactions **20.31–20.33**
payments **20.27**
Pension Benefit Guaranty Corporation **20.09**
planning the audit **20.20–20.21**
quality control reviews of ERISA audits **20.04–20.05**
receivables **20.26–20.27**
reporting on **20.34–20.38**
representation letter **20.33**
subject to ERISA **20.04–20.05**
tax status **20.33**
trust established under **20.37–20.38**
trusteed assets **20.22–20.24**
types of **20.03**
Employee health and welfare benefit plans. *See* Employee benefit plans
Employee Retirement Income Security Act of 1974 (ERISA) **20.03–20.05, 20.36**
Encumbrances **24.05, 24.15**
Engagement. *See specific types of engagement*
Engagement letter **5.10–5.11**
   agreed-upon procedures engagement **17.08, 17.20**
   interim financial information engagement **13.06–13.07**
Enterprise fund **23.07–23.08**
Equipment. *See also* Property
   construction contractors **18.14**
   health care providers **21.07–21.08, 21.14, 21.17–21.18**
Equity
   credit unions **19.11, 19.24**
Equity method, long-term investments **8.39–8.41**
Equity Method of Accounting for Investments in Common Stock. See APB Opinion No. 18
Equity securities
   Accounting for Certain Investments in Debt and Equity Securities. See FAS-115

ERISA. *See* Employee Retirement Income
  Security Act of 1974
Errors, correction of   **3.20, 11.22**
Errors and irregularities. *See also* Deviations
  auditor's responsibility to detect and
    report. *See* SAS-53
  communication of   **7.45–7.46**
  definition of
    SAS-53   **7.40**
  detection of   **7.40**
  discovering   **7.45**
  governmental units   **24.19**
  material v. immaterial   **7.40–7.42**
  maximum tolerable rate of   **9.12, 9.14**
  nature of   **7.41–7.42**
  nonsampling   **8.11–8.12**
  possibility of   **7.40**
  reporting   **7.46**
  risk related to   **7.42–7.44**
Escheat property   **23.33**
Estimates
  auditing. *See* SAS-57
  changes to   **3.19**
    construction contractors   **18.10**
    cumulative catch-up method   **18.10**
    reallocation method   **18.11**
    and standard auditor's report   **11.26**
  circumstances giving rise to   **8.44**
  construction contractors   **18.10–18.11**
  definition   **8.42**
  development of   **8.43**
  establishing   **8.43**
  evaluating   **8.44–8.46**
  evidence for   **8.44**
  generally accepted accounting prin-
    ciples   **8.46**
  internal control   **8.43**
  *Reasonable Estimation of the Amount of a
    Loss. See* FIN-14
  reasonableness of, evaluating   **8.44–8.46**
  SAS-57   **8.42**
Ethics rulings   **24.40–24.62**
Events subsequent to the balance sheet date.
  See Subsequent events
Evidence
  for accounting estimates   **8.42–8.43**
  accounts, unconfirmed   **8.34–8.35**
  accounts receivable, confirmation
    of   **8.35–8.36**
  from analytical procedures   **8.59–8.64**
    applicability of   **8.62**
    application of   **8.59, 8.62**
    auditor's expectations   **8.59, 8.63**

deviations, significant   **8.63–8.64**
    materiality thresholds   **8.63**
    planning   **8.60–8.61**
    precision of the established
      expectation   **8.63**
    quality of data   **8.63**
    substantive tests   **8.61–8.63**
  for attest engagement   **16.17–16.20**
  audit procedures   **8.27–8.77**
    when using the work of another
      auditor   **8.55–8.59**
  audit risk   **8.11–8.12, 8.17–8.22**
  competency of   **8.08**
    SAS-31   **8.08**
  confirmations   **8.28–8.36**
    accounts receivable   **8.35–8.36**
    characteristics of respondents   **8.32**
    design of   **8.29–8.32**
    form   **8.30–8.31**
  control risk   **7.23–7.24, 7.30–7.31, 8.20**
  detection risk   **8.20–8.21**
  dual-purpose tests   **8.77**
  estimates
    circumstances giving rise to   **8.44**
    development of   **8.42–8.43**
    evaluating   **8.44–8.46**
    internal control   **8.43**
    management responsibility for   **8.43**
    presentation in accordance with
      GAAP   **8.46**
    reasonableness of, evaluating   **8.44–
      8.46**
    SAS-57   **8.42**
  Evidential Matter. See SAS-31
  fieldwork standard   **4.10**
  financial statement assertions   **8.09**
  going-concern concept   **8.69–8.75**
  inherent risk   **8.19**
  for interim financial information   **13.16–
    13.19**
  and internal auditors   **8.52**
  interrelationship of   **7.29**
  inventories   **8.36–8.39**
    counted by others   **8.38–8.39**
    held by others   **8.37–8.38**
  long-term investments   **8.39–8.42**
    cost method   **8.41–8.42**
    equity method   **8.39–8.41**
    other   **8.42**
  materiality   **8.17–8.18**
  other auditor, using the work of   **8.55–
    8.59**

Evidence, *cont.*
for prospective financial statements 15.21–15.23
qualities of 8.07–8.08
related party transactions 8.64–8.69
audit approach 8.66–8.67
conditions that increase the possibility of 8.65–8.66
disclosures 8.68–8.69
examples of 8.65
identifying 8.64–8.66
for review of interim financial information 13.16–13.19
risk 8.11–8.12, 8.17, 8.18–8.22
sampling 8.10–8.17
segment information 8.52–8.59
client's refusal to disclose 8.55
design factors for testing of 8.53–8.54
sources of 7.27
specialist
evidence obtained from 8.46–8.52
qualifications of 8.48–8.49
subsequent events 8.76
substantive tests 8.13–8.17
sufficiency of 8.08–8.09, 8.10–8.12
tests of controls 8.12–8.13
third party, evaluation of information received from 8.34
timeliness of 7.27–7.28
workpapers 8.22–8.27
Examination engagement
attest engagement 16.18–16.19
of credit unions 19.04, 19.25
for partial presentations 15.17–15.18
for pro forma financial information 16.34–16.35
for prospective financial information 15.17–15.18, 15.19–15.27
assumptions, sufficient evidence for 15.21–15.23
attestation risk 15.20
evidence 15.23–15.24
independence 15.20
materiality 15.19
planning and supervision 15.20–15.21
purpose of 15.17–15.18
report 15.24–15.25
training and proficiency 15.20
uncertainty, degree of 15.19
Expenditures. *See also* Capital expenditures
governmental units 23.14–23.15
Expense recognition principles 3.08–3.09

Expenses
functional classification of 22.05, 22.13–22.14, 22.17–22.18
fund-raising 22.13–22.14
health care providers 21.11–21.12, 21.15, 21.19
not-for-profit organizations 22.13–22.14, 22.17–22.18
voluntary health and welfare organizations 22.05, 22.11, 22.17
Exposure Draft
on fraud 7.75–7.80
on new auditing standards 8.39

F

FAF. *See* Financial Accounting Foundation
Fair value concept 20.06, 20.19–20.20
Fair value disclosures, reporting on 8.46, 11.45–11.48
FAS-107 11.45
False advertising 24.36
Family relationships, effect on independence 24.14–24.16
FAS-5 4.06, 7.50, 10.06, 10.09, 11.35–11.36, 21.06, 21.09–21.10
FAS-14 8.52–8.55, 11.20–11.21
FAS-15 19.08
FAS-16 3.20, 21.06
FAS-19 10.19
FAS-21 8.53
FAS-25 10.19
FAS-35 20.03, 20.05–20.10, 20.29
FAS-47 19.11
FAS-57 8.64–8.66, 8.68, 20.31, 21.13, 22.07, 23.34
FAS-65 19.09
FAS-71 3.20
FAS-87 8.49
FAS-93 21.08
FAS-94 21.10, 21.12, 22.07
FAS-95 11.19, 22.06
FAS-105 19.07, 20.19–20.20
FAS-107 11.45, 19.07, 20.19–20.20
FAS-109 8.46, 18.10
FAS-110 20.03, 20.07, 20.20
FAS-114 19.08
FAS-115 8.41, 19.06
FAS-116 21.11–21.12, 22.08, 22.11–22.12
FAS-117 21.04–21.05, 22.03, 22.04–22.06, 22.08, 22.16

FAS-124 **21.05–21.06, 22.09**
FASB. *See* Financial Accounting Standards Board
FASB Concepts Statement No. 1 **16.10**
FASB Concepts Statement No. 2 **8.17**
FCPA. *See* Foreign Corrupt Practices Act
Federal Credit Union Act of 1934 **19.03, 19.04**
Federal financial assistance/awards internal control structure **16.63**
Federal funds
  credit unions **19.10**
  state governments **23.32–23.33**
Federal Reserve System **19.10**
Federal securities statutes, filings under **13.27–13.30**
  document review of filings **13.30**
  predecessor auditor's responsibilities **13.29**
  registration statement **13.28**
  SAS-37 **13.27**
  Securities Act of 1933 **13.27–13.28**
  subsequent-events period **13.29**
  unaudited financial statements **13.30**
Fiduciary funds **23.30**
Fieldwork
  completion of, and report date **11.07–11.08**
  standards **4.08–4.10**
FIFO to LIFO change **11.19**
Filings Under Federal Securities Statutes. See SAS-37
FIN-18 **13.05**
FIN-35 **8.39**
Financial Accounting Foundation (FAF) **3.12**
Financial Accounting Standards Board (FASB)
  authority of **24.26–24.27**
  publications **3.12**
  Statements and Interpretations **3.12**
  Technical Bulletins **3.12**
Financial data, selected. *See* Condensed financial statements
Financial forecast. *See* Forecasts, financial
Financial Forecasts and Projections **15.03**
Financial information
  interim. *See* Interim financial information
  pro forma. *See* Pro forma financial information
Financial institutions. *See also* Credit unions
  as clients, loans from **24.10–24.12**
Financial projections. *See* Forecasts, financial; Prospective financial statement

Financial Report Survey **3.17**
Financial statements. *See also* Disclosures
  assertions **7.17**
  association with **11.08–11.09.** *See also* SAS-26
  audited, other data and information in a document containing **11.41–11.42**
  basic **3.09–3.11**
  comparability of **3.07**
  comparative. *See* Comparative financial statements
  component, for not-for-profit organizations **22.23–22.24**
  condensed. *See* Condensed financial statements
  consolidated, as auditor-submitted documents **11.49–11.50**
    health care providers **21.12–21.13**
  construction contractors **18.03–18.07, 18.11**
  current-value **12.06–12.07**
  credit unions **19.05–19.12, 19.24**
  deficiencies in. *See* Reporting
  defined benefit pension plans **20.06–20.09**
  defined by SSARS-1 **14.05–14.06**
  defined contribution pension plans **20.11–20.12**
  departure from GAAP **3.17**
  employee benefit plans **20.05–20.20**
  employee health and welfare plans **20.14–20.18**
  errors, correction of **11.22**
  examples of **14.07**
  fair value disclosures **11.45–11.48**
  FAS-117 **22.16**
  health care providers **21.04–21.13**
  historical-cost **12.06**
  illegal acts with direct effects on **7.47–7.48**
  illegal acts with indirect effects on **7.48–7.49**
  information included with, responsibilities for **10.17–10.21**
  insurance regulators, based on standards established by **12.22**
  interim, summarized **13.11–13.12**
  internal control policies and procedures and **7.07–7.11**
  irregularities and **7.45–7.46**
  liquidation basis of accounting **12.03, 12.26–12.27**
  material misstatements on **7.40–7.42**

Financial statements, *cont.*
  misstated, by predecessor auditor **5.08–5.09**
  not-for-profit organizations **22.04–22.06, 22.16**
  OCBOA **12.05–12.08**
  opinion on. *See* Opinions; Reporting
  other countries, for use in **12.33–12.39**
    auditing standards **12.34–12.35**
    fieldwork standards **12.35**
    general standards **12.34–12.35**
    reporting standards **12.35–12.39**
  preparation of, and auditor **2.04**
  prepared for use in another country, reporting on **12.33–12.39**
  prepared to comply with contracts or regulations **12.18–12.24**
  presentation and disclosure on **7.17**
  prospective. *See* Prospective financial statements
  relationship with tests of controls **7.25–7.26**
  review of. *See* Review engagement
  special-purpose, reporting on **12.18**
    for not-for-profits **22.22–22.23**
  standards of reporting **4.10–4.13**
  statement of cash flows, change in format of **11.19–11.20**
  submission of, defined by SSARS-7 **14.10–14.12**
  summarized interim **13.11–13.12**
  supplementary information, reporting on **11.42–11.45**
  and trial balance, factors differentiating **14.07–14.08**
  unaudited. *See* Unaudited financial statements—public companies
    and SEC filings **13.30**
  unaudited condensed interim **13.43–13.44**
  use of computer processing for **4.06**
  voluntary health and welfare organizations **22.05–22.06**
Findings, evaluation of **10.15–10.17**
  compliance attestation **17.26–17.27**
Fixed assets. *See* Assets
Flowcharts for documenting internal control **7.21–7.22**
Forecasts, financial. *See also* Prospective financial statements
  agreed-upon procedures engagement **17.28**
  SEC registration **13.41–13.42**
Foreign Corrupt Practices Act (FCPA) **7.72–7.74, 16.63**

Foreign countries. *See* Other countries, financial statements for use in
Form of organization **24.38–24.40**
Former practitioner, and independence **24.09**
Forward-looking information **15.06**
Fraud. *See* Errors and irregularities, Exposure Draft
Full disclosure concept **3.06**
Fund accounting
  definition and discussion of **23.05**
  for not-for-profit organizations **22.04, 22.06**
Fund balances
  governmental units **23.29**
Fund-raising costs
  not-for-profit organizations **22.13–22.14**
Funds. *See specific types of funds*

G

GAAP. *See* Generally accepted accounting principles
GAAS. *See* Generally accepted auditing standards
Gains **3.10**
  health care providers **21.11–21.12, 21.15, 21.19**
GAO. *See* General Accounting Office
Gas. *See* Oil and gas activities
GASB. *See* Governmental Accounting Standards Board
GASB-1 **3.13, 23.10**
GASB-3 **23.24**
GASB-6 **23.06**
GASB-10 **23.26**
GASB-14 **23.09, 23.31, 24.17**
GASB-20 **23.03, 23.30**
GASB-21 **23.33**
GASB-24 **23.33**
GASB-25 **23.07**
GASB-26 **23.07**
GASB-27 **23.07**
GASB-28 **23.24**
GASB Technical Bulletin 87-1 **23.24**
GASB Technical Bulletin 94-1 **23.24**
Gas companies. *See* Oil and gas activities
General Accounting Office. *See also Government Auditing Standards*
  state and local governments **23.03–23.04**
General fixed assets account group **23.05, 23.08**
General fund **23.05**

General long-term debt account group   **23.05,
   23.08**
Generally accepted accounting principles
   (GAAP)
   accounting changes   **3.18–3.19**
   assumptions   **3.04, 3.05–3.09**
   authoritative support for   **3.13–3.17**
   basic principles   **3.04, 3.05–3.09**
   basic financial statements   **3.09–3.11**
   broad principles   **3.04, 3.09–3.11**
   comparability   **3.07**
   conservatism   **3.06**
   consistency   **3.07, 3.18–3.19**
   continuity   **3.06**
   current performance   **3.07–3.08**
   defined   **3.03**
   departure from   **3.17, 11.14–11.15**
   detailed principles   **3.05, 3.11–3.13**
   disclosure, full   **3.06**
   and error correction   **3.20**
   estimates, changes in   **3.19**
   expense recognition   **3.08–3.09**
   full disclosure   **3.06**
   going concern   **3.06**
   hierarchy   **3.13–3.17**
      private-sector   **3.15**
      public-sector   **3.16**
   internal control and   **7.07–7.11**
   matching   **3.05**
   materiality   **3.06**
   neutrality   **3.07**
   objectivity   **3.07**
   operating cycle   **3.06–3.07**
   pervasive principles   **3.04, 3.05–3.09**
   prior-period adjustments   **3.20**
   and regulated industries   **3.20–3.21**
   representational faithfulness   **3.05–3.06**
   and review of interim financial
      information   **13.11–13.12**
   separate entity   **3.05**
   sources of   **3.03–3.04**
   and specialized industries   **3.21**
   substance over form. *See* Representational
      faithfulness
   and unaudited financial statements of
      nonpublic companies   **14.18–14.19**
Generally accepted auditing standards
   (GAAS)   **4.03**
   auditor characteristics   **4.05–4.08**
      independence   **4.07**
      proficiency   **4.05–4.07**
      training of   **4.05–4.07**

   auditor's opinion   **4.12–4.13**
   broad nature of   **4.13**
   due professional care   **4.07–4.08**
   evidence   **4.10**
   fieldwork standards   **4.08–4.10**
   general standards   **2.04–2.06, 4.03.** *See also*
      SAS-1
   planning   **4.08–4.09**
   reporting standards   **4.10–4.13**
   and review of interim financial
      information   **13.12–13.13**
   supervision   **4.08–4.09**
   and unaudited financial statements of
      nonpublic companies   **14.19–14.20**
   understanding internal control   **4.09**
Gifts. *See* Contributions; Support
Going concern   **3.06**
   audit procedures   **8.69–8.70**
   auditor's consideration of. *See* SAS-59
   concept   **8.69**
   credit unions   **19.15**
   disclosures   **8.73–8.74**
   examples of conditions   **8.70–8.71**
   financial statements, liquidation
      basis   **8.69, 8.74**
   information related to   **8.70–8.71**
   management's plans   **8.71–8.73**
   prospective financial statements   **8.72**
   report, example of   **8.74–8.75**
      using conditional language in   **8.74**
   reporting on   **8.74–8.75, 11.37–11.39,
      12.38–12.39**
   SAS-59   **8.69–8.71**
   uncertainties related to   **11.37–11.39**
Government Auditing Standards   **7.35, 12.15,
   16.63, 21.20, 23.03–23.40**
Governmental Accounting Standards Board
   (GASB)
   authority of   **3.12–3.13, 24.26–24.27**
   Statements and Interpretations   **3.12–3.13**
Governmental Audit Guide   **23.03**
Governmental GAAP, and independence   **24.16–24.18**
Governmental units
   account groups   **23.08**
   accounting for   **23.09–23.16, 23.24**
   accounting hierarchy   **23.11**
   agency fund   **23.06**
   auditing   **23.16–23.41**
   basis of accounting   **23.13–23.14**
   budgetary accounts   **23.05**
   budgets   **23.18–23.19**

Governmental units, *cont.*
capital expenditures   23.14–23.15, 23.27–23.28
capital projects fund   23.06
cash   23.23–23.25
compliance with laws and regulations   23.19–23.21
SAS-74   23.19–23.21
component units   23.09
debt   23.15–23.16, 23.28–23.29
debt service fund   23.06
encumbrances   23.05, 23.15
enterprise fund   23.07–23.08
errors, irregularities, and illegal acts   23.19
escheat property   23.33
expenditures   23.14–23.15, 23.26, 23.27–23.28
fiduciary funds   23.30
fund, defined   23.05
fund accounting   23.05
fund balances   23.29
funds of   23.05–23.08, 23.16
GASB-14   23.09, 23.30
general fixed assets account group   23.05, 23.08
general fund   23.05
general long-term debt account group   23.05, 23.08
going concern   23.34–23.35
Government Auditing Standards   23.03–23.04, 23.40
grants, pass-through   23.32–23.33
and independence   24.16–24.18
interfund transactions   23.29
internal control   23.17–23.18
internal service fund   23.07
investments   23.23–23.24
letter of audit inquiry   23.33
measurement focus   23.13–23.14
NCGA pronouncements   23.10, 23.12
nonexpendable trust funds   23.06–23.07, 23.16
pass-through grants   23.32–23.33
pension trust fund   23.07
planning the audit   23.16–23.17
proprietary accounts   23.05
proprietary funds   23.16, 23.30
receivables   23.25–23.26
related party transactions   23.34
reporting entity   23.08–23.09, 23.31, 24.17
reports   23.35–23.41

modifications   23.39–23.40
special   23.40–23.41
standard   23.35–23.38
representation letter   23.33–23.34
revenues   23.14
special revenue fund   23.05–23.06
state   23.31–23.33
aid to local governments   23.32
escheat property   23.33
income taxes   23.32
independence   23.32
joint audits   23.32
lotteries   23.31
Medicaid   23.31–23.32
pass-through grants   23.32–23.33
reporting entity   23.31
revenue sharing   23.31
subsidiary ledgers   23.05
tests
of controls   23.22
of controls over compliance with laws and regulations   23.22
substantive   23.22–23.23
trust fund   23.06–23.07, 23.16
Governments. *See* Governmental units
Grants   22.19–22.20, 23.32–23.33. *See also* Contributions; Support

H

Haphazard sampling   9.11
Health and welfare benefit plans. *See* Employee benefit plans
Health and welfare organizations. *See* Voluntary health and welfare organizations
Health maintenance organizations (HMOs). *See* Health care providers
Health Care Guide   21.03
Health care providers
accounting for   21.05–21.13
advance fees   21.07
assets   21.07–21.08, 21.14, 21.17–21.18
auditing   21.15–21.21
auditor's report   21.21
cash and cash equivalents   21.05
contingencies   21.09–21.11, 21.14, 21.18–21.19
continuing care contracts   21.07, 21.11
commitments   21.09–21.11, 21.14, 21.18–21.19
equipment   21.07–21.08, 21.14, 21.17–21.18

expenses **21.11–21.12, 21.15, 21.19**
FAS-124 **21.05–21.06**
Financial Accounting and Reporting by Providers of Prepaid Health Care Services. See SOP 89-5
financial statements **21.04–21.13**
gains **21.11–21.12, 21.15, 21.19**
industry practices **21.13–21.15**
internal control **21.13–21.15**
investments **21.05–21.06, 21.13, 21.15–21.16**
obligations **21.08–21.09, 21.18**
losses **21.11–21.12, 21.15, 21.19**
malpractice **21.09–21.11, 21.14, 21.18–21.19**
property **21.07–21.08, 21.14, 21.17–21.18**
receivables **21.06–21.07, 21.14, 21.16–21.17**
related organizations **21.12–21.13, 21.15, 21.20**
reporting entity **21.12–21.13, 21.15**
reports **21.21**
revenues **21.11–21.12, 21.15, 21.19**
SOP 92-9 **21.21**
supplies **21.07–21.08, 21.14, 21.17–21.18**
types of **21.04**
Hierarchy. *See* Accounting hierarchy
Historical-cost financial statements **12.06**
Hospitals. *See* Health care providers

I

Illegal acts **7.47–7.52**
and audit report **7.51**
communicating
to audit committee **7.50–7.51**
to third parties **7.50–7.51**
definition **7.47**
discovery of **7.50–7.52**
effects on audit procedures **7.49–7.50**
effects on financial statements **7.50**
governmental units **24.19**
information indicating existence of **7.48–7.49**
reporting **7.51**
SAS-54 **7.47**
no suspicion of, audit procedures **7.49**
suspicion of, audit procedures **7.49–7.50**
Illegal Acts by Clients. See SAS-54
Immediate recognition **3.08**
Income
current operating performance v. all-inclusiveness **3.07–3.08**

recognition methods
completed contract method **18.05–18.07, 18.19–18.21**
completed contract method based on immateriality justification **18.19, 18.20**
percentage-of-completion method **18.03–18.04, 18.19–18.21**
percentage-of-completion method with a zero profit basis **18.19, 18.20**
statement, for credit unions **19.11–19.12, 19.24–19.25**
Income tax. *See also* Tax
in interim periods, accounting for. *See* FIN-18
Incomplete presentation **12.18–12.21**
Independence (Rule 101) **24.05–24.20**
and attest engagements **24.18–24.18**
of auditor **2.05, 2.06–2.07, 4.07**
circumstances that impair **24.08**
circumstances that impair during an attest engagement **24.19–24.20**
comfort letters **13.42–13.43**
and cooperative agreements with clients **24.20**
engagements that require **24.06–24.07**
ethics rulings **24.40–24.62**
financial interests in a nonclient that has relationship with the client **24.12–24.14**
former practitioner **24.09**
GAAS general standards **2.04–2.06**
governmental GAAP **24.16–25.18**
honorary director or trustee **24.09–24.10**
in fact as well as appearance **16.13**
interpretations, Code of Professional Conduct **24.08–24.20**
joint venture relationship **24.13**
litigation, effect on **24.12**
loans between a CPA and a client **24.10–24.12**
other accounting services **24.09**
and pre-engagement planning **5.09**
quality control of **2.06–2.08**
scope of terms *member* and *member's firm* **24.14**
and Statements on Standards for Attestation Engagements **24.18–24.20**
terminology **24.14–24.16**
underwriters, letters to **13.42–13.43**
Independent, used in report title **11.05**
Independent auditor. *See* Auditor
Industry, characteristics of, and audit risk **7.42–7.43**

Inherent risk   **7.23, 8.19, 19.14**
    attestation engagements   **16.15**
    definition
        SAS-47   **8.19**
        SAS-55   **7.24**
Initial year reporting
    comparative-years presentation   **12.27–12.28**
    single-year presentation   **12.27**
Inspection, quality control and   **2.10**
Institute. *See* American Institute of Certified
    Public Accountants
Integrity and objectivity (Rule 102)   **24.20–24.22**
Interest
    on receivables and payables. *See* APB
        Opinion No. 21
    pooling of
        changes resulting from   **11.26–11.27**
        reporting by successor auditor
            for   **11.34**
    rate risk   **19.15**
Interest-free loans   **22.16, 22.20**
Interest on Receivables and Payables. See APB
    Opinion No. 21
Interfund transactions   **23.29**
Interim date, and substantive testing   **8.15–8.16**
Interim financial information
    accompanying audited financial
        statements, reports on   **13.25–13.27**
    accountant's report   **13.19–13.27**
        GAAP modification   **13.22–13.23**
        going-concern modification   **13.24**
        inadequate disclosure modifica-
            tion   **13.23–13.24**
        inconsistency modification   **13.24**
        marked "Unaudited"   **13.20**
        responsibilities after the report
            date   **13.25**
        scope modification   **13.21**
        standard report, contents of   **13.19–13.20**
        subsequent events   **13.24–13.25**
        uncertainty modification   **13.24**
        using the work of another accoun-
            tant   **13.21–13.22**
    analytical procedures   **13.16–13.18**
    audit committee, communication
        with   **13.18–13.19**
    condensed   **13.43–13.44**
    differs from audit   **13.05**
    engagement letter   **13.06–13.08**

evidential material   **13.16–13.19**
    and GAAP   **13.08–13.12**
        accounting changes, report-
            ing   **13.10–13.11**
        accounting for other costs and
            expenses   **13.09–13.10**
        accounting practices, modi-
            fied   **13.08–13.09**
        estimates   **13.09**
        financial statements, summarized
            interim   **13.11–13.12**
        inventory, exceptions to valuation
            of   **13.08–13.09**
        uncertainties   **13.09**
    and GAAS   **13.12–13.13**
        evidential material   **13.13**
        independence, concept of   **13.12**
        internal control   **13.12–13.13**
        planning and supervision   **13.12–13.13**
        reporting, standards of   **13.13**
    internal control, consideration of   **13.15–13.16**
    interval of   **13.04**
    limited assurance   **13.05**
    planning   **13.13–13.15**
        centralization of client's accounting
            function   **13.14**
        new accounting standard   **13.14**
    pre-engagement planning   **13.06**
    purpose of   **13.05–13.06**
    reporting. *See* APB Opinion No. 28
    SAS-71. *See* SAS-71
Internal audit function
    agreed-upon procedures engage-
        ment   **17.10–17.11, 17.22**
    auditor's consideration of. *See* SAS-65
    construction contractors   **18.14–18.15**
    degree of reliance on   **7.55–7.56**
    effect on audit planning   **7.54–7.55**
    internal auditors
        assessing objectivity and competence
            of   **7.53–7.54**
        evaluating work of   **7.56–7.57**
        and evidential matter   **8.52**
    internal control   **7.54**
    organizational status of   **7.53–7.54**
    SAS-65   **7.52–7.57**
Internal Control—Integrated Framework. See
    Committee of Sponsoring Organizations
*Internal Control Structure, Consideration of, in a
    Financial Statement Audit. See* SAS-55

Internal control
  adequacy of   2.03–2.04
  agreed-upon procedures engagement
    17.10
  application of concepts to small/midsized
    entities   7.13–7.14
  audit and accounting guide   7.05
  and audit risk   8.11–8.12
  consideration of
    governmental units   23.17–23.18
    in review of interim financial
      information   13.16–13.19
  construction contractors   18.12
  control environment   7.08–7.11
  control procedures   7.08
  control risk   7.21–7.24
    determine   7.21–7.24
    document   7.29–7.30
    evaluate   7.27–7.30
  COSO definitions   7.07–7.13, 16.38
  credit unions   19.13–19.14
  design
    deficiencies in   7.32
    evaluation of   7.25–7.26
    other factors   7.15
    and prevention of errors and
      irregularities   7.41–7.42
  documenting auditor's understanding
    of   7.21–7.23
    flowcharts   7.21–7.22
    internal control questionnaire   7.22
    narrative descriptions   7.22–7.23
  employee benefit plans   20.21–20.22
  errors and irregularities   7.40–7.47
  failure in operation of   7.31–7.33
  five components of   7.07–7.13, 16.38
  governmental units   23.17–23.18
  health care providers   21.13–21.15
  illegal acts   7.47–7.52
  internal audit function   7.52–7.57
  internal auditors   7.52–7.57
  limitations of   7.15
  management letter   7.38
  nature of   7.07–7.13
  objectives of   7.17
  operational effectiveness, evaluation
    of   7.25–7.26
  policies and procedures of   7.16–7.17,
    7.24–7.26
  PPPO/TOE report   7.62–7.66
  questionnaire   7.22
  reportable conditions   7.31–7.38, 16.49

  reporting on   16.37–16.63
    accepting engagement   16.37–16.38
    agreed-upon procedures   16.63
    compliance   16.63
    COSO   16.38, 16.46
    disagreements with manage-
      ment   16.51–16.53
    evaluating   16.42
    examination procedures   16.39–16.44
    expressing opinion on management's
      assertions   16.39
    federal awards   16.63
    federal financial assistance   16.63
    forming opinion   16.44
    management reports on   7.38–7.40
    management's assertions   7.38, 16.37
    management's responsibilities   16.37
    material inconsistency   16.62
    material misstatement   16.62
    material weakness   16.48–16.53
    operational effectiveness   16.42–16.44
    other information   16.62
    planning the engagement, examina-
      tion   16.40–16.42
    reference to another report   16.54–
      16.55
    report modifications   16.48–16.60
    representation letter   16.46–16.47
    scope limitation   16.53–16.54
    segment   16.57
    separate report   16.45–16.46
    subsequent event   16.56
    testing   16.42–16.44
    understanding internal control   7.16–
      7.21, 16.42
    written representations   16.61–16.62
  risk   7.21–7.24, 7.27, 7.43–7.44
  service organizations   7.51–7.72
  standards of fieldwork   4.09
  substantive tests   7.30–7.31
  tests of   7.24–7.26
  understanding   4.09, 7.16–7.21, 16.42
  workpapers   7.72
Internal Revenue Service Form 990   12.25
Internal service fund   23.07
Internal use statements. *See* Prospective
  financial statements
Inventories
  counted by others   8.38–8.39
  evidential material for   8.36–8.38
  FIFO to LIFO change   11.19
  financial statements related to   7.16–7.17

Inventories, *cont.*
    gross-profit method at interim
        date   **13.05, 13.08**
    held by others   **8.37–8.38**
    public warehouses   **8.37–8.38**
    review of interim financial informa-
        tion   **13.08–13.10**
Investments. *See also specific types of*
    investments
    cost method   **8.41–8.42**
    credit unions   **19.05–19.07, 19.17–19.18**
    employee benefit plans   **20.22–20.26**
    equity method   **8.39–8.41**
    evidence for   **8.39**
    exposure draft **8.39**
    governmental units   **23.23–23.24**
    health care providers   **21.05–21.06, 21.13,**
        21.15–21.16
    long-term   **8.39–8.42**
    not-for-profit organizations   **22.09, 22.14**
    performance statistics, reporting
        on   **16.05**
Irregularities. *See* Errors and irregularities
IRS. *See* Internal Revenue Service Form 990

J

Joint ventures
    construction contractors   **18.08–18.09**

L

Labor unions. *See* Not-for-profit organizations
Lawyer. *See* Attorney
Letters
    audit inquiry   **10.07–10.10, 23.33**
    attorney   **10.07–10.10**
    comfort. *See* SAS-72; Underwriters, letters
        for
    engagement   **5.10–5.11**
        agreed-upon procedures   **17.08, 17.20**
        interim financial information   **13.06–**
            13.07
        internal control considerations   **7.38**
        management   **7.38**
        representation
            agreed-upon procedures engage-
                ment   **17.15**
            comfort letter engagements   **13.33**
            construction contractors   **18.22**
            contents of   **8.76, 10.12–10.15**
            credit unions   **19.16**
            employee benefit plans   **20.33**
            governmental units   **23.33–23.34**

    internal control engagements   **16.46–**
        16.47
    SAS-19   **10.12**
    for underwriters. *See* SAS-72; Underwrit-
        ers, letters for
Liabilities
    construction contractors   **18.17–18.18**
    existence or occurrence of   **7.16**
    not-for-profit organizations   **22.21**
    as obligations of entity   **7.17**
    offsetting of   **3.10**
Life income funds, for colleges and
    universities   **22.10–22.11**
LIFO, change to, from FIFO   **11.19**
Limited reporting engagement   **12.06**
Line-of-credit loans   **19.19**
Liquidation basis of accounting, reporting
    on   **12.04, 12.26–12.28**
    comparative-years presentation   **12.27–**
        12.28
    single-year presentation   **12.27**
    uncertainty   **12.27**
Liquidity risk   **19.15–19.16**
Litigation
    FAS-5   **10.06, 10.09**
    and independence   **24.12**
    procedures to identify   **10.05–10.10**
Litigation support services   **16.05–16.06**
Loans. *See also specific types of loans*
    credit unions   **19.07–19.09, 19.18–19.20**
    definition of   **24.11**
    federal funds. *See* Federal funds
    and independence   **24.10–24.12**
    impairment of, accounting by creditor. *See*
        FAS-114
    interest-free, to not-for-profit organiza-
        tions   **22.16, 22.20**
    not-for-profit organizations   **22.16, 22.20**
    participations   **19.09, 19.20**
Local governments. *See* Governmental units
Loss contingency. *See* Contingencies
Loss reserves, auditing. *See* SOP 92-4
Losses   **3.10**
    credit unions   **19.07–19.09, 19.20–19.22**
    health care providers   **21.11–21.12, 21.15,**
        21.19
Lotteries   **24.31**

M

Malpractice   **21.09–21.11, 21.14, 21.18–21.19**
Management
    assertions of   **17.18–17.19**
        about compliance   **17.24–17.25**

about internal control **17.28**
  definition of **17.18**
  examples of **17.19**
  presentation of **17.19**
  characteristics of, and audit risk **7.42**
  and control environment **7.38–7.40**
  letter **7.38**
Management Consulting Services Executive Committee **24.24**
Marketable securities
  accounting for. *See* FAS-12; FAS-115
Matching concept **3.05**
Material misstatements. *See* Misstatements
Material weakness **7.36–7.38**
  defined **7.36**
  internal control **7.36–7.38, 16.48–16.53**
    report on **7.36–7.37**
    SAS-60 **16.48**
Materiality **3.06**
  attest engagements **16.12–16.13, 16.16**
  and audit risk, relationship between **8.17–8.18**
  basis for
    limited-scope audit **12.11–12.12**
    incomplete presentations **12.18–12.21**
  concept of **3.06**
  factor, establishment of **8.18**
  SAS-47 **8.18**
  thresholds **8.63**
MCSEC. *See* Management Consulting Services Executive Committee
Meaning of "Present Fairly in Conformity with Generally Accepted Accounting Principles," in the Independent Auditor's Report. See SAS-69
Measurement focus **23.13–23.14**
Medicaid **23.31–23.32**
Medical care. *See* Health care providers
Medicare **21.06**
Misrepresentations in the financial statements **24.21**
Misstatements
  accumulation of **10.15–10.17**
  of fact, material **11.42–11.43**
  on financial statements **7.39–7.42**
  intentional **7.40**
  internal control assertions **16.62**
  known **10.15**
  likely **10.15**
  planning for **7.42–7.44**
  in review of interim financial information **13.17–13.18**

  risk of material **10.15–10.16**
  unintentional **7.40**
Modifications to the auditor's report
  accounting changes **11.09–11.10**
  accounting conditions **11.09, 11.11–11.17**
  departure from GAAP **11.11–11.15**
  disclosures, inadequate **11.15–11.17**
  emphasis of a matter **11.39–11.40**
  negative assurance **11.51**
  other data and information in a document containing audited financial statements **11.41–11.42**
  piecemeal opinions **11.51**
  to report on pro forma financial information **16.36–16.37**
  reporting when not independent **11.40–11.41**
  required supplementary information **11.42–11.45**
  to review report, interim financial information **13.21–13.24**
  scope conditions **11.10, 11.28–11.35**
  to special reports **12.25–12.26**
  uncertainty conditions **11.10, 11.35–11.39**
Mortgage banking activities, accounting for. *See* FAS-65
Mortgage loans
  credit unions **19.19**
  investments in **20.26**
Museums. *See* Not-for-profit organizations

N

NAARS. *See* National Automated Accounting Research System
National Automated Accounting Research System (NAARS) **3.17**
National Council on Governmental Accounting (NCGA) **3.13**
  pronouncements **23.10, 23.12**
National Credit Union Administration (NCUA) **19.03, 19.06, 19.10, 19.13**
National Credit Union Share Insurance Fund (NCUSIF) **19.03, 19.04**
NCGA. *See* National Council on Governmental Accounting
NCUA. *See* National Credit Union Administration
NCUSIF. *See* National Credit Union Share Insurance Fund
Negative assurance **11.51, 13.21**
  comfort letters **13.46–13.47**
Negligence **24.34**

Net assets
  statement of available
    for defined benefit pension
      plan   20.06–20.07
    for defined contribution pension
      plan   20.11
    for employee health and welfare
      plan   20.14
  statement of changes in
    for defined benefit pension
      plan   20.07
    for defined contribution pension
      plan   20.11
    for employee health and welfare
      plan   20.14
Neutrality   3.07
Nonexpendable trust funds   23.06–23.07,
  23.16
Nonmonetary items, donated, to not-for-
  profit organizations   22.16, 22.19–22.20
Nonpublic entity, defined by SSARS-1   14.05
Nonsampling risk   9.05
Nonstatistical sampling. *See* Sampling
Normal operating cycle concept   18.04
Not-for-profit organizations. *See also* Colleges
  and universities; Governmental units;
  Health care providers; Voluntary health and
  welfare organizations
  accounting for   22.03–22.12
  affiliated organizations   22.22
  annuities   22.10–22.11
  assets   22.05, 22.16, 22.20–22.21
    permanently restricted   22.05
    temporarily restricted   22.05
    unrestricted   22.05
  audit procedures   22.17–22.26
  auditor's report   22.22
  auditor's special report   22.22–22.23
  basis of accounting   22.04
  capital additions   22.15–22.16, 22.19–
    22.20
  collections   22.11–22.12
  contributions   22.08–22.09, 22.15–22.16
    audit procedures   22.19
    cash   22.15
    future interests   22.16, 22.20
    interest-free loans   22.16, 22.20
    nonmonetary items   22.16, 22.19–
      22.20
    securities   22.16, 22.19–22.20
    services   22.15–22.16, 22.19
  depreciation   22.11–22.12
  donated services   22.15–22.16, 22.19

expenses   22.13–22.14, 22.17–22.18
    classification of   22.13–22.14, 22.17–
      22.18
  FAS-116   22.11–22.12
  FAS-117   22.16
  FAS-124   21.05–21.06, 22.09
  financial statements   22.04–22.06, 22.16
  fund accounting   22.04, 22.06
  fund-raising   22.13–22.14
  industry practices   22.12–22.16
  interest-free loans   22.16, 22.20
  internal control   22.12–22.16
  investments   22.09, 22.14
  liabilities   22.21
  life income fund   22.10–22.11
  liquidity of   22.04
  receipt of federal awards   21.21, 22.25–
    22.26, 23.41
  reimbursements, third-party   22.14–22.15
  related entities, reporting   22.06–22.08
  reports   22.22–22.26
  revenue   22.08–22.09, 22.14–22.15, 22.18–
    22.19
  sale of products   22.14
  service fees   22.14
  SOP 92-9   21.21, 22.25–22.26, 23.41
  SOP 94-3   22.06–22.07
  support   22.15–22.16, 22.19–22.20
Notes payable, credit unions   19.10
Notice to Practitioners, definition of   11.57
Nursing homes. *See* Health care providers

O

Obligations   21.08–21.09, 21.18
Objectives, determining, for sampling tests of
  controls   9.07–9.08
Objectivity   3.07. *See also* Integrity and
  objectivity (Rule 102)
OCBOA. *See* Basis of accounting, other than
  GAAP
Office of Management and Budget (OMB)
  state and local governments   23.17, 23.20
Offsetting   3.10
Oil and gas activities
  Financial Accounting and Reporting by
    Oil and Gas Producing Companies. *See*
    FAS-19
  required supplementary informa-
    tion   10.19–10.21
OMB. *See* Office of Management and Budget
OMB Circular A-133, applicability of   21.21,
  22.26

Omitted procedures **10.23–10.24**
consideration of, after the report date. *See*
SAS-46
*Omnibus Statement on Auditing Standards—
1983. See* SAS-45
*Omnibus Statement on Auditing Standards—
1987. See* SAS-52
*Omnibus Statement on Auditing Standards—
1990. See* SAS-64
*Omnibus Statement on Standards for Accounting
and Review Services—1992. See* SSARS-7
Operating cycle **3.06–3.07**
Operating expenditures, for governmental
units **23.27**
Opinions
adverse. *See* Adverse opinion
disclaimer of. *See* Disclaimer of opinion
emphasizing a matter without qualifying **11.39–11.40**
piecemeal **11.51**
qualified
based on another auditor's report **11.32–11.35**
on going concern **8.74–8.75**
in review of interim financial
information **13.21–13.22**
"subject to" no longer permis-
sible **8.75**
shopping for **12.28**
Oral advice
on application of accounting principles **12.29**
Organization, name and form of **24.38–25.40**
Other auditor, using the work of **8.55–8.59**
Other countries, financial statements for use
in. *See also* Financial statements, other
countries
reporting purposes **12.33–12.39**
*Other Information in Documents Containing
Audited Financial Statements. See* SAS-8
Ownership, of practice **24.39–24.40**

P

*Part of Audit Performed by Other Independent
Auditors. See* SAS-1, Section 543
Partial presentations **15.15–15.18**. *See also*
SOP 90-1
compilation **15.16–15.17**
definition of **15.15**
with disclosures **15.15**
engagement, procedures and conditions
for **15.16**
examination **15.17–15.18**
procedures **15.15**

reporting on **15.16**
Party-in-interest transactions **20.31–20.33**
Pass-through grants **23.32–23.33**
Payments, benefit, for benefit plans **20.27**
Peer reviews. *See* Quality reviews
Pension and Welfare Benefits Administration
(PWBA) **20.04–20.05**
Pension plans. *See* Employee benefit plans
Pension trust funds **23.07**
Percentage-of-completion method of income
recognition **18.03–18.04, 18.21**
Permanently restricted gifts **22.05**
Pervasive principles. *See* Generally accepted
accounting principles, pervasive principles
Physicians. *See* Health care providers
Piecemeal opinions **11.51**
Planning **6.03–6.10**
agreed-upon procedures engagements **17.06–17.08, 17.20–17.21, 17.26**
analytical procedures **6.08, 8.60–8.61**
appointment of auditor **6.04**
attest engagement **16.14–16.17**
checklist **6.08–6.10**
computer environment **6.05–6.06**
employee benefit plans **20.20–20.21**
governmental units **23.16–23.17**
interim financial information **13.13–
13.15**
nature, timing, and extent of procedures **6.06–6.07**
supervision **6.07**
Planning and Supervision. See SAS-22
Plant and equipment fund. *See* Equipment;
Property
Pledges **22.08–22.09, 22.15**
Political parties. *See* Not-for-profit organizations
Pooled life income funds **22.11**
Pooling of interests
accounting change **11.26–11.27**
pro forma financial information **16.36–
16.37**
reporting by successor auditor **11.34**
Post-audit procedures **10.22–10.24**
PPPO/TOE report. *See* Reports on policies
and procedures in operation and tests of
operating effectiveness
PPS sampling **9.24**
Practice, name and form of **24.38–24.40**
Practitioners, Notice to, definition of **11.57**
Predecessor accountant/auditor
communication with. *See* SAS-7; SSARS-4
definition of **14.15**

Predecessor accountant/auditor, *cont.*
  reporting by **11.55–11.62**
  responsibilities of, SEC filings **13.27–13.30**
  that has ceased operations **5.07–5.09**
  reporting when **11.56–11.62**
Predecessor and Successor Auditors, Communications Between. See SAS-7
Pre-engagement planning **5.03–5.12**
  agreed-upon procedures engagement **17.06–17.08, 17.20–17.21**
  attest engagement **16.08–16.14**
  audit engagement
    client acceptance/continuation **5.03–5.04, 5.11–5.12**
    communication with predecessor auditor **5.04–5.06**
    documentation **5.11**
    engagement letter **5.10–5.11**
    independence **5.09**
  review of interim financial information **13.04–13.05**
  unaudited financial statements of nonpublic companies **14.13–14.18**
    communication with the predecessor accountant **14.14–14.16**
    engagement letters **14.17–14.18**
    evaluation of the client **14.13–14.14**
    independence **14.17**
Prescribed forms or schedules, reporting on **12.24–12.26**
Presentations, partial. *See* Partial presentations
Preventive controls **9.08**
Primary government. *See* Reporting entity
Prior-period adjustments **3.20.** *See also* FAS-16
  health care providers **21.06**
Pro forma financial information **16.28–16.37**
  accountant's responsibilities **16.30–16.31**
  attest engagement **16.28–16.37**
  audit and review procedures **16.31–16.33**
  comfort letter **13.46–13.47**
  examination engagement **16.30, 16.34–16.35**
  modifications **16.36–16.37**
  pooling-of-interests **16.37**
  relative level of assurance **16.30–16.31**
  reporting on **16.33–16.37**
  review engagement **16.30–16.31, 16.35–16.36**

Probability-proportional-to-size (PPS) technique **9.24**
Procedures. *See* Audit procedures
Professional development. *See* Training
Projections, financial. *See* Forecasts, financial; Prospective financial statements
Promissory notes, credit unions **19.10**
Property
  health care providers **21.07–21.08, 21.14, 21.17–21.18**
Proprietary funds **23.16, 23.30**
Prospective financial statements
  agreed-upon procedures **15.27**
  compilation **15.27–15.31**
    procedures **15.28–15.30**
    professional standards **15.28**
    reporting on **15.30–15.31**
  definition of **15.03**
  evidence **15.21–15.24**
  examination engagement **15.17–15.18, 15.19–15.27**
  forecast, definition of **15.03**
  hypothetical assumptions **15.09–15.10**
  internal use only **15.12–15.15**
    accountant's transmittal letter **15.15**
    if accountant is not independent **15.14–15.15**
    example of **15.14**
    format **15.14**
    report based on the performance of another service **15.14**
  intended use **15.04**
  partial presentations **15.15–15.18**
    compilation engagement **15.16–15.17**
    definition of **15.15**
    engagement, procedures and conditions for **15.16**
    examination engagement **15.17–15.18**
    included disclosures **15.15**
    reporting standards, general **15.16**
  preparation **15.07–15.10**
    accounting principles **15.08**
    appropriate assumptions **15.09**
    appropriate care **15.08**
    assumption sensitivity **15.10**
    best information **15.08**
    comparison of results **15.10**
    consistency of information **15.08–15.09**
    documentation **15.10**
    good faith **15.08**

key factors **15.09**
  review and approval **15.10**
professional standards **15.20–15.21**
purpose **15.17–15.18**
reporting on
    compilation engagement **15.30–15.31**
    examination engagement **15.24–15.25**
responsible party **15.04**
safe harbor consideration **15.06–15.07**
standards **15.10–15.12**
    assumptions to be disclosed **15.11**
    corrections and updates **15.11–15.12**
    hypothetical assumptions **15.09**
    materiality **15.19**
    minimum **15.05**
    reporting **15.24–15.25, 15.30–15.31**
Prospectus. *See* Registration statement
Public accountant. *See* Auditor
Public broadcasting stations. *See* Not-for-profit organizations
Public-sector accounting hierarchy **23.11**
PWBA. *See* Pension Welfare Benefits Administration

Q

Qualified opinion. *See* Opinions, qualified
Qualitative Characteristics of Accounting Information. See FASB Concepts Statement No. 1
Quality-control system
    acceptance and continuance of clients **2.08**
    administration of **2.09**
    advancement of personnel **2.07–2.08**
    assignment of personnel **2.07–2.08**
    components of **2.07–2.08**
    hiring policies **2.07–2.08**
    independence **2.07**
    inspection **2.10**
    monitoring **2.09–2.11**
    professional development **2.07–2.08**
    standards of **2.06–2.08**
Questions and Answers on the Term Reasonably Objective Basis and Other Issues Affecting Prospective Financial Statements. See SOP 92-2
Questions Concerning Accountants' Services on Prospective Financial Statements. See SOP 89-3

R

Random-number sampling **9.10**

Ratio approach to sampling **9.24**
Rational and systematic allocation **3.08**
Real estate
    investments in **20.26**
Realization principle **3.05**
Reasonable assurance, concept of **7.73**
Reasonable Estimation of the Amount of a Loss. See FIN-14
Receivables
    employee benefit plans **20.26–20.27**
    governmental units **23.25–23.26**
    health care providers **21.06–21.07, 21.14, 21.16–21.17**
Recognition, immediate **3.08**
Recognition of expenses **3.08–3.09**
Record retention **24.34**
Referral fees. *See* Commissions
Registration statement **13.27–13.30**
    shelf, definition of **13.28, 13.37–13.38**
Regulated industries, GAAP and **3.20–3.21**
Regulations, compliance with
    financial statements to comply with **12.15–12.18**
    governmental units **23.22**
    reporting on **16.05, 16.63, 16.64–16.82**
Regulatory agencies
    examination by, for credit unions **19.04, 19.25**
    reportable conditions and **7.34–7.35**
    workpapers and **8.24–8.27**
Rejection, incorrect, risk of (substantive tests) **9.06**
Related party transactions **8.64–8.69**
    audit approach **8.66–8.67**
    audit procedures **8.66–8.67**
    conditions that increase the possibility of **8.65–8.66**
    disclosures **8.68–8.69**. *See also* FAS-57
    examples of **8.65**
    FAS-57 **8.64–8.65, 8.66–8.68**
    health care providers **21.12–21.13, 21.15, 21.20**
    identifying **8.64–8.66**
    SAS-45 **8.64–8.66**
    skepticism associated with **8.64–8.65**
Relationship of GAAS and Quality Control Standards. See SAS-25
Relatives, effect on independence **24.14–24.16**
Repo. *See* Repurchase agreements
Reportable conditions **7.31–7.38**
    and agreed-upon procedures **7.34**

Reportable conditions, *cont.*
  defined **7.31**
  internal control **7.31–7.38, 16.48**
  and material weaknesses **7.35–7.38**
  reporting **7.34**
  in review of interim financial informa-
    tion **13.16–13.19**
  SAS-60 **7.31–7.38, 16.48**
Reporting
  on accounting changes **11.09–11.10,
    11.17–11.28**
    to acceptable principle **11.21–11.22**
    accounting estimates **11.25**
    error correction **11.22**
    FIFO to LIFO **11.19**
    inappropriate treatment of **11.23–
      11.24**
    lack of consistency **11.17–11.19**
    no justification for **11.24–11.25**
    pooling of interest **11.26–11.27**
    reporting entity **11.26**
    segment information **11.20–11.21**
    statement of cash flows for-
      mat **11.19–11.20**
    to unacceptable principle **11.22–
      11.23**
  on agreed-upon procedures engage-
    ment **17.11–17.14, 17.22–17.24**
    combined reports **17.16**
    compliance attestation **17.27**
    forecasts **17.28**
    included reports **17.16**
    projections **17.28**
    responsibility to update report **17.14**
  on application of accounting prin-
    ciples **12.28–12.33, 14.69**
    performance standards **12.31–12.33**
    reporting standards **12.31–12.33**
    SAS-50 **12.28–12.33**
  association with financial state-
    ments **11.08–11.09**
  on attest engagements **16.21–16.27**
    agreed-upon procedures **16.21–
      16.22, 16.24, 16.26**
    deficiencies, presentation **16.25–
      16.26**
    deficiencies, scope **16.25–16.25**
    examination and reviews **16.22–
      16.23**
  auditor-submitted documents **11.48–
    11.51**
  client-prepared documents **11.48**

on comparative financial statements. *See*
  Comparative financial statements,
  reporting on
on comparative information **15.31**
on compilations, for prospective financial
  statements
    comparative information **15.31**
    departure from presentation
      guidelines **15.31**
    emphasis of a matter **15.31**
    independence, lack of **15.31**
    reporting standards **15.30–15.31**
on compliance
    with contracts/regulations **12.15–
      12.18**
      report added to standard
        report **12.17–12.18**
      reporting standards **12.16–12.18**
      separate report **12.16–12.17**
on compliance attestation, agreed-upon
  procedures engagement **17.27**
components **22.23–22.24**
on condensed financial statements and
  selected financial data **13.55–13.58**
  SAS-42 **13.55–13.58**
on conformity with a comprehensive basis
  of accounting other than GAAP **12.04–
  12.11**
    adequate disclosure **12.07–12.08**
    reporting standards **12.08–12.11**
    summary of significant accounting
      policies **12.08**
on construction contractors **18.22–18.23**
on credit unions **19.25–19.28**
on departure from GAAP **11.11–11.15**
disclosures
    on fair value **11.45–11.48**
    inadequate **11.15–11.17**
emphasis of a matter **11.39–11.40**
employee benefit plans **20.34–20.38**
on examination engagements, for
  prospective financial statements
    comparative information **15.26**
    departure from presentation
      guidelines **15.25**
    emphasis of a matter **15.26**
    lack of reasonable basis **15.25–15.26**
    scope limitation **15.26**
    use of another accountant **15.26**
    when a part of a larger engage-
      ment **15.26–15.27**
evidence, insufficient **11.27–11.30**
fair value disclosures **11.45–11.48**

FAS-5 **11.36, 11.37**
filings under federal securities statutes **13.27–13.30**
on financial presentations
in prescribed forms or schedules **12.24–12.26**
to comply with contracts/regulations **12.18–12.24**
to comply with grants **22.24–22.25**
on financial statements
prepared for use in other countries **12.33–12.39**
prepared on the liquidation basis of accounting **12.04, 12.26–12.28**
on forecasts, agreed-upon procedures engagements **17.28**
on going concern **8.74–8.75, 11.36–11.37, 11.39**
on governmental units **23.35–23.41**
on health care organizations **21.21**
on internal control
COSO **16.38, 16.46**
errors and irregularities **7.46**
examination procedures **16.39–16.44**
illegal acts **7.51**
management's assertions on **16.37–16.63.** *See also* SSAE-2
material weaknesses **7.35–7.38, 16.48–16.53**
report modifications **16.48–16.60**
reportable conditions **7.31–7.38, 16.48**
of service organizations **7.66–7.71**
written representations **16.61–16.62**
letters for underwriters **13.31–13.55**
on limited reporting engagements **11.30–11.31**
negative assurance **11.51**
newly discovered information **10.10–10.11, 10.22–10.23**
on not-for-profit organizations **22.22–22.26**
related entities **22.06–22.08**
piecemeal opinions **11.51**
predecessor auditor **11.54–11.62**
on prescribed forms **12.24–12.26**
on projections, agreed-upon procedures engagements **17.28**
on prospective financial statements **15.16, 15.18–15.19, 15.24–15.25, 15.30–15.31**
compilation engagement **15.30–15.31**
examination engagement **15.24–15.25**

related entities **22.06–22.08**
responsibilities after report date **8.75, 13.25**
required supplementary information **11.42–11.45**
on review of interim financial information **13.13–13.14, 13.19–13.25**
GAAP modification **13.22–13.23**
going-concern modification **13.24**
inadequate disclosure modification **13.23–13.24**
inconsistency modification **13.24**
marked "Unaudited" **13.20**
responsibilities after the report date **13.25**
scope modification **13.21**
standard report, contents of **13.19–13.21**
subsequent events **13.24–13.25**
uncertainty modification **13.24**
using the work of another accountant **13.21–13.22**
SAS-62 **12.04**
SAS-77 **11.38**
SAS-79 **11.36–11.37**
scope conditions **11.10, 11.28–11.35**
insufficient evidence **11.28–11.30**
limited reporting engagements **11.31–11.32**
opinion based on other auditor's report **11.32–11.34**
scope limitations **11.30–11.31**
unaudited financial statements, public companies **11.35**
on selected financial data **13.55–13.58**
SAS-42 **13.55–13.58**
on service organizations **7.66–7.71**
on specified elements, accounts, or items **12.11–12.15**
potential conflict **12.14–12.15**
standards of **12.12–12.15**
standard auditor's report **11.04–11.08**
contents **11.04–11.08**
date of **11.07–11.08**
example of **11.06–11.07**
of a foreign country **12.38**
format of **11.04–11.05**
introductory paragraph **11.06**
modifications to **11.09–11.62, 12.25–12.26, 20.35–20.38**
opinion paragraph **11.06**
SAS-58 **11.03, 11.05**
scope paragraph **11.06**

Reporting, *cont.*
    should not contain **11.07**
    standards of **11.04–11.06**
    for special reports **12.22**
    on uncertainties **11.10, 11.36–11.37**
        related to going concern **11.37–11.39**
        unrelated to going concern **11.35–11.37**
    uncertainty modification **7.51–7.52, 11.36–11.37**
    unqualified opinion, assurances made by **11.07–11.08**
    when not independent **11.41**
    on work of another auditor **8.58–8.59**
Reporting engagements, limited **11.31–11.32**
Reporting entity
    change in **11.26**
    fund accounting **23.05**
    GASB-14 **23.09, 23.31**
    governmental units **23.08–23.09, 23.31**
    health care providers **21.12–21.13, 21.15**
    related entities, not-for-profit organizations **22.06–22.08**
Reporting on Comparative Financial Statements. See SSARS-2
Reporting on Compiled Financial Statements. See SSARS-5
Reporting on Condensed Financial Statements and Selected Financial Data. See SAS-42
Reporting on Financial Statements Prepared for Use in Other Countries. See SAS-51
Reporting on Information Accompanying the Basic Financial Statement in Auditor-Submitted Documents. See SAS-29
Reporting on Personal Financial Statements included in Written Personal Financial Plans. See SSARS-6
Reporting on Pro Forma Financial Information **16.28–16.31**
Reporting Repurchase-Reverse Repurchase Agreements and Mortgage-Backed Certificates by Savings and Loan Associations. See SOP 86-1
Reporting standards **4.10–4.13**
Reports on Audited Financial Statements. See SAS-58
Reports on policies and procedures placed in operation and tests of operating effectiveness **7.62–7.71**
    formatting of **7.66–7.68**
    qualified **7.69–7.71**
    sample of **7.66–7.67**
Reports on the Application of Accounting Principles. See SAS-50

Representation letters **8.76, 10.12–10.15**. *See also* Letters, representation
    agreed-upon procedures engagement **17.15**
    for comfort letter engagements **13.32–13.34**
    for construction contractors **18.22**
    contents of **10.12–10.13**
    for employee benefit plans **20.26**
    for internal control engagements **16.46–16.47**
    for management's assertions about internal control **16.46–16.47**
    obtaining **10.12–10.15**
    materiality **10.13**
    reliability of **10.12**
    underwriters **13.33–13.35**
Representational faithfulness **3.05–3.06**
Representations, client **8.76**
    agreed-upon procedures engagement **17.15**
    internal control assertions **16.37–16.39**
Representations, substantiating **10.07**
Repurchase agreements
    accounting for. *See* SOP 85-2
    credit unions **19.18**
    reverse
        credit unions **19.10–19.11**
Required supplementary information
    audit procedures **10.17–10.19**
    in compilations **14.46**
    deviation in measurement or presentation **11.43**
    limited procedures not applied to **11.44**
    oil and gas reserves **10.19–10.21**
    omitted **11.43**
    reporting standards **11.43–11.45**
    required by FASB or GASB **11.43**
    responsibility for **10.17–10.21**
    in reviews **14.53–14.54**
    SAS-8 **10.19**
    SAS-52 **10.17–10.18**
    substantial doubt about conformance **11.44–11.45**
Responsibility. *See* Auditor, responsibility and function
Responsible party, definition of **15.04**
Restatement, retroactive **11.18–11.19**
Restricted gifts **22.05**
Restructuring. *See* Troubled debt restructuring
Retirement communities. *See* Health care providers

Retroactive restatement **11.18**
*Return of Organizations Exempt from Income
Tax. See* Internal Revenue Form 990
Revenue
    construction contractors **18.14**
    health care providers **21.11–21.12, 21.15,
    21.19**
    governmental units, basis of account-
      ing **23.14**
    not-for-profit organizations **22.08–22.09,
    22.14–22.15, 22.18–22.19**
Revenue sharing, and audits of state
    governments **23.31**
Review engagement
    attest engagement **16.19–16.20, 16.21–
    16.22, 16.23–16.24, 16.30–16.31**
    client representations **14.32**
    emphasis of a matter **14.52**
    incomplete review **14.31**
    inquiry and analytical procedures **14.29–
    14.30**
    interim financial information **13.04–
    13.27**
    internal control, consideration of **14.33–
    14.34**
    knowledge of accounting principles and
      practices **14.28**
    knowledge of client's business **14.28–
    14.29**
    necessity for additional proce-
      dures **14.30–14.31**
    planning **14.32–14.33**
    of pro forma financial informa-
      tion **16.35–16.36**
    report modification, inadequacy of **14.52**
    reporting obligations **14.34–14.37**
    reporting on **14.48–14.54**
      disclosure, inadequate **14.51–14.52**
      GAAP, departure from **14.50–14.51,
      14.52**
      incomplete review **14.49–14.50**
      inconsistency **14.52**
      independence **14.50**
      uncertainty **14.52**
    review standards **14.27–14.28**
    subsequent discovery **14.53**
    supplementary information **14.53–14.54**
    withdrawing from engagement **14.54–
    14.55**
    workpapers **14.31–14.32**
Risk. *See also specific types of risk*
    assessing
      account balance or class of transac-
      tions level **7.54–7.55**

      financial statement level **7.54**
    attestation **16.15–16.16**
    audit, assessing **8.21–8.22**
    control **8.20**
      determining planned assessed
      level **7.23–7.24**
      documenting assessed level **7.29–
      7.30**
      evaluating assessed level **7.27–7.29**
    for credit unions **19.14–19.16**
    detection **7.30, 8.20–8.21**
    inherent **8.19**
    maximum level **7.24**
    overall audit **7.30–7.31**
    sampling **8.10–8.12, 9.05–9.06, 9.12, 9.18–
    9.20.** *See also* Sampling
      acceptable **9.26–9.27**
      agreed-upon procedures engage-
      ment **17.14**
      allowance for **9.18–9.20**
      of assessing control risk too
      low **9.05, 9.12**
      of assessing control risk too
      high **9.05**
      of incorrect acceptance **9.05**
      of incorrect rejection **9.06**
      nonstatistical sampling **9.20**
      projecting misstatement to the
      population **9.29**
      statistical sampling **9.18–9.20**
    SAS-55 definitions **7.23–7.24**

S

Sampling
    attribute sampling **9.04**
    audit risk **8.10–8.12, 9.05–9.06**
    block sampling **9.11**
    conclusions **9.20–9.21, 9.29**
    deviations **9.08–9.09**
      calculating rate **9.17–9.18**
      expected rate **9.14**
      qualitative aspects **9.20**
    documenting **9.21, 9.30**
    evidence **8.10–8.12**
    fixed plan **9.15**
    guidance for **9.04**
    haphazard sampling **9.11**
    misstatement **9.29, 9.30**
    nonstatistical sampling **9.16–9.17**
      and sample size **9.17**
      and sampling risk **9.20**

Sampling, *cont.*
  probability-proportionate-to-size **9.24**
  purpose of **9.03**
  random number sampling **9.10**
  ratio approach **9.24**
  risk
    agreed-upon procedures engagement **17.14**
    classifications **9.05–9.06**
    effect of sample size **9.11–9.12**
    and evaluating results **9.17–9.18, 9.30**
    and nonstatistical sampling **9.20**
    and statistical sampling **9.18–9.20**
  sample size **8.12–8.13, 9.11–9.17, 9.24**
  statistical sampling
    plans **9.04–9.05**
    and sample size **9.15**
    and sampling risk **9.18–9.20**
    techniques **9.23–9.24**
  substantive tests **7.29–7.31, 8.13–8.17, 9.21–9.30**
    documentation of **9.30**
    objectives, determining **9.22**
    performance of **9.28–9.29**
    population, defining **9.22–9.23**
    results, evaluation of **9.29**
    risk of incorrect acceptance or rejection **9.05–9.06**
    sample, determining size **9.24–9.28**
    sample, selecting **9.28**
    technique, choosing **9.23–9.24**
    timing of **8.14–8.17**
  systematic sampling **9.10–9.11**
  tests of controls **8.12–8.13, 9.06–9.21**
    deviation conditions, defining **9.08–9.09**
    documentation of **9.21**
    objectives, determining **9.07–9.08**
    performance of **9.17**
    population, defining **9.09–9.10**
    results, evaluation of **9.17–9.21**
    risk of assessing control risk too high or low **9.05, 9.12**
    sample, determining size **9.11–9.17**
    sample, selecting **9.10–9.11**
    tolerable rate **9.12–9.14**
    units **9.09, 9.23**
  variable sampling **9.04–9.05, 9.24**
SAS-1 **1.03–1.04, 2.03, 4.03–4.04, 7.61, 8.06, 8.38, 8.42, 8.76, 10.03, 10.04, 10.10–10.11, 10.23**
  Section 543 **5.08, 7.61, 13.21–13.22, 24.17**

Section 560 **13.30**
Section 561 **5.05, 11.22, 11.58, 14.44, 14.53, 15.12**
SAS-7 **5.03, 5.04–5.06, 6.03, 6.04, 12.31**
SAS-8 **7.38–7.40, 10.03, 10.04, 10.21, 11.03, 11.04, 11.41–11.42, 13.56–13.57, 16.29, 19.26, 20.33**
SAS-11 **8.47.** *See also* SAS-73
SAS-12 **2.04, 4.06, 8.23, 10.03–10.04, 10.05–10.10, 21.19, 23.33**
SAS-19 **8.76, 10.03, 10.04, 10.12–10.13, 10.14, 16.62, 18.22, 19.16, 20.33, 23.33**
SAS-20 **7.31**
SAS-21 **8.05, 8.07, 8.55**
SAS-22 **5.03, 5.04, 6.03–6.04, 6.06–6.08, 8.20, 8.23, 14.32, 23.16**
SAS-25 **2.03, 2.06, 8.20**
SAS-26 **2.05, 11.03, 11.04, 11.08, 11.35, 14.60**
SAS-29 **10.03, 10.04, 10.21, 11.03, 11.04, 11.48, 19.26, 20.35, 23.38**
SAS-31 **7.16, 8.05, 8.06, 8.08, 8.09–8.10, 8.29, 17.06**
SAS-32 **11.03, 11.04, 11.15**
SAS-35. *See* SAS-75
SAS-37 **13.03, 13.04, 13.27–13.30, 13.57, 16.29**
SAS-39 **7.63, 8.05, 8.06, 8.10–8.11, 8.13, 8.20, 9.03, 19.23**
  applicability of **9.03, 9.12–9.14, 9.24**
SAS-41 **7.05, 7.72, 8.05, 8.06, 8.22–8.23, 9.21, 9.30, 13.18, 23.21**
SAS-42 **13.03, 13.04**
SAS-43 **11.19**
SAS-45 **8.05, 8.06, 8.15, 8.29, 8.63–8.68, 10.19, 18.09**
SAS-46 **10.03, 10.04**
SAS-47 **7.05, 8.05, 8.06, 8.17–8.20, 10.03, 10.04, 15.21, 19.14**
SAS-49 **13.31.** *See also* SAS-72
SAS-50 **12.03, 12.28–12.32, 14.71**
SAS-51 **12.03–12.04, 12.33–12.34, 12.38–12.39**
SAS-52 **10.03, 10.04, 10.17, 10.19**
SAS-53 **6.03, 7.05, 7.40–7.46, 23.19, 23.22**
SAS-54 **7.05, 7.47–7.52, 16.68, 19.13, 20.32–20.33, 23.19**
SAS-55 **7.05–7.06, 7.08, 7.12–7.16, 7.18–7.20, 7.23–7.24, 7.29, 7.63, 8.77, 9.14, 16.62, 20.21–20.22, 23.17, 23.21**
SAS-56 **8.05, 8.59–8.60, 10.03–10.05, 19.17, 19.24**
SAS-57 **8.05, 8.06, 8.42, 11.45**
SAS-58 **8.55, 10.12, 11.03, 11.05, 11.16, 11.28, 11.30, 11.35, 11.52, 12.14, 12.39, 19.26, 19.28, 21.21, 22.22**

SAS-59 7.43, 8.05, 8.07, 8.69–8.74, 11.03, 11.04, 11.37, 11.39, 14.43, 19.15

SAS-60 2.04, 7.05, 7.31–7.38, 8.23, 16.48, 16.73, 20.22, 23.21

SAS-61 7.05, 10.03, 10.04, 10.24–10.27, 13.19

SAS-62 11.09, 12.03, 12.04, 12.04–12.25, 14.06, 16.64, 17.05, 17.17, 18.23, 19.27, 21.21, 22.22, 23.40

   comprehensive basis other than GAAP 12.04–12.11

   modifications to standard report 12.25–12.26

   reporting on

      compliance with contracts/ regulations 12.15–12.18

      financial information presented in prescribed forms and schedules 12.24–12.26

      financial presentations to comply with contract/regulation 12.18–12.24

      special report format 12.09

      specified elements, accounts, or items 12.11–12.15

SAS-64 8.05, 8.07, 8.74, 11.03, 11.04, 11.34, 11.38

SAS-65 5.06, 7.05, 7.52–7.57, 8.05–8.07, 8.33, 8.52, 16.41, 16.71

SAS-67 8.05, 8.06, 8.28–8.36, 23.26

SAS-68. *See* SAS-74

SAS-69 3.13, 3.14, 11.06, 12.07, 12.30, 14.18, 19.05, 21.21, 23.03, 23.10–23.11

SAS-70 6.05, 7.05, 7.58–7.72, 17.17, 19.13, 20.22, 20.24

SAS-71 13.03, 13.04–13.06, 13.13–13.18, 14.05

SAS-72 13.03, 13.04, 13.31–13.55, 16.64, 17.05, 17.17

SAS-73 2.04, 4.06, 5.06, 6.06, 8.05, 8.07, 8.46–8.51, 15.24, 16.71, 18.19, 20.23, 20.28

SAS-74 12.15, 16.63, 17.04, 17.17, 23.19–23.21

SAS-75 12.15, 13.33, 14.06, 17.03, 17.04–17.17, 20.25, 24.18–24.19

SAS-76 13.03–13.0413.33

SAS-77 8.06, 8.07, 8.74, 11.03, 11.04, 12.03

SAS-78 7.05–7.06

SAS-79 11.03, 11.04, 11.36–11.37

SAS. *See specific SASs*

Savings accounts

   credit unions 19.09–19.10, 19.22–19.23

Scope

   deficiencies in special reports 12.25–12.26

   evidential matter, insufficient 11.28–11.31

   limitations 8.54, 11.10, 11.30–11.31

   in internal control engagements 16.53–16.54

   limited reporting engagements 11.31–11.32

   opinion based on another auditor's report 11.32–11.35

   reporting by successor auditor for a pooling of interests 11.34

Securities. *See also specific types of securities*

   credit unions 19.05–19.07, 19.12

Securities Act of 1933 13.27, 13.30–13.31

   document review of filings 13.30

   letters for underwriters and other requesting parties 13.31–13.55

   predecessor auditor's responsibilities under 13.28–13.29

   specific duties and responsibilities under 13.27–13.28

   subsequent-events period 13.29

   unaudited financial statements 13.30

Securities and Exchange Commission, reports to

   letters for underwriters and other requesting parties 13.31–13.55

   registration with 13.27–13.30, 13.37

Segment information

   audit procedures to test 8.54

   disclosures 8.55

   evidence for 8.52–8.55

   FAS-14 8.54

   Financial Reporting for Segments of a Business Enterprise 8.52

   internal control 16.57

   nonpublic companies 11.20–11.21

   reporting on 8.54

   SAS-21 8.54

   Segment Information. See SAS-21

Segmental reporting. *See* FAS-114

Selected financial data. *See* Condensed financial statements

Separate entity concept 3.05

Service auditor

   evaluation by user auditor 7.61

   illegal acts, irregularities, or errors; awareness of 7.60

   role of 7.62–7.66

   written representation from the service organization 7.71–7.72

Service fees, not-for-profit organizations 22.14

Service organization

   defined 7.57–7.58

   internal control 7.58

Service organization, *cont.*
  reporting on   7.62–7.66
  SAS-70   7.58–7.72
  written representation to the service
    auditor   7.71–7.72
*Service Organizations, Reports on the Processing
  of Transactions by. See* SAS-70
Services, donated or contributed, to not-for-
  profit organizations   22.15–22.16, 22.19
Shelf registration   13.37
"Shopping for opinions"   12.28
Single-year presentation   12.27
Social clubs. *See* Not-for-profit organizations
Solicitation. *See* Advertising and Code of
  Professional Conduct
Solvency
  agreed-upon procedures engage-
    ment   17.05
  attest engagements   16.26
SOP 78-1   21.03
SOP 81-1   18.03–18.23
SOP 81-2   21.03
SOP 82-1   14.71
SOP 85-1   21.03
SOP 85-2   23.24
SOP 87-1   21.03
SOP 87-2   22.14
SOP 89-5   21.03
SOP 90-3   19.04
SOP 90-5   19.03, 19.25
SOP 90-8   21.03, 21.07
SOP 90-11   19.04
SOP 92-2   15.03
SOP 92-3   19.04, 23.12
SOP 92-4   8.47
SOP 92-7   23.03
SOP 92-9   21.20, 21.21, 22.26, 23.41
SOP 93-3   3.11
SOP 94-2   3.13–3.14
SOP 94-3   22.06–22.07
SOP 94-4   20.03, 20.13–20.14
Special assessments   23.06
  GASB-6   23.06
Special-purpose financial presentation, not-
  for-profit organizations   22.24–22.25
Special revenue funds   23.05–23.06
Specialists
  agreed-upon procedures engage-
    ment   17.10, 17.21
  evaluation of   8.48–8.49
  evidence obtained from   8.46–8.52
  qualifications of   8.48–8.49

responsibilities of   8.48
using the work of. *See* SAS-73
*Special-Purpose Reports on Internal Accounting
  Control at Service Organizations. See* SAS-44
Special reports. *See* Reporting; SAS-62
Specialized industries, GAAP and   3.21
Specified elements, accounts, or items   12.11–
  12.15. *See also* Agreed-upon procedures
  engagement
Spouses, effect on independence   24.15–24.16
SQCS-1   2.06, 5.03, 5.12, 6.03, 13.03
SQCS-2   2.06–2.07, 4.04, 14.11, 14.13–14.14
SQCS-3   2.10–2.11
SSAE-1   16.05, 16.06, 16.07, 16.12, 16.14–
  16.20, 16.28–16.37, 17.03, 17.04
SSAE-2   16.06, 16.07, 16.37–16.63, 17.03, 17.04
  examination procedures   16.39–16.44
  professional services, other   16.62–16.63
  report modifications   16.48–16.61
  written representations   16.61–16.62
SSAE-3   16.06, 16.07, 16.64–16.82, 17.03,
  17.04, 17.25–17.26
  agreed-upon procedures engage-
    ment   16.82
  client representation   16.74–16.75
  examination engagement   16.66–16.82
  materiality   16.69–16.70
  risk assessment   16.67–16.69
  subsequent events   16.74
SSAE-4   17.03, 17.17–17.24, 17.28
SSAE-5   16.06, 16.27
SSAE-6   16.06
SSARS-1   14.11, 14.17, 14.54, 14.66, 14.69–
  14.70
SSARS-2   14.11, 14.66
SSARS-3   14.11, 14.46–14.48
SSARS-4   14.11, 14.14–14.16, 14.62
SSARS-6   14.11–14.12, 14.69–14.70
SSARS-7   14.10–14.11, 14.12, 14.16, 14.18–
  14.19
SSARS Interpretations
  (December 1979)   14.20, 14.35, 14.51
  (November 1980)   14.40, 14.45, 14.53
  (August 1981)   14.12, 14.38
  (November 1981)   14.06
  (May 1982)   14.40, 14.48
  (November 1982)   14.09
  (December 1982)   14.43
  (March 1983)   14.26
  (September 1990)   14.06, 14.19, 14.35
  (May 1991)   14.10, 14.70
SSASPFI   15.03

SSCS **16.27–16.28**
State governments. *See* Governmental units
Statement of cash flows. *See* FAS-95
Statement on Standards for Consulting Services (SSCS). *See* SSCS
Statements on Auditing Procedures **1.03–1.04**
Statements on Auditing Standards (SAS). *See specific SASs*
Statements on Quality Control Standards (SQCS). *See specific SQCSs*
Statements on Standards for Accountant's Services on Prospective Financial Information **15.03**
Statements on Standards for Attestation Engagements. *See specific SSAEs*
Statements on Standards for Consulting Services **16.27–16.28**
Statistical sampling. *See* Sampling
Statutory basis of accounting **12.20**
Subordination of judgment **24.21–24.22**
Subpoenas, for workpapers **8.26**
Subsequent Discovery of Facts Existing at the Date of the Auditor's Report. See SAS-1, Section 561
Subsequent events
    audit procedures **7.72, 10.10–10.12**
    identifying **10.10–10.12**
    internal control engagement **16.56**
    review of interim financial information **13.25**
    SAS-1 **10.10–10.12**
    SEC filings **13.27–13.30**
Subservice organizations **7.72**
Subsidiary ledgers **23.05**
Substance over form. *See* Representational faithfulness
Substantial doubt. *See* Going concern
Substantive procedures, designing **7.30–7.31**
Substantive tests. *See also* Sampling
    analytical procedures in **8.60–8.61**
    based on control risk, designing **7.27–7.31**
    cost effectiveness **8.15–8.16**
    governmental units **23.22–23.23**
    sampling **8.13–8.14, 9.21–9.30**
    timing of **8.14–8.17**
    types of **8.15**
Substantive tests of details **9.21–9.30**
Successor auditor. *See* Communication with predecessor auditor
Supervision
    planning audit engagement and **6.07**. *See also* SAS-22

    and quality control **2.08**
    and standards of fieldwork **4.08–4.10**
Support
    definition of **22.15**
    for not-for-profit organizations **22.15–22.16, 22.19–22.20**
Suspension of Certain Accounting Requirements for Oil and Gas Producing Companies. See FAS-25
Systematic and rational allocation **3.08**
Systematic sampling **9.10–9.11**

T

Tax. *See also* Income tax
    construction contractors **18.10**
    employee benefit plans **20.26**
    health care providers **21.08–21.09**
    prospective financial statements **15.23**
    shelters **15.23**
    treasury, credit unions **19.10**
    unrelated business income (UBI) **21.08–21.09**
Technical Bulletins, FASB **3.12**
Temporarily restricted gifts/assets **22.05**
Tests. *See also specific types of tests*
    of compliance with laws and regulations **23.22**
    of controls **7.25–7.27**
        for governmental units **23.22**
        sample sizes for **8.12–8.13**
        and sampling **8.12–8.13, 9.06–9.21**
        and timeliness of evidential matter **7.27**
    of details of transactions **7.27, 9.21–9.30**
    dual-purpose **8.77**
    substantive **7.29–7.31, 8.13–8.17, 9.21–9.30**
Tolerable misstatement **9.27**
Tolerable rate **9.12, 9.14**
Training
    of auditor **2.05**
    standards **4.05–4.08**
    quality control and **2.07–2.08**
Transactions
    completeness of **7.17**
    hypothetical **12.29**
    tests of details of. *See* Tests, of details of transactions
Treadway Commission **16.38, 16.46**
Troubled debt restructuring. *See also* FAS-15
    for credit unions **19.08**

Trust funds **23.06–23.07, 23.16**
Trusteed assets, for benefit plans **20.22–20.24**

U

Unacceptable principle, changing to **11.22–11.23**
Unaudited financial statements—nonpublic companies
  comparative financial statements, reporting on **14.56–14.69**
  compilation of financial statements **14.20–14.26**
  engagement letter **14.17–14.18**
  evaluation of client **14.13–14.14**
  financial statement defined by SSARS-1 **14.06**
  and GAAP **14.18–14.19**
  and GAAS **14.19–14.20**
  independence **14.17**
  internal control, consideration of **14.33–14.34**
  level of engagement, change in **14.55–14.56**
  nonpublic entity defined by SSARS-1 **14.05**
  planning **14.33–14.34**
  pre-engagement planning **14.13–14.18**
  predecessor accountant **14.14–14.16**
  reporting
    on compilations **14.37–14.48**
    obligations **14.34–14.37**
    on personal financial statements **14.69–14.72**
    on reviews **14.48–14.54**
  responsibility and function of the accountant **14.12–14.13**
  review of financial statements **14.26–14.32**
  withdrawing from engagement **14.54–14.55**
Uncertainty conditions **11.35–11.39**
  going concern **11.35–11.39**
  in liquidation-based financial statements **12.27**
  prospective financial statements **15.19**
  unrelated to going concern **11.35–11.37**
Uncertainty modifications, elimination of **7.51**
Underwriters, letters for **13.31–13.55**
  addressee **13.39**
  alternative letter **13.32–13.33**
  applicability of SAS-72 **13.32–13.35**
    capsule financial information **13.44–13.45**
    changes, subsequent **13.46–13.48, 13.50**
    compliance **13.41–13.42**
    concluding paragraph **13.50**
    contents **13.38–13.50**
    date of **13.39**
    example of **13.50–13.54**
    financial forecasts **13.46**
    independence **13.41**
    introductory paragraph **13.39–13.40**
    other accountants **13.36–13.37**
    other information in letter **13.42–13.48**
    pro forma financial information **13.45–13.46**
    reference to other reports **13.40**
    representation letter **13.33–13.34**
    SAS-71 **13.44**
    SAS-72 **13.31, 13.34**
    sample **13.50–13.54**
    SEC **13.41–13.42**
    shelf registrations **13.37**
    subsequent changes **13.47–13.48, 13.50**
Unrestricted gifts **22.05**
User auditor, role of in service organization **7.58–7.61**
    evaluation of service auditor **7.61**
    PPPO report, use of **7.66**
Using the Work of a Specialist. See SAS-73

V

Valuation **7.17**
    assertion of **8.09**
    reporting, fair value disclosures **11.45–11.48**
Variable sampling **9.04–9.05, 9.24**
Voluntary Health and Welfare Guide **22.03**
Voluntary health and welfare organizations. *See also* Not-for-profit organizations
    functional expense classification **22.05, 22.13–22.14, 22.17–22.18**

W

"Wash" sales **19.07**
Wheat Committee **3.12**
Work of another auditor **8.55–8.59**
Work-product privilege, attorney's, and letter of audit inquiry **10.07, 10.08**
Working capital **3.10**
Working Papers. See SAS-41

Workpapers **8.22–8.27, 13.18**
  access to by regulators **8.24–8.27**
  agreed-upon procedures engagement **17.17**
  "bridging" **7.72**
  content of **8.22**
  internal control **7.72**
  misstatements **10.15–10.17**
  of predecessor auditor, unavailability of **5.07–5.08**
  professional standards relative to **8.23**
  quality control **2.10**
  regulators and **8.24–8.27**
  review of **2.10**
  sampling **9.21, 9.30**
  SAS-41 **7.72, 8.22–8.23**
  SSAE-5 **16.27**

Y

Yellow Book. *See Government Auditing Standards*